Understanding Globalization Through the Lens of Gravity

Understanding Globalization Through the Lens of Gravity

Editor

Jeffrey H. Bergstrand

University of Notre Dame, USA

World Scientific

NEW JERSEY • LONDON • SINGAPORE • BEIJING • SHANGHAI • HONG KONG • TAIPEI • CHENNAI • TOKYO

Published by

World Scientific Publishing Co. Pte. Ltd.
5 Toh Tuck Link, Singapore 596224
USA office: 27 Warren Street, Suite 401-402, Hackensack, NJ 07601
UK office: 57 Shelton Street, Covent Garden, London WC2H 9HE

Library of Congress Cataloging-in-Publication Data
Names: Bergstrand, Jeffrey H, editor.
Title: Understanding globalization through the lens of gravity / edited by Jeffrey H. Bergstrand (UNIVERSITY OF NOTRE DAME, USA).
Description: New Jersey : World Scientific, [2019] | "A curated collection of Bergstrand's published papers over the 30 years since his first paper on the theme of gravity."
Identifiers: LCCN 2019013767 | ISBN 9789811202261 (hc)
Subjects: LCSH: Gravity model of international trade. | Free trade. | Investments, Foreign--Law and legislation. | Treaties.
Classification: LCC HF1008 .U53 2019 | DDC 382.01--dc23
LC record available at https://lccn.loc.gov/2019013767

British Library Cataloguing-in-Publication Data
A catalogue record for this book is available from the British Library.

For any available supplementary material, please visit
https://www.worldscientific.com/worldscibooks/10.1142/11332#t=suppl

Desk Editors: Anthony Alexander/Daniele Lee

Typeset by Stallion Press
Email: enquiries@stallionpress.com

To Cyndee,
for your support, patience, and love for more than 40 years,

and to Kirsten, Lauren, and Jason,
to understand what I was doing all those years at the office
as you grew up.

About the Author

Professor Jeffrey H. Bergstrand has taught economics and international finance in the undergraduate, MBA, and Executive MBA programs since 1986 when he joined the Notre Dame faculty, winning awards for his MBA and Executive MBA teaching. He earned his B.A. in Economics and Political Science from Northwestern University in 1974 and his Ph.D. in Economics from the University of Wisconsin at Madison in 1981 with specializations in international and macroeconomics, and worked as an economist at the Federal Reserve Bank of Boston from 1981 to 1986. He has authored over 60 papers on determinants of international trade flows, foreign direct investment, multinational firm behavior, and real exchange rates in prominent journals in economics such as the *American Economic Review* and *Journal of International Economics*. Professor Bergstrand is best known for his early formal theoretical foundations for the "gravity equation" in international trade, which is now the empirical workhorse for studying international trade, foreign direct investment, and migration flows, and the effects of natural and policy frictions on these flows. More recently, he has explored factors that explain the probability that pairs of countries have economic integration agreements, the timing of the formation of such agreements, and the impact of such agreements on countries' trade. He has consulted with the U.S., European Union, and Swiss governments on the impacts of economic integration agreements on international trade and foreign direct investment flows and his methodologies continue to influence governments' policy analyses. His research impact has placed him in the top two percent of economists in the world, as measured by the Research Papers in Economics (RePEc) project. Also, he is a former president of the International Economics and Finance Society, a global professional society of international trade and finance economists.

Acknowledgments

I would like to thank the following publishers and journals for granting their permissions to reproduce the articles in this volume:

Publishers
Elsevier Science
Oxford University Press
The MIT Press
Wiley

Journals
Economic Inquiry
Economic Journal
European Economic Review
Journal of International Economics
Review of Economics and Statistics
Review of International Economics

Contents

Introduction

Jeffrey H. Bergstrand

There are two major paths one often embarks upon in parallel during their adult life. One is personal, marriage to a lifelong partner; the other is professional, one's career. Both of mine started during the first week of July 1978. My wife, Cyndee, and I were wed on July 1, 1978; we have been happily married for over forty years. Following a romantic week-long honeymoon in the Bahamas, we returned to the University of Wisconsin at Madison on July 8, where I started my summer employment as a research assistant (RA) for a newly-minted assistant professor named Andre Sapir, having just completed my first 2 years of Ph.D. work in economics. This was my first RA position and my responsibilities were to collect data on bilateral international trade flows from the Organization for Economic Cooperation and Development (OECD) along with other macroeconomic data (gross domestic products, populations, etc.) and to run regressions using something referred to as the "gravity equation in international trade." Andre Sapir, now a renowned Belgian economist at the Universite Libre de Bruxelles, was implementing an econometric evaluation of the partial (treatment) effects of the Generalized System of Preferences on gross trade creation of the members of the European Economic Community (EEC), cf., Sapir (1981). Acceptance of his empirical methodology benefited partly from a decade-earlier *American Economic Review* article that used the gravity equation similarly to study the partial effects of the EEC and European Free Trade Association on European trade flows, cf., Aitken (1973). The Aitken (1973) paper benefited from earlier papers by Tinbergen (1962), Poyhonen (1963a), Poyhonen (1963b), and Pulliainen (1963), and a book on this subject by Linnemann (1966). Poyhonen, Pulliainen, and Linnemann were all students of Nobel laureate Jan Tinbergen.

Yet, common to all of these studies was an *ad hoc* theoretical economic explanation for estimating the gravity equation by ordinary least squares (OLS), which was generally specified as either:

$$\ln X_{ijt} = \beta_0 + \beta_1 \ln Y_{it} + \beta_2 \ln Y_{jt} + \beta_3 \ln \text{DIST}_{ij} + \beta_4 \text{EIA}_{ijt} + \ln \epsilon_{ijt} \tag{1}$$

or:

$$\ln X_{ijt} = \beta_0 + \beta_1 \ln Y_{it} + \beta_2 \ln N_{it} + \beta_3 \ln Y_{jt} + \beta_4 \ln N_{jt} + \beta_5 \ln \text{DIST}_{ij} + \beta_6 \text{EIA}_{ijt} + \ln \epsilon_{ijt}, \tag{2}$$

where ln denotes the natural logarithm, X_{ijt} is the value (typically, in U.S. dollars) of the nominal trade flow from i to j in year t, Y_{it} is nominal gross domestic product (GDP) in i (typically, in U.S. dollars), N_{it} is population in i, Y_{jt} is nominal GDP in j, N_{jt} is population in j, DIST_{ij} is (time-invariant) bilateral distance between economic centers of i and j, EIA_{ijt} is a binary (or dummy) variable representing the presence or absence of an economic integration agreement (EIA) between i to j in year t, and ϵ_{ijt} is a log-normally distributed error term.[1] The studies by Tinbergen, Linnemann, Aitken, and Sapir all assumed that GDPs in the exporting and importing countries represented economic "masses." In the case of equation (2), exporter and importer population was interpreted as negatively affecting potential export supply and potential import demand, respectively, owing to "economies of scale;" the larger the population, "the larger will be the domestic market to foreign market ratio" and the smaller the potential export supply or import demand. Bilateral distance was a proxy

[1]Throughout this book, the term EIA may refer to one-way preferential trade agreements, two-way preferential trade agreements, free trade agreements, customs unions, common markets, and economic unions; for each paper, we will clarify use of the term.

for transportation costs and the dummy variables for EIAs explained relative tariff rates. General price levels were assumed to adjust due to commodity arbitrage, and hence were ignored and consequently set equal to unity.

However, I found this explanation *ad hoc*, and — facing the task of a 3rd-year dissertation proposal — I embarked in 1978 on providing a "formal" theoretical microeconomic foundation for the gravity equation in international trade, encouraged sequentially (and fortunately!) by advisors J. David Richardson (my chair), Andre Sapir, Robert Baldwin, and Rachel McCulloch. Some of the questions that arose are:

1. Why was the best fit empirically for the gravity equation multiplicative in levels, or linear in the logarithms of the underlying variables?
2. Why were the GDP elasticities precisely unity or — in some cases — not unity?
3. Having been the "stepchild" of the international trade literature, how did the gravity equation "fit in" with the (then) established Heckscher–Ohlin model of international trade, and what role did populations *really* play?
4. And why were prices altogether absent (noting that relative wage rates were important in the migration literature using gravity equations)?

Such questions formed the basis for my first three papers on theoretical foundations for the gravity equation, which are discussed in Part 1 of this book, along with three more papers on the theoretical foundations for the gravity equation in trade.

Over time, growing interest and use of the gravity equation sparked even more questions. With increasing application of the gravity equation, partial effects for the EIA dummy variables varied considerably, and often had counterintuitive coefficient signs. Why was that? Working with Scott Baier, we argued that *endogeneity bias* was likely present in many gravity-equation applications, obscuring the true partial effects of EIAs. But if EIAs were determined contemporaneously with trade flows, wouldn't it be useful to know *what explains* EIAs? This question led to the series of papers in Part 2 (two with Scott Baier and one with Peter Egger and Mario Larch) that examined theoretically and empirically economic determinants of bilateral EIAs.

Once we had a better understanding of the economic determinants of EIAs, we could then investigate the appropriate econometric approach to estimate with consistency and precision the partial effects of EIAs, such as free trade agreements (FTAs). In Part 3, I discuss the contributions to this literature of four papers with various coauthors (three with Baier and one with Mario Larch and Yoto Yotov).

Moreover, the gravity equation has not been used just for studying determinants of bilateral trade flows and migration flows; it has also been used to explain bilateral foreign affiliate sales of multinational firms and foreign direct investment (FDI). This inspired Peter Egger and me to pursue a research agenda on the theoretical foundations for the gravity equations of bilateral foreign affiliate sales and of bilateral FDI. Adapting the two-factor, two-country, two-good Knowledge–Capital model of James Markusen and various coauthors, we introduced a third factor (physical capital) and third country (rest-of-world) to create a Knowledge-and-Physical-Capital model of multinational firm behavior. In Part 4, I discuss how this model helped to provide a formal theoretical foundation for the gravity equations of foreign affiliate sales and of FDI in a world with identical factor endowments and then, in a second paper, in a world with different relative factor endowments. This part concludes with a paper that synthesizes much of this entire research agenda by modeling formally the economic determinants of bilateral investment treaties *and* bilateral trade agreements in a world with differing relative factor endowments, consistent with the existence of gravity equations of trade, foreign affiliate sales, and FDI.

Since those papers were written, the most notable innovation in the international trade literature has been the Melitz model of trade that allows firms to be "heterogeneous" in their productivities (also introduced in the Eaton–Kortum model) and to face export fixed costs for every market. In the conclusion to this introduction, I will discuss briefly three of my most recent (and two not yet published) papers that address the topics of determinants of bilateral international trade flows, determinants of bilateral FDI stocks, and effects of EIAs on bilateral trade flows — in the context of a Melitz model with firm heterogeneity and export (or FDI) fixed costs.

I chose the title of this book for two reasons: First, as already surmised from the previous paragraphs, the concept of "gravity" obviously plays a central role. Second, for the non-economist, a central theme throughout this volume of papers is to help the reader better "understand globalization." Citing Wikipedia, globalization is the "process of interaction and integration between people, companies, and governments worldwide." One aspect of globalization — and a very important one — is *economic* globalization, via the movement internationally of goods and services (trade), capital (FDI and portfolio investment), and workers (skilled and unskilled migration). Just focusing on trade for a moment, international trade flows are influenced (exhaustively) by natural and unnatural factors. Examples of natural variables are nations' economic sizes and their geography. "Unnatural" variables are "man-made," notably trade (and even domestic) policies set by governments. As suggested above, the papers in the first three parts of this book deal with helping us to better understand *logically, consistently, and quantitatively* — wedding theory and empirical work — natural and policy variables affecting trade flows, natural and policy variables affecting (policy-oriented) economic integration agreements, and then the effects of EIAs on trade flows.

However, capital flows and migration flows are also major forces of economic globalization. In the papers in Part 4, I examine (with coauthors) the determinants of bilateral foreign affiliate sales, foreign direct investment stocks, and multinational firms' behaviors — but not in isolation from trade-flow determinants and national exporting firms' behaviors. Trade and FDI flows are determined simultaneously by the behaviors of consumers, firms, and governments, given natural factors such as absolute factor endowments, relative factor endowments, and geography. To make concepts tractable, throughout the book the reader should note that trade flows, economic integration agreements, FDI stocks, bilateral FDI treaties, and the like are all influenced by three sets of factors: nations' economic sizes and similarities (based upon absolute factor endowments), natural and policy-based bilateral trade and FDI costs, and relative factor endowments. Moreover, even after 40 years of research, I have not yet had time to extend this analysis in a substantive (and similar in-depth) manner to portfolio investment behavior and migration flows. I leave this work for future generations.[2]

Finally, several papers in this volume were coauthored. I am deeply grateful for the valued collaborations and friendships with Scott Baier, Peter Egger, Mario Larch, Yoto Yotov, Ronald Mariutto, and Michael Feng.[3]

1. Determinants of International Trade Flows

The six papers in this section all relate to microeconomic foundations for the gravity equation in international trade. The first three of these were sole-authored in the 1980s and are related to my dissertation completed at the University of Wisconsin at Madison in 1981. The lapse in time until publication of some of these three reflects the first 5 years of my career as an economist at the Federal Reserve Bank of Boston writing several *New England Economic Review* articles on exchange rates and international monetary issues; my academic career started at the University of Notre Dame in 1986. Following a respite from gravity and instead writing on international finance topics in the 1990s, I returned to the topic of the gravity equation after the turn of the century with the two papers coauthored with Scott Baier and one with Peter Egger and Mario Larch.

[2]There is also a sub-text to the title starting with "Understanding Globalization. . . ." The chair of my dissertation committee, J. David Richardson, who incessantly inspired my work on this subject and mentored me with incredible support and grace, wrote a textbook titled *Understanding International Economics: Theory and Practice*. This is a tribute to Dave.

[3]Moreover, several other published papers (about 35) not included in this volume have benefitted from valuable collaborations and friendships with Ronald Balvers, Koen Berden, Thomas Bundt, Matthew Clance, Stephen Cray, Mitch Gainer, Antoine Gervais, Patrick McLaughlin, Eva van Etten, Erika Vidal, and Tao Xu.

Chapter 1 is my most cited article and probably will always remain so. This paper, "The Gravity Equation in International Trade: Some Microeconomic Foundations and Empirical Evidence," or Bergstrand (1985), was based largely on the first (substantive) chapter of my dissertation. This paper is frequently cited alongside Anderson (1979) as two of the earliest formal theoretical economic foundations for the gravity equation in international trade including positive trade costs cf., Head and Mayer (2014).[4] Three points are worth noting: First, Anderson (1979) obviously preceded Bergstrand (1985); moreover, Anderson (1979) influenced my paper. Second, Anderson (1979) and Bergstrand (1985) made different contributions to understanding the trade gravity equation in economic terms; each had its contributions and each had its limitations, which I will discuss. Third, the two papers (models) are actually mutually compatible and consistent with the seminal paper by Anderson and van Wincoop (2003). In fact, I will show formally how the two are compatible with Anderson and van Wincoop (2003) and the notion of "structural gravity" as now known, cf., Head and Mayer (2014) and Baier *et al.* (2017).

Since the notion of the gravity equation is central to this volume, it is relevant in this first chapter to understand the important basic contributions found in the papers by Anderson (1979) and Bergstrand (1985). The beauty of the frictionless model in the paper by Anderson (1979) is its elegant simplicity. Anderson's paper impressed me by a finding in its earliest section based upon so few assumptions that yielded such an important result. Four plausible assumptions generated the basic frictionless gravity equation. First, assume every country i produces a unique differentiated good. Second, assume preferences across all importing countries are identical and homothetic. Third, assume no trade frictions; hence, prices are identical for all goods (and can have any common value, including unity). Then, the nominal trade flow demanded from exporter i to importer j (X_{ij}) is:

$$X_{ij} = \theta_i Y_j, \tag{3}$$

[4]Krugman (1979) assumed costless trade.

where θ_i is every importer's demand for good i as a share of its total expenditures and Y_j is nominal gross output (and income and expenditures).[5] Fourth, assume all output must be consumed either at home or by foreigners (implicitly, trade balance holds):

$$Y_i = \sum_{j=1}^{N} X_{ij} = \sum_{j=1}^{N} \theta_i Y_j = \theta_i \sum_{j=1}^{N} Y_j = \theta_i Y_W, \tag{4}$$

where Y_W is world income and output. Equation (4) is equivalent to:

$$\theta_i = Y_i / Y_W. \tag{5}$$

Substituting equation (5) in equation (3) yields:

$$X_{ij} = Y_i Y_j / Y_W. \tag{6}$$

Only four assumptions yield one of the most durable empirical relationships in international trade: bilateral trade between two countries is related multiplicatively to the two countries' incomes and with unit income elasticities (all else constant).

I will just offer a couple of more insights from Anderson (1979). The two subsequent sections introduce first a tradable goods share of expenditures as an *ad hoc* function of a country's income and population (with minimal motivation), and then address estimation issues of efficiency and bias. The penultimate section introduces many goods, tariff rates, and bilateral distances. The elegance of the first section is diminished in later sections by a large set of assumptions to generate a gravity equation that is multiplicative in incomes and a function of bilateral distance. Moreover, in this exercise as well as the appendix using constant-elasticity-of-substitution (CES) preferences, he assumes all prices are unity, which cannot hold in the presence of trade frictions. The assumption of setting all prices to unity in the presence of trade frictions is the main limitation in Anderson (1979). This limitation was overcome in Anderson and van Wincoop (2003), where the authors show that trade flows in a gravity equation are indeed functions of (non-constant) prices and set the stage for structural gravity as we now understand it.

[5]This equation holds also for intranational trade, i.e., X_{jj}.

In contrast to Anderson (1979), the main motivation behind Bergstrand (1985) was to address the role of prices in the gravity equation, both theoretically and empirically. Unlike Anderson (1979), Bergstrand (1985) started with a CES utility function to emphasize that products from various markets were imperfect substitutes, as originally hypothesized by Armington. Moreover, I nested a CES utility function among importables inside a CES utility function between importables and the domestic good. On the supply side, I chose not to use the convention of constant marginal costs. Rather, I introduced a constant-elasticity-of-transformation (CET) function for producing output in the domestic market and foreign market, allowing a cost (in terms of labor) for output to be transformed between home and foreign markets.[6] I also used a CET function to allow a cost for foreign output to be transformed between various export markets. I nested the latter CET function inside the former CET function. This formulation motivated upward-sloping supply curves (increasing marginal costs) *for each bilateral market.* Assuming bilateral import demand values equaled bilateral export supply values in general equilibrium, this generated a system of $4N^2 + 3N$ equations in the same number of unknowns.

Assuming each bilateral market was small relative to the other $N^2 - 1$ markets and identical utility and production functions, I derived the trade gravity equation shown in equation (14) of Chapter 1. This gravity equation was estimated using various (imperfect) proxies for the bilateral trade-cost terms and for the four "multilateral price" terms. The results suggested certain insights about the elasticities of substitution in consumption and of transformation in production, including that it was not costless for producers to substitute goods between markets.

To my knowledge, comparing and contrasting the final gravity equation in the CES appendix to Anderson (1979) and equation (14) from Bergstrand (1985) was never done; authors since then only cited both works. Head and Mayer (2014) made a cursory (but

[6]Interestingly, the plausibility of this assumption resurfaced only recently in Feenstra (2010).

correct) correspondence between the two approaches, alongside other approaches, in their excellent survey. However, the two models are mutually compatible, and consistent with that of Anderson and van Wincoop (2003) and the notion of "structural gravity equations" discussed by Baier *et al.* (2017). The limitation in Anderson (1979) was the assumption of "prices of unity" in the presence of transport costs; the limitation in Bergstrand (1985) was the absence of a "market-clearing" assumption, due to the complexity of equation (14) in Chapter 1.

However, a straightforward simplification of the model and gravity equation (14) in Bergstrand (1985) — along with incorporating the market-clearing (or multilateral trade balance) assumption — yields a structural gravity model *identical* to the one finally obtained in Anderson and van Wincoop (2003). The simplification involves three easy steps: First, starting with equation (14) in Chapter 1, simplify the model by allowing the elasticities of substitution in consumption to be identical ($\sigma = \mu$) and the elasticities of transformation in production to be identical ($\gamma = \eta$) and simplify notation by denoting $\tau_{ij} \equiv C_{ij}T_{ij}/E_{ij}$. This yields:

$$X_{ij} = Y_i^{\frac{\sigma-1}{\gamma+\sigma}} Y_j^{\frac{\gamma+1}{\gamma+\sigma}} (\tau_{ij})^{(1-\sigma)\frac{\gamma+1}{\gamma+\sigma}} \left[\left(\sum_{j=1}^{N} p_{ij}^{1+\gamma}\right)^{\frac{1}{1+\gamma}}\right]^{-\frac{(\sigma-1)(1+\gamma)}{\gamma+\sigma}}$$

$$\times \left[\left(\sum_{i=1}^{N} (p_{ij}\tau_{ij})^{1-\sigma}\right)^{\frac{1}{1-\sigma}}\right]^{-\frac{(1-\sigma)(1+\gamma)}{\gamma+\sigma}}, \tag{7}$$

where I have replaced some notation in the original article in this introduction.[7] Second, assume production is costlessly transformed between markets (i.e., $\gamma = \infty$). This yields:

$$X_{ij} = Y_j \left(\frac{p_i \tau_{ij}}{P_j}\right)^{1-\sigma}, \tag{8}$$

[7] I use X_{ij} for the nominal trade flow rather than PX_{ij}, and I use p_{ij} rather than P_{ij} to denote bilateral prices.

where p_{ij} is replaced by p_i since output is now costlessly transformed between markets and:

$$P_j \equiv \left[\sum_{i=1}^{N} (p_i \tau_{ij})^{1-\sigma} \right]^{1/(1-\sigma)}. \tag{9}$$

Equation (8) is identical to equation (6) in Anderson and van Wincoop (2003) (ignoring the arbitrary preference parameter β_i) and to the bilateral import demand functions in structural gravity equations discussed in Baier *et al.* (2017). Hence, structural gravity follows once one assumes market clearance (trade balance), $Y_i = \sum_{j=1}^{N} X_{ij}$. Following derivations in Anderson and van Wincoop (2003) and Baier *et al.* (2017):

$$X_{ij} = \frac{Y_i Y_j}{Y_W} \left(\frac{\tau_{ij}}{\Pi_i P_j} \right)^{1-\sigma}, \tag{10}$$

where:

$$\Pi_i = \left[\sum_{j=1}^{N} \theta_j \left(\frac{\tau_{ij}}{P_j} \right)^{1-\sigma} \right]^{1/(1-\sigma)}, \tag{11}$$

and:

$$P_j = \left[\sum_{i=1}^{N} \theta_i \left(\frac{\tau_{ij}}{\Pi_i} \right)^{1-\sigma} \right]^{1/(1-\sigma)}. \tag{12}$$

Thus, two simplifications of equation (14) from Bergstrand (1985) along with adding in the market-clearing condition yields the same structural gravity equation as in Anderson and van Wincoop (2003) and Baier *et al.* (2017).

Chapter 2 addresses the specification noted in equation (2) above, which includes exporter and importer populations as well. In the late 1970s, the Heckscher–Ohlin model still dominated the trade literature as the work of Krugman (1979) on intra-industry trade had just surfaced. The empirical importance of exporter and importer populations in the gravity equations of Linnemann (1966), Aitken (1973), and Sapir (1981) — and the implied roles of exporter and importer per capita GDPs — did not have a satisfactory explanation in my view. Nor was the specification of the gravity equation in equation (2) linked to the established Heckscher–Ohlin (H–O) model. Although Elhanan Helpman and Paul Krugman established formally the interface between the Heckscher–Ohlin factor-proportions inter-industry trade model and the emerging Krugman model of intra-industry trade in the absence of trade costs, they did not motivate a theoretical foundation for a gravity equation including exporter and importer GDPs and per capita GDPs in the presence of positive trade costs, cf., Helpman and Krugman (1985). The absence then of a theoretical foundation for the gravity equation typically specified as in equation (2) motivated the second (substantive) chapter of my dissertation, which provided a foundation for Chapter 2's "The Generalized Gravity Equation, Monopolistic Competition, and the Factor-Proportions Theory in International Trade" or (Bergstrand, 1989).

I decided to wed a two-good, two-factor, N-country version of the H–O model with the Helpman–Krugman monopolistic competition model of intra-industry trade allowing for positive trade costs. Once again, I nested utility functions. I nested CES preferences for each of the two goods inside a Cobb–Douglas utility function, but also incorporated a minimum consumption requirement for one good (the Stone–Geary aspect) to generate non-homothetic tastes. The non-homotheticity in the utility function generated a role for per capita income in bilateral importer demands, alongside aggregate income and relative prices. On the production side, each firm in each of the two industries used labor and capital in production but I included a fixed cost as in Krugman (1979) to allow monopolistically competitive firms to benefit from economies of scale internal to the firm. I assumed as in Bergstrand (1985) that output was not costlessly substitutable across the N markets using a CET function for each firm's output in each industry. I assumed factor markets cleared, but as in Bergstrand (1985) I did not include the trade-balance clearing condition, due to the complexity of the reduced-form gravity equation.

The solution to the system of equations generated gravity equation (12) in Bergstrand (1989). First, the gravity equation derived included the term $(\beta_{KA}\beta_{LB} - \beta_{KB}\beta_{LA})^{-1}[\beta_{LB} - \beta_{KB}(K_i^*/L_i^*)^{-1}]^{\frac{\sigma^A-1}{\gamma^A+\sigma^A}}$, where β_{mn} denotes the input requirement of factor m in production of a good in industry n and K_i^* (L_i^*) denotes the stock of capital (labor) in country i used in production. Assuming across countries that per capita GDPs are highly correlated with their K^*/L^* (which they are), then country i per capita GDP's effect on output of good n and trade flow X_{ijn} would be positive or negative depending upon relative factor intensities in production. For instance, if industry A is relatively capital intensive in production, then a higher level of K^*/L^* in country i (proxied by its per capita GDP) will increase output of good A in i and exports of good A from i to j.

The second distinguishing theoretical result from gravity equation (12) in Bergstrand (1989) is the inclusion of the term $(1 - y_j^{-1})^{\frac{\gamma^A+1}{\gamma^A+\sigma^A}}$, where y_j is per capita income in j. This term reflects the non-homotheticity in the demand function. Higher levels of per capita income in the importing country will raise demand for good A in the importing country, if A is a luxury good. While not shown in the original paper, if then good B is the necessity, the gravity equation for good B is slightly different, with import demand a negative function of the importer's per capita income.

As with Bergstrand (1985), I took the model to the data. In this case, I used one-digit Standard Industrial Trade Classification (SITC) trade flows. Noting that the theory applied to a two-good framework and data had 10 goods (SITC 0-9), I also wrote a proof generalizing the Rybczynski-theorem's theoretical results undergirding my exporter per capita GDP hypotheses. That unpublished proof is appended to the end of Chapter 2, showing that — in an N good, two-factor world — an increase in capital will *tend* to increase output of the good that is relatively capital intensive in production.

The empirical results revealed that for several years' cross-sections higher exporter per capita GDPs were associated significantly with higher exports from i to j in raw materials, chemicals, and manufactures. This suggested such industries were relatively capital intensive in production, which is plausible. Higher exporter per capita GDP was associated with lower exports in beverages and tobacco, which is also plausible. On the demand side, higher importer per capita GDPs were associated significantly with higher imports from i to j

in beverages and tobacco, manufactures classified chiefly by material, and miscellaneous manufactures, which is plausible. Higher importer per capita GDP was associated significantly with lower imports from i to j in fuels, which is plausible as energy is a necessity.

In the 1980s, the growing theoretical and empirical interest in intra-industry trade persuaded me to pursue a paper using the gravity equation as a pedagogical device for better understanding of the economic determinants of the shares of industries' bilateral trade flows that were "intra-industry trade" (IIT). Having just completed Bergstrand (1989) and having published earlier Bergstrand (1983) on measurement and determinants of intra-industry trade, I wrote Chapter 3, "The Heckscher–Ohlin–Samuelson Model, the Linder Hypothesis and the Determinants of Bilateral Intra-Industry Trade" (Bergstrand, 1990). The paper was a natural fit for me. Bergstrand (1983) had established theoretically the importance of measuring IIT shares *bilaterally* instead of multilaterally, since in a multi-country, multi-commodity, two-factor, factor-price non-equalized world, the commodity version of the H–O theorem need not hold for a country's multilateral trade but *will* hold for any pair of countries. Hence, multilateral IIT is unsurprising, but bilateral IIT is surprising if the world is governed by H–O trade. In the 1980s, several empirical studies had examined econometrically the determinants of bilateral IIT using cross-sections. However, a unified theoretical framework for understanding the empirical relationships between the share of IIT between two countries and the average levels of and differences between their GDPs, per capita GDPs, *and* tariff rates had not yet been established. Moreover, several empirical studies in the 1980s had interpreted a larger difference in per capita incomes between a country-pair as taste differences, in the spirit of the Linder hypothesis. Yet, formal theoretical models of IIT interpreted per capita GDP differences between two countries as reflecting capital–labor endowment-ratio differences, cf., Helpman and Krugman (1985). Similarly, higher average per capita GDPs could be influencing IIT shares via non-homothetic tastes and demand or through higher average capital–labor ratios and supply. Finally, some empirical relationships — such as that between IIT shares and average tariff-rate levels — had no formal theoretical rationale. All these considerations motivated this paper.

The theoretical model generating the gravity equation undergirding the disaggregate trade flows was nearly identical to that in Bergstrand (1989), expediting the study. One theoretical innovation was that I solved for the endogenous number of firms in the differentiated goods industry for each country. The theoretical contribution was largely in the derivation of eight comparative statics predicting for the differentiated goods industry the effect on bilateral IIT shares of average levels of and differences between GDPs, capital–labor endowment ratios, per capita GDPs, and tariff rates, which motivated expected coefficient signs for these variables for the empirical analysis.

Using data for the three two-digit SITC categories in SITC 7 (Machinery and Transport Equipment), I estimated the model. Conforming to the theoretical comparative statics, I provided evidence that larger differences in pairs of countries' capital–labor endowment ratios, per capita GDPs, GDPs, and tariff rates all reduced intra-industry trade for these manufactured products (as expected), with relative factor endowment differences reflecting factor-proportion (H–O) considerations on the supply side and per capita GDP differences reflecting taste (Linder) considerations on the demand side. Also, average GDP, per capita GDP, and tariff rates increased IIT, as expected; higher average capital–labor endowment ratios lowered IIT, indicating that these manufactured products were relatively labor intensive in production.

After a respite from work on the gravity equation, during much of the 1990s to spend time on international finance papers and the beginning of work on economic determinants of economic integration agreements (to be discussed in Part 2), I worked on three more gravity-equation papers published after the turn of the century. Chapter 4, "The Growth of World Trade: Tariffs, Transport Costs, and Income Similarity" coauthored with Scott Baier, or Baier and Bergstrand (2001), was motivated by reading Krugman (1995). In an influential survey of the terrain of international trade circa 1995, among several topics Krugman asked the simple question: "Why has world trade grown?" Krugman argued that journalistic discussion tended to focus on technological change and that falling transport and communication costs had been the driving factor, but international trade economists tended to argue that policy factors — trade-policy liberalization under the General Agreement on Tariffs and Trade (GATT) and proliferating economic integration agreements — were the driving force. However, Krugman provided no quantitative evidence one way or the other.

This paper inspired us to look quantitatively at the growth of world trade. With the gravity equation having acquired greater traction in the trade literature during the 1990s based upon theoretical economic foundations in the 1980s by Anderson, Helpman, Krugman, and myself, we turned to the gravity equation to examine the economic determinants of the *change* in country-pairs' bilateral trade flows using data from the late 1950s to the late 1980s.

The theoretical gravity model was based upon a simplification of Bergstrand (1985), but incorporating the monopolistic competition model of Krugman (1980). We eliminated the nested CES utility functions and nested CET functions in Bergstrand (1985), and even showed under costless transformation of output between markets, that the gravity equation simplified to the RHS being the product of Y_iY_j/Y^W and a relative price term. However, this paper, completed in 2000 and published in 2001, preceded the Anderson-van Wincoop notion of "structural gravity" articulated in the paper by Anderson and van Wincoop (2003) using outward and inward multilateral price (resistance) terms.

The main contribution of the paper was the assembly of a data set of tariff rates and transport cost factors from the late 1950s and late 1980s combined with the microeconomic-founded gravity-equation methodology to provide sharp quantitative evidence of the relative contributions of growth in output, income similarity, tariffs, and transport costs for the growth of bilateral trade flows. We found that aggregate income growth (not surprisingly) explained 67 percent of the growth of world trade, reductions in tariffs explained 25 percent, reductions in c.i.f.-f.o.b. factors explained 8 percent, and income-similarity growth explained virtually none of the growth. Hence, the role of trade-policy liberalizations contributed three times as much as transport-cost reductions in explaining world trade growth. This paper earned the (third) *Bhagwati Award* from the *Journal of International Economics* for the best paper in the 2-year period 2001–2002.

By the mid 2000s, theoretical foundations for the gravity equation in trade were accepted using different underlying theoretical approaches, such as Ricardian (Eaton and Kortum, 2002), Armington (Anderson and van Wincoop, 2003), Krugman-type monopolistic competition (Baier and Bergstrand, 2001), and Melitz (Chaney, 2008). However, all the approaches were faced empirically with the difficult task of quantifying *multilateral price* terms. As mentioned above, Baier and Bergstrand (2001) used producer and consumer price indexes as proxies. Eaton and Kortum (2002) used a method of "normalizing import shares" to avoid computation of multilateral price terms, and then employed (assumed exogenous) retail prices in their sample of countries to generate a measure of relative prices for empirical work. Using nonlinear least squares (NLLS), Anderson and van Wincoop (2003) estimated a structural gravity equation of trade flows and multilateral price terms. However, the NLLS approach has typically provided biased estimates relative to using exporter and importer fixed effects. Feenstra (2004) illustrates the extent of the bias, and has motivated many gravity studies to use exporter and importer fixed effects in cross section (or exporter-year and importer-year fixed effects with panel data). Although the use of exporter and importer fixed effects readily solves the problem of measuring multilateral price terms (and, for that matter, exporter and importer expenditures) allowing consistent and precise estimates of coefficients for bilateral variables, a problem remains if the researcher is interested in the coefficient estimates for any multilateral variables, such as exporter and importer incomes or whether or not the importer is a member of the World Trade Organization. This dilemma led to Chapter 5, "*Bonux vetus* OLS: A Simple Method for Approximating International Trade-Cost Effects using the Gravity Equation" coauthored with Scott Baier (Baier and Bergstrand, 2009a).[8]

[8]The Latin phrase denoted "Good Old OLS."

Theoretically, we started with the Anderson and van Wincoop (2003) model. We took a first-order log-linear Taylor series expansion of the multilateral price terms (allowing asymmetric terms). We centered the expansion around symmetric *ad valorem* bilateral trade costs (i.e., $t_{ij} = t$). This led to the multilateral price (MR) term approximations (under the assumption of symmetric bilateral trade costs):

$$\ln P_i = \sum_{j=1}^{N} \theta_j \ln t_{ij} - 0.5 \sum_{i=1}^{N} \sum_{j=1}^{N} \theta_i \theta_j \ln t_{ij}; \tag{13}$$

and

$$\ln P_j = \sum_{i=1}^{N} \theta_i \ln t_{ij} - 0.5 \sum_{i=1}^{N} \sum_{j=1}^{N} \theta_i \theta_j \ln t_{ij}, \tag{14}$$

where θ_i is the share of country i's income in world income and the second RHS terms in equations (13) and (14) are constants (in cross-section analysis). This MR approximation could be used for any bilateral variable.

Using data from McCallum (1995) on U.S. states and Canadian provinces, we estimated the effects of distance and border dummies. We found that the coefficient estimates using either the Anderson–van Wincoop NLLS method or our MR approximations yielded biased estimates relative to exporter and importer fixed effects, because estimates were sensitive to the measurement of internal distance. To capture the estimation biases of our method and Anderson–van Wincoop's relative to fixed effects, we needed to exclude mis-measurement and mis-specification biases. We pursued two Monte Carlo studies, where we established the "true models." The first used the Canadian–U.S. data set. Devoid of measurement and specification biases, we showed that our method and the Anderson–van Wincoop method yielded coefficient estimates nearly identical to the fixed effects estimates, confirming the relevance of our technique (subsequently termed in the literature "BV-OLS"). We then conducted a second Monte Carlo study, constructing the true trade flows among 88 countries using data on GDPs, bilateral distances, and a dummy variable "No Adjacency." Again, the Monte

Carlo simulations generated coefficient estimates using the BV-OLS technique with nearly identical coefficient estimates to those using exporter and importer fixed effects.

This paper also examined quantitatively the usefulness of the BV approach for conducting comparative statics. In the first set of comparative statics for the Canadian–U.S. border effect, our approximation method yielded that the general equilibrium effect of the national border caused trade to be 78 percent of that without the border. Using the Anderson–van Wincoop technique, the national border caused trade to be 56 percent of that without the border. However, comparative static estimates for world trade flows fared better for the BV technique. 74 percent of the comparative statiscs using the approximation method were within 5 percent of the true values (as determined by the Anderson–van Wincoop technique). 92 percent of the comparative statics using the BV technique were within 20 percent of the true values.

Nearly 30 years after publishing my first gravity-equation paper, Chapter 1, I returned to the gravity equation again with Chapter 6, "Gravity *Redux*: Estimation of Gravity Equation Coefficients, Elasticities of Substitution, and General Equilibrium Comparative Statics" coauthored with Peter Egger and Mario Larch (Bergstrand *et al.*, 2013). The purpose of this paper was to show — in the context of a standard structural gravity equation framework — that one could estimate *with consistency and precision* the infamous "trade elasticity" — even without any *ad valorem* measures of bilateral trade costs.

We started with a standard Krugman model of monopolistic competition with one sector and N countries. The theoretical model yielded a system of N^2 intra-national and international trade flow equations along with N market-clearing conditions (i.e., trade-balance conditions) in N^2 unknown intra-national and international trade flows and N unknown levels of nominal income. The system was represented by:

$$X_{ij} = Y_i Y_j \frac{(Y_i/L_i)^{-\sigma} t_{ij}^{1-\sigma}}{\sum_{k=1}^{N} Y_k (Y_k/L_k)^{-\sigma} t_{kj}^{1-\sigma}} \epsilon_{ij}, \tag{15}$$

where ϵ_{ij} is an error term. Market-clearance is ensured by assuming N equations:

$$Y_i = \sum_{j=1}^{N} X_{ij}, \quad i = 1, \ldots, N. \tag{16}$$

With the wage rate in each country i equal to its per capita GDP (Y/L), all individual prices, wage rates, and numbers of products were determined endogenously. Moreover, this framework benefited from three further aspects: First, with the system having N^2 X_{ij} and N Y_i unknowns, initial conditions had observable values and these variables could be compared to observed data. Second, with the number of firms/products in a country a function of its observable labor force and the wage rate determined by per capita GDP, individual prices (p_i) were determined, unlike the Anderson–van Wincoop framework. Third, the system allows asymmetric bilateral trade costs.

The true novelty of the study, however, was offering a new methodology for calculating the *trade elasticity* in the absence of *ad valorem* measures of bilateral trade costs; in the context of this Krugman-type model, the trade elasticity corresponded to the elasticity of substitution in consumption.[9] One purpose of this new methodology was to avoid weak and incomplete measures of bilateral trade costs, such as c.i.f./f.o.b. factors or tariff-rate data. Another purpose of this new methodology was to avoid estimating the elasticity of substitution of $(Y_i/L_i)^{-\sigma}$ as shown in equation (15) owing to possible correlation of $(Y_i/L_i)^{-\sigma}$ with the error term. The new methodology was to estimate a gravity equation with standard bilateral trade-cost proxies and exporter and importer fixed effects to obtain estimates $\widehat{t_{ij}^{1-\sigma}}$. Then, using equation (15) for the ratio $\hat{X}_{ij}/\hat{X}_{mj}$ (where $\hat{X}$ denotes the predicted value from the regression), one could determine an estimate of the trade elasticity, $\hat{\sigma}$. The trade elasticity estimate $\hat{\sigma}$ could then be used to calculate comparative statics also.

[9]Given the recent theoretical results in Baier *et al.* (2017), our methodology likely generalizes to other theoretical economic foundation models as well.

First, we applied our methodology to the famous Anderson and van Wincoop (2003) data set on Canadian–U.S. trade. Unlike previous papers, our methodology allowed estimation of σ. Since our first stage gravity-equation regressions used exporter and importer fixed effects, our coefficient estimates for distance and the border dummy were consistent. Our estimation implied an elasticity of substitution of 6.98. This value close to 7 was much larger than the *assumed* elasticity of substitution of 5 made in Anderson and van Wincoop (2003). Not surprisingly, with a larger elasticity of substitution estimate, the welfare gains from eliminating the Canadian–U.S. border were notably smaller.

Second, we also ran Monte Carlo experiments to show differential effects of estimation methodologies for coefficient estimates, general equilibrium comparative statics, and welfare from various techniques. Under the assumption of symmetric bilateral trade costs and the same trade elasticity, our suggested model had lower mean absolute errors for coefficient estimates than either OLS or the Anderson–van Wincoop NLLS technique, under either correlated or uncorrelated error terms in the Monte Carlo exercise. The mean absolute errors of the suggested model's general equilibrium trade effects and economic welfare were also lower than those using Anderson–van Wincoop, especially when the error terms were correlated. Even with uncorrelated errors and using fixed effects for both sets of estimation, under the assumption of asymmetric bilateral trade costs the suggested model had lower mean absolute errors for the welfare calculations.

Thus, Chapter 6 brought together several elements of earlier work, establishing in the context of the Krugman monopolistic competition model both a theoretical foundation for the gravity equation and a method for calculating estimates of the trade elasticity, general equilibrium comparative statics, and economic welfare in a consistent manner and using only observed data on trade flows and incomes. This work provided foundations for subsequent work on economic determinants of economic integration agreements, estimating effects of economic integration agreements on trade flows, and determinants of FDI stocks.

2. Determinants of Economic Integration Agreements

In 1996, Scott Baier also joined the Department of Finance at the University of Notre Dame and we started working on three research paths, the topics of which span Parts 1, 2, and 3. Motivated by trying to find consistent and precise estimates of economic integration agreements (EIAs) on trade flows using gravity equations, it occurred to us that such attempts were faced with endogeneity bias, i.e., country-pairs' trade flows are influenced by EIAs but also country-pairs that have considerable trade select into EIAs. This motivated us to first examine economic determinants of EIAs.

The main premise behind the three papers in this section is that the probability of a country-pair forming an EIA is related to the potential net welfare gains to the two countries' representative consumers from such an agreement. The first paper in this trilogy is Chapter 7, "Economic Determinants of Free Trade Agreements" with Scott Baier (Baier and Bergstrand, 2004). Guided by the qualitative choice framework in two papers by McFadden (1975, 1976), we let y^* denote the unobservable difference in utility levels from the formation of an EIA. We assumed y^* could be explained by a vector of explanatory economic characteristics, x, where $y^* = \beta_0 + x\beta + e$ where β is a vector of parameters and e is an error term with standard normal distribution. With y^* unobservable, we defined an indicator variable, FTA, which takes the value one if two countries have an FTA (indicating $y^* = min(\Delta U_i, \Delta U_j) > 0$), and 0 otherwise. The response probability, P, for FTA is $P(FTA = 1) = P(y^* > 0) = G(\beta_0 + x\beta)$, where $G()$ is the standard normal distribution.[10]

With this as background, our first task was to develop a theoretical model that suggested economic variables that explained the net welfare gains from an FTA (which was modeled as a reduction in tariff rates). A series of papers by Jeffrey Frankel with various coauthors — Frankel, Stein, and Wei (1995), Frankel, Stein, and Wei (1996), and Frankel, Stein, and Wei (1998) — and a book — Frankel (1997) — showed based upon a simple, one-sector

[10] In this paper, we focused on free trade agreements, or FTAs, and customs unions; we used FTA to capture both.

Krugman-type model with tariffs and intercontinental (but not intra-continental) transport costs the net welfare gains from natural (i.e., continental) and unnatural (i.e., different continents) FTAs. Inspired by these works, Baier and I extended their framework to include intra-continental transport costs, two sectors, and two factors in a world with three continents and two countries on each continent. Thus, we constructed a Krugman-type monopolistic competition structure inside a Heckscher–Ohlin framework with explicit tariffs, intra-continental transport costs, and intercontinental transport costs. All together, the model (including clearing conditions) had 204 equations in 204 unknowns.

Using a numerical version of the theoretical model, the theory suggested six empirically testable hypotheses: First, the net (welfare) gain from a bilateral FTA increases as distance between the countries decreased, as lower transport costs cause a larger trade volume which causes consumers to benefit more from an FTA. Second, the net gain for two continental trading partners (from a bilateral FTA) increased as their remoteness from the rest-of-world (ROW) increased, because the pair traded more. Third, the net gain increased as their economic sizes increased, as larger economies traded a larger number of varieties of goods. Fourth, the net gain increased the more similar their economic sizes. Fifth, the net gain decreased the larger the economic size of the ROW, due to trade diversion. Sixth, the net gain increased the larger are relative factor endowment differences (i.e., traditional Heckscher–Ohlin trade), but might eventually decline due to increased specialization.

After constructing a data base for pairings of 54 countries using 1996 data (and for robustness, 1960 data), we evaluated the hypotheses using our probit model.[11] All of the six theoretical hypotheses were supported. The probability of a bilateral FTA increased with lower distance, greater remoteness, larger and more similar economic sizes, greater bilateral relative factor endowments (up to a point), and smaller relative factor endowment differences relative to the ROW. The results held up under several robustness analyses. Finally, we

[11] The empirical model included FTAs and customs unions.

showed that the empirical probit model predicted correctly 85 percent of the 286 FTAs in our sample of 1431 pairs, and predicted correctly 97 percent of the remaining 1145 pairs with no FTA.

Baier and I returned to the topic a decade later in Chapter 8 with "Economic Determinants of Free Trade Agreements Revisited: Distinguishing Sources of Interdependence" along with Ronald Mariutto (Baier *et al.*, 2014). In 2008, Egger and Larch (2008) found empirical evidence of *interdependence* among FTA formations, in the spirit of Richard Baldwin's "domino effects," cf., Baldwin (1995), which is that the formation of an FTA begets subsequent FTA formations. Baldwin and Jaimovich (2012) provided further support for FTA contagion. However, Baier *et al.* (2014) delved deeper empirically into the *sources* of the interdependence. Two countries forming an FTA could be attributable to "own effects" associated with both countries already having FTAs with other countries; this would be associated with a "domino theory." Alternatively, a country-pair may respond to FTAs forming among countries in the ROW (with which neither has an FTA), which we refer to as a "cross effect" and is motivated by "competitive liberalization," as argued in Bergsten (1996). These provided two contrasting sources of "contagion."

The paper consisted of three major contributions: First, we used the same basic model of a one-sector Krugman monopolistic competition model with intra-continental and intercontinental transport costs among two countries on each of three continents as in Chapter 7. We considered first the cross effect. If two countries on continent 2 ($2A$ and $2B$) have an FTA, then when $1A$ and $1B$ on continent 1 form an FTA, the latter gain more from trade than if $FTA_{2A,2B}$ did not exist due to a larger volume of trade owing to trade diversion arising from $FTA_{2A,2B}$. However, the relative gain from the existence of $FTA_{2A,2B}$ is dampened by the real income (or terms-of-trade) loss for $1A$ and $1B$ from that initial trade diversion. Thus, we expect the "competitive liberalization" motive exists, but may be small. By contrast, if $FTA_{1A,2A}$ exists initially, then the gain from $FTA_{1A,1B}$ is greater than if $FTA_{1A,2A}$ was absent. Although the existence of $FTA_{1A,2A}$ lowers the volume of trade and gains from $FTA_{1A,1B}$, the higher real income and terms-of-trade from $FTA_{1A,2A}$ has a positive benefit on the gains from $FTA_{1A,1B}$. These factors are analogous to the notion of "tariff complementarity" in Bagwell and Staiger (1998). For plausible values of the model's few parameters, our simulations indicated that the own effect could be *30 times* that of the cross effect. We then turned to an empirical analysis to determine the relative size of these effects.

Second, we extended Chapter 7's data set from 54 countries for 1 year to 146 countries for 46 years (1960–2005).[12] Referring to Chapter 8 for details, we found that the increase in the (response) probability of FTA_{ijt} of either i or j having one more FTA with another country k was *50 times* that of the increase in the probability of FTA_{ijt} from one more FTA among another pair kl, which is consistent both qualitatively and quantitatively with our theoretical model.

Third, we introduced a Sensitivity–Specificity analysis to determine the ability of the model to predict correctly true positives (predicting an FTA for ij when one existed) and true negatives (predicting no FTA for ij when none existed). Noting that due to our very large panel of over 350,000 observations the unconditional probability of an FTA existing is only 3 percent (the share of 1's in our FTA sample). Using the cutoff probability of 0.03, our Sensitivity–Specificity analysis showed that our empirical model predicted an FTA correctly 91 percent of the time and predicted no-FTA correctly also 91 percent of the time. Thus, the empirical model supported the theoretical model, and the results implied that the own effect ("domino theory") tended to explain the growth of regionalism via contagion considerably more than the cross effect ("competitive liberalization").

While the previous two papers tended to explain the existence of preferential trade agreements (or PTAs) in a given year or years and the relative sources of PTA contagion, they did not provide guidance toward understanding the "timing" of the formation and enlargement of PTAs, which is the subject of Chapter 9, "Economic Determinants of the *Timing* of Preferential Trade Agreement Formations and Enlargements" with Peter Egger and Mario Larch (Bergstrand,

[12] In this paper, the term FTA denoted broadly free trade agreements, customs unions, common markets, and economic unions.

Egger, and Larch, 2016).[13] Like the previous two papers, this paper included a theoretical model and empirical work.[14] The empirical work was the main focus of this study as it departed from the previous two papers just discussed because it tried to explain the actual *year* that two countries formed an agreement; thus, we were trying to explain "events" for pairs of countries. In a data set of 10,518 pairings of 146 countries over 57 years (potentially, 463,289 observations), we were trying to explain only 1,560 events. Thus, we were trying to explain in-sample *very rare events.*

The econometric methodology chosen for our study was "duration analysis." In our context, the use of duration analysis is motivated in the following way. We assumed in a "No-PTA" state that two governments of i and j receive utility associated with trade flows (and consumption). Upon receiving the possibility to conclude a PTA at random intervals, the governments then decide about when to form one. The decision will depend on the comparison of the expected gains from membership with the reservation gains. Country-pair ij's transition rate from No-PTA to PTA in year t is reflected in the product of a constant (exogenous) rate at which PTAs become possible in any year (g) and the probability that they are acceptable in year t, $P_{ij}(t)$. The "hazard rate" for the duration analysis is then a function of the exogenous constant g and the probability of entering a PTA in year t, $P_{ij}(t)$.

The next step in the analysis was to motivate the economic, political, historical, and interdependence factors that influence the hazard rate; we will leave that discussion to the reader to explore in Chapter 9. Table 3 in the paper provides the results of the duration analysis, with the best specification for the hazard rate generating a pseudo-R^2 value of 0.36, keeping in mind that — due to data limitations — we were explaining 1,560 rare events in a sample of 340,726 observations.

The next part of the paper examined the success of predicting the 1,560 PTA events, either in the year of the event or during

[13]In this paper, PTAs included FTAs, customs unions, common markets, and economic unions, as in Chapter 8.

[14]The theoretical supplement is available at the publisher's web-site.

alternative windows (up to 10 years) preceding the event. To summarize, we found that our preferred specification of the empirical model could predict (in-sample) correctly 601 of the 1,560 rate events, or 39 percent, *in the actual year of the event.* Moreover, the preferred specification could predict correctly 1,076 of the 1,560 events, or 69 percent, within a window of 10 years leading up to the event. And in one of several robustness analyses, we showed that — using data only from 1970 onwards (or 37 years) — the model predicted correctly *77 percent* of the 1,560 events.

Finally, we pursued some out-of-sample predictions. First, using data up to year 2000, we could predict out-of-sample for 2001–2006 50 percent of the events correctly. The original Canadian–U.S. Free Trade Agreement, formed in 1989, was predicted to form in the window 1976–1989. The North American Free Trade Agreement, formed in 1994, was correctly predicted in 1994. The European Union (EU) started with the original European Economic Community (EEC) and incurred seven enlargements between 1973 and 2013. Six of the founding ten bilateral pairings (counting Belgium-Luxembourg as one country) were predicted in 1958, the first year of the EEC. All pairings of subsequent enlargements were correctly predicted in windows of 8–13 years prior to the enlargements. Moreover, for seven of the ten most likely post-2006 out-of-sample events, either a PTA formed during the period 2007–2013 or one had been proposed. Thus, economic factors can explain — and even predict — the timing of PTA formations and enlargements.

3. Estimating the Effects of Economic Integration Agreements

Around the turn of the millennium, I pursued with various coauthors the study of estimating the (partial) effects of economic integration agreements (EIAs) on trade flows. Having established economic factors that tended to explain EIA events, a major focus of the next four papers was to try to estimate *consistent and precise* partial (treatment) effects of EIAs. Later, Head and Mayer (2014) and Baier *et al.* (2017) would confirm *ex post* the importance of this undertaking. The trade-gravity-equation empirical literature, going back to Tinbergen

(1962), revealed enormous variance in estimates of partial effects of EIAs. Although there is good reason to expect variance in partial effects across different specific EIAs due to the variance in degrees of liberalization as well as interactions between the liberalizations and levels of variable trade costs, fixed trade costs, and development,[15] the instability and inconsistency of partial effect estimates suggested the presence of endogeneity bias.

In Chapter 10, "Do Free Trade Agreements Actually Increase Members' International Trade?" coauthored with Scott Baier (Baier and Bergstrand, 2007), we examined methodologically how to estimate consistent and precise partial effects of EIAs.[16] In the context of equation (1) or (2) above, partial effect estimates for the dummy variable representing EIA_{ijt} will be biased if the error term (ϵ_{ijt}) is correlated with EIA_{ijt}. What might cause these variables to be correlated? In light of papers in Part 2, many of the observable factors explaining empirically the likelihood of EIA_{ijt} are also observable factors that explain trade flows, X_{ijt}. Yet, ϵ_{ijt} may well include unobservable factors (to the econometrician) — such as policy barriers (cf., non-tariff barriers) tending to reduce trade between i and j — that are not accounted for by standard gravity equation RHS covariates, but may be correlated with the decision to form an EIA. As an example, suppose two countries have extensive unmeasurable domestic regulations (e.g., internal shipping regulations) that inhibit trade (causing ϵ_{ijt} to be negative). The likelihood of the two countries' governments selecting into an EIA may be high if there is a large expected welfare gain from potential bilateral trade creation if the EIA deepens liberalization beyond tariff barriers into domestic regulations (and other non-tariff barriers). Thus, EIA_{ijt} and the intensity of domestic regulations may be positively correlated in a cross-section of data, but the gravity equation error term ϵ_{ijt} and the intensity of domestic regulations may be negatively correlated.

[15] See Baier *et al.* (2018).

[16] In the empirical work, EIAs included FTAs, customs unions, common markets, and economic unions.

This reason suggests that EIA_{ijt} and ϵ_{ijt} are negatively correlated, and the EIA coefficient estimate will tend to be underestimated.

The traditional method to turn to in cross-section analysis for this issue is instrumental variables (IV). However, identification was a serious problem. Most of the factors that tend to explain EIAs in the first stage also tend to be factors that explain trade flows. Baier and Bergstrand (2007) concluded that it is virtually impossible to identify factors that explain EIAs that also do not explain trade flows, precluding identification.

However, panel data avoids these problems. If the unobservable factors that tend to cause EIA_{ijt} are slow moving (hence, essentially time-invariant), then panel data techniques using either bilateral fixed effects or first differencing can account for the endogeneity bias. In light of the theoretical foundations for trade gravity equations discussed earlier, Baier and Bergstrand (2007) suggested estimating the effects of EIAs using:

$$\ln X_{ijt} = \beta_0 + \beta_1(EIA_{ijt}) + \eta_{ij} + \delta_{it} + \psi_{jt} + \epsilon_{ijt}, \tag{17}$$

where η_{ij} is a country-pair fixed effect to capture all time-invariant unobservable bilateral factors influencing nominal trade flows, and δ_{it} and ψ_{jt} are exporter-time and importer-time fixed effects, respectively, to capture time-varying exporter and importer GDPs as well as all other time-varying country-specific unobservables in i and j influencing trade, *including* the exporter's and importers' "multilateral price/resistance" terms. We refer to this as the fixed-effects (FE) specification. It is important to note that in most gravity-equation applications using a comprehensive set of RHS variables, the vast bulk of "bilateral" trade-cost variables are time-invariant, such as bilateral distance, common border, common language, etc. Baier and Bergstrand (2007) showed that the partial effect of the typical EIA on nominal trade flows was about 0.76, implying that the typical EIA increased bilateral trade by about 114 percent after 10–15 years.

Baier and Bergstrand (2007) also employed an alternative specification using first-differencing (FD):

$$\Delta_5 \ln X_{ijt} = \beta_0 + \beta_1(\Delta_5 EIA_{ijt}) + \delta_{5,it} + \psi_{5,jt} + \upsilon_{5,ijt}, \tag{18}$$

where Δ_5 refers to first-differencing over 5 years. Note that the bilateral country-pair fixed effects are eliminated; however, the exporter-time ($\delta_{5,it}$) and importer-time ($\psi_{5,jt}$) fixed effects are retained to capture *changes* in the time-varying exporter and importer GDPs and multilateral price terms over the same 5-year period. Baier and Bergstrand (2007) showed that the partial effect of the typical EIA on nominal trade flows was about 0.61 using this approach, with the different estimate likely attributable to different assumptions regarding the error-term processes for ϵ_{ijt} and $v_{5,ijt}$.[17]

While Chapter 10 addressed consistent and precise measurement of average treatment effects (ATE) using a traditional parametric approach, an alternative *non-parametric* approach to estimating such effects is using "matching econometrics," which incorporates the use of "propensity scores." Chapter 11, "Estimating the Effects of Free Trade Agreements on International Trade Flows using Matching Econometrics" coauthored with Scott Baier (Baier and Bergstrand, 2009b), addressed this alternative. While the approach in Baier and Bergstrand (2007) mandated panel data, a matching-econometrics approach allowed the possibility of estimating (long-run) average treatment effects needing only cross-sectional data. A non-parametric matching approach addresses two issues that potentially complicate standard parametric approaches as in Baier and Bergstrand (2007). First, nonlinearities may exist; that is, the effects of EIAs on trade flows may be functions of levels of trade flows and of RHS covariates. Matching provides an alternative approach to log-linear gravity equations to estimate treatment effects without knowing *a priori* the functional relationship. Second, matching estimators allow ready estimation of average treatment effects when EIA treatment effects are subject to self-selection bias. Matching econometrics provide a simple method to form treatment and control groups by selecting on observable covariates and comparing observations drawn from the "same" distribution. For each country pair with an EIA, we constructed a control group of country-pairs with nearly identical economic characteristics but having no EIA; the average difference in

[17]Essentially, $v_{5,ijt} = \epsilon_{ijt} - \epsilon_{ij,t-5}$.

trade flows between the pairs with EIAs and their control groups provides an average estimate of "treatment." This methodology allowed us to provide the very first cross-sectional non-parametric matching estimates of long-run partial (treatment) effects on trade flows.[18]

We summarize the two main findings from the study: First, we found across many settings and years that the matching estimates of treatment effects are much more stable and economically plausible than typical cross-sectional OLS treatment effects. Moreover, we estimated average treatment effects on the "treated" (ATTs) as well as just average treatment effects, or ATEs (on treated and untreated). The ATT estimates indicated that EIAs increased members' trade by economically and statistically significant amounts for each of the 9 years of our sample.

Next, we used this approach to evaluate the trade effects of two historically prominent EIAs. First, the average treatment effects for a typical pair of members of the original European Economic Community, or EEC, (that is, the ATT) were positive and economically significant from 1960 to 1970. By 1970, the EEC's Treaty of Rome had more than doubled on average the six members' bilateral trade. However, the enlargements of the Community in the early 1970s, the EC-EFTA free trade agreements, and the economic liberalization of Central and Eastern European countries and their subsequent EIAs with EC and EFTA members in the early 1990s reduced the *original* six members' bilateral trade significantly (i.e., trade diversion). Second, we found that the treatment effects for a typical pair of countries in the original Central American Common Market (CACM) were positive and rose monotonically until 1970. However, in the early 1970s and early 1980s, the treatment effects were considerably lower, rebounding only in the 1990s. These estimates supported anecdotal evidence that the CACM flourished in the 1960s, but as some member countries faced considerable political instability and cross-border armed conflicts that had begin in 1969 and then again in 1979,

[18]While the paper's title used the term free trade agreement, the sample was similar to that in Baier and Bergstrand (2007) and included FTAs, customs unions, common markets, and economic unions.

CACM became less effective between 1970 and 1990, reinvigorated by the nations' presidents in the 1990s.

With our enormous data set on all economic integration agreements for 37,830 pairings of 195 countries (in both directions) from 1950 through 2005 categorized by the six different types of agreements — one-way preferential, two-way preferential, FTA, customs union, common market, and economic union — Scott Baier and I, along with Michael Feng, decided to pursue analyzing partial (treatment) effects *by type of agreement.* Moreover, by 2010 the importance of distinguishing between *extensive margin* versus *intensive margin* (trade) effects of trade policies and costs, as emphasized in Melitz (2003) and Chaney (2008), had taken hold. With the insight in Arkolakis, Costinot, and Rodriguez-Clare (2012) that the gravity equation was a critical and central element to help quantify the gains from trade, we pursued a comprehensive examination of the extensive margin, intensive margin, and overall trade effects of economic integration agreements in Chapter 12, "Economic Integration Agreements and the Margins of International Trade" (Baier *et al.*, 2014).

Although numerous studies have examined empirically the margins and overall trade effects of individual (country-specific) trade-policy liberalizations, there is not yet a comprehensive study of EIAs' effects on the various margins of trade. Our paper provided the first evidence using gravity equations of both extensive and intensive (*goods*) margins being affected by EIAs employing a panel data set with a large number of country pairs (pairings of 149 countries), product categories, and EIAs from 1960 to 2000, using the Hummels and Klenow (2005) methodology for constructing extensive and intensive (goods) margins. The paper provided the first evidence of the differential (partial) effects on these margins of various "types" of EIAs; we differentiated EIAs by one-way preferential agreements, two-way preferential agreements, free trade agreements, and deeper integration agreements (which combined customs unions, common markets, and economic unions, due to the few numbers of agreements within each of these categories). Moreover, given our long time series, we were able to differentiate the "timing" of intensive versus extensive margin effects.

Theoretically, we motivated our empirical gravity equation with a Melitz model as summarized in the work of Arkolakis, Costinot, and Rodriguez-Clare (2012):

$$X_{ijt}^m = N_{it}^m Y_{jt}^m \left(\frac{(a_{Lit}^m)^{-\gamma^m} w_{it}^{-\gamma^m} \tau_{ijt}^{-\gamma^m} f_{ijt}^{-[\gamma^m/(\sigma^m-1)-1]}}{\sum_{k=1}^K N_{kt}^m (a_{Lkt}^m)^{-\gamma^m} w_{kt}^{-\gamma^m} \tau_{kjt}^{-\gamma^m} f_{kjt}^{-[\gamma^m/(\sigma^m-1)-1]}} \right), \tag{19}$$

where X_{ijt}^m is the trade flow from i to j in year t in "good" m, N_{it}^m is the number of firms in i (exporting and non-exporting) that produce output in good m, Y_{jt}^m is the expenditure in j on good m, a_{Lit}^m (defined as unit input requirements of labor) is the lower bound of the Pareto distribution of productivities in m in i, γ^m is an index of productivity heterogeneity among firms in good m, w_{it} is the wage rate in i, τ_{ijt} is variable trade costs of exporting i's products into j, f_{ijt} is fixed export costs from i to j, and σ^m is the elasticity of substitution in consumption. Note that the relative price term in large parentheses is a standard representation of relative prices in the gravity equation as discussed earlier in Chapter 6, but now also reflecting productivity heterogeneity (through a_{Lit}^m and γ^m) and fixed exporting costs (f_{ijt}), cf., Arkolakis *et al.* (2012).

In the context of these models, variable trade costs, τ_{ijt}, affect X_{ijt}^m via both the intensive and extensive margins. As Chaney (2008) demonstrates in his Melitz-type model, $\gamma^m = (\sigma^m - 1) + [\gamma^m - (\sigma^m - 1)]$. $\sigma^m - 1$ represents the intensive margin elasticity of variable trade costs, whereas, $\gamma^m - (\sigma^m - 1)$ is the extensive margin elasticity of variable trade costs. For finite means in the theory, $\gamma^m/(\sigma^m - 1)$ must exceed one. Empirically, Chaney (2008) notes empirical estimates of $\gamma^m/(\sigma^m - 1)$ range between 1.5 and 2. Hence, these models suggest that the intensive margin variable-trade-cost elasticity *should be larger* than the extensive margin variable-trade-cost elasticity. For instance, if $\gamma = 1.5(\sigma - 1)$, the intensive margin elasticity is twice as large as the extensive margin elasticity; if $\gamma = 2(\sigma - 1)$, the intensive margin elasticity is equal to the extensive margin elasticity.[19]

The theoretical model allowed using specifications similar to equations (17) and (18) above. As in the paper, we focus on FD specifications. The main results were the following. First, we found that extensive margins, intensive margins, and overall trade were all significantly related to the various types of EIAs, with the magnitudes of the effects in line with expectations: deeper EIAs had larger effects on all margins. For instance, including current and lagged effects, one-way PTAs increased (overall) trade by 41 percent, FTAs increased trade by 60 percent, and deep EIAs (with customs unions, common markets, and economic unions) increased trade by 101 percent after 10 years.

Second, as the theory discussed above predicted, intensive margin effects tended to dominate extensive margin effects. For one-way PTAs, intensive and extensive effects were 0.273 and 0.128, respectively. For FTAs, intensive and extensive margin effects were 0.302 and 0.169, respectively. For deep agreements, intensive and extensive margins were 0.460 and 0.237, respectively.[20]

Third, as expected, intensive margin (or trade of existing firms) effects tended to arise earlier than extensive margin (trade of new firms), since new firms require start-up costs. For all four types of agreements, the size of the current effect on the intensive margin (extensive margin) tended to exceed (be below) the size of the lagged effect.

The final paper in this section brings together three strands of the literature in international trade that, up to 2015, had been largely treated separately. Chapter 13, "Economic Integration Agreements,

[19]However, f_{ijt} works entirely through the extensive margin, so that there is no clear theoretical hypothesis for the relative sizes of intensive and extensive margin effects of a given EIA formation. Yet, in light of estimates of $\gamma/(\sigma-1)$ between 1.5 and 2, this additional fixed-trade-cost elasticity can range feasibly only between 0.5 and 1. Such an effect is dwarfed by the intensive margin elasticity $(\sigma-1)$ with likely values between 4 and 9 (if σ ranges between 5 and 10), under certain assumptions. The key assumption pertains to the effect of an EIA on fixed costs versus variable costs and is discussed more fully in the paper.

[20]These estimates were the Set 2 estimates in the paper's Table 1.

Border Effects, and Distance Elasticities in the Gravity Equation" coauthored with Mario Larch and Yoto V. Yotov (Bergstrand, Larch, and Yotov, 2015), addressed three issues. First, consider the gravity equation described by equation (19) above. Baier and Bergstrand (2007) and Baier *et al.* (2014) assumed that variation *over time* in τ_{ijt} and in f_{ijt} could only occur from trade-policy changes, such as free trade or deeper agreements.[21] Most bilateral non-policy trade costs are captured by the inclusion of time-invariant variables such as bilateral distance, adjacency dummy, language dummy, etc. or by time-invariant bilateral fixed effects. However, there may exist unobservable (to the econometrician) *time-varying bilateral* variables that influence τ_{ijt} and f_{ijt} and consequently influence international relative to intra-national trade. To address this, we augmented specification (17) in the following way: We included measures of *intra-national* trade in our sample. Since gross output data is available for manufactures, we could subtract a country's manufactures exports (which are measured on a gross, not value-added, basis) to obtain intra-national trade in manufactures. Next, we included a dummy variable for unobservable time-varying bilateral variation in international relative to intranational trade. We multiplied the time-invariant dummy $INTERNATIONAL_{ij}$ with a dummy variable for each year D_t to obtain $INTER_{ijt}$, which captured unobserved changes in international relative to intra-national trade costs.[22]

Second, one of the side benefits of this augmented specification is that the coefficient estimate for $INTER_{ijt}$ reveals the changing effect of international borders over time. Estimates of the well-known "(international) border effect" have been have been scrutinized for decades following the publication of McCallum (1995). Researchers have questioned the very large cross-section estimates of the border effect for years. Our methodology addresses measuring only *changes* in the barrier effect of an international border over time, allowing

[21] Baier and Bergstrand (2007) and Baier *et al.* (2014) allowed for the effects of (most) currency unions, as such unions frequently occur in economic unions (such as the Eurozone).

[22] We also allowed a specification for trend effects of bilateral unobserved heterogeneity.

the bilateral fixed effects to capture the pair-varying effects of an international border on the level of trade.

Third, we pursued a battery of robustness analyses for our findings. In one particular robustness analysis, we replaced our novel $INTER_{ijt}$ variable with an interaction of the log of bilateral distance $DIST_{ij}$ with the year dummies D_t as well as various other time-invariant proxies for transaction costs such as the language dummy with the year dummies. One of the side benefits of this alternative specification is that one can estimate whether the "distance elasticity" is changing over time. Meta analyses of the distance elasticity as in Disdier and Head (2008) suggest that distance elasticities have not fallen; our specification allows a panel-data based evaluation in contrast to typical cross-section analyses of this issue.

We found three interesting empirical results in this paper: First, we found evidence that the partial effect estimates of EIAs from specifications such as those in Baier and Bergstrand (2007) and Baier *et al.* (2014) were biased upward by not including the $INTER_{ijt}$ variables to account for unobservable changes in international relative to intra-national trade costs. Second, our results suggested that previous estimates of the declining effect (in absolute terms) of international borders had been biased upward. We found that the depressing effect (on trade) of international borders was only about 2.4 percent annually from 1990 to 2002. Third, we found that earlier estimates of the declining effect of distance on international trade found in Yotov (2012) were biased upward (in absolute terms) by not accounting for the effects of endogenous EIAs and unobserved bilateral heterogeneity. Our estimates suggested that the effect of distance on international trade declined about 1.2 percent annually from 1990 to 2002.

4. Foreign Direct Investment, Foreign Affiliate Sales, and Multinational Enterprises

With the turn of the century and increased attention worldwide to "globalization," I became increasingly interested in broadening our understanding of economic forces behind globalization and decided to turn to acquiring a better understanding of FDI alongside international trade, two of the three major forces of economic globalization (alongside migration). The gravity equation had also been used frequently to explain bilateral FDI stocks (and occasionally flows). However, there was a much smaller empirical literature on this. Moreover, even by year 2000 — in sharp contrast to the trade literature — there was no theoretical foundation for the gravity equation for FDI (or foreign affiliate sales) akin to the types of models discussed in Part 1 of this book. In fact, even as late as 2011, James Anderson wrote, "Foreign Direct Investment has been successfully explained by gravity structures without theoretical foundation" (Anderson, 2011, p. 155).[23] Motivated by these considerations, Peter Egger and I pursued a research agenda on the gravity equation for FDI. The three papers in this section address determinants of international trade flows, FDI stocks, foreign affiliate sales, free trade agreements, and bilateral investment treaties in a three-country, three-factor world with national and multinational firms.

The first paper in this section, Chapter 14, "A Knowledge-and-Physical-Capital Model International Trade Flows, Foreign Direct Investment, and Multinational Enterprises" coauthored with Peter Egger (Bergstrand and Egger, 2007), focused predominantly on generating a theoretical foundation simultaneously for gravity equations of international trade flows, FDI stocks, and foreign affiliate sales. Two seminal papers published in 1984 laid the groundwork for formal theoretical foundations for foreign affiliate sales and the role of multinational firms. Helpman (1984) had laid down a formal theoretical foundation for the existence of vertical multinational enterprises and Markusen (1984) had laid down a formal theoretical foundation for the existence of horizontal multinational firms. Markusen along with various coauthors (such as Keith Maskus and Anthony Venables) fleshed out more economic details of multinational firm behavior in the 1990s, utilizing numerical general equilibrium models to capture the complexities of a world with two countries, two

[23]Later, Anderson adds that "More recent work has made progress. . . ." (p. 155). Moreover, as part of this recent work he cites the first paper in this section.

goods, two factors (skilled and unskilled labor), international policy and non-policy trade costs, national firms, and multinational firms, often referred to as the "Knowledge–Capital" model. The bulk of this is expertly summarized in Markusen (2002).

However, Peter Egger and I noticed two prominent shortcomings of the $2 \times 2 \times 2$ Knowledge–Capital model: First, one of the implications of the model is that — in a $2 \times 2 \times 2$ world with identical absolute and relative factor endowments — multinational firms would *completely displace* national (exporting) firms; international trade between two identical economies would be zero. This puzzling theoretical finding appeared to "fly in the face" of the enormous empirical trade gravity equation literature that showed that bilateral trade between a pair of countries would be *at a maximum* when their economies were identical in economic size (all else constant). Second, although simulations of the $2 \times 2 \times 2$ Knowledge–Capital model showed that the country-pair's foreign affiliate sales were positively related to the sum of their GDPs and negatively related to differences in their economic sizes, this literature had not yet provided a theoretical foundation for the gravity relationship between bilateral foreign affiliate sales and the product of their GDPs. Moreover, as Markusen noted frankly in his book, "the models in this book are addressed more closely to affiliate output and sales than to investment stocks" (Markusen, 2002, p. 8). Hence, the Knowledge–Capital model could provide no formal theoretical foundation for the gravity equation for *FDI stocks.*[24]

In our extension of the "Knowledge–Capital" (KC) model, Egger and I introduced a third factor (physical capital) and a third country (Rest-of-World, or ROW). Physical capital served several purposes for our theoretical findings. In the KC model, unskilled labor was internationally mobile with no transport costs and used singularly in producing a homogeneous good, produced in a perfectly competitive market with constant returns to scale. Multinational enterprises

[24]The "trade" literature, working in (long-run) general equilibrium, has generally focused only on explaining bilateral FDI stocks, not flows. The analysis of FDI flows has been more the purview of (dynamic) international finance models.

(MNEs) were distinguished by the ability to share costlessly across international borders the "knowledge capital" of its skilled workers (except for a fixed setup cost of an affiliate); hence, the knowledge capital of skilled labor was *non-rival* across geographic markets. By contrast, claims on physical capital introduced in our model were assumed to be *rival* and could only be transferred across markets with a cost. In the context of our model, FDI was a claim abroad on physical capital, for which factor rewards would be paid to the home country. Moreover, in the KC model without physical capital, actual *plants* could not exist; in our model physical capital was necessary to setup a "plant."

The importance of a third factor, physical capital, to resolve the puzzle in Markusen (2002) — that MNEs of identical countries completely displace trade of national exporting firms (NEs) — is readily shown, as long as MNEs require both skilled labor and physical capital in setting up foreign affiliates (and a plant setup requiring physical capital). In the KC model, setups of firms and plants both require skilled labor. If transport costs of goods between two countries are sufficiently high and the ratio of headquarters scale economies (fixed costs) relative to plant scale economies (fixed costs) is large (small), then the relative cost for headquarters country i of supplying a foreign market j is low relative to exporting from i. In a two-country world with identical absolute and relative factor endowments and differentiated goods produced by i and j, only MNEs will exist to serve each other's markets and trade must be totally displaced (due to the scarcity of skilled labor).[25] By contrast, in our model *plant setups* require physical capital. Hence, as two countries i and j become more similar in economic size, the replacement of NEs by MNEs does require more skilled labor for affiliate setups but the net demand for skilled labor falls due to the need for physical capital by MNEs to setup plants in foreign markets. With the relative demand for skilled labor falling, and hence lowering its price, this allows NEs to coexist

[25] Only for a (highly unlikely) unique combination of trade costs and ratio of national-to-multinational firm setup costs can MNEs and national firms coexist.

with MNEs — even when both countries are identical in absolute and relative factor endowments.[26]

The introduction of a third country (ROW) into the model also helped to resolve two limitations of the two-country model. First, in a world with only two countries, bilateral and multilateral trade flows and balances are the same; one needs a third country (we introduce the Rest-of-World) to generate differential behavior of bilateral and multilateral trade. Second, in our two-country world with the third factor, exports between two countries are *non*-monotonic functions of GDP similarity, which conflicts with empirical evidence. By adding the third country, bilateral trade flows, bilateral foreign affiliate sales, and bilateral FDI are all monotonic functions of GDP similarity. Simulations showed gravity-like relationships between bilateral trade flows, bilateral foreign affiliates sales, and bilateral FDI with GDP sizes and similarities.

Although most of the equations describing the underlying theoretical model are presented in the paper, we attach Appendix A to the end of Chapter 14 to provide the remaining equations for conditional factor demands, factor-market clearing, and multilateral current account balances. The same model structure undergirded Chapters 15 and 16.[27]

A prominent shortcoming of Bergstrand and Egger (2007) was the assumption of identical relative factor endowments and thus no vertical MNEs.[28] Moreover, at the same time, the international trade/MNE literature had been struggling to "find evidence" of vertical MNEs (VMNEs). For instance, Markusen and Maskus (2002) reject the KC model in favor of bilateral foreign affiliate sales being driven by horizontal MNEs (HMNEs). In fact, in a summary of the empirical literature, Blonigen (2005) concludes that, "It seems clear

[26]Consequently, MNEs and NEs can coexist for a wide range of parameter values for transport costs and the ratio of national-to-multinational firm setup costs; the proof is in the paper.

[27]In Bergstrand and Egger (2007), there is a typo in the free entry and exit conditions (14a)–(14c); on the RHS of each condition, the term $(\epsilon - 1)$ should be replaced by the term (-1), since $\epsilon < 0$.

[28]Anderson (2011) noted this limitation.

that vertical motivations are not prevalent in the general FDI patterns." One of the main goals of writing Chapter 15, "Shouldn't Physical Capital *Also* Matter for Multinational Enterprise Activity?" with Peter Egger (Bergstrand and Egger, 2013a), was to find evidence of VMNEs.[29] A second goal of this paper, more closely associated with its title, is that — despite the empirical prominence of home country physical capital–labor ratios for explaining bilateral FDI flows — physical capital had been ignored in the theoretical literature based largely on the KC model in the first decade of the 2000s. Consequently, our goal in Chapter 15 was to determine if a third factor — physical capital — was important theoretically and empirically in finding evidence of VMNE activity. We adopted the same theoretical model as in Bergstrand and Egger (2007) but now allowed relative factor endowment differences.[30]

Before exploring the implications of our theoretical model, we first explained why it was difficult to find evidence for VMNEs in the context of Markusen's $2 \times 2 \times 2$ KC model. The limitation of the $2 \times 2 \times 2$ framework largely precluded finding — in Edgeworth box space — relative factor endowment configurations where VMNE headquarters could be clearly distinguished from HMNE headquarters, and thus quelched from the start the ability of the KC model to guide predictions of VMNE activity.

Using a numerical version of the $3 \times 3 \times 2$ Bergstrand and Egger (2007) model calibrated to allow relative factor endowment differences, we were able to show that horizontal and vertical MNEs' headquarters surface in different parts of the Edgeworth box relating the parent country's skilled labor share (of the parent's and host's endowments) relative to its physical capital share. The key economic insight was that horizontal MNE headquarters will be relatively more abundant than vertical MNE headquarters in countries that are abundant in physical capital relative to skilled labor, because of the multi-plant (single-plant) structure of horizontal (vertical) MNEs — assuming

[29] In fact, a previously circulated unpublished version of this paper was originally titled, "Finding Vertical Multinational Enterprises."

[30] The appendix attached to the end of Chapter 15 describes the calibration of the numerical model for this paper.

plants (headquarters) use physical capital (skilled labor) relatively intensively in their setups. The theoretical relationships suggested augmenting empirical foreign affiliate sales gravity equations with fourth-order polynomials of the parent's skilled labor share alongside those of the parent's physical capital share.

Interestingly, the empirical model worked very well. First, the parent country's skilled labor share (of the two countries' skilled labor endowment) had the expected fourth-order polynomial relationship with bilateral foreign affiliate sales. All of the polynomial's coefficient estimates had the expected signs and were statistically significant. Second, the parent country's physical capital share also had the expected fourth-order polynomial relationship with bilateral foreign affiliate sales. All of this polynomial's coefficient estimates had the expected signs and were statistically significant. Third, the parent's unskilled labor share had the expected negative relationship with foreign affiliates sales and was statistically significant. Finally, empirically predicted values (from the regressions) of bilateral foreign affiliates sales matched well the theoretically predicted foreign affiliate sales generated from the numerical general equilibrium model.

The final chapter in this book, Chapter 16, "What Determines BITs?" with Peter Egger (Bergstrand and Egger, 2013b), returns to a research agenda that began almost a decade prior. "What Determines BITs?" is a paper about theoretical and empirical economic determinants of bilateral investment treaties (BITs). With the previous two papers published, the gravity equation for FDI now had formal theoretical foundations that would make it feasible for analyzing the effects of BITs on bilateral FDI stocks and potentially on economic welfare. However, empirically the same endogeneity bias that contaminated earlier gravity-equation analyses using EIA dummies was likely also present for BITs and FDI stocks. Before proceeding, it was important first to understand the economic determinants of BITs.

The theoretical models just discussed in Chapters 14 and 15 made it clear that international trade flows and FDI stocks were determined simultaneously and both were functions of similar economic variables. Moreover, the model of Chapters 14 and 15 was composed of two goods — one a differentiated manufactured good produced under increasing returns in a monopolistically competitive market *a la* Krugman and the other a homogeneous good — with national exporting firms along with vertical and horizontal MNEs in multiple countries. The model lent itself well to the approach used in Baier and Bergstrand (2004) in Chapter 7 because of the core elements common to most of the papers in this volume. The key elements affecting trade flows, foreign affiliate sales, and FDI stocks fell into three categories: (1) economic size and similarity, (2) bilateral trade and investment costs, and (3) relative factor endowments. Consequently, the economic factors that would likely predict the net benefits from an economic integration agreement (in this paper, referred to as a PTA) and/or a BIT would be among these three groups, and thus we organized our theoretical hypotheses and numerical simulations around these.

The numerical general equilibrium model suggested six clear hypotheses: First, the net utility gain from (and consequently the likelihood of) a PTA and a BIT between two countries is a positive function of their economic size. Second, the net utility gain from a PTA and a BIT between two countries is a positive function of the similarity of their economic sizes. Third, the net utility gain from a PTA between two countries is a negative function of their natural bilateral trade costs and a positive function of their natural bilateral investment costs. Fourth, the net utility gain from a BIT between two countries is a negative function of their bilateral investment costs and a positive function of their natural trade costs. Fifth, the net utility gain from a PTA between two countries is decreasing in the difference between the two countries' ratios of physical capital to unskilled labor. Sixth, the net utility gain from a BIT between two countries is increasing in the abundance of skilled labor relative to physical capital and unskilled labor in either country.

Empirically, the first two hypotheses were relatively easy to test since they employed GDP data. Both of these hypotheses were confirmed strongly. GDP sizes and similarities had positive and statistically significant effects on the likelihood of a PTA and of a BIT. Larger and more similarly sized economies benefited more from a PTA on a larger number of varieties of goods traded. Larger and more similarly sized economies benefitted more from a BIT on a larger number of varieties of goods produced by HMNEs and their affiliates.

The second two hypotheses were slightly more difficult to test as there are no direct measures of bilateral *ad valorem* natural trade costs τ_{ij} and of bilateral *ad valorem* natural investment costs γ_{ij}. In the model, *ad valorem* tariffs on imports were represented by a variable b_{ij} and a PTA would reduce that to zero; expropriation risk — which a BIT would reduce to zero — was represented by a variable g_{ij}. As in most trade gravity studies, natural trade costs were proxied empirically by bilateral distance and dummies for adjacency and common language were expected to be negatively related to natural trade costs. Natural investment costs were proxied for by a measure of political instability. As expected, the likelihood of a PTA was negatively related to natural trade costs, proxied by distance,[31] and positively related to the political instability proxy for natural investment costs. As expected, the likelihood of a BIT was positively related to political stability (hence, negatively related to natural investment costs) and negatively related to adjacency and common language (and hence positively related to natural trade costs).

The third two hypotheses were the most difficult to test. Of these two, the fifth hypothesis was the easier to address. We could use our data on factor shares to generate a variable, $KURatio_{ij}$, that measured the absolute differences in the natural logs of the ratios of physical capital to unskilled labor of the two countries i and j; this was expected to have a negative relationship to the likelihood of a PTA. A larger difference between capital-unskilled labor ratios raises the volume of trade of NEs, but this is more than offset by the utility loss from fewer HMNEs. $KURatio_{ij}$ did have a negative and statistically significant relationship with the probability of a PTA. The sixth hypothesis required creating a novel variable. The net utility gain from a BIT between two countries is increasing in the abundance of skilled labor relative to physical capital and unskilled

[31]Adjacency and common language dummies had positive effects, as expected, since these are inversely related to trade costs.

labor in either country. As discussed in the paper, this relationship is represented by a positive correlation between the probability of a BIT and the variable $KUDiff_{ij}$ where:

$$KUDiff_{ij} \equiv \ln \mid (k_i^2 + u_i^2)^{1/2}\mu_{ij} - (k_j^2 + u_j^2)^{1/2}\mu_{ij} \mid, \qquad (20)$$

and

$$\mu_{ij} \equiv \frac{1}{(k_i^2 + u_i^2)^{1/2} + (k_j^2 + u_j^2)^{1/2}}, \qquad (21)$$

where k_i (u_i) is country i's share of the two countries physical capital (unskilled labor) endowment. Intuitively, VMNEs and HMNEs will be prominent when skilled labor is abundant relative to physical capital and to unskilled labor, because such a country would have a comparative advantage in setting up headquarters and a comparative disadvantage in production at home. The probability of a BIT was positively and statistically significantly related to $KUDiff_{ij}$. The empirical work provided strong support for the paper's theoretical hypotheses.

5. Conclusions and Future Directions

Hopefully the reader has appreciated the logic, consistency, and quantitative approach of this set of papers aimed toward improving our "understanding globalization." As mentioned in the introduction, I am deeply indebted to my multiple coauthors for their contributions to this research agenda and this set of papers. Moreover, I am grateful that we have been able to build upon the "shoulders of giants" and whose papers I have cited throughout this book.

However, the task of developing a logical, consistent, and quantitative theoretical and empirical foundation for understanding economic globalization will never end. Needless to say, the trade flow, trade policy, foreign affiliate sales, and FDI literatures continued to evolve in the subsequent years since the latest publication of this book. Notably, the trade and FDI literatures have embraced the notion that firms' productivities are heterogeneous and that there are fixed costs to export to (or produce in) foreign markets. In the following, I will assume that readers are familiar with the "Melitz model" of international trade, summarized expertly in Redding (2011). With this in mind, I briefly describe three papers that provide direction for the literatures.

The first paper, tentatively titled "Distorted Gravity *Redux*: Firm Heterogeneity, Increasing Costs, and the Gravity Equation in International Trade" coauthored with Stephen Cray and Antoine Gervais, returns to the theoretical foundations for the gravity equation in the context of a Melitz model — but allowing for increasing marginal costs *a la* Bergstrand (1985). The "trade elasticity" is central to the analysis of the trade and welfare effects of changes in trade costs. With the Melitz model of international trade, trade economists now focus on two key parameters determining this elasticity: the elasticity of substitution in consumption determines the intensive margin elasticity and the index of heterogeneity of firms' productivities (less the substitution elasticity in consumption) determines the extensive-margin elasticity. Yet, all such models assume constant marginal (production) costs. In reality, the brunt of recent empirical evidence confirms increasing marginal costs, cf., Hottman *et al.* (2016). With this in mind, we will extend the Melitz model to allow variable marginal costs and show how the extensive-margin and intensive-margin elasticities are modified to capture the degree of curvature of the marginal cost curve. Furthermore, we can extend the Feenstra (2010) extension of the Melitz model and show how the curvature of each economy's transformation curve between domestic and export outputs and the levels national wage rates are altered. The main point is that there are now *three* important empirically motivated parameters in the Melitz model likely determining the general equilibrium effects of trade-cost changes on trade flows and economic welfare.

The second paper, "Heterogeneous Effects of Economic Integration Agreements" coauthored with Scott Baier and Matthew Clance (Baier *et al.*, 2018), in the *Journal of Development Economics* returns to the topic of estimating the partial (and general) equilibrium effects of EIAs. It is now widely accepted that EIAs and other trade-policy liberalizations contribute to nations' economic growth and development and help alleviate poverty. However, the economic effects of such policies vary across countries' economic structures; for instance, developing countries face higher fixed trade costs (partly due to higher government border-crossing costs and weaker port infrastructures). Extending a standard Melitz general equilibrium trade model with firm heterogeneity, we show how variable-cost and fixed-cost "trade elasticities" associated with trade liberalizations are heterogeneous and endogenous to *levels* of country-pairs' bilateral policy and non-policy, variable and fixed trade costs — even allowing for CES preferences and an untruncated Pareto distribution of productivities. Using associated comparative statics, we provide several explicit predictions of the heterogeneous (variable- *and* fixed-cost) bilateral extensive-margin, intensive-margin, and trade elasticities and provide empirical support for the theoretical hypotheses. Finally, we demonstrate the relevance of these theoretical and empirical results for *ex ante* trade-flow predictions of potential EIAs.

The third paper, tentatively titled "The Gravity Equation for Foreign Direct Investment: Some Microeconomic Foundations and Empirical Evidence" coauthored with Scott Baier, Mitch Gainer, and Tao Xu, addresses three issues at the nexus of the theoretical and empirical literatures on long-run economic determinants of bilateral FDI stocks using the "gravity equation." First, FDI and foreign affiliates production and sales (FAS) — though related — are *not* the same. Despite a developed literature on theoretical relationships between two countries' GDP sizes and their bilateral FAS, there is *no* (closed-form) formal theoretical foundation for a gravity equation of FDI explained by home and host GDPs with *unit GDP elasticities*. We introduce a second factor — capital (alongside labor) — into a Melitz model of multinational production (and also allow an endogenous home-versus-host financing decision) and generate a theoretical gravity equation of FDI and the product of both countries' GDPs — with unit elasticities. Moreover, we introduce a non-parametric quantile regression econometric approach — that is robust to heteroskedasticity and misspecification bias — to confirm empirically the unit elasticities across ventiles. Second, despite a prominent survey's claim that (capital-scarce) developing economies "are more likely" to be the destination of FDI, a recent Bayesian statistical analysis suggests that FDI is explained well by a parsimonious log-linear specification *without* host per capita GDP. Our novel two-factor Melitz model of FAS and FDI generates a role for home and host per capita GDPs (reflecting capital–labor ratios) with asymmetric, varying elasticities. Our quantile regression approach allows for varying home and host per capita GDP elasticities across ventiles, sensitive to the endogenous shares of local (versus parent) financing and consequently the *level* of FDI. Third, while FAS must be positive or zero, FDI can be positive, zero, *or negative*; affiliates can be net lenders to parents. Our quantile regression analysis allows estimation of the FDI gravity equation at the lowest ventile — where FDI is *negative*.

References

Aitken, N. D. (1973): The Effect of EEC and EFTA on European Trade: A Temporal Cross-Section Analysis, *American Economic Review* 63 (5), 881–892.

Anderson, J. (1979): A Theoretical Foundation for the Gravity Equation, *American Economic Review*, 69 (1), 106–116.

Anderson, J. (2011): The Gravity Model, *Annual Review of Economics* 3, 133–160.

Anderson, J. and van Wincoop, E. (2003): Gravity with Gravitas: A Solution to the Border Puzzle, *American Economic Review* 93 (1), 170–192.

Arkolakis, C., Costinot, A. and Rodriguez-Clare, A. (2012): New Trade Models, Same Old Gains?, *American Economic Review* 102 (1), 94–130.

Bagwell, K. and Staiger, R. (1998): Regionalism and Multilateralism Tariff Cooperation, in J. Pigott and A. Woodland (eds.) *International Trade Policy and the Pacific Rim* (St. Martin's Press, New York).

Baier, S. and Bergstrand, J. (2001): The Growth of World Trade: Tariffs, Transport Costs, and Income Similarity, *Journal of International Economics* 53 (1), 1–27.

Baier, S. and Bergstrand, J. (2004): Economic Determinants of Free Trade Agreements, *Journal of International Economics* 64 (1), 29–63.

Baier, S. and Bergstrand, J. (2007): Do Free Trade Agreements Actually Increase Members' International Trade?, *Journal of International Economics* 71 (1), 72–95.

Baier, S. and Bergstrand, J. (2009a): *Bonus Vetus* OLS: A Simple Method for Approximating International Trade-Cost Effects using the Gravity Equation, *Journal of International Economics* 77 (1), 77–85.

Baier, S. and Bergstrand, J. (2009b): Estimating the Effects of Free Trade Agreements on International Trade Flows using Matching Econometrics, *Journal of International Economics* 77 (1), 63–76.

Baier, S., Bergstrand, J. and Clance, M. (2018): Heterogeneous Effects of Economic Integration Agreements, *Journal of Development Economics* 135, 587–608.

Baier, S., Bergstrand, J. and Feng, M. (2014): Economic Integration Agreements and the Margins of International Trade, *Journal of International Economics* 93 (2), 339–350.

Baier, S., Bergstrand, J. and Mariutto, R. (2014): Economic Determinants of Free Trade Agreements Revisited: Distinguishing Sources of Interdependence, *Review of International Economics* 22 (1), 31–58.

Baier, S., Kerr, A. and Yotov, Y. (2017): Gravity, Distance, and International Trade, in W. Wesley and B. Blonigen (eds.) *Handbook of International Trade and Transportation* (Edward Elgar Publishing).

Baldwin, R. (1995): A Domino Theory of Regionalism, in: R. E., Baldwin, P. Haaparanta and Kiander, J. (eds.), *Expanding Membership in the European Union* (Cambridge University Press).
Baldwin and Jaimovich

Baldwin, R. and Jaimovich, D. (2012): Are Free Trade Agreements Contagious?, *Journal of International Economics* 66 (1), 1–16.

Bergsten, C. F. (1996): *Competitive Liberalization and Global Free Trade: A Vision for the Early 21st Century.* (Peterson Institute for International Economics, Washington, DC).

Bergstrand, J. (1983): Measurement and Determinants of Intra-Industry International Trade, in P. Tharakan (ed.) *Intra-Industry Trade: Empirical and Methodological Aspects*, pp. 201–253. (Elsevier Science Publishing, Amsterdam).

Bergstrand, J. (1985): The Gravity Equation in International Trade: Some Microeconomic Foundations and Empirical Evidence, *Review of Economics and Statistics* 67 (3), 474–481.

Bergstrand, J. (1989): The Generalized Gravity Equation, Monopolistic Competition, and the Factor-Proportions Theory in International Trade, *Review of Economics and Statistics* 71 (1), 143–153.

Bergstrand, J. (1990): The Heckscher-Ohlin-Samuelson Model, the Linder Hypothesis and the Determinants of Bilateral Intra-industry Trade, *Economic Journal* 100 (403), 1216–1229.

Bergstrand, J., and Egger, P. (2007): A Knowledge-and-Physical-Capital Model of International Trade Flows, Foreign Direct Investment, and Multinational Enterprises, *Journal of International Economics* 73, 278–308.

Bergstrand, J., and Egger, P. (2013a): Shouldn't Physical Capital *Also* Matter for Multinational Enterprise Activity?, *Review of International Economics* 21, 945–965.

Bergstrand, J., and Egger, P. (2013b): What Determines BITs?, *Journal of International Economics* 90, 107–122.

Bergstrand, J., Egger, P. and Larch, M. (2016): Economic Determinants of the Timing of Preferential Trade Agreement Formations and Enlargements, *Economic Inquiry* 54 (1), 315–341.

Bergstrand, J., Larch, M. and Yotov, Y. (2015): Economic Integration Agreements, Border Effects, and Distance Elasticities in the Gravity Equation, *European Economic Review* 78, 307–327.

Bergstrand, J. H., Egger, P. and Larch, M. (2013): *Gravity Redux*: Estimation of Gravity-Equation Coefficients, Elasticities of Substitution and General Equilibrium Comparative Statics under Asymmetric Bilateral Trade Costs, *Journal of International Economics* 89 (1), 110–121.

Blonigen, B. (2005): A Review of the Empirical Literature on FDI Determinants, *Atlantic Economic Journal* 33 (4), 383–403.

Chaney, T. (2008): Distorted Gravity: The Intensive and Extensive Margins of International Trade, *American Economic Review* 98 (4), 1707–1721.

Disdier, A. and Head, K. (2008): The Puzzling Persistence of the Distance Effect on Bilateral Trade, *Review of Economics and Statistics* 90 (1), 37–48.

Eaton, J. and Kortum, S. (2002): Technology, Geography and Trade, *Econometrica* 70 (5), 1741–1779.

Egger, P. and Larch, M. (2008): Interdependent Preferential Trade Agreement Memberships: An Empirical Analysis, *Journal of International Economics* 76 (2), 384–399.

Feenstra, R. (2004): *Advanced International Trade: Theory and Evidence.* (Princeton University Press, Princeton, New Jersey).

Feenstra, R. (2010): *Product Variety and the Gains from International Trade.* (MIT Press, Cambridge, MA).

Frankel, J. (1997): *Regional Trading Blocs.* (Institute for International Economics, Washington, DC).

Frankel, J., Stein, E. and Wei, S. (1998): Continental Trading Blocs: Are They Natural or Supernatural?, in J. A. Frankel (ed.) *The Regionalization of the World Economy*, ed. by J. A. Frankel pp. 91–113. (The University of Chicago Press, Chicago, IL).

Frankel, J., Stein, E. and Wei, S.-J. (1995): Trading Blocs and the Americas, *Journal of Development Economics* 47 (1), 61–95.

Frankel, J., Stein, E. and Wei, S.-J. (1996): Regional Trading Arrangements: Natural or Supernatural?, *American Economic Review, Papers and Proceedings* 86 (2), 52–56.

Head, K. and Mayer, T. (2014): Gravity Equations: Workhorse, Toolkit, and Cookbook, in G. Gopinath, E. Helpman, and K. Rogoff (eds.) *Handbook of Interantional Economics, Volume 4* (Elsevier, Amsterdam).

Helpman, E. (1984): A Simple Theory of International Trade with Multinational Corporations, *Journal of Political Economy* 32 (3), 451–471.

Helpman, E. and Krugman, P. (1985): *Market Structure and Foreign Trade — Increasing Returns, Imperfect Competition and the International Economy.* (The MIT Press, Cambridge, Massachusetts).

Hottman, C., Redding, S. and Weinstein, D. (2016): Quantifying the Sources of Firm Heterogneity, *Quarterly Journal of Economics* 131 (3), 1291–1364.

Hummels, D. and Klenow, P. (2005): The Variety and Quality of a Nation's Exports, *American Economic Review* 95 (3), 704–723.

Krugman, P. (1979): Increasing Returns, Monopolistic Competition and International Trade, *Journal of International Economics* 9 (4), 469–479.

Krugman, P. (1980): Scale Economies, Product Differentiation, and the Pattern of Trade, *American Economic Review* 70 (5), 950–959.

Krugman, P. (1995): Growing World Trade: Causes and Consequences, *Brookings Papers on Economic Activity* 1995 (1), 327–377.

Linnemann, H. (1966): *An Econometric Study of International Trade Flows.* (North-Holland Publishing, Amsterdam).

Markusen, J. (1984): Multinationals, Multi-Plant Economies, and the Gains from Trade, *Journal of International Economics* 16 (3–4), 205–226.

Markusen, J. (2002): *Multinational Firms and the Theory of International Trade.* (The MIT Press, Cambridge, Massachusetts).

Markusen, J. and Maskus, K. (2002): Discriminating Among Alternative Theories of the Multinational Enterprise, *Review of International Economics* 10 (4), 694–707.

McCallum, J. (1995): National Borders Matter, *American Economic Review* 85 (3), 615–623.

McFadden, D. (1975): The Revealed Preferences of a Government Bureaucracy: Theory, *Bell Journal of Economics* 6, 401–416.

McFadden, D. (1976): Quantal Choice Analysis: A Survey, *Annals of Economic and Social Measurement* 5, 363–390.

Melitz, M. (2003): The Impact of Trade on Intra-Industry Reallocations and Aggregate Industry Productivity, *Econometrica* 71 (6), 1695–1725.

Poyhonen, P. (1963a): A Tentative Model for the Volume of Trade between Countries, *Weltwirtschaftliches Archiv* 90 (1), 93–100.

Poyhonen, P. (1963b): Toward a General Theory of International Trade, *Economiska Samfundets Tidskrift* 16, 69–77.

Pulliainen, K. (1963): A World Trade Study: An Econometric Model of the Pattern of the Commodity Flows of International Trade in 1948-60, *Economiska Samfundets Tidskrift* 16, 78–91.

Redding, S. (2011): Theories of Heterogeneous Firms, *Annual Review of Economics* 3, 77–105.

Sapir, A. (1981): Trade Benefits under the EEC Generalized System of Preferences, *European Economic Review* 15, 339–355.

Tinbergen, J. (1962): *Shaping the World Economy: Suggestions for an International Economic Policy.* (The Twentieth Century Fund, New York).

Yotov, Y. V. (2012): A Simple Solution to the Distance Puzzle in International Trade, *Economics Letters* 117 (3), 794–798.

PART 1

Determinants of International Trade Flows

Chapter 1

THE GRAVITY EQUATION IN INTERNATIONAL TRADE: SOME MICROECONOMIC FOUNDATIONS AND EMPIRICAL EVIDENCE

Jeffrey H. Bergstrand*

Abstract—Despite the gravity equation's empirical success in "explaining" trade flows, the model's predictive potential has been inhibited by an absence of strong theoretical foundations. A general equilibrium world trade model is presented from which a gravity equation is derived by making certain assumptions, including perfect international product substitutability. If, however, trade flows are differentiated by origin as evidence suggests, the typical gravity equation is misspecified, omitting certain price variables. The last section presents empirical evidence supporting the notion that the gravity equation is a reduced form from a partial equilibrium subsystem of a general equilibrium model with nationally differentiated products.

THE "gravity equation" has been long recognized for its consistent empirical success in explaining many different types of flows, such as migration, commuting, tourism, and commodity shipping. Typically, the log-linear equation specifies that a flow from origin i to destination j can be explained by economic forces at the flow's origin, economic forces at the flow's destination, and economic forces either aiding or resisting the flow's movement from origin to destination.

In international trade, bilateral gross aggregate trade flows are explained commonly using the following specification:

$$PX_{ij} = \beta_0 (Y_i)^{\beta_1} (Y_j)^{\beta_2} (D_{ij})^{\beta_3} (A_{ij})^{\beta_4} u_{ij} \quad (1)$$

where PX_{ij} is the U.S. dollar value of the flow from country i to country j, Y_i (Y_j) is the U.S. dollar value of nominal GDP in i (j), D_{ij} is the distance from the economic center of i to that of j, A_{ij} is any other factor(s) either aiding or resisting trade between i and j, and u_{ij} is a log-normally distributed error term with $E(\ln u_{ij}) = 0$. This specification was used in Tinbergen (1962), Poyhonen (1963a, 1963b), Pulliainen (1963), Geraci and Prewo (1977), Prewo (1978), and Abrams (1980).[1] Table 1 presents results from estimating a gravity equation similar to (1) for 15 OECD countries' trade flows.[2] Coefficient estimates are stable across years and are representative of trade gravity equations.

Despite the model's consistently high statistical explanatory power, its use for predictive purposes has been inhibited owing to an absence of strong theoretical foundations. The most common justification—used in Linnemann (1966), Aitken (1973), Geraci and Prewo (1977), Prewo (1978), Abrams (1980), and Sapir (1981)—was developed by Linnemann and asserts that the gravity model is a reduced form from a four-equation partial equilibrium model of export supply and import demand. Prices are always excluded since "they merely adjust to equate supply and demand."[3] However, critics have argued that this approach is "loose" and does not explain the multiplicative functional form.[4]

This study addresses these and other issues in developing further the microeconomic foundations of the gravity equation. The "looseness" critique is addressed by systematically describing assumptions necessary to generate a gravity equation similar to (1) from a general equilibrium framework. Specific, yet intuitively plausible, functions for utility and production generate the equation's multiplicative form. Section I presents a general equilibrium model of world trade derived from utility- and profit-maximizing agent behavior in N countries assuming a single factor of production in

Received for publication June 16, 1983. Revision accepted for publication December 12, 1984.

* Federal Reserve Bank of Boston.

The author is very grateful to J. David Richardson, Robert Baldwin, Rachel McCulloch, James Alm, Saul Schwartz and two anonymous referees for helpful comments on earlier drafts, and Doug Cleveland for research assistance. All errors remain the author's responsibility. The views expressed do not necessarily reflect the views of the Federal Reserve Bank of Boston or the Federal Reserve System.

[1] Linnemann (1966), Aitken (1973), Sattinger (1978) and Sapir (1981) used the same general specification, but also included exporter and importer populations. Microeconomic foundations of this alternative specification are discussed in Bergstrand (1984).

[2] The countries are Canada, United States, Japan, Belgium-Luxembourg, Denmark, France, West Germany, Italy, Netherlands, United Kingdom, Austria, Norway, Spain, Sweden, and Switzerland. The adjacency, EEC, and EFTA dummies are explained in the appendix.

[3] Linnemann (1966), p. 41; Leamer and Stern (1970), p. 146; Geraci and Prewo (1977), p. 68; Prewo (1978), p. 344; and Sapir (1981), p. 341.

[4] See, for example, Anderson (1979), p. 106 and Leamer and Stern (1970), p. 158.

*Originally Published in *The Review of Economics and Statistics*, 67(3), pp. 474–481.

TABLE 1.—TYPICAL GRAVITY EQUATION COEFFICIENT ESTIMATES FOR AGGREGATE TRADE FLOWS

Variables	1965	1966	1975	1976
Country i's Income	0.80[b]	0.80[b]	0.83[b]	0.84[b]
	(20.10)	(20.70)	(19.03)	(18.95)
Country j's Income	0.65[b]	0.66[b]	0.69[b]	0.69[b]
	(16.14)	(17.11)	(15.83)	(15.45)
Distance	−0.72[b]	−0.69[b]	−0.71[b]	−0.72[b]
	(12.15)	(12.11)	(10.35)	(10.21)
Adjacency Dummy	0.61[b]	0.63[b]	0.69[b]	0.74[b]
	(4.35)	(4.61)	(5.13)	(5.36)
EEC Dummy	0.35[a]	0.41[b]	0.24[a]	0.30[a]
	(2.02)	(2.46)	(1.80)	(2.23)
EFTA Dummy	0.69[b]	0.73[b]	0.66[b]	0.69[b]
	(4.94)	(5.40)	(3.35)	(3.46)
Constant	1.90[b]	1.54[b]	0.64	0.56
	(2.82)	(2.36)	(0.89)	(0.77)
Adjusted R^2	0.80	0.81	0.80	0.79
Root Mean Square Error	0.639	0.616	0.607	0.615
Number of Observations	210	210	210	210

Sources of data: See appendix.
Notes: All variables except dummies are expressed in natural logarithms; estimation is by ordinary least squares. t-statistics are in parentheses.
[a] Significant at the 5% level, one-tail test.
[b] Significant at the 1% level, one-tail test.

each. The reduced form from this system specifies the trade flow from i to j as a function of all countries' resource availabilities for a given year as well as trade barriers and transport-cost factors among all pairs of countries. However, this is not a "gravity equation." A bilateral trade flow equation must include exporter and importer incomes as exogenous variables to be a gravity model, by definition. Section II demonstrates that a gravity model similar to (1) can be explicitly derived from this system by making certain simplifying assumptions, including perfect substitutability of goods across countries. Yet if aggregate trade flows are differentiated by national origin, (1) misspecifies the gravity model by omitting certain price variables. In light of strong evidence implying the existence of nationally differentiated products, section III presents estimates of a gravity equation that includes price variables. The results support the notion that the gravity equation is a reduced form from a partial equilibrium subsystem of a general equilibrium trade model with nationally differentiated products.

I. A General Equilibrium Model of World Trade

Demand

In each country j in each year, consumers are assumed to share the constant-elasticity-of-substitution (CES) utility function:

$$U_j = \left\{ \left[\left(\sum_{\substack{k=1 \\ k \neq j}}^{N} X_{kj}^{\theta_j} \right)^{1/\theta_j} \right]^{\psi_j} + X_{jj}^{\psi_j} \right\}^{1/\psi_j}, \qquad j = 1, \ldots, N \quad (2)$$

where X_{kj} (X_{jj}) is the amount of k's aggregate good (j's domestically produced good) demanded by j's consumers, $\psi_j = (\mu_j - 1)/\mu_j$ where μ_j is the CES between domestic and importable goods in j ($0 \leqq \mu_j \leqq \infty$), and $\theta_j = (\sigma_j - 1)/\sigma_j$ where σ_j is the CES among importables in j ($0 \leqq \sigma_j \leqq \infty$). This specification allows the elasticity of substitution between domestic and importable goods and that among importables to differ.[5] Equation (2) simplifies to a standard CES function when μ_j and σ_j are constrained to be equal. Expenditures in j are constrained by income:

$$Y_j = \sum_{k=1}^{N} \bar{P}_{kj} X_{kj}, \qquad j = 1, \ldots, N \quad (3)$$

and $\bar{P}_{kj} = P_{kj} T_{kj} C_{kj} / E_{kj}$ where P_{kj} is the k-currency price of k's product sold in the jth market,

[5] Some have argued that this "two-level" form suggests consumers first choose between domestic and importable goods according to relative aggregate (domestic/import) prices, and then choose among various foreign suppliers according to relative (bilateral) prices among importables. See Hickman and Lau (1973) and Geraci and Prewo (1982).

T_{kj} is one plus j's tariff rate on k's product ($T_{jj} = 1$), C_{kj} is the transport-cost (c.i.f./f.o.b.) factor to ship k's product to j ($C_{jj} = 1$), and E_{kj} is the spot value of j's currency in terms of k's currency ($E_{jj} = 1$). Henceforth, Σ'' will denote summation over $k = 1, \ldots, N$, $k \neq j$. Maximizing (2) subject to (3) generates $N(N+1)$ first-order conditions that are solvable for $N(N-1)$ bilateral aggregate import demand equations:

$$X_{ij}^D = Y_j \bar{P}_{ij}^{-\sigma_j} \left[\left(\Sigma'' \bar{P}_{kj}^{1-\sigma_j} \right)^{1/(1-\sigma_j)} \right]^{\sigma_j - \mu_j} \times \left\{ \left[\left(\Sigma'' \bar{P}_{kj}^{1-\sigma_j} \right)^{1/(1-\sigma_j)} \right]^{1-\mu_j} + P_{jj}^{1-\mu_j} \right\}^{-1} \quad i, j = 1, \ldots, N \; (i \neq j) \quad (4)$$

and N domestic demand equations:

$$X_{jj}^D = Y_j P_{jj}^{-\mu_j} \left\{ \left[\left(\Sigma'' \bar{P}_{kj}^{1-\sigma_j} \right)^{1/(1-\sigma_j)} \right]^{1-\mu_j} + P_{jj}^{1-\mu_j} \right\}^{-1}, \quad j = 1, \ldots, N. \quad (5)$$

Derivations, for above and below, are available from the author upon request.

Supply

In each country i in each year, firms maximize the profit function:

$$\Pi_i = \sum_{k=1}^{N} P_{ik} X_{ik} - W_i R_i, \quad i = 1, \ldots, N \quad (6)$$

where R_i is the amount available of the single, internationally immobile resource in a given year in i (e.g., labor hours) to produce the various outputs and W_i is the i-currency value of a unit of R_i. R in each country is allocated according to the constant-elasticity-of-transformation (CET) joint production surface:

$$R_i = \left\{ \left[\left(\sum_{\substack{k=1 \\ k \neq i}}^{N} X_{ik}^{\phi_i} \right)^{1/\phi_i} \right]^{\delta_i} + X_{ii}^{\delta_i} \right\}^{1/\delta_i}, \quad i = 1, \ldots, N \quad (7)$$

where $\delta_i = (1 + \eta_i)/\eta_i$ where η_i is i's CET between production for home and foreign markets ($0 \leq \eta_i \leq \infty$) and $\phi_i = (1 + \gamma_i)/\gamma_i$ where γ_i is i's CET for production among export markets ($0 \leq \gamma_i \leq \infty$). This specification allows the elasticity of transformation of supply between home and foreign markets and that among foreign markets to differ.[6] Equation (7) simplifies to a standard CET function when η_i and γ_i are constrained to be equal. Henceforth, Σ' will denote summation over $k = 1, \ldots, N$, $k \neq i$. Substituting (7) into (6) and maximizing the resulting equation yields N^2 first-order conditions that are solvable for $N(N-1)$ bilateral aggregate export supply equations:

$$X_{ij}^S = Y_i P_{ij}^{\gamma_i} \left[\left(\Sigma' P_{ik}^{1+\gamma_i} \right)^{1/(1+\gamma_i)} \right]^{-(\gamma_i - \eta_i)} \times \left\{ \left[\left(\Sigma' P_{ik}^{1+\gamma_i} \right)^{1/(1+\gamma_i)} \right]^{1+\eta_i} + P_{ii}^{1+\eta_i} \right\}^{-1} \quad i, j = 1, \ldots, N \; (i \neq j) \quad (8)$$

and N domestic supply equations:

$$X_{ii}^S = Y_i P_{ii}^{\eta_i} \left\{ \left[\left(\Sigma' P_{ik}^{1+\gamma_i} \right)^{1/(1+\gamma_i)} \right]^{1+\eta_i} + P_{ii}^{1+\eta_i} \right\}^{-1}, \quad i = 1, \ldots, N \quad (9)$$

where, with one factor of production, national income in i is constrained by

$$Y_i = W_i R_i, \quad i = 1, \ldots, N. \quad (10)$$

Equilibrium

Assume N^2 equilibrium conditions:

$$X_{ij} = X_{ij}^D = X_{ij}^S, \quad i, j = 1, \ldots, N \quad (11)$$

where X_{ij} is the actual trade flow volume from i to j. Equations (3)–(5) and (7)–(11) produce a general equilibrium model of world trade with $4N^2 + 3N$ equations and endogenous variables.

The reduced form for X_{ij} from this system would be a function of every R_i ($i = 1, \ldots, N$), T_{ij} and C_{ij} ($i, j = 1, \ldots, N$; $i \neq j$). Yet such a function is not a gravity equation, since this reduced form necessarily excludes endogenous exporter and importer incomes. The next section demonstrates that a gravity equation similar to (1), including incomes as exogenous variables, can nevertheless be derived from this system using certain additional assumptions.

II. Solving for the Gravity Equation: A Partial Equilibrium Approach

Assumption 1

The first assumption is that the market for the aggregate trade flow from i to j is small relative to

[6] Some have argued that this form suggests a "two-level" decision for producers analogous to that for consumers.

the other $N^2 - 1$ markets. This is analogous to the small open economy assumption frequently used in international finance studies, which implies that the foreign price level, the foreign interest rate, and foreign income can be treated as exogenous. The small market assumption implies that variations in X_{ij} and P_{ij} to equilibrate X_{ij}^D and X_{ij}^S have negligible impacts on Y_i, Y_j, P_{ii}, P_{jj}, $\Sigma' P_{ik}^{1+\gamma_i}$, and $\Sigma'' \overline{P}_{kj}^{1-\sigma_j}$. The general equilibrium system of $4N^2 + 3N$ equations can then be considered N^2 partial equilibrium subsystems of 4 equations each in 4 endogenous variables (X_{ij}, X_{ij}^D, X_{ij}^S, P_{ij}) and $3N$ constraints. Combining one each of (4) and (8) with one of (11) yields:

$$P_{ij} = \Big\{ Y_i^{-1} Y_j C_{ij}^{-\sigma_j} T_{ij}^{-\sigma_j} E_{ij}^{\sigma_j} \times \Big(\sum{}' P_{ik}^{1+\gamma_i}\Big)^{(\gamma_i - \eta_i)/(1+\gamma_i)} \times \Big(\sum{}'' \overline{P}_{kj}^{1-\sigma_j}\Big)^{(\sigma_j - \mu_j)/(1-\sigma_j)} \times \Big[\Big(\sum{}' P_{ik}^{1+\gamma_i}\Big)^{(1+\eta_i)/(1+\gamma_i)} + P_{ii}^{1+\eta_i}\Big] \times \Big[\Big(\sum{}'' \overline{P}_{kj}^{1-\sigma_j}\Big)^{(1-\mu_j)/(1-\sigma_j)} + P_{jj}^{1-\mu_j}\Big]^{-1} \Big\}^{1/(\gamma_i + \sigma_j)} \tag{12}$$

and

$$X_{ij} = \Big\{ Y_i^{\sigma_j} Y_j^{\gamma_i} C_{ij}^{-\gamma_i \sigma_j} T_{ij}^{-\gamma_i \sigma_j} E_{ij}^{\gamma_i \sigma_j} \times \Big(\sum{}' P_{ik}^{1+\gamma_i}\Big)^{-\sigma_j(\gamma_i - \eta_i)/(1+\gamma_i)} \times \Big(\sum{}'' \overline{P}_{kj}^{1-\sigma_j}\Big)^{\gamma_i(\sigma_j - \mu_j)/(1-\sigma_j)} \times \Big[\Big(\sum{}' P_{ik}^{1+\gamma_i}\Big)^{(1+\eta_i)/(1+\gamma_i)} + P_{ii}^{1+\eta_i}\Big]^{-\sigma_j} \times \Big[\Big(\sum{}'' \overline{P}_{kj}^{1-\sigma_j}\Big)^{(1-\mu_j)/(1-\sigma_j)} + P_{jj}^{1-\mu_j}\Big]^{-\gamma_i} \Big\}^{1/(\gamma_i + \sigma_j)}$$

$$i, j = 1, \ldots, N \ (i \neq j). \tag{13}$$

The small market assumption yields a reduced-form bilateral trade equation with Y_i and Y_j treated exogenously. A consequence of this assumption is that certain price terms are also treated exogenously.

Assumption 2

An assumption of identical utility and production functions across countries ensures that parameters in (12) and (13) are constant across all country pairings. This assumption is common to trade analyses, including the Heckscher-Ohlin-Samuelson model of interindustry trade and recent formal models of intraindustry trade, cf., Dixit and Norman (1980).[7] Combining (12), (13), and this assumption yields:

$$PX_{ij} = Y_i^{(\sigma-1)/(\gamma+\sigma)} Y_j^{(\gamma+1)/(\gamma+\sigma)} C_{ij}^{-\sigma(\gamma+1)/(\gamma+\sigma)} \times T_{ij}^{-\sigma(\gamma+1)/(\gamma+\sigma)} E_{ij}^{\sigma(\gamma+1)/(\gamma+\sigma)} \times \Big(\sum{}' P_{ik}^{1+\gamma}\Big)^{-(\sigma-1)(\gamma-\eta)/(1+\gamma)(\gamma+\sigma)} \times \Big(\sum{}'' \overline{P}_{kj}^{1-\sigma}\Big)^{(\gamma+1)(\sigma-\mu)/(1-\sigma)(\gamma+\sigma)} \times \Big[\Big(\sum{}' P_{ik}^{1+\gamma}\Big)^{(1+\eta)/(1+\gamma)} + P_{ii}^{1+\eta}\Big]^{-(\sigma-1)/(\gamma+\sigma)} \times \Big[\Big(\sum{}'' \overline{P}_{kj}^{1-\sigma}\Big)^{(1-\mu)/(1-\sigma)} + P_{jj}^{1-\mu}\Big]^{-(\gamma+1)/(\gamma+\sigma)} \tag{14}$$

where PX_{ij} is the value of the trade flow from i to j ($PX_{ij} = P_{ij} X_{ij}$). Equation (14) is termed the "generalized" gravity equation. Given data limitations, (14) can be estimated by ordinary least squares (OLS) when a constant and log-normally distributed error term are appended. The specification is "general" because it treats exporter and importer incomes as *exogenous* yet imposes no restrictions on parameter values other than being identical across all country pairings.

Assumptions 3–6

A gravity model more similar to (1) that excludes all price terms can be obtained with four additional assumptions. Assuming perfect substitutability of goods internationally in production and consumption, perfect commodity arbitrage, zero tariffs, and zero transport costs (and normalizing all exchange rates to unity) implies $C_{ij} = T_{ij} = 1$ and $\overline{P}_{ij} = P$ for all $i, j = 1, \ldots, N$. Since $\sigma = \mu = \gamma = \eta = \infty$, (14) simplifies to

$$PX_{ij} = (1/2) Y_i^{1/2} Y_j^{1/2} \tag{15}$$

which is similar to the gravity equation in (1).

[7]Likewise, Anderson (1979) assumed identical expenditure functions across countries in his theoretical foundation.

III. An Empirical Model of the Generalized Gravity Equation

While each of the previous six assumptions should be tested, this paper focuses on only the last four. Numerous studies over the past decade have revealed large and persistent deviations of national price levels from purchasing power parity (PPP). Isard (1977) found that for even the most disaggregated manufactured commodities for which U.S. and foreign prices could be matched, "relative price behavior... marks them as differentiated products, rather than near-perfect substitutes" (p. 942). Richardson (1978) found that commodity arbitrage did occur, but neither significantly for every commodity group nor at all for many groups. When commodity arbitrage did occur, it was imperfect. Kravis and Lipsey (1984) recently concluded, "we are pretty sure that equality of price levels among countries (PPP) will not turn out to be the norm, even in the long run" (p. 5). Thus, substantive deviations from PPP seem to persist even in the absence of tariffs and transport costs; the existence of these barriers only complicates problems.

This evidence suggests that assumptions 3–6 are restrictive and the generalized gravity equation would be more appropriate to estimate. This section presents an econometric version of (14) and discusses the results of its estimation.

Econometric Issues

The econometric analogue to (14) is distinguished from (1) predominantly by the former including price and exchange rate variables. The tariff variable in (14) can be proxied by dummy variables indicating the presence of preferential trading arrangements as in the basic gravity equation. The transport-cost factor can be proxied by the distance between economic centers of i and j and a dummy for adjacency.

Calculating the complex price terms in (14) is beyond this paper's scope; however, cross-country differences in aggregate price levels can be approximated by cross-country variation in aggregate price (or unit value) indexes. If (local-currency-denominated) export price indexes are calculated similarly for several countries using a common base period—the latter "well chosen" to avoid large divergences from PPP—then variation across countries in these indexes in a given year can approximate the cross-country variation of export price levels, that is, of $(\Sigma' P_{ik}^{1+\gamma})^{1/(1+\gamma)}$ across all i. Likewise, j's import price index can approximate $(\Sigma'' \overline{P}_{kj}^{1-\sigma})^{1/(1-\sigma)}$;[8] i's GDP deflator can approximate

$$\left[\left(\sum{}' P_{ik}^{1+\gamma}\right)^{(1+\eta)/(1+\gamma)} + P_{ii}^{1+\eta}\right];$$

and j's GDP deflator can approximate

$$\left[\left(\sum{}'' \overline{P}_{kj}^{1-\sigma}\right)^{(1-\mu)/(1-\sigma)} + P_{jj}^{1-\mu}\right].^{9}$$

The exchange rate index will indicate changes in the i-currency value of a unit of j's currency since the common base period. A rise in this index implies an appreciation (depreciation) of the importer's (exporter's) currency from the base.[10]

As before, the generalized gravity model is estimated for 1965, 1966, 1975 and 1976. This will help indicate the stability of parameter estimates from year to year, from one decade to another, and from "fixed" to "floating" exchange rates.

Previous partial-equilibrium time-series studies have suggested that price changes have multiyear effects on trade flows. Magee (1975) noted evidence of significant effects of price changes on the volume of traded goods five years after the price change. Base years 1960 for 1965/1966 estimates and 1970 for 1975/1976 estimates not only allow a generous lag length but also reflect years of "normal" economic activity—that is, neither years of recession troughs or expansion peaks nor years of exchange rate regime changes.[11]

[8] Export/import unit value indexes were used rather than export/import price indexes because the former were available for all 15 countries whereas the latter were available for only 4.

[9] Such considerations form the analytical basis for comparing internationally unit labor cost, unit value and aggregate price indexes in the IMF's *International Financial Statistics* (Cost and Price Comparisons). Critics may argue that construction and commodity composition of national price indexes varies widely across countries. Yet the aggregation/composition problem in cross-country index comparisons is no more severe than in time-series import and export demand studies. Country j's wholesale price index will also be used as a proxy for the weighted average of j's domestic and import prices.

[10] Local-currency-denominated import unit value indexes and importer GDP deflators implicitly reflect variations in exchange rates and tariff rates influencing $(\Sigma'' \overline{P}_{kj}^{1-\sigma})^{1/(1-\sigma)}$.

[11] Critics may argue that 1970 was not a year of "normal" economic activity. However, real GDP growth among industrial countries in 1970 was only 1 percentage point below the average for 1961–80. Consumer prices rose in 1970 only 0.4 percentage points below the average for the same period. 1970 avoided the 9-year global economic boom of the 1960s, yet preceded the 1971–73 transition to floating rates as well as the 1973–74 oil shock and its aftermath. Data are from the IMF's *International Financial Statistics Yearbook* (1983).

TABLE 2.—GENERALIZED GRAVITY EQUATION COEFFICIENT ESTIMATES FOR AGGREGATE TRADE FLOWS

Variables	1965	1966	1975	1976
Country *i*'s Income	0.75[b]	0.76[b]	0.80[b]	0.84[b]
	(16.95)	(17.24)	(16.04)	(15.79)
Country *j*'s Income	0.63[b]	0.66[b]	0.54[b]	0.56[b]
	(14.03)	(14.63)	(9.12)	(9.34)
Distance	−0.78[b]	−0.75[b]	−0.76[b]	−0.77[b]
	(12.70)	(12.47)	(11.22)	(10.92)
Adjacency Dummy	0.58[b]	0.59[b]	0.74[b]	0.76[b]
	(4.23)	(4.43)	(5.54)	(5.62)
EEC Dummy	0.32[a]	0.35[a]	0.18	0.18
	(1.82)	(2.07)	(1.37)	(1.35)
EFTA Dummy	0.67[b]	0.73[b]	0.62[b]	0.73[b]
	(4.92)	(5.45)	(3.20)	(3.67)
Exchange Rate (E_{ij})	0.58	0.30	0.74[a]	0.73
	(0.40)	(0.23)	(1.76)	(1.62)
i's Export Unit Value Index	−1.39[b]	−1.14[b]	−0.55	−0.96
	(3.03)	(2.83)	(0.90)	(1.55)
j's Import Unit Value Index	0.78	0.61	2.32[b]	1.85[b]
	(0.94)	(0.77)	(4.15)	(4.14)
i's GDP Deflator	−1.91[b]	−1.46[a]	−0.79	−0.05
	(2.37)	(2.00)	(1.17)	(0.07)
j's GDP Deflator	−1.28	−0.41	−1.13	−1.12[a]
	(1.43)	(0.50)	(1.55)	(1.67)
Constant	30.19[b]	19.62[a]	4.06	4.50
	(3.11)	(2.22)	(0.68)	(0.95)
Adjusted R^2	0.81	0.82	0.81	0.81
Root Mean Square Error	0.619	0.603	0.583	0.591
Number of Observations	210	210	210	210

Sources of data: See appendix.
Notes: See table 1.

Empirical Results

Some remarks are first in order regarding expected coefficient signs. Four variables have unambiguous expected impacts. A rise in *j*'s income, an appreciation of *j*'s currency, adjacency, and the presence of preferential trading arrangements should increase the trade flow from *i* to *j*; greater distance between these countries should reduce this flow. Remaining variables have ambiguous expected effects. If the elasticity of substitution among importables (σ) exceeds unity, *i*'s income and GDP deflator will have positive and negative coefficients, respectively. If, additionally, the elasticity of transformation among exportables (γ) exceeds that between production for the domestic market and for abroad (η), *i*'s export unit value index will have a negative coefficient. Country *j*'s import unit value index will have a positive coefficient if the elasticity of substitution among importables exceeds that between domestic and imported products (μ). Finally, *j*'s GDP deflator coefficient will be negative or positive depending upon whether μ is less than or greater than unity, respectively.

All coefficient estimate signs conform to those suggested above in all four years, as shown in table 2. Importer income, adjacency, and preferential trading arrangements have positive coefficient signs as in the basic gravity model; distance has a negative coefficient sign. An appreciation of the importer's currency increases the trade flow from *i* to *j*. A rise in exporter's income increases the trade flow, implying that σ exceeds unity. The negative coefficient estimate for *i*'s GDP deflator supports this conclusion about σ. The negative coefficient estimate for *i*'s export unit value index is consistent with σ greater than one and γ greater than η. The positive coefficient estimate for *j*'s import unit value index is consistent with σ greater than μ. The negative coefficient estimate for *j*'s GDP deflator suggests that μ is less than one. All these elasticity conclusions are intuitively plausible.

Most coefficient estimates for traditional gravity equation variables—incomes, distance, and dummies—are statistically significant in one-tail *t*-tests in all four years and are similar in value to estimates shown in table 1. Among price and exchange rate variables, 40% have statistically significant coefficient estimates in one-tail *t*-tests.

Interestingly, the exchange rate index coefficient estimate, which was insignificant under fixed exchange rates, became statistically significant in 1975 under flexible exchange rates, as this index became more volatile. The stability of coefficient estimates across years within decades suggests that the generalized gravity equation is rather robust.[12]

F-tests were conducted upon restrictions implied by assumptions 3–6, i.e., to test equation (15) versus (14). The restrictions imposed by these assumptions were overwhelmingly rejected.

Finally, what can be inferred about (1)? This equation cannot be explicitly derived from the theoretical model. Yet with the coefficients in (1) not constrained a priori, the specification implies that the elasticities of substitution and transformation are not expected to equal infinity. But if these elasticities do not equal infinity a priori, (14) is clearly more appropriate to estimate. Given the theoretical framework, (1) would not sensibly be estimated over (14), except in the absence of data for price and exchange rate variables. To be complete, F-tests rejected (1) relative to (14), i.e., that all price and exchange rate variables had zero coefficient estimates, at the 5% significance level in all four years and at the 1% level in three years.

IV. Conclusion

For twenty years, the gravity equation applied to international aggregate trade flows has been estimated in a specification represented by equation (1). The equation's empirical success induced curiosity about its underlying "behavior." Over the years, theories—with and without economic content—surfaced to explain this equation.

In this study, a general equilibrium model of world trade was introduced from which a gravity equation similar to (1) could be derived under certain assumptions. Many of these—such as perfect substitutability of goods internationally in consumption and production and perfect commodity arbitrage—have been refuted by recent empirical evidence, however. Because these assumptions were refutable, a "generalized" gravity equation could be derived. This methodology for understanding the trade gravity equation mirrors that used to augment understanding the gravity equation for migration flows. As Greenwood (1975) noted:

> Empirically based studies that have examined place-to-place migration within this framework have almost universally adopted for estimation purposes a modified gravity-type model of gross migration. The models are "gravity-type" in that migration is hypothesized to be directly related to size of the relevant origin and destination populations, and inversely related to distance. The models are "modified" in the sense that the variables of the basic gravity model are given behavioral content, and additional variables that are expected to importantly influence the decision to migrate are included in the estimated relationships. The additional variables are typically suggested as proxies for various arguments of individual utility functions. (p. 398)

Incomes make our generalized equation a "gravity-type" model. Yet price terms, derived from underlying utility and production functions, importantly influence trade flows and lend behavioral content to the gravity equation.

Empirically, the price and exchange rate variables have plausible and significant effects on aggregate trade flows. Coefficient estimates suggest that products are differentiated by national origin and commodity arbitrage is imperfect. Moreover, within the context of the theoretical model, these results imply that the elasticity of substitution among importables exceeds unity, the elasticity of substitution between domestic and imported products is below unity, and the elasticity of transformation among export markets exceeds that between production for domestic and foreign markets.

APPENDIX

Bilateral trade flows are from OECD, *Statistics of Foreign Trade, Series C, Trade by Commodities*, various issues (c.i.f. import values; U.S. and Canadian f.o.b. values modified to conform). Incomes are GDPs in U.S. dollars from OECD *National Accounts*, various issues. For distance, sea distances are from U.S. Naval Oceanographic Office, *Distance Between*

[12] The generalized gravity equation was also estimated for all four years substituting j's wholesale price index for j's GDP deflator. The results do not differ substantively from those in table 2. The small markets assumption enables the error term in the generalized gravity equation to be assumed uncorrelated with incomes, export and import price terms, and domestic price terms. If P_{ij} or X_{ij} significantly influences any of these variables, a simultaneous equations bias arises. The generalized gravity model was reestimated using (one-year) lagged values of incomes, unit value indexes, domestic price indexes, and the exchange rate index. The results do not differ substantively from those in table 2. However, this was not a powerful test since current and lagged values of these variables were highly correlated. Both sets of results are available from the author upon request.

Ports, H.O. Publication No. 151, U.S. Government Printing Office, 1965, and land distances are from *Rand McNally Road Atlas of Europe*, Rand McNally and Co., 1974. Land distances were multiplied by a factor of two following W. H. Gruber and R. Vernon, "The Technology Factor in a World Trade Matrix," in R. Vernon (ed.), *The Technology Factor in International Trade* (New York: National Bureau of Economic Research, 1970). Countries' economic centers are specified in Linnemann (1966). Exchange rates and export/import unit value indexes are from IMF *International Financial Statistics*, various issues. GDP deflators were calculated from nominal and real GDPs in OECD *National Accounts*. Wholesale price indexes are from UN *Statistical Yearbook*, 1968, 1977. The adjacency dummy equals 1 if both countries share a land border, 0 otherwise. The EEC (EFTA) dummy equals 1 if both countries are members of the European Economic Community (European Free Trade Association), 0 otherwise.

REFERENCES

Abrams, Richard K., "International Trade Flows under Flexible Exchange Rates," *Economic Review*, Federal Reserve Bank of Kansas City (Mar. 1980), 3–10.

Aitken, Norman D., "The Effect of EEC and EFTA on European Trade: A Temporal Cross-Section Analysis," *American Economic Review* 63 (Dec. 1973), 881–892.

Anderson, James E., "A Theoretical Foundation for the Gravity Equation," *American Economic Review* 69 (Mar. 1979), 106–116.

Bergstrand, Jeffrey H., "The Gravity Equation and the Factor-Proportions Theory of International Trade: A Theoretical and Empirical Synthesis," processed paper, Federal Reserve Bank of Boston, 1984.

Dixit, Avinash K., and Victor Norman, *Theory of International Trade* (London: Nisbet and Company, Ltd., 1980).

Geraci, Vincent J., and Wilfried Prewo, "Bilateral Trade Flows and Transport Costs," this REVIEW 59 (Feb. 1977), 67–74.

______, "An Empirical Demand and Supply Model of Multilateral Trade," this REVIEW 64 (Aug. 1982), 432–441.

Greenwood, Michael J., "Research on Internal Migration in the U.S.: A Survey," *Journal of Economic Literature* 13 (June 1975), 397–435.

Hickman, Bert G., and Lawrence J. Lau, "Elasticities of Substitution and Export Demands in a World Trade Model," *European Economic Review* 4 (1973), 347–380.

Isard, Peter, "How Far Can We Push the 'Law of One Price'?" *American Economic Review* 67 (Dec. 1977), 942–948.

Kravis, Irving B., and Robert E. Lipsey, "The Study of International Price Levels," research summary for the NBER Conference on Research on Recent and Prospective U.S. Trade Policy (Mar. 1984).

Leamer, Edward E., and Robert Stern, *Quantitative International Economics* (Chicago: Aldine Publishing Co., 1970).

Linnemann, Hans, *An Econometric Study of International Trade Flows* (Amsterdam: North-Holland Publishing Co., 1966).

Magee, Stephen P., "Prices, Incomes, and Foreign Trade," in P. B. Kenen (ed.), *International Trade and Finance* (Cambridge: Cambridge University Press, 1975).

Poyhonen, Pentti, "A Tentative Model for the Volume of Trade between Countries," *Weltwirtschaftliches Archiv*, Band 90, Heft 1 (1963a), 93–100.

______, "Toward a General Theory of International Trade," *Economiska Samfundets Tidskrift* 16 (1963b), 69–77.

Prewo, Wilfried, "Determinants of the Trade Pattern among OECD Countries from 1958 to 1974," *Jahrbucher fur Nationalekonomie und Statistik* 193 (Aug. 1978), 341–358.

Pulliainen, Kyosti, "A World Trade Study: An Econometric Model of the Pattern of the Commodity Flows of International Trade in 1948–60," *Economiska Samfundets Tidskrift* 16 (1963), 78–91.

Richardson, J. David, "Some Evidence on Commodity Arbitrage and the Law of One Price," *Journal of International Economics* 8 (May 1978), 341–352.

Sapir, Andre, "Trade Benefits under the EEC Generalized System of Preferences," *European Economic Review* 15 (1981), 339–355.

Sattinger, Michael, "Trade Flows and Differences between Countries," *Atlantic Economic Journal* 6 (July 1978), 22–29.

Tinbergen, Jan, *Shaping the World Economy: Suggestions for an International Economic Policy* (New York: The Twentieth Century Fund, 1962).

Chapter 2

THE GENERALIZED GRAVITY EQUATION, MONOPOLISTIC COMPETITION, AND THE FACTOR-PROPORTIONS THEORY IN INTERNATIONAL TRADE

Jeffrey H. Bergstrand*

Abstract—A general equilibrium model of world trade with two differentiated-product industries and two factors is developed to illustrate how the gravity equation, including exporter and importer populations as well as incomes, "fits in" with the Heckscher-Ohlin model of inter-industry trade and the Helpman-Krugman-Markusen models of intra-industry trade. The study extends the microeconomic foundations for a generalized gravity equation in Bergstrand (1985) to incorporate relative factor-endowment differences and non-homothetic tastes. Empirical estimates of this generalized gravity equation for single-digit SITC industry groups yield plausible inferences of their capital–labor intensities.

IN international trade gross bilateral trade flows across pairs of countries are explained commonly using the gravity equation:

$$PX_{ij} = \Psi_0(Y_i)^{\Psi_1}(Y_i/L_i)^{\Psi_2}(Y_j)^{\Psi_3} \times (Y_j/L_j)^{\Psi_4}(D_{ij})^{\Psi_5}(A_{ij})^{\Psi_6}e_{ij} \quad (1)$$

where PX_{ij} is the U.S. dollar value of the flow from country i to country j, $Y_i(Y_j)$ is the U.S. dollar value of nominal GDP in $i(j)$, $L_i(L_j)$ is the population in $i(j)$, D_{ij} is the distance from the economic center of i to that of j, A_{ij} is any other factor(s) either aiding or resisting trade between i and j, and e_{ij} is a log-normally distributed error term. Estimates of Ψ_1, Ψ_2, Ψ_3 and Ψ_4 are typically positive; estimates of Ψ_5 are negative.[1] Formal theoretical foundations for the gravity equation have been provided in Anderson (1979), Bergstrand (1985), and Helpman and Krugman (1985, ch. 8). Although all three studies linked bilateral trade flows to exporter and importer incomes multiplicatively, exporter and importer per capita incomes (or populations) were ignored. Moreover, no one has attempted to fully integrate the gravity equation into the factor-proportions theory of trade.[2]

This study extends the microeconomic foundations for the gravity equation presented in Bergstrand (1985) to incorporate factor-endowment variables in the spirit of Heckscher-Ohlin (H-O) and taste variables in the spirit of Linder. The paper provides an explicit theoretical foundation for exporter and importer incomes and per capita incomes consistent with traditional (and newer) trade theories. Section I describes the taste assumptions. Section II describes the technology assumptions. Section III derives the "generalized" gravity equation. Section IV presents empirical

Received for publication August 24, 1987. Revision accepted for publication May 24, 1988.

*College of Business Administration, University of Notre Dame.

The author is grateful to Robert Baldwin, J. David Richardson, Rachel McCulloch, Saul Schwartz, James Grant, Ronald Balvers, Thomas Bundt, Carl Davidson, participants at the Spring 1987 meeting of the Midwest International Economics Group, and two anonymous referees for helpful comments on earlier drafts, and to Marina Hatsopoulos for excellent research assistance.

[1] Bergstrand (1985) and Brada and Mendez (1985) cite previous empirical studies. An alternative specification to (1) uses L_i and L_j instead of Y_i/L_i and Y_j/L_j, respectively. Estimated coefficients of this alternative (denoted with asterisks) are related to (1)'s coefficients as $\Psi_2^* = -\Psi_2$, $\Psi_4^* = -\Psi_4$, $\Psi_1^* = \Psi_1 + \Psi_2$, and $\Psi_3^* = \Psi_3 + \Psi_4$.

[2] Linnemann (1966) and Leamer (1974) are the exceptions. Each *added* a variable(s) to reflect the commodity composition of the trade flow. In chapter 6, Linnemann added a variable representing the "goodness of fit" of i's exports to j's imports. Leamer estimated a modified gravity equation for various 2-digit SITC commodity classifications. While incorporating income and population variables, Leamer included *separate* measures of relative factor endowments as independent variables. Although income and population in Leamer's equations had no economic interpretation beyond being "stage-of-development" variables, income and population consistently outperformed the resistance variables (tariff, distance) and resource variables (per capita factor endowments). To capture the spirit of Linder (1961), two studies *added* the absolute difference between the two countries' per capita incomes as an explanatory variable to the basic gravity equation. Gruber and Vernon (1970) appended absolute per capita income differences to a specification like (1) as a "crude index of the difference in consumption patterns" (p. 256). Similarly, Thursby and Thursby (1987) added absolute per capita income differences to a generalized gravity equation without populations (see Bergstrand, 1985); Thursby and Thursby added this variable to "reflect differences in importer j's tastes" (p. 490). By contrast, this paper attempts to identify specifically the roles of income and population in a gravity equation like (1) for a particular commodity (group) using a Heckscher-Ohlin-Chamberlin-Linder framework *without* including additional measures of relative factor endowments (like Leamer) or taste differences (like Gruber and Vernon or Thursby and Thursby).

*Originally Published in *The Review of Economics and Statistics*, 71(1), pp. 143–153.

estimates for a two-factor, multi-industry, multi-country world. Section V concludes.

I. The Consumer

The representative consumer's behavior is modeled as a bilateral version of the one in Markusen (1986). The consumer is assumed to maximize a "nested" Cobb-Douglas–CES–Stone-Geary utility function subject to an income constraint; the resulting demand curves relate bilateral trade flows to national income, per capita income, and (c.i.f.) prices. Countries with similar per capita incomes will have similar demands, as suggested in Linder (1961, p. 94).

The utility function of consumer l in country j (U_{jl}) is

$$U_{jl} = \left[\left(\sum_{n=1}^{N}\sum_{h=1}^{H_{An}} X_{Ahnjl}^{\theta^A}\right)^{1/\theta^A}\right]^{\delta} \times \left[\left(\sum_{n=1}^{N}\sum_{h=1}^{H_{Bn}} X_{Bhnjl}^{\theta^B}\right)^{1/\theta^B} - \bar{X}_B\right]^{1-\delta}$$
$$-\infty < \theta^A, \theta^B < 1;\ 0 < \delta < 1 \quad (2)$$

where X_{Ahnjl} (X_{Bhnjl}) is the amount of the *manufactured* (*non-manufactured*) output of industry A's (B's) firm h in country n demanded by consumer-worker l in country j and $\bar{X}_B$ is the minimum consumption requirement of good B by any consumer (common to a Stone-Geary utility function). Expenditures are constrained by the consumer's nominal income measured on an aggregate expenditure basis (Y_{jl}):

$$Y_{jl} = \sum_{a=A,B}\sum_{n=1}^{N}\sum_{h=1}^{H_{an}} (P_{anj}T_{anj}/E_{nj})X_{ahnjl} \quad (3)$$

where T_{anj} is one plus the exogenous tariff rate on industry a ($a = A, B$) exports from n to j, E_{nj} is the exogenous exchange rate between the two countries defined as n's currency per unit of j's currency, and P_{anj} is the f.o.b. price of firm h's output of industry a exported from country n to country j; for simplicity, assume that all firms in country n in an industry charge the same price in market j. Prices are denominated in j in a common monetary unit (the numeraire), the market for which is eliminated by Walras' Law (see Krugman, 1980). Henceforth Σ_n denotes the summation over $n = 1, \ldots, N$ and $\Sigma_h^A(\Sigma_h^B)$ denotes the summation over $h = 1, \ldots, H_{An}(H_{Bn})$.

Maximizing (2) subject to (3) yields a set of Armington-like bilateral import demand functions. Since consumers in country j are identical, we can aggregate demand curves across consumers and derive country j's (inverse) market demand curve for the output of A produced by firm g in country i:

$$P_{Aij} = \delta^{1/\sigma^A} X_{Agij}^{-1/\sigma^A}(Y_j)^{1/\sigma^A}(1 - y_j^{-1})^{1/\sigma^A} T_{Aij}^{-1}E_{ij} \times \left[\sum_n \sum_h^A (P_{Ahjn}T_{Anj}/E_{nj})^{1-\sigma^A}\right]^{-1/\sigma^A},$$
$$i = 1, \ldots, N \quad (4)$$

where $\sigma^A = 1/(1 - \theta^A)$, Y_j is j's nominal GDP and y_j is j's "per capita" GDP, where "capita" is expressed in terms of the minimum consumption requirement of B by the population. That is, $y_j = Y_j/(p_{Bj}\bar{X}_B)L_j$ where $p_{Bj} = [\Sigma_n\Sigma_h^B(P_{Bnj} \times T_{Bnj}/E_{nj})^{1-\sigma^B}]^{1/(1-\sigma^B)}$. Analogous demand curves for industry B's output exist with $(1 - y_j^{-1})$ replaced by $(1 + [\delta/(1 - \delta)]y_j^{-1})$. These functions imply that the national income elasticity of demand for $A(B)$ will be greater (less) than one if per capita income rises.

II. The Firm

The representative firm in country i is assumed to maximize profits in an environment similar to other recent models explaining the simultaneous existence of intra-industry and inter-industry trade. Each firm h in each of the two industries produces a uniquely differentiated product in a market that can be characterized as Chamberlinian monopolistic competition, using two factors of production, labor (L) and capital (K). The technology takes the linear form:

$$L_{agi} = \alpha_{La} + \beta_{La}X_{agi} \quad (5)$$

$$K_{agi} = \alpha_{Ka} + \beta_{Ka}X_{agi}$$
$$g = 1, \ldots, H_{ai};\ a = A, B;\ i = 1, \ldots, N \quad (6)$$

where $L_{agi}(K_{agi})$ is the labor (capital) required by firm g in industry a in country i to produce output X_{agi}, the α's are fixed setup costs, and the β's are the constant input requirements to produce a unit of output. All firms and countries share identical technology. The associated cost function for firm g in industry a:

$$\begin{aligned} S_{agi}(W_i, R_i, X_{agi}) &= W_i L_{agi} + R_i K_{agi} \\ &= (W_i \alpha_{La} + R_i \alpha_{Ka}) \\ &\quad + W_i \beta_{La} X_{agi} + R_i \beta_{Ka} X_{agi} \end{aligned}$$

$$g = 1, \ldots, H_{ai}; \quad a = A, B; \quad i = 1, \ldots, N \quad (7)$$

where W_i and R_i are the given wage rate for labor and rental rate for capital, respectively (determined in competitive markets and denominated in i's currency), satisfies all the properties recommended in Helpman (1981). Assume labor and capital are in fixed supply in each country i:

$$L_i = \sum_h^A L_{Ahi} + \sum_h^B L_{Bhi} \quad (8a)$$

$$K_i = \sum_h^A K_{Ahi} + \sum_h^B K_{Bhi}. \quad (8b)$$

Following Geraci and Prewo (1982), each firm's output is assumed to be distributed among domestic and foreign markets according to the constant-elasticity-of-transformation (CET) function:

$$X_{agi} = \left[\sum_n (C_{ain} X_{agin})^{\phi^a} \right]^{1/\phi^a},$$

$$1 < \phi^a < \infty; \quad g = 1, \ldots, H_{ai};$$

$$a = A, B; \quad i = 1, \ldots, N \quad (9)$$

where C_{ain} is the c.i.f./f.o.b. factor (> 1) to ship output in industry a from country i to country n; hence, only a portion of a shipment arrives at its destination with the part lost in transit representing the resources exhausted to ship the output, as in Krugman (1980). For $\phi^a > 1$, the transformation curve for output between domestic and foreign markets and among foreign markets is concave (like the typical production possibility frontier between two goods). Intuitively, each firm's behavior can be considered as a two-stage process. First, each firm *produces* a uniquely differentiated commodity under increasing returns to scale. In the second stage, each firm *distributes* its product to N markets (including the home market) under diminishing returns, similar to Krugman (1987).

Maximizing profit function:

$$\begin{aligned} \pi_{agi} &= \sum_n P_{ain} X_{agin} - (W_i \alpha_{La} + R_i \alpha_{Ka}) \\ &\quad - W_i \beta_{La} \left[\sum_n (C_{ain} X_{agin})^{\phi^a} \right]^{1/\phi^a} \\ &\quad - R_i \beta_{Ka} \left[\sum_n (C_{ain} X_{agin})^{\phi^a} \right]^{1/\phi^a} \end{aligned}$$

$$g = 1, \ldots, H_{ai}; \quad a = A, B; \quad i = 1, \ldots, N \quad (10)$$

for the representative firms in industries A and B yields equations for the marginal cost of exporting to any market j. For industry A:

$$\begin{aligned} X_{Agij} &= H_{Ai}^{-1} (\beta_{KA} \beta_{LB} - \beta_{KB} \beta_{LA})^{-1} \\ &\quad \times (\beta_{LB} K_i^* - \beta_{KB} L_i^*)(P_{Aij}/C_{Aij})^{\gamma^A} \\ &\quad \times C_{Aij}^{-1} \left[\sum_n (P_{Ain}/C_{Ain})^{1+\gamma^A} \right]^{-\gamma^A/(1+\gamma^A)} \end{aligned}$$

$$g = 1, \ldots, H_{Ai}; \quad i = 1, \ldots, N \quad (11)$$

where $\gamma^A = 1/(\phi^A - 1)$ and $K_i^*(L_i^*)$ is country i's capital (labor) stock net of resources consumed by set-up costs, e.g., $K_i^* = K_i - H_{Ai}\alpha_{KA} - H_{Bi}\alpha_{KB}$. Analogous marginal cost functions for industry B's firms exist with $(\beta_{LB} K_i^* - \beta_{KB} L_i^*)$ replaced by $(-\beta_{LA} K_i^* + \beta_{KA} L_i^*)$.

III. The Gravity Equation

Sections I and II provide an analytical framework for generating the gravity equation, as specified in (1). The "usual monopolistic competition assumption" that firms view the marginal utility of income as fixed is made; Y_j, y_j, and the bracketed price terms in (4) are treated as exogenous. The representative firm in A, for example, maximizes profits by supplying exports according to (11) given demand curve (4). Making the appropriate substitutions, solving for reduced forms, summing up across all firms in industry A in country i, and some mathematical manipulation yields the "generalized" gravity equation:

$$
\begin{aligned}
PX_{Aij} \\
&= \delta^{(\gamma^A+1)/(\gamma^A+\sigma^A)} \left(Y_i^K\right)^{(\sigma^A-1)/(\gamma^A+\sigma^A)} \\
&\times (\beta_{KA}\beta_{LB} - \beta_{KB}\beta_{LA})^{-1} \\
&\times \left[\beta_{LB} - \beta_{KB}(K_i^*/L_i^*)^{-1}\right]^{(\sigma^A-1)/(\gamma^A+\sigma^A)} \\
&\times (Y_j)^{(\gamma^A+1)/(\gamma^A+\sigma^A)} \\
&\times \left(1 - y_j^{\,1}\right)^{(\gamma^A+1)/(\gamma^A+\sigma^A)} \\
&\times C_{Aij}^{-(\sigma^A-1)(1+\gamma^A)/(\gamma^A+\sigma^A)} \\
&\times T_{Aij}^{-\sigma^A(\gamma^A+1)/(\gamma^A+\sigma^A)} \\
&\times E_{ij}^{\sigma^A(\gamma^A+1)/(\gamma^A+\sigma^A)} \\
&\times \left\{\left[\sum_n (P_{Ain}/C_{Ain})^{1+\gamma^A}\right]^{1/(1+\gamma^A)}\right\}^{-\gamma^A(\sigma^A-1)/(\gamma^A+\sigma^A)} \\
&\times \left\{\left[\sum_n (P_{Anj}T_{Anj})/E_{nj}\right]^{1-\sigma^A}\right\}^{-(\gamma^A+1)/(\gamma^A+\sigma^A)}
\end{aligned}
\tag{12}
$$

where PX_{Aij} is the value of the trade flow from i to j in industry A and Y_i^K is i's national output in terms of units of capital ($Y_i^K = K_i^* = \Sigma_h^A \beta_{KA} X_{Ahi} + \Sigma_h^B \beta_{KB} X_{Bhi}$).

Exporter i's national output and capital–labor ratio and importer j's income and per capita income enter explicitly with theoretically interpretable coefficients. In the typical gravity equation estimated, exporter GDP is a proxy of i's national output expressed in terms of units of capital. Exporter per capita GDP is a proxy of i's capital–labor endowment ratio. Importer GDP is j's national income. Importer per capita GDP is j's per capita income. Distance in the typical gravity equation is interpreted as the c.i.f./f.o.b. factor. Hence, A_{ij} should include measures of j's tariff rate on i's exports, the bilateral exchange rate, and the two complex price terms.

Typical gravity equations coefficient estimates for exporter and importer incomes and per capita incomes using specification (1) are all positive when aggregate trade flows are examined. If good A is the luxury in consumption, good A is capital intensive in production, and good A's elasticity of substitution exceeds unity, the theoretical coefficients for exporter and importer incomes and per capita incomes in equation (12) are all positively signed. Thus, typical gravity equation coefficient estimates for these variables in aggregate trade flow regressions suggest that the products exchanged tend to be capital intensive in production and luxuries in consumption; these are feasible inferences since estimation usually involves trade flows among major industrialized countries. Of course, expected coefficient signs would change as one or more of these assumptions change. Moreover, only in this special case of two industries and two factors can the capital or labor intensity of an industry be *inferred*.

IV. The Gravity Equation in a Multi-Industry World

Efforts to generalize the H-O model beyond two industries and two factors have usually failed. Moreover, empirical efforts to infer the relative factor abundance of a country given its technology matrix and its net exports have been shown recently to be flawed. Similarly, as Leamer and Bowen (1981, p. 1041) suggest, one cannot infer relative factor intensities of industries using the preceding gravity equation framework when there are more then two factors and two industries.

Yet Deardorff (1982) provided a "weak" generalization of the H-O theorem by proving that "countries tend to export those goods which use intensively their abundant factors" (p. 684). Analogously, the Rybczynski theorem can be generalized to show that in a multi-industry world an increase in a country's endowment of capital (labor) *tends* to increase the output of relatively capital-intensive (labor-intensive) industries; the proof is available upon request. Thus, the coefficient for exporter's per capita income (as a proxy for the exporter's K/L ratio) will have a certain *tendency* linked to whether the gravity equation is estimated for a capital- or labor-intensive industry. Consequently, a weak inference of the relative factor intensity of the industry can be made using exporter per capita income coefficient estimates from a gravity equation.

The empirical analysis of the generalized gravity equation here distinguishes industries by single-digit Standard Industrial Trade Classifications (SITCs) 0 through 8. The tariff variable is proxied by dummy variables indicating the presence of preferential trading arrangements, as is common. The transport-cost factor is proxied by the distance between economic centers of i and j and a dummy for adjacency.[3] The calculation of the complex price terms of (12) is beyond this paper's scope. However, as discussed in Bergstrand (1985) cross-country differences in such price levels can be approximated by cross-country variation in price indexes, if the latter are calculated similarly using a common base period "well chosen" to avoid large divergences from purchasing power parity. Aggregate wholesale price indexes (WPIs) are used.[4] The exchange rate index will indicate changes in the i-currency value of a unit of j's currency since the common base period. A rise in this index implies an appreciation (depreciation) of the importer's (exporter's) currency from the base. As in Bergstrand (1985), base years 1960 for 1965 and 1966 estimates and 1970 for 1975 and 1976 estimates were chosen. Estimation used the heteroskedasticity-consistent covariance-matrix estimator of White (1980), given cross-country data and the possibility of heteroskedastic error terms.

Some remarks are in order regarding expected coefficient signs. Four variables have unambiguous expected effects. A rise in j's income, an appreciation of j's currency, adjacency, and the presence of preferential trading arrangements should increase (the value of) the trade flow from i to j; greater distance between these countries should reduce this flow. If the elasticity of substitution in consumption for the industry (σ) exceeds unity, i's income, i's WPI, and j's WPI will have positive, negative, and positive coefficient estimates, respectively; conversely, if σ is less than one. If σ exceeds one, then a positive (negative) coefficient for exporter per capita income indicates a tendency for the industry to be capital (labor) intensive. Finally, a positive (negative) coefficient for importer per capita income indicates that the industry's output is a luxury (necessity) in consumption.

Tables 1–4 present coefficient estimates and t-statistics from the generalized gravity equations. Exporter and importer income coefficient estimates here conform to typical gravity equation results for aggregate trade flows in previous studies. Additionally, positive and statistically significant coefficient estimates for exporter income for each industry and year imply each industry's elasticity of substitution exceeds unity.

The coefficient estimate for exporter per capita income is positive and statistically significant for raw materials (SITC 2) in all four years, for chemicals (SITC 5) and machinery and transport equipment (SITC 7) in 1965, 1966, and 1975, for manufactures classified chiefly by material (SITC 6) in 1965 and 1966, and for food products (SITC 0) in 1975 and 1976, suggesting that these products *tend* to be capital intensive in production. This coefficient estimate is negative and statistically significant for beverages and tobacco (SITC 1) in all four years and miscellaneous manufactures (SITC 8) in 1975 and 1976, suggesting these products *tend* to be labor intensive. All of these results seem plausible.

The coefficient estimate for importer per capita income is positive and statistically significant for beverages and tobacco, manufactures classified chiefly by material, and miscellaneous manufactures in all four years, and for machinery and transport equipment in 1975 and 1976, suggesting that these products are luxuries. This coefficient estimate is negative and statistically significant for raw materials in 1975 and 1976, for fuel and fuel products (SITC 3) in 1965, and for chemicals in 1976, suggesting that these products are necessities. These results also seem plausible.

Traditional nonactivity variables, such as distance and dummies for adjacency, EC member-

[3] The countries are the United States, Canada, Japan, Austria, Belgium-Luxembourg, Denmark, France, Germany, Italy, Netherlands, Norway, Portugal, Spain, Sweden, Switzerland, and the United Kingdom. The sources for all data except populations are in Bergstrand (1985). Populations are from OECD *Annual Main Economic Indicators, 1955–71* for 1965 and 1966 and OECD *Monthly Main Economic Indicators*, January 1979 for 1975 and 1976. The adjacency dummy equals 1 if both countries share a common land border; 0 otherwise. The *EC* (*EFTA*) dummy assumes a value of 1 if both countries are members of the *EC* (*EFTA*); 0 otherwise. The *ECEFTA* dummy is for participation in the EC-EFTA free trade pact which applies to 1975 and 1976 trade flows; this dummy assumes a value of 1 if both countries are members of these trade groups and 0 otherwise.

[4] Aggregate wholesale price indexes are available for a wide range of countries whereas product price indexes by 1-digit SITC groups are not. OECD *Main Economic Indicators* (later monthly issues) publish producer price indexes by industry groups, and groups varying according to country. Nevertheless, cross-country variation in aggregate wholesale price indexes capture variation in these producer price indexes reasonably well, except for fuel. Cross-country correlation coefficients between 1976 wholesale price indexes and the respective 1976 industry-group producer price index (both based to 1970) when the latter had at least 7 observations are reported (the number of observations for each correlation is in parentheses): agriculture (7), 0.98; food products (11), 0.95; textiles (7), 0.93; metals (7), 0.89; chemicals (10), 0.87; fuel (13), 0.15. The poor correlation for fuel is not surprising since the OPEC shock of 1974 came between 1976 and the base year, 1970.

TABLE 1.—GENERALIZED GRAVITY EQUATION ESTIMATED FOR ONE-DIGIT SITC TRADE FLOWS, 1965

	SITC 0	SITC 1	SITC 2	SITC 3	SITC 4	SITC 5	SITC 6	SITC 7	SITC 8
Right-Hand-Side Variables	Food & Live Animals	Beverages & Tobacco	Raw Materials	Fuels	Animal & Vegetable Oils & Fats	Chemicals	Manufactures Classified Chiefly by Material	Machinery & Transport Equipment	Miscellaneous Manufactures
Exporter Income	0.75[b]	1.67[b]	0.61[b]	1.87[b]	0.94[b]	0.92[b]	0.61[b]	0.95[b]	0.89[b]
	(8.80)	(13.81)	(8.83)	(11.81)	(7.46)	(14.49)	(10.76)	(15.31)	(14.65)
Exporter Per Capita Income	−0.12	−1.64[b]	0.73[b]	0.20	−0.25	0.41[b]	0.30[a]	1.40[b]	0.07
	(−0.68)	(−5.65)	(4.52)	(0.59)	(−0.90)	(2.68)	(2.34)	(8.61)	(0.47)
Importer Income	0.77[b]	0.76[b]	0.76[b]	0.68[b]	0.89[b]	0.67[b]	0.62[b]	0.54[b]	0.63[b]
	(8.45)	(6.00)	(10.87)	(4.42)	(6.60)	(10.69)	(10.59)	(7.51)	(9.63)
Importer Per Capita Income	0.32	1.13[b]	−0.08	−0.79[a]	−0.40	−0.22	0.48[b]	0.17	0.86[b]
	(1.46)	(3.94)	(−0.55)	(−2.34)	(−1.37)	(−1.53)	(3.89)	(1.17)	(6.03)
Distance	−0.84[b]	−1.77[b]	−0.70[b]	−2.80[b]	−1.10[b]	−0.93[b]	−0.86[b]	−0.70[b]	−0.67[b]
	(−6.24)	(−8.53)	(−7.15)	(−11.57)	(−5.62)	(−9.35)	(−9.89)	(−6.64)	(−6.72)
Adjacency Dummy	0.62[b]	−0.03	0.68[b]	0.99[a]	0.85[a]	0.60[b]	0.45[b]	0.75[b]	0.83[b]
	(2.80)	(−0.10)	(3.30)	(2.06)	(2.41)	(3.63)	(2.92)	(4.20)	(5.12)
EEC Dummy	0.43	−0.002	0.22	0.13	0.12	0.32[a]	0.57[b]	0.69[b]	0.62[a]
	(1.50)	(−0.005)	(0.98)	(0.25)	(0.37)	(1.97)	(3.39)	(3.12)	(2.52)
EFTA Dummy	0.33	0.96[b]	0.14	1.20[a]	0.56	0.73[b]	0.82[b]	0.42[a]	1.05[b]
	(1.28)	(2.64)	(0.59)	(2.50)	(1.37)	(4.08)	(5.20)	(2.33)	(6.50)
Appreciation of Importer's Currency	7.83[b]	2.49	12.15[b]	−15.93[b]	−5.33	−5.62[a]	−1.36	−7.91[b]	−6.66[b]
	(3.54)	(0.72)	(5.71)	(−3.35)	(−1.33)	(−2.52)	(−0.88)	(−4.19)	(−3.10)
Exporter WPI	0.62	0.12	−2.08	−6.05	−4.03	−2.41	−6.73[b]	0.88	−2.47
	(0.36)	(0.05)	(−1.59)	(−1.69)	(−1.64)	(−1.73)	(−5.61)	(0.53)	(−1.80)
Importer WPI	2.93	−4.62	0.07	−3.46	3.62	−0.17	0.65	0.95	−0.57
	(1.38)	(−1.61)	(0.04)	(−1.11)	(1.33)	(−0.13)	(0.56)	(0.74)	(−0.37)
Constant	−25.57	25.71	13.71	66.78	−2.37	17.19	45.96[b]	−14.07	18.80
	(−1.16)	(0.88)	(0.82)	(1.73)	(−0.09)	(1.08)	(3.45)	(−0.82)	(1.14)
Adjusted R^2	0.53	0.58	0.66	0.63	0.38	0.72	0.73	0.78	0.73
Root Mean Square Error	1.394	1.978	1.084	2.464	2.043	0.977	0.879	1.017	0.986
Number of Observations	240	240	240	240	240	240	240	240	240

Notes: All variables except dummies are expressed in natural logarithms. Estimation uses White's heteroskedasticity-consistent covariance matrix estimator. t-statistics are in parentheses.
[a] Significant in two-tail t-tests at the 5% level.
[b] Significant in two-tail t-tests at the 1% level.

TABLE 2.—GENERALIZED GRAVITY EQUATION ESTIMATED FOR ONE-DIGIT SITC TRADE FLOWS, 1966

	SITC 0	SITC 1	SITC 2	SITC 3	SITC 4	SITC 5	SITC 6	SITC 7	SITC 8
Right-Hand-Side Variables	Food & Live Animals	Beverages & Tobacco	Raw Materials	Fuels	Animal & Vegetable Oils & Fats	Chemicals	Manufactures Classified Chiefly by Material	Machinery & Transport Equipment	Miscellaneous Manufactures
Exporter Income	0.79[b]	1.68[b]	0.60[b]	1.93[b]	0.99[b]	0.89[b]	0.58[b]	0.93[b]	0.89[b]
	(9.58)	(13.98)	(9.14)	(12.71)	(7.44)	(13.89)	(10.65)	(14.16)	(14.64)
Exporter Per Capita	−0.01	−1.64[b]	0.84[b]	0.12	−0.09	0.46[b]	0.30[a]	1.28[b]	−0.06
Income	(−0.06)	(−5.47)	(5.29)	(0.33)	(−0.31)	(3.01)	(2.46)	(7.59)	(−0.35)
Importer Income	0.76[b]	0.82[b]	0.77[b]	0.74[b]	1.00[b]	0.69[b]	0.65[b]	0.60[b]	0.65[b]
	(8.90)	(6.72)	(11.08)	(4.86)	(6.92)	(10.92)	(11.83)	(8.23)	(10.45)
Importer Per Capita	0.33	1.06[b]	−0.12	−0.33	−0.28	−0.24	0.41[b]	0.07	0.79[b]
Income	(1.57)	(3.71)	(−0.82)	(−0.98)	(−0.92)	(−1.70)	(3.43)	(0.48)	(5.59)
Distance	−0.73[b]	−1.60[b]	−0.65[b]	−2.63[b]	−1.07[b]	−0.89[b]	−0.85[b]	−0.77[b]	−0.69[b]
	(−5.57)	(−7.74)	(−6.66)	(−10.83)	(−5.27)	(−9.20)	(−10.32)	(−7.16)	(−7.06)
Adjacency Dummy	0.65[b]	0.03	0.70[b]	0.88	0.69	0.61[b]	0.41[b]	0.71[b]	0.79[b]
	(3.26)	(0.09)	(3.38)	(1.82)	(1.81)	(3.56)	(2.72)	(4.12)	(4.56)
EEC Dummy	0.56[a]	0.28	0.30	0.20	0.65[a]	0.45[b]	0.69[b]	0.63[b]	0.72[b]
	(2.15)	(0.76)	(1.32)	(0.40)	(2.00)	(2.70)	(4.46)	(2.88)	(2.92)
EFTA Dummy	0.40	0.97[b]	0.03	0.97[a]	0.58	0.72[b]	0.88[b]	0.67[b]	1.17[b]
	(1.70)	(2.63)	(0.14)	(1.99)	(1.28)	(3.93)	(5.72)	(3.98)	(7.80)
Appreciation of	6.60[b]	2.72	10.16[b]	−10.57[a]	−7.23	−4.53[a]	−0.59	−7.69[b]	−5.55[b]
Importer's Currency	(3.58)	(0.93)	(5.69)	(−2.37)	(−1.84)	(−2.33)	(−0.47)	(−4.74)	(−2.94)
Exporter WPI	4.30[b]	4.08	−0.57	2.11	0.40	−3.94[b]	−7.47[b]	−2.61	−3.92[b]
	(2.88)	(1.57)	(−0.44)	(0.59)	(0.16)	(−2.85)	(−6.66)	(−1.56)	(−2.92)
Importer WPI	1.79	−2.90	1.36	−5.54	3.95	0.11	0.80	0.75	−0.31
	(0.91)	(−1.05)	(0.94)	(−1.80)	(1.32)	(0.09)	(0.72)	(0.58)	(−0.20)
Constant	−44.85[a]	−16.24	−6.50	21.62	−38.00	25.79	50.06[b]	11.85	27.24
	(−2.29)	(−0.56)	(−0.43)	(0.57)	(−1.32)	(1.69)	(3.89)	(1.68)	(1.66)
Adjusted R^2	0.56	0.58	0.68	0.62	0.40	0.72	0.74	0.77	0.73
Root Mean Square Error	1.309	1.946	1.046	2.444	2.146	0.974	0.834	1.030	0.974
Number of Observations	240	240	240	240	240	240	240	240	240

Notes: See table 1.

TABLE 3.—GENERALIZED GRAVITY EQUATION ESTIMATED FOR ONE-DIGIT SITC TRADE FLOWS, 1975

	SITC 0	SITC 1	SITC 2	SITC 3	SITC 4	SITC 5	SITC 6	SITC 7	SITC 8
Right-Hand-Side Variables	Food & Live Animals	Beverages & Tobacco	Raw Materials	Fuels	Animal & Vegetable Oils & Fats	Chemicals	Manufactures Classified Chiefly by Material	Machinery & Transport Equipment	Miscellaneous Manufactures
Exporter Income	0.63[b]	1.29[b]	0.60[b]	1.59[b]	1.10[b]	1.08[b]	0.92[b]	1.26[b]	1.15[b]
	(8.22)	(10.32)	(7.31)	(9.46)	(7.30)	(17.84)	(15.29)	(21.59)	(18.58)
Exporter Per Capita Income	0.47[a]	−1.54[b]	1.21[b]	0.58	0.34	0.33[a]	−0.10	0.32[a]	−0.85[b]
	(2.36)	(−4.68)	(5.81)	(1.27)	(0.87)	(2.20)	(−0.70)	(2.07)	(−5.03)
Importer Income	0.79[b]	0.92[b]	1.05[b]	1.04[b]	1.07[b]	0.84[b]	0.75[b]	0.67[b]	0.69[b]
	(9.40)	(5.71)	(11.57)	(5.23)	(7.13)	(13.21)	(13.36)	(10.88)	(11.34)
Importer Per Capita Income	0.001	1.71[b]	−0.54[b]	0.25	−0.45	−0.12	0.41[b]	0.32[a]	0.75[b]
	(0.01)	(5.20)	(−2.68)	(0.59)	(−1.15)	(−0.76)	(3.25)	(2.27)	(5.28)
Distance	−0.76[b]	−1.85[b]	−0.84[b]	−1.67[b]	−1.32[b]	−0.72[b]	−0.56[b]	−0.43[b]	−0.37[b]
	(−6.07)	(−6.65)	(−6.92)	(−5.87)	(−5.16)	(−7.19)	(−5.91)	(−4.22)	(−3.81)
Adjacency Dummy	0.83[b]	−0.02	0.66[b]	1.31[b]	0.78[a]	0.71[b]	0.71[b]	0.73[b]	0.93[b]
	(4.18)	(−0.06)	(3.16)	(2.77)	(2.05)	(3.53)	(4.68)	(4.52)	(5.30)
EEC Dummy	0.79[b]	−0.11	0.08	0.88	0.93[a]	0.90[b]	0.85[b]	1.11[b]	1.09[b]
	(2.90)	(−0.22)	(0.36)	(1.60)	(2.08)	(4.65)	(4.60)	(5.68)	(5.48)
EFTA Dummy	0.36	0.56	0.71[a]	0.12	0.30	1.04[b]	1.82[b]	1.69[b]	1.82[b]
	(1.22)	(1.17)	(2.08)	(0.15)	(0.43)	(3.79)	(9.83)	(6.86)	(7.47)
ECEFTA Dummy	−0.21	−0.80	0.56[a]	1.38[b]	0.72	0.92[b]	1.18[b]	1.25[b]	1.08[b]
	(−0.96)	(−1.88)	(2.38)	(2.70)	(1.74)	(4.97)	(7.86)	(7.58)	(5.87)
Appreciation of Importer's Currency	1.44	−1.99	5.07[b]	6.39[b]	0.51	0.76	−0.30	−1.83[b]	−2.65[b]
	(1.86)	(−1.52)	(6.20)	(3.31)	(0.36)	(1.24)	(−0.54)	(−3.26)	(−4.87)
Exporter WPI	0.67	5.07[b]	−1.62	−3.71	−0.17	−3.04[b]	−0.66	1.26	0.96
	(0.54)	(2.63)	(−1.29)	(−1.24)	(−0.08)	(−3.35)	(−0.78)	(1.59)	(1.19)
Importer WPI	2.58[a]	0.91	5.66[b]	11.19[b]	−0.61	1.19	0.94	−0.87	−2.78[b]
	(2.29)	(0.44)	(4.50)	(3.88)	(−0.27)	(1.26)	(1.09)	(−1.07)	(−3.14)
Constant	−25.40[b]	−48.39[b]	−33.95[b]	−66.88[b]	−3.33	6.17	−7.04	−12.21[a]	4.88
	(−3.31)	(−3.69)	(−4.11)	(−3.57)	(−0.21)	(0.86)	(−1.22)	(−2.22)	(0.80)
Adjusted R^2	0.65	0.61	0.63	0.55	0.49	0.78	0.76	0.81	0.77
Root Mean Square Error	1.064	1.809	1.132	2.482	2.009	0.848	0.734	0.760	0.803
Number of Observations	240	240	240	240	240	240	240	240	240

Notes: See table 1.

TABLE 4.—GENERALIZED GRAVITY EQUATION ESTIMATED FOR ONE-DIGIT SITC TRADE FLOWS, 1976

	SITC 0	SITC 1	SITC 2	SITC 3	SITC 4	SITC 5	SITC 6	SITC 7	SITC 8
Right-Hand-Side Variables	Food & Live Animals	Beverages & Tobacco	Raw Materials	Fuels	Animal & Vegetable Oils & Fats	Chemicals	Manufactures Classified Chiefly by Material	Machinery & Transport Equipment	Miscellaneous Manufactures
Exporter Income	0.70[b]	1.22[b]	0.72[b]	1.54[b]	1.32[b]	1.05[b]	0.94[b]	1.35[b]	1.16[b]
	(8.77)	(8.63)	(9.13)	(8.88)	(8.17)	(16.81)	(14.89)	(20.29)	(16.91)
Exporter Per Capita Income	0.62[b]	−1.39[b]	1.36[b]	1.57[b]	0.49	0.26	−0.21	0.21	−0.95[b]
	(3.03)	(−3.91)	(6.14)	(2.93)	(1.20)	(1.57)	(−1.38)	(1.15)	(−4.93)
Importer Income	0.72[b]	1.20[b]	0.91[b]	1.21[b]	0.93[b]	0.96[b]	0.79[b]	0.69[b]	0.72[b]
	(8.04)	(7.16)	(10.23)	(6.12)	(5.70)	(15.04)	(13.25)	(9.74)	(10.57)
Importer Per Capita	0.12	1.68[b]	−0.56[b]	0.50	−0.53	−0.36[a]	0.37[b]	0.45[b]	0.82[b]
	(0.62)	(4.76)	(−2.74)	(1.08)	(−1.33)	(−2.07)	(2.74)	(2.70)	(4.67)
Distance	−0.79[b]	−1.85[b]	−0.88[b]	−2.07[b]	−1.42[b]	−0.77[b]	−0.57[b]	−0.44[b]	−0.36[b]
	(−6.01)	(−6.93)	(−7.94)	(−7.74)	(−5.27)	(−7.95)	(−6.07)	(−3.94)	(−3.58)
Adjacency Dummy	0.83[b]	−0.09	0.64[b]	1.36[b]	0.77[a]	0.62[b]	0.70[b]	0.78[b]	0.97[b]
	(4.20)	(−0.25)	(3.40)	(3.01)	(2.04)	(3.16)	(4.66)	(4.61)	(5.36)
EEC Dummy	0.73[b]	0.09	0.002	1.01	0.97[a]	1.04[b]	1.05[b]	1.32[b]	1.23[b]
	(2.69)	(0.19)	(0.01)	(1.84)	(2.00)	(5.31)	(5.61)	(6.26)	(5.87)
EFTA Dummy	0.26	0.85	0.80[b]	0.59	0.53	1.25[b]	1.93[b]	1.90[b]	1.81[b]
	(0.86)	(1.62)	(2.67)	(0.78)	(0.79)	(4.57)	(10.40)	(7.11)	(6.61)
ECEFTA Dummy	−0.26	−0.56	0.52[a]	1.54[b]	0.76	1.09[b]	1.34[b]	1.44[b]	1.20[b]
	(−1.17)	(−1.27)	(2.46)	(2.96)	(1.74)	(5.93)	(8.68)	(7.80)	(6.03)
Appreciation of Importer's Currency	0.37	1.77	1.74[a]	7.14[b]	−2.42	2.14[b]	−0.41	−1.86[b]	−2.04[b]
	(0.40)	(1.10)	(2.05)	(3.46)	(−1.55)	(3.31)	(−0.64)	(−2.78)	(−3.28)
Exporter WPI	1.36	−0.19	1.19	−4.28	4.92[a]	−4.00[b]	−0.22	1.77[a]	0.88
	(1.03)	(−0.08)	(0.92)	(−1.41)	(2.20)	(−4.38)	(−0.24)	(1.97)	(0.96)
Importer WPI	1.25	4.32[a]	2.30[a]	11.72[b]	−4.16	2.66[b]	0.43	−1.05	−2.05[a]
	(1.06)	(2.00)	(2.02)	(4.12)	(−1.92)	(2.85)	(0.49)	(−1.14)	(−2.29)
Constant	−21.19[b]	−37.98	−29.92[b]	−68.39[b]	−15.26	2.36	−7.08	−16.13[b]	−0.34
	(−3.32)	(−3.26)	(−4.67)	(−4.68)	(−1.27)	(0.41)	(−1.55)	(−3.25)	(−0.06)
Adjusted R^2	0.66	0.62	0.63	0.60	0.52	0.79	0.77	0.79	0.75
Root Mean Square Error	1.043	1.824	1.058	2.471	1.990	0.840	0.736	0.827	0.857
Number of Observations	240	240	240	240	240	240	240	240	240

Notes: See table 1.

ship, EFTA membership, and the EC-EFTA trade pact, generally have the expected coefficient signs and are often significant. Distance's coefficient estimate sign is negative and statistically significant in all 36 regressions. Adjacency's coefficient estimate is positive in all industries but beverages and tobacco, and is positive and statistically significant in all but beverages and tobacco, fuels, and animal and vegetable oil and fats (some years). The dummies for trade-preference membership are positive in 84 and 90 cases and are statistically significant in 56 cases.

Nontraditional nonactivity variables—exporter and importer WPI's and the exchange rate—do not fare as well; coefficient estimates have mixed signs and are usually statistically insignificant. Aggregate WPIs— being crude proxies for industry-specific producer price indexes—may explain these poor results. Finally, the coefficient estimate for the appreciation of the importer's currency—anticipated to be positive—is positive and statistically significant in 9 (of 36) cases, but is negative and statistically significant in 12 cases. Although the latter results can be discounted for 1965 and 1966 because of little variation in this variable during the pre-1973 regime of "fixed" exchange rates, the remaining negative and statistically significant exchange rate coefficient estimates in 1975 and 1976 for two industries, machinery and transport equipment and miscellaneous manufactures, cannot be so readily explained.

V. Conclusion

The purpose of this study was to offer an analytical framework for understanding the gravity equation that is consistent with modern theories of inter-industry and intra-industry trade. Using a two-factor, two-industry, *N*-country Heckscher-Ohlin-Chamberlin-Linder model, exporter income and per capita income could be interpreted as national output in terms of units of capital and the country's capital–labor endowment ratio, respectively. Changes in importer income and per capita income could be interpreted as alterations of expenditure capabilities and taste preferences á la Linder, respectively.

The generalized gravity equation explains empirically between 40% and 80% of the variation across countries in one-digit SITC trade flows. Exporter and importer income coefficients match those from typical and generalized gravity equations estimated for aggregate trade flows. Exporter per capita income coefficient estimates suggest that raw materials, chemicals, machinery and transport equipment, manufactures classified chiefly by material, and food products tend to be capital intensive in production and that beverages and tobacco and miscellaneous manufactures tend to be labor intensive in production. Importer per capita income coefficient estimates suggest that manufactures tend to be luxuries and that raw materials, fuels, and chemicals tend to be necessities in consumption. Since price and exchange rate coefficients have mixed signs probably owing to the crudeness of the proxies, future research should refine the proxies for the complex theoretical price terms, perhaps along the line suggested in Kravis, Heston and Summers (1982); moreover, such research should extend the level of disaggregation.

REFERENCES

Anderson, James E., "A Theoretical Foundation for the Gravity Equation," *American Economic Review* 69 (Mar. 1979), 106–116.

Bergstrand, Jeffrey H., "The Gravity Equation in International Trade: Some Microeconomic Foundations and Empirical Evidence," this REVIEW 67 (Aug. 1985), 474–481.

Brada, Josef C., and José A. Méndez, "Economic Integration Among Developed, Developing and Centrally Planned Economies: A Comparative Analysis," this REVIEW 67 (Nov. 1985), 549–556.

Deardorff, Alan, "The General Validity of the Heckscher-Ohlin Theorem," *American Economic Review* 72 (Sept. 1982), 683–694.

Geraci, Vincent J., and Wilfried Prewo, "An Empirical Demand and Supply Model of Multilateral Trade," this REVIEW 64 (Aug. 1982), 432–441.

Gruber, William H., and Raymond Vernon, "The Technology Factor in a World Trade Matrix," in Raymond Vernon (ed.), *The Technology Factor in International Trade* (New York: Columbia University Press, 1970), 233–272.

Helpman, Elhanan, "International Trade in the Presence of Product Differentiation, Economies of Scale and Monopolistic Competition: A Chamberlin-Heckscher-Ohlin Approach," *Journal of International Economics* 11 (1981), 305–340.

Helpman, Elhanan, and Paul Krugman, *Market Structure and Foreign Trade* (Cambridge, MA: MIT Press, 1985).

Kravis, Irving B., Alan Heston and Robert Summers, *World Product and Income: International Comparisons of Real Gross Product* (Baltimore: Johns Hopkins University Press, 1982).

Krugman, Paul, "Scale Economies, Product Differentiation, and the Pattern of Trade," *American Economic Review* 70 (Dec. 1980), 950–959.

———, "Pricing to Market when the Exchange Rate Changes," in Sven W. Arndt and J. David Richardson (eds.), *Real-Financial Linkages Among Open Economies* (Cambridge, MA: MIT Press, 1987).

Leamer, Edward E., "The Commodity Composition of International Trade in Manufactures: An Empirical Analysis," *Oxford Economic Papers* 26 (1974), 350–374.

Leamer, Edward E., and Harry P. Bowen, "Cross-Section Tests of the Heckscher-Ohlin Theorem: Comment," *American Economic Review* 71 (Dec. 1981), 1040–1043.

Linder, Staffan Burenstam, *An Essay on Trade and Transformation* (New York: John Wiley and Sons, 1961).

Linnemann, Hans, *An Econometric Study of International Trade Flows* (Amsterdam: North-Holland Publishing Co., 1966).

Markusen, James R., "Explaining the Volume of Trade: An Eclectic Approach," *American Economic Review* 76 (Dec. 1986), 1002–1011.

Thursby, Jerry G., and Marie C. Thursby, "Bilateral Trade Flows, the Linder Hypothesis, and Exchange Risk," this REVIEW 69 (Aug. 1987), 488–495.

White, Halbert, "A Heteroskedasticity-Consistent Covariance Matrix Estimator and a Direct Test for Heteroskedasticity," *Econometrica* 48 (May 1980), 817–838.

SUPPLEMENTARY PROOF

A Weak Generalization of the Rybczynski Theorem

Assume that a country can produce M goods using two factors of production, capital (K) and labor (L). Let ρ_m equal the (exogenous) capital-labor ratio for producing good m ($m = 1, \ldots, M$); ℓ_m is the share of labor used in producing good m. Both factors are assumed to be fully employed. Relative factor and commodity prices are fixed so that the optimum capital-labor ratio to produce any commodity does not change. Under these conditions, the following theorem holds:

Theorem. If the capital stock increases, a good's output will tend to rise (fall) if that good is relatively capital (labor) intensive in production; if the labor stock increases, a good's output will tend to rise (fall) if that good is relatively labor (capital) intensive in production.

Proof. Full employment ensures

$$\sum_{m=1}^{M} \ell_m = 1 \quad \text{and} \quad \sum_{m=1}^{M} \rho_m \ell_m = K/L.$$

Suppose the national capital stock increases from K to K^*, then:

$$(K/L)^* - (K/L) = \sum_{m=1}^{M} \rho_m \ell_m^* - \sum_{m=1}^{M} \rho_m \ell_m = \sum_{m=1}^{M} \rho_m \hat{\ell}_m > 0,$$

where $\hat{\ell}_m = \ell_m^* - \ell_m \gtreqless 0$. In vector notation:

$$\underline{\rho}' \cdot \hat{\underline{\ell}} > 0$$

where "$\cdot$" denotes the inner product, $\underline{\rho}$ is an Mx1 vector of $K - L$ intensities for the M goods, and $\hat{\underline{\ell}}$ is an Mx1 vector of differences between the new and old shares of labor used to produce the M goods. Using an approach similar to Deardorff (Journal of Political Economy, 1980), a positive correlation between the factor intensity (ρ_m) of a good and the corresponding change in its factor share ($\hat{\ell}_m$) is sufficient to establish that if a good is relatively capital (labor) intensive in production the good's output will tend to rise (fall) as the capital endowment increases. The correlation between factor intensities and changes in factor shares is defined as:

$$\mathrm{Corr}(\underline{\rho}, \hat{\underline{\ell}}) = \mathrm{Cov}(\underline{\rho}' \cdot \hat{\underline{\ell}})/[\mathrm{Var}(\underline{\rho})\mathrm{Var}(\hat{\underline{\ell}})]^{1/2}, \tag{1}$$

where

$$\mathrm{Cov}(\hat{\underline{\rho}}, \hat{\underline{\ell}}) = \sum_{m=1}^{M} (\rho_m - \overline{\rho})(\hat{\ell}_m - \overline{\hat{\ell}}),$$

$$\mathrm{Var}(\underline{\rho}) = \sum_{m=1}^{M} (\rho_m - \overline{\rho})^2, \qquad \mathrm{Var}(\hat{\underline{\ell}}) = \sum_{m=1}^{M} (\hat{\ell}_m - \overline{\hat{\ell}})^2,$$

$$\mathrm{Mean}\,(\underline{\rho}) = \overline{\rho} = \left(\sum_{m=1}^{M} \rho_m\right)/M, \quad \mathrm{Mean}\,(\hat{\underline{\ell}}) = \overline{\hat{\ell}} = \left(\sum_{m=1}^{M} \hat{\ell}_m\right)/M.$$

The denominator of equation (1) is nonnegative when the correlation is defined and positive when variances are nonzero; this is assumed. Hence, the correlation and the covariance must have the same sign. The covariance, however, can be written as:

$$\mathrm{Cov}(\underline{\rho}, \hat{\underline{\ell}}) = \underline{\rho}' \cdot \hat{\underline{\ell}} - M\overline{\rho}\overline{\hat{\ell}}.$$

Yet, the assumption of full employment ensures:

$$\sum_{m=1}^{M} \hat{\ell}_m = \sum_{m=1}^{M} (\ell_m^* - \ell_m) = 0$$

which implies

$$\bar{\hat{\ell}} = \left(\sum_{m=1}^{M} \hat{\ell}_m \right) / M = 0.$$

Hence,

$$\mathrm{Corr}(\underline{\rho}, \underline{\hat{\ell}}) = \underline{\rho}' \cdot \underline{\hat{\ell}} > 0.$$

□

By analogy, if the labor stock increases, a good's output will tend to rise (fall) if that good is relatively labor (capital) intensive in production.

Chapter 3

THE HECKSCHER–OHLIN–SAMUELSON MODEL, THE LINDER HYPOTHESIS AND THE DETERMINANTS OF BILATERAL INTRA-INDUSTRY TRADE*

Jeffrey H. Bergstrand

In the past ten years, several econometric studies of intra-industry trade have examined the determinants of the degree of this trade between pairs of countries for a particular industry, cf., Balassa and Bauwens (1987). These cross-country studies have found systematic empirical relationships between the share of intra-industry trade between two countries and the average levels of and inequalities between their gross domestic products (GDPs), per capita GDPs, and tariffs.

Although these relationships are robust across econometric studies, a unified theoretical framework for including each one of these particular variables has not yet been established. This paper extends the theoretical work of Dixit and Norman (1980), Helpman (1981, 1987), Krugman (1979, 1980, 1981), Helpman and Krugman (1985), and Markusen (1986) by analysing how each of the six determinants noted above, as well as the average level of and inequality between their capital-labour endowment ratios, specifically influences their share of intra-industry trade in a given commodity group. Empirical results are provided to evaluate the theoretical propositions.

Section I provides a motivation. Section II summarises the theoretical model developed in Bergstrand (1989) and extended here to address these particular issues. Section III describes the determinants of the volume and pattern of bilateral trade. Section IV presents the empirical results. Section V summarises the paper's results and qualifies them.

I. MOTIVATION

Theoretical rationales for the robust empirical relationships between the share of intra-industry trade between two countries and the average levels of and inequalities between their GDPs, per capita GDPs, and tariffs have either varied or not been demonstrated formally. In the case of inequality between per capita incomes, rationales have varied. Pagoulatos and Sorensen (1975), Loertscher and Wolter (1980), Toh (1982), Lundberg (1982) and Havrylyshyn and Civan (1983) interpret the inequality between two countries' per capita incomes as taste differences, as suggested by Linder (1961); the share of

* The author is grateful to Ronald Balvers, Peter Lloyd, two anonymous referees, an associate editor, and participants at the April 1988 meeting of the Midwest International Economics Group in Minneapolis, Minnesota and at the May 1989 'Symposium on Intra-Industry Trade' organised by P. K. M. Tharakan at the European Institute for Advanced Studies in Management in Brussels for helpful comments on earlier drafts.

*Originally Published in *The Economic Journal*, 100(403), pp. 1216–1229.

bilateral intra-industry trade is lower the greater the difference in their per capita incomes. Yet formal theoretical models of intra-industry trade, such as Helpman (1981), Krugman (1981) and Helpman and Krugman (1985), explain this negative correlation by interpreting per capita income differences as capital-labour endowment ratio differences. Helpman (1981) notes this has the 'flavor of the Linder hypothesis', but adds that his framework reflects supply considerations whereas Linder's hypothesis is 'based on the assumption that relative demands change with per capita income' (p. 337).

Similarly, most econometric studies have explained the positive relationship between the share of intra-industry trade and average level of per capita income using Linder (1961). Higher average per capita income represents a higher 'level of economic development', raising the extent of demand for differentiated products, increasing the share of intra-industry trade, cf., Loertscher and Wolter (1980), Havrylyshyn and Civan (1983), Balassa (1986*a*, *b*), and Balassa and Bauwens (1987). Yet theoretical models, such as Helpman and Krugman (1985), suggest that higher average per capita income represents a higher average capital-labour endowment ratio. On the assumption that industries that are capital intensive tend to have 'relatively more production of differentiated products', countries with higher average capital-labour ratios will experience a greater share of intra-industry specialisation. Along similar lines, Markusen (1986) argues that if capital intensity in production is positively correlated with a high income elasticity of demand in consumption, relatively capital-rich countries will have a higher share of intra-industry trade, although he notes that this 'empirical connection between factor intensities and income elasticities has not yet been established' (p. 1011).

On the other hand, some of the empirical correlations have no formal theoretical rationale. Some econometric studies have found a negative (positive) correlation between countries' average tariff and/or nontariff barrier levels (custom union dummies) and the share of intra-industry trade, cf., Pagoulatos and Sorensen (1975), Loertscher and Wolter (1980), Caves (1981), Toh (1982), Bergstrand (1983), Havrylyshyn and Civan (1983), Balassa (1986*a*, *b*) and Balassa and Bauwens (1987). Although Falvey (1981) showed theoretically that the volume of intra industry trade should vary inversely with the average level of trade restrictions, Balassa (1986*b*) notes 'the question is if tariffs will affect intra-industry trade more than inter-industry trade' (p. 29). Similarly, a formal justification for the inequality between countries' tariff levels is lacking.

This literature is extended in three directions. First, the analytical framework uses familiar utility and production assumptions, except that the high income-elasticity good need not be capital intensive in production. Second, the gravity equation plays a prominent role; other studies have typically ignored this device.[1] Greenaway and Milner (1986) suggest that gravity equations provide

[1] Dixit and Norman (1980) and Markusen (1986) do not discuss gravity models; Helpman and Krugman (1985) derive one where bilateral trade flows are a multiplicative function of exporter and importer GDPs only. Helpman and Krugman (1985) note that 'gravity equations tend to fit the trade pattern better, the more important are increasing returns' (p. 167).

all relevant empirical phenomena 'even if they are not able to tell us precisely how they are relevant' (p. 109). Extending Bergstrand (1989), the gravity equation is shown to be a tractable pedagogical tool for explaining simultaneously the impacts of larger and widening national incomes, per capita incomes, capital-labour ratios, and tariffs on the degree of intra-industry trade between pairs of countries. Third, empirical work confirms several formally-presented theoretical propositions.

II. THEORETICAL ISSUES

This section summarises the behaviour of the representative consumer and firm. Since the theoretical foundation follows Bergstrand (1989) fairly closely, only essential differences vis-à-vis that study will be highlighted.

The representative consumer-worker maximises a 'nested' Cobb-Douglas-CES-Stone-Geary utility function subject to an income constraint. The consumer-worker has Cobb-Douglas preferences between two tradeable goods (X, Z). Industry X produces differentiated manufactured commodities which are symmetric, but imperfect, substitutes in demand; products are differentiated by country of origin $(i = 1, \ldots, N)$ and by firm within each country $(h = 1, \ldots, H_{Xi})$. The sub-utility function for good X has a constant elasticity of substitution (CES). Industry Z produces a homogeneous non-manufactured commodity for which the representative consumer-worker has a minimum consumption requirement, common to the Stone-Geary utility function which is used as the sub-utility function for Z.

The constrained utility maximisation yields bilateral import demand function:

$$X_{hij} = \delta Y_j(1-y_j^{-1})\,(P_{hij}D_{ij}\,T_{ij}/E_{ij})^{-\sigma}(\bar{P}_j)^{-1} \tag{1}$$

where X_{hij} is aggregate demand in country j for output of country i's firm h, Y_j is j's national income, y_j is j's per capita income (where 'capita' is expressed in terms of the value of the minimum consumption requirement of Z), P_{hij} is the f.o.b. i-currency price of firm h's output of X sold in j, D_{ij} is the exogenous transport-cost (c.i.f.-f.o.b.) factor to ship X from i to j, T_{ij} is one plus the exogenous tariff rate on exports of X from i to j, E_{ij} is the exogenous exchange rate defined as i's currency per unit of j's currency, $\bar{P}_j$ is an index of the c.i.f. prices of good X supplied by all firms in all countries to j, and σ is the elasticity of substitution in consumption $(\sigma > 1)$. Equation (1) differs from the typical Armington (1969) bilateral import demand function only by the addition of y_j; this term implies an income elasticity of demand for X (Z) greater (less) than one. Hence, X (Z) is the luxury (necessity) by assumption.

The representative firm in industry X in country i maximises profits subject to technology constraints in a market characterised by Chamberlinian monopolistic competition using two factors of production, labour and capital, which are in fixed supply. The firm faces (internal) increasing returns to scale because of fixed setup costs and constant marginal costs; this is captured by the standard linear cost function, as used by Helpman, Krugman, and Markusen.

Different from their models, output of each firm is considered a 'composite commodity' here.

Recent empirical evidence on the price responsiveness of firms substituting output between domestic and foreign markets is inconsistent with the notion that such substitution is costless. As in Geraci and Prewo (1982), Bergstrand (1985, 1989), Deardorff and Stern (1986) and de Melo and Robinson (1985, 1989), shipments by the firm to domestic and foreign markets are considered imperfect substitutes, represented here by a constant-elasticity-of-transformation (CET) function.

Two conditions characterise Chamberlinian monopolistic competition, profit maximisation by firms and zero economic profits in equilibrium. Profit maximisation by the firm given demand function (1) yields mark-up pricing function:

$$P_{hij} = [(1-\sigma^{-1})^{-1}(X_{hij}/X_{hi})^{1/\gamma}](W_i\beta_{LX}+R_i\beta_{KX}) \tag{2}$$

where W_i (R_i) is the wage (rental) rate for labour (capital) in country i, determined in competitive factor markets and taken as given by the firm, β_{LX} (β_{KX}) is the constant marginal input requirement of labour (capital) to produce a unit of X, X_{hij} is the output of firm h in country i exported to country j, X_{hi} is the (composite) output of firm h, and γ is the elasticity of transformation of output among all domestic and foreign markets, i.e.,

$$X_{hi} = [\Sigma_{j=1}^{N} X_{hij}^{(\gamma+1)/\gamma}]^{\gamma/(\gamma+1)}, \quad \gamma > 0.$$

Price is a markup over marginal cost $(W_i\beta_{LX}+R_i\beta_{KX})$. While the markup is characteristically a negative function of the elasticity of substitution in consumption, it is uncharacteristically a positive function of the share of the firm's output exported to market j. If output was costlessly substitutable among markets ($\gamma = \infty$), $(X_{hij}/X_{hi})^{1/\gamma}$ would be unity, leaving the standard markup.

Second, setting profits equal to zero allows solving for the equilibrium (composite) output of the firm:

$$X_{hi} = (\sigma-1)[(W_i\alpha_{LX}+R_i\alpha_{KX})/(W_i\beta_{LX}+R_i\beta_{KX})] \tag{3}$$

where $(W_i\alpha_{LX}+R_i\alpha_{KX})$ is the fixed cost of the firm and recall $\sigma > 1$. That the firm's output is a positive (negative) function of fixed (marginal) costs is common, cf., Krugman (1981) and Markusen (1986).

The value of the bilateral trade flow exported by firm h in country i to country j is determined by substituting output function (3) and demand function (1) into markup pricing function (2), then solving for equilibrium price and quantity. To find the value of the aggregate trade flow from i to j in X, the number of producers (and products) in industry X in i needs to be determined. Assuming labour ($\bar{L}_i$) and capital ($\bar{K}_i$) in each country i are in fixed supply and fully employed:

$$\bar{L}_i = (\alpha_{LX}H_{Xi}+\beta_{LX}H_{Xi}X_{hi})+\beta_{LZ}H_{Zi}Z_{hi} \tag{4a}$$

$$\bar{K}_i = (\alpha_{LX}H_{Xi}+\beta_{KX}H_{Xi}X_{hi})+\beta_{KZ}H_{Zi}Z_{hi} \tag{4b}$$

where the first (second) RHS term in each equation represents the amount of the respective factor used up by industry X (Z). Homogeneous non-manufactured good Z is produced under constant returns to scale; its setup costs are zero. With X_{hi} determined by equation (3), equations (4a) and (4b) can be solved for the number of firms in X in country i (H_{Xi}) and the output of Z in country i ($H_{Zi}Z_{hi}$).

The equilibrium number of firms producing X in country i is:

$$H_{Xi} = \{[(\beta_{KX}\beta_{LZ}-\beta_{KZ}\beta_{LX})(\sigma-1)(W_i\alpha_{LX}+R_i\alpha_{KX})/(W_i\beta_{LX}+R_i\beta_{KX})] + (\alpha_{KX}\beta_{LZ}-\beta_{KZ}\alpha_{LX})\}^{-1}(\beta_{LZ}\bar{K}_i-\beta_{KZ}\bar{L}_i). \quad (5)$$

At given factor prices, changes in factor endowments alter the number of goods produced in industry X, not the level of output of the representative firm, as common to these models. The effect of augmenting a factor's endowment on the equilibrium number of firms depends on relative factor intensities in production, a 'Rybczynski-like' result. Equation (5) readily illustrates that if $X(Z)$ is relatively capital (labour) intensive in production and $\sigma > 1$, a higher capital (labour) stock in country i would increase (decrease) the number of firms producing X in i.[2] In the context of a monopolistically competitive market for X, these results are analogous to the Rybczynski effect in a perfectly competitive market. In perfectly competitive industry Z, conventional Rybczynski results hold.

III. DETERMINANTS OF THE VOLUME AND PATTERN OF BILATERAL TRADE

The value of the bilateral trade flow from i to j in X (PX_{ij}) is determined by multiplying the value of the flow of firm h by the number of firms, equation (5). This yields 'gravity equation' (6) which is similar, but not identical, to that in Bergstrand (1989) because here the number of firms is endogenous:

$$\begin{aligned} PX_{ij} = {} & \sigma^{-\gamma(\sigma-1)/(\gamma+\sigma)}(\sigma-1)^{(\gamma+1)(\sigma-1)/(\gamma+\sigma)}\delta^{(\gamma+1)/(\gamma+\sigma)}\bar{K}_i \\ & \times\{[(\beta_{KX}\beta_{LZ}-\beta_{KZ}\beta_{LX})(\sigma-1)(W_i\alpha_{LX}+R_i\alpha_{KX})/(W_i\beta_{LX}+R_i\beta_{KX}) \\ & +(\alpha_{KX}\beta_{LZ}-\beta_{KZ}\alpha_{LX})]^{-1}[\beta_{LZ}-\beta_{KZ}(\bar{K}_i/\bar{L}_i)^{-1}]\}\,Y_j^{(\gamma+1)/(\gamma+\sigma)} \\ & \times(1-y_j^{-1})^{(\gamma+1)/(\gamma+\sigma)}D_{ij}^{-\sigma(1+\gamma)/(\gamma+\sigma)}T_{ij}^{-\sigma(\gamma+1)/(\gamma+\sigma)}E_{ij}^{\sigma(\gamma+1)/(\gamma+\sigma)} \\ & \times[(W_i\beta_{LX}+R_i\beta_{KX})^{-(\gamma+1)}(W_i\alpha_{LX}+R_i\alpha_{KX})]^{(\sigma-1)/(\gamma+\sigma)}(\bar{P}_j)^{-(\gamma+1)/(\gamma+\sigma)}. \quad (6) \end{aligned}$$

The share of intra-industry trade between i and j in industry X is usually measured using a bilateral version of the Grubel-Lloyd index:

$$GL_{Xij} = 1-[|PX_{ij}-PX_{ji}|/(PX_{ij}+PX_{ji})], \quad 0 \leqslant GL_{Xij} \leqslant 1. \quad (7)$$

Substitution of (6) for PX_{ij} and its analogue for PX_{ji} in (7) yields a complex function (not shown here, but available from the author on request) illustrating

[2] X is considered capital (labour) intensive in production when $\beta_{KX}\beta_{LZ}-\beta_{KZ}\beta_{LX} > 0$ (< 0) and $\alpha_{KX}\beta_{LZ}-\beta_{KZ}\alpha_{LX} > 0$ (< 0). The equilibrium number of firms producing X in i, H_{Xi} will be assumed to be positive; this implies that, if X is relatively capital (labour) intensive in production, then $\beta_{LZ}\bar{K}_i-\beta_{KZ}\bar{L}_i$ ($-\beta_{LZ}\bar{K}_i+\beta_{KZ}\bar{L}_i$) is positive. Unlike Helpman and Krugman (1985) and Markusen (1986), differentiated manufactures industry X is neither assumed to be capital nor labour intensive.

explicitly how average levels of and inequalities between two countries' GDPs, per capita GDPs, capital-labour ratios, and tariffs influence their degree of intra-industry trade. For brevity, only relevant comparative statics are presented. Since these are complex, assume initially an equilibrium where countries i and j are identical in all respects, i.e., identical capital stocks, labour, incomes, factor prices, etc., as in Helpman (1981). In this initial equilibrium, $GL_{Xij} = 1$; all trade is intra-industry in nature. Though some propositions are not new, they have not yet been derived together from a common formal theoretical model.

PROPOSITION 1. *The share of intra-industry trade between countries i and j* (GL_{Xij}) *will be lower the greater the inequality between their relative capital-labour endowment ratios.*

A marginal reallocation of the (initially equal) capital stocks from j to i and of the labour stocks from i to j that alters their relative factor endowments, but not their incomes, commodity prices, factor prices, or per capita incomes (the last restriction to be relaxed shortly) yields:

$$GL_{Xij} = 1 - \left|\frac{\beta_{LZ}\bar{K}_i - \beta_{KZ}\bar{L}_i}{\beta_{LZ}\bar{K}_j - \beta_{KZ}\bar{L}_j} - 1\right| \bigg/ \left(\frac{\beta_{LZ}\bar{K}_i - \beta_{KZ}\bar{L}_i}{\beta_{LZ}\bar{K}_j - \beta_{KZ}\bar{L}_j} + 1\right) < 1. \tag{8}$$

The new inequality between relative factor endowments has created Heckscher-Ohlin-Samuelson trade. This accords with a proposition in Helpman (1981), in a similar model, 'if we reallocate the world's labour and capital stock in a way which [widens the two countries' capital-labour ratios] without disturbing commodity prices and factor rewards, then the share of intra-industry trade...will decline' (p. 325).

PROPOSITION 2. *The share of intra-industry trade will be lower the greater the inequality between per capita incomes because of a greater divergence in tastes.*

In this model, per capita income seems to influence the volume and pattern of trade via two channels, one supply and one demand. On the supply side, national income is attributable ultimately to capital or labour; a larger capital-labour endowment ratio must be associated with higher per capita income, as cross-country empirical comparisons reveal. Greater inequality between two countries' per capita incomes reflects greater inequality between their capital-labour ratios, and the smaller should be their intra-industry trade, as shown above. However, in Helpman (1981), tastes were homothetic. In this model, tastes are nonhomothetic, as in Markusen (1986). Consequently, wider per capita income differences can reduce the share of intra-industry trade here by widening taste differences, even after removing the effect of greater inequality in their capital-labour ratios. Consider the initial equilibrium. A marginal adjustment creating an inequality between per capita incomes of i and j, without altering relative capital-labour ratios or other variables (including average per capita income) yields:

$$GL_{Xij} = 1 - \frac{|(1-y_j^{-1})^{(\gamma+1)/(\gamma+\sigma)} - (1-y_i^{-1})^{(\gamma+1)/(\gamma+\sigma)}|}{[(1-y_j^{-1})^{(\gamma+1)/(\gamma+\sigma)} + (1-y_i^{-1})^{(\gamma+1)/(\gamma+\sigma)}]} < 1. \quad (9)$$

The observed negative empirical correlation between greater inequality between two countries' per capita GDPs and the share of intra-industry trade potentially has both supply and demand explanations. Since econometric studies have not explicitly included capital-labour ratio differences as an independent variable along with per capita income differences, these two channels have not been able to be distinguished empirically. The empirical results in the next section will show that both channels have influence on the degree of intra-industry trade.

PROPOSITION 3. *The share of intra-industry trade will be higher or lower the greater the average capital-labour endowment ratio of the two countries, depending upon relative factor intensities in production.*

If X is capital intensive in production, equation (8) can be more usefully rewritten as:

$$GL_{Xij} = 1 - |\beta_{LZ}(\bar{K}_i - \bar{K}_j) - \beta_{KZ}(\bar{L}_i - \bar{L}_j)| / [\beta_{LZ}(\bar{K}_i + \bar{K}_j) - \beta_{KZ}(\bar{L}_i + \bar{L}_j)].$$

Consider an epsilon (ϵ) increase in both countries' capital stocks that does not alter the difference between their capital stocks (nor consequently between their capital-labour ratios), i.e., $(K_i+\epsilon)-(K_j+\epsilon) = K_i - K_j$. Since X is capital intensive, the capital stocks' augmentation will enlarge the number of differentiated products in each country's industry X, raising the denominator of the second RHS term, and increasing the share of intra-industry trade.

But if X is labour intensive, equation (8) can be more usefully rewritten as:

$$GL_{Xij} = 1 - |-\beta_{LZ}(\bar{K}_i - \bar{K}_j) + \beta_{KZ}(\bar{L}_i - \bar{L}_j)| / [-\beta_{LZ}(\bar{K}_i + \bar{K}_j) + \beta_{KZ}(\bar{L}_i + \bar{L}_j)].$$

The epsilon increase in both capital stocks, without altering the difference between their capital stocks, reduces the number of differentiated products in each country's industry X, decreasing the share of intra-industry trade.

The effect of a higher average capital-labour ratio on GL_{Xij} depends on relative factor intensities. In this regard, this model departs from Helpman and Krugman (1985) and Markusen (1986) which assumed the differentiated manufactured goods industry was capital intensive. In Markusen (1986), the higher the average capital-labour endowment ratio of two countries, the higher would be their share of intra-industry trade because capital-intensive manufactured goods were assumed to have income elasticities greater than one. In this model, the effects of higher average capital-labour endowment ratio and higher average per capita income of two countries on the share of intra-industry trade are 'uncoupled'. As will be empirically shown, for some manufacturing industries a higher average capital-labour endowment ratio for two countries can lower the share of intra-industry trade, even though a higher average per capita income can raise it.

PROPOSITION 4. *The share of intra-industry in the luxury (necessity) good will be higher (lower) the higher the average level of economic development.*

Although I do not assume that the differentiated (homogeneous) good is capital (labour) intensive in production, I do assume that the differentiated good (homogeneous commodity) is the luxury (necessity) in consumption. Hence, the share of intra-industry trade between two countries should rise unambiguously the larger is their average per capita income because, as equation (6) suggests, the volume of bilateral trade will be augmented in industry X, assuming no change in the difference between their per capita incomes. To illustrate, consider an epsilon increase in both countries' per capita incomes that does not alter the difference between their per capita incomes. Only the denominator of the second RHS term in equation (9) changes; the increase in the denominator raises GL_{Xij}.

PROPOSITION 5. *The share of intra-industry trade will be lower the greater the inequality between their economic sizes.*

From the initial equilibrium, a marginal reallocation of the two countries' capital and labour stocks (say, from j to i) that does not alter the countries' combined capital and labour stocks, combined incomes, relative factor endowments, per capita incomes, etc., yields:

$$GL_{Xij} = 1 - |\bar{K}_i Y_j^{(\gamma+1)/(\gamma+\sigma)} - \bar{K}_j Y_i^{(\gamma+1)/(\gamma+\sigma)}| / [\bar{K}_i Y_j^{(\gamma+1)/(\gamma+\sigma)} + \bar{K}_j Y_i^{(\gamma+1)/(\gamma+\sigma)}] < 1. \tag{10}$$

The new inequality of economic sizes lowers the share of intra-industry trade below unity. The reallocation of capital and labour from j to i has expanded the number of firms producing and varieties produced of X in one country and reduced them in the other country; which country's industry X expands and which contracts is indeterminate *a priori* without knowing relative factor intensities in production at prevailing wage-rental ratios. The rise in $\bar{K}_i$ relative to $\bar{K}_j$ is dampened by the fall in Y_j relative to Y_i; however, since $\sigma > 1$, the fall (rise) in $Y_j^{(\gamma+1)/(\gamma+\sigma)}$ ($Y_i^{(\gamma+1)/(\gamma+\sigma)}$) is less than proportionate to the rise (fall) in $\bar{K}_i$ ($\bar{K}_j$). This proposition illustrates formally the notion that the scope for exchange of product diversity is narrowed the greater the inequality between two countries' economic sizes, and corroborates a proposition in Helpman (1987), in a similar context, 'the more similar countries are in size the larger the share of intra-industry trade.'

PROPOSITION 6. *The share of intra-industry trade will be higher the greater their average economic size.*

For convenience, equation (10) can be rewritten as:

$$GL_{Xij} = 1 - |kY_j^{(\gamma+1)/(\gamma+\sigma)} - Y_i^{(\gamma+1)/(\gamma+\sigma)}| / [kY_j^{(\gamma+1)/(\gamma+\sigma)} + Y_i^{(\gamma+1)/(\gamma+\sigma)}]$$

where $k = \bar{K}_i/\bar{K}_j$. Consider an epsilon increase in both countries' capital and labour stocks that leaves unchanged their capital-labour ratios, per capita incomes, relative capital stocks (k), and absolute difference between their incomes (specifically, the numerator of the second RHS term). In this case, only the denominator of the second RHS term rises with both countries' incomes, causing the share of intra-industry trade to rise.

PROPOSITION 7. *The share of intra-industry trade will be lower the greater the inequality between their tariff levels.*

From the initial equilibrium, suppose T_{ij} (T_{ji}) is raised (lowered) slightly without altering their average tariff rate. The share of intra-industry trade falls below unity:

$$GL_{Xij} = 1 - \frac{|T_{ij}^{-\sigma(\gamma+1)/(\gamma+\sigma)} - T_{ji}^{-\sigma(\gamma+1)/(\gamma+\sigma)}|}{[T_{ij}^{-\sigma(\gamma+1)/(\gamma+\sigma)} + T_{ji}^{-\sigma(\gamma+1)/(\gamma+\sigma)}]} < 1. \tag{11}$$

PROPOSITION 8. *The share of intra-industry trade between two countries will be lower the greater their average tariff level, i.e., artificial barriers to trade.*

Consider an epsilon increase in tariff levels in both countries that lowers the denominator of equation (11), without altering the absolute difference between their tariffs (specifically, the numerator of the second RHS term in (11)). The lower denominator will decrease the share of intra-industry trade.

IV. EMPIRICAL EVIDENCE

Although inequalities between and average levels of national incomes, per capita incomes, and tariffs have been included in previous cross-country econometric analyses, inequalities between and average levels of capital-labour endowment ratios have not. Only two regressions will be estimated: one including all eight variables mentioned above (along with three dummies) and one excluding the two capital-labour ratio variables.

The dependent variable in both regressions is the logit of an average of three-digit SITC bilateral Grubel-Lloyd intra-industry trade indexes calculated for each two-digit SITC industry grouping in SITC 7. Formally:

$$GL_{Xij} = 1 - \frac{1}{M}\sum_{m=1}^{M} [|PX_{ijm} - PX_{jim}|/(PX_{ijm} + PX_{jim})] \tag{12}$$

where M is the number of three-digit SITC industries in two-digit SITC industry group X and PX_{ijm} is the U.S. dollar value of the bilateral trade flow from country i to country j in three-digit SITC industry m. The three-digit SITC classification is typically considered an 'industry' for econometric purposes. This particular unweighted average of three-digit SITC intra-industry trade indexes to generate an 'average' two-digit SITC index for cross-country econometric analysis is also found in this literature, cf., Greenaway and Milner (1986, pp. 62–5).

Calculating bilateral intra-industry trade indexes for all three-digit SITC industries is far beyond the scope of this paper. However, the industry groups comprising SITC 7 – nonelectrical machinery (71), electrical machinery (72), and transportation equipment (73) – possess several characteristics summarised in Bergstrand (1983, p. 210) that make them suitably representative of most manufacturing industries.

Using equation (12), the dependent variable was calculated for each two-digit industry group in SITC 7 for each possible pairing of fourteen major industrialised countries using 1976 data; this yielded 91 indexes for each industry group, or 273 when pooled. Before calculating these indexes, each three-digit SITC bilateral trade flow was 'adjusted' to reflect multilateral aggregate trade balance. The methodology and rationale for this adjustment is discussed in Bergstrand (1983, pp. 206–9); see Greenaway and Milner (1986, pp. 70–1) and Kol (1989) for support.

A unique aspect of this empirical study is the inclusion of capital-labour endowment ratios to help distinguish between the supply and demand influences of per capita incomes. Leamer (1984, Appendix B) provides measures of capital stocks, labour stocks, and GNP for each of the fourteen countries for 1975. Population data for each country for 1975 were collected from the World Bank's *World Tables* (1983). Average tariff levels for the countries were collected from the GATT's *Basic Documentation for Tariff Study* (1970). That study provides post-Kennedy Round nominal tariff data for fourteen major industrialised countries (the constraint behind the countries chosen for this empirical work), disaggregated by industry categories (for SITC 7, such categories correspond to 71, 72 and 73).[3]

Three dummy variables were appended. A dummy variable captured 'border trade,' assuming a value of one if two countries shared a common land border and zero otherwise. Two dummy variables accounted for differences across industry groups in their average levels of intra-industry trade owing to innate differences in industry characteristics. The regressions are estimated using weighted least squares. Although the logit of an intra-industry trade index, GL_{Xij}, yields unbiased estimates, the variance of the error terms associated with OLS estimation would be $[GL_{Xij}(1-GL_{Xij})]^{-1}$. To avoid heteroskedasticity, all variables are weighted first by $[GL_{Xij}(1-GL_{Xij})]^{\frac{1}{2}}$, cf., Bergstrand (1983) or Balassa (1986*a*).

Regression 1 is distinguished from regression 2 by the former omitting the average of and inequality between each pair of countries' capital-labour endowment ratios. Propositions 2, 5, and 7 suggest unambiguously that the share of intra-industry trade will be *lower* the greater the inequality between two countries' per capita GDPs, national incomes, and tariffs, respectively. Empirical results for regression 1 in table 1 confirm this; using one-tailed *t*-tests, all three coefficient estimates are statistically significant at the 10% level at least. Proposition 6 (8) suggests unambiguously that the share of intra-industry trade will be higher (lower) the higher the average level of the countries' GDPs

[3] The inequality between two countries' GDPs, etc., was calculated using the 'inequality' measure used in Balassa (1986*a*) and Balassa and Bauwens (1987). This measure, *INEQY*, shown below for the inequality between GDPs in i and j, Y_i and Y_j, has values between 0 and 1:

$$INEQY_{ij} = 1 + \{[Y_i/(Y_i+Y_j)] \ln [Y_i/(Y_i+Y_j)] + [Y_j/(Y_i+Y_j)] \ln [Y_j/(Y_i+Y_j)]\}/\ln 2$$

Table 1

Coefficient Estimates of Determinants of Cross-Country Bilateral Intra-Industry Trade Indexes (t-statistics in parentheses)

Independent variable	Regression 1	Regression 2	Expected coefficient sign for Regression 2
Inequality of capital-labour endowment ratio		−0·86 (−0·64)	−
Inequality of per capita GDPs	−1·42* (−1·30)	−1·21 (−0·82)	−
Inequality of GDPs	−0·69*** (−3·60)	−0·50*** (−2·58)	−
Inequality of tariff levels	−0·91* (−1·30)	−0·90* (−1·31)	−
Average capital-labour endowment ratio		−1·19*** (−3·14)	?
Average per capita GDP	−0·46** (−1·95)	0·46 (1·18)	+
Average GDP	0·37*** (6·10)	0·27*** (4·00)	+
Average tariff level	−0·34*** (−6·57)	−0·34*** (−6·53)	−
Adjacency dummy	0·30*** (3·00)	0·31*** (3·16)	+
Dummy for SITC 71	−0·08 (−0·96)	−0·08 (−0·95)	?
Dummy for SITC 73	−0·76*** (−8·05)	−0·77*** (−8·30)	?
WLS Intercept	1·31 (0·14)	5·38** (2·01)	?
R^2	0·41	0·44	
Adjusted R^2	0·39	0·42	
S.E.E.	0·28	0·27	
Number of observations	273	273	
Degrees of freedom	263	261	

Note: *, **, *** denote statistical significance in one-tail t-tests at the 10%, 5%, and 1% levels, respectively.

(tariffs). The results for regression 1 confirm this; these results are statistically significant at the 1% level.

However, the expected coefficient sign in regression 1 for the average level of the countries' per capita GDPs is ambiguous. Proposition 4 suggests that the share of intra-industry trade will be higher (lower) among two countries the higher their average per capita GDP if the good is the luxury (necessity). But Proposition 3 claims that the share of intra-industry trade will be higher (lower) among two countries the higher their average capital-labour ratio if the good is capital (labour) intensive in production. Since capital-labour ratios and per capita incomes across countries are highly correlated, the exclusion of average capital-labour ratios in regression 1 may cause per capita income variation across countries to reflect both demand and supply channels of influence. Even if goods in SITC 7 were luxuries, the coefficient estimate for average per capita GDPs may be negative if SITC 7 industries are labour intensive in production, i.e., an omitted variables bias may be present. Indeed, in regression 1, average per capita GDP has a statistically significant negative coefficient estimate; in the model's context, this is consistent with SITC 7 goods being necessities in consumption or labour intensive in production or both.

The addition of the average of and inequality between capital-labour ratios in regression 2 is intended to distinguish empirically between the demand and supply influences of per capita income. Coefficient estimates for the average of and inequality between GDPs and tariffs need no discussion as these estimates are not significantly different between regressions 1 and 2. Instead, note that the addition of the average of and inequality between capital-labour ratios has significantly altered the coefficient estimates of the average of and inequality between per capita incomes in a consistent and economically meaningful way.

First, Proposition 1 suggests that the share of intra-industry trade between two countries should be unambiguously lower the greater the inequality of their capital-labour endowment ratios. The coefficient estimate for this variable in regression 2 is negative, although statistically insignificant at conventional levels. Note the coefficient estimate for the inequality in per capita incomes, while still negative, is smaller in regression 2 than in regression 1. This reduction is consistent with the model's hypothesis that wider per capita income differences tend to reduce the share of intra-industry trade as a proxy both for wider taste differences (demand) and wider relative factor endowments (supply); the coefficient estimate for per capita income inequality falls because some of that variable's explanatory power has shifted to the capital-labour ratio inequality variable. The coefficient estimates, however, are not statistically significant.

Second, the addition of the average capital-labour endowment ratio in regression 2 has reversed the coefficient estimate sign for average per capita GDP. The average per capita income coefficient estimate changes from a statistically significant negative value to a positive value, the latter having statistical significance only at a 15% level in a one-tailed test. But the average capital-labour ratio coefficient estimate is negative and statistically significant at the 1% level, suggesting that machinery and transport equipment is relatively labour intensive in production. Thus, the explicit inclusion of average capital-labour ratios has 'released' the variation of average per capita incomes across countries from reflecting both demand and supply influences. In the context of the theoretical model, average per capita income variation now influences only demand and its (statistically insignificant) positive coefficient estimate in regression 2 modestly suggests that differentiated manufactured machinery and transport equipment products are luxuries in consumption.

The coefficient estimate for land adjacency is positive and statistically significant; this is consistent with other empirical evidence that the share of intra-industry trade between two countries is influenced by 'cross-border' trade. The industry dummies' coefficient estimates suggest that the average degree of intra-industry trade in electrical machinery (SITC 72) is not significantly different from that in nonelectrical machinery (SITC 71), but is significantly greater than that in transport equipment (SITC 73).

Summarising, the regression results generally support the propositions addressed in section III. The data suggest that the share in intra-industry trade between two countries in SITC 7 tends to be significantly lower the greater their average capital-labour ratio (Proposition 3), implying – in the context of the theoretical model – that these manufactured products are labour intensive in production. The data modestly suggest that the share of intra-industry trade between two countries in SITC 7 tends to be higher the greater their average per capita income (Proposition 4), consistent in the model's context with these products being luxuries in consumption. These results are economically plausible. Moreover, the analysis here suggests that the assumption in Helpman and Krugman (1985) and Markusen (1986) that the differentiated manufactures industry is capital intensive in production may not be necessary to demonstrate a relationship between per capita income and the share of intra-industry trade. Finally, the explanatory power here ($R^2 = 0{\cdot}44$ in regression 2) using only 273 observations is equal to that in other studies using 62,000 observations, cf. Balassa and Bauwens (1987).

V. CONCLUSIONS

Prominent systematic empirical relationships between the share of intra-industry trade between pairs of countries and the average levels of and inequalities between their national incomes, per capita incomes, capital-labour endowment ratios, and tariffs were rationalized theoretically using a synthesised framework. The model revealed that a greater similarity of two countries' per capita incomes would be associated with more intra-industry trade both for supply (Heckscher-Ohlin-Samuelson) and demand (Chamberlin-Linder) reasons simultaneously. Several other testable propositions evolved from the model, which used a gravity-like equation as a pedagogical device.

It should be emphasised, however, that these propositions evolve from a restricted set of assumptions. Intra-industry trade in this model evolves only among horizontally differentiated products; other models have shown such trade among homogenous goods under different market structures. Heckscher-Ohlin-Samuelson models have predicted two-way trade in vertically differentiated goods.

In structuring the empirical model, emphasis was given to selecting an SITC industry grouping that was representative of the bulk of OECD trade. Our empirical results generally confirm the theoretical propositions. However, the lack of statistical significance in all of the suggested relationships suggests a path for future research in this area.

University of Notre Dame

Date of receipt of final typescript: June 1990

References

Anderson, J. E. (1979). 'A theoretical foundation for the gravity equation.' *American Economic Review*, vol. 69, March, pp. 106–16.

Armington, P. S. (1969). 'A theory of demand for products distinguished by place of production.' *IMF Staff Papers*, vol. 16, March, pp. 159–77.

Balassa, B. (1986*a*). 'Intra-industry trade among exporters of manufactured goods.' In *Imperfect Competition and International Trade: The Policy Aspects of Intra-Industry Trade* (ed. D. Greenaway and P. K. M. Tharakan). Brighton: Wheatsheaf Press.

—— (1986*b*). 'Intra-industry specialization: a cross-country analysis.' *European Economic Review*, vol. 30, pp. 27–42.

—— and Bauwens, L. (1987). 'Intra-industry specialization in a multi-country and multi-industry framework.' Economic Journal, December, vol. 97, pp. 923–39.

Bergstrand, J. H. (1983). 'Measurement and determinants of intra-industry international trade.' In *Tharakan* (1983), pp. 201–53.

—— (1985). 'The gravity equation in international trade: some microeconomic foundations and empirical evidence.' *Review of Economics and Statistics*, vol 67, August, pp. 474–81.

—— (1989). 'The generalized gravity equation, monopolistic competition, and the factor-proportions theory in international trade,' *Review of Economics and Statistics*, vol. 71, February, pp. 143–53.

Deardorff, A. V. and Stern, R. M. (1986). *The Michigan Model of World Production and Trade: Theory and Application*. Cambridge, MA: MIT Press.

de Melo, J. and Robinson, S. (1985). 'Product differentiation and trade dependence of the domestic price system in computable general equilibrium trade models.' In *International Trade and Exchange Rates in the Late Eighties* (ed. T. Peeters, *et al.*). Amsterdam: North-Holland.

—— (1989). 'Product differentiation and the treatment of foreign trade in computable general equilibrium models of small economies.' *Journal of International Economics*, vol. 27, August, pp. 47–68.

Dixit, A. and Norman, V. (1980). *Theory of International Trade*. Cambridge. Cambridge University Press.

Falvey, R. E. (1981). 'Commercial policy and intra-industry trade.' *Journal of International Economics, vol.* 11, pp. 495–511.

Geraci, V. J. and Prewo, W. (1982). 'An empirical demand and supply model of multilateral trade.' *Review of Economics and Statistics*, vol. 64, August, pp. 432–41.

Greenaway, D. and Milner, C. (1986). *The Economics of Intra-Industry Trade*. Oxford: Basil Blackwell.

Grubel, H. G. and Lloyd, P. J. (1975). *Intra-Industry Trade*. New York: John Wiley.

Havrylyshyn, O. and Civan, E. (1983). 'Intra-industry trade and the stage of development: a regression analysis of industrial and developing countries.' In *Tharakan* (1983), pp. 111–40.

Helpman, E. (1981). 'International trade in the presence of product differentiation, economies of scale and monopolistic competition: a Chamberlin–Heckscher–Ohlin approach.' *Journal of International Economics*, vol 11, pp. 305–40.

—— (1987). 'Imperfect competition and international trade: evidence from fourteen industrial countries.' *Journal of the Japanese and International Economies*, vol. 1, March, pp. 62–81.

—— and Krugman, P. (1985). *Market Structure and Foreign Trade*. Cambridge, Massachusetts: MIT Press.

Kol, J. (1989). 'Corrections for trade imbalance: a survey.' *Weltwirtschaftliches Archiv*, vol. 125, pp. 703–16.

Krugman, P. (1979). 'Increasing returns, monopolistic competition, and international trade.' *Journal of International Economics*, vol. 9, pp. 469–79.

—— (1980). 'Scale economies, product differentiation, and the pattern of trade.' *American Economic Review*, vol. 70, December, pp. 950–9.

—— (1981). 'Intra-industry specialization and the gains from trade.' *Journal of Political Economy*, vol. 89, October, pp. 959–73.

Leamer, E. E. (1984). *Sources of International Comparative Advantage*. Cambridge, MA: MIT Press.

Linder, S. B. (1961). *An Essay on Trade and Transformation*. New York: John Wiley.

Loertscher, R. and Wolter, F. (1980). 'Determinants of intra-industry trade: among countries and across industries.' *Weltwirtschaftliches Archiv*, vol. 116, pp. 281–93.

Lundberg, L. (1982). 'Intra-industry trade: the case of Sweden.' *Weltwirtschaftliches Archiv*, vol. 118, pp. 302–16.

Markusen, J. R. (1986). 'Explaining the volume of trade: an eclectic approach.' *American Economic Review*, vol 76 (December), pp. 1002–11.

Pagoulatos, E. and Sorensen, R. (1979). 'Two-way international trade: an econometric analysis.' *Weltwirtschaftliches Archiv*, vol. 111, pp. 454–65.

Tharakan, P. K. M. (1983). *Intra-Industry Trade: Empirical and Methodological Aspects*. Amsterdam: North-Holland.

Toh, K. (1982). 'A cross-section analysis of intra-industry trade in U.S. manufacturing industries.' *Weltwirtschaftliches Archiv*, vol. 118, pp. 281–300.

Chapter 4

The growth of world trade: tariffs, transport costs, and income similarity

Scott L. Baier, Jeffrey H. Bergstrand*

Department of Finance and Business Economics, University of Notre Dame, Notre Dame, IN 46556-0399, USA

Received 6 October 1997; accepted 9 November 1999

Abstract

In the 25th anniversary issue of the *Brookings Papers on Economic Activity*, Paul Krugman [Krugman, P., 1995. Growing world trade: Causes and consequences. Brookings Papers on Economic Activity (1), 327–377] stated that the answer to the fundamental question "Why has world trade grown?" remains surprisingly disputed. He noted that journalistic discussion tends to view the growth of world trade as due to technology-led declines in transportation costs, while economists argue that policy-led multilateral and bilateral trade liberalization has spurred this growth. A third potential explanation raised by Elhanan Helpman [Helpman, E., 1987. Imperfect competition and international trade: Evidence from fourteen industrial countries. Journal of the Japanese and International Economies 1 (1) 62–81] and Hummels and Levinsohn (1995) [Hummels, D., Levinsohn, J., 1995. Monopolistic competition and international trade: Reconsidering the evidence. Quarterly Journal of Economics 110 (3) 799–836] is increased similarity of countries' incomes. The purpose of this study is to disentangle from one another (and from income growth) the relative effects of transport-cost reductions, tariff liberalization, and income convergence on the growth of world trade among several OECD countries between the late 1950s and the late 1980s. In the context of the model, the empirical results suggest that income growth explains about 67%, tariff-rate reductions about 25%, transport-cost declines about 8%, and income convergence virtually none of the average world trade growth of our post World War II sample.

Keywords: Trade; Tariffs; Transport Costs; Imperfect Competition; Gravity Equation

JEL classification: F12

*Corresponding author. Tel.: + 1-219-631-6761; fax: + 1-219-631-5255.
E-mail address: bergstrand.1@nd.edu (J.H. Bergstrand).

*Originally Published in *Journal of International Economics*, 53(2001), pp. 1–7.

1. Introduction

In the 25th anniversary issue of the *Brookings Papers on Economic Activity*, which focused on international economic issues, Krugman (1995) asked two very fundamental questions: Why has world trade grown, and what are the consequences of that growth? Both topics, he claimed, are surprisingly disputed. Regarding the first question, he noted that:

> Most journalistic discussion of the growth of world trade seems to view growing integration as driven by a technological imperative – to believe that improvements in transportation and communication technology constitute an irresistible force dissolving national boundaries. International economists, however, tend to view much, though not all, of the growth of trade as having essentially political causes, seeing its great expansion after World War II largely as a result of the removal of the protectionist measures that had constricted world markets since 1913 (p. 328).

With one of the leading international economists of our time raising this disputed issue to the fore, an empirical examination of the predominant sources of postwar growth of world trade seems warranted.

In the spirit of Krugman's article, Feenstra (1998) suggests four possible factors to explain the growth of world trade. Like Krugman, he notes the two sources that 'come to mind immediately' are trade liberalization and falling transportation costs. A third possible explanation is that trade has grown because economies have converged in economic size, as suggested in Helpman (1987) and Hummels and Levinsohn (1995). A fourth possibility is increased outsourcing; as the production process 'disintegrates' internationally and multinational firms become more vertically specialized, intermediate goods cross borders multiple times increasing world trade relative to output.

The primary purpose of this study is to disentangle from one another the relative empirical contributions of transport-cost reductions, trade liberalization, income convergence, and income growth to the expansion of world trade in the post WWII period.[1] We hope to provide a benchmark for the cross-sectional determinants of

[1] The possible role of increased vertical specialization is beyond the scope of this paper as the theoretical foundation for our empirical work is a standard trade model in *final* goods. See Hummels et al. (1998) and Feenstra (1998) on the role of increased vertical specialization.

trade growth.[2] The methodology employs the gravity equation, which Bayoumi and Eichengreen (1997) termed the 'workhorse for empirical studies of the pattern of trade' (p. 142) and Rauch (1999) noted is the 'standard empirical framework used to predict how countries match up in international trade' (p. 10).

In the context of Krugman's quote, the conclusion for the impatient reader is an interesting one: while neither side can take full credit, *economists have the edge!* In the context of our theoretical model, tariff-rate reductions have had roughly three times the impact upon the growth of world trade as transport-cost declines, other factors held constant. The remainder of this paper is as follows. Section 2 describes the empirical methodology used and the analytical justification for its use. Section 3 discusses econometric issues. Section 4 describes the data. Section 5 provides the empirical results on the relative economic impacts of transport-cost declines, tariff reductions, income convergence, and income growth on the enlargement of world trade among OECD countries based upon a reduced-form equation from a standard general equilibrium model of international trade in final goods and using bilateral trade flows. Section 6 concludes.

2. Methodological issues

As noted by Eichengreen and Irwin (1995), 'a standard framework for investigating the pattern of trade is the gravity model, which relates the value of bilateral flows to national income, population, distance, and contiguity' (p. 8). The empirical success of the gravity model for explaining and predicting cross-sectional international trade pattern levels is well documented and has a rich history beginning with Nobel laureate Jan Tinbergen (1962); see Baldwin (1994); Oguledo and MacPhee (1994); Frankel (1997, Ch. 4), and Deardorff (1998) for useful surveys.[3] The gravity equation is a log-linear cross-sectional specification, relating the nominal bilateral trade flow from exporter i to importer j in any year (PX_{ij}) to the exporting and importing countries' nominal gross domestic products (GDP_i and GDP_j, respectively), distance between their economic centers (D_{ij}), and

[2]This is not, of course, the first paper to examine empirically the sources of post-WWII trade growth. Rose (1991) examines numerous factors in a reduced-form regression to explain trade growth among 14 countries. For the small economies, he finds that changing industrial structure and tariffs, but not transport costs, have contributed to the growth of trade (relative to output). However, Rose uncovers no significant trade growth determinants for large economies. Rose's empirical findings are not addressed though in the context of an explicit general equilibrium model. Also, Bayoumi and Eichengreen (1997) examine the effects of the creation of preferential trade agreements on the growth in bilateral trade flows.

[3]Work by Tinbergen developed from early foundations established in Walter Isard (1954a,b).

typically an array of dummy variables reflecting the presence or absence of a preferential trading agreement (PTA_{ij}) or of a common land border (A_{ij}). The basic gravity equation has the econometric specification:

$$PX_{ij} = \beta_0(GDP_i)^{\beta 1}(GDP_j)^{\beta 2}(D_{ij})^{\beta 3}e^{\beta 4(PTAij)}e^{\beta 5(Aij)}\varepsilon_{ij} \tag{1}$$

where e is the natural logarithm base and ε_{ij} is a log-normally distributed error term.

Empirical investigations in international trade using the gravity equation typically note that formal theoretical foundations for the model have been provided in Anderson (1979), Krugman (1979), Helpman and Krugman (1985), and Bergstrand (1985, 1989, 1990), and are now well established.[4] In these studies, the gravity equation is derived theoretically as a reduced form from a general equilibrium model of international trade in final goods. Exporter and importer GDPs can be interpreted in these models as the production and absorption capacities of the exporting and importing countries, respectively. Bilateral distance between the two countries is generally associated with transportation costs; more distance suggests greater transit costs.[5]

These papers are usually offered as theoretical substitutes; choose your preferred set of assumptions and model. We provide a brief discussion to show that these theoretical foundations are complementary, each a special case of a more general model. We use this framework to motivate a simple novel econometric specification to estimate the relative contributions of income growth, income convergence, trade liberalization, and transport-cost declines for explaining the growth of world trade.

2.1. Theories without tariffs, transportation costs, and distribution costs

Anderson (1979) provided a formal theoretical foundation for the gravity equation based upon the properties of expenditure systems. Assuming that each country specializes completely in the production of its own good, there is one good for each country and assume its price is normalized to unity. Assuming identical homothetic preferences, the volume of trade from country i to country j (X_{ij}) can be represented by:

$$X_{ij} = \theta_i Y_j \tag{2a}$$

[4]Baldwin (1994) noted that, 'The gravity model used to have a poor reputation among reputable economists. Starting with Wang and Winters (1991), it has come back into fashion. One problem that lowered its respectability was its oft-asserted lack of theoretical foundations. In contrast to popular belief, it does have such foundations . . .' (p. 82).

[5]As many authors have noted, the 'costs' of distance may extend well beyond freight charges, including cultural dissimilarities and other barriers measured with difficulty (cf., Anderson and Marcouiller, 1999). Thus, while distance has always been an important variable in gravity equations, authors have never been sure exactly what 'costs' distance represents.

or

$$\theta_i = X_{ij}/Y_j \tag{2b}$$

where θ_i denotes the fraction of income spent on country i's product (the fraction identical across importers) and Y_j denotes real GDP in importing country j. Since production of every country i must equal the volume of exports and domestic consumption of the good, then:

$$Y_i = \sum_{j=1}^{N} X_{ij} = \sum_{j=1}^{N} \theta_i Y_j = \theta_i \left(\sum_{j=1}^{N} Y_j \right) \tag{3a}$$

or

$$\theta_i = Y_i / \left(\sum_{j=1}^{N} Y_j \right) = Y_i / Y^W \tag{3b}$$

where $Y^W = \Sigma_{j=1}^{N} Y_j$ is world real GDP, which is constant across country pairs. Substituting Eq. (3b) into Eq. (2a) yields:

$$X_{ij} = Y_i Y_j / \left(\sum_{j=1}^{N} Y_j \right) = Y_i Y_j / Y^W. \tag{4}$$

This simple gravity equation relies only upon the (adding-up) constraints of an expenditure system combined with identical homothetic preferences and the specialization of each country in one good.

A limitation of this model is that product differentiation is constrained arbitrarily by the number of *countries*. The models of Krugman (1979, 1980) and Helpman and Krugman (1985) relax this strong restriction by offering instead a market structure. Using the Dixit and Stiglitz (1977) framework, they assume monopolistically competitive firms producing slightly differentiated final goods under increasing returns to scale in production. In the absence of transportation costs and tariff barriers, the Helpman-Krugman model leads to a simple gravity equation identical to Eq. (4), but where the number of goods produced differs across countries of different economic size and depends endogenously upon the level of fixed costs in production, the taste for variety, and factor endowments.[6]

[6]Monopolistic competition is not the only market structure compatible with a gravity model. For instance, Feenstra et al. (1998) derive a gravity equation from a reciprocal-dumping model of trade with homogeneous goods and Deardorff (1998) derives a gravity equation from a model with perfectly competitive markets (see footnote 8). However, Evenett and Keller (1998) show empirically that the monopolistic competition/increasing-returns-to-scale based theories of trade 'are an important reason why the gravity equation fits trade flows among industrialized countries well' (p. 2).

A limitation of both models, however, is the absence of natural (i.e., geographic) and artificial (i.e., policy-induced) impediments to trade, such as transportation costs and tariff barriers, respectively.

2.2. Theories with tariff barriers, transportation costs, and distribution costs

In reality, of course, economies are dispersed geographically in an asymmetric fashion, governments impose tariff and nontariff barriers asymmetrically, and firms face costs in distributing, marketing, and tailoring products to each country. Anderson (1979) and Bergstrand (1985) introduced bilateral trade barriers, such as tariffs and transportation costs, explicitly in their respective gravity models.[7] In both cases, bilateral trade flows are influenced by the absolute level of bilateral transaction costs *and* the level of bilateral transaction costs relative to an income-weighted average of the exporter's bilateral costs to all markets (including the home market), as discussed in Deardorff (1998) and Bergstrand (1998).[8]

Bergstrand (1985) differs from Anderson (1979) by also allowing potentially for the costs of distributing, marketing, and tailoring each country's product to each national market.[9] These potential distribution costs are captured formally by a constant-elasticity-of-transformation function that allows each country's producer to treat export supplies to each market as imperfect substitutes; Bergstrand finds empirical support for a finite elasticity of transformation of output among export markets. As in Anderson though, each country produces one (arbitrarily) differentiated good. Bergstrand (1989,1990) extends his earlier model to incorporate Dixit-Stiglitz preferences, monopolistically-competitive markets, and increasing returns to scale in production and nests this in a two-industry, two-factor, Heckscher-Ohlin context.

---

[7]Krugman (1980) and Helpman and Krugman (1985, Ch. 10) discuss transport costs using 'iceberg' technology, but do not solve for a gravity equation.

[8]Deardorff (1998) discusses a theoretical foundation for the gravity equation considering a similar decomposition: frictionless trade and impeded trade. With frictionless trade, the gravity model can be motivated even in the context of a Heckscher-Ohlin world with homogeneous goods and perfect competition. With impediments, his theory requires complete specialization (as in the other theories) and 'every good is produced by a different country'; hence, each good is identified with the country that produces it and then 'enter them into a utility function as imperfect substitutes' (pp. 17–18).

[9]One can interpret these as nation-by-nation 'specific factors.' Rauch (1999) and Rauch and Feenstra (1999) discuss such costs in the context of 'networks' in international trade. Engel and Rogers (1998) found recently that the degree of relative price dispersion across locations suggested that 'consumer markets are, to a great degree, national markets,' arguing that distribution efforts are 'organized nationally' (p. 18).

2.3. The theoretical framework

The gravity equation to be estimated is based upon a synthesis and generalization of these theories. Within this framework, the relative importance of expenditure constraints emphasized by Anderson, market structure emphasized by Helpman and Krugman, and distribution costs emphasized by Bergstrand becomes transparent.

2.3.1. Consumers and bilateral import demand

In each country, the representative consumer maximizes a constant-elasticity-of-substitution (CES) utility function subject to a budget constraint where prices of the imported products reflect 'iceberg' transportation costs and ad valorem tariffs. The constrained utility maximization yields the import demand function of country j for the product of the representative firm in country i (x_{ij}):

$$x_{ij} = (I_j / P_j^C)(\boldsymbol{p}_{ij} / P_j^C)^{-\sigma} \tag{5}$$

where I_j is nominal income in j, σ is the elasticity of substitution in consumption ($\sigma>1$), P_j^C is the standard Dixit-Stiglitz price index, $(\Sigma_{i=1}^{N} \Sigma_{k=1}^{ni} \boldsymbol{p}_{ijk}^{1-\sigma})^{1/(1-\sigma)}$, and $\boldsymbol{p}_{ijk}$ is the landed price in country j of the product of firm k in country i inclusive of tariffs. Assuming identical producers k in country i ($k = 1, \ldots, n_i$), $\boldsymbol{p}_{ij} = p_{ij}(1 + t_{ij})$ where p_{ij} is the c.i.f. price expressed in terms of the numeraire ($p_{jj} = 1$) and t_{ij} is the ad valorem tariff rate.[10] Eq. (5) also represents the domestic demand function when $i = j$, for which $t_{ij} = 0$.

2.3.2. Firms

The representative firm in country i maximizes profits subject to two technology constraints. First, the production of goods has fixed (α) and constant marginal (ϕ) costs given by the linear cost function:

$$l_i = \alpha + \phi y_i \tag{6}$$

where l_i denotes labor used by the representative firm in country i and y_i denotes output of the firm.

Second, the potential presence of costs in distributing the product to each market causes the representative firm to treat each potential market's supply as an

[10]Alternatively, the ad valorem tariff rate may be applied to the f.o.b. value of each good. Both methods have been used in the literature, cf., Frankel (1997) and Frankel et al. (1998). The approach used here follows the European Union approach, attaching tariff rates to c.i.f. values, while the United States uses f.o.b. values.

imperfect substitute, captured formally by the constant-elasticity-of-transformation (CET) function:

$$y_i = \left[\sum_{j=1}^{N} y_{ij}^{(1+\gamma)/\gamma} \right]^{\gamma/(1+\gamma)} \tag{7}$$

where y_{ij} is output supplied to country j by the representative firm in i and γ is the elasticity of transformation of production ($\gamma > 0$).[11] Assuming iceberg transport costs, a fraction δ_{ij} of the goods 'falls into the ocean' so that only $x_{ij} = (1 - \delta_{ij})y_{ij}$ arrives and is sold in country j (assume $\delta_{ii} = 0$). It will be convenient to assume that $a_{ij} \equiv \delta_{ij}/(1 - \delta_{ij})$, so that $(1 - \delta_{ij}) \equiv 1/\{1 + [\delta_{ij}/(1 - \delta_{ij})]\} \equiv 1/(1 + a_{ij})$.

While Eq. (6) is standard to this class of models, only a few studies have employed Eq. (7), in particular, Geraci and Prewo (1982); Bergstrand (1985, 1989); de Melo and Tarr (1992); Gould (1994), and Weyerbrock (1999). The motivation for this additional condition is simply that output of the representative firm in a differentiated-product industry is not likely be substituted *costlessly* between foreign markets, due to the costs of distributing, marketing, and tailoring a product to any foreign market. Rauch and Feenstra (1999) argue that differentiated-product industries tend to need networks to help match the 'multifarious characteristics of buyers and sellers' (p. 4). As a study by the European Commission (1989) noted, a survey of successful exporters found that half of them tailored their products to destination markets. Most trade models ignore these costs, assuming production is perfectly substitutable between home and export markets and among export markets (i.e., a linear transformation function as in Anderson and in Helpman and Krugman). At the other extreme, Deardorff and Stern (1986, 1990) in the Michigan World Trade Model assume that production for home and export markets is *completely separate*, resulting 'from locational requirements or from the need to tailor products to national markets'; they assume 'certain fixed factors of production that cannot easily be transferred between the sectors' (1990, p. 19).

The CET function provides an analytically and empirically tractable means of letting the data determine the degree of transformability, or substitutability, of production among markets. Estimates of γ can range theoretically from 0 to ∞. If γ equals infinity, output is perfectly substitutable across home and foreign markets as in most trade models; Eq. (7) reduces then to the simple expenditure constraint in Anderson (1979), as in Eq. (3a). Conversely, if γ equals 0, production is not substitutable across home and foreign markets, or among export markets, as in Deardorff and Stern (1986, 1990). In fact, our empirical evidence discussed later implies that γ is positive but finite, suggesting that exports are imperfectly substitutable across markets. By incorporating the CET function, our econometric

[11] See Powell and Gruen (1968) on the theoretical foundations for the CET function.

model can estimate how much world trade growth has been diminished by the resources absorbed in allocating production among various markets.[12]

2.3.3. Equilibrium, bilateral export supply, and full employment

Two conditions characterize equilibrium in this class of models. First, profit maximization ensures that prices are a markup over marginal costs:

$$P_i^F = [\sigma/(\sigma-1)]\phi W_i \tag{8}$$

where ϕW_i is the marginal production cost of the representative firm, W_i is the wage rate, and P_i^F is a CET index of the firm's prices, i.e., $P_i^F = [\Sigma_{j=1}^N [p_{ij}/(1 + a_{ij})]^{1+\gamma}]^{1/(1+\gamma)}$. Second, under monopolistic competition firms earn zero profits which implies:

$$y_i = \left[\sum_{j=1}^{N} y_{ij}^{(1+\gamma)/\gamma}\right]^{\gamma/(1+\gamma)} = (\alpha/\varphi)(\sigma-1) \equiv \psi \tag{9}$$

Hence, as is typical to these models, the firm's output is determined parametrically by the cost and utility functions.

Unlike other models in this class where exporters are assumed to face zero nationally-specific distribution costs, the presence of a potentially *finite* elasticity of transformation of output among destination markets allows this model to be solved for the bilateral export supply functions of the representative firm. Combining, from the firm's first-order conditions, $x_{ij} = (1 + a_{ij})^{-(\gamma+1)}(p_{ij}/p_{ii})^{\gamma}x_{ii}$ with $x_{ij} = y_{ij}/(1 + a_{ij})$, Eq. (9), and some algebra yields:

$$x_{ij} = \psi(p_{ij}/P_i^F)^{\gamma}(1 + a_{ij})^{-(\gamma+1)} \tag{10}$$

where the domestic supply function follows analogously for $j = i$ (assume $a_{ii} = 0$).

The assumption of full employment of labor in each country ensures that the size of the factor endowment (L_i) determines the number of varieties (n_i) produced, as is common to this class of models. Combining Eqs. (6) and (7) with $x_{ij} = (1 + a_{ij})^{-(\gamma+1)}(p_{ij}/p_{ii})^{\gamma}\ x_{ii}$ yields:

$$L_i = \sum_{k=1}^{n_i} l_{ik} = \alpha\sigma n_i \quad \text{or} \quad n_i = (\alpha\sigma)^{-1}L_i \tag{11}$$

[12]Some recent empirical studies in international trade have emphasized implicitly the costs of distribution to bring buyers and sellers of differentiated products together better. Gould (1994), Head and Ries (1998), and Dunlevy and Hutchinson (1999) provide evidence that stocks of immigrants enhance the export opportunities of the immigrants' home countries by providing exporters with knowledge about the host country. Rauch (1999) provides evidence that business networks enhance trade more in differentiated product industries than in homogeneous product industries.

2.3.4. The gravity equation

The solution for a gravity equation from this model is obtained by setting Eq. (5) equal to Eq. (10) for all pairs (i, j) including $i = j$ and noting that there are n_i producers in each country i (i.e., Eq. (11)). This yields the real bilateral trade flow relationship:

$$X_{ij} = n_i x_{ij} = \psi^{-\gamma/(\gamma+\sigma)} Y_i Y_j^{\gamma/(\gamma+\sigma)} (1 + a_{ij})^{-\sigma(\gamma+1)/(\gamma+\sigma)} (1 + t_{ij})^{-\sigma\gamma/(\gamma+\sigma)} \times \left[(P_i^F/P_j^C)^{-\sigma}(P_j^F/P_j^C)\right]^{\gamma/(\gamma+\sigma)} \tag{12}$$

where X_{ij} is the quantity of imports of country j from country i, Y_i is aggregate output of exporter i, and Y_j is aggregate output of importer j (where $Y_j = I_j/P_j^F = n_j y_j$). If distribution costs are zero as typically assumed, then $\gamma = \infty$ and the coefficient of Y_j above equals 1 as in Anderson (1979) and Helpman and Krugman (1985).[13]

Since country i's aggregate output is a CET function of its bilateral exports (including sales to itself), one can alternatively derive the gravity equation in the form:

$$X_{ij} = \frac{Y_i Y_j}{Y^W} \left[\frac{\theta_j^{-\sigma}(1 + a_{ij})^{-\sigma(\gamma+1)/\gamma}(1 + t_{ij})^{-\sigma}(P_i^F/P_j^C)^{-\sigma}(P_j^F/P_j^C)}{\left(\sum_{j=1}^{N} \left[\theta_j (1 + a_{ij})^{1-\sigma}(1 + t_{ij})^{-\sigma}(P_i^F/P_j^C)^{-\sigma}(P_j^F/P_j^C)\right]^{(\gamma+1)/(\gamma+\sigma)} \right)^{(\gamma+\sigma)/(\gamma+1)}} \right]^{\gamma/(\gamma+\sigma)} \tag{13}$$

which is the analogue to Eq. (4), where Y^W is a constant and $\theta_j = Y_j/Y^W$. In the context of this model, a particular exporter i that is either more (less) distant from importers or facing a higher (lower) tariff rate will have a lower (higher) P_i^F in general equilibrium. An exporter with a larger economic size will have a higher P_i^F in general equilibrium, as in Krugman (1980). Consequently, it can be shown that $(\Sigma_{j=1}^{N} [\theta_j(1 + a_{ij})^{1-\sigma}(1 + t_{ij})^{-\sigma}(P_i^F/P_j^C)^{-\sigma}(P_j^F/P_j^C)]^{(\gamma+1)/(\gamma+\sigma)})^{(\gamma+\sigma)/(\gamma+1)} = \psi/Y^W$, which is a constant in Eq. (13).

Eq. (13) is a generalized version of Eq. (4) that allows transport costs and tariff barriers to be non-zero, prices to be non-unity, and the elasticity of transformation to be non-infinity. In the special case when the elasticity of transformation (γ) is set equal to infinity and prices are set equal to unity, Eq. (13) reduces to Eqs. (16) and (18) in Anderson (1979) and Deardorff (1998), respectively. Moreover, when

[13]The complex bracketed relative price term has the following interpretation. The first part reflects terms of trade effects: for instance, P_i^F/P_j^C may be high for some country pairs due to a larger market in i, tending to reduce demand in j for i's products. The second part reflects an income effect: for instance, P_j^F/P_j^C may be high for country j due to lower tariffs in j, tending to raise real income and imports (as tariff revenue is not redistributed to consumers in our model).

$a_{ij} = t_{ij} = 0$ as well, Eq. (13) reduces further to Eq. (4), the frictionless gravity equation.

Eqs. (12) and (13) help to highlight the importance of output-expenditure constraints emphasized by Anderson, market structure emphasized by Helpman and Krugman, and distribution costs emphasized by Bergstrand. The model above incorporates the output-expenditure constraints emphasized in Anderson (1979), but allows potentially for costly transformation of output across markets, as suggested in Bergstrand (1985). We provide empirical evidence later that exports are not perfectly substitutable across markets. Furthermore, we allow for relative price levels to depart from unity, as documented by Summers and Heston (1991) and others. In the context of this class of models with economies of scale, monopolistic competition, asymmetric country sizes, and positive transport costs, relative price and wage levels will not likely be unity; consequently, the common assumption of setting all prices to unity is not innocuous. The model thus incorporates explicitly into the gravity equation the notion emphasized in Krugman (1980) that larger markets will tend to have relatively higher price and wage rate levels.

3. Econometric issues

The purpose of the econometric model is to evaluate empirically the absolute and relative roles of real income growth, real income convergence, tariff reductions, and falling transportation costs in explaining the growth of world trade between the late 1950s and the late 1980s. Gravity Eqs. (12) and (13) were derived to describe in the context of a general equilibrium model long-run determinants of bilateral trade flow *levels*. If one assumes that the elasticities of substitution in consumption (σ) and of transformation of production (γ) are stable over this period, then the growth of trade can be described by changes in the RHS variables in Eqs. (12) and (13).

We note two estimation issues. First, at the level of aggregation being investigated, the quantity of goods exported from i to j (X_{ij}) is unobservable. In fact, gravity equations are usually estimated across countries using nominal bilateral trade flow *values* (and nominal GDPs) for which data exist, because the gravity model has been used traditionally to explain the *level* of trade. Since we are interested in the growth of real trade flows, it is appropriate to deflate nominal trade flows by a price index. Since bilateral trade flow price deflators are unavailable, we employ nominal trade flows adjusted for changes in the firm's price index (P_i^F). As in Bayoumi and Eichengreen (1997), we use the exporter's GDP deflator; since the exporter's income variable is deflated by the GDP deflator, the model suggests this is the appropriate deflator for the trade flows. Second, the relative roles of real income growth versus real income convergence are not readily transparent from Eqs. (12) and (13).[14] The appendix details the algebra used to yield a form of Eq. (12) specified below that is more conducive to potential econometric evaluation of the rates of real income growth, real income convergence, and declining tariff rates and transport costs in explaining real trade flow growth:

$$X_{ij}^{cif} = \psi^{-(\gamma+1)/(\gamma+\sigma)}(Y_i + Y_j)^2(s_i s_j)(1 + a_{ij})^{(1-\sigma)(\gamma+1)/(\gamma+\sigma)} \cdot(1 + t_{ij})^{-\sigma(\gamma+1)/(\gamma+\sigma)} Y_j^{(1-\sigma)/(\gamma+\sigma)}\left[(P_i^F/P_j^C)(P_j^F/P_j^C)^{-1/\sigma}\right]^{-\sigma(\gamma+1)/(\gamma+\sigma)} \tag{14}$$

where X_{ij}^{cif} denotes the real trade flow (the nominal c.i.f. value of the trade flow divided by the exporter's deflator), $Y_i(Y_j)$ denotes real GDP of country $i(j)$, and $s_i(s_j)$ denotes i's(j's) share of the two countries real incomes (e.g., $s_i = Y_i/[Y_i + Y_j]$).

Similar to Bayoumi and Eichengreen (1997), we study the growth of world trade by examining the first-difference logarithmic form of Eq. (14):

$$\begin{aligned}\Delta \log X_{ij}^{cif} = {} & \beta_0 + 2\Delta \log(Y_i + Y_j) + \Delta \log(s_i s_j) \\ & +[(1-\sigma)(\gamma+1)/(\gamma+\sigma)]\,\Delta \log(1 + a_{ij}) \\ & +[-\sigma(\gamma+1)/(\gamma+\sigma)]\,\Delta \log(1 + t_{ij}) \\ & +[(1-\sigma)/(\gamma+\sigma)]\,\Delta \log(Y_j) \\ & +[-\sigma(\gamma+1)/(\gamma+\sigma)]\,\Delta \log([P_i^F/P_j^C][P_j^F/P_j^C]^{-1/\sigma})\end{aligned} \tag{15}$$

where log denotes the natural logarithm. The potential gains in estimating Eq. (15) are fivefold.

First, all variables are in real terms, which are the factors of interest for growth. Second, the effect of bilateral income growth is captured by variation in the term $(Y_i + Y_j)$; world income growth is captured in the constant.[15] Third, the effect of income convergence is captured by variation in $s_i s_j$. In the context of this model, the convergence of incomes of country pairs augments trade flow growth. Income convergence is monotonically positively related to $s_i s_j$, which can vary theoretically from 0 to 0.25. Fourth, the effects of transport-cost and tariff-rate changes are captured by the gross c.i.f.-f.o.b. factor $(1+a_{ij})$ and gross tariff rate $(1+t_{ij})$,

[14] Note that $Y_i Y_j = (Y_i + Y_j)^2(s_i s_j)$. In the context of this class of models, the trade flow is proportional to the product of the country incomes. Even though these terms are equivalent, we choose to include the latter because the coefficient estimates on the components of $(Y_i + Y_j)$ and $(s_i s_j)$ reflect *explicitly* the relative roles of income growth and income convergence, respectively.

[15] In the context of this model, $\beta_0 = -[(\gamma+1)/(\gamma+\sigma)][\Delta \log \psi] = -[(\gamma+1)/(\gamma+\sigma)][\Delta \log (\alpha/\phi)(\sigma-1)] = -[(\gamma+1)/(\gamma+\sigma)][\Delta \log (\alpha\sigma) + \Delta \log (Y^W/L^W)]$. Even though ψ, Y^W, and L^W are constant across country pairs within any year, these constants may be different *between* two periods. β_0 is likely to be negative, reflecting (although not equal to) the growth in world per capita real GDP due to technological change.

respectively. Fifth, the coefficient estimate of Y_j indicates whether or not the elasticity of transformation of output across markets is finite; if $\gamma=\infty$ as commonly assumed, Y_j's coefficient estimate will be 0.

Since some of the growth of trade may have resulted from the initial period (1958–60) not being one of 'general equilibrium,' we estimate the model including additionally the natural logarithm of the initial period's trade flow level, log $PX_{ij,1958-60}$.[16] Hence, the econometric model to be estimated is:

$$\begin{aligned}\Delta \log X_{ij}^{cif} = {} & \beta_0 + \beta_1 \Delta \log(Y_i + Y_j) + \beta_2 \Delta \log(s_i s_j) \\ & + \beta_3 \Delta \log(1 + a_{ij}) + \beta_4 \Delta \log(1 + t_{ij}) + \beta_5 \Delta \log(Y_j) \\ & + \beta_6 \Delta \log\left([P_i^F / P_j^C][P_j^F / P_j^C]^{-1/\sigma}\right) \\ & + \beta_7 \log(PX_{ij,1958-60}) + \varepsilon_{ij} \end{aligned} \tag{16}$$

where ε_{ij} is a normally distributed random error. Given the theoretical model, linear constraints can be evaluated for coefficient estimates of β_1 and β_2 and nonlinear constraints for coefficient estimates of β_3, β_4, β_5, and β_6.

As the next section of the paper will discuss, data for all variables except P_i^F / P_j^C and P_j^F / P_j^C are readily available. Since P_j^C is a Dixit-Stiglitz price index of landed prices in country j of products from all N markets (including j), the presence of P_j^C is problematic econometrically because the variable is a function of one of the model's parameters to be estimated (σ). Similarly, P_i^F and P_j^F are Dixit-Stiglitz indexes and are functions of another model parameter (γ). One possible solution is to estimate (16) using nonlinear least squares with values of the p_{ijk}s; however, cross-country data on the p_{ijk}s do not exist.

While we do not expect to capture the effects of these variables well, we attempt at least to capture some of the variation in the countries' relative price levels, P_i^F / P_j^C. Since the theoretical model separates nominal GDPs into real GDPs (Y_i,Y_j) and price levels, the natural choice for the proxies are the two countries' GDP deflators. We create a proxy for the relative price variable, P_i^F / P_j^C, employing the ratio of the countries' deflators (adjusted for the exchange rate), maintaining a low expectation that the coefficient estimates of β_6 will accord with the theory. There is no reasonable proxy for P_j^F / P_j^C; however, if tariff revenue is redistributed to households, the role of this factor diminishes. Moreover, changes in this ratio from the late 1950s to the late 1980s likely had little effect empirically on the growth of

[16] Since the initial period's trade flow enters as a log *level* cross-sectionally, it is meaningless to adjust the initial period's nominal trade flow levels by the exporter's deflator (an index). The model was also estimated without the initial period's log-level trade flow; the empirical results are qualitatively and quantitatively similar and are omitted here only due to space constraints of the journal.

country j's real income $(P_j^F Y_j / P_j^C)$. Finally, the mis-measurement of $(P_i^F / P_j^C)(P_j^F / P_j^C)^{-1/\sigma}$ is likely to bias its coefficient estimate toward zero.

4. Data issues

Bayoumi and Eichengreen (1997) note that a common concern in some previous estimates of international trade gravity equations is the pooling of data for industrial and developing countries. The concern arises because the relationship 'between trade and economic characteristics may vary between the two groups of countries' (p. 143). For this reason and tariff data limitations (see below), our cross section includes bilateral trade flows and economic characteristics among 16 OECD countries (listed in Table 1). Systematically-measured bilateral trade flow data from the International Monetary Fund (IMF, 1958/62) begins in 1958 (see *Direction of Trade, Annual 1958–62*). Bilateral trade flow data from the OECD begins earlier, but excludes Japan, Australia and Finland (as the OEEC, the precursor to the OECD, was smaller in the early and mid 1950s). Consequently, we used the IMF's *Direction of Trade* bilateral trade flow import-measured data for the years 1958–1960, averaged over the three years. To avoid the consolidation of East and West Germany and the phased-in introduction of the Canada-U.S. Free Trade Agreement but to recognize fully-phased-in Tokyo Round tariff reductions, OECD (1992) bilateral trade data for the years 1986–1988, averaged over the

Table 1
Gross CIF-FOB factors for 16 OECD countries[a]

Country	1958–1960	1986–1988
Canada	1.0321	1.0250
United States	1.1148	1.0442
Japan	1.2005	1.0681
Belgium-Luxembourg	1.0700	1.0310
Denmark	1.0581	1.0464
France[b]	1.1461	1.0336
(W.) Germany	1.0702	1.0261
Italy	1.0993	1.0690
Netherlands	1.0600	1.0560
United Kingdom	1.1272	1.0438
Austria	1.0260	1.0470
Norway	1.0279	1.0270
Sweden	1.0710	1.0230
Switzerland	1.0140	1.0100
Australia	1.1258	1.0872
Finland	1.0702	1.0450

[a] Source: IMF International Financial Statistics (1995).
[b] For France, 1958–60 data was unavailable; 1960–62 data was used.

three years, were used.[17] OECD data for 1986–88 matched with corresponding IMF data, but the former were measured in thousands rather than millions of U.S. dollars.

In the context of Eq. (16), the effect of transportation-cost reductions on trade growth is reflected in the change in the gross cif-fob factor and the effect of policy-induced trade liberalization is reflected in the change in the gross tariff rate. Regarding c.i.f.-f.o.b. factors, the IMF's *Direction of Trade* statistics and the OECD's *Trade Series C-Foreign Trade by Commodities* both provide f.o.b.-valued export data and c.i.f.-valued import data on bilateral trade flows. In a perfectly measured world, all the f.o.b.-valued exports, say, from Canada to Belgium-Luxembourg would arrive in Belgium-Luxembourg so that the ratio of Belgium-Luxembourg's c.i.f.-valued imports from Canada to Canada's f.o.b.-valued exports to Belgium-Luxembourg would reveal the gross bilateral c.i.f.-f.o.b. transport-cost factor. In reality, not all of Canada's exports to Belgium-Luxembourg are imported by Belgium-Luxembourg. For instance, in 1986–88 the average annual f.o.b. value of Canada's exports to Belgium-Luxembourg was US$705.7 million while the average annual c.i.f. value of Belgium-Luxembourg's imports from Canada was US$470.2 million – only two-thirds of the value of the trade flow exported from Canada to Belgium-Luxembourg. This problem arose for several trade flows, suggesting that c.i.f.-f.o.b. factors for bilateral flows were not reliable estimates of bilateral transportation costs.

However, the IMF's *International Financial Statistics* (1995) provide estimates of countries' multilateral gross c.i.f.-f.o.b. factors (i.e., the ratio of c.i.f.-valued imports to f.o.b.-valued imports). The use of multilateral c.i.f.-f.o.b. factor changes assumes that declines over the (approximately) 30-year period in an importing country's transportation and insurance costs were proportionate among the suppliers.[18] Table 1 shows each country's gross (multilateral) c.i.f.-f.o.b. factor in 1958–60 and 1986–88. The average c.i.f.-f.o.b. factor was 8.21% in 1958–60 and declined 48% to 4.27% by 1986–88.

Some constraints were faced also estimating gross tariff-rate reductions. Ideally, we want to have bilateral measures of changes in ad valorem tariff rates (or their equivalents) as suggested by Eq. (16). The only source of such measures is data prepared for Prewo (1978). Prewo calculated annual bilateral average tariff rates for 18 OECD countries (the 16 countries listed in Table 1 and Portugal and Spain) for years 1958 through 1974, the last year being one in which Kennedy Round tariff reductions had been fully phased in but Tokyo Round tariff reductions had not yet been implemented. Deardorff and Stern (1986, 1990) provide measures of pre- and post-Tokyo Round average (multilateral) tariff rates for 18 OECD countries (the 16 listed in Table 1 and Ireland and New Zealand). Using the

[17] The data cutoff of 1988 also precludes the influence of the rapid decline in communication costs in the 1990s, for which measurement is difficult.

[18] Moreover, use of these data assumes the composition of imports changes little over time.

changes in average multilateral tariff rates from Deardorff and Stern (1986, 1990), we extended the Prewo (1978) average bilateral tariff rate data to 1987 (the year in which Tokyo Round tariff reductions had been fully phased in). This extension of bilateral tariff rates was not severely restricted by the use of the multilateral average tariff changes because, by 1987, 12 of the 16 countries in our sample had a free trade arrangement with each other (i.e., EC, EFTA, or the EC–EFTA pact).[19] Consequently, for 1986–1988 more than 132 of 240 bilateral trade relations had a zero tariff rate (or gross tariff rate of unity). The average bilateral tariff rate in the sample was 11.2% in 1958–1960 and declined 81% to 2.1% in 1986–1988; the low average tariff rate in the latter period, of course, reflects the large share of bilateral free trade arrangements.[20]

The remaining income and price variables needed to estimate Eq. (16) were obtained from the IMF *International Financial Statistics* (1995). Nominal and real GDP values and exchange rates for 1958–1960 and 1986–1988 were readily available. Bilateral exchange rates were measured using annual average values (*IFS* series rf) to express relative prices and real GDPs in terms of a common currency.

For later reference, Table 2 reports the mean, standard deviation, and coefficient of variation of the logarithmic difference (i.e., growth rate) of each of the variables and the log-level of the initial period's trade flow.

Table 2
Statistics for the growth rates and log-level of selected variables[a]

Variable	Mean (%)	Stand. Dev. (%)	Coeff. of variation
First-difference log of:			
Nominal Trade Flow (PX_{ij}^{cif})	327.1	86.7	0.27
Exporter's GDP Deflator (P_i^F)	179.5	30.5	0.17
Real Trade Flow (X_{ij}^{cif})	147.6	76.0	0.51
Average Real GDP ($Y_i + Y_j$)	105.0	24.3	0.23
Product of Real GDP Shares ($s_i s_j$)	−3.3	21.6	−6.55
Importer's Real GDP (Y_j)	103.3	23.9	0.23
Gross c.i.f./f.o.b. factor ($1 + a_{ij}$)	−3.6	3.7	−1.03
Gross Tariff Rate ($1 + t_{ij}$)	−8.5	4.1	−0.48
Relative Price Level (P_i^F / P_j^C)	0.0	44.6	na
Log-level of:			
Nominal Trade Flow ($PX_{ij,1958-60}$)	1108.3	159.5	0.14

[a] Sources: See text; 'na' denotes not applicable.

[19]We used the 1958–1960 average of the bilateral tariff rates in Prewo (1978). The Tokyo Round tariff reductions were phased in fully by 1987. The rates calculated for 1987 are used for the 1986–1988 variable.

[20]Regrettably, no such comparable measures exist of nontariff barriers, in order to consider their possible effect.

5. Empirical results

The empirical results are reported in four parts. In the first section, we report estimates of a simple regression of trade flow growth on the changes in the gross c.i.f.-f.o.b. factor and gross tariff rate – a specification suggested by intuition rather than an explicit general equilibrium model. Second, we estimate the first-difference logarithmic version of Eq. (4) to determine whether the basic 'frictionless' gravity equation holds. Third, we estimate Eq. (16) to evaluate empirically the absolute and relative effects of real income growth, real income convergence, falling transport costs, and declining tariffs on the growth of world trade. Fourth, we re-estimate Eq. (16) imposing restrictions implied by the theory that are not rejected statistically, use these coefficients to estimate the elasticities of substitution in consumption and of transformation of production among national markets, and then compare these elasticity estimates to others in the literature.

5.1. Preliminary results

Before reporting the results of estimating Eq. (16), we present some preliminary regression findings of a specification suggested by intuition discussed in the introduction. It is worth noting that an ordinary least squares (OLS) regression of changes in real bilateral trade flows from 1958–60 to 1986–88 on a constant and changes in the gross c.i.f.-f.o.b. factors and gross tariff rates over this period yields:

$$\begin{aligned} \Delta \log X_{ij}^{cif} &= \underset{(9.65)}{1.09} - \underset{(-3.38)}{4.41}\,\Delta \log(1 + a_{ij}) - \underset{(-2.29)}{2.71}\,\Delta \log(1 + t_{ij}) \\ R^2 &= 0.080, \text{ Adjusted } R^2 = 0.072, \text{ SEE} = 0.733, N = 240 \end{aligned} \tag{17}$$

where SEE is the standard error of the regression and t-statistics are in parentheses.

Three results emerge from this regression. First, the reduction over these 28 years in transportation costs and in tariff rates had the expected effects, both factors contributing to the growth of world trade (148 percentage points on average in this sample). However, these factors only explain 7% of the growth of trade (adjusted $R^2 = 0.07$), which is not surprising given the absence of income growth as an explanatory variable. Second, both factors had economically and statistically significant effects on world trade growth; also, since both measures are calculated comparably, a 1% reduction in tariff rates had a smaller impact on trade growth than did a 1% reduction in the transport-cost factor. Third, the average tariff reduction in our sample explains 23 percentage points of the 148 percentage point growth of world trade (approximately 16%) while the average transport-cost decline explains only 16 percentage points (approximately 11%). Although the coefficient estimate of tariffs is below that of transport costs, the average logarithmic change of gross tariffs (−8.5 percentage points for our sample) is almost $2\frac{1}{2}$ times higher than that of transport costs (−3.6 percentage points for our sample).[21]

5.2. Results from the 'frictionless' model

As Section 2 discusses, the frictionless Anderson and Helpman-Krugman models suggest Eq. (4) holds. We estimated the first-difference logarithmic version of Eq. (4):

$$\Delta \log X_{ij}^{cif} = -\Delta \log Y^{W} + \beta_1(\Delta \log Y_i + \Delta \log Y_j) + \varepsilon_{ij} \tag{18}$$

where, in the context of their models, $\beta_1 = 1$ and the constant should approximate the negative of the growth of world real GDP. Estimation of Eq. (18), without restricting β_1 to 1, yields:

$$\begin{gathered} \Delta \log X_{ij}^{cif} = -\underset{(-4.54)}{1.19} + \underset{(10.29)}{1.29}(\Delta \log Y_i + \Delta \log Y_j) \\ R^2 = 0.308, \text{ Adjusted } R^2 = 0.305, \text{ SEE} = 0.634, N = 240 \end{gathered} \tag{19}$$

This frictionless model explains 31% of the growth of world trade (adjusted $R^2 = 0.31$), more than the previous specification. The frictionless gravity model implies that the single coefficient estimate for both countries' income growth should not differ significantly from unity. This linear restriction cannot be rejected at the 1% significance level [$F(1,238) = 5.40$]. Moreover, the constant is negative and significant, consistent with theory; the intercept estimate of −1.19 suggests world output growth of 119%, close to the actual 103% world income growth of this sample.

We also estimated the frictionless model separating explicitly the effects of income growth and income convergence. The resulting regression was:

$$\begin{gathered} \Delta \log X_{ij}^{cif} = -\underset{(-2.14)}{0.67} + \underset{(6.73)}{2.06}\,\Delta \log(Y_i + Y_j) + \underset{(1.03)}{0.35}\,\Delta \log(s_i s_j) \\ R^2 = 0.332, \text{ Adjusted } R^2 = 0.326, \text{ SEE} = 0.624, N = 240 \end{gathered} \tag{20}$$

The income growth and income convergence variables' coefficient estimates have the expected signs. However, the joint hypothesis that the income growth

[21] Since any free trade agreement between a country pair would be captured by a gross bilateral tariff rate of unity, it seemed redundant to include a separate dummy variable to reflect the introduction of a preferential trading arrangement (PTA). However, one might argue that greater trade might be induced by the creation of a PTA *beyond* the effects of zero tariffs. To anticipate this concern, we added a dummy variable to the specification in (17) that had a value of 1 if a PTA was introduced between 1958 and 1988 (i.e., both countries became members of the EC or EFTA, or one EC and one EFTA), and zero otherwise. In this specification, the coefficient estimate of this dummy variable was negative, but trivially small (−0.18), and was statistically insignificant at the 1% level (t-statistic equal to 1.69). Thus, the trade-creating benefits were apparently captured by the bilateral tariff rate, as expected.

coefficient estimate is 2 and the income convergence coefficient estimate is 1 can be rejected at the 1% significance level [$F(2,237)=7.01$].

5.3. Results from the unrestricted model with tariffs, transport costs, and distribution costs

Estimation of Eq. (16) including the logarithm of the initial period's trade flow yields:

$$\begin{aligned}\Delta \log X_{ij}^{cif} = & \underset{(0.09)}{0.05} + \underset{(6.29)}{2.37} \Delta \log(Y_i + Y_j) + \underset{(1.74)}{0.60} \Delta \log(s_i s_j) \\ & - \underset{(-2.71)}{3.19} \Delta \log(1 + a_{ij}) - \underset{(-4.48)}{4.49} \Delta \log(1 + t_{ij}) - \underset{(-2.83)}{0.68} \Delta \log Y_j \\ & - \underset{(-2.69)}{0.25} \Delta \log(P_i^F / P_j^C) - \underset{(-2.62)}{0.08} \log PX_{ij,1958-60}\end{aligned}$$

$$R^2 = 0.400, \text{ Adjusted } R^2 = 0.388, \text{ SEE} = 0.584, N = 240 \tag{21}$$

5.3.1. Summary of the regression results

Specification (21) has greater explanatory power (adjusted $R^2=0.39$) than either the simple frictionless trade model or the preliminary regression. All coefficient estimates have signs consistent with the theoretical model. The coefficient estimate for income growth has a value close to 2 and the coefficient estimate for income convergence has a value close to 1, as expected; results of statistical tests for these values are provided later. The coefficient estimates for transportation costs and tariff rates have negative signs and the estimate for the transport-cost factor is smaller (in absolute value) than that for tariffs, as expected given Eq. (15). The coefficient estimate for importer's real GDP is negative as expected and statistically significantly different from zero, indicating that the elasticity of transformation of output across national markets may be finite. The coefficient estimate for the growth rate of the relative price level is negative and statistically significant as expected. Not surprisingly, the coefficient estimate is close to zero, since the relative price level is likely mis-measured. Finally, the coefficient estimate for the initial trade flow has a significant negative effect with a plausible magnitude.

5.3.2. Explaining the mean growth of world trade

The results indicate that income growth, tariff rate reductions, and transport-cost declines all contributed nontrivially to the real growth of world trade. Using the results from specification (21), we estimate the contribution of each of these three factors for explaining the 148 percentage points mean growth of trade. First, income growth explains about 100 percentage points of this growth (or 67% of the total). This result is quite plausible since most estimates for OECD countries over the same period find that the share of merchandise trade in GDP increased about

2% annually.[22] Second, tariff-rate reductions explain 38 percentage points (or roughly 26%) of the growth of trade. This is obtained from the product of the mean logarithmic change of the tariff variable, −8.5 percentage points, and its coefficient estimate, −4.49. Third, transport-cost reductions explain 12 percentage points (or roughly 8%) of the growth. The mean logarithmic change of the gross c.i.f./f.o.b. factor was −3.6 percentage points and its coefficient estimate was −3.19.

However, income convergence explains virtually none of the mean growth of trade in our sample. Importantly, note that the *relationship* between trade and income convergence raised in Helpman (1987) does hold; that is, the coefficient estimate for $s_i s_j$ is not significantly different from unity, as expected. But the degree of income convergence measured is trivial in our sample. In fact, as Table 2 reveals the degree of income similarity in our sample of the richest industrialized countries fell by 3% over the 28-year period; in a broader sample of all OECD countries, we found an increase in income similarity of 4%. For our sample, the index of income convergence contributed a trivial −2 percentage points to world trade growth; this is the product of the mean growth rate of the index of similarity of real GDPs (−3.3 percentage points) and the coefficient of 0.60. Together, these four factors explain all 148 percentage points of the growth in world trade of this sample, since the mean logarithmic change in the relative price variable is zero.[23]

In the context of Krugman's quote earlier, the international economists seem to

[22]The estimate of 100 percentage points is determined by three factors. First, mean growth of the sum of the countries' real incomes, $\Delta \log (Y_i + Y_j)$, was 1.05 (or 105 percentage points); multiplying this by its coefficient of 2.37 yields a contribution of 2.49. Second, if γ is finite, mean growth in importer income (1.03) will have a dampening effect on trade growth by a factor of −0.68, the importer's income coefficient. The product of 1.03 and −0.68 yields −0.70; subtracting 0.70 from 2.49 yields 1.79. Third, as noted in footnote 15, the constant is related to the negative of the logarithmic change in world per capita real GDP in the context of the model (excluding the lagged log-level of the trade flow). However, the constant contributes only 0.05, inconsistent with the growth of world per capita real GDP (0.80 in our sample). The reason is the presence of the lagged log-level trade flow. As Table 2 indicates, this variable had little variation compared with the growth rates; note the coefficient of variation of 0.14. Consequently, it is nearly perfectly collinear with the constant (a partial correlation coefficient of 0.99), which can bias the intercept's value. (In the comparable specification *without* the log-level trade flow, the constant was −1.04.) Combining the intercept estimate (0.05) with the effect from the lagged trade flow (−0.84 = −0.08 × 11.08) yields −0.79; this suggests growth of world per capita real GDP growth of 0.79, close to the actual value for this sample of 0.80. Subtracting 0.79 from 1.79 yields 1.00, or 100 percentage points, as the estimate of the overall effect of income growth on trade growth.

[23]Since every pair of countries enters twice (each country as exporter and as importer), the mean logarithmic change in the relative price level is zero by construction. Using each pair of countries once, the mean growth rate of the relative price level provides an estimate of the average long-run departure from relative purchasing power parity. The absolute value of the mean logarithmic change of the relative price level using each pair once ($N = 120$) was a trivial 8.5 percentage points, consistent with other empirical evidence for industrialized countries that relative purchasing power parity holds on average between similar economies in the long run (cf., Frankel and Rose, 1996).

have been right! Using these estimates, trade liberalization appears to have contributed about 75% of the (approximately) 2% average annual growth of world merchandise trade as a share of income in the postwar period compared with transport-cost declines, which have contributed only 25% of the growth in trade relative to income.[24]

5.4. Estimating the values of the elasticities of substitution and transformation

Table 3 provides a summary of the F-statistics and results for the various linear and nonlinear restrictions imposed on Eq. (16) by theoretical Eq. (15). To summarize, the restrictions imposed by the theory – with the exception of one – could *not* be rejected. The restriction *systematically* rejected whenever included was that on the coefficient estimate for the relative price level [$\beta_6 = -\sigma(\gamma+1)/$

Table 3
Hypothesis test results for restrictions imposed by the theoretical model

Null hypothesis	F-statistic	F-critical	Accept or reject[a]
1. β_1	0.97	6.75	Accept
2. β_2	1.39	6.75	Accept
3. β_1, β_2	5.55	4.70	**Reject**
4. $\beta_3, \beta_4, \beta_5$	0.32	6.75	Accept
5. $\beta_1, \beta_3, \beta_4, \beta_5$	0.56	4.70	Accept
6. $\beta_2, \beta_3, \beta_4, \beta_5$	0.87	4.70	Accept
7. $\beta_1, \beta_2, \beta_3, \beta_4, \beta_5$	3.81	3.87	Accept
8. $\beta_3, \beta_4, \boldsymbol{\beta_6}$	30.63	6.75	**Reject**
9. $\beta_1, \beta_3, \beta_4, \boldsymbol{\beta_6}$	15.42	4.70	**Reject**
10. $\beta_2, \beta_3, \beta_4, \boldsymbol{\beta_6}$	16.36	4.70	**Reject**
11. $\beta_1, \beta_2, \beta_3, \beta_4, \boldsymbol{\beta_6}$	13.35	3.87	**Reject**
12. $\beta_3, \beta_5, \boldsymbol{\beta_6}$	9.74	6.75	**Reject**
13. $\beta_1, \beta_3, \beta_5, \boldsymbol{\beta_6}$	8.05	4.70	**Reject**
14. $\beta_2, \beta_3, \beta_5, \boldsymbol{\beta_6}$	4.70	4.70	**Reject**
15. $\beta_1, \beta_2, \beta_3, \beta_5, \boldsymbol{\beta_6}$	9.55	3.87	**Reject**
16. $\beta_4, \beta_5, \boldsymbol{\beta_6}$	22.71	6.75	**Reject**
17. $\beta_1, \beta_4, \beta_5, \boldsymbol{\beta_6}$	11.93	4.70	**Reject**
18. $\beta_2, \beta_4, \beta_5, \boldsymbol{\beta_6}$	10.03	4.70	**Reject**
19. $\beta_1, \beta_2, \beta_4, \beta_5, \boldsymbol{\beta_6}$	8.15	3.87	**Reject**
20. $\beta_3, \beta_4, \beta_5, \boldsymbol{\beta_6}$	19.16	4.70	**Reject**
21. $\beta_1, \beta_3, \beta_4, \beta_5, \boldsymbol{\beta_6}$	11.98	3.87	**Reject**
22. $\beta_2, \beta_3, \beta_4, \beta_5, \boldsymbol{\beta_6}$	14.01	3.87	**Reject**
23. $\beta_1, \beta_2, \beta_3, \beta_4, \beta_5, \boldsymbol{\beta_6}$	11.96	3.40	**Reject**

[a] 'Accept' denotes we could not reject the null hypothesis at the 1% significance level.

[24] One might argue that we have ignored important dynamic effects of tariff-rate and transport-cost declines on world trade growth. However, in an earlier version of this paper, we show that the dynamic effects of tariff-rate and transport-cost declines only contributed about 2 percentage points and 3 percentage points, respectively, to the growth of world trade.

$(\gamma + \sigma)$]; this restriction is boldfaced in Table 3. However, as previously discussed, the use of exporter and importer GDP deflators as proxies for the two theoretical Dixit-Stiglitz prices indexes and the likely associated mis-measurement could explain this result.

Given the results of the hypothesis tests, we re-estimated Eq. (16) imposing the 'accepted' linear and nonlinear constraints for coefficients β_1, β_2, β_3, β_4, and β_5. This yielded:

$$\Delta \log X_{ij}^{cif} = \underset{(1.40)}{0.54} + 2\Delta \log(Y_i + Y_j) + 1\Delta \log(s_i s_j)$$
$$- 3.46\Delta \log(1 + a_{ij}) - 4.10\Delta \log(1 + t_{ij}) - 0.36\Delta \log Y_j$$
$$- \underset{(-2.29)}{0.21}\, \Delta \log\left(P_i^F / P_j^C\right) - \underset{(-4.26)}{0.11}\, \log PX_{ij,1958-60}$$
$$R^2 = 0.399, \text{Adjusted } R^2 = 0.389, \text{SEE} = 0.594, N = 240 \qquad (22)$$

Restricted regression (22)'s coefficient estimates are similar to those for unrestricted regression (21) with a minor increase (in absolute value) in the coefficient estimate for the transport-cost factor relative to that for the tariff rate. Moreover, the adjusted R^2 of the restricted regression slightly exceeded that of the unrestricted regression. The decomposition of the growth of world trade for restricted regression (22) consequently is similar to that for unrestricted regression (21). Of the 148 percentage points mean growth of trade, 103 percentage points are accounted for by income growth (versus 100 points for the unrestricted regression), 35 percentage points by the tariff rate (vs. 38), 13 percentage points by the transport-cost factor (vs. 12), and −3 percentage points by income convergence (vs. −2). Tariff reductions still explain almost three times as much trade growth as transport-cost declines.

Unlike regression (21), restricted regression (22) allows the construction of point estimates and confidence intervals for the elasticities of substitution in consumption (σ) and of transformation of production among national markets (γ). Using regression (22), the point estimate of σ is 6.43 with a 90% confidence interval of 2.44 to 10.42. These estimates are well in line with other estimates from recent trade analyses of the elasticity of substitution among imports, cf., Harrigan (1993), Feenstra (1994), and Head and Ries (1999). These estimates are also in the range used in recent studies of the regionalization of trade policy using monopolistically-competitive market structures, cf., Krugman (1991), Frankel (1997), and Frankel et al. (1995, 1996, 1998); for instance, Krugman (1991) used a range of 2 to 10.

By contrast, many previous trade analyses typically assume that the elasticity of transformation in production among markets (γ) is either infinity (e.g., Helpman and Krugman, 1985) or zero (e.g., Deardorff and Stern, 1986, 1990). Using specification (22), the point estimate of γ is 8.56 with a 90% confidence interval of 1.37 to 15.75. These estimates suggest that exports are imperfectly substitutable across national markets, closer to the construct in Deardorff and Stern (1986, 1990). The implication that exports are not perfect substitutes is consistent with the conclusions of Engel and Rogers (1998), who noted that the degree of relative price dispersion observed suggested that consumer markets are national markets and that distribution efforts are 'organized nationally,' as well as empirical evidence of Gould (1994), Head and Ries (1998), and Rauch (1999). Without any benchmark for comparison, future research into estimating this transformation elasticity seems warranted.

6. Conclusions

In 'Growing World Trade,' Krugman (1995) noted that the answer to the question, 'Why has world trade grown?' remains 'surprisingly disputed.' Journalists have argued that technology-led declines in transportation costs have been the major source, while international economists tend to argue that policy-induced trade liberalization has been the critical factor. Feenstra (1998) notes that these two sources 'come to mind immediately,' and he argues that increased convergence in economic size and greater vertical specialization and outsourcing may have contributed as well.

This paper has attempted to provide an empirical benchmark for this issue. Using a standard theoretical general equilibrium model of international trade in final goods and the empirical workhorse for studying trade flow volumes, we estimated the relative contributions of income growth, income convergence, tariff reductions, and transport-cost declines in explaining the mean growth in real bilateral trade flows among a group of 16 OECD countries for which data was available. In this sample, the mean logarithmic growth of trade was 148 percentage points. We found that approximately 67–69% of this growth could be explained by real GDP growth, 23–26% by tariff-rate reductions and preferential trade agreements, 8–9% by transport-cost declines, and virtually none by real GDP convergence. Thus, the relative contribution of trade liberalization was three times that of transport costs, giving economists the edge in the debate articulated by Krugman.

Finally, the model explains approximately 40% of the variation in trade flow growth in the sample. Although income growth and convergence, tariff-rate decreases, and transport-cost declines are represented, increased vertical specialization and outsourcing of intermediate production was beyond the scope of this particular final-goods model. Future research might incorporate this aspect into the framework used here to try to explain some of the remaining variation in the sample left unexplained.

Acknowledgements

The authors thank Ralph Chami, Donald Davis, Simon Evenett, Robert Feenstra, David Hummels, Wolfgang Keller, Rafael Tenorio, Kei-Mu Yi, two anonymous referees, and participants at the Empirical Investigations in International Trade Conference III at Purdue University in 1996, American Economic Association in Chicago in 1998, CEPR conference on 'New Issues in Trade and Location' at Lund University in Sweden in 1998, and seminars at Indiana University at Bloomington, IU at Indianapolis, and Western Michigan University for helpful comments on earlier drafts. We are grateful to Gwen Bartscherer, Cynthia Cicon, Sean Cocchia, and Bethany Marquis for valuable research assistance and the Notre Dame Center for Research in Business for financial support.

Appendix A

This appendix details the solution for a gravity equation from this model for real bilateral trade flows, using nominal bilateral trade flows scaled by the exporter's price level. First, setting Eq. (5) equal to Eq. (10) for all pairs (i, j) including $i = j$ and noting that there are n_i producers in each country i (i.e., Eq. (11)) yields the bilateral trade flow relationship in nominal terms:

$$\begin{aligned} PX_{ij} = n_i p_{ij} x_{ij} &= \psi^{-(\gamma+1)/(\gamma+\sigma)} Y_i Y_j^{(\gamma+1)/(\gamma+\sigma)} \\ &\cdot (1 + a_{ij})^{(1-\sigma)(\gamma+1)/(\gamma+\sigma)} (1 + t_{ij})^{-\sigma(\gamma+1)/(\gamma+\sigma)} \\ &\cdot (P_i^F)^{\gamma(1-\sigma)/(\gamma+\sigma)} (P_j^C)^{\sigma(\gamma+1)/(\gamma+\sigma)} \left[(P_j^F / P_j^C)\right]^{(\gamma+1)/(\gamma+\sigma)} \end{aligned} \tag{A.1}$$

where PX_{ij} is the value of imports of country j from country i.

Second, to convert the nominal trade flow into a real trade flow, divide each side by P_i^F:

$$\begin{aligned} X_{ij}^{cif} = PX_{ij} / P_i^F &= \psi^{-(\gamma+1)/(\gamma+\sigma)} (Y_i Y_j) Y_j^{(1-\sigma)/(\gamma+\sigma)} \\ &\cdot (1 + a_{ij})^{(1-\sigma)(\gamma+1)/(\gamma+\sigma)} (1 + t_{ij})^{-\sigma(\gamma+1)/(\gamma+\sigma)} \\ &\cdot \left[(P_i^F / P_j^C)(P_j^F / P_j^C)^{-1/\sigma}\right]^{-\sigma(\gamma+1)/(\gamma+\sigma)} \end{aligned} \tag{A.2}$$

where X_i^{cif} is the real c.i.f. imports of country j from country i.

Finally, since $Y_i Y_j = (Y_i + Y_j)^2 s_i s_j$, where $s_i = Y_i / (Y_i + Y_j)$ and $s_j = 1 - s_i$, we substitute $(Y_i + Y_j)^2 \cdot (s_i\ s_j)$ for $Y_i\ Y_j$ in Eq. (A.2) above to yield Eq. (14) in the text.

References

Anderson, J.E., 1979. A theoretical foundation for the gravity equation. American Economic Review 69 (1), 106–116.

Anderson, J.E., Marcouiller, D., SJ, 1999. Trade, location and security: an empirical investigation. NBER Working Paper No. 7000.

Baldwin, R.E. 1994. Towards an Integrated Europe. Centre for Economic Policy Research, London.

Bayoumi, T., Eichengreen, B., 1997. Is regionalism simply a diversion? Evidence from the EU and EFTA. In: Ito, T., Kreuger, A. (Eds.), Regionalism versus Multilateral Trade Arrangements. The University of Chicago Press, Chicago.

Bergstrand, J.H., 1985. The gravity equation in international trade: Some microeconomic foundations and empirical evidence. Review of Economics and Statistics 67 (3), 474–481.

Bergstrand, J.H., 1989. The generalized gravity equation, monopolistic competition, and the factor-proportions theory in international trade. Review of Economics and Statistics 71 (1), 143–153.

Bergstrand, J.H., 1990. The Heckscher-Ohlin-Samuelson model, the Linder hypothesis, and the determinants of bilateral intra-industry trade. Economic Journal 100 (4), 1216–1229.

Bergstrand, J.H., 1998. Comments on Determinants of bilateral trade flows: Does gravity work in a neoclassical world. In: Frankel, J.A. (Ed.), The Regionalization of the World Economy. The University of Chicago Press, Chicago, pp. 23–28.

Deardorff, A.V., 1998. Determinants of bilateral trade flows: Does gravity work in a neoclassical world. In: Frankel, J.A. (Ed.), The Regionalization of the World Economy. The University of Chicago Press, Chicago, pp. 7–22.

Deardorff, A.V., Stern, R.M., 1986. The Michigan Model of World Production and Trade. MIT Press, Cambridge, MA.

Deardorff, A.V., Stern, R.M., 1990. Computational Analysis of Global Trading Arrangements. University of Michigan Press, Ann Arbor, MI.

de Melo, J., Tarr, D., 1992. A General Equilibrium Analysis of U.S. Foreign Trade Policy. MIT Press, Cambridge, MA.

Dixit, A., Stiglitz, J.E., 1977. Monopolistic competition and optimum product diversity. American Economic Review 67 (3), 297–308.

Dunlevy, J.A., Hutchinson, W.K., 1999. The impact of immigration on American import trade in the late nineteenth and early twentieth centuries. Journal of Economic History 59 (4), 1043–1062.

Eichengreen, B., Irwin, D., 1995. Trade blocs, currency blocs and the reorientation of world trade in the 1930s. Journal of International Economics 38 (1/2), 1–24.

Engel, C., Rogers, J.H. 1998. Relative price volatility: What role does the border play? International Finance Discussion Paper No. 623, Board of Governors of the Federal Reserve System.

European Commission, 1989. The Participation of Small- and Medium-Sized Enterprises in Exporting Outside the Community. Vol. 1, Main Report – Summary and Recommendations. Netherlands, January.

Evenett, S., Keller, W. 1998. On theories explaining the success of the gravity equation. Unpublished manuscript, May.

Feenstra, R.C., 1994. New product varieties and the measurement of international prices. American Economic Review 84 (1), 157–177.

Feenstra, R.C., 1998. Integration of trade and disintegration of production in the global economy. Journal of Economic Perspectives 12 (4), 31–50.

Feenstra, R.C., Markusen, J.A., Rose, A.K. 1998. Understanding the home market effect and the gravity equation: The role of differentiating goods. NBER Working Paper No. 6904.

Frankel, J.A., 1997. Regional Trading Blocs in the World Economic System. Institute for International Economics, Washington, DC.

Frankel, J.A., Stein, E., Wei, S.-J., 1995. Trading blocs and the Americas: The natural, the unnatural, and the super-natural. Journal of Development Economics 47 (1), 61–95.

Frankel, J.A., Stein, E., Wei, S.-J., 1996. Regional trading arrangements: Natural or supernatural? American Economic Review 86 (2), 52–56.

Frankel, J.A., Stein, E., Wei, S.-J., 1998. Continental trading blocs: Are they natural or supernatural. In: Frankel, J.A. (Ed.), The Regionalization of the World Economy. University of Chicago Press, Chicago.

Frankel, J.A., Rose, A.K., 1996. A panel project on purchasing power parity: Mean reversion within and between countries. Journal of International Economics 40 (CHR.4.17;), 209–224.

Geraci, V.J., Prewo, W., 1982. An empirical demand and supply model of multilateral trade. Review of Economics and Statistics 64 (3), 432–441.

Gould, D.M., 1994. Immigrant links to the home country: Empirical implications for US. bilateral trade flows. Review of Economics and Statistics 76, 302–316.

Harrigan, J., 1993. OECD imports and trade barriers in 1983. Journal of International Economics 35 (1), 91–111.

Head, K., Ries, J., 1998. Immigration and trade creation: Econometric evidence from Canada. Canadian Journal of Economics 31, 47–62.

Head, K., Ries, J., 1999. Armington vs. Krugman: A test of two trade models. Unpublished manuscript, November.

Helpman, E., 1987. Imperfect competition and international trade: Evidence from fourteen industrial countries. Journal of the Japanese and International Economies 1 (1), 62–81.

Helpman, E., Krugman, P., 1985. Market Structure and Foreign Trade. MIT Press, Cambridge, MA.

Hummels, D., Levinsohn, J., 1995. Monopolistic competition and international trade: Reconsidering the evidence. Quarterly Journal of Economics 110 (3), 799–836.

Hummels, D., Rapoport, D., Yi, K.-M., 1998. Vertical specialization and the changing nature of world trade. Federal Reserve Bank of New York Economic Policy Review 4 (2), 79–99.

International Monetary Fund, 1958/62. Direction of Trade, Annual 1958–62. International Monetary Fund, Washington, DC.

International Monetary Fund, 1995. International Financial Statistics, CD-ROM (June). International Monetary Fund, Washington, DC.

Isard, W., 1954a. Location theory and international and interregional trade. Quarterly Journal of Economics 68, 97–114.

Isard, W., 1954b. Location theory and trade theory: Short-run analysis. Quarterly Journal of Economics 68, 305–320.

Krugman, P., 1979. Increasing returns, monopolistic competition, and international trade. Journal of International Economics 9, 469–479.

Krugman, P., 1980. Scale economies, product differentiation, and the pattern of trade. American Economic Review 70 (5), 950–959.

Krugman, P., 1991. Is bilateralism bad. In: Helpman, E., Razin, A. (Eds.), International Trade and Trade Policy. MIT Press, Cambridge, MA.

Krugman, P. 1995. Growing world trade: Causes and consequences. Brookings Papers on Economic Activity (1), 327–377.

Oguledo, V.I., MacPhee, C.R., 1994. Gravity models: A reformulation and an application to discriminatory trade arrangements. Applied Economics 26, 107–120.

OECD, 1992. Trade Series C–Foreign Trade by Commodities, 1991. Organization for Economic Cooperation and Development, Paris.

Powell, A.A., Gruen, F.H.G., 1968. The constant elasticity of transformation production frontier and linear supply system. International Economic Review 9 (3), 315–328.

Prewo, W., 1978. Determinants of the trade pattern among OECD countries from 1958 to 1974. Jahrbucher fur Nationalekonomie und Statistick 193, 341–358.
Rauch, J.E., 1999. Networks versus markets in international trade. Journal of International Economics 48 (1), 7–35.
Rauch, J.E., Feenstra, R.C., 1999. Introduction to symposium on Business and Social Networks in International Trade. Journal of International Economics 48 (1), 3–6.
Rose, A.K., 1991. Why has world trade grown faster than income? Canadian Journal of Economics 24, 417–427.
Summers, R., Heston, A., 1991. The Penn world table (mark 5): An expanded set of international comparisons, 1950–1988. Quarterly Journal of Economics 106 (2), 327–368.
Tinbergen, J., 1962. Shaping the World Economy. Twentieth Century Fund, New York.
Wang, Z.K., Winters, L.A., 1991. The trading potential of eastern Europe. Centre for Economic Policy Research Discussion Paper No. 610, London.
Weyerbrock, S., 1999. East-West European integration: A general equilibrium analysis of alternative agricultural policies. Review of International Economics, forthcoming.

Chapter 5

Bonus vetus OLS: A simple method for approximating international trade-cost effects using the gravity equation☆

Scott L. Baier [a,b,1], Jeffrey H. Bergstrand [c,d,e,*]

[a] John E. Walker Department of Economics, Clemson University, Clemson, SC 29634, USA
[b] Federal Reserve Bank of Atlanta, Atlanta, GA 30309, USA
[c] Department of Finance, Mendoza College of Business, University of Notre Dame, Notre Dame, IN 46556, USA
[d] Kellogg Institute for International Studies, University of Notre Dame, Notre Dame, IN 46556, USA
[e] CESifo, Munich, Germany

ARTICLE INFO

Article history:
Received 17 April 2006
Received in revised form 10 October 2008
Accepted 13 October 2008

Keywords:
International trade
Gravity equation
Multilateral resistance terms
Border barriers

JEL classification:
F1

ABSTRACT

Using a Taylor-series expansion, we solve for a simple reduced-form gravity equation revealing a transparent theoretical relationship among bilateral trade flows, incomes, and trade costs, based upon the model in Anderson and van Wincoop [Anderson, James E., and van Wincoop, Eric. "Gravity with Gravitas: A Solution to the Border Puzzle." American Economic Review 93, no. 1 (March 2003): 170–192.]. Monte Carlo results support that virtually identical coefficient estimates are obtained easily by estimating the reduced-form gravity equation including theoretically-motivated exogenous multilateral resistance terms. We show our methodology generalizes to many settings and delineate the economic conditions under which our approach works well for computing comparative statics and under which it does not.

1. Introduction

For nearly a half century, the gravity equation has been used to explain econometrically the *ex post* effects of economic integration agreements, national borders, currency unions, immigrant stocks, language, and other measures of "trade costs" on bilateral trade flows. Until recently, researchers typically focused on a simple specification akin to Newton's Law of Gravity, whereby the bilateral trade flow from region i to region j was a multiplicative (or log-linear) function of the two countries' gross domestic products (GDPs), their bilateral distance, and an array of bilateral dummy variables assumed to reflect the bilateral trade costs between that pair of regions; we denote this the "traditional" gravity equation.

However, the traditional gravity equation has come under scrutiny, partly because it ignores that the volume of trade from region i to region j should be influenced by trade costs between regions i and j *relative* to those of the rest-of-the-world (ROW), and the economic sizes of the ROW's regions (and prices of their goods) matter as well. While two early formal theoretical foundations for the gravity equation with trade costs – first Anderson (1979) and later Bergstrand (1985) – addressed the role of "multilateral prices," Anderson and van Wincoop (2003) refined the theoretical foundations for the gravity equation to emphasize the importance of accounting properly for the endogeneity of prices. Two major conclusions surfaced from the seminal Anderson and van Wincoop (henceforth, A-vW) study, "Gravity with *Gravitas*." First, traditional cross-section empirical gravity equations have been misspecified owing to the omission of theoretically-motivated endogenous multilateral (price) resistance terms for exporting and importing regions. Second, to estimate properly the general equilibrium comparative statics of a national border or an EIA, one needs to estimate these multilateral resistance (MR) terms for any two regions with *and* without a border, in a manner consistent with theory. Due to the nonlinearity of the structural relationships, A-vW applied a custom nonlinear least squares (NLS) program to account for the endogeneity of prices and estimate the general equilibrium comparative statics.

Another – and computationally less taxing – approach to estimate unbiased gravity equation coefficients, which also acknowledges the influence of theoretically-motivated MR terms, is to use region-

☆ The authors are grateful for financial support under National Science Foundation grants SES-0351018 (Baier) and SES-0351154 (Bergstrand). The authors are also grateful for excellent comments on previous drafts from Eric van Wincoop, Jim Anderson, Tom Cosimano, Peter Egger, two anonymous referees, and participants at presentations at the University of Munich (CESifo), University of Nottingham (Leverhulme Center), University of Groningen, Vanderbilt University, and the 2006 Southern Economic Association annual meeting in Charleston, SC.

* Corresponding author. Tel.: +1 574 631 6761; fax: +1 574 631 5255.
E-mail addresses: Sbaier@Clemson.edu (S.L. Baier), Bergstrand.1@nd.edu (J.H. Bergstrand).
[1] Tel.: +1 864 656 4534.

*Originally Published in *Journal of International Economics*, 77(2009), pp. 77–85.

specific fixed effects, as noted by A-vW, Eaton and Kortum (2002), and Feenstra (2004). An additional benefit is that this method avoids the measurement error associated with measuring regions' "internal distances" for the MR variables. Indeed, van Wincoop himself – and nearly every gravity equation study since A-vW – has employed this simpler technique of fixed effects for determining gravity-equation parameter estimates, cf., Rose and van Wincoop (2001) and Baier and Bergstrand (2007a). Yet, without the structural system of nonlinear equations, one still cannot generate region- or pair-specific general equilibrium (GE) comparative statics; fixed effects estimation precludes estimating MR terms with *and* without EIAs. Empirical researchers can use fixed effects to obtain the key gravity-equation parameter estimates, and then simply construct a system of nonlinear equations to estimate multilateral price terms with and without the "border." But they don't.

Consequently, the empirical researcher faces a tradeoff. A customized NLS approach can potentially generate consistent, efficient estimates of gravity-equation coefficients *and* comparative statics, but it is computationally burdensome relative to ordinary least squares (OLS) and subject to measurement error associated with internal distance measures. Fixed-effects estimation uses OLS and avoids internal distance measurement error for MR terms, but one cannot retrieve the multilateral price terms necessary to generate quantitative comparative-static effects without also employing the structural system of equations. Is there a third way to estimate gravity equation parameters using *exogenous* measures of multilateral resistance and "good old" ("*bonus vetus*") OLS and/or compute region-specific resistance terms that can be used to approximate MR terms for comparative statics or other purposes (to be discussed later) without using a nonlinear solver? This paper suggests a method that may be useful.

Following some background, this paper has three major parts: theory, estimation, and comparative statics. First, we suggest a method for "approximating" the MR terms based upon theory. We use a simple first-order log-linear Taylor-series expansion of the MR terms in the A-vW system of equations to motivate a reduced-form gravity equation that includes theoretically-motivated exogenous MR terms that can be estimated potentially using OLS. However – unlike fixed-effects estimation – this method can *also* generate theoretically-motivated general equilibrium comparative statics without using a system of nonlinear equations or assuming symmetric bilateral trade costs.

Second, we show that our first-order log-linear approximation method provides *virtually identical* coefficient estimates for gravity-equation parameters to those in A-vW. For tractability, we apply our technique first to actual trade flows using the same context and Canadian–U.S. data sets as used by McCallum (1995), A-vW, and Feenstra (2004). However, the insights of our paper have the potential to be used in numerous contexts, especially estimation of the effects of tariff reductions and free trade agreements on world trade flows – the most common usage of the gravity equation in trade. Using Monte Carlo techniques, we show that the linear approximation approach works in the context of regional (intra-continental) and world (intra- and inter-continental) trade flows.

Third, we demonstrate the economic conditions under which our approximation method works well to calculate comparative-static effects of key trade-cost variables… and when it does not. We compare the comparative statics generated using our approach versus those using A-vW's approach both for the Canadian–U.S. context and for world trade flows using Monte Carlo simulations. We find that the largest comparative static changes in multilateral price terms (and largest approximation errors) tend to be among – not just small GDP-sized economies (and consequently those with large trading partners) as emphasized in A-vW – but small countries that are *physically close.* Using a fixed-point iterative matrix manipulation, the approximation errors can be eliminated using an $N \times N$ matrix of GDP shares *relative to* bilateral distances, that is, measures of economic "density." Since our approximation method can generate MR terms even when trade costs are bilaterally asymmetric, our method can yield lower average absolute biases of comparative statics than the A-vW method (which only addresses average border barriers under asymmetry).

The remainder of the paper is as follows. Section 2 reviews the A-vW analysis. Section 3 uses a first-order log-linear Taylor-series expansion to motivate a simple reduced-form gravity equation. In Section 4, we apply our estimation technique to the McCallum–A-vW–Feenstra data set and compare our coefficient estimates to these papers' findings. Section 5 examines the economic conditions under which our approach approximates the comparative statics of trade-cost changes well and under which it does not. Section 6 concludes.

2. Background: the gravity equation and prices

2.1. The A-vW theoretical model

To understand the context, we initially describe a set of assumptions to derive a gravity equation; for analytical details, see A-vW (2003). First, assume a world endowment economy with N regions and N (aggregate) goods, each good differentiated by origin. Second, assume consumers in each region j have identical constant-elasticity-of-substitution (CES) preferences. Maximizing utility subject to a budget constraint yields a set of first-order conditions that can be solved for the demand for the nominal bilateral trade flow from i to j (X_{ij}):

$$X_{ij} = \left(\frac{p_i t_{ij}}{P_j}\right)^{1-\sigma} Y_j \tag{1}$$

where p_i is the exporter's price of region i's good, t_{ij} is the gross trade cost (one plus the *ad valorem* trade cost) associated with exports from i to j, Y_j is GDP of country j, and P_j is the CES price index given by:

$$P_j = \left[\sum_{i=1}^{N} (p_i t_{ij})^{1-\sigma}\right]^{1/(1-\sigma)}. \tag{2}$$

A third assumption of market-clearing and some algebraic manipulation yields:

$$X_{ij} = \left(\frac{Y_i Y_j}{Y^T}\right)\left(\frac{t_{ij}}{\Pi_i P_j}\right)^{1-\sigma} \tag{3}$$

where

$$\Pi_i = \left[\sum_{j=1}^{N} \left(\theta_j / t_{ij}^{\sigma-1}\right) P_j^{\sigma-1}\right]^{1/(1-\sigma)} \tag{4}$$

$$P_j = \left[\sum_{i=1}^{N} \left(\theta_i / t_{ij}^{\sigma-1}\right) \Pi_i^{\sigma-1}\right]^{1/(1-\sigma)} \tag{5}$$

Y^T denotes total income of all regions, which is constant across region pairs, and θ_i (θ_j) denotes Y_i/Y^T (Y_j/Y^T). It will be useful now to define the term "economic density." For i, the bilateral "economic density" of a trading partner j is the amount of economic activity in j relative to the cost of trade between i and j, or $\theta_j / t_{ij}^{\sigma-1}$.

To solve this system of equations, A-vW employed a strong fourth assumption: trade costs are symmetric bilaterally, implying $t_{ij} = t_{ji}$. Under this fourth assumption, their model simplifies to a system of N^2 equations in $N(N-1)$ endogenous trade flows and N endogenous price terms (P).

2.2. The A-vW econometric model

As is common to this literature, for an econometric model we assume the log of the observed trade flow ($\ln\mathbf{X}_{ij}$) is equal to the log of the true trade flow ($\ln X_{ij}$) plus a log-normally distributed error term (ε_{ij}). Y_i can feasibly be represented empirically by observable $\mathbf{GDP}_i$. However, the world is not so generous as to provide observable measures of bilateral

S.L. Baier, J.H. Bergstrand / Journal of International Economics 77 (2009) 77–85 79

trade costs t_{ij}. Following the literature, a fifth assumption is that the gross trade cost factor is a log-linear function of (boldfaced) *observable* variables, such as bilateral distance ($\mathbf{DIS}_{ij}$) and dummy variable $e^{-\alpha \mathbf{EIA}_{ij}}$:

$$t_{ij} = \mathbf{DIS}_{ij}^{\rho} e^{-\alpha \mathbf{EIA}_{ij}} \tag{6}$$

where equals $e^{-\alpha \mathbf{EIA}_{ij}}$ equals $e^{-\alpha}$ (<1) if the two regions are in an economic integration agreement (assuming $\alpha > 0$). One could also include a language dummy, an adjacency dummy, etc.; for brevity, we ignore these.

In the McCallum–A-vW–Feenstra context of Canadian provinces and U.S. states, $\mathbf{EIA}_{ij} = 1$ if the two regions are in the same country, and 0 otherwise. A-vW describe one customized nonlinear procedure for estimating Eqs. (3)–(6) to generate unbiased estimates in a two-country world with 10 Canadian provinces, 30 U.S. states and an aggregate rest-of-U.S. (the other 20 states plus the District of Columbia), or 41 regions total. A-vW also estimate a multicountry model; we discuss that later. This procedure minimized the sum-of-squared residuals of:

$$\ln\left[\mathbf{X}_{ij}/(\mathrm{GDP}_i\mathrm{GDP}_j)\right] = a_0 + a_1 \ln \mathbf{DIS}_{ij} + a_2 \mathbf{EIA}_{ij} - \ln P_i^{1-\sigma} - \ln P_j^{1-\sigma} + \varepsilon_{ij} \tag{7}$$

subject to the 41 market-equilibrium conditions ($j = 1, \ldots, 41$):

$$P_j^{1-\sigma} = \sum_{k=1}^{41} P_k^{\sigma-1}\left(\mathrm{GDP}_k/\mathrm{GDP}^T\right) e^{a_1 \ln \mathbf{DIS}_{kj} + a_2 \mathbf{EIA}_{kj}} \tag{8}$$

to estimate a_0, a_1, and a_2 where $a_0 = -\ln \mathbf{GDP}^T$, $a_1 = -\rho(\sigma-1)$, $a_2 = -\alpha(\sigma-1)$, and trade costs are bilaterally symmetric.

2.3. Estimating comparative-static effects

MR terms $P_i^{1-\sigma}$ and $P_j^{1-\sigma}$ are "critical" to understanding the impact of border barriers on bilateral trade. Once estimates of a_0, a_1, and a_2 are obtained, one can retrieve estimates of $P_j^{1-\sigma}$ for all $j = 1, \ldots, 41$ regions in the presence and absence of a national border. Let $\mathbf{P}_i^{1-\sigma}$ ($\mathbf{P}_i^{*1-\sigma}$) denote the estimate of the MR region i with (without) an EIA following NLS estimation of Eqs. (7) and (8). A-vW and Feenstra (2004) both show that the ratio of bilateral trade between any two regions with an EIA ($\mathbf{X}_{ij}$) and without an EIA ($\mathbf{X}_j$) is given by:

$$\mathbf{X}_{ij}/\mathbf{X}_{ij}^{*} = e^{a_2 \mathbf{EIA}_{ij}}\left(\mathbf{P}_i^{*1-\sigma}/\mathbf{P}_i^{1-\sigma}\right)\left(\mathbf{P}_j^{*1-\sigma}/\mathbf{P}_j^{1-\sigma}\right). \tag{9}$$

However, while fixed effects can determine gravity equation parameters consistently, as A-vW note, estimation of country-specific border effects still requires construction of the structural system of nonlinear price equations to distinguish MR terms with *and* without borders. Moreover, the procedure works only under the case of bilaterally symmetric trade costs. We demonstrate in this paper a simple technique that yields virtually identical estimates of gravity-equation parameters *and* (in many instances) the comparative statics by applying a Taylor-series expansion to the theory, allowing asymmetric bilateral trade costs ($t_{ij} \neq t_{ji}$).

3. Theory

In this section, we apply a first-order log-linear Taylor-series expansion to the system of price equations Π_i and P_j in Eqs. (4) and (5) above to generate a reduced-form gravity equation — including theoretically-motivated exogenous multilateral resistance (MR) terms — that can be estimated using OLS. A first-order Taylor-series expansion of any function $f(x_i)$, centered at x, is given by $f(x_i) = f(x) + [f'(x)](x_i - x)$.[2] Since the solution to a Taylor-series expansion is sensitive to how it is centered, we use in our static trade context the natural choice of an expansion "centered" around a world with symmetric trade frictions ($t_{ij} = t$).[3] However, we note that our method will yield approximations of Π_i and P_j as functions of asymmetric GDP shares and asymmetric bilateral trade costs.

We begin with N Eq. (4) from Section 2.1. It will be useful to divide both sides of Eq. (4) by a constant $t^{1/2}$, yielding:

$$\begin{aligned} \Pi_i/t^{1/2} &= \left[\sum_{j=1}^{N} \theta_j\left(t_{ij}/t^{1/2}\right)^{1-\sigma}/P_j^{1-\sigma}\right]^{1/(1-\sigma)} \\ &= \left[\sum_{j=1}^{N} \theta_j\left(t_{ij}/t\right)^{1-\sigma}/\left(P_j/t^{1/2}\right)^{1-\sigma}\right]^{1/(1-\sigma)}. \end{aligned} \tag{10}$$

Define $\tilde{\Pi}_i = \Pi_i/t^{1/2}$, $\tilde{P}_j = P_j/t^{1/2}$ and $\tilde{t}_{ij} = t_{ij}/t$. Substituting these expressions into Eq. (10) yields:

$$\tilde{\Pi}_i = \left[\sum_{j=1}^{N} \theta_j\left(\tilde{t}_{ij}/\tilde{P}_j\right)^{1-\sigma}\right]^{1/(1-\sigma)} \tag{11}$$

for $i = 1, \ldots, N$. It will be useful for later to rewrite Eq. (11) as:

$$e^{(1-\sigma)\ln \tilde{\Pi}_i} = \sum_{j=1}^{N} e^{\ln \theta_j} e^{(\sigma-1)\ln \tilde{P}_j} e^{(1-\sigma)\ln \tilde{t}_{ij}} \tag{12}$$

where e is the natural logarithm operator. In a world with symmetric trade costs ($t > 0$), $t_{ij} = t$, implying $\tilde{t}_{ij} = 1$. In this world, the latter implies:

$$\tilde{\Pi}_i^{1-\sigma} = \sum_{j=1}^{N} \theta_j \tilde{P}_j^{\sigma-1} \tag{13}$$

for all $i = 1, \ldots, N$. Multiplying both sides of Eq. (13) by $\tilde{\Pi}_i^{\sigma-1}$ yields:

$$1 = \sum_{j=1}^{N} \theta_j\left(\tilde{\Pi}_i \tilde{P}_j\right)^{\sigma-1}. \tag{14}$$

As noted in Feenstra (2004, p. 158, footnote 11), the solution to Eq. (14) is $\tilde{\Pi}_i = \tilde{P}_j = \tilde{P}_j = 1$. Hence, under symmetric trade costs ($t_{ij} = t$), $\tilde{t}_{ij} = \tilde{\Pi}_i = \tilde{P}_j = 1$ and it follows that $\Pi_i = P_j = t^{1/2}$.

A first-order log-linear Taylor-series expansion of Eq. (12) and its analogue for $\tilde{P}_j$, centered at $\tilde{t} = \tilde{\Pi} = \tilde{P} = 1$ (and $\ln \tilde{t} = \ln \tilde{\Pi} = \ln \tilde{P} = 0$) yields $2N$ equations:

$$\ln \Pi_i = -\sum_{j=1}^{N} \theta_j \ln P_j + \sum_{j=1}^{N} \theta_j \ln t_{ij} \tag{15}$$

and

$$\ln P_j = -\sum_{i=1}^{N} \theta_i \ln \Pi_i + \sum_{i=1}^{N} \theta_i \ln t_{ij} \tag{16}$$

using $d[e^{(1-\sigma)\ln \tilde{x}}]/d(\ln \tilde{x}) = (1-\sigma)e^{(1-\sigma)\ln \tilde{x}}$ and some algebraic manipulation (which generates an expression using the original "pre-transformed" variables). A solution to this system of equations (normalizing $P_1 = 1$) is:

$$\ln \Pi_i = \sum_{j=1}^{N} \theta_j \ln t_{ij} + \sum_{k=1}^{N} \theta_k \ln t_{k1} - \sum_{k=1}^{N}\sum_{m=1}^{N} \theta_k \theta_m \ln t_{km}, \quad i = 2, \ldots, N \tag{17}$$

$$\ln P_j = \sum_{i=1}^{N} \theta_i \ln t_{ij} - \sum_{k=1}^{N} \theta_k \ln t_{k1}, \quad j = 2, \ldots, N. \tag{18}$$

See Appendix A for derivations.

Eqs. (17) and (18) are critical to understanding this analysis; they are clearly "multilateral resistance" terms. Consider first Eq. (18). The

[2] We find using a Monte Carlo robustness analysis that a first-order Taylor series works well for estimating gravity equation coefficients. Higher-order terms are largely unnecessary for estimation. However, such terms are relevant for subsequent comparative statics; we address this later in Section 5.

[3] We are grateful to a referee that suggested this center that collapsed two cases into one more general case.

first term on the RHS is a GDP-share-weighted (geometric) average of the gross trade costs facing importer j across all exporters i. The higher this average, the greater overall multilateral resistance in importer j. Holding constant bilateral determinants of trade, the larger is j's multilateral resistance, the lower are bilateral trade costs relative to multilateral trade costs. Hence, the larger the bilateral trade flow from i to j will be. The second term on the RHS (which is constant across all P_j, $j=2,\ldots, N$) scales each P_j to account for normalizing country 1's "inward" multilateral price, $P_1=1$.

Consider now Eq. (17). The first term on the RHS is a GDP-share-weighted (geometric) average of the gross trade costs facing exporter i across all importers j. The higher this average, the greater overall multilateral resistance facing exporter i. Holding constant bilateral determinants of trade, the larger is i's multilateral resistance, the lower are bilateral trade costs relative to multilateral trade costs. Hence, the *larger* the bilateral trade flow from i to j will be. The second term on the RHS scales each $\prod_i$ to account for country 1's inward multilateral resistance term being normalized, as for Eq. (17). The third term on the RHS of "outward" multilateral resistance Eq. (17) (which is also constant across all $\prod_i$, $i=2,\ldots, N$) scales each $\prod_i$ to account for the normalization applying to an "inward" price, P. While the second and third and the second terms on the RHS of Eqs. (17) and (18), respectively, are constant in estimation, under asymmetry comparative statics will be sensitive to the choice of numeraire.

Under the assumption of bilaterally symmetric trade costs, a solution to Eqs. (15) and (16) is easier to derive. Under symmetry, the solution is:

$$\ln P_i=\left[\sum_{j=1}^{N}\theta_j \ln t_{ij}-(1/2)\sum_{k=1}^{N}\sum_{m=1}^{N}\theta_k\theta_m \ln t_{km}\right] \tag{19}$$

and:

$$\ln P_j=\left[\sum_{i=1}^{N}\theta_i \ln t_{ij}-(1/2)\sum_{k=1}^{N}\sum_{m=1}^{N}\theta_k\theta_m \ln t_{km}\right] \tag{20}$$

where the multilateral prices are normalized by (the square root of) GDP-weighted average trade costs, cf., Baier and Bergstrand (2006, 2007b).

In the remainder of this paper, we focus on coefficient estimation and comparative statics under the case of bilaterally symmetric trade costs, which implies $\prod_i=P_i$. In the context of the theory just discussed and bilaterally symmetric trade costs, we can obtain consistent estimates of the gravity equations' coefficients – accounting for the endogenous multilateral price variables – by estimating *using OLS* reduced form:

$$\begin{aligned}\ln X_{ij}&=\beta_0'+\ln GDP_i+\ln GDP_j-(\sigma-1)\ln t_{ij}\\&+(\sigma-1)\left[\left(\sum_{k=1}^{N}\theta_k \ln t_{ik}\right)-\frac{1}{2}\left(\sum_{k=1}^{N}\sum_{m=1}^{N}\theta_k\theta_m \ln t_{km}\right)\right]\\&+(\sigma-1)\left[\left(\sum_{k=1}^{N}\theta_k \ln t_{kj}\right)-\frac{1}{2}\left(\sum_{k=1}^{N}\sum_{m=1}^{N}\theta_k\theta_m \ln t_{km}\right)\right]\end{aligned} \tag{21}$$

where $\beta_0'=-\ln Y^T$ is a constant across country pairs, as is $\sum_{k=1}^{N}\sum_{m=1}^{N}\theta_k\theta_m \ln t_{km}$. Thus, in the context of the theoretical model, the influence of the endogenous multilateral price variables can be accounted for – once we have measures of t_{ij} – using these theoretically-motivated *exogenous* multilateral resistance variables.

We close this section noting that it is useful to exponentiate Eq. (21). After some algebra, this yields:

$$\frac{X_{ij}}{Y_iY_j/Y^T}=\left(\frac{t_{ij}}{t_i(\theta)t_j(\theta)/t^T(\theta)}\right)^{-(\sigma-1)} \tag{22}$$

where $t_i(\theta)=\prod_{k=1}^{N}t_{ik}^{\theta_k}$, $t_j(\theta)=\prod_{k=1}^{N}t_{kj}^{\theta_k}$, $t^T(\theta)=\prod_{k=1}^{N}\prod_{m=1}^{N}t_{km}^{\theta_k\theta_m}$ and recall $\theta_i=Y_i/Y^T$ and $t_{ij}=t_{ji}$ (by assumption). Our use of the Taylor-series expansion simplifies further the "significantly simplified" gravity equation implied by A-vW's Eqs. (7)–(9), cf., A-vW (2003, p. 176). Eq. (22) is a simple reduced-form equation capturing the theoretical influences of bilateral and multilateral trade costs on bilateral trade (relative to GDPs). Given data on bilateral trade flows, national incomes, and bilateral trade costs, Eq. (21) can be estimated by "good old" OLS, noting the possible endogeneity bias introduced by GDP-share weights in RHS variables.[4]

4. Estimation

The goal of this section is to show that one can generate virtually identical gravity equation coefficient estimates ("partial" effects) to those generated using the technique in A-vW but using instead OLS with exogenous multilateral-resistance terms suggested in the previous section. While the approach should work in numerous contexts, we apply it first empirically in Section 4.1 to McCallum's U.S.–Canadian case, a popular context. In Section 4.2, to avoid measurement and specification biases, we provide Monte Carlo analyses for two contexts: Canadian–U.S. flows and world trade flows among 88 countries. In both cases, we assume symmetric bilateral trade costs; we discuss another case of asymmetry later.[5]

Before implementing Eq. (21) econometrically, one issue needs to be addressed. We need to replace the unobservable theoretical trade-cost variable t_{ij} in Eq. (21) with an *observable* variable. Eq. (6) earlier suggests two typical observable variables likely influencing unobservable t_{ij} – bilateral distance ($\mathbf{DIS}_{ij}$) and a dummy representing the presence or absence of an economic integration agreement ($\mathbf{EIA}_{ij}$). We define a dummy variable, $\mathbf{BORDER}_{ij}$, which assumes a value of 1 if regions i and j are *not* in the same nation; hence, $\mathbf{EIA}_{ij}\equiv 1-\mathbf{BORDER}_{ij}$.[6] Taking the logarithms of both sides of Eq. (6) and then substituting the resulting equation for $\ln t_{ij}$ into Eq. (21) yields:

$$\begin{aligned}\ln \mathbf{x}_{ij}&=\beta_0'-\rho(\sigma-1)\ln \mathbf{DIS}_{ij}-\alpha(\sigma-1)\mathbf{BORDER}_{ij}+\rho(\sigma-1)\mathbf{MRDIS}_{ij}\\&+\alpha(\sigma-1)\mathbf{MRBORDER}_{ij}+\varepsilon_{ij}\end{aligned} \tag{23}$$

where

$$\begin{aligned}\mathbf{MRDIS}_{ij}&=\left[\left(\sum_{k=1}^{N}\theta_k \ln \mathbf{DIS}_{ik}\right)+\left(\sum_{m=1}^{N}\theta_m \ln \mathbf{DIS}_{mj}\right)\right.\\&\left.-\left(\sum_{k=1}^{N}\sum_{m=1}^{N}\theta_k\theta_m \ln \mathbf{DIS}_{km}\right)\right],\\ \mathbf{MRBORDER}_{ij}&=\left[\left(\sum_{k=1}^{N}\theta_k \mathbf{BORDER}_{ik}\right)+\left(\sum_{m=1}^{N}\theta_m \mathbf{BORDER}_{mj}\right)\right.\\&\left.-\left(\sum_{k=1}^{N}\sum_{m=1}^{N}\theta_k\theta_m \mathbf{BORDER}_{km}\right)\right],\end{aligned}$$

and $\mathbf{x}_{ij}\equiv X_{ij}/\mathbf{GDP}_i\mathbf{GDP}_j$. To conform to our theory, coefficient estimates for ln**DIS** (**BORDER**) and **MRDIS** (**MRBORDER**) are restricted to have identical but oppositely-signed coefficient values.

As readily apparent, Eq. (23) can be estimated using OLS, once data on trade flows, GDPs, bilateral distances, and borders are provided. We

[4] We ignore here the possibility of "zero" trade flows. Such issues have been dealt with by various means; see, for example, Felbermayer and Kohler (2006) and Santos Silva and Tenreyro (2006).

[5] Note that since the second RHS terms in Eqs. (17)–(20) (and the third RHS term in Eq. (18)) are constants in estimation, the MR approximation terms are effectively identical under symmetric or asymmetric bilateral trade costs.

[6] It will be useful now to distinguish "regions" from "countries." We assume that a country is composed of regions (which, for empirical purposes later, can be considered states or provinces). We will assume N regions in the world and n countries, with $N>n$. Our theoretical model applies to a two-country or multi-country ($n>2$) world. We will assume $n\geq 2$. A "border" separates countries. Also, we use **BORDER** rather than **EIA** so that the coefficient estimates for **DIS** and **BORDER** are both negative and therefore are consistent with A-vW (2003) and Feenstra (2004). The model is isomorphic to being recast in a monopolistically-competitive framework.

Table 1
Estimation results: Canada–U.S

Parameters	(1) OLS w/o MR terms	(2) A-vW NLS-2	(3) A-vW NLS-3	(4) OLS with MR terms	(5) Fixed effects	(6) A-vW NLS-2-a	(7) OLS with MR terms-a
$-\rho(\sigma-1)$ for	−1.06	−0.79	−0.82	−0.82	−1.25	−0.92	−1.02
distance	(0.04)	(0.03)	(0.03)	(0.04)	(0.04)	(0.03)	(0.03)
$-\alpha(\sigma-1)$ for	−0.71	−1.65	−1.59	−1.11	−1.54	−1.65	−1.24
border	(0.06)	(0.08)	(0.08)	(0.07)	(0.06)	(0.07)	(0.07)
Avg. error terms							
US–US	−0.21	0.06	0.06	0.39	0.00	0.05	0.27
CA–CA	1.95	−0.17	−0.02	−0.34	0.00	−0.22	−0.23
US–CA	0.00	−0.05	−0.04	−0.50	0.00	−0.04	−0.35
R^2	0.42	n.a.	n.a.	0.36	0.66	n.a.	0.60
No. of obs.	1511	1511	1511	1511	1511	1511	1511

Numbers in parentheses are standard errors of the estimates. n.a. denotes not applicable.

note that the inclusion of these additional MR terms appears reminiscent of early attempts to include – what A-vW term – "atheoretical remoteness" variables, typically GDP-weighted averages of each country's distance from all of its trading partners. However, there are two important differences here. First, our additional (the last two) terms are motivated by theory. Second, previous atheoretical remoteness measures included only multilateral *distance*, ignoring other multilateral "border" variables (such as adjacency, language, etc.).

4.1. Estimation using the McCallum–A-vW–Feenstra data set for actual Canadian–U.S. trade flows

We follow the A-vW procedure (for the two-country model) of estimating the gravity equation for trade flows among 10 Canadian provinces and 30 U.S. states. As in A-vW, we do not include trade flows internal to a state or province. We calculate the distance between the aggregate U.S. region and the other regions in the same manner as A-vW. We also compute and use the internal distances as described in A-vW for **MRDIS**. Some trade flows are zero and, as in A-vW, these are omitted. As in A-vW and Feenstra (2004), we have 1511 observations for trade flows from year 1993 from Robert Feenstra's website.

Table 1 provides the results. For purposes of comparison, column (1) of Table 1 provides the benchmark model (McCallum) results estimating Eq. (23) except *omitting* **MRDIS** and **MRBORDER**. Columns (2) and (3) provide the model estimated using NLS as in A-vW for the two-country and multi-country cases, respectively. Column (4) provides the results from estimating Eq. (23). For completeness, column (5) provides the results from estimating Eq. (23), but using region-specific fixed effects instead of **MRDIS** and **MRBORDER**.

Column (1)'s coefficient estimates for the basic McCallum regression, ignoring multilateral resistance terms, are biased, as expected. This specification can be compared with Feenstra (2004, Table 5.2, column 3), since it uses US–US, CA–CA, and US–CA data for 1993. Note, however, that Feenstra did not constrain the GDP elasticities to be unity and we report the border dummy's coefficient estimate ("Indicator border") whereas Feenstra reports instead the implied "Country Indicator" estimates.[7] Columns (2) and (3) in Table 1 report the estimates (using *GAUSS*) of the A-vW benchmark coefficient estimates; these correspond exactly to those in A-vW's Table 2 and (for the two-country case) Feenstra's Table 5.2, column (4). The coefficient estimates from our OLS specification (23) are reported in column (4) of Table 1. Both our coefficient estimates in column (4) and the NLS estimates in columns (2) and (3) differ from the estimates using fixed effects in column (5). Recall that – as both A-vW and Feenstra note – fixed effects should provide unbiased coefficient estimates of the bilateral distance and bilateral border effects, accounting fully for multilateral-resistance influences in estimation. Our column (5) estimates match exactly those in A-vW and Feenstra (2004).[8]

We now address the difference between coefficient estimates in columns (2)–(5). As A-vW (2003, p. 188) note, the bilateral distance coefficient estimate using their NLS program is quite sensitive to the calculation of "internal distances." In their sensitivity analysis, they provide alternative coefficient estimates when the internal distance variable values are doubled (or, 0.5 minimum capitals' distance). These are reported in column (6) of our Table 1; note that the absolute value of the distance coefficient increases. These results confirm A-vW's suspicion that the NLS estimation technique is sensitive to measurement error in internal distances.

However, adjustment for internal distance measurement error cannot explain entirely the difference between coefficient estimates in columns (2) and (3) and those in column (5). As A-vW (2003, p. 180) note, potential specification error can also bias the coefficient estimates in columns (2)–(4). In particular the trade-cost function from Eq. (6) may be misspecified. Classic omitted variables bias may exist. As noted above, with GDPs on both the LHS and RHS of Eq. (23), endogeneity bias may arise. When GDP coefficients are not constrained to unity, the coefficient estimates in all the specifications change; column (7) reports the estimates just for the distance and border coefficients using our Eq. (23) allowing unconstrained GDP elasticities.

The differences between the coefficient estimates in Table 1 suggest that an alternative approach is needed to compare the consistency of estimates using A-vW's method, our approach, and fixed effects. Is there a way to compare the estimation results of A-vW and our approach *excluding* mis-measurement and specification biases?

4.2. Monte Carlo analyses

In this section, we employ a Monte Carlo approach to show that our OLS method yields estimates of border and distance coefficient estimates that are *virtually identical* to those using A-vW's NLS method when we know the "true" model. To do this, in Section 4.2.1 we construct the "true" bilateral international trade flows among 41 regions using the theoretical model of A-vW described in Section 2. We assume the world is described precisely by Eqs. (7) and (8), assuming various arbitrary values for α, ρ, and σ. Using Canadian–U.S. province and state data on GDPs and bilateral distances and dummy variables for borders, we can compute the "true" bilateral trade flows *and* "true" multilateral resistance terms associated with these economic characteristics for given values of parameters α, ρ, and σ. We then assume that there exists a log-normally distributed error term for each trade flow equation. We make 1000 draws for each trade equation and run various regression specifications 1000 times.[9] We use *GAUSS* in all estimates. In Section 4.2.2, to show that this approach works in the more traditional context of world trade flows, we employ the same Monte Carlo approach and provide the results.

4.2.1. Monte Carlo analysis #1: Canada–U.S.

We consider five specifications. Specification (1) is the basic gravity model ignoring multilateral resistance terms, as used by McCallum. In

[7] In Feenstra's Table 5.2, column 3, he does not report the actual dummy variable's coefficient estimate (comparable to our estimate of 0.71). Instead, he reports only the implied "Indicator Canada" and "Indicator US" estimates of 2.75 and 0.40, respectively. The implied Indicator Canada and Indicator US estimates from our regression are 2.66 and 0.48, respectively; the difference is that we restrict the GDP elasticities to unity. When we relax the constraints on GDP elasticities, our estimates match those in Feenstra's Table 5.2, column 3 and A-vW's Table 1 exactly.

[8] The coefficient estimates from the fixed-effects regression in A-vW's Table 6, column (viii) are not reported. However, they were generously provided by Eric van Wincoop in e-mail correspondence, along with the other coefficient estimates associated with their Table 6. A-vW's Distance (Border) coefficient estimate using fixed effects was −1.25 (−1.54).

[9] The error terms' distribution is such that the R^2 (and standard error of the estimate) from a regression of trade on GDP, distance, and borders using a standard gravity equation is similar to that typically found (an R^2 of 0.7 to 0.8).

Table 2
Monte Carlo simulations: Canada–U.S

Specification	Coefficient estimate average	Standard deviation	Fraction within 2 standard errors of true value
(1) McCallum			
Border	−0.799	0.054	0.000
Distance	−0.569	0.036	0.000
(2) OLS with atheoretical remoteness terms			
Border	−1.139	0.057	0.000
Distance	−0.958	0.042	0.042
(3) A-vW			
Border	−1.648	0.061	0.955
Distance	−0.791	0.028	0.954
(4) Fixed effects			
Border	−1.648	0.069	0.953
Distance	−0.793	0.045	0.937
(5) OLS with MR approximations			
Border	−1.639	0.069	0.962
Distance	−0.850	0.042	0.744

True border coefficient = −1.65.
True distance coefficient = −0.79.

the context of the theory, we should get biased estimates of the true parameters since we intentionally omit the true multilateral price terms or fixed effects. Specification (2) is the basic gravity model augmented with "atheoretical remoteness" terms ($\mathbf{REMOTE}_i$ and $\mathbf{REMOTE}_j$), as in McCallum (1995) and Helliwell (1998). Eq. (7) would include $\mathbf{REMOTE}_i$ and $\mathbf{REMOTE}_j$, instead of P_i and P_j, where $\mathbf{REMOTE}_i = \ln\Sigma_j^N(\mathbf{DIS}_{ij}/\mathbf{GDP}_j)$ and analogously for $\mathbf{REMOTE}_j$. In the context of the theory, we should get biased estimates of the true parameters since we are using atheoretical measures of remoteness. This specification also ignores other multilateral trade costs. For Specification (3), we take the system of equations described in Eq. (8) to generate the "true" multilateral resistance terms associated with given values of $-\rho(\sigma-1)$ and $-(\sigma-1)$. We then estimate the regression (7) using the true values of the multilateral resistance terms. In the presence of the true MR terms, we expect the coefficient estimates to be virtually identical to the true parameters. Specification (4) uses region-specific fixed effects. As discussed earlier, region-specific fixed effects should also generate unbiased estimates of the coefficients. Specification (5) is our OLS Eq. (23). If our hypothesis is correct, these parameter estimates should be virtually identical to those estimated using Specifications 3 and 4.

We run these five specifications for values for $a_1 = -\rho(\sigma-1) = -0.79$ and $a_2 = \alpha(\sigma-1) = -1.65$ (the values obtained empirically in A-vW using NLS). We report three statistics in Table 2. First, we report the average coefficient estimates for a_1 and a_2 from the 1000 regressions for each specification. Second, we report the standard deviation of these 1000 estimates. In the last column, we report the fraction of times (from the 1000 regressions) that the coefficient estimate for a variable was within two standard errors of the true coefficient estimate.[10]

Table 2 reports the estimated values for the five specifications under this scenario in columns (2)–(4). There are two major results worth noting. First, the first two specifications provide biased estimates of the border and distance coefficient estimates, as expected. Second, both fixed effects and our approximation method provide estimates very close to those using Specification 3, as expected. While the approximation method's average coefficient estimates depart slightly from the average A-vW estimates, 96 (74) percent of the border (distance) coefficient estimates in Specification 5 are within two standard errors of true values.

4.2.2. Monte Carlo analysis #2: gravity equations for world trade flows

Of course, the gravity equation has been used over the past four decades to analyze economic and political determinants of a wide range of aggregate "flows." However, the most common usage of the gravity equation has been for explaining *world* (intra- and inter-continental) bilateral trade flows. The issues raised in A-vW (2003) and in this paper have potential relevance for estimating effects of EIAs and of tariff rates on world trade flows.

We constructed a set of "artificial" aggregate bilateral world trade flows among 88 countries for which data on the exogenous RHS variables discussed above were readily available. Three exogenous RHS variables that typically explain world trade flows are countries' GDPs, their bilateral distances, and a dummy representing the presence (0) or absence (1) of a common land border ("NoAdjacency"). We then estimate the relationship among bilateral trade flows, national incomes, bilateral distances and NoAdjacency among 88 countries using our OLS method. We simply redo Section 4.2.1's Monte Carlo simulations.[11] In short, the main finding is that the estimation biases for coefficients remain small; results are omitted for brevity.

A full multi-country empirical analysis of world trade flows using our approach is beyond the space constraints of this paper. However, two recent empirical gravity equation studies examining determinants of world trade flows have found that the coefficients estimated using our approach are *virtually identical* to the respective coefficient estimates using fixed effects, cf., Adam and Cobham (2007) and Dolman (2008).

5. Comparative statics

In this section, we examine the potential usefulness of our approximation approach for conducting comparative statics.[12] In Section 5.1, our linearization method implies we can compute the comparative statics analytically and provide intuition for why the approach provides a "good approximation" of the comparative-static (overall) country effects for Canada and the United States provided in A-vW (2003), but a poor one of region-pair-specific (such as Alberta–Alabama) comparative statics. In Section 5.2, we move to the most common context — gravity equations of international trade flows among large numbers of countries with symmetric bilateral trade costs — to examine under what conditions the approximation method works well for comparative statics — and when it does not. We find that the approximation method works best the smaller is the comparative-static effect, as would be expected from any linear Taylor-series expansion of a nonlinear equation. However, extending A-vW, the effects of trade costs on multilateral price terms are not simply the greatest for economically small countries (with consequently large trading partners), but for small countries *that are close* in distance. Using the concept of economic "density," or $\theta_j/t_{ij}^{\sigma-1}$

[10] Note that the standard deviation refers to the square root of the variance of all the coefficient estimates for a specification. We also calculated the standard errors of each coefficient estimate. The last column in each table refers to the fraction of the 1000 regressions that the estimated coefficient is within two standard errors of the true value.

[11] Naturally, we could also introduce in this exercise an array of other typical bilateral dummies, such as common language, common EIA, etc. However, this would have no bearing on the generality of our results.

[12] Other potential uses exist also. For instance, recent analyses of the effects of free trade agreements (FTAs) on trade using *nonparametric* (matching) econometric techniques require theory-based indexes of multilateral resistance, cf., Egger et al. (2008) and Baier and Bergstrand (2009); an approach such as ours is needed. Also, recent estimation of economic and political determinants of EIAs between country pairs using probit models of the likelihoods of FTAs requires theory-based (exogenous) measures of multilateral resistance, cf., Mansfield and Reinhardt (2003), Baier and Bergstrand (2004), and Mansfield et al. (2008).

from Eqs. (4) and (5), we show that a simple fixed-point iterative matrix manipulation can eliminate the approximation errors of our multilateral resistance approximations.[13] Finally, since our approximation method was derived allowing bilaterally asymmetric trade costs, our approach may generate lower biases in comparative statics (relative to "true" values) than the A-vW method under bilaterally asymmetric trade costs, as the latter method only addresses "average" border effects (cf., A-vW, 2003, Footnote 12), and we discuss one implementation of our approach under bilateral asymmetry in Section 5.3.

5.1. Analytical estimates of country-specific comparative statics using the approximation approach

Our procedure allows one to estimate the country-specific border effects without employing the nonlinear system of equations. Recall Eq. (9) to calculate (region-specific) border effects for $\mathbf{x}_{ij}$, using its log-linear form:

$$BB_{ij} = \ln \mathbf{x}_{ij} - \ln \mathbf{x}^*_{ij} = a_2 - \ln P_i^{1-\sigma} + \ln P_i^{*1-\sigma} - \ln P_j^{1-\sigma} + \ln P_j^{*1-\sigma} \quad (24)$$

where $\mathbf{x}_{ij} = \mathbf{X}_{ij}/\mathbf{Y}_i\mathbf{Y}_j$, a_2 is the estimate of $-\alpha(\sigma-1)$, and $a_2<0$. We substitute Eq. (6) into Eqs. (19) and (20) to find the MR terms with *and* without national borders. Substituting these results into Eq. (24) yields:

$$BB_{ij} = \ln \mathbf{x}_{ij} - \ln \mathbf{x}^*_{ij} = a_2\left\{\left[1 - \left(\sum_{k=1}^{N} \theta_k \mathbf{BORDER}_{ik}\right) - \left(\sum_{m=1}^{N} \theta_m \mathbf{BORDER}_{mj}\right) + \left(\sum_{k=1}^{N}\sum_{m=1}^{N} \theta_k\theta_m \mathbf{BORDER}_{km}\right)\right]\right\} \quad (25)$$

where $\mathbf{BORDER}_{ij}=1$ if regions i and j are not in the same nation and 0 otherwise (distance components cancel out).[14]

For the simple Canadian–U.S. case, Eq. (25) can be calculated analytically once we have data on Canadian province and U.S. state GDPs and an estimate of a_2; we use $a_2=-1.65$. Given the definition of $\mathbf{BORDER}_{ij}$, it turns out that the second term in the large brackets on the RHS in Eq. (25) is simply Canada's share of Canadian and U.S. GDPs (0.08) and the third term in the brackets is simply the U.S. share of Canadian and U.S. GDPs (0.92). Consequently, the sum of these terms cancels out the 1 and the effect is −1.65 times the last term in the brackets; the last term simplifies to $2\times0.08\times0.92$, or 0.147. Hence, the general equilibrium comparative static effect of the national border on the trade between a Canadian province and U.S. state, using our linear approximation method, is $-1.65\times0.147=-0.243$, implying that the ratio of trade with the barrier (BB) to trade without the barrier (NB) is 0.78 ($=e^{-0.243}$). This is larger than the A-vW multi-country (two-country) estimate of 0.56 (0.41).

While our approximation method can generate border-effect estimates similar to those reported in the recent "border-puzzle" debate, a more demanding test of the method is to evaluate the comparative statics for *specific pairs* of regions. In this particular context, our method provides only a crude approximation, since Canada's share and the U.S. share of the two countries' joint GDP are identical for every region-pair. Consequently, the "country-wide" border effects are identical to the region-pair border effects. However, using A-vW's NLS system, the region-pair border effects vary from 0.32 to 0.49 with an average of 0.41 (using the A-vW two-country technique). Consequently, for particular pairs of Canadian provinces and U.S. states, our method cannot capture the aspect of A-vW that regions within smaller countries face larger multilateral resistance than regions within larger countries.

5.2. Comparative statics using world trade flows and symmetric bilateral trade costs

A-vW motivated the importance of estimating appropriate comparative statics in the context of one specific case: McCallum's Canadian–U.S. "border puzzle." However, for nearly half a century, the gravity equation in international trade has been used most commonly to analyze bilateral aggregate international trade flows and – in particular – the effects of free trade agreements (FTAs) on such flows.

In this section we use the same Monte Carlo approach used earlier for our 88-country world (see Section 4.2). We calculated the "true" trade flows using the A-vW NLS specification including real GDPs, bilateral distance, an adjacency dummy, a language dummy, and a dummy variable representing the presence or absence of an EIA. To keep the approach similar to the literature, we define "NoEEA" as one if the two countries are not members of the European Economic Area (EEA), and zero if they are; the ratios calculated are then interpreted similar to the effects of "border barriers" discussed earlier. We calculated the comparative statics by pairs of countries of NoEEA using A-vW. We then calculated the same comparative statics using our (GDP-share-weighted) approximation method.

5.2.1. The European economic area

The most important economic integration agreement in post-WWII history has been European economic integration. Consequently, an important context to evaluate the approximation method's accuracy is measuring the trade-cost effects of removing the "European Economic Area," or "NoEEA." Among our 88 countries, the potential number of country-pairs that are directly affected by EEA include 165 of the 3872 country-pairs in our sample. Reporting the results for all 165 pairs – much less the *other* 3707 pairs is prohibitive in terms of space. Consequently, we can only summarize the results.

The most notable result from this Monte Carlo experiment is that *74%* of the comparative statics using the approximation method are within 5% of the "true" (here, A-vW-method-determined) comparative statics. Another 9% of the comparative statics using the approximation method have biases between 5 and 10% of the A-vW values. Ninety two percent of the approximation-method comparative statics are within 20% of the A-vW values. As expected using a Taylor approximation, the largest biases are for country pairs with the largest changes in their MR terms (and hence in the comparative statics).

Eight percent of the approximation-method comparative statics differ from the A-vW values by more than 20%. The largest error is 38%. Yet, *every single one* of the country-pairs with a bias greater than 20% includes either Austria, Belgium, Denmark, Ireland, or Switzerland in the pair. Moreover, every single pair where the approximation method performs poorly involves economically small EEA countries that are *close* to one another (and to large trading partners), that is, where countries' multilateral economic densities ($\theta_j/t_{ij}^{\sigma-1}$) are large, cf., Footnote 13.[15]

We find in our general setting of world trade flows that our approximation method for computing pair-specific general equilibrium comparative statics is accurate within 10% of the A-vW values in *83%* of our 3872 country pairings. This result – demanding only OLS – is clearly an improvement over simply using the coefficient estimate (or "partial" effect) of an FTA dummy variable, as is typically done.

[13] Economic density refers, in general, to the amount of economic activity for a given physical area; a large literature exists on its measurement, cf., Ciccone and Hall (1996). In the trade context, a country's multilateral economic density is high when there is a strong negative correlation between partners' sizes and bilateral distances. For instance, Switzerland has a very high multilateral economic density; its largest trading partners are quite close.

[14] In reality, GDP shares will change also. However, as in A-vW, such changes are very small. Consequently, these GDP changes are ignored here.

[15] Since Switzerland is in EFTA, which has an FTA with the EU, it is considered in the EEA here.

5.2.2. A method to eliminate the approximation errors

The Monte Carlo analysis above indicated that the largest MR term changes (from trade costs) were not just for the economically small countries (with consequently large trading partners) as A-vW emphasized, but for small countries that are *physically close*.[16] We discuss a simple fixed-point iteration procedure that eliminates the approximation errors without using NLS estimation or a higher-order Taylor expansion (which, as for modern dynamic macroeconomic models, is very difficult and outside the paper's scope). A simple "fixed-point" iteration on a matrix equation can generate precise estimates of the A-vW MR terms. The key matrix in the equation is an $N \times N$ matrix of GDPs *scaled* by bilateral trade costs, $\theta_j / t_{ij}^{\sigma-1}$, that is, a measure of multilateral economic "densities."[17] We summarize the process briefly, referring the reader to a technical appendix for details (available on request). First, calculate initial estimates of every $P_i^{1-\sigma}$ ($P_i^{*1-\sigma}$) using OLS, denoted $P_i^{1-\sigma}{}_0$ ($P_i^{*1-\sigma}{}_0$), for every region ($i=1,\ldots, N$); * denotes "without borders." Denote the $N \times 1$ vector of these MR terms V_0 (V_0^*) and the $N \times 1$ vector of the inverses of each of these MR terms V_0^- (V_0^{-*}). Second, define an $N \times N$ matrix of GDP-share-weighted trade costs, B, where each element, b_{ij}, equals $\theta_j / t_{ij}^{\sigma-1}$. Third, compute V_{k+1} (with borders) according to:

$$V_{k+1} = zBV_k^- + (1-z)V_k \tag{26}$$

starting at $k=0$ until successive approximations are less than a predetermined value of ε (say, 1×10^{-9}), where $\varepsilon = \max|V_{k+1} - V_k|$ and z is a dampening factor with $z \in (0,1)$, and analogously for V_k^* (without borders). Given the initial estimates of $P_i^{1-\sigma}$ ($P_i^{*1-\sigma}$) using OLS ($i=1,\ldots, N$), this fixed-point iteration process will converge to the set of multilateral price terms identical to those generated using A-vW's NLS quasi-Newton program (which uses a second-order Taylor series).[18] We have run this set of matrix calculations and the correlation coefficient between our MR terms (using fixed-point iteration) and A-vW's MR terms (using NLS) is 1.0 (reported to seven decimal places) in both the Canadian–U.S. context and the 88-country context.

5.3. Comparative statics using world trade flows and asymmetric bilateral trade costs

Finally, even though previous cases assume bilaterally symmetric trade costs, our MR approximations were derived under the more general case of bilaterally asymmetric trade costs. In reality, many trade costs are bilaterally asymmetric, such as tariff rates (cf., Bergstrand et al., 2007) and preferential trade agreements (such as the Generalized System of Preferences). As A-vW (2003, Footnote 12) note, in the case of bilaterally asymmetric trade costs, one must interpret the border barriers in their approach as an average of the barriers in both directions. Consequently, comparative static computations will reflect this constraint.

Since our MR approximations were derived allowing for bilaterally asymmetric trade costs, it is possible that general equilibrium comparative static estimates using our approach could be more accurate than those computed using A-vW's technique under the case of bilateral asymmetry. There is a trade-off: while our method is a first-order approximation of the MR terms, the average absolute errors in estimates may be lower than those generated using A-vW's method because the latter approach constrains the barrier to be an average of bilaterally asymmetric barriers.

Space constraints prevent a full Monte Carlo analysis of this issue. However, in a separate Monte Carlo study, Bergstrand et al. (2007, Table 2) computed similar comparative statics in a setting with asymmetric bilateral trade costs using our method alongside the A-vW method (assuming either symmetry *or* asymmetry). In their analysis, the "true" values were computed from a fully-specified general equilibrium model. That analysis confirms that the average absolute errors from the "true" values using our approximation method are lower than those using the A-vW method (assuming symmetry or asymmetry). Thus, while A-vW's technique outperforms our approach for computing comparative statics under bilaterally symmetric trade costs, one context in which our method can generate lower average absolute errors is under bilaterally asymmetric trade costs.

6. Conclusions

Six years ago, theoretical foundations for the gravity equation in international trade were enhanced to recognize the systematic bias in coefficient estimates of bilateral trade-cost variables from omitting theoretically-motivated endogenous "multilateral (price) resistance" (MR) terms. This paper has attempted to make four potential contributions. First, we have demonstrated that a first-order log-linear Taylor series expansion of the system of nonlinear price equations suggests an alternative OLS log-linear specification that introduces theoretically-motivated *exogenous* MR terms. Second, Monte Carlo simulations suggest that the method yields virtually identical coefficient estimates to fixed effects and NLS estimation. Third, we have shown using Monte Carlo simulations that – in the case of symmetric bilateral trade costs – the comparative statics associated with our approximation method have a bias of no more than 5% in 74% of the 3872 country pairings of 88 countries examined; moreover, we identified the size of countries relative to their bilateral trade costs as the key economic variable explaining the approximation errors. Finally, in the case of asymmetric bilateral trade costs, the linear approximation method can actually have lower average absolute comparative-static errors (compared to the "true" values) than the A-vW method, when the latter assumes either symmetric or asymmetric bilateral trade costs.

Appendix A

Because of the complexity of allowing asymmetric bilateral trade costs and the matrix inversion needed, we assume a three-country world ($i=1, 2, 3$). In such a world, the system of $2N$ Eqs. (15) and (16) simplifies to:

$$\begin{bmatrix} \theta_1 & \theta_2 & \theta_3 & 1 & 0 & 0 \\ \theta_1 & \theta_2 & \theta_3 & 0 & 1 & 0 \\ \theta_1 & \theta_2 & \theta_3 & 0 & 0 & 1 \\ 1 & 0 & 0 & \theta_1 & \theta_2 & \theta_3 \\ 0 & 1 & 0 & \theta_1 & \theta_2 & \theta_3 \\ 0 & 0 & 1 & \theta_1 & \theta_2 & \theta_3 \end{bmatrix} \begin{bmatrix} \ln P_1 \\ \ln P_2 \\ \ln P_3 \\ \ln \Pi_1 \\ \ln \Pi_2 \\ \ln \Pi_3 \end{bmatrix} = \begin{bmatrix} ext_1 \\ ext_2 \\ ext_3 \\ imt_1 \\ imt_2 \\ imt_3 \end{bmatrix} \tag{A1}$$

where we define $ext_i \equiv \sum_{j=1}^{N} \theta_j \ln t_{ij}$ and $imt_j \equiv \sum_{i=1}^{N} \theta_i \ln t_{ij}$. To solve the system of equations for $\ln P_1$, $\ln P_2$, $\ln P_3$, $\ln \Pi_1$, $\ln \Pi_2$ and $\ln \Pi_3$, we need to invert the LHS 6×6 matrix. However, the determinant of this matrix is zero, implying a redundant equation (because $\theta_1 + \theta_2 + \theta_3 = 1$ is imposed). We set P_1 ($=1$) as the numeraire and also eliminate one equation, $\theta_1 \ln P_1 + \theta_2 \ln P_2 + \theta_3 \ln P_3 + \ln \Pi_1 = ext_1$ leaving a system of 5 equations in 5 unknowns. Since the determinant of the LHS 5×5

[16] A-vW's emphasis on relative size of trading partners (θ_j), of course, is not inconsistent with our emphasis on $\theta_j / t_{ij}^{\sigma-1}$.

[17] One advantage of the fixed-point method is that it is computationally much less resource-intensive than used by A-vW, as it does not require computation of the Jacobian of the system of equations, nor does it even require that the inverse of the Jacobian exists.

[18] We use Eq. (6) to measure $t_{ij}^{\sigma-1}$ using bilateral distance and a coefficient estimate. The results are robust to alternative initial values of $P_i^{1-\sigma}$ ($P_i^{*1-\sigma}$).

matrix is nonzero (and equal to θ_1), we can invert this matrix. Consequently, we find:

$$\begin{bmatrix} \ln P_2 \\ \ln P_3 \\ \ln \Pi_1 \\ \ln \Pi_2 \\ \ln \Pi_3 \end{bmatrix} = \begin{bmatrix} 0 & 0 & -1 & 1 & 0 \\ 0 & 0 & -1 & 0 & 1 \\ -\theta_2/\theta_1 & -\theta_3/\theta_1 & 2-\theta_1 & \theta_2(\theta_2+\theta_3)/\theta_1 & \theta_3(\theta_2+\theta_3)/\theta_1 \\ 1 & 0 & \theta_2+\theta_3 & -\theta_2 & -\theta_3 \\ 0 & 1 & \theta_2+\theta_3 & -\theta_2 & -\theta_3 \end{bmatrix} \begin{bmatrix} ext_2 \\ ext_3 \\ imt_1 \\ imt_2 \\ imt_3 \end{bmatrix}. \tag{A2}$$

Since good 1 is the numeraire, we ignore $\ln P_1$ and $\ln \prod_1$. Focusing on countries 2 and 3, we have:

$$\ln P_2 = imt_2 - imt_1 = \sum_{i=1}^{3} \theta_i \ln t_{i2} - \sum_{i=1}^{3} \theta_i \ln t_{i1} \tag{A3}$$

$$\ln P_3 = imt_3 - imt_1 = \sum_{i=1}^{3} \theta_i \ln t_{i3} - \sum_{i=1}^{3} \theta_i \ln t_{i1} \tag{A4}$$

$$\begin{aligned} \ln \Pi_2 &= ext_2 + \theta_2(imt_1 - imt_2) + \theta_3(imt_1 - imt_3) \\ &= \sum_{j=1}^{3} \theta_j \ln t_{2j} + \sum_{i=1}^{3} \theta_i \ln t_{i1} - \sum_{i=1}^{3}\sum_{j=1}^{3} \theta_i\theta_j \ln t_{ij} \end{aligned} \tag{A5}$$

$$\begin{aligned} \ln \Pi_3 &= ext_3 + \theta_2(imt_1 - imt_2) + \theta_3(imt_1 - imt_3) \\ &= \sum_{j=1}^{3} \theta_j \ln t_{3j} + \sum_{i=1}^{3} \theta_i \ln t_{i1} - \sum_{i=1}^{3}\sum_{j=1}^{3} \theta_i\theta_j \ln t_{ij}. \end{aligned} \tag{A6}$$

It is clear that this will generalize to N countries, such that for any two countries i and j $(i, j \neq 1)$:

$$\ln \Pi_i = \sum_{j=1}^{N} \theta_j \ln t_{ij} + \sum_{k=1}^{N} \theta_k \ln t_{k1} - \sum_{k=1}^{N} \sum_{m=1}^{N} \theta_k \theta_m \ln t_{km}, \quad i = 2, \ldots, N \tag{17}$$

$$\ln P_j = \sum_{i=1}^{N} \theta_i \ln t_{ij} - \sum_{k=1}^{N} \theta_k \ln t_{k1}, \quad j = 2, \ldots, N \tag{18}$$

where t_{ij} need not equal t_{ji}, and the second and third RHS terms in Eq. (17) and second RHS term in Eq. (18) are constant across the N countries.

References

Adam, Christopher, Cobham, David, 2007. Modelling multilateral trade resistance in a gravity model with exchange rate regimes. Oxford University working paper. August.

Anderson, James E., 1979. A theoretical foundation for the gravity equation. American Economic Review 69 (no. 1), 106–116 March.

Anderson, James E., van Wincoop, Eric, 2003. Gravity with gravitas: a solution to the border puzzle. American Economic Review 93 (no. 1), 170–192 March.

Baier, Scott L., Bergstrand, Jeffrey H., 2004. Economic determinants of free trade agreements. Journal of International Economics 64 (no. 1), 29–63 October.

Baier, Scott L., Bergstrand, Jeffrey H., 2006. *Bonus vetus* OLS: a simple approach for addressing the "border puzzle" and other gravity-equation issues. working paper. March.

Baier, Scott L., Bergstrand, Jeffrey H., 2007a. Do free trade agreements actually increase members' international trade? Journal of International Economics 71 (no. 1), 72–95 March.

Baier, Scott L., Bergstrand, Jeffrey H., 2007b. *Bonus vetus* OLS: a simple method for approximating international trade-cost effects using the gravity equation. working paper. October.

Baier, Scott L., Bergstrand, Jeffrey H., 2009. Estimating the Effects of Free Trade Agreements on International Trade flows using Matching Econometrics. Journal of International Economics 77, 63–76.

Bergstrand, Jeffrey H., 1985. The gravity equation in international trade: some microeconomic foundations and empirical evidence. Review of Economics and Statistics 67 (no. 3), 474–481 August.

Bergstrand, Jeffrey H., Egger, Peter, Larch, Mario, 2007. Gravity *redux*: structural estimation of gravity equations with asymmetric bilateral trade costs. working paper.

Ciccone, Antonio, Hall, Robert E., 1996. Productivity and density of economic activity. American Economic Review 86 (no. 1), 54–70 March.

Dolman, Ben, 2008. Migration, trade and investment. Australian Government Productivity Commission Staff Working Paper. February, http://ssrn.com/abstract=1154910.

Eaton, Jonathan, Kortum, Samuel, 2002. Technology, geography, and trade. Econometrica 70 (no. 5), 1741–1779 September.

Egger, Harmut, Egger, Peter, Greenaway, David, 2008. The Trade Structure Effects of Endogenous Regional Trade Agreements. Journal of International Economics 74 (no. 2), 278–298.

Feenstra, Robert C., 2004. Advanced International Trade: Theory and Evidence. Princeton Univ Press, Princeton, NJ.

Felbermayer, Gabriel J., Kohler, Wilhelm, 2006. Exploring the intensive and extensive margins of world trade. Review of World Economics 142, 642–674.

Helliwell, John F., 1998. How Much Do National Borders Matter? Brookings Institution, Washington, DC.

Mansfield, Edward D., Reinhardt, Eric, 2003. Multilateral determinants of regionalism: the effects of GATT/WTO on the formation of preferential trading arrangements. International Organization 57 (no. 4), 829–862 Fall.

Mansfield, Edward D., Milner, Helen, C., Pevehouse, Jon C., 2008. Democracy, Veto Players, and the Depth of Regional Integration. The World Economy 31 (no. 1), 67–96.

McCallum, John, 1995. National borders matter: Canada–U.S. regional trade patterns. American Economic Review 85 (no. 3), 615–623 (June).

Rose, Andrew, van Wincoop, Eric, 2001. National money as a barrier to international trade: the real case for currency union. American Economic Review Papers and Proceedings 91 (no. 2), 386–390 May.

Silva Santos, J.M.C., Tenreyro, Silvana, 2006. The log of gravity. Review of Economics and Statistics 88 (no. 4), 641–658 November.

Chapter 6

Gravity *Redux*: Estimation of gravity-equation coefficients, elasticities of substitution, and general equilibrium comparative statics under asymmetric bilateral trade costs

Jeffrey H. Bergstrand [a,b,c,*], Peter Egger [c,d,e,f,g,h], Mario Larch [c,f,i]

[a] Department of Finance, Mendoza College of Business, University of Notre Dame, Notre Dame, IN 46556, USA
[b] Kellogg Institute for International Studies, University of Notre Dame, USA
[c] CESifo Munich, Germany
[d] ETH University, KOF, Zurich, Switzerland
[e] CEPR, United Kingdom
[f] Ifo Institute, Germany
[g] WIFO, Austria
[h] Centre for Globalization and Economic Policy, University of Nottingham, United Kingdom
[i] Department of Law and Economics, University of Bayreuth, Universitaetsstrasse 30, 95447 Bayreuth, Germany

ARTICLE INFO

Article history:
Received 7 November 2008
Received in revised form 12 January 2012
Accepted 11 May 2012
Available online 24 May 2012

JEL classification:
F10
F12
F13

Keywords:
International trade
Gravity equation
Trade costs
Structural estimation

ABSTRACT

A large class of models with CES utility and iceberg trade costs are now known to generate isomorphic "gravity equations." Economic interpretations of these gravity equations vary in terms of two basic elements: the exporter's "mass" variable and the elasticity of trade with respect to true ad valorem "trade costs." In this paper, we offer three potential contributions. First, we formulate and estimate a structural gravity equation based on the standard Krugman model of monopolistic competition and increasing returns. In the context of this model, a key parameter, the elasticity of substitution in consumption (σ), can be estimated precisely – even without observable true ad valorem trade-cost measures – using exporter's population and observable variables that influence trade costs. Second, in the empirical context of the well-known McCallum Canadian–U.S. "border puzzle," our approach – allowing estimation of σ – yields considerably different general equilibrium comparative static trade-flow and economic welfare effects than those in an Armington endowment economy and assumed values of σ. Moreover, our predicted trade flows and GDPs are highly correlated with their respective observed values in the case of bilaterally symmetric or asymmetric Canadian–U.S. border effects. Third, a Monte Carlo analysis confirms unbiased and precise estimates of all coefficients, the elasticity of substitution, and comparative statics using our approach.

1. Introduction

For half a century, the "gravity equation" has been used to estimate econometrically the ex post partial (or direct) effects of economic integration agreements, national borders, currency unions, language, and other measures of trade costs on bilateral international trade flows (cf., Anderson, 2011 and Bergstrand and Egger, 2011 for recent surveys). While two early formal theoretical foundations for the gravity equation with trade costs – first Anderson (1979) and later Bergstrand (1985) – addressed the role of "multilateral prices," Anderson and van Wincoop (2003) refined the theoretical foundations for the gravity equation to emphasize the importance of accounting properly for the endogeneity of prices in a structural gravity model. Eaton and Kortum (2002), Melitz (2003), Helpman et al. (2008), and Chaney (2008) refined the theoretical foundations further for firm heterogeneity in productivity and zero trade flows. As Eaton and Kortum (2002) and Arkolakis et al. (2012) note, there is a large class of models with constant-elasticity-of-substitution (CES) preferences, iceberg trade costs, and complete specialization that generate isomorphic gravity equations.

In Anderson and van Wincoop (2003), or AvW, a complete derivation of a standard Armington ("conditional," in AvW terms) general equilibrium endowment-economy model of bilateral trade in a multi-region ($N>2$) setting with one good per region and iceberg trade costs suggests that traditional cross-section empirical gravity equations have been misspecified owing to the omission of theoretically motivated nonlinear multilateral price terms for exporting and importing regions. Their model yields the bilateral trade "structural" gravity model allowing asymmetric bilateral trade costs (ABTC):

$$X_{ij} = \frac{Y_i Y_j}{Y_W} \frac{t_{ij}^{1-\sigma}}{\Pi_i^{1-\sigma} P_j^{1-\sigma}}, \tag{1}$$

where $\Pi_i^{1-\sigma} = \sum_{j=1}^{N} \frac{Y_j}{Y_W} \frac{t_{ij}^{1-\sigma}}{P_j^{1-\sigma}}$, $P_j^{1-\sigma} = \sum_{i=1}^{N} \frac{Y_i}{Y_W} \frac{t_{ij}^{1-\sigma}}{\Pi_i^{1-\sigma}}$,

* Corresponding author at: Department of Finance, Mendoza College of Business, University of Notre Dame, Notre Dame, IN 46556, USA.
E-mail addresses: bergstrand.1@nd.edu (J.H. Bergstrand), egger@kof.ethz.ch (P. Egger), mario.larch@uni-bayreuth.de (M. Larch).

*Originally Published in *Journal of International Economics*, 89(2013), pp. 110–121.

where X_{ij} is the nominal trade flow from region i to region j, Y_i (Y_j) is the nominal GDP in i (j), Y_W is world GDP, t_{ij} is one plus the iceberg trade costs (the latter expressed as an ad valorem rate) on goods exported from i to j, and σ is the elasticity of substitution in consumption. In the special case of symmetric bilateral trade costs (SBTC), $t_{ij}=t_{ij}$, the system of Eq. (1) reduces to:

$$X_{ij} = \frac{Y_i Y_j}{Y_W} \frac{t_{ij}^{1-\sigma}}{P_i^{1-\sigma} P_j^{1-\sigma}}, \text{ where } P_i^{1-\sigma} = \sum_{j=1}^{N} \frac{Y_j}{Y_W} \frac{t_{ij}^{1-\sigma}}{P_j^{1-\sigma}}. \tag{2}$$

Owing to the nonlinearities in both sets of structural relationships, AvW employ a nonlinear least squares (NLS) program for estimation, focusing on Eq. (2) with SBTC. In the absence of observable measures of t_{ij}, AvW assume $t_{ij}^{1-\sigma} = d_{ij}^{(1-\sigma)\rho} e^{[(1-\sigma) lnb_{US,\,CA}]Border_{ij}}$ where d_{ij} is bilateral distance, $Border_{ij}$ is a dummy variable with a value of 1 (0) if the two regions are separated by a national border, σ, ρ, and $lnb_{US,\,CA}$ are unknown parameters, and e is the natural log base. Consequently, the system of equations does not permit identification of σ separately from ρ and $lnb_{US,\,CA}$.[1] Hence, for general equilibrium comparative static estimates, they *assume* values of σ. Moreover, all estimation of parameters and calculation of comparative statics were conducted under the assumption of SBTC, even though many bilateral trade costs are asymmetric. For instance, based on bilateral tariff data from the Global Trade Analysis Project (GTAP) on 67 countries in 2001, there is a large heterogeneity bilaterally in tariff rates. Fifty-eight percent of the bilateral tariff rates are asymmetric; moreover, the asymmetry can be as large as 150%.[2]

Eaton and Kortum (2002), or EK, introduced an alternative Ricardian framework to generate a structural gravity equation where the key parameter, θ, governs the heterogeneity in firms' productivities (or comparative advantages):

$$X_{ij} = \frac{T_i Y_j \left(w_i t_{ij}\right)^{-\theta}}{\sum_{k=1}^{N} T_k \left(w_k t_{kj}\right)^{-\theta}}, \tag{3}$$

where T_i is an index of country i's "state of technology" and w_i is labor's wage rate.[3] While preferences are also modeled using CES utility, the elasticity of substitution in consumption (σ) does not have a role in determining equilibrium bilateral trade flows. The structure of the model implies that the key parameter for estimation (and subsequently for comparative statics) is the supply-side measure of firm heterogeneity (θ). To identify θ, EK used two alternative approaches, one using retail price data and another using wage data.[4]

However, as Arkolakis et al. (2012) note, the perfect competition models in AvW and EK and the monopolistic competition models in Krugman (1980) and Melitz (2003) are all in a broad class of models sharing Dixit–Stiglitz preferences, one factor of production, linear cost functions, complete specialization, and iceberg trade costs. Arkolakis et al. (2012) show that if three "macro-level" restrictions hold, then all four models will share a common estimator of the gains from trade — which depends only on the import-penetration ratio and a gravity-equation-based estimate of the "trade-cost" elasticity of trade flows (of which σ is a measure of in many models).

In this paper, we first formulate a structural gravity equation based on Krugman (1980) monopolistic competition and increasing returns to scale (MC-IR) model as an alternative framework to AvW and EK for estimating gravity-equation coefficients, the elasticity of substitution in consumption (σ), and general equilibrium comparative statics, allowing ABTC.[5] We show in the context of this model that σ (the key parameter for welfare analysis) can be identified *precisely* — even without observable ad valorem trade-cost measures. The reason is that the exporter's absolute factor endowment – related to the number of varieties produced – helps identify (or "pin down") individual exporters' price levels (p_i), which allows identification of σ (not possible in the AvW framework). In reality, unlike in the AvW framework with one good per region, most regions produce a variety of products and evidence suggests that the *number* of varieties/producers – that is, the extensive margin of varieties produced per region – is related to the absolute factor endowment size of the region (cf., Bernard et al., 2009).[6]

Second, in the empirical context of the well-known "McCallum border puzzle," we apply our approach for estimating gravity-equation coefficients, the elasticity of substitution, and general equilibrium comparative statics. Since our *estimated* σ differs from the one assumed in AvW, our general equilibrium comparative statics differ significantly from those in AvW. However, our estimate of approximately 7 is in the middle of the range of typical estimates for σ of 5–10 discussed in Anderson and van Wincoop (2004).

Third, we use a Monte Carlo analysis to confirm precise and unbiased estimates of all coefficients, the elasticity of substitution, and general equilibrium comparative statics using our approach, even in small samples. We also demonstrate using this analysis that the comparative static effects on trade flows of a given trade-cost change can be *very sensitive* to the elasticity of substitution, with such effects for $\sigma=10$ more than 40 times those for $\sigma=3$. We show that our approach and the AvW approach under ABTC can also be used for general equilibrium comparative statics for *real* economic variables, such as economic welfare. However, these results are very sensitive – even qualitatively – to σ, providing further motivation for finding a technique that identifies σ precisely.

The remainder of this paper is as follows. Section 2 presents the well-known Krugman MC-IR model to derive a structural gravity model that allows estimation of the elasticity of substitution (given consistently estimated gravity equation parameters) and of comparative static effects. Section 3 provides an empirical analysis of our approach and compares it to the results from other approaches, including AvW, in the well-known context of the McCallum Canadian–U.S. border puzzle. Section 4 presents Monte Carlo results demonstrating – in the absence of specification and measurement error – that we can obtain precise and unbiased estimates of the elasticity of substitution and of comparative statics using our approach. Section 5 concludes.

[1] Of course, this issue generalizes for any number of determinants of $t_{ij}^{1-\sigma}$.

[2] Balistreri and Hillberry (2007) first showed that allowing for asymmetric bilateral trade costs influences the results of estimating the Canadian–U.S. "border effect."

[3] For conciseness, we ignore intermediate goods in this specification, a component of the original EK model.

[4] In one approach, they employed cross-country disaggregate retail price level data to approximate bilateral ad valorem trade costs (t_{ij}). Assuming commodity price arbitrage, the maximum difference between two countries' prices for similar goods bounds ad valorem bilateral trade costs. Second, they used wage rate data (and alternatively instruments for w_i) to estimate θ. Using wage rate data (wage instruments), EK found an estimate for θ of 2.86 (3.60). Using the disaggregated price data and the commodity-price-arbitrage condition, EK found estimates of θ ranging between 2.44 and 12.86 depending upon OLS or two-stage least squares estimation.

[5] As noted above, AvW could only assume values for σ. Waugh (2007) also notes the importance of asymmetric bilateral trade costs for explaining observed bilateral trade flow patterns and relative price and real per capita income differences between countries.

[6] An earlier related paper to ours is Lai and Trefler (2002), which examines using panel data the MC-IR model. With regard to model specification issues, Lai and Trefler find that the MC-IR model works well, explaining about 78% of the variation in bilateral (aggregate manufacturing) trade flows and they also use their model to estimate welfare effects of tariff liberalizations. Our approach also has parallels to Redding and Venables (2004), where the authors derive a gravity equation based upon the MC-IR model. They estimate the model and the predicted trade flows are then used to construct market-access and supply-access variables, which are then used (as generated regressors) in a wage (per capita income) equation to explain sources of wage variation. They do not address comparative statics, estimation of any nonlinear price terms, nor estimation of the elasticity of substitution.

2. Methodology

In Section 2.1, we summarize the Krugman MC-IR model and describe the structural gravity equation it implies. In Section 2.2, we show how to use the approach to estimate the elasticity of substitution in consumption, general equilibrium comparative static trade-flow effects of a reduction in trade costs, and economic welfare effects of trade-cost reductions (i.e., the "gains from trade").

2.1. The monopolistic competition-increasing returns model

2.1.1. Aggregate bilateral trade flows

Following Krugman (1980), we assume there exists a single industry where preferences are constant-elasticity-of-substitution (CES). We assume iceberg transport costs and symmetric firms within each region, and hence all products in region i sell at the same price, p_i. As in Krugman (1980) and Feenstra (2004), the value of aggregate bilateral exports from region i to region j, X_{ij}, equals $n_i p_i t_{ij} c_{ij}$, where n_i is the number of firms (varieties produced) in i, $t_{ij} \geq 1$ are ad valorem iceberg trade costs, and c_{ij} is demand in j for output of each firm in i. As standard, X_{ij} is determined by:

$$X_{ij} = n_i \left(\frac{p_i t_{ij}}{P_j}\right)^{1-\sigma} Y_j, \text{ where } P_j = \left[\sum_{i=1}^{N} n_i \left(p_i t_{ij}\right)^{1-\sigma}\right]^{\frac{1}{1-\sigma}} \tag{4}$$

which is identical to Eq. (5.26) in Feenstra (2004, p. 153). We assume the t_{ij}s are the *true* – but empirically unobservable – ad valorem trade costs.

2.1.2. Production

The assumption of a monopolistically competitive market with increasing returns to scale in production (internal to the firm) and a single factor (labor) is sufficient to identify the exporting region's number of varieties. The representative firm in region i is assumed to maximize profits subject to the workhorse linear cost function:

$$l_i = \alpha + \phi y_i, \tag{5}$$

where l_i denotes labor used by the representative firm in country i, y_i denotes the output of the firm, α denotes the labor requirement necessary to setup a firm, and ϕ denotes the amount of labor necessary to produce one unit of output. We assume that these labor requirements are homogeneous across all countries, as standard in the Krugman MC-IR model.

Two conditions characterize equilibrium in this class of models. First, profit maximization ensures that prices are a markup over marginal costs:

$$p_i = \frac{\sigma}{\sigma - 1}\phi w_i, \tag{6}$$

where w_i is the wage rate in country i and ϕw_i determines the marginal cost of production.[7] Second, under monopolistic competition, zero economic profits in equilibrium ensure:

$$y_i = \frac{\alpha}{\phi}(\sigma - 1) = y, \tag{7}$$

so that the output of each firm in each country is the same ($y_i = y$). An assumption of full employment of labor in each region ensures that the size of the exogenous factor endowment, L_i, determines the number of firms/varieties (the extensive margin), using Eq. (7):

$$n_i = \frac{L_i}{\alpha + \phi_i y} = \frac{L_i}{\alpha\sigma}. \tag{8}$$

[7] The wage rate in country 1 serves as the numéraire.

2.1.3. The gravity equation

We can now formulate an (estimable) gravity equation. First, the trade flow from i to j is a function of GDPs, labor endowments, and trade costs. With labor being the only factor of production, $Y_i = w_i L_i$ or $w_i = Y_i / L_i$. Using Eqs. (6) and (8), we can substitute $\sigma\phi w_i/(\sigma - 1)$ for p_i and $L_i/(\alpha\sigma)$ for n_i in Eq. (4) and substitute Y_i/L_i for w_i in the resulting equation. Allowing bilateral trade flows to be measured with multiplicative error ϵ_{ij}, this yields:

$$X_{ij} = Y_i Y_j \frac{(Y_i/L_i)^{-\sigma} t_{ij}^{1-\sigma}}{\sum_{k=1}^{N} Y_k (Y_k/L_k)^{-\sigma} t_{kj}^{1-\sigma}} \epsilon_{ij} \Rightarrow \frac{X_{ij} Y_W}{Y_i Y_j} = \frac{Y_W (Y_i/L_i)^{-\sigma} t_{ij}^{1-\sigma}}{\sum_{k=1}^{N} Y_k (Y_k/L_k)^{-\sigma} t_{kj}^{1-\sigma}} \epsilon_{ij}. \tag{9}$$

Second, the deterministic part of stochastic Eq. (9) is identical to the gravity equation in Feenstra (2004, p. 154) with GDPs and prices, after noting that Y_i/L_i is proportional to the producer price p_i.[8] However, a missing element in Eq. (9) is the market-clearance (or multilateral trade-balance) condition, as in AvW or EK. Market-clearance is ensured by assuming N equations:

$$Y_i = \sum_{j=1}^{N} X_{ij} \quad i = 1, \ldots, N. \tag{10}$$

Hence, our structural gravity model is based on Eq. (9) subject to Eq. (10). The latter allows solving for N endogenous GDPs, Y_i; because of this, we can later assess how well the solutions for Y_i in the model $\left(\hat{Y}_i\right)$ "match" the corresponding observed data on GDP (Y_i).[9]

Finally, we note three results. First, the system of Eq. (9) subject to Eq. (10) allows ABTC. Second, all endogenous variables (X_{ij}, Y_i, and Y_i/L_i) have observable values for initial conditions. Third, since n_i is proportional to observable L_i and w_i is pinned down by Y_i/L_i, then p_i (proportional to w_i) is identified, which was not possible in the AvW model.

2.2. Estimating the elasticity of substitution in consumption and general equilibrium comparative statics

While AvW focused on structural estimation of Eq. (2) using an NLS program, the literature since then has adopted as a norm (in the absence of zeros in trade flows) the estimation of a log-linear form of their equation for X_{ij} in Eq. (2) using region-specific fixed effects for the nonlinear multilateral price terms to avoid omitted variables bias and ensure consistent gravity equation coefficient estimates. In the context of our model above, replacing $Y_i (Y_i/L_i)^{-\sigma}$ and $\frac{Y_j}{\sum_{k=1}^{N} Y_k (Y_k/L_k)^{-\sigma} t_{kj}^{1-\sigma}}$ in Eq. (9) with exporter and importer fixed effects, respectively, yields the log-linear gravity equation:

$$lnX_{ij} = \lambda + \eta_i + \zeta_j + (1-\sigma) lnt_{ij} + u_{ij}, \tag{11}$$

where $u_{ij} = ln\ \epsilon_{ij}$ and one would substitute observable bilateral trade-cost variables to proxy for the unobservable bilateral ad valorem trade-cost variable t_{ij}.[10]

Few have gone further to compute general equilibrium (GE) comparative statics. The two notable studies that estimated GE comparative

[8] Moreover, this equation is isomorphic to Eq. (3) above from EK.

[9] We are grateful to a referee for this suggestion. In our empirical work later using bilateral trade flows among 10 Canadian provinces and 30 U.S. states, we note now that our 40 *observed* (or actual) GDPs (Y_i) will not match our 40 endogenous predicted GDPs $\left(\hat{Y}_i\right)$ owing to multilateral trade imbalances. In the spirit of Dekle et al. (2007), we will also generate later endogenous predicted GDPs and trade flows (including predicted trade flows with *ROW*) to calculate a correction for these imbalances to demonstrate whether or not our general equilibrium comparative static estimates for trade flows and economic welfare are sensitive to such imbalances.

[10] For instance, as noted earlier, AvW assumed $(1-\sigma)lnt_{ij} = (1-\sigma)\rho lnd_{ij} + [(1-\sigma) lnb_{US,CA}]Border_{ij}$.

statics are AvW and EK. AvW did not provide a method to solve for σ in their framework; for comparative statics they simply assumed a range for σ from 2 to 20. EK instead estimated their key structural parameter, θ, a Ricardian index of product heterogeneity on the supply side, using alternatively price and wage rate data discussed earlier. EK found estimates of θ ranging from 2 to 13.

2.2.1. Estimating σ

There are three alternative ways to estimate σ here, and we denote them as Methods 1, 2, and 3:

2.2.1.1. Method 1. If ad valorem bilateral tariff rates and cif-fob ratios were correctly measured, σ could be estimated directly as a parameter on the true observable ad valorem bilateral trade costs (t_{ij}), even with exporter and importer fixed effects.[11] However, most gravity models do not use such measures. Moreover, it is well known that ad valorem bilateral cif-fob ratios and tariff rates are prone to considerable measurement error; see Anderson and van Wincoop (2004) and Hummels and Lugovskyy (2006) on the former and Fisman and Wei (2004) and Javorcik and Narciso (2008) on the latter.

2.2.1.2. Method 2. In a structural version of our model's Eqs. (9) and (10), σ may be estimated as a parameter on potentially observable Y_i/L_i without observable values of t_{ij}. However, given Eq. (9) proper estimation would require using observed values of Y_i/L_i to estimate σ in the first step of an iterative process, then updating endogenous Y_i from solving Eq. (10), estimating σ again, updating Y_i again, etc., until convergence is achieved.[12] Yet, such a procedure may yield biased estimates of σ owing to correlation of the error terms with observed Y_i/L_i. To ensure consistent estimation of parameters in the first stage, one would need exporter and importer fixed effects. However, in that case, Y_i/L_i would be subsumed in the exporter's fixed effect, precluding estimation of σ.

2.2.1.3 . Method 3. We suggest an approach that allows unbiased and precise estimates of σ (and then of general equilibrium comparative statics) allowing ABTC. Estimation of Eq. (11) using observable determinants of bilateral trade costs generates estimates $\widehat{t_{ij}^{1-\sigma}}$.[13] We can then utilize the structure of the model ex post to generate an estimate of σ. Substituting $\widehat{t_{ij}^{1-\sigma}}$ in Eq. (9) to generate $\hat{X}_{ij}$, $\widehat{t_{mj}^{1-\sigma}}$ in its analog to generate $\hat{X}_{mj}$, and taking the resulting equations' ratio implies:

$$\frac{\hat{X}_{ij}}{\hat{X}_{mj}} = \frac{Y_i}{Y_m}\left(\frac{Y_i/L_i}{Y_m/L_m}\right)^{-\sigma}\frac{\widehat{t_{ij}^{1-\sigma}}}{\widehat{t_{mj}^{1-\sigma}}} \tag{12}$$

$$\Rightarrow \hat{\sigma} = -\left[\ln\left(\frac{\hat{X}_{ij}}{\hat{X}_{mj}}\frac{Y_m}{Y_i}\frac{\widehat{t_{mj}^{1-\sigma}}}{\widehat{t_{ij}^{1-\sigma}}}\right)/\ln\left(\frac{Y_i/L_i}{Y_m/L_m}\right)\right],$$

where Y_i, Y_m, L_i and L_m are observable also.[14] We can then calculate $N^2(N-1)$ such values of σ by using all combinations i, j, and m ($m \neq i$). In our empirical investigation later using the Canadian–U.S. border-puzzle data set with $N=40$ regions, this results in $40^2(40-1)=62{,}400$ values. As a measure of central tendency, we use the median value of σ as our (summary) estimate, since the distribution of σ estimates is skewed to the right in that context (and the mean is slightly higher than the median). Standard errors for σ are obtained via bootstrapping.[15]

The advantage of Method 3 over Methods 1 and 2 is that $\widehat{t_{ij}^{1-\sigma}}$ is estimated without bias from its possible correlation with region-specific omitted variables as the estimates are obtained from Eq. (11) with i-specific and j-specific fixed effects. In the remainder of the paper, we use Method 3 for computing $\hat{\sigma}$.[16]

2.2.2. Comparative statics methodology

In the next section, we will estimate gravity-equation coefficients, elasticities of substitution, and two comparative static effects, the GDP-scaled nominal trade flow $\left(\frac{X_{ij}Y_W}{Y_iY_j}\right)$ and the economic welfare (EV_i) effects of a change in trade costs. For our "Suggested Model" (MC-IR), the comparative static effect on GDP-scaled nominal trade flows in percent where c denotes counter-factual values is:

$$\Delta\frac{X_{ij}Y_W}{Y_iY_j} = 100\left[\frac{\left[Y_W^c(Y_i^c/L_i)^{-\hat{\sigma}}\left(\widehat{t_{ij}^{1-\sigma}}\right)^c\right]/\left[\sum_{k=1}^N Y_k^c(Y_k^c/L_k)^{-\hat{\sigma}}\left(\widehat{t_{kj}^{1-\sigma}}\right)^c\right]}{\left[Y_W(Y_i/L_i)^{-\hat{\sigma}}\left(\widehat{t_{ij}^{1-\sigma}}\right)\right]/\left[\sum_{k=1}^N Y_k(Y_k/L_k)^{-\hat{\sigma}}\left(\widehat{t_{kj}^{1-\sigma}}\right)\right]} - 1\right]. \tag{13}$$

where we let $\Delta\frac{X_{ij}Y_W}{Y_iY_j}$ denote a *percentage* change (deleting henceforth "hat" notation for X_{ij} and Y_i). The corresponding equivalent variation for country i (EV_i, in percentage change) is defined as:

$$EV_i = 100\left[\frac{Y_i^c/\left[\sum_{k=1}^N Y_k^c(Y_k^c/L_k)^{-\hat{\sigma}}\left(\widehat{t_{ki}^{1-\sigma}}\right)^c\right]^{\frac{1}{1-\hat{\sigma}}}}{Y_i/\left[\sum_{k=1}^N Y_k(Y_k/L_k)^{-\hat{\sigma}}\left(\widehat{t_{ki}^{1-\sigma}}\right)\right]^{\frac{1}{1-\hat{\sigma}}}} - 1\right]. \tag{14}$$

3. Empirical evidence

We now apply our technique to actual data on trade flows, populations, GDPs, bilateral distances, and dummy variables for national borders. We consider a well-known empirical context: the U.S.–Canadian "border puzzle" case as examined in AvW. We will address it in the presence of either symmetric *or* asymmetric bilateral trade costs. In Section 3.1, we re-estimate the same specifications addressed in that literature, initially assuming SBTC (as assumed there). We show that if coefficient estimates are identical from the first stage (using fixed-effects parameter estimation) then our approach and that of AvW lead to identical comparative static effects *if* the elasticity of substitution is assumed to be the same. However, if one uses the estimated elasticity generated using Method 3 in our approach, significantly different comparative statics will result. In Section 3.2, we allow bilaterally *asymmetric* (direct) border effects for Canada and the United States, resulting in some different findings relative to those under SBTC.

3.1. Symmetric Canadian–U.S. national border barriers

In this section, we present the results of re-evaluating the Canadian–U.S. "border puzzle" empirical analysis retaining the assumption of SBTC but using alternative estimation techniques: traditional ordinary least squares (OLS), the Baier and Bergstrand (2009, 2010) linear approximation methods (*BV-OLS-1* and *BV-OLS-2*), AvW using non-linear least squares (NLS), AvW using fixed effects in estimation, and our "Suggested (MC-IR) Model" (also using fixed effects in estimation and following Method 3 for estimating σ). All data on Canadian–U.S.

[11] The term "cif-fob" ratios refer to bilateral trade flows measured "cost-insurance-freight" and "free-on-board."

[12] This procedure can be done with or without the correction for multilateral trade imbalances.

[13] For instance, in the AvW context, $\widehat{t_{ij}^{1-\sigma}}$ would be determined by the exponentiated value of $\widehat{[(1-\sigma)\rho]}\ Ind_{ij} + \widehat{[(1-\sigma)\ln b_{US,CA}]}\ Border_{ij}$.

[14] Alternatively, we can use the predicted Ys from the model. We show in our empirical results that the correlation coefficient between observed and predicted Ys is 0.992.

[15] Standard errors for all other parameters are the analytical standard errors of the corresponding models. However, the bootstrapped standard errors of those parameters are very similar to the analytical ones.

[16] The Monte Carlo analysis later will demonstrate in the absence of measurement and specification errors that all parameter estimates and comparative statics using Method 3 are unbiased and precise.

trade flows, GDPs, bilateral distances, and border dummies are from James Anderson's website. The only other variable needed was populations of Canadian provinces and U.S. states; these data came from Statistics Canada and the U.S. Census Bureau, respectively. We assume that $t_{ij}^{1-\sigma} = d_{ij}^{(1-\sigma)\rho} e^{[(1-\sigma)lnb_{US,CA}]\text{Border}_{ij}}$ where d_{ij} is symmetric bilateral distance between the economic centers of regions i and j, Border_{ij} is a dummy variable with a value of 1 (0) if the two regions are separated by a national border, and σ, ρ and $lnb_{US,CA}$ are unknown parameters.

Hence, our OLS specification refers to:

$$ln\frac{X_{ij}Y^W}{Y_iY_j} = \lambda + [(1-\sigma)\rho]lnd_{ij} + \left[(1-\sigma)lnb_{US,CA}\right]\text{Border}_{ij} + u_{ij}, \qquad (15)$$

with all variables and parameters defined earlier. *BV-OLS-1* and *BV-OLS-2* refer to the linear approximation method introduced for estimating gravity equations with multilateral price terms in Baier and Bergstrand (2009). In this method, linear approximations of the (exogenous components of the) nonlinear multilateral price terms in AvW are introduced as exogenous RHS variables in estimation, and general equilibrium comparative statics of trade flows can be approximated allowing for multilateral influences. Specifications using *BV-OLS-1* employ simple averages of the exogenous bilateral resistance terms, whereas specifications using *BV-OLS-2* employ GDP-weighted averages of the bilateral resistance terms. As explained in Baier and Bergstrand (2010), parameter estimates are expected to be less biased using *BV-OLS-1* than *BV-OLS-2* because the simple-weighted averages in *BV-OLS-1* work similar to region fixed effects. However, comparative static estimates using *BV-OLS-2* are likely to approximate non-linear estimates better due to the GDP weights, as discussed in Baier and Bergstrand (2009, 2010). SBTC-AvW NLS refers to the nonlinear estimation of Eq. (2), after substituting in bilateral distance and the border dummy, as in AvW (2003). SBTC-AvW fixed effects refers to a specification similar to Eq. (15) above, but including fixed effects terms η_i and ξ_j as in Eq. (11) earlier; multilateral prices P_i are calculated as in AvW using a nonlinear solver (following Eq. (2)). Finally, for our suggested (MC-IR) model, we also estimate parameters first using the same fixed-effects specification as above; predicted trade flows, GDPs, prices, and the elasticity of substitution are calculated for our MC-IR approach as described earlier.

Table 1 presents four panels with the alternative estimation techniques described across columns (2)–(7). In the four panels, we provide coefficient (parameter) estimates of the gravity equation, correlation coefficients of observed and predicted trade flows and GDPs (for our approach), GDP-scaled nominal trade-flow comparative statics, and – for the AvW and MC-IR approaches – (real) economic welfare comparative statics. In the top panel, we have estimates of the coefficients for bilateral distance ($(1-\sigma)\rho$), the border dummy ($(1-\sigma)lnb_{US,CA}$), and – only for our MC-IR model in column (7) – of σ. We start with the results in column (2). As expected, the coefficient estimates for OLS in column (2) are biased, owing to the absence of multilateral price terms (or fixed effects). Coefficient estimates using *BV-OLS-1* in column (3) are essentially the same as those using fixed effects estimations for AvW in column (6) and for our model in column (7) as expected. Also as expected, coefficient estimates using *BV-OLS-2* are biased. And those for AvW using NLS are biased – as in AvW (2003) – whenever trade costs are correlated with the region-specific error components. In column (7), the estimate of σ is 6.982. This value is in the middle of the range of typical estimates of σ of 5–10, as suggested in Anderson and van Wincoop (2004). Note the R^2 values are highest in columns (6) and (7) using fixed effects and are lowest using OLS and AvW with NLS due to correlated errors.

The second panel reports correlation coefficients between observed and model-predicted (GDP-scaled) nominal trade flows and between observed and predicted GDPs for our approach. Two results are worth noting. First, the highest correlation coefficient estimate between observed and predicted trade flows is for our suggested MC-IR model at 0.808. Interestingly, the next highest correlations are for the two *BV-OLS* approaches. Second, only our MC-IR method allows GDPs (and per capita GDPs) to be endogenous in the benchmark equilibrium so that we can report a correlation coefficient between observed and predicted values for our model. As noted in column (7), the correlation coefficient for observed and predicted GDPs from our model is extremely high at 0.992, providing strong

Table 1
Estimation results for the AvW data-set assuming symmetric border barrier effects.

	SBTC-AvW					
Estimates	OLS	*BV-OLS-1*	*BV-OLS-2*	NLS	Fixed effects	Suggested model
(1)	(2)	(3)	(4)	(5)	(6)	(7)
Parameters						
$(1-\sigma)\rho$	−1.057	−1.261	−1.191	−0.788	−1.252	−1.252
	(0.039)	(0.043)	(0.043)	(0.032)	(0.037)	(0.037)
$(1-\sigma)lnb_{US,CA}$	−0.714	−1.526	−1.317	−1.646	−1.551	−1.551
	(0.058)	(0.069)	(0.068)	(0.077)	(0.059)	(0.059)
σ	–	–	–	–	–	6.982
						(0.048)
R^2	0.425	0.513	0.480	0.435	0.664	0.664
σ^2	1.148	0.972	1.038	1.062	0.841	0.841
Correlation (corr.) of baseline predictions with data						
$\frac{X_{ij}Y_W}{Y_iY_j}$ (corr.)	0.324	0.716	0.788	0.374	0.684	0.808
Y_i (corr.)	–	–	–	–	–	0.992
Comparative static trade effects of border barrier abolition (average change in percent; $\Delta\frac{X_{ij}Y_W}{Y_iY_j}$*)*						
Intra-US trade	0.000	−17.363	−3.827	8.173	13.027	−5.140
Intra-CA trade	0.000	−82.030	−85.484	22.476	55.186	−52.248
Inter-trade	104.136	77.207	39.475	112.823	155.505	217.972
Comparative static welfare effects of border barrier abolition (average equivalent variation in percent; EV_i*)*						
US	–	–	–	1.428	1.179	0.973
CA	–	–	–	39.654	23.105	12.577

Table 2
Estimation results for the AvW data-set allowing for asymmetric border barrier effects.

	ABTC-AvW						
Estimates	OLS	*BV-OLS-1*	*BV-OLS-2*	NLS	Fixed effects	Suggested model	Suggested model, MTI
(1)	(2)	(3)	(4)	(5)	(6)	(7)	(8)
Parameters							
$(1-\sigma)\rho$	−1.058	−1.252	−1.191	−0.788	−1.252	−1.252	−1.252
	(0.039)	(0.037)	(0.043)	(0.008)	(0.037)	(0.037)	(0.037)
$(1-\sigma)lnb_{US}$	−0.540	−0.470	−0.151	−0.264	−0.470	−0.470	−0.470
	(0.072)	(0.046)	(0.300)	(0.173)	(0.046)	(0.046)	(0.046)
$(1-\sigma)lnb_{CA}$	−0.891	−0.825	−2.485	−3.028	−0.825	−0.825	−0.825
	(0.073)	(0.047)	(0.301)	(0.104)	(0.047)	(0.047)	(0.047)
σ	-	-	-	-	-	7.101	7.101
						(0.087)	(0.087)
R^2	0.431	0.664	0.485	0.435	0.664	0.664	0.664
σ^2	1.137	0.841	1.028	1.062	0.841	0.841	0.841
Correlation (corr.) of baseline predictions with data							
$\frac{X_{ij}Y_W}{Y_iY_j}$ (corr.)	0.321	0.574	0.786	0.380	0.684	0.810	0.642
Y_i (corr.)	-	-	-	-	-	0.992	1.000
Comparative static trade effects of border barrier abolition (average change in percent; $\Delta\frac{X_{ij}Y_W}{Y_iY_j}$)							
Intra-US trade	0.000	−7.774	−3.831	85.796	−2.099	−2.548	−1.745
Intra-CA trade	0.000	−51.729	−85.510	33.540	−6.687	−36.486	−26.719
Inter-trade	107.227	27.479	41.183	160.630	28.218	60.624	119.291
Comparative static welfare effects of border barrier abolition (average equivalent variation in percent; EV_i)							
US	-	-	-	−1.183	−0.394	0.519	0.409
CA	-	-	-	28.667	10.917	6.764	2.417

Notes: the model in the last column controls for multilateral trade imbalances.

evidence of the relevance of our model, even without adjustment yet for multilateral trade imbalances.[17]

The third panel reports the estimates of the (GDP-scaled) nominal trade-flow comparative statics from all the models. The most interesting result from this panel concerns the "Intra-US trade" and "Intra-Canadian trade" comparative statics. Our prior would be that the elimination of the border would decrease intra-national trade and increase international trade. In Table 1, only our MC-IR approach and the two *BV-OLS* approaches predict decreases in intra-national trade *and* increases in international trade. Assuming SBTC, both AvW using NLS and using fixed effects predict increases in international trade but *increases* in intra-national trade, suggesting that the income effects of trade liberalization in these approaches dominate the price effects (captured by P_i and P_j).

The fourth panel reports the estimates of the (real) economic welfare comparative static effects of removing the border. The difference in welfare effects between the two AvW techniques is attributable to different parameter estimates, not to different σs (assumed equal to 5 in both). The AvW NLS parameter estimates are likely biased by correlated errors, whereas the AvW fixed effects parameter estimates are not. However, the difference between the AvW fixed-effects welfare effects and the MC-IR model's welfare effects is due primarily to differing σs. Our model uses a higher *estimated* elasticity of about 7, whereas the AvW fixed-effects model assumed $\sigma = 5$. Consequently, as expected, the welfare effects estimated by our model are lower.[18]

[17] The low values for the trade-flow correlation coefficients for the AvW approach are attributable to non-linearities embedded in the calculations of P_i and P_j.

[18] Note in Table 1 that the higher U.S. and Canadian welfare effects for model 6 relative to model 7 are due to a lower σ in model 6. However, the higher U.S. and Canadian welfare effects for model 5 relative to model 6 are due to a larger direct (border) effect in model 5.

3.2. Asymmetric Canadian–U.S. national border effects

In this section, all specifications allow the direct (or partial) effect of the national border to be bilaterally *asymmetric*. To accomplish this, we introduce separate dummy variables and coefficients for the border's effect on U.S. imports from Canada and on Canadian imports from the United States. Other than this change, Table 2's format is the same as Table 1's, except that we add a column (8) of numbers associated with estimating the robustness of our results to allowing for multilateral trade imbalances in our sample, which we discuss later.

The top panel in Table 2 reports the estimates of the coefficients for bilateral distance ($(1-\sigma)\rho$), the impact of the border on U.S. imports from Canada ($(1-\sigma)lnb_{US}$), and the impact of the border on Canadian imports from the United States ($(1-\sigma)lnb_{CA}$). The first result is that the border's direct effect is considerably asymmetric; this notable difference holds across all specifications. The direct trade-reducing effect of the Canadian-U.S. border is much larger for Canadian imports from the United States relative to U.S. imports from Canada. However, the distance coefficient estimates are identical to those in Table 1.

The second panel reports estimates of correlation coefficients between observed and predicted (GDP-scaled) nominal trade flows and between observed and predicted GDPs for our model. First, we find that the highest correlation coefficient estimate between observed and model-predicted trade flows is for the suggested MC-IR model in column (7) at 0.810, consistent with the finding in Table 1. As before, the next highest correlation coefficient is for *BV-OLS-2*. Second, as in Table 1, the correlation coefficient estimate is very high for GDPs using our model (0.992), shown in column (7). By design, GDPs as predicted by the model in column (8) are perfectly correlated with observed GDPs (in the benchmark equilibrium) when accounting for multilateral trade imbalances; we discuss this in more detail shortly.

The third panel reports the estimates of the (GDP-scaled) nominal trade-flow comparative statics from all the models. The most interesting result from this panel again concerns the "Intra-US trade" and "Intra-Canadian trade" comparative statics. Our prior is that the elimination of the border would decrease intra-national trade and increase international trade. In Table 2, our MC-IR approach, the two *BV-OLS* approaches, and the AvW approach using fixed effects predict increases in international trade *and* decreases in intra-national trade. Only the AvW approach using NLS predicts increases in intra-national trade. However, the quantitative differences between the estimates of comparative static effects of the preferred AvW model (in this case, AvW using fixed effects) and the MC-IR model remain economically quite significant.

The fourth panel reports the estimate of the (real) economic welfare comparative static effects of removing the border. The difference in welfare effects between the two AvW techniques is attributable to different parameter estimates, not to different σs (assumed equal to 5 in both). The AvW NLS parameter estimates are as before likely compromised by correlated errors, whereas the AvW fixed effects parameter estimates are not. However, the difference between the AvW fixed-effects welfare effects and our model's welfare effects is due solely to differing σs. Our model under ABTC estimates an elasticity of approximately 7.1, whereas the AvW fixed-effects model assumed $\sigma=5$. We discuss this in more detail below.

Finally, we note one more specification in Table 2, labeled (8). In reality, observed GDPs of any province or state i would not likely equal observed internal absorption plus exports, due to multilateral trade imbalances (MTIs). Hence, market-clearing condition (10) is likely violated in reality, which potentially influences all comparative statics. Ideally, it would be simple to account for this influence using observed MTIs for each region i (MTI_i). However, as AvW note, although data exist for Canadian provinces' trade flows with ROW implying observable MTIs for the provinces, no such data exists for U.S. states trade with the *ROW*, precluding observed MTIs for U.S. states.[19]

Hence, we adjust for MTIs in the following way to generate a set of comparative statics where predicted GDPs equal *exactly* observed GDPs (satisfying market-clearing). Since we have data on GDPs and populations and estimated values of $\hat{\sigma}$ and $\widehat{t_{ij}^{1-\sigma}}$ for all region-pairs *including* province and state trade flows with *ROW*, we can predict X_{ij} for all region-pairs including every region's trade with *ROW* using Eq. (9). Using these $\hat{X}_{ij}$, we can compute estimates of MTI_i using $\hat{MTI}_i=\sum_j \hat{X}_{ij}-\sum_j \hat{X}_{ji}$. We then add $\hat{MTI}_i$ to each region i's market-clearing condition (10) to eliminate any violations (in the benchmark equilibrium).[20] We then re-estimate the (GDP-scaled) nominal trade flows for the benchmark equilibrium and all trade-flow and economic welfare comparative statics. We note three results in column (8). First, the predicted scaled trade flows in the second panel of Table 2 are not as highly correlated with observed scaled trade flows as in our benchmark model, column (7). However, by design, predicted GDPs are perfectly correlated with observed GDPs. Second, there are some minor changes quantitatively in the comparative static trade-flow effects of eliminating the Canadian–U.S. border with the adjustment relative to those in column (7), but the results are qualitatively the same. Third, comparative static effects for welfare of eliminating the border are also qualitatively the same in columns (7) and (8), but lower in column (8) than in column (7).

We summarize now the key findings from our empirical analysis under ABTC. First, coefficient estimates for specifications (6), (7), and (8) in Table 2 are unbiased owing to the use of the exporter and importer fixed effects. By allowing ABTC, the (partial) effects of a national border are different for Canadian province imports from the United States relative to U.S. state imports from Canada. Specification (7) is preferred because our MC-IR model allows estimation of the key parameter, the elasticity of substitution (σ).[21] Another notable finding is that the estimate of σ is higher than assumed in the AvW models and only slightly higher than in column (7) of Table 1, where we assumed SBTC. We will use a Monte Carlo analysis in the next section to show that our methodology generates unbiased and precise estimates of σ.

Second, the MC-IR model in column (7) (or (8)) allows real GDPs to be estimated in the benchmark and counterfactual equilibria, whereas the other approaches use observed real GDPs in the benchmark. Nevertheless, our model's predicted real GDPs are highly correlated with observed real GDPs (0.992). Moreover, the results hold up qualitatively when adjusted for multilateral trade imbalances.

Third, in the presence of ABTC, all the specifications in Table 2, with the exception of AvW using NLS, yield economically plausible trade-flow changes in responses to elimination of the Canadian–U.S. border. Intra-national trade flows decline in both countries (except using AvW-NLS), more in Canada than in the United States as expected. International trade flows increase in all specifications and by plausible magnitudes.

Fourth, even more interesting is the difference between the MC-IR model and the two AvW models in terms of the economic welfare effects. Specifications (6) and (7) share common (first-stage) gravity-equation coefficient estimates, since both are estimated using exporter and importer fixed effects. However, our approach, based on the MC-IR model, allows estimation of σ. There result two substantive differences between the two specifications' welfare effects in Table 2. For Canada, eliminating the U.S. border improves welfare in Canada by much less using the MC-IR model with an estimated σ of 7.1 than using the AvW model with an assumed $\sigma=5$. This result is because, in the AvW model with a lower elasticity of substitution, there is a greater "love-of-variety." Consequently, there is a larger welfare gain for Canada from lowering trade costs due to importing a larger volume of highly differentiated goods from the United States.

The other substantive difference concerns the relative U.S. and Canadian economic welfare effects. The differences can be explained by examining the equivalent variation (*EV*) comparative-static formula in Eq. (14). The change in welfare from abolishing the border barrier is the ratio of the change in nominal income to the change in the price index. A fall in iceberg trade costs creates excess labor supply, tending to lower nominal wages (relative to the numéraire). However, with lower trade costs real income is higher, tending to raise demand, prices (p), and wages (w). Since Canada is a much smaller economy than the United States and consequently relies much more on traded goods, Canada's wage rate (w_{CA}) rises on net and its price index (P_{CA}) falls, relative to their U.S. counterparts. Accordingly, both w_{CA} and P_{CA} react much more to abolishing the border than their counterparts in the United States (w_{US} and P_{US}); smaller countries benefit relatively more from trade liberalization. This effect is exacerbated with larger partial trade cost effects in Canada than in the United States $\left[(1-\hat{\sigma})lnb_{CA}-(1-\hat{\sigma})lnb_{US}<0\right]$. Moreover, the discrepancy of welfare gains in Canada relative to the U.S. is larger the smaller is σ, due to the stronger love of variety and less elastic demand in that case. For that reason, the difference in welfare gains of Canada relative to the United States is larger in model 6 with an assumed $\sigma=5$ than in model 7 with an estimated $\sigma=7.1$.[22]

Finally, it would be useful to know if the economic welfare changes using the two alternative approaches – fixed-effects AvW and our suggested approach – would be the same if the elasticities were identical. However, that exercise requires comparing the two

[19] See the discussions in footnote 22 on page 181 and Appendix A of AvW.

[20] Note that this approach has the additional advantage that the world trade balance is zero as $\sum_i\sum_j\hat{X}_{ij}-\sum_i\sum_j\hat{X}_{ji}=0$ when summed over all 41 regions including titROW.

[21] Specification (8) is slightly less preferred due to the lower correlation between predicted and observed scaled trade flows, relative to specification (7).

[22] Of course, whether the comparative static effect on any endogenous variable is positive or negative in one country on average (or in a given state or province) depends on the choice of the numéraire. Of interest effectively is the *relative* difference in changes between U.S. and Canadian variables.

welfare estimates in a "laboratory" setting. In the next section, we use a Monte Carlo analysis to show that estimates of σ, comparative static trade-flow changes, and economic welfare comparative static effects are unbiased and precise using our approach. Moreover, in this setting we show that – when both approaches use identical elasticities of substitution – the welfare effects from trade-cost reductions are indeed identical.

4. Monte Carlo analysis

Although fixed effects ensure unbiased estimates of gravity equation parameters, we need a Monte Carlo analysis to confirm unbiased and precise estimates for σ using Method 3 and the associated general equilibrium (GE) comparative statics using the MC-IR model in comparison to some other models. The Monte Carlo analysis is able also to shed light on whether comparative static effects (of bilateral trade flows or welfare) are sensitive to σ, in the absence of measurement and specification error, for alternative models.

Among numerous results, we show that Method 3 provides unbiased and precise estimates of σ and GE comparative statics. While the empirical findings of AvW suggested that nominal trade-flow comparative statics were insensitive to the value of σ, our Monte Carlo analysis demonstrates that this is not generally true. Trade-flow and economic welfare comparative static estimates appear highly sensitive to the value of the elasticity of substitution, motivating the importance of a method providing unbiased and precise estimates of σ. In fact, an incorrect value of σ in AvW can suggest even the wrong *direction* of economic welfare estimates. Finally, irrespective of SBTC or ABTC, comparative static effects of trade costs are biased when using linearized versions of AvW's model, but the bias declines as the number of countries in the world increases and the value of σ decreases.

4.1. Monte Carlo design

We use alternative sets of parameter values described below to generate sets of all endogenous variables in the MC-IR model – X_{ij}, Y_i, and Y_i/L_i – as functions of exogenous endowments L_i, exogenous bilateral trade costs g_{ij}, and the model's parameters in the baseline equilibrium. This also determines the endogenous variables in the AvW system in a baseline equilibrium. We then change exogenous trade costs holding constant the model's parameters and all endowments to obtain *counterfactual* values for all endogenous variables in a "laboratory" setting.

We specify nine different configurations (or scenarios) of the world economy for robustness. We consider three alternative values for $\sigma \in \{3, 5, 10\}$ to allow us to study the role of "curvature" for estimation of parameters, elasticities, and comparative statics.[23] Moreover, we consider three alternative sizes of the number of countries in the world, $N \in \{10, 20, 40\}$, to study the performance of alternative techniques for estimation and comparative statics as sample size increases. This gives nine parameter configurations.

For each of these configurations, we use 10 different draws from a set of empirical observations for populations (as a proxy for endowments, L_i) for 207 countries from *World Development Indicators* (2003) and from measurable cif-fob ratios (as a proxy for t_{ij}), from the International Monetary Fund's *Direction of Trade Statistics* (2003). We assume *true* – but unobservable – bilateral trade costs, t_{ij}, are determined as $t_{ij}^{1-\sigma} = g_{ij}^{(1-\sigma)\rho}$, where g_{ij} is a cif-fob factor and assume arbitrarily $\rho = 2$ (without loss of generality). Hence, employing g_{ij} does not allow for direct estimation of $1-\sigma$.[24] Bilateral cif-fob factors g_{ij} are drawn from empirical realizations of the cif-fob factors in the 25th–75th percentiles of the empirical distribution for the same 207 countries.[25] The 10 draws from these data along with the nine parameter combinations generate 90 alternative *baseline* equilibria (9 scenarios × 10 draws per scenario) of X_{ij} and Y_i (and, hence, Y_i/L_i) in the MC-IR model and of X_{ij}, Y_i, $\Pi^{1-\sigma}$, and $P_i^{1-\sigma}$ in the AvW model consistent with general equilibrium (before stochastic error terms are introduced). For each of those 90 equilibria we determine a counterfactual equilibrium which corresponds to an arbitrary alternative draw of g_{ij} (under SBTC or ABTC).

To each of the obtained 90 baseline configurations and equilibria, we add a stochastic error to the bilateral trade equation (as in empirical gravity-equation settings). We do so independently 2000 times assuming random disturbances which are uncorrelated with the determinants of aggregate nominal bilateral trade in the model and, alternatively, 2000 times assuming disturbances which are correlated with trade costs. We can then *estimate* parameters and comparative static effects in Monte Carlo simulations using 4000 runs per scenario, treating the 90 parameter configurations and equilibria as fixed in repeated samples (totaling 360,000 simulations).

4.2. Error structure

In Eq. (9) we introduced a multiplicative stochastic term ϵ_{ij}, and in Eq. (11) defined the log-additive disturbance term $u_{ij} \equiv \ln \epsilon_{ij}$. The two alternative error structures in the Monte Carlo simulations are specified as follows. In general, we assume that the error terms u_{ij} in the log-linearized bilateral trade equations are given by $u_{ij} = \mu_i + \nu_j + \xi_{ij}$.[26] In all cases, ξ_{ij} is drawn from a normal distribution with $\mathcal{N}\left(0, s_\xi^2\right)$ and $s_\xi = 0.35 s_x$, where s_x denotes the standard deviation of true log bilateral exports.[27] First, we assume that the error terms (u_{ij}) are uncorrelated with the right-hand-side variables. In the tables, this error structure is labeled "uncorrelated." In this case, μ_i and ν_j are each distributed as $\mathcal{N}\left(0, s_\mu^2\right)$ with $s_\mu = 0.15 s_x$. Then, AvW's iterative non-linear least squares (NLS) estimation approach is consistent, as is fixed effects estimation. We made 2000 draws for the error terms under this structure. Second, we also consider an error structure where we know the u_{ij} are correlated with the observable bilateral trade cost variable, g_{ij}.[28] In the tables, this error structure is labeled "correlated." In the latter case, AvW's iterative NLS approach is inconsistent, but fixed effects is consistent. We made 2000 draws for the error terms under this structure also.

4.3. Monte Carlo results assuming symmetric bilateral trade costs

Table 3a reports information about true and estimated *parameters* from a gravity equation, where we report the mean, standard deviation, and mean absolute error (MAE) of each parameter estimate under the assumption that SBTC holds.[29] The MAEs are reported as

---

[23] We set both α (the fixed cost in the production function) and ϕ (the labor unit input coefficient) to unity, without loss of generality.

[24] The reason we chose this particular distribution is that it includes both bilaterally symmetric observations as well as bilaterally asymmetric ones, which is not possible if we used instead bilateral distance (because $d_{ij} = d_{ji}$).

[25] In the interquartile range, the average cif-fob ratio is $\frac{1}{N(N-1)} \sum_i^N \sum_{j \neq i} g_{ij} = 1.196$, the standard deviation of that measure is 0.067, and the corresponding minimum and maximum are 1.010 and 1.455, respectively.

[26] An additive log-linear error term is conventional to the general-equilibrium-based literature on gravity-model estimation (cf., Anderson and van Wincoop, 2003). In particular, it seems to be a suitable assumption in the absence of zero trade flows, as in our application. We have chosen to add the stochastic error term in only the trade flow equation. GDP could potentially have measurement error as well. However, because we estimate the trade flow equation with region-specific fixed effects, region-specific measurement error or correlation of trade costs with the region-specific error components will not bias our parameter estimates.

[27] We scale the variance of the error term (ξ) to a fraction of the variance of exports (0.35) in order for the Monte Carlo simulations of the gravity equations to have R^2 values of approximately 0.65.

[28] To do this, we added ten times the average exporter-specific trade cost variable $\left(g_{i.} \equiv (1/N) \sum_{j=1} g_{ij}\right)$ to the respective μ_i and ten times the average importer-specific trade cost variable $\left(g_{.j} \equiv (1/N) \sum_{i=1} g_{ij}\right)$ to the respective ν_j.

[29] Recall that one cannot solve for an estimate of σ in the AvW approach or in reduced forms.

Table 3a
Monte Carlo results for gravity-equation parameters in the case of a $\sigma = 5$ and symmetric trade costs.

Estimates	True	OLS		*BV-OLS-1*		*BV-OLS-2*		AvW		Suggested model	
		Uncorr.	Corr.	Uncorr.	Corr.	Uncorr.	Corr.	Uncorr.	Corr.	Uncorr.	Corr.
(1)	(2)	(3)	(4)	(5)	(6)	(7)	(8)	(9)	(10)	(11)	(12)
10-country-world, $\sigma = 5$											
$\rho\,(1-\sigma)$											
Mean	−8	−7.6241	−6.8319	−8.0214	−8.0354	−7.7444	−7.8193	−8.0149	−7.5514	−8.0214	−8.0354
Std.	–	0.5502	0.6785	0.3232	0.3205	0.6343	0.6395	0.4738	0.5197	0.3232	0.3205
MAE	–	6.7748	14.7083	3.2207	3.2069	6.6943	6.5789	4.6685	6.7944	3.2207	3.2069
σ											
Mean	5	–	–	–	–	–	–	–	–	5.0177	5.0264
Std.	–	–	–	–	–	–	–	–	–	0.2487	0.2467
MAE	–	–	–	–	–	–	–	–	–	3.7163	3.7071
20-country-world, $\sigma = 5$											
$\rho\,(1-\sigma)$											
Mean	−8	−7.7905	−7.206	−8.0107	−8.0087	−7.8510	−7.7691	−8.0107	−7.6167	−8.0107	−8.0087
Std.	–	0.2655	0.3237	0.1558	0.1559	0.2712	0.2235	0.2570	0.2333	0.1558	0.1559
MAE	–	3.5705	9.9623	1.5518	1.5545	3.0960	3.2839	2.5415	4.8903	1.5518	1.5545
σ											
Mean	5	–	–	–	–	–	–	–	–	5.0092	5.0078
Std.	–	–	–	–	–	–	–	–	–	0.1249	0.1248
MAE	–	–	–	–	–	–	–	–	–	1.8199	1.8232
40-country-world, $\sigma = 5$											
$\rho\,(1-\sigma)$											
Mean	−8	−7.7949	−7.4301	−8.0029	−8.0026	−7.7537	−7.7207	−8.0106	−7.8565	−8.0029	−8.0026
Std.	–	0.1205	0.1547	0.0764	0.0776	0.1944	0.2150	0.1359	0.1305	0.0764	0.0776
MAE	–	2.5981	7.1239	0.7633	0.7733	3.2803	3.5994	1.3514	2.0033	0.7633	0.7733
σ											
Mean	5	–	–	–	–	–	–	–	–	5.0008	5.0003
Std.	–	–	–	–	–	–	–	–	–	0.0780	0.0789
MAE	–	–	–	–	–	–	–	–	–	1.0884	1.1039

Notes: the mean absolute error (MAE) is expressed as a percent of the true value.

a percent of the true parameter value. Since $\sigma = 5$ for all results in Table 3a, the findings pertain to 2000 draws for "world" sizes of $N \in \{10, 20, 40\}$ each.

Table 3b reports information about general equilibrium (GE) *comparative static* estimates. This table provides information about the true and estimated percent changes of (GDP-scaled nominal bilateral) trade flows and of real economic welfare (equivalent variation), in percent. As with parameter estimates, we report the means, standard deviations, and MAEs of the true and estimated (GE) comparative static effects across all country-pairs, Monte Carlo runs, and N-configurations at $\sigma = 5$, corresponding to Table 3a. Since the true comparative static effects are already expressed in percent, the MAEs in Table 3b are measured as an average absolute percentage point deviation from the true comparative static percentage change. Both Tables 3a and 3b are divided horizontally into three blocks of estimates, each corresponding to a different scenario of N. Supplemental tables for values of $\sigma \in \{3, 10\}$ are reported in the Appendix Tables A1a, A1b and A2a, A2b.

Tables 3a and 3b have 12 columns each. In Table 3a, column (1) lists the two parameters, $(1-\sigma)\rho$ and σ. In Table 3b, column (1) lists the two endogenous variables relevant for comparative static estimates, the trade flow and the equivalent variation (EV). Column (2) specifies the true values of the parameters assumed in the simulations, $(1-\sigma)\rho = 8$ and $\sigma = 5$ in Table 3a, and the true values of the comparative static effects, $\Delta(X_{ij}Y_W/Y_iY_j)$ and EV_i, in Table 3b. Columns (3)–(12) provide estimates of the parameters and comparative statics using various estimation techniques which we will describe.[30] For brevity, we discuss only the bottom third of each table, that is, the 40-country-world.

Columns (3) and (4) in Tables 3a and 3b present the estimates using traditional OLS gravity equations *ignoring* entirely the role of endogenous prices; hence, this specification follows Eq. (2) omitting region fixed effects for the P_is and P_js, as in McCallum (1995).[31] Columns (3) and (4) present the OLS results assuming uncorrelated and correlated errors, respectively. The purpose of these specifications is to confirm the extent of bias of traditional gravity-equation parameter estimates when ignoring multilateral price terms as suggested by AvW, or even regions' fixed effects. The parameter-estimate bias is large under both error structures, and especially large under correlated errors. Not surprisingly, in Table 3b the means of the trade-flow comparative static effects indicate considerable bias and the MAEs are quite large.

Columns (5)–(8) provide estimates using linear approximations for $lnP_i^{1-\sigma}$ and $lnP_j^{1-\sigma}$ in the log-transformed model of AvW as derived in Baier and Bergstrand (2009). In this method, linear approximations of the (exogenous components of the) nonlinear multilateral resistance terms are introduced as exogenous RHS variables and consequently comparative statics of trade flows can be conducted, respecting multilateral resistances. Specifications (5) and (6) – labeled *BV-OLS-1* – employ simple averages of bilateral trade costs for the multilateral price terms, whereas specifications (7) and (8) – labeled *BV-OLS-2* – employ GDP-weighted averages of bilateral trade costs for the multilateral terms, the latter used in Baier and Bergstrand (2009). As explained in Baier and Bergstrand (2010), coefficient estimates are expected to be less biased using *BV-OLS-1* than *BV-OLS-2* in Table 3a because the simple-weighted averages work similar to region fixed effects. Trade-flow comparative static estimates are biased in the BV-OLS specifications in Table 3b because comparative statics are based on linear approximations of the nonlinear price terms in

[30] Since only the structural MC-IR model can estimate σ, we leave the corresponding discussion until columns (11) and (12) of Tables 3a and 3b.

[31] Consequently, there will be no EV comparative static estimates for the OLS results.

Table 3b
Monte Carlo results for predicted trade flow and welfare comparative statics in the case of a $\sigma=5$ and symmetric trade costs.

Estimates	True	OLS		BV-OLS-1		BV-OLS-2		AvW		Suggested model	
		Uncorr.	Corr.	Uncorr.	Corr.	Uncorr.	Corr.	Uncorr.	Corr.	Uncorr.	Corr.
(1)	(2)	(3)	(4)	(5)	(6)	(7)	(8)	(9)	(10)	(11)	(12)
10-country-world, $\sigma=5$											
$\Delta\frac{X_{ij}Y_W}{Y_iY_j}$											
Mean	15.6348	21.2083	16.9485	14.6863	14.7388	20.9057	21.2467	15.7720	13.7475	15.7586	15.8197
Std.	67.7946	73.8767	61.3019	63.0199	63.1647	81.6642	82.1467	68.4578	62.1077	68.2929	68.4372
MAE	–	26.4978	24.1339	19.0619	19.0723	22.7052	22.8996	2.5982	3.7948	1.8482	1.8396
EV_i											
Mean	1.7030	–	–	–	–	–	–	1.7038	1.6365	1.7011	1.6972
Std.	9.1959	–	–	–	–	–	–	9.1918	9.0527	9.1915	9.1818
MAE	–	–	–	–	–	–	–	0.1483	0.2054	0.2234	0.2213
20-country-world, $\sigma=5$											
$\Delta\frac{X_{ij}Y_W}{Y_iY_j}$											
Mean	23.3920	24.3130	20.7552	19.0991	19.0883	26.1341	25.4988	23.4934	21.2079	23.4703	23.4569
Std.	90.5346	84.9751	75.3124	80.1990	80.1646	96.5163	94.8488	90.9789	83.7935	90.8372	90.7944
MAE	–	22.2170	21.7635	17.9046	17.9053	14.7770	14.2352	1.8146	3.3970	1.1651	1.1674
EV_i											
Mean	0.8988	–	–	–	–	–	–	0.8997	0.8486	0.8984	0.8986
Std.	7.2242	–	–	–	–	–	–	7.2294	7.0372	7.2194	7.2202
MAE	–	–	–	–	–	–	–	0.0903	0.1692	0.0788	0.0789
40-country-world, $\sigma=5$											
$\Delta\frac{X_{ij}Y_W}{Y_iY_j}$											
Mean	23.8155	18.9762	17.0660	19.2797	19.2779	25.0291	24.7589	23.8913	22.9440	23.8488	23.8473
Std.	89.7503	78.7336	73.0796	78.7351	78.7310	92.7942	91.6696	90.0318	87.0564	89.8462	89.8410
MAE	–	23.5040	23.5699	20.6474	20.6487	11.3734	11.2878	0.9867	1.4566	0.7160	0.7260
EV_i											
Mean	−0.0880	–	–	–	–	–	–	−0.0878	−0.0941	−0.0906	−0.0909
Std.	7.7841	–	–	–	–	–	–	7.7914	7.6844	7.7875	7.7880
MAE	–	–	–	–	–	–	–	0.0587	0.0878	0.0658	0.0668

Notes: the mean absolute error (MAE) is expressed in percentage points of the true value (as scaled trade flows and EVs are in percentage points already).

Table 4a
Monte Carlo results for gravity-equation parameters in the case of a $\sigma=5$ and asymmetric trade costs.

Estimates	True	OLS	BV-OLS-1	BV-OLS-2	SBTC-AvW, FE	ABTC-AvW, FE	Suggested model, FE
		Uncorr.	Uncorr.	Uncorr.	Uncorr.	Uncorr.	Uncorr.
(1)	(2)	(3)	(4)	(5)	(6)	(7)	(8)
10-country-world, $\sigma=5$							
$\rho(1-\sigma)$							
Mean	−8	−7.3749	−8.0382	−7.7583	−8.0382	−8.0382	−8.0382
Std.	–	0.6668	0.3156	0.54048	0.3156	0.3156	0.3156
MAE	–	8.8907	3.1563	5.9763	3.1563	3.1563	3.1563
σ							
Mean	5	–	–	–	–	–	5.0203
Std.	–	–	–	–	–	–	0.1939
MAE	–	–	–	–	–	–	2.8983
20-country-world, $\sigma=5$							
$\rho(1-\sigma)$							
Mean	−8	−7.7019	−8.0098	−7.7381	−8.0098	−8.0098	−8.0098
Std.	–	0.3093	0.1640	0.3348	0.1640	0.1640	0.1640
MAE	–	4.5091	1.6493	4.2320	1.6493	1.6493	1.6493
σ							
Mean	5	–	–	–	–	–	5.0063
Std.	–	–	–	–	–	–	0.0951
MAE	–	–	–	–	–	–	1.5143
40-country-world, $\sigma=5$							
$\rho(1-\sigma)$							
Mean	−8	−7.7564	−8.0002	−7.7129	−8.0002	−8.0002	−8.0002
Std.	–	0.1234	0.0738	0.3207	0.0738	0.0738	0.0738
MAE	–	3.0832	0.7190	3.8906	0.7190	0.7190	0.7190
σ							
Mean	5	–	–	–	–	–	5.0003
Std.	–	–	–	–	–	–	0.0472
MAE	–	–	–	–	–	–	0.7339

Notes: the mean absolute error (MAE) is expressed as a percent of the true value.

Table 4b
Monte Carlo results for predicted trade flow and welfare changes in the case of a $\sigma = 5$ and asymmetric trade costs.

Estimates	True	OLS	*BV-OLS-1*	*BV-OLS-2*	SBTC-AvW, FE	ABTC-AvW, FE	Suggested model, FE
		Uncorr.	Uncorr.	Uncorr.	Uncorr.	Uncorr.	Uncorr.
(1)	(2)	(3)	(4)	(5)	(6)	(7)	(8)
10-country-world, $\sigma = 5$							
$\Delta \frac{X_{ij} Y_W}{Y_i Y_j}$							
Mean	20.6721	15.5437	16.2140	25.6395	19.9104	20.9153	20.9538
Std.	87.9681	73.5495	66.1239	99.9547	85.6286	89.0451	89.1178
MAE	-	30.4533	23.7172	17.2115	7.0729	2.0564	2.1426
EV_i							
Mean	−0.0872	-	-	-	0.6541	−0.0872	−0.0913
Std.	7.1420	-	-	-	10.3313	7.1578	7.1357
MAE	-	-	-	-	4.2611	0.1145	0.1286
20-country-world, $\sigma = 5$							
$\Delta \frac{X_{ij} Y_W}{Y_i Y_j}$							
Mean	23.8479	17.135	18.7285	27.9349	23.2814	23.9096	23.9158
Std.	91.909	77.1394	73.4616	99.3701	90.3398	92.1191	92.1374
MAE	-	30.9097	27.6675	15.4569	4.4997	1.1872	1.2932
EV_i							
Mean	−0.0894	-	-	-	0.8445	−0.0890	−0.0900
Std.	7.1531	-	-	-	10.5091	7.1519	7.1522
MAE	-	-	-	-	4.4064	0.0639	0.0522
40-country-world, $\sigma = 5$							
$\Delta \frac{X_{ij} Y_W}{Y_i Y_j}$							
Mean	21.8075	18.1371	19.3053	22.1782	21.9812	21.8084	21.8109
Std.	88.5205	77.9766	80.7079	88.7955	88.1429	88.5378	88.5429
MAE	-	23.7442	20.5455	11.0263	2.3084	0.5078	0.5361
EV_i							
Mean	−0.0144	-	-	-	−0.6080	−0.0138	−0.0142
Std.	5.2335	-	-	-	7.0521	5.2333	5.2341
MAE	-	-	-	-	3.7975	0.0210	0.0182

Notes: The mean absolute error (MAE) is expressed in percentage points of the true value (as scaled trade flows and EVs are in percentage points already).

AvW. However, the bias is small in the 40-country case using GDP-weighted averages in the linear approximations (*BV-OLS-2*) compared to simple averages (*BV-OLS-1*), and the bias of *BV-OLS-2* in particular diminishes as the number of countries in the world (N) increases.[32]

Columns (9) and (10) in Tables 3a and 3b present estimates using the NLS estimation procedure used in AvW (2003), assuming uncorrelated errors in column (9) and correlated errors in column (10). Since we are assuming SBTC, we estimate the AvW model as in (2) using NLS. Under uncorrelated errors, column (9) reveals that the AvW coefficient estimates and comparative statics are unbiased. The purpose of estimating the same model with correlated errors is to verify that the iterative SBTC-AvW procedure actually used in AvW (2003) yields biased gravity-equation coefficient estimates and comparative statics in the presence of such errors. Thus, if there exists any possibility in an empirical application of correlated errors, one would be better off using region fixed effects in estimation and then subsequently using a nonlinear solver for estimating comparative statics.

The final specifications in columns (11) and (12) are estimates using our ("Suggested") structural MC-IR model. First, parameters are estimated using fixed effects. Consequently, regardless of uncorrelated or correlated errors, these coefficient estimates are unbiased. Second, as discussed previously, only the MC-IR approach generates an estimate of σ; columns (11) and (12) report unbiased and precise estimates of σ using Method 3. Third, as shown in Table 3b, we find that both AvW's (uncorrelated errors) approach and our approach deliver unbiased and precise estimates of comparative statics. Of course, in AvW, we have *assumed* knowledge of the true $\sigma = 5$ whereas our approach *estimates* σ. In sum, both AvW's and our approach provide unbiased and precise parameter and comparative static estimates, and ours also provides unbiased and precise estimates of σ.

Finally, in their sensitivity analysis for empirical results, AvW (2003) found their trade-flow comparative statics were insensitive to varying σ between 2 and 20. Our Monte Carlo analysis can be used to examine the sensitivity of trade-flow and *EV* comparative statics to varying σ under laboratory conditions. Appendix Tables A1a, A1b and A2a, A2b provide comparable information to that in Tables 3a, 3b for values of $\sigma \in \{3, 10\}$. The notable finding is that the trade-flow and *EV* comparative static estimates are *highly* sensitive to the value of the elasticity of substitution. For the 40-country-world for a given trade-cost shock, the trade-flow elasticity is almost 200% for $\sigma = 10$ whereas the trade-flow elasticity is only 5% for $\sigma = 3$; the former is *40 times* the latter.[33] Both the comparative static trade-flow and the *EV* estimates vary considerably depending upon the value of σ. The key difference here is that our approach *estimates* the value of σ and AvW uses an *assumed* value. So if the true elasticity differs from the assumed one, our approach can capture this whereas the comparative static estimates from AvW will be biased.

4.4. Monte Carlo results assuming asymmetric bilateral trade costs

For asymmetric trade costs (ABTC), we summarize the findings from the Monte Carlo analysis in Tables 4a and 4b. Table 4a reports information about true and estimated parameters from a gravity equation as before, and Table 4b reports the comparative static estimates. For brevity, we assume errors to be uncorrelated with trade costs in all the estimates, as the previous analysis explained the

[32] The biases of *BV-OLS-2* for trade-flow comparative statics also diminish as σ decreases.

[33] See Appendix Tables A1b and A2b at the mean of $\Delta \frac{X_{ij} Y_W}{Y_i Y_j}$.

impact of correlated errors. Also, in both AvW specifications – one using the approach based upon Eq. (1) labeled ABTC-AvW and one using the approach based upon Eq. (2) labeled SBTC-AvW – we estimate the trade-cost parameter using country fixed effects (FE), since NLS and FE will yield identical estimates with uncorrelated errors. Again, we focus on the bottom third of each table, the 40-country-world.

For brevity, the main results from this Monte Carlo exercise are summarized. First, regarding parameter estimates in Table 4a, the alternative methods perform comparably to their respective counterparts for uncorrelated errors under SBTC in Table 3a. This is not surprising, even for SBTC-AvW, since we have estimated the AvW model using region fixed effects. The MC-IR model permits an unbiased and precise estimate of the elasticity of substitution, σ, for ABTC as well as SBTC. Second, ABTC-AvW provides unbiased and precise estimates of trade-flow comparative statics — under the *assumption* that we know the true value of σ (in Table 4b, the true $\sigma = 5$). However, we know from the previous section that the trade-flow comparative static estimates will be much different if the assumed value of σ is incorrect, and such trade-flow comparative statics can increase by as much as 40 times as the value of σ increases from 3 to 10. Third, Table 4b indicates that – when trade costs are bilaterally asymmetric – only our method and ABTC-AvW (when σ is *known*) provide unbiased and precise estimates of *EV* changes. However, as Appendix Tables 1b and 2b report, such comparative statics are biased using AvW with an assumed value of σ different from the true one.

5. Conclusions

Theoretical foundations for estimating gravity equations were enhanced recently in Eaton and Kortum (2002), Anderson and van Wincoop (2003), and Helpman et al. (2008). Though elegant and isomorphic, not all of the approaches provide unbiased estimates of the trade-cost elasticity, a key parameter in computing general equilibrium comparative statics. We use the workhorse Krugman monopolistic competition and increasing returns model of trade to motivate estimating gravity equation coefficients, the elasticity of substitution in consumption, and general equilibrium trade-flow and economic welfare comparative statics. In applying our framework empirically to the well-known McCallum "border-puzzle" as in Anderson and van Wincoop (2003), we generate an unbiased estimate of the elasticity of substitution and economically plausible trade-flow and economic welfare comparative statics that differ significantly from those provided using AvW's technique (which *assumes* an elasticity of substitution) and are sensitive to using bilaterally symmetric or asymmetric trade costs.

However, the paper has not addressed several issues, which should be examined in future research. Notably, the model should be extended to incorporate heterogeneous productivities and fixed market entry costs as in Melitz (2003) and zeros in trade flows as in Helpman et al. (2008). Moreover, future work should extend the analysis to multiple sectors and multiple factors, subjects also beyond the scope of the present paper.

Acknowledgments

We are grateful to the editor, Jonathan Eaton, and two anonymous referees for excellent comments that have substantively improved the manuscript. We are also grateful for useful comments at seminars or conferences at CESifo, ETH Zurich, the European Economic Association, Georgia Tech, the German Economic Association, University of Groningen, University of Innsbruck, University of Mainz, University of Munich, University of Nottingham, University of Oxford, Purdue University (EIIT conference), and University of Warsaw. Bergstrand, Egger, and Larch are grateful for financial supports under U.S. National Science Foundation grant SES-0351154, under Austrian Science Fund grant P17713-G05, and from the Leibniz-Gemeinschaft (WGL) under project Pakt 2009 Globalisierungsnetzwerk, respectively, and from CESifo.

Appendix A. Supplementary data

Supplementary data to this article can be found online at http://dx.doi.org/10.1016/j.jinteco.2012.05.005.

References

Anderson, J.E., 1979. A theoretical foundation for the gravity equation. The American Economic Review 69, 106–116.
Anderson, James E., 2011. The gravity model. Annual Review of Economics.
Anderson, J.E., van Wincoop, E., 2003. Gravity with gravitas: a solution to the border puzzle. The American Economic Review 93, 170–192.
Anderson, J.E., van Wincoop, E., 2004. Trade costs. Journal of Economic Literature 42, 691–751.
Arkolakis, Costas, Costinot, Arnaud, Rodriguez-Clare, Andres, 2012. New trade models, same old gains? American Economic Review. 102, 94–130.
Baier, S.L., Bergstrand, J.H., 2009. Bonus vetus OLS: a simple method for approximating international trade-cost effects using the gravity equation. Journal of International Economics 77, 77–85.
Baier, S.L., Bergstrand, J.H., 2010. Approximating general equilibrium impacts of trade liberalizations using the gravity equation. In: Brakman, S., van Bergeijk, P. (Eds.), The Gravity Equation in International Trade: Advances and Applications. Cambridge University Press, Cambridge, UK.
Balistreri, E.J., Hillberry, R.H., 2007. Structural estimation and the border puzzle. Journal of International Economics 72, 451–463.
Bergstrand, J.H., 1985. The gravity equation in international trade: some microeconomic foundations and empirical evidence. The Review of Economics and Statistics 67, 474–481.
Bergstrand, J.H., Egger, P., 2011. Gravity equations and economic frictions in the world economy. In: Bernhofen, D., Falvey, R., Kreickemeier, U. (Eds.), Palgrave Handbook of International Trade. Palgrave Macmillan, London, UK.
Bernard, A.B., Jensen, J.B., Redding, S.J., Schott, P.K., 2009. The margins of U.S. trade. The American Economic Review 99, 487–493.
Chaney, T., 2008. Distorted gravity: the intensive and extensive margins of international trade. The American Economic Review 98, 1707–1721.
Dekle, R., Eaton, J., Kortum, S., 2007. Unbalanced trade. American Economic Review: Papers and Proceedings 97, 351–355.
Eaton, J., Kortum, S., 2002. Technology, geography, and trade. Econometrica 70, 1741–1779.
Feenstra, R., 2004. Advanced International Trade: Theory and Evidence. Princeton University Press, Princeton, NJ.
Fisman, R., Wei, S.-J., 2004. Tax rates and tax evasion: evidence from 'missing imports' in China. Journal of Political Economy 112, 471–496.
Helpman, E., Melitz, M., Rubinstein, Y., 2008. Estimating trade flows: trading partners and trading volumes. Quarterly Journal of Economics 123, 441–487.
Hummels, D.L., Lugovskyy, V., 2006. Are matched partner trade statistics usable measures of transportation costs? Review of International Economics 14, 69–86.
Javorcik, B., Narciso, G., 2008. Differentiated products and evasion of import tariffs. Journal of International Economics 76, 208–222.
Krugman, P.R., 1980. Scale economies, product differentiation, and the pattern of trade. The American Economic Review 70, 950–959.
Lai, H., Trefler, D., 2002. The gains from trade with monopolistic competition: specification, estimation, and mis-specification. NBER Working Paper 9169. September.
McCallum, J., 1995. National borders matter: Canada–U.S. regional trade patterns. The American Economic Review 85, 615–623.
Melitz, M., 2003. The impact of trade on intra-industry reallocations and aggregate industry productivity. Econometrica 71, 1695–1725.
Redding, S., Venables, A.J., 2004. Economic geography and international inequality. Journal of International Economics 62, 53–82.
Waugh, Michael E. (2007). Bilateral trade, relative prices, and trade costs, unpublished manuscript, University of Iowa, November.

Appendix

Table A1a: Monte Carlo results for model parameters in the case of a $\sigma = 3$ and symmetric trade costs.

		OLS		BV-OLS-1		BV-OLS-2		AvW		Suggested Model	
Estimates (1)	True (2)	Uncorr. (3)	Corr. (4)	Uncorr. (5)	Corr. (6)	Uncorr. (7)	Corr. (8)	Uncorr. (9)	corr. (10)	Uncorr. (11)	Corr. (12)
						10-country-world, $\sigma = 3$					
$\rho(1-\sigma)$											
mean	−4	−3.7571	−3.2041	−4.0136	−4.0194	−3.9321	−4.0462	−4.0119	−4.0035	−4.0136	−4.0194
std.	—	0.2799	0.3539	0.1698	0.1690	0.3235	0.3411	0.3167	0.2881	0.1698	0.1690
MAE	—	7.5737	19.9271	3.3738	3.3803	6.5394	7.0723	6.2824	5.8070	3.3738	3.3803
σ											
mean	3	—	—	—	—	—	—	—	—	3.0080	3.0129
std.	—	—	—	—	—	—	—	—	—	0.1153	0.1153
MAE	—	—	—	—	—	—	—	—	—	3.0183	3.0335

(Continued)

Table A1a: (*Continued*)

Estimates (1)	True (2)	OLS Uncorr. (3)	OLS Corr. (4)	BV-OLS-1 Uncorr. (5)	BV-OLS-1 Corr. (6)	BV-OLS-2 Uncorr. (7)	BV-OLS-2 Corr. (8)	AvW Uncorr. (9)	AvW corr. (10)	Suggested Model Uncorr. (11)	Suggested Model Corr. (12)
20-country-world, $\sigma = 3$											
$\rho(1-\sigma)$											
mean	−4	−3.7878	−3.1911	−4.0034	−4.0043	−3.9528	−3.9859	−4.0033	−3.8925	−4.0034	−4.0043
std.	—	0.1631	0.2800	0.0787	0.0785	0.2024	0.1871	0.1926	0.1841	0.0787	0.0785
MAE	—	5.5451	20.2220	1.5676	1.5565	4.0657	3.7943	3.7673	4.3525	1.5676	1.5565
σ											
mean	3	—	—	—	—	—	—	—	—	3.0032	3.0044
std.	—	—	—	—	—	—	—	—	—	0.0926	0.0919
MAE	—	—	—	—	—	—	—	—	—	2.1690	2.1483
40-country-world, $\sigma = 3$											
$\rho(1-\sigma)$											
mean	−4	−3.8842	−3.5452	−4.0021	−4.0017	−3.9462	−3.9459	−4.0011	−3.9242	−4.0021	−4.0017
std.	—	0.0694	0.1030	0.0380	0.0382	0.0975	0.0972	0.0868	0.0997	0.0380	0.0382
MAE	—	2.9590	11.3697	0.7595	0.7626	2.1731	2.2230	1.7105	2.6967	0.7595	0.7626
σ											
mean	3	—	—	—	—	—	—	—	—	3.0016	3.0013
std.	—	—	—	—	—	—	—	—	—	0.0286	0.0288
MAE	—	—	—	—	—	—	—	—	—	0.7539	0.7585

Notes: The mean absolute error (MAE) is expressed as a percent of the true value.

Table A1b: Monte Carlo results for predicted trade flow and welfare changes in the case of a $\sigma = 3$ and symmetric trade costs.

		OLS		BV-OLS-1		BV-OLS-2		AvW		Suggested Model	
Estimates (1)	True (2)	Uncorr. (3)	Corr. (4)	Uncorr. (5)	Corr. (6)	Uncorr. (7)	Corr. (8)	Uncorr. (9)	Corr. (10)	Uncorr. (11)	Corr. (12)
					10-country-world, $\sigma = 3$						
$\Delta \frac{X_{ij} Y_W}{Y_i Y_j}$											
mean	6.6662	3.2435	2.3500	3.5120	3.5190	8.2709	9.3040	6.6014	6.8860	6.7489	6.7416
std.	36.9948	27.8818	23.5375	27.7128	27.7392	41.0057	44.4533	37.1356	38.1079	37.2688	37.2623
MAE	—	17.8267	17.6405	15.2644	15.2651	4.4485	5.3880	1.6633	1.5481	0.9934	0.9887
EV_i											
mean	0.2351	—	—	—	—	—	—	−0.0611	−0.0875	0.2304	0.2317
std.	14.1707	—	—	—	—	—	—	7.4562	7.5313	14.1729	14.1630
MAE	—	—	—	—	—	—	—	4.3464	4.3028	0.1355	0.1352

(*Continued*)

Table A1b: (*Continued*)

Estimates (1)	True (2)	OLS Uncorr. (3)	OLS Corr. (4)	BV-OLS-1 Uncorr. (5)	BV-OLS-1 Corr. (6)	BV-OLS-2 Uncorr. (7)	BV-OLS-2 Corr. (8)	AvW Uncorr. (9)	AvW Corr. (10)	Suggested Model Uncorr. (11)	Suggested Model Corr. (12)
20-country-world, $\sigma = 3$											
$\Delta \frac{X_{ij} Y_W}{Y_i Y_j}$											
mean	5.4797	3.7566	2.5930	4.4173	4.4194	6.0417	6.0668	5.4408	5.1722	5.4923	5.4933
std.	35.3275	31.1362	25.9515	31.3472	31.3551	36.6611	36.8558	35.4044	34.3500	35.3767	35.3852
MAE	—	13.1648	13.4517	11.3259	11.3260	3.7866	3.7163	1.0460	1.1888	0.4772	0.4750
EV_i											
mean	0.1196	—	—	—	—	—	—	−0.0231	−0.0290	0.1184	0.1187
std.	9.8557	—	—	—	—	—	—	5.2396	5.1146	9.8611	9.8581
MAE	—	—	—	—	—	—	—	3.4358	3.5203	0.1346	0.1339
40-country-world, $\sigma = 3$											
$\Delta \frac{X_{ij} Y_W}{Y_i Y_j}$											
mean	4.7364	4.5261	3.7749	4.4345	4.4335	4.7299	4.7390	4.6834	4.5225	4.7431	4.7416
std.	33.7559	31.2879	28.2547	31.4914	31.4874	34.1411	34.1706	33.7530	33.0860	33.7794	33.7748
MAE	—	9.8183	9.9459	9.0524	9.0524	2.2595	2.2712	0.4662	0.7302	0.2050	0.2058
EV_i											
mean	0.4752	—	—	—	—	—	—	0.1975	0.1907	0.4748	0.4749
std.	7.0784	—	—	—	—	—	—	3.7986	3.7388	7.0774	7.0777
MAE	—	—	—	—	—	—	—	2.5146	2.5626	0.0190	0.0191

Notes: The mean absolute error (MAE) is expressed in percentage points of the true value (as scaled trade flows and EVs are in percentage points already).

Table A2a: Monte Carlo results for model parameters in the case of a $\sigma = 10$ and symmetric trade costs.

		OLS		BV-OLS-1		BV-OLS-2		AvW		Suggested Model	
Estimates (1)	True (2)	Uncorr. (3)	Corr. (4)	Uncorr. (5)	Corr. (6)	Uncorr. (7)	Corr. (8)	Uncorr. (9)	Corr. (10)	Uncorr. (11)	Corr. (12)
					10-country-world, $\sigma = 10$						
$\rho(1-\sigma)$											
mean	−18	−18.0739	−17.4395	−18.1151	−18.0950	−16.4232	−16.3901	−18.0302	−17.3963	−18.1151	−18.0950
std.	—	1.0715	1.1069	0.7788	0.7756	2.6003	2.5866	0.8402	0.7863	0.7788	0.7756
MAE	—	4.7878	5.4869	3.4823	3.4579	13.1853	13.1519	3.7112	4.4491	3.4823	3.4579
σ											
mean	10	—	—	—	—	—	—	—	—	10.0318	10.0207
std.	—	—	—	—	—	—	—	—	—	0.5865	0.5889
MAE	—	—	—	—	—	—	—	—	—	4.1089	4.0843

(Continued)

Table A2a: (*Continued*)

		OLS		BV-OLS-1		BV-OLS-2		AvW		Suggested Model	
Estimates (1)	True (2)	Uncorr. (3)	Corr. (4)	Uncorr. (5)	Corr. (6)	Uncorr. (7)	Corr. (8)	Uncorr. (9)	Corr. (10)	Uncorr. (11)	Corr. (12)
20-country-world, $\sigma = 10$											
$\rho(1-\sigma)$											
mean	−18	−17.6570	−17.0613	−18.0253	−18.0327	−15.6098	−15.5545	−18.0037	−17.5787	−18.0253	−18.0327
std.	—	0.6485	0.6821	0.3721	0.3759	2.1116	2.0400	0.4886	0.5454	0.3721	0.3759
MAE	—	3.3918	5.6584	1.6554	1.6777	14.1517	13.9282	2.1710	3.1475	1.6554	1.6777
σ											
mean	10	—	—	—	—	—	—	—	—	10.0001	9.9912
std.	—	—	—	—	—	—	—	—	—	0.7965	0.7933
MAE	—	—	—	—	—	—	—	—	—	4.3285	4.3509
40-country-world, $\sigma = 10$											
$\rho(1-\sigma)$											
mean	−18	−17.5999	−17.2310	−18.0035	−18.0024	−15.4103	−15.4223	−17.7132	−17.4493	−18.0035	−18.0024
std.	—	0.3311	0.3615	0.1831	0.1838	0.8177	0.8364	0.3260	0.3568	0.1831	0.1838
MAE	—	2.3740	4.2745	0.8119	0.8141	14.3872	14.3203	1.9529	3.1321	0.8119	0.8141
σ											
mean	10	—	—	—	—	—	—	—	—	9.9974	10.0029
std.	—	—	—	—	—	—	—	—	—	1.0969	1.0989
MAE	—	—	—	—	—	—	—	—	—	5.5566	5.5380

Notes: The mean absolute error (MAE) is expressed as a percent of the true value.

Table A2b: Monte Carlo results for predicted trade flow and welfare changes in the case of a $\sigma = 10$ and symmetric trade costs.

		OLS		BV-OLS-1		BV-OLS-2		AvW		Suggested Model	
Estimates (1)	True (2)	Uncorr. (3)	Corr. (4)	Uncorr. (5)	Corr. (6)	Uncorr. (7)	Corr. (8)	Uncorr. (9)	Corr. (10)	Uncorr. (11)	Corr. (12)
10-country-world, $\sigma = 10$											
$\Delta \frac{X_{ij} Y_W}{Y_i Y_j}$											
mean	123.3248	129.9514	116.2394	91.1245	90.9670	227.5535	233.1863	125.6036	113.0115	127.7351	127.5996
std.	469.3185	521.3890	453.9210	293.4474	293.1617	1128.8546	1204.7017	485.1469	432.9379	494.9210	495.4916
MAE	—	92.7117	85.5440	74.4546	74.4805	214.5082	219.7298	15.3387	16.9658	17.5295	17.4202
EV_i											
mean	0.1390	—	—	—	—	—	—	0.9072	0.9780	0.1034	0.1056
std.	7.0641	—	—	—	—	—	—	15.5048	15.6467	7.0674	7.0776
MAE	—	—	—	—	—	—	—	5.4158	5.6047	0.3054	0.3043

(*Continued*)

Table A2b: (*Continued*)

		OLS		BV-OLS-1		BV-OLS-2		AvW		Suggested Model	
Estimates (1)	True (2)	Uncorr. (3)	Corr. (4)	Uncorr. (5)	Corr. (6)	Uncorr. (7)	Corr. (8)	Uncorr. (9)	Corr. (10)	Uncorr. (11)	Corr. (12)
						20-country-world, $\sigma = 10$					
$\Delta \frac{X_{ij} Y_W}{Y_i Y_j}$											
mean	137.9529	139.7465	125.7076	129.4379	129.5752	136.3740	133.9121	139.2621	129.7217	139.7014	139.9970
std.	509.0532	536.1079	474.6907	471.1198	471.2312	531.6067	509.3490	516.0786	476.7905	516.9189	517.5073
MAE	—	79.3370	76.5853	80.4346	80.4387	116.1598	114.3426	10.0604	13.7876	11.2513	11.3483
EV_i											
mean	0.5568	—	—	—	—	—	—	1.6953	1.6870	0.5251	0.5120
std.	6.5455	—	—	—	—	—	—	14.3039	14.3381	7.0969	6.6141
MAE	—	—	—	—	—	—	—	5.5801	5.6378	0.2931	0.2868
						40-country-world, $\sigma = 10$					
$\Delta \frac{X_{ij} Y_W}{Y_i Y_j}$											
mean	192.7730	160.0134	149.9590	154.7657	154.7352	177.6109	177.6029	185.2525	177.1900	196.6792	196.5124
std.	714.2798	574.2420	532.3568	574.5780	574.4365	787.0798	792.4892	686.9376	652.4061	736.2606	735.6959
MAE	—	111.2852	111.3648	112.1997	112.2014	146.8040	146.9326	11.3912	17.6107	19.2990	19.1996
EV_i											
mean	0.2995	—	—	—	—	—	—	1.2536	1.2613	0.1826	0.1867
std.	7.4031	—	—	—	—	—	—	16.2158	16.1786	7.6870	7.6855
MAE	—	—	—	—	—	—	—	6.5144	6.5101	0.5404	0.5367

Notes: The mean absolute error (MAE) is expressed in percentage points of the true value (as scaled trade flows and EVs are in percentage points already).

PART 2

Determinants of Economic Integration Agreements

Chapter 7

Economic determinants of free trade agreements

Scott L. Baier[a,b], Jeffrey H. Bergstrand[c,*]

[a] *John E. Walker Department of Economics, Clemson University, Clemson, SC 29634, USA*
[b] *Research Department, Federal Reserve Bank of Atlanta, Atlanta, GA 30309, USA*
[c] *Department of Finance and Business Economics, Mendoza College of Business, Kellogg Institute for International Studies, University of Notre Dame, Notre Dame, IN 46556, USA*

Received 29 June 2001; received in revised form 27 June 2002; accepted 4 December 2002

Abstract

The purpose of this study is to provide the first systematic empirical analysis of the economic determinants of the formation of free trade agreements (FTAs) and of the likelihood of FTAs between pairs of countries using a qualitative choice model. We develop this econometric model based upon a general equilibrium model of world trade with two factors of production, two monopolistically-competitive product markets, and explicit intercontinental and intracontinental transportation costs among multiple countries on multiple continents. The empirical model correctly predicts, based solely upon economic characteristics, 85% of the 286 FTAs existing in 1996 among 1431 pairs of countries and 97% of the remaining 1145 pairs with no FTAs.

Keywords: Free trade agreements; International trade; Qualitative choice models

JEL classification: F11; F12; F15

1. Introduction

> Free trade areas may well be an endogenous variable—that is, a response to, rather than a source of, large trade flows.... Presumably, (governments) are more likely to form free trade areas, (if) the benefits outweigh the costs. (Lawrence, 1998, p. 59)

Ever since Viner (1950), international economists have debated whether or not free trade agreements (FTAs)—on net—enhance or reduce economic agents' welfare. While

* Corresponding author. Tel.: +1-574-631-6761; fax: +1-574-631-5255.
E-mail address: bergstrand.1@nd.edu (J.H. Bergstrand).

*Originally Published in *Journal of International Economics*, 64(2004), pp. 29–63.

most of the literature has focused on theoretical welfare gains or losses from FTAs for member (and nonmember) countries, there is no study in the literature that has tried to explain—or predict—FTAs between pairs of countries. As the quote above notes, FTAs may well be an endogenous variable. Lawrence's remark should come as no surprise to trade economists as there is a large literature in international economics on endogenous trade policy. While a large literature exists explaining empirically tariff and nontariff barriers cross-sectionally, no study has analyzed econometrically cross-sectional determinants of FTAs—much less one based upon a formal economic model.

The goal of this paper is to determine key economic factors influencing the likelihood of pairs of countries forming an FTA in a given year, based upon a qualitative choice methodology. We hope to provide an empirical benchmark for the determinants of FTAs, upon which strategic and political factors can be embedded subsequently. Qualitative choice models were designed to provide economists with the ability to evaluate decision behavior when choices are discrete (e.g. voting 'yes' or 'no') and characteristics of the population are unobservable (e.g. utility gain or loss from a policy decision). The decision to form an FTA is essentially a binary choice by a pair of countries' governments since, according to the GATT's Article XXIV, only complete (no partial) FTAs can be formed between a pair of countries. Qualitative choice models provide a framework to estimate the probability that a pair of governments are making a decision as if maximizing their respective agents' utilities.

What economic factors should influence the likelihood of an FTA? In his seminal survey of the theory of customs unions, Lipsey (1960) stated: "If one wishes to predict the welfare effects of a customs union it is necessary to predict the relative strengths of the forces causing trade creation and trade diversion (p. 498)". For the impatient reader, we find that trade-creating and trade-diverting economic characteristics matter considerably in explaining the probability of an FTA. Pairs of countries with FTAs tend to have the particular economic characteristics that the theory suggests should enhance the two countries' net trade creation and welfare (though possibly reducing nonmembers' net welfare). We find strong evidence that pairs of countries' governments tend to form FTAs: (i) the closer are two countries in distance; (ii) the more remote a pair of continental trading partners is from the rest of the world (ROW); (iii) the larger and more similar in economic size are two trading partners; (iv) the greater the difference of capital–labor ratios between two partners; and (v) the smaller the difference of the members' capital–labor ratios with respect to the ROW's capital–labor ratio. In the case of our framework, these 'pure economic' characteristics can predict accurately 85% of the 286 FTAs existing among 1431 country pairs in 1996 for which data were available and 97% of the remaining 1145 country pairs with no FTAs.

The remainder of the paper is as follows. Section 2 motivates the analysis. Section 3 presents the theoretical model. Section 4 discusses the econometric methodology and data requirements. Section 5 discusses simulations demonstrating theoretical relationships between the utility changes from an FTA and intercontinental and intracontinental transport costs, countries' real GDPs, and relative factor endowments, and presents empirical results on 'testable' hypotheses. Section 6 presents an evaluation of the robustness of the empirical results. Section 7 presents estimates of quantitative effects of typical changes in various economic characteristics on probabilities of FTAs. Section 8 interprets the results. Section 9 concludes.

2. Motivation and related literature

> The pure economic theory of trading blocs is essentially part of the broader theory of preferential trading arrangements. This theory... is a subject of inherent complexity and ambiguity; theory per se identifies the main forces at work, but offers few presumptions about what is likely to happen in practice. To make any headway, one must either get into detailed empirical work, or make strategic simplifications and stylizations that one hopes do not lead one too far astray. Obviously *detailed empirical work is the right direction...* (Krugman, 1993, p. 60; italics added)

Krugman (1991b) delineated sharply for the 1990s the debate on the relative merits of regional FTAs. In that paper, he appropriately separated discussions of the (pure) 'economics of trading blocs' and the 'political economy of FTAs'. In the 1990s, the debate about regional FTAs has subsequently followed these tracks. The 'economics' of trading blocs literature addresses FTAs in a competitive framework, either perfect or monopolistic competition. Baldwin and Venables (1995) discuss the economics of FTAs in terms of competitive frameworks[1]. Rodrik's (1995) survey addresses political economy frameworks. We discuss each approach in turn, with our focus on the former.

In addressing the economics of FTAs, Krugman (1991a,b) addressed the relative merits of FTAs in a static monopolistically-competitive framework, but emphasized economic geography. With zero intercontinental transport costs, continental FTAs decrease welfare unambiguously. With prohibitive intercontinental transport costs, such agreements increase welfare unambiguously. Krugman (1991b) concluded that, because most FTAs are among 'natural' trading partners, the likelihood of much trade diversion was small and "prospective moves toward regional free trade would almost surely do more good than harm to the members of the free trade areas" (p. 21). However, in a subsequent commentary, Bergsten (1991) noted: "This is an empirical question on which Krugman offers little supportive evidence" (p. 48). Our paper is concerned with providing supportive evidence.

The Krugman work led Frankel (1997), Frankel et al. (1995, 1996, 1998) to investigate the continuum between zero and prohibitive intercontinental transport costs. First, for high intercontinental transport costs, FTAs between countries geographically close—that is, continental or natural FTAs—are welfare enhancing on net and should lead social planners in these countries to adopt FTAs, because large intracontinental trade creation would

[1] The static effects are the net gains to a country's representative household from an FTA due to changes in trade volumes, trade distortion costs, or terms of trade that would arise in a perfectly competitive framework (with constant returns). These potential gains would be supplemented in the monopolistically competitive framework with scale and variety effects. The potential dynamic gains arise once factor accumulation is allowed, leading to potential investment creation and diversion.

dominate small intercontinental trade diversion. However, as intercontinental transport costs fall, continental FTAs may become welfare decreasing. Second, for any level of intercontinental transport costs, FTAs between countries geographically distant or on separate continents—that is, unnatural FTAs—are welfare decreasing and should lead countries' social planners to avoid FTAs, as the welfare loss from intracontinental trade diversion exceeds the welfare gain from intercontinental trade creation.

In the context of a qualitative choice framework with social planners, the FSW analysis suggests two hypotheses. First, all else constant, the more remote from the ROW are continental trading partners, the more likely an FTA will be formed due to less potential trade diversion. Second, the more natural (i.e. closer in distance) are two trading partners, the more likely an FTA will be formed by the countries' governments due to more potential trade creation. Consequently, the FSW model suggests two economic factors that could predict FTAs.

However, the Krugman and FSW theoretical results were generated in a model with identical economies, one industry and zero intracontinental transport costs. In reality, the world is not so generous as to make countries identical in terms of economic size or relative factor endowments, nor are intracontinental transport costs zero. As even noted in comments on Frankel et al. (1998) by Krugman (1998), the restriction of identical economic sizes may not be innocuous:

> My second, more analytical, concern is with the way Frankel, Stein, and Wei map the theoretical model onto the real world... there is a crucial assumption in the model that is not nearly true of the real world: that countries themselves are of equal economic size. In reality, of course, the size distribution of GDPs is highly unequal, and this surely makes a major difference when we try to model the effects of integration. (p. 115)

See Srinivasan (1998) and Panagariya (2000) for more on the problems raised by the symmetry assumption.

Second, the models in Krugman and FSW assume a world with one factor and one industry. As noted in Deardorff and Stern (1994) and Haveman (1996), such a model precludes trade in traditional comparative advantages, such as Heckscher–Ohlin trade. By eliminating traditional comparative advantages, the model may be relying too heavily on imperfect substitution among products that 'stacks the cards' against bilateralism.

Third, the Krugman and FSW models assume intra-continental transport costs are zero. Just as FSW noted Krugman's conclusions are sensitive to intercontinental transport costs, Nitsch (1996) challenged the FSW work by noting that the results are sensitive to intracontinental transport costs. Nitsch argued that introducing an intra-continental transport cost may cause the FSW phenomenon of 'supernatural' FTAs to disappear[2]. In FSW, the assumption of zero intracontinental transport costs is not innocuous; the trade diversion effect on welfare of a continental FTA is enhanced with zero intracontinental transport costs.

[2] In Frankel et al. (1995), the term 'supernatural FTA' refers to a continental FTA that is welfare-reducing on net due to low intercontinental transport costs.

Our paper generalizes the Krugman–FSW model to allow for economies with different absolute and relative factor endowments, and intra- as well as inter-continental transport costs. In our framework, governments are assumed to maximize their citizens' economic welfare. The net welfare gain or loss of two countries from forming an FTA depends on the trade creation versus trade diversion of the members. Economic determinants of trade creation and diversion can be categorized into three groups. The first is economic geography factors. Trade creation is greater the closer are two countries, and trade diversion is less the more remote two (continental) trading partners are from the ROW. The second category is intra-industry trade determinants. Trade creation is greater the larger and more similar are two countries' economic sizes, and trade diversion is less the smaller is the economic size of the ROW. The third category is inter-industry trade determinants. Trade creation is greater the wider are relative factor endowments between two countries, and trade diversion is less the smaller the difference between the relative factor endowments of the pair and that of the ROW. We find empirical support for all three groups of characteristics in predicting FTAs.

We now discuss briefly issues that we do not address to make our analysis tractable and to limit the paper's scope and length. First, as noted, the alternative track to the 'pure economics' of FTAs is the literature on the 'political economy' of FTAs. The latter literature is concerned largely with explaining theoretically the level of trade liberalization in general, or an FTA in particular, based on the relevant economic actors in an imperfect market structure with little competition. In the absence of special interest lobbies or distributional preferences, a government would act as a social planner, maximizing welfare of the country's agent.

As this paper is the first attempt to explain empirically the determinants of FTAs, we choose here to assume a social planner for each country that maximizes consumer welfare. While political lobbies and government distributional preferences may well influence FTA decisions, we intentionally ignore these factors initially to limit the scope and enhance the tractability of our analysis[3]. We find empirical support for our approach in Goldberg and Maggi (1999) which found "the weight of (consumer economic) welfare in the government's objective function is many times larger than the weight of (political) contributions" (p. 1135; italics added). Specifically, they estimated the weight of consumer welfare (political contributions) in government trade policy decisions to be 98% (2%)[4]. Our empirical investigation of select economic determinants of FTAs, based upon a model with monopolistically competitive firms and a social planner maximizing consumer welfare, consequently complements the political economy literature on empirical determinants of trade protection. Our paper intends to develop an empirical 'benchmark' for economic factors, hoping future research will address empirically political economy factors.

Second, we assume that the decision for a pair of countries' governments to form an FTA is based upon the welfare of only representative agents of the country pair, and ignore the possible net welfare loss to nonmember countries. We assume a social planner for each

[3] Moreover, we do not create any explicit coalition-formation structure in the model, as in Bond and Syropoulos (1996).

[4] Using a similar framework, Gawande and Bandyopadhyay (2000) estimated an even higher relative weight for consumer welfare versus contributions; their estimate ($a = 3175$) implies a welfare weight of 99%.

country, not for the world. In the (more restrictive) symmetric models of Krugman and FSW, inferences could be made about world welfare, and whether FTAs were good or bad for the world. We cannot attempt to address world welfare empirically; we restrict our analysis to the net welfare gain or loss of trade creation versus trade diversion for member countries. As in Baldwin and Venables (1995), tension between trade creation versus trade diversion makes the net welfare gain ambiguous for nonmember and member countries[5].

Third, we treat the decision to enter an FTA as a bilateral, rather than multilateral, one. While the decision of a country to form an FTA with the European Union (EU), for instance, may appear to be a multilateral one, every country in the EU has the ability to veto an FTA with a nonmember. In effect, every country in the EU decides bilaterally whether the net national welfare gain from an FTA with another country warrants formation[6].

Fourth, as we are interested in explaining empirically the cross-sectional variation in FTAs for a given year (1996), we assume that each country pair makes a decision in 1996 to form or not form an FTA, or to enforce or not enforce an FTA formed prior to 1996. This 'static' approach is in conformity with most cross-sectional 'gravity' analyses of bilateral trade flows where the presence or absence of an FTA is determined exogenously annually based upon government documentation. In theory, the presence or absence of an FTA in a given year depends only upon the economic characteristics in that year, similar to empirical cross-sectional endogenous trade-policy studies. Dynamic issues are important, but are outside the scope of the present paper and are left for future research.

3. The Model

In this section, we generalize the model in Frankel et al., (1995, 1996, 1998), Frankel (1997) to allow for asymmetries between countries and sectors, and intra- versus inter-continental transport costs. We use this theoretical model in Section 5 as the basis for a computable general equilibrium (CGE) model to illustrate the relationships between net utility gains (losses) from an FTA and relative transport costs, national outputs, and factor-endowment ratios. These relationships are employed to motivate the likely key empirical economic determinants of the probabilities of FTAs between pairs of countries.

International trade within each of two monopolistically-competitive sectors is generated by the interaction of consumers having tastes for diversity and production being characterized by economies of scale. Assume two factors of production, capital and labor, each perfectly mobile between sectors and each immobile internationally. We label the two sectors goods and services. Initially, these labels are arbitrary. Only much later will we differentiate the two sectors along conventional Balassa–Samuelson lines: goods (services) will be capital (labor) intensive in production and more (less) tradable. Within each

[5] As Baldwin and Venables (1995) note, "Perhaps the most important conclusion to be drawn is that—despite theoretical ambiguities—RIAs (regional integration agreements) seem to have generated welfare gains for the participants, with small, but possibly negative spillovers onto the rest of the world" (p. 1638).

[6] However, a bilateral decision does not imply a pair of countries ignores economic factors external to the pair. We address these considerations later.

S.L. Baier, J.H. Bergstrand / Journal of International Economics 64 (2004) 29–63 35

sector, taste for diversity is captured formally by Dixit–Stiglitz preferences. Increasing returns to scale internal to the firm are captured with fixed costs and linear cost functions.

To capture the effects of asymmetries on regionalism, we assume three continents (indexed by 1, 2, 3) with two countries on each continent (countries indexed by A and B). Each country is allowed potentially to have different absolute and relative factor endowments of capital and labor. The two sectors are allowed potentially to differ in terms of relative factor intensities, tastes for variety, and trade barriers (transportation costs and/or tariffs). While earlier CGE models address the relative welfare benefits of regionalism, they do not explore these effects with explicit intercontinental and intracontinental transport costs, emphasizing—in the spirit of the Krugman and FSW frameworks—world geography.

3.1. Consumers

Each country i has a representative consumer who derives utility from consuming goods and services (g and s, respectively), based upon Cobb–Douglas preferences. Within each sector, the consumer has a taste for diversity captured formally by Dixit–Stiglitz (CES) preferences. The representative consumer for each of the six countries (i = 1A, 1B, 2A, 2B, 3A, 3B) has a nested utility function:

$$U_i = [(\Sigma_{k=1}^{n_i^g} g_{iik}^{\theta^g} + \Sigma_{k=1}^{n_{i'}^g} g_{ii'k}^{\theta^g} + \Sigma_{j \neq i,i'} \Sigma_{k=1}^{n_{j \neq i,i'}^g} g_{ijk}^{\theta^g})^{1/\theta^g}]^{\gamma}[(\Sigma_{k=1}^{n_i^s} s_{iik}^{\theta^s} + \Sigma_{k=1}^{n_{i'}^s} s_{ii'k}^{\theta^s} + \Sigma_{j \neq i,i'} \Sigma_{k=1}^{n_{j \neq i,i'}^s} s_{ijk}^{\theta^s})^{1/\theta^s}]^{1-\gamma} \tag{1}$$

where U_i denotes the utility of the representative household in i. Let g_{iik} (s_{iik}) be consumption in country i of differentiated good (service) k produced in the home country (i), $g_{ii'k}(s_{ii'k})$ is consumption in country i of good (service) k produced in the foreign country on the same continent (i'), and g_{ijk} (s_{ijk}) is consumption in country i of good (service) k produced in each of the four foreign countries on other continents (j). Let θ^g (θ^s) denote the parameter determining the elasticity of substitution in consumption in goods (services) with $0<\theta^g, \theta^s<1$. Let γ $(1-\gamma)$ be the Cobb–Douglas preference parameter for goods (services). Finally, let n_i^g (n_i^s) be the number of varieties of goods (services) produced in the home country, $n_{i'}^g$ ($n_{i'}^s$) the number of varieties of goods (services) produced in the foreign country on the same continent, and n_j^g (n_j^s) the number of varieties of goods (services) produced by a foreign country on another continent.

Within any country, households and firms are assumed symmetric; with symmetry, subscript k can be eliminated. Consequently, the budget constraint for the representative consumer in country i is:

$$w_i + r_i\left(\frac{K_i}{L_i}\right) + T_i = n_i^g p_i^g g_{ii} + n_i^g p_{ii'}^g g_{ii'} + \sum_{j \neq i,i'} n_j^g p_{ij}^g g_{ij} + n_i^s p_i^s s_{ii} + n_{i'}^s p_{ii'}^s s_{ii} + \sum_{j \neq i,i'} n_j^s p_{ij}^s s_{ij} \tag{2}$$

where w_i is the wage rate of the representative consumer–worker (or household) in country i, r_i is the rental rate on capital per household, K_i/L_i is the amount of capital exogenously supplied (or endowed) per household, T_i is tariff revenue redistributed back to households in a lump sum, p_i^g (p_i^s) is the price of the good (service) produced in the home country, $p_{ii'}^g$ ($p_{ii'}^s$) is country i's c.i.f. price of the good (service) produced in the foreign country on the same continent, and p_{ij}^g (p_{ij}^s) is country i's c.i.f. price of the good (service) produced in a foreign country on another continent.

Following FSW, c.i.f. prices differ from home prices due to Samuelson-type 'iceberg' transportation costs and ad valorem tariffs. Let a (b) represent the fraction of output exported by a country that is 'consumed' (or lost) due to intra- (inter-) continental transport[7]. Let $t_{ii'}$ and t_{ij} denote the ad valorem tariff rates in country i (that can potentially differ by trading partner). In the presence of positive tariffs and transport costs, country i's price of the good (service) produced by the foreign country on the same continent, $p_{ii'}^g$ ($p_{ii'}^s$), is

$$p_{ii'}^g = p_{i'}^g \left[\frac{1}{(1-a^g)}\right] + p_{i'}^g t_{ii'}^g \tag{3}$$

$$p_{ii'}^s = p_{i'}^s \left[\frac{1}{(1-a^s)}\right] + p_{i'}^s t_{ii'}^s \tag{4}$$

Country i's price of the good (service) produced by a foreign country on a different continent, p_{ij}^g (p_{ij}^s), is:

$$p_{ij}^g = p_j^g \left\{\frac{1}{[(1-a^g)(1-b^g)]}\right\} + p_j^g t_{ij}^g \tag{5}$$

$$p_{ij}^s = p_j^s \left\{\frac{1}{[(1-a^s)(1-b^s)]}\right\} + p_j^s t_{ij}^s \tag{6}$$

Tariff rates and transport costs can differ across sectors[8]. For each country's consumer, maximizing Eq. (1) subject to Eqs. (2)–(6) yields a set of demand equations which, for brevity, are omitted here.

3.2. Firms

Each firm in the goods industry is assumed to produce output subject to the technology

$$g_i = z_i^g (k_i^g)^{\alpha g} (l_i^g)^{1-\alpha g} - \varphi^g \tag{7}$$

where g_i denotes output of the representative firm in this industry in country i, z_i^g is an exogenous productivity term for goods producers, k_i^g is the amount of capital used by this

[7]Note these transport costs are of the hub-and-spoke variety discussed in Frankel et al. (1995) where each continent represents a hub. For intercontinental shipments, costs are broken down into two components. The cost of transporting a good (service) from one hub to another is given by b^g (b^s) and the cost to distribute the good (service) to each spoke is a^g (a^s).

[8]Asymmetries in transport costs across pairs of countries is beyond the scope of the present model; thus, a change in a or b changes transport costs for all country pairs. Note that a and b both contribute to total "inter-continental" transport costs.

firm, l_i^g is the amount of labor used by this firm, and φ^g represents a fixed cost facing each firm (e.g. marketing costs absorbing both capital and labor), the latter assumed identical across countries for simplicity. Each firm in the services industry is assumed to have a similar technology:

$$s_i = z_i^s (k_i^s)^{\alpha s} (l_i^s)^{1-\alpha s} - \varphi^s \tag{8}$$

where s_i denotes output of the representative firm, z_i^s, k_i^s, l_i^s, and φ^s are defined analogously for services, and factor intensities α^g and α^s can differ.

Firms in each industry in each country maximize profits subject to the technology defined in Eqs. (7) and (8), given the demand schedules implied by Section 3.1 above. Equilibrium in these types of models is characterized by two conditions. First, profit maximization ensures that prices are a markup over marginal production costs:

$$p_i^g = (\theta^g)^{-1}\left[\left(\frac{C}{z_i^g}\right) r_i^{\alpha g} w_i^{1-\alpha g}\right] \tag{9}$$

$$p_i^s = (\theta^s)^{-1}\left[\left(\frac{D}{z_i^s}\right) r_i^{\alpha s} w_i^{1-\alpha s}\right] \tag{10}$$

where $C=(\alpha^g)^{-\alpha g}(1-\alpha^g)^{-(1-\alpha g)}$ and $D=(\alpha^s)^{-\alpha s}(1-\alpha_s)^{-(1-\alpha s)}$. Second, firms earn zero economic profits which implies:

$$g_i = \frac{\theta^g \varphi^g}{(1-\theta^g)} \tag{11}$$

$$s_i = \frac{\theta^s \varphi^s}{(1-\theta^s)} \tag{12}$$

Common to such models, output of the representative firm in each industry is determined parametrically.

3.3. Factor endowment constraints

As standard, we assume that endowments of capital (K_i) and labor (L_i) are exogenous, with both factors internationally immobile. Assuming full employment

$$K_i = K_i^g + K_i^s = n_i^g k_i^g + n_i^s k_i^s \tag{13}$$

$$L_i = L_i^g + L_i^s = n_i^g l_i^g + n_i^s l_i^s \tag{14}$$

3.4. Equilibrium

The number of firms and product varieties in each industry and country, factor employments and prices in each industry and country, consumptions of each good, and product prices can be determined uniquely given parameters of the model (γ, θ^g, θ^s, α^g, α^s,

φ^g, φ^s) and initial transport costs, tariffs, and factor endowments. All together, the model includes 204 equations in 204 endogenous variables; the remaining equations are described in a technical appendix available from the corresponding author on request.

3.5. The social planner

To enable comparison with FSW, we assume that the social planner in each country sets tariffs initially at 30%. The formation of an FTA eliminates tariffs between members, leaving the members' tariffs on nonmember countries' products at 30%[9]. If the changes in utility for two countries' agents from an FTA are positive, we assume each social planner would choose to enter an FTA with the other country's planner. Thus, for a bilateral FTA to be formed, it must be the case that the change in utility is positive for both countries' agents. If the change in utility is negative for either country, we assume an FTA is not formed.

4. Econometric issues and data

4.1. Econometric issues

The econometric framework we employ is the qualitative choice model of McFadden (1975, 1976). A qualitative choice model can be derived from an underlying latent variable model. For instance, let y^* denote an unobserved (or latent) variable, where for simplicity we ignore the observation subscript. As in Wooldridge (2000), let y^* in the present context represent the difference in utility levels from an action (the formation of an FTA), where

$$y* = \beta_0 + x\beta + e \tag{15}$$

where x is a vector of explanatory variables (i.e. economic characteristics), β is a vector of parameters, and error term e is assumed to be independent of x and to have a

[9] The calibration exercise later requires initial (or pre-integration) and post-integration tariffs. We use 0.30 as our initial tariffs and as our post-integration tariff rates on nonmember imports, similar to FSW. Frankel (1997, pp. 167–168) discusses the empirical rationale for using 0.30. The ideal approach would be to consider the Nash equilibrium tariffs; the Nash equilibrium tariffs in a post-integration situation are likely to differ from those in the pre-integration situation. Addressing this limitation, however, is beyond the scope of the present paper, especially due to the emphasis here on asymmetric economies with intra- and inter-continental transport costs; many papers solving for Nash equilibrium tariffs benefit from a symmetry assumption, such as Krugman (1991a). Bond and Syropoulos (1996) address how the Nash equilibrium tariffs change between pre- and post-integration situations; the authors show conditions under which the Nash equilibrium tariffs of FTA members with nonmembers may even fall. Bond and Syropoulos also show when the Krugman (1991a) approach is a limiting case; in the symmetric trading-blocs model in Krugman, the optimal tariff is $1/(\varepsilon - 1)$ where ε is the elasticity of demand for the country's exports, and this (in his model) is a function of the representative bloc's absolute economic size or number of blocs and the elasticity of substitution, $1/(1-\theta)$. Yi (2000) shows in a model with "taste-for-variety" preferences that an FTA could alter the Nash equilibrium tariffs of members with nonmembers downward to "balance" the varieties of imported goods. Ornelas (2001) shows that the Nash equilibrium tariffs of members with nonmembers may fall due to rent dissipation. See Bagwell and Staiger (1999) also for a detailed discussion of Nash equilibrium tariff structures in the presence of preferential and multilateral trade policies.

standard normal distribution. In the context of our model formally, $y^* = \min(\Delta U_i, \Delta U_j)$. Hence, both countries' consumers need to benefit from an FTA for their governments to form one.

Since y^* is unobservable, we define an indicator variable, FTA, which takes the value 1 if two countries have a FTA (indicating $y^*>0$), and 0 otherwise (indicating $y^* \leq 0$). The response probability, P, for FTA is

$$P(\text{FTA} = 1) = P(y* > 0) = G(\beta_0 + x\beta) \tag{16}$$

where $G(\cdot)$ is the standard normal cumulative distribution function, which ensures that $P(\text{FTA}=1)$ lies between 0 and 1. The standard errors of the estimates of β are asymptotically normally distributed and z-statistics reported in Section 5 will indicate whether estimates of β are statistically significant (see Wooldridge, 2000). While the statistical significance of the probit estimates can be determined, the coefficient estimates can only reveal the signs of the partial effects of changes in x on the probability of an FTA, due to the nonlinear nature of $G(\cdot)$. Letting $E(\cdot)$ denote the expectation of a variable, the direction of the effect of variable x_j on $E(y^*|x)=\beta_0+x\beta$ is only qualitatively (not quantitatively) identical to the effect of x_j on $E(\text{FTA}|x)=G(\beta_0+x\beta)$. We estimate directly the partial effects on the response probabilities in Section 7. In Section 8, we compare predicted FTAs to actual FTAs.

4.2. Data issues

Since Linnemann (1966), a plethora of trade studies have measured the presence or absence of an FTA between a pair of countries using a binary variable; see Frankel (1997, Ch. 4) for a survey. Following those studies, variable FTA_{ij} will have the value 1 for a pair of countries (i, j) with an FTA in 1996, and 0 otherwise. This variable was constructed for the pairings of 54 countries (hence, $(54 \times 53)/2$ or 1431 pairings) using appendices in Lawrence (1996) and Frankel (1997) and FTAs notified to the GATT/WTO under GATT Article XXIV or the Enabling Clause for developing economies as of May 2002 (WTO, 2002). We included only full (no partial) FTAs or customs unions.

In the Krugman and FSW models, the dichotomy between inter- and intra-continental transport costs was simply an abstraction to emphasize that two countries that are closer geographically will tend to have lower transport costs. The lower are transport costs between two countries (ignoring their distance from the ROW), the more each country can consume the other's varieties, enhancing trade creation regionally. As the primary factor influencing such costs is bilateral distance, this task amounted to calculating 1431 bilateral distances among 54 countries' economic centers. Similar to Bergstrand (1985, 1989), distances were calculated in nautical miles using US Department of the Navy Oceanographic Office (1965) for sea distances and Road Atlas of Europe (1988) for land distances (the latter multiplied by a standard factor of 2 for the transport-cost differential between land and sea transport). We used Linnemann (1966) for identifying countries' economic centers. NATURAL_{ij} (denoting natural trading partners) is the natural logarithm of the inverse of the distance between the economic centers of i and j.

While measuring closeness is straightforward, measuring the 'remoteness' of a pair of continental trading partners from the ROW is not. We constructed REMOTE as

$$\mathrm{REMOTE}_{ij} = \mathrm{DCONT}_{ij} \times \left\{ \frac{\left[\log\left(\sum_{k=1,k\neq j}^{N} \mathrm{Distance}_{ik}/N-1\right) + \log\left(\sum_{k=1,k\neq i}^{N} \mathrm{Distance}_{jk}/N-1\right)\right]}{2} \right\}$$

The interpretation of REMOTE is as follows. First, DCONT is a binary variable assuming the value 1 if both countries are on the same continent, and 0 otherwise. If two countries (i,j) are on the same continent, REMOTE measures the simple average of (the natural logarithms of) the mean distance of country i from all of its trading partners except j and the mean distance of country j from all of its trading partners except i. If two countries (i, j) are on different continents, REMOTE has the value 0. This measure captures the spirit of b for natural FTAs because it measures how far two countries on the same continent are from other countries, but it has no value for unnatural trading partners. As will be discussed in Section 5 below, for any given value of intracontinental transport costs, only the welfare gains from a continental FTA increase monotonically with increases in intercontinental transport costs (b) in our model.

Other economic variables were readily measurable. Data on real GDPs and per worker physical capital stocks (all in international dollars) are from Baier et al. (2000), assembled from primary data in Mitchell (1992, 1993, 1995); availability of capital stock data determined the sample of countries[10]. Data on tariff rates for countries are from World Bank (2000). Despite the cross-sectional nature of the decision, an issue of potential endogeneity arises. In the context of our theoretical model, the decision between two countries to have an FTA or not in 1996 depends upon economic characteristics in 1996. However, income and factor endowments vary over time and have likely been influenced by trade liberalization. For many pairs, an FTA between two countries in 1996 was formed well before 1996, the earliest (the original six-member EEC) phased in over 10 years beginning in 1958. Since an FTA formed several years prior to 1996 likely influenced subsequent trade—which then influenced economic growth—incomes and capital stocks in 1996 may well be endogenous. To account for this, we used the earliest data on incomes and capital and labor stocks in Baier et al. (2000) for a wide sample, namely, 1960 data.

5. Numerical analysis and empirical results

This section offers seven theoretical hypotheses about the relationships between the net gains from an FTA and various economic characteristics of country pairs, using a calibrated CGE model based upon the theoretical model in Section 3. Following each hypothesis (except

[10] The 54 countries include Algeria, Egypt, Nigeria, South Africa, Hong Kong, Iran, Iraq, Japan, Singapore, Austria, Belgium, Denmark, France, Germany (W. Germany in 1960), Greece, Ireland, Italy, Netherlands, Norway, Portugal, Spain, Sweden, Switzerland, Turkey, United Kingdom, Canada, Costa Rica, El Salvador, Guatemala, Honduras, Mexico, Nicaragua, Panama, United States, Argentina, Bolivia, Brazil, Chile, Colombia, Ecuador, Paraguay, Peru, Uruguay, Venezuela, Bulgaria, Czech Republic (Czechoslovakia in 1960), Hungary, Poland, Romania, South Korea, Philippines, Thailand, Indonesia, and Australia.

one), we evaluate empirically the relationship between the likelihood of an FTA and the various economic characteristics using the qualitative choice framework outlined in Section 4.

Hypothesis 1. The net gain from an FTA between two countries increases as the distance between them decreases.

One of the key implications from Krugman (1991b), Frankel et al. (1995, 1996, 1998) is that natural FTAs are unambiguously welfare superior to unnatural FTAs; hence, the two countries' social planners will form an FTA the smaller the distance between them. For a given distance between country pair and the ROW (other things equal), the closer are two countries, the lower their transport costs of international trade and consequently the higher is their trade volume. Elimination of the ad valorem tariff between close members alleviates the price distortion on a large amount of trade, improving utility of consumers more in continental FTAs[11].

As a benchmark, consider initially a special case of our model where countries and continents are identical in factor endowments ($K_i = L_i = 100$ for $i = 1A, \ldots, 3B$) and industries are identical, analogous to FSW's single-industry case[12]. Fig. 1 illustrates the relationship between intercontinental transport costs, intracontinental transport costs, and net benefits from either a natural FTA or an unnatural FTA. The top (bottom) surface is the net welfare gain from a natural (unnatural) FTA. Consistent with FSW, the welfare effects of a natural FTA exceed (or equal) those of an unnatural FTA for any levels of inter- and intra-continental transport costs. Frankel et al. (1995) Fig. 2 is a special case of our Fig. 1 evaluated at $a = 0$; this special case is shown in Fig. 1 by the plane relating 'Percent Change in Welfare' to 'Intercontinental T.C. Factor'. Thus, the FSW relationship is robust to varying intracontinental transport costs (a).

In the context of our qualitative choice framework and theoretical model, two countries will have a higher probability of an FTA if the welfare benefits outweigh the welfare costs. The first testable hypothesis is that the probability of an FTA is higher as the distance between the countries' economic centers falls. Specification (column) 1 in Table 1 shows that the first hypothesis is supported; the likelihood of an FTA is larger the more natural are two countries as trading partners.

Hypothesis 2. The net welfare gain from an FTA for two continental trading partners increases as their remoteness from the ROW increases.

A second important implication from the FSW model is that the net welfare gains from a continental FTA increase the greater are intercontinental transport costs (b) relative to intracontinental transport costs (a). As relative intercontinental transport costs increase, the volume of trade with remote countries (on other continents) decreases and that with near countries (on the same continent) increases. With less trade with remote countries, the

[11] We use "continental" and "natural" interchangeably, "intercontinental" and "unnatural" interchangeably.

[12] With perfect symmetry, tariff rates between sectors and countries (t_{ij}^g, t_{ij}^g, t_{ij}^s, t_{ij}^s) are identical, transport costs between continents (b^g, b^s) and countries on the same continent (a^g, a^s) are identical between sectors, factor intensities (α^g, α^s) are identical, CES preference parameters θ^g and θ^s are identical and equal to 0.75 as in FSW (implying elasticities of substitution in consumption in both sectors of four), and preferences for goods versus services are identical ($\gamma = 1 - \gamma = 1/2$). For simplicity, fixed costs in each sector (φ^g, φ^s) are unity, tariff rates are 0.30 initially in both sectors as in FSW (see [9]), and total factor productivity is normalized to unity ($z_i^g = z_i^s = 1$).

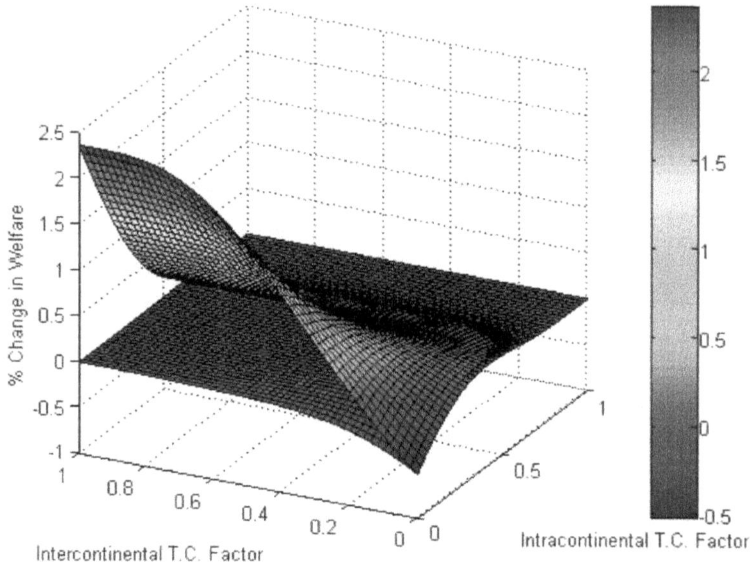

Fig. 1. Net welfare gains from natural and unnatural FTAs.

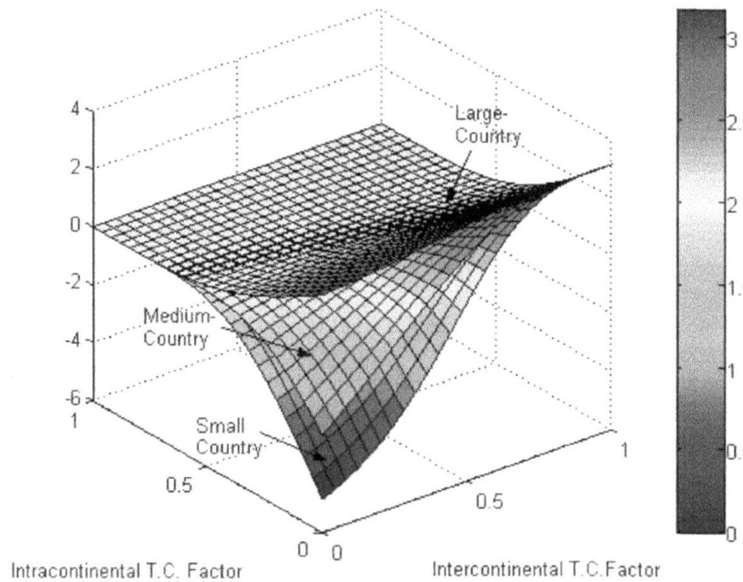

Fig. 2. Net welfare gains from natural FTAs and economic size.

Table 1
Probit results for the probability of an FTA

Variable:	Specification						
	1	2	3	4	5	6	7
Constant	13.42[a] (20.29)	9.76[a] (12.46)	4.31[a] (3.48)	3.49[a] (2.72)	4.22[a] (3.05)	4.22[a] (3.05)	7.90[a] (4.92)
NATURAL	1.74[a] (21.21)	1.36[a] (14.29)	1.49[a] (13.97)	1.52[a] (13.74)	1.64[a] (13.59)	1.65[a] (13.59)	1.76[a] (13.43)
REMOTE		0.15[a] (10.37)	0.15[a] (9.86)	0.16[a] (9.98)	0.17[a] (10.28)	0.17[a] (10.24)	0.18[a] (10.03)
RGDP			0.19[a] (5.33)	0.23[a] (5.94)	0.22[a] (5.28)	0.22[a] (5.27)	0.17[a] (3.67)
DRGDP				− 0.25[a] (-4.29)	− 0.27[a] (− 4.68)	− 0.28[a] (− 4.69)	− 0.34[a] (− 5.45)
DKL					0.43[a] (5.42)	0.49[b] (2.10)	0.85[a] (7.37)
SQDKL						− 0.02 (− 0.27)	
DROWKL							− 1.29[a] (− 5.53)
Pseudo R^2	0.571	0.647	0.668	0.683	0.704	0.704	0.728
Log likelihood	− 306.9	− 252.5	− 237.4	− 227.1	− 211.7	− 211.7	− 194.4
Number of observations	1431	1431	1431	1431	1431	1431	1431

[a] Denotes statistically significant z-statistic at 1% level in two-tailed test.
[b] Denotes statistically significant z-statistic at 5% level in two-tailed test.

relative tariff distortion with remote countries has less impact on utility; in Vinerian terms, there is less 'trade diversion'. With more trade with near countries, the elimination of the tariff distortion has greater utility gains.

The top surface in Fig. 1 reveals clearly for any level of a the monotonic relationship between greater intercontinental transport costs (b) and the larger net welfare benefits from a natural FTA. At $a=0$, the welfare effect of a regional FTA increases monotonically with b, and replicates (in the left-hand-side plane at $a=0$) FSW's Fig. 2 natural FTA line[13].

At higher values of a, the shape of this relationship remains monotonic, but 'flattens' considerably. The intuition is the following. First, suppose b is low. If a is zero, the utility loss of consumption of varieties intercontinentally (trade diversion) from a continental FTA exceeds the utility gain from more intracontinental trade (trade creation); with a equal to zero, there is no cost to transporting goods intracontinentally. However, at high levels of a, there is relatively little international trade, so there is relatively little welfare loss from increased relative discrimination against remote trading partners as well as little welfare gain from the continental FTA.

Next, suppose b is high. Even if a is zero, there is little intercontinental and much intracontinental trade, and hence little potential loss of trade volume intercontinentally (trade diversion) from a continental FTA. If a increases, intracontinental trade is dampened, decreasing the welfare gains from a continental FTA. Thus, the relationship between b and welfare from a continental FTA flattens as a increases[14].

The second testable hypothesis from the theory is that—for a given distance of two countries from one another—two continental trading partners will have a higher probability of forming an FTA the more remote the countries are from the ROW, measured by $REMOTE_{ij}$. Column 2 in Table 1 demonstrates that REMOTE is positively related to the probability of an FTA as expected and the coefficient estimate is statistically significant at the 1% level.

Hypothesis 3. The net welfare gain from an FTA between a pair of countries increases the larger are their economic sizes (i.e. average real GDPs).

We now introduce asymmetric sizes in terms of absolute factor endowments to determine scale-economies effects and address concerns raised earlier in Krugman (1998). We examine this in two exercises, first for natural trading partners and second for unnatural partners. In the first exercise, we allow countries on continent 1 (1A, 1B) to have larger absolute endowments of capital and labor than countries on continent 2 (2A, 2B), and 2A and 2B to have larger absolute endowments than countries on continent 3 (3A,

[13] FSW also showed that the net welfare loss from an unnatural FTA decreases unambiguously as intercontinental transport costs increase, possibly suggesting another testable hypothesis. However, in a world with asymmetric economies, this theoretical conclusion is not robust. We show, in the discussion below of Hypothesis 3, the ambiguous relationship between the net gains (losses) from an unnatural FTA and b.

[14] This result is in contrast to Nitsch (1996). Like Nitsch, we find that—for a given b—the welfare cost of a continental FTA decreases as a rises; however, FSW's "supernatural" region of welfare loss does not disappear. Only for higher values of a (such as 0.2–0.4) does the supernatural effect disappear. Moreover, Nitsch found that the entire two-dimensional line shifted up. We found this result counterintuitive. At high intercontinental transport costs, there is little intercontinental trade, and so a continental FTA generates large trade creation intracontinentally relative to little trade diversion intercontinentally. Thus, higher intracontinental transport costs should, on net, reduce the trade and welfare gains from a continental FTA as our figure confirms, counter to Nitsch's findings.

3B). Countries on the same continent have identical factor endowments. Moreover, for now relative factor endowments (capital–labor ratios) in every country are identical. Intuitively, the welfare gains from natural FTAs should be higher for countries with larger absolute factor endowments (and thus larger real GDPs). An FTA between two large partners (1A, 1B) increases the volume of trade in more varieties than an FTA between two small partners (3A, 3B), and reduces trade in fewer varieties from nonmembers than two small natural partners would, improving utility more in large countries relative to small countries. Second, the consequent larger increase in trade among two large economies causes a larger net expansion of demand and hence a larger rise in real income. Small countries 3A and 3B face considerable trade diversion when 1A and 1B form an FTA; the excess relative supply of factors in the small countries causes an erosion of terms of trade[15]. Fig. 2 illustrates that—for any values of a or b—the welfare gains from natural FTAs on all three continents are monotonically higher the larger the endowments of the countries.

Analogous reasoning applies to an unnatural FTA, the second exercise. Fig. 3 confirms the monotonic relationship—for any given values of a and b—between economic size and the welfare benefits of an unnatural FTA; net welfare gains (losses) increase (decrease) monotonically with economic size.

The third testable hypothesis is that the probability of an FTA is higher the larger economically are the trading partners, after accounting for distance and remoteness. $RGDP_{ij}$ measures the sum of the logs of real GDPs of countries i and j in 1960. Column 3 in Table 1 reveals that pairs of countries with larger average real GDPs have a higher probability of an FTA, in accordance with Hypothesis 3.

Figs. 2 and 3 also lend insight into the previous hypothesis about remoteness and FTA welfare gains. Fig. 2 illustrates also that—for a natural FTA—for a given economic size, net welfare gains (losses) increase (decrease) as remoteness (b) increases. However, Fig. 3 illustrates that such a monotonic relationship does not exist for unnatural FTAs. For $a = b = 0$, larger economies on net gain from an unnatural FTA due to trade in a larger number of varieties and favorable terms-of-trade effects. However, as b increases (relative to a) these relative benefits for the largest economies erode. By contrast, for smaller economies, the loss of consumption of varieties from discriminating against natural and other unnatural trading partners by introducing an FTA offsets the gain in trade with an unnatural partner, but the welfare losses of this distortion decrease as b rises[16]. In some

[15] This is a theoretical argument for the potential endogeneity of incomes in the subsequent empirical work. Simulations of real income confirm this.

[16] Note that the formation of an FTA is symmetric; each pair of countries on each continent is assumed to form an FTA, as in Krugman and FSW. However, in the empirical work that will follow, we are more interested in the likely effect of an increase in the economic size of a pair of countries on the formation of an FTA between that pair of countries (i.e. probit analysis). We find that the effect on net welfare of a single natural or unnatural FTA still increases monotonically with the countries' absolute factor endowment sizes; figures are not shown but are available on request. Welfare effects are qualitatively similar but quantitatively larger; with one pair of countries forming an FTA, there is less trade diversion. As this discussion suggests, the net welfare gains (losses) from an FTA are sensitive to what other bilateral decisions are being made. That is, the net welfare gain from an FTA between country 1A and 1B is sensitive to whether country 1A is considering one with (in a broader context) another country on the continent. While this issue important, it is beyond the scope of the present theoretical analysis which focuses on "bilateral" decisions, not multilateral ones; we leave this issue for future theoretical research. However, we do address this issue of bilateral decisions empirically in a limited fashion in the econometric analysis.

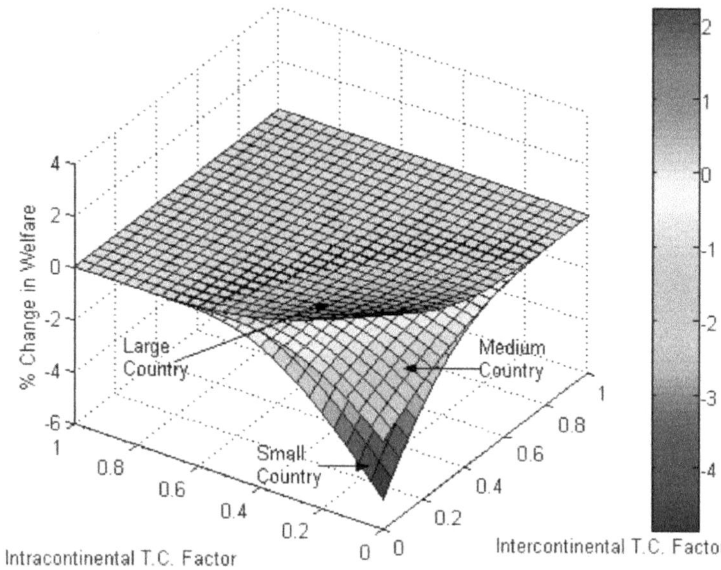

Fig. 3. Net welfare gains from unnatural FTAs and economic size.

cases, we can show the relationship between net welfare gains (losses) from an unnatural FTA and b is even quadratic.

Hypothesis 4. The net welfare gain from an FTA between a pair of countries increases the more similar are their economic sizes (i.e. real GDPs).

In this class of models, the more similar are the two countries' market sizes the larger the gains from an FTA. In the context of the first exercise, suppose 1A and 1B have identical shares of the two countries' factor endowments. The formation of a natural FTA provides gains from an increase in the volume of trade as the tariff distortion is eliminated on much continental trade. By contrast, if 1A has virtually all of the capital and labor on continent 1, formation of an FTA provides little welfare increase since there is virtually no trade between 1A and 1B. Similar reasoning applies to unnatural FTAs.

Fig. 4 illustrates the relationship between disparity in country sizes and the welfare benefits from a natural FTA for any given values of a and b (here, assuming $a = 0$). As disparity increases, the loss of trade vis-a-vis the ROW for the larger country rises relative to its diminishing trade being created with a smaller and smaller FTA partner. Since one of the countries' net welfare declines with size disparity, the likelihood of an FTA decreases with disparity.

The fourth testable hypothesis is that the probability of an FTA is higher the more similar economically are the trading partners. $DRGDP_{ij}$ measures the absolute value of the difference between the logs of real GDPs of countries i and j in 1960. Column 4 in Table 1

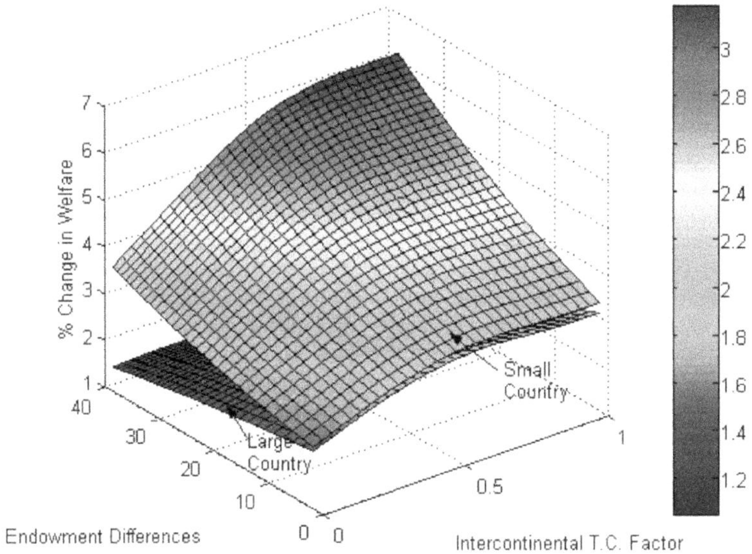

Fig. 4. Net welfare gains from a natural FTA for disparate economic sizes.

reveals that pairs of countries with smaller differences in real GDPs have a higher probability of an FTA.

Hypothesis 5. The net welfare gain from an FTA between a pair of countries decreases the larger is the economic size of countries outside the FTA (i.e. ROW real GDP).

The previous two hypotheses address the economic sizes of only those two countries. Surely the economic size of the ROW matters also. We can demonstrate (figure not shown) that the trade diversion from an FTA between a country pair is less the smaller the absolute factor endowment size of the ROW. As the ROW shrinks, the loss of consumption of varieties from the ROW due to an FTA is diminished. Moreover, the terms of trade effect is enhanced.

Unfortunately, the fifth hypothesis is difficult to evaluate empirically. In a cross-section of country pairs, the ROW's GDP does not vary much across the 1431 observations. Not surprisingly, the variance of this variable is trivial (coefficient of variation of 0.002) and consequently it was excluded.

Hypothesis 6. The net welfare gain from an FTA between a pair of countries increases with wider relative factor endowments, but might eventually decline due to increased specialization (if intercontinental transport costs are low).

At this point, asymmetries have been introduced between economies, but not between industries; a limitation of the Krugman–FSW model raised by Deardorff and Stern (1994) is the assumption of only one factor and one industry. As suggested in

Haveman (1998), the only paper in the literature that attempts to synthesize the complementary approaches of traditional Hecksher–Ohlin comparative advantage under perfect competition with the Krugman–FSW approach featuring imperfect competition to analyze the welfare benefits of regional FTAs in the presence of transport costs is Spilimbergo and Stein (1998). The limitation of Spilimbergo and Stein's two-factor two-industry extension is that each industry uses only one factor of production (capital in manufactures, labor in agriculture); in their framework, countries' factor endowments "differ only in their capital endowment" (p. 128). Consequently, differing capital–labor ratios only create differences in per capita income through scale-economies effects, not traditional comparative advantages. Changes in relative factor endowments cannot influence production shares and relative employment of capital and labor in sectors, since factors are immobile between sectors (an uncommon assumption to capture traditional Heckscher–Ohlin effects). Haveman (1998) notes that the Spilimbergo–Stein model "is really a world full of endowment economies" (p. 147). By contrast, our model allows endogenous adjustment of capital and labor between sectors (perfect factor mobility between sectors but not between countries) and endogenous determination of numbers of varieties of products in each industry. Our model can potentially separate differences between countries in per capita incomes due to scale-economies effects as well as specialization due to traditional comparative advantages; we allow also for differences in per capita incomes due to productivity differences.

Following most work, we assume 'goods' are capital-intensive and 'services' are labor-intensive in production in the spirit of the Balassa–Samuelson model, cf. Bergstrand (1991). As in Roland-Holst et al. (1994), we set $\alpha_g = 0.36$ and $\alpha_s = 0.27$ (capital shares in production). All other parameters for the two sectors are assumed identical. Starting with countries initially having identical capital and labor endowments, we increase the capital stock of country 1A to initiate a difference between the capital–labor ratios of 1A and 1B, but reduce 1A's productivity proportionately in both sectors (z^g, z^s) to hold 1A's real GDP fixed (to suppress scale-economies effects).

In traditional trade models (ignoring transport costs), the benefits of an FTA between a pair of countries should be enhanced the wider their relative factor endowments because traditional comparative advantages would be exploited more fully. Fig. 5 illustrates the relationship between differences in capital–labor endowment ratios and the net welfare benefits from a natural FTA for the capital-abundant country (1A). At high intercontinental transport costs, the relationship is positive and monotonic. At high values of b, there is little intercontinental trade. Consequently, most variety is exchanged intra-continentally. As relative factor endowments widen, both countries specialize more in the industries where they have comparative advantages and enjoy more net welfare gains from an FTA. There is little loss of variety (trade diversion) for 1A due to high intercontinental transport costs.

However, at low intercontinental transport costs, the net gains from an FTA increase at first with wider relative factor endowments, but eventually decline. At low values of b, there is considerable intercontinental trade in goods and services. As relative factor endowments widen, country 1A gains initially from specialization in goods. Yet, at high levels of specialization, 1A relies more on intra- and inter-continental trade to

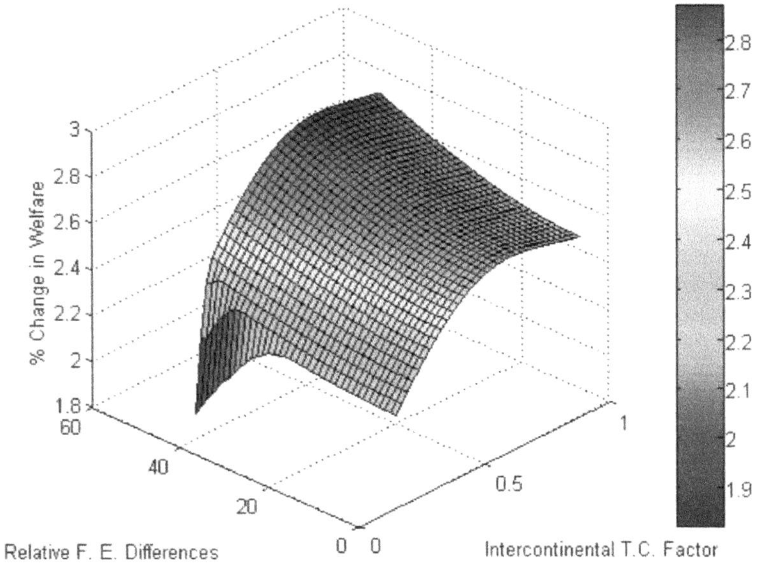

Fig. 5. A natural FTA and relative factor-endowment differences.

meet its demand for varieties of services. A natural FTA causes considerable trade diversion of services intercontinentally. With increasing specialization, the net welfare gains from inter-industry trade are eventually offset by the net trade diversion due to intra-industry trade. A qualitatively similar relationship holds for an unnatural FTA (figure not shown).

The sixth hypothesis is that the probability of an FTA is higher the larger the difference between two countries relative factor endowments, but possibly only up to a point. If intercontinental transport costs are not very low or relative factor endowment differences not high, the quadratic term may be unimportant. DKL_{ij} measures the absolute value of the difference between the logs of the capital–labor ratios of countries i and j in 1960; $SQDKL_{ij}$ measures the square of DKL. DKL should be positively related to $P(FTA=1)$ while SQDKL should be negatively related to it. Column 5 in Table 1 reveals that DKL has the expected positive effect. Larger relative factor endowment differences between country pairs have a positive and statistically significant relationship with the probability of an FTA.

Column 6 reveals that the variables have the expected quadratic relationship with $P(FTA=1)$, but the statistical significance of the coefficient estimate of DKL erodes and the coefficient estimate for the quadratic term—while having the expected negative sign—is statistically insignificant. The overall explanatory power from adding the quadratic term is negligible; the pseudo-R^2 of specification 6 is virtually identical to that of specification 5. Hence, for parsimony, we omitted the quadratic term in subsequent regressions.

Hypothesis 7. The net welfare gain from an FTA between a pair of countries decreases the larger is the difference between the relative factor endowment of the pair and that of the ROW.

The previous hypothesis concerns only trade between the country pair and the pair's capital–labor ratios. The loss in welfare from an FTA for the country pair will be higher the more Heckscher–Ohlin trade is foregone with the ROW (up to a point). We can demonstrate readily (figure not shown) that the loss of gains from specialization from an FTA between a country pair is less the smaller the difference between the pair's relative factor endowment size and that of the ROW.

The last testable hypothesis is that the probability of an FTA declines the wider is the (absolute) difference between the capital–labor ratios of the member countries and the ROW's capital–labor ratio, due to potential trade diversion. This variable—DROWKL_{ij}—is measured as

$$\text{DROWKL}_{ij} = \frac{\left\{\left|\log\left[\left(\sum_{k=1,k\neq j}^{N} K_k\right)/\left(\sum_{k=1,k\neq i}^{N} L_k\right)\right] - \log[K_i/L_i]\right| + \left|\log\left[\left(\sum_{k=1,k\neq j}^{N} K_k\right)/\left(\sum_{k=1,k\neq i}^{N} L_k\right)\right] - \log[K_j/L_j]\right|\right\}}{2}$$

Column 7 in Table 1 reveals that DROWKL has a negative relationship with the probability of an FTA and its coefficient estimate is statistically significant, likely due to the potential inter-industry trade diversion.

On net, the probit model works well. All six RHS variables in specification 7 have the expected sign and their coefficient estimates are statistically significant. Using the pseudo-R^2 term as a summary measure of explanatory power, specification 7 'explains' 73% of the variation of FTAs among 1431 country pairings in 1996. The pseudo-R^2 measure is the one discussed in Wooldridge (2000), one minus the ratio of the log-likelihood value for the estimated model to that for the model with only an intercept.

An alternative measure of goodness-of-fit for probit models is the 'percent correctly predicted,' also discussed in Wooldridge (2000). If the estimated probability of the pair exceeds 0.5, we define a variable *PredFTA* to be one; if the probability is less than 0.5, *PredFTA* takes on the value zero. The percentage of times that *PredFTA* matches FTA (which equals 1 if an FTA exists, and 0 otherwise) is an alternative measure of goodness-of-fit. However, Wooldridge notes that it is even more useful to report the percentage correctly predicted for each of the two possible outcomes, for the following reason. With 1431 country pairs and 286 FTAs, a probit specification of FTA on a constant only would result in predicted values of FTA of 0.2 for every observation (i.e. 286/1431). In this naive specification, however, *PredFTA* would still match FTA for 1145 of the 1431 cases, or 80% of the time. Even if the model failed to predict even one FTA correctly, this goodness-of-fit measure would suggest a predictive power of 80%.

Consequently, we report the percentage correctly predicted for each of the two possible outcomes. In our sample of 1431 pairs, 286 pairs have an FTA and 1145 pairs do not have an FTA. Using the rule described, 243 of the 286 FTAs are predicted correctly, or 84.97%. Also, 1114 of the 1145 pairs without an FTA are predicted correctly, or 97.29%. Thus, using alternative criteria the model appears to have a reasonably good fit.

6. Robustness of the empirical results

In this section, we evaluate the sensitivity of the results to several potential econometric issues.

6.1. Clustering and heteroskedasticity

First and foremost, the specifications assume that FTA_{ij} is independent across observations. In reality, a FTA between the United States and Mexico is not independent of such an agreement between the United States and Canada. Certain pairings of countries belong to a group or 'cluster'. The lack of independence of observations can influence the econometric results in several ways. First, it might influence the variance-covariance matrix of the econometric model. Akin to adjusting for heteroskedasticity, we re-estimated the specification in column 7 to adjust for possible interdependence of bilateral observations. This correction has an effect only on the standard errors, not the coefficient estimates. We assumed that pairs of countries within certain clusters (e.g. EU members) were interdependent, but clusters were independent. Clusters had three major categories: both countries belong to an FTA, one of the countries in a pair belongs to an FTA, or neither country belongs to one. We defined 99 clusters. Interdependence of observations within clusters had no significant effect on standard errors and thus was not a major concern. Hence, in the following empirical work, this adjustment was ignored[17].

6.2. Bloc size and bias

The fact that certain countries form a cluster might also introduce bias in coefficient estimates. For instance, Turkey may enter an FTA with the EU not to gain with respect to every member but to gain with respect to members on average. This possibility suggests that the results in specification 7 may be biased by the omission of a variable representing economic characteristics of the 'bloc,' such as the share of world GDP of the bloc's other members. We re-estimated the model adding two variables: the average share of world GDP of the other members of the trading bloc or blocs (if either or both of a country pair were in an FTA) and the absolute difference in these shares. The larger the relative economic size of the other members, the more likely an FTA existed between a country pair. The smaller the difference in these shares, the more likely an FTA existed. The variable representing the relative economic size of other trading bloc members had a positive and statistically significant coefficient estimate, as expected. Also, the variable representing the relative economic size difference had a negative and statistically significant coefficient estimate, as expected. The additional presence of these variables affected the other coefficients' quantitatively, but not qualitatively; the only RHS variable's coefficient estimate that became statistically insignificant—not surprisingly—

[17] We also re-estimated the model correcting for general heteroskedasticity; this had little effect on standard errors.

was the sum of the two countries' GDPs. In fact, the pseudo-R^2 rose from 0.73 to 0.80. The percent of FTAs (No FTAs) correctly predicted rose from 85 to 88% (97–98%).

Thus, the argument that multilateral, not bilateral, characteristics matter has merit; moreover, these empirical results are consistent with our theoretical model. However, we reserve caution about coefficient estimates from this specification due to potential endogeneity. If the econometric model is to 'explain' the likelihood of an FTA between a country pair using economic characteristics, it seems that a RHS variable constructed using a priori knowledge of bloc members (to determine the economic characteristics of the other bloc members) introduces an endogenous RHS variable. To err on the side of caution, we retained specification 7 in Table 1 as the primary specification for later analysis to preclude this potential endogeneity (with the other results available on request).

6.3. Sample bias

One might argue that the importance of bilateral distance and remoteness in explaining the likelihood of an FTA may well be driven by the presence of the EU and the size of the EU (in real GDP and number of countries). Moreover, as just discussed, countries that have obtained an FTA with the EU (say, Turkey) may be driven by the attractive market size of the entire EU, rather than by the economic size of individual EU member countries (say, Denmark). To address these issues, we re-estimated specification 7 for three subsamples of our entire 1431 observations. The results are qualitatively identical to those in Table 1 (not shown for brevity), and most of the coefficient estimates remain statistically significant at the 1% significance level. Similar results are obtained when the sample excludes any country pair that includes a Western European country or a European country. Thus, results for specification 7 are robust to the exclusion of Europe, the most geographically-clustered country group.

6.4. Tariffs of nonmembers

The net welfare gains (losses) from an FTA should be sensitive to the levels of tariffs among nonmembers. The higher are tariffs in the ROW, the larger will be the volume of trade created within the FTA. We can demonstrate readily (figure not shown) that the net welfare gains (losses) increase (decrease) with higher ROW tariffs. We evaluated the hypothesis that the probability of an FTA increases the higher are tariff levels in the ROW. However, variation in this variable was virtually negligible (coefficient of variation of 0.04) as with ROW's GDP for country pairs; inclusion of ROW's tariffs had an effect only on the intercept's value and statistical significance. The percentage correctly predicted of FTAs (and No FTAs) changed trivially. Hence, we also excluded ROW's tariffs in the remaining analysis.

6.5. Endogeneity of GDPs and capital stocks

As noted earlier, time-varying RHS economic variables were measured using 1960 data to ensure predetermined values; 1996 values of incomes and capital stocks would be potentially endogenous. We implemented the test for endogeneity of the 1996 values of income and capital stocks proposed by Rivers and Vuong (1988). The test for endogeneity is a Wald test. The test statistic is a chi-squared (χ^2) statistic with four restrictions; the critical value is 13.28 at the 1% level. The χ^2 statistic was 51.67. The null hypothesis of exogeneity of 1996 values of incomes and capital stocks was rejected. This is consistent with our theory that trade policy, by influencing terms of trade and other factors, influences income and capital investment. This is consistent with empirical evidence in Frankel and Romer (1999).

6.6. Omitted institutional and political-economy variables

Consistent with our assumption that FTAs are formed by governments maximizing consumer welfare, we have not yet introduced any 'political' variables. In the context of our theory, such variables' inclusion would be ad hoc. However, readers may be concerned that—despite the theory—some political, institutional, social, and cultural factors may be correlated with other RHS variables and with FTA, resulting in biased coefficient estimates of the economic determinants. An exhaustive examination of all such potential non-economic variables is clearly outside our scope.

Nevertheless, we considered several variables. We introduced three measures of 'institutional' characteristics that might affect the likelihood of an FTA: an index of the countries' average degrees of 'market orientation,' a dummy variable to reflect shared legal origins (i.e. British law, etc.), and a dummy for having a common language. Governments also pay attention to national security issues, the environment, and labor standards in deciding on the formation of an FTA. We included, respectively, the share of GDP of the countries in defense expenditures and the (absolute value of the) difference in their shares, the per capita level of CO_2 emissions in the countries and the difference in these values, and the (average) fraction of children in a country aged 10–14 in the country's labor force and the difference in these fractions. Of all these nine variables, only one variable was significant; per capita CO_2 emissions in a country pair had a negative and statistically significant relationship with the probability of an FTA.

As Trefler (1993) notes, common across many cross-industry endogenous tariff protection studies is the empirical result that protection tends to be higher in industries with greater import penetration. When the bilateral trade between the country pairs was the sole RHS variable in a probit regression, the coefficient estimate was positive and significant; however, the pseudo-R^2 (0.082) was considerably smaller than in any of Table 1's specifications. The addition of the level of trade between a country pair to specification 7—already holding constant the pair's economic size (and other economic determinants)—can be a crude proxy for import 'penetration'; the expected coefficient is negative. In this enhanced specification, the countries' bilateral trade in 1958–1960 had a negative relationship with the FTA probability, consistent with the endogenous protection literature. The coefficient estimate was -0.20 and was significant at 1% ($z = -2.96$). Yet, other coefficient estimates did not change materially.

Finally, Grossman and Helpman (1995) addressed the 'politics' of FTAs. In their theoretical political economy analysis, the formation of an FTA by two governments is more likely when there are substantial economic welfare gains for each country's average voter, similar to our model. Moreover, in their model with specific factors owned by a few concentrated firms, political pressure to prevent an FTA is reduced the more 'balanced' is potential trade between the partner countries, due to offsetting political pressures from exporters and importers. To try to capture the spirit of Grossman–Helpman's analysis, we also re-estimated specification 7 adding the absolute value of the difference in the logarithms of the two countries' average trade flows in 1958–1960. The result was that differences in trade volumes had a negative relationship with the probability of an FTA, but was statistically insignificant. However, with both trade variables included, only the bilateral trade level was significant (at the 1% level).

In sum, the inclusion of CO2 emissions, the level of trade, and the imbalance of trade had no perceptible impact on the coefficient estimates of main specification 7 (or their statistical significance). None of the estimated FTA predictions were altered materially; even with all three additional variables, the model predicted 238, rather than 243, of the existing FTAs, and 1115, rather than 1114, of the 'No FTAs'. This evidence is consistent with the Goldberg and Maggi (1999) result that consumers' welfare had predominant weight in US trade policy. In the interest of parsimony and to focus on 'pure economic' determinants, we ignored including these variables subsequently.

7. Partial effects of RHS variables on response probabilities

As discussed earlier, the probit estimates cannot reveal the quantitative effect of a change in any RHS variable on the probability of an FTA. Given the standard normal cumulative distribution function, G(·), the partial effect on the response probability of FTA (denoted p_{xj}) to a one standard deviation (S.D.) change in any variable x_j, $\hat{\sigma}_{xj}$, is

$$p_{xj} = G\left[\hat{\beta}_o + \sum_{i \neq j} \hat{\beta}_i \bar{x}_i + \hat{\beta}_j(\bar{x}_j \pm \hat{\sigma}_{xj})\right] - G\left[\hat{\beta}_o + \sum_{i \neq j} \hat{\beta}_i \bar{x}_i + \hat{\beta}_j \bar{x}_j\right]$$

where $\bar{x}_i$ denotes the mean level of x_i.

Note that p_{xj} is sensitive to the levels of the elements of x. This accords with our theoretical model. This issue is illustrated most transparently by reconsidering Fig. 1 in Section 5. The net welfare gain from an FTA from being natural rather than unnatural trading partners is sensitive to the level of intercontinental transport costs (b). Analogous nonlinearities arise in our generalization of the FSW model. For instance, we expect a one S.D. increase in economic size to have a larger effect on the probability of an FTA for natural partners than unnatural ones[18]. Similarly, the effects of an increase in economic size disparities, differences in capital–labor ratios, bilateral distance, and remoteness are

[18] Consider how the effect of an increase in economic size on the net welfare gain from FTAs is sensitive to whether the countries are natural or unnatural trading partners. Figs. 2 and 3 in Section 5 illustrate this. In Figs. 2 and 3, assuming $b = 0.10$ and $a = 0.05$, the net welfare gain from a natural or unnatural FTA for the medium-sized countries is negative. Suppose absolute factor endowments increase for each country pair (from 75 to 250). The percentage net welfare gain from an FTA from the increase in the factor endowment rises from −1.38 to 2.06%, or by 3.44%, for the natural pair. By contrast, the percentage net welfare gain from an FTA from increasing the factor endowment rises from −1.60 to 1.44%, or by only 3.04%, for the unnatural pair.

Table 2

Response probabilities to a one S.D. (σ) change in RHS variables for natural trading partners (evaluated at the mean level of remote)[a]

Variable	P(FTA = 1|natural partners) = 0.867	
	$-\sigma$	$+\sigma$
NATURAL	0.384 (0.302, 0.472)	0.994 (0.984, 0.998)
REMOTE	0.859 (0.804, 0.903)	0.873 (0.814, 0.911)
RGDP	0.780 (0.693, 0.850)	0.926 (0.873, 0.961)
DRGDP	0.938 (0.895, 0.966)	0.751 (0.663, 0.825)
DKL	0.663 (0.568, 0.749)	0.964 (0.930, 0.983)
DROWKL	0.952 (0.909, 0.977)	0.712 (0.615, 0.796)

[a] Values in parentheses denote the 95% confidence interval for the associated response probability estimate.

sensitive to levels of other variables. Following convention, mean values of the RHS variables are used for levels.

One complication arises in estimating the partial effects on the response probabilities for the particular vector of RHS variables, x, in our model by using mean values for the levels. One of the RHS variables, REMOTE, is the product of a continuous variable and a binary variable. Thus, the variable has the value of two countries' distance from the ROW when the pair share a continent, but 0 if not on the same continent. The mean value of this variable is economically meaningless. To account for this, we estimate the partial effects on the response probabilities for two scenarios, one with the mean value of NATURAL and the mean value of REMOTE when the two countries are on the same continent, and one with the mean value of NATURAL and 0 as the value of REMOTE when they are not.

Tables 2 and 3 present the response probabilities under these two alternative scenarios for a one S.D. change in each of the RHS variables along with (in parentheses) the 95% confidence interval associated with the respective response probability. Table 2 presents the response probabilities for continental trading partners. For ease of reference, we note that at the mean level of all RHS variables the probability of an FTA among natural partners is 0.867[19]. A one S.D. increase (decrease) in the closeness of such partners increases (decreases) this probability by 0.127 (0.483). The differential partial effect is due, of course, to the nonlinear functional relationships. Not surprisingly, a S.D. change in distance has an economically and statistically significant effect on the probability of an FTA among natural partners. A S.D. increase (decrease) in the remoteness of two natural partners from the ROW increases (decreases) the probability of an FTA by 0.006 (0.008).

Geographic proximity is not the only factor influencing the probability of an FTA. Changes in the level of or disparity between countries' real GDPs have economically and statistically significant impacts on P(FTA = 1). For instance, a S.D. increase in the level of real GDPs increases the response probability by 5.9% points, approximately half the effect of a S.D. increase in closeness. S.D. changes in the difference between real GDPs and the differences between capital–labor ratios all have economically and statistically significant impacts of approximately the same magnitudes as real GDP levels.

[19] For NATURAL and REMOTE, we used the means of the variables only for natural partners.

Table 3
Response probabilities to a one S.D. (σ) change in RHS variables for unnatural trading partners (evaluated at remote = 0)[a]

Variable	P(FTA = 1|unnatural partners) = 0.012	
	$-\sigma$	$+\sigma$
NATURAL	0.000014 (0.000001, 0.00010)	0.086 (0.057, 0.126)
RGDP	0.005 (0.002, 0.012)	0.028 (0.015, 0.050)
DRGDP	0.071 (0.045, 0.107)	0.010 (0.004, 0.022)
DKL	0.0009 (0.0002, 0.0033)	0.041 (0.023, 0.069)
DROWKL	0.013 (0.006, 0.028)	0.0007 (0.0002, 0.0024)

[a] Values in parentheses denote the 95% confidence interval for the associated response probability estimate.

Table 3 reports the response probabilities for unnatural country pairs. Not surprisingly, at the mean level of all RHS variables the probability of an unnatural FTA is about 1%[20]. A S.D. increase in closeness causes this probability to rise from 0.012 to 0.086, reinforcing the importance of economic geography in the likelihood of an FTA; this effect is statistically significant. Economic factors still manage a role in influencing the likelihood of an unnatural FTA. A S.D. rise in the level of real GDPs increases the response probability of an FTA by 1.6% points; this effect is economically and statistically significant. A S.D. decrease in the absolute difference between real GDPs of unnatural partners has a similar economically and statistically significant positive effect on the probability of an FTA (6% points). Increases in the differences between capital–labor ratios also have economically and statistically significant effects on P(FTA = 1).

Thus, the response probability estimates confirm that economic characteristics as well as geography have economically and statistically significant impacts on the probability of an FTA.

8. Interpreting the results

> If governments maximized the welfare of their citizens, prospective moves toward regional free trade would almost surely do more good than harm to the members of the free trade areas. (Krugman, 1991b, p. 21)

> This is an empirical question on which Krugman offers little supportive evidence. (Bergsten 1991, p. 48)

The original 'Krugman vs. Krugman' debate yielded unambiguous conclusions. In a world with symmetric economies and no transport costs, bilateralism was bad; in the same world with prohibitive intercontinental transport costs, bilateralism was good. FSW illustrated that the outcome depends upon the degree of intercontinental transport costs.

[20] For REMOTE we used zero, and for NATURAL we used the mean of the variable only for unnatural partners. Response probabilities are not reported for REMOTE in Table 3 since this has a value of zero here.

Drawing upon empirical data for intercontinental transport costs (external to the model), FSW concluded that regionalization may have become excessive.

In a world with asymmetric economies, we cannot make sweeping statements that bilateralism is 'good' or 'bad'. The focus of this paper has been on explaining and predicting FTAs bilaterally based upon pure economic characteristics (of member and nonmember countries). However, as Krugman's quote suggests, we can make limited statements about the net welfare gain or loss for the member countries.

In the context of McFadden's motivation of qualitative choice models, predicted probabilities of an FTA suggest whether particular pairs of countries should have an FTA based upon economic characteristics that—in the context of the theory—enhance welfare. If the predicted probability of an FTA for a country pair exceeds one-half, this suggests—in this framework—that there is a net welfare gain for the country pair. As the empirical results show, the probability of an FTA exceeded one-half for 243 of the 286 country pairs with FTAs, or 84.97%. The results suggest—in the model's context—that bilateralism is good for these pairs (though not necessarily for non-members).

Second, although 243 of the FTAs were predicted, 43 of the remaining 286 country pairs with FTAs were not predicted. In the context of the model, this suggests that 15% of the FTAs in our sample were welfare-reducing for the two countries. One might say, for these country pairs, bilateralism was 'excessive'.

Third, our qualitative choice model also allows us to identify for which country pairs bilateralism might be considered 'insufficient'. Bilateralism is termed 'insufficient' if an FTA is predicted but does not exist (yet). Of 1145 country pairs without an FTA, 1114 pairs were predicted correctly, or 97.29%. We note that 31 country pairs that had no FTA should have such an agreement (according to the model's predictions); these are shown in Table 4 along with each pair's predicted probability in parenthesis[21].

Table 5 shows the 43 cases where bilateralism was 'excessive,' that is, where an FTA existed in 1996 but the model's prediction probability was less than one-half. Five cases involve agreements between Algeria with EC members and ten cases involve agreements between Egypt and EC members; these agreements went into force in 1976 and 1977, respectively, although evidence suggests that Algeria's and Egypt's imports from the EC still face high tariffs. Eight cases involve Turkey with EC members; the EC-Turkey agreement was notified to the GATT/WTO in 1995, legally entered into force January 1996, and is still 'under examination'. Evidence suggests this agreement is effective[22]. Thus, although 15% of the FTAs in existence were not predicted, it is

[21] Of these 31 cases, 11 would become members of an FTA if the Free Trade Agreement of the Americas (FTAA) evolves into an FTA. Six cases involve members of the Asian Pacific Economic Cooperation (APEC) forum. While APEC is not considered an FTA, discussion has centered around members forming an FTA by 2020. Finally, seven cases involve Romania and Bulgaria, which became members of the Central European Free Trade Agreement (CEFTA) in 1997 and 1998, respectively. Thus, 24 of the 31 cases are pairs involved in potential (or, in the 2 years after 1996, actual) FTAs.

[22] We thank Francois Benaroya of the French Trade Ministry for information on Algeria, Egypt and Turkey.

Table 4
Cases of insufficient bilateralism

1	Panama–Venezuela (0.792)
2	Costa Rica–Ecuador (0.539)
3	Costa Rica–Venezuela (0.764)
4	Mexico–Honduras (0.556)
5	Mexico–Guatemala (0.863)
6	Mexico–El Salvador (0.756)
7	Mexico–Nicaragua (0.619)
8	Venezuela–Guatemala (0.604)
9	Venezuela–Brazil (0.645)
10	Peru–Chile (0.948)
11	Peru–Argentina (0.507)
12	Japan–South Korea (0.924)
13	Japan–Philippines (0.728)
14	Hong Kong–Singapore (0.646)
15	Hong Kong–South Korea (0.805)
16	Hong Kong–Philippines (0.716)
17	South Korea–Philippines (0.578)
18	Bulgaria–Czechoslovakia (0.763)
19	Bulgaria–Hungary (0.946)
20	Bulgaria–Poland (0.756)
21	Bulgaria–Romania (0.998)
22	Bulgaria–Turkey (0.514)
23	Romania–Poland (0.756)
24	Romania–Hungary (0.926)
25	Switzerland–Algeria (0.919)
26	Switzerland–Egypt (0.758)
27	Iraq–Turkey (0.711)
28	Iran–Iraq (0.988)
29	Iran–Indonesia (0.557)
30	Iran–Turkey (0.938)
31	Nigeria–South Africa (0.682)

important to note that 23 of the 43 cases of 'excessive' bilateralism can be explained solely by FTAs between the EC and Algeria, Egypt and Turkey.

We close this section addressing three points. First, with the literature on FTAs having been largely a theoretical one, empirical evaluation of FTAs has largely fallen into two camps: CGE models of trade and trade policy, and econometric analyses of the trade flow impacts of FTAs. Common to both approaches—and different from ours—is that FTAs are exogenous. CGE analyses generally focus on the trade creation and trade diversion impacts of an FTA, calculating the impacts in terms of a share of GDP. As is well known, however, CGE studies are essentially, as Baldwin and Venables (1995) note, 'theory with numbers'. Such analyses provide a quantitative articulation of what the underlying theoretical model suggests, but do not explain the formation of FTAs.

Econometric analyses of the impacts of FTA tend largely to explore the ex post effect of an FTA on trade flows, often using 'gravity equations,' such as in Bergstrand, (1985), Bergstrand (1989) and Frankel (1997). While these models have indicated successfully gross trade creation and diversion from an FTA, one still cannot make welfare statements. As with CGE models, gravity equations do not explain the endogenous

Table 5
Cases of excessive bilateralism

1	Algeria–Denmark (0.417)
2	Algeria–Germany (0.275)
3	Algeria–Ireland (0.465)
4	Algeria–Sweden (0.199)
5	Algeria–UK (0.321)
6	Egypt–Iraq (0.031)
7	Egypt–Belgium (0.356)
8	Egypt–Denmark (0.308)
9	Egypt–France (0.497)
10	Egypt–Germany (0.169)
11	Egypt–Ireland (0.164)
12	Egypt–Netherlands (0.364)
13	Egypt–Portugal (0.088)
14	Egypt–Spain (0.224)
15	Egypt–Sweden (0.178)
16	Egypt–UK (0.195)
17	Turkey–Norway (0.125)
18	Turkey–Belgium (0.379)
19	Turkey–Denmark (0.254)
20	Turkey–Germany (0.186)
21	Turkey–Netherlands (0.387)
22	Turkey–UK (0.214)
23	Turkey–Portugal (0.033)
24	Turkey–Spain (0.244)
25	Turkey–Sweden (0.226)
26	Portugal–Hungary (0.336)
27	Portugal–Bulgaria (0.481)
28	Portugal–Romania (0.384)
29	Chile–Mexico (0.022)
30	Chile–Brazil (0.174)
31	Chile–Paraguay (0.318)
32	Chile–Ecuador (0.468)
33	Bolivia–Brazil (0.097)
34	Bolivia–Ecuador (0.334)
35	Bolivia–Colombia (0.163)
36	Bolivia–Mexico (0.004)
37	Colombia–Nicaragua (0.147)
38	Colombia–Mexico (0.194)
39	Argentina–Venezuela (0.484)
40	Brazil–Paraguay (0.248)
41	Philippines–Singapore (0.412)
42	Philippines–Indonesia (0.400)
43	Thailand–Indonesia (0.105)

formation of FTAs. We see our approach as a complement to these alternative approaches in providing quantitative insight about FTAs.

Second, we note that our statements about whether bilateralism is excessive or insufficient abstract from the issue of bilateralism versus multilateralism. Given the model, when all countries are symmetric forming natural FTAs on all continents is welfare inferior to multilateral tariff liberalization. However, one can also show that (for certain transport costs) a natural FTA between a country pair may be welfare superior for that pair to their elimination of tariffs on imports from all countries, or even to world free trade. Our econometric analysis does not address this issue.

Third, we note Leamer's quote, "Give me data or give me death". Leamer (1998) noted that answers to questions such as the one in this paper should "be sought using four different methodologies: theory, calibration, indirect estimation, and direct observation" (p. 149). This paper has attempted intentionally to address the issue of bilateralism using all four methodologies. We have constructed a fairly parsimonious model of international trade with intra-industry trade as well as Heckscher–Ohlin trade in a setting with explicit transportation costs. Despite parsimony, the complexity of the model requires calibration to determine qualitative theoretical relationships. Turning to the qualitative choice framework, we apply observations on FTAs and economic characteristics of countries to determine the predictability of FTAs for particular pairs and to draw inferences about the net welfare gain or loss for these pairs. We find that country pairs that have bilateral FTAs tend to have those economic characteristics that should enhance economic welfare for the pair. Using direct observations, we find evidence that individual cases of 'excessive' bilateralism are constrained to a few plausible pairs of countries.

9. Conclusions

The main purpose of this study was to develop an econometric model that explains the 'pure economic' determinants of FTAs and that also predicts successfully the likelihood of pairs of countries forming FTAs. This is the first econometric model, to our knowledge, that predicts FTAs based upon an explicit general equilibrium model of world trade of multiple countries on multiple continents. It provides a economic benchmark for future political economy models to enhance the explanation of FTA determinants.

The main conclusions of the study are that the potential welfare gains and likelihood of a FTA between a pair of countries are higher: (i) the closer in distance are two trading partners; (ii) the more remote a natural pair is from the ROW; (iii) the larger and more similar economically (i.e. real GDPs) are two trading partners by exploiting economies of scale in the presence of differentiated products; (iv) the greater the difference in capital–labor endowment ratios between two countries due to the gains from traditional comparative advantages (i.e. Heckscher–Ohlin trade); and (v) the less is the difference in capital–labor endowment ratios of the member countries relative to that of the ROW due to less inter-industry trade diversion. These factors have economically and statistically significant effects on the probability of an FTA.

One measure of overall fit of a probit model is how well the model predicts correctly the outcome. Of the 1431 country pairs in our sample, 286 country pairs had an FTA and 1145 pairs did not have an FTA in 1996. We predicted correctly 243 of the 286 FTAs, or 84.97%. Also, 1114 of the 1145 pairs without an FTA are predicted correctly, or 97.29%.

Is bilateralism good? Unlike the restrictive symmetric models of Krugman and FSW, we cannot make any sweeping statement. While we predict 85% of FTAs in our sample in 1996, we find that 43 of the 286 FTAs in 1996 were not predicted, suggesting that 15% of the FTAs in that year were 'excessive' in a strict interpretation of the results. Yet, two important caveats are worth noting. First, of these 43 cases, 23 are agreements between the EC with Algeria, Egypt, and Turkey. Thus, half of the cases of excessive bilateralism are limited to three particular countries (and the Algeria and Egypt agreements may not even be effective). Second, we found 31 cases where agreements should exist (in the model's context) but none did, suggesting for these pairs bilateralism is insufficient.

Acknowledgements

We are grateful for helpful comments from two anonymous referees, Robert Staiger, Richard Baldwin, Francois Benaroya, Daniel Benjamin, William Dougan, Peter Egger, Antoni Estevadeordal, Robert Feenstra, Jeffrey Frankel, Mark Hallerberg, David Hummels, Chris Magee, Emanuel Ornelas, Mika Saito, Dieter Schumacher, Curtis Simon, Ernesto Stein, Ernesto Talvi, Robert Tamura, Jerry Thursby, Shang-Jin Wei, Eduardo Zambrano, and participants at presentations at the Austrian Institute of Economic Research (WIFO) in Vienna, German Institute for Economic Research (DIW) in Berlin, inaugural conference of the Regional Integration Network in Uruguay, second annual European Trade Study Group conference at the University of Glasgow, Midwest International Economics conference at the University of Minnesota, Clemson University, DePaul University, Indiana University, Purdue University, University of Notre Dame, and West Virginia University. Baier thanks the Center for International Trade at Clemson University and Bergstrand thanks the Mendoza College of Business and Kellogg Institute for International Studies at the University of Notre Dame for financial support.

References

Bagwell, K., Staiger, R., 1999. An economic theory of GATT. American Economic Review 89 (1), 215–248.

Baier, S.L., Dwyer, G., Tamura, R., 2000. The Growth and Development of Nations. Clemson University and Federal Reserve Bank of Atlanta, Manuscript.

Baldwin, R.E., Venables, A., 1995. Regional economic integration. In: Grossman, G.M., Rogoff, K. (Eds.). Handbook of International Economics, vol. 3. Elsevier, Amsterdam, pp. 1597–1644.

Bergsten, C.F., 1991. Comment on: Paul Krugman, the move toward free trade Zones. In: Policy Implications of Trade and Currency Zones, proceedings of a Federal Reserve Bank of Kansas City symposium, pp. 43–58.

Bergstrand, J.H., 1985. The Gravity equation in international trade: some microeconomic foundations and empirical evidence. Review of Economics and Statistics 67 (3), 474–481.

Bergstrand, J.H., 1989. The Generalized Gravity equation, monopolistic competition, and the factor-proportions theory in international trade. Review of Economics and Statistics 71 (1), 143–153.

Bergstrand, J.H., 1991. Structural determinants of real exchange rates and national price levels: some empirical evidence. American Economic Review 81 (1), 325–334.

Bond, E.W., Syropoulos, C., 1996. The size of trade blocs: market power and world welfare effects. Journal of International Economics 40 (3/4), 411–437.

Deardorff, A.V., Stern, R.M., 1994. Multilateral trade negotiations and preferential trading arrangements. In: Deardorff, A.V., Stern, R.M. (Eds.), Analytical and Negotiating Issues in the Global Trading System. University of Michigan Press, Ann Arbor, pp. 27–85.

Frankel, J.A., 1997. Regional Trading Blocs. Institute for International Economics, Washington, DC.

Frankel, J.A., Romer, D., 1999. Does trade cause growth? American Economic Review 89 (3), 379–399.

Frankel, J.A., Stein, E., Wei, S.-J., 1995. Trading Blocs and the Americas: the natural, the unnatural, and the super-natural. Journal of Development Economics 47 (1), 61–95.
Frankel, J.A., Stein, E., Wei, S.-J., 1996. Regional trading arrangements: natural or supernatural. American Economic Review 86 (2), 52–56.
Frankel, J.A., Stein, E., Wei, S.-J., 1998. Continental trading blocs: are they natural or supernatural. In: Frankel, J.A. (Ed.), The Regionalization of the World Economy. University of Chicago Press, Chicago, pp. 91–113.
Gawande, K., Bandyopadhyay, U., 2000. Is protection for sale? Evidence on the Grossman–Helpman theory of endogenous protection. Review of Economics and Statistics 82 (1), 139–152.
Goldberg, P.K., Maggi, G., 1999. Protection for sale: an empirical investigation. American Economic Review 89 (5), 1135–1155.
Grossman, G.M., Helpman, E., 1995. The politics of Free-Trade agreements. American Economic Review 85 (4), 667–690.
Haveman, J., 1996. Some welfare effects of sequential customs union formation. Canadian Journal of Economics 24 (4), 941–958.
Haveman, J., 1998. Comment on: Antonio Spilimbergo, Ernesto Stein, the welfare implications of trading blocs among countries with different endowments. In: Frankel, J.A. (Ed.), The Regionalization of the World Economy. University of Chicago Press, Chicago, pp. 145–149.
Krugman, P., 1991a. Is bilateralism bad. In: Helpman, E., Razin, A. (Eds.), International Trade and Trade Policy. MIT Press, Cambridge, pp. 9–23.
Krugman, P., 1991b. The Move Toward Free Trade Zones. In: Policy Implications of Trade and Currency Zones, proceedings of a Federal Reserve Bank of Kansas City symposium, pp. 7–41.
Krugman, P., 1993. Regionalism versus multilateralism: analytical notes. In: de Melo, J., Panagariya, A. (Eds.). New Dimensions in Regional Integration. Cambridge University Press, Cambridge, pp. 58–89.
Krugman, P., 1998. Comment on: Jeffrey A. Frankel, Ernesto Stein, Shang-Jin Wei, continental trading blocs: are they natural or supernatural? In: Frankel, J.A. (Ed.), The Regionalization of the World Economy. University of Chicago Press, Chicago, pp. 114–115.
Lawrence, R.Z., 1996. Regionalism, Multilateralism, and Deeper Integration. Brookings Institution, Washington, DC.
Lawrence, R.Z., 1998. Comment on: Barry Eichengreen, Douglas A. Irwin, the role of history in bilateral trade flows. In: Frankel, J.A. (Ed.), The Regionalization of the World Economy. University of Chicago Press, Chicago, pp. 57–59.
Leamer, E.E., 1998. Comment on: Antonio Spilimbergo, Ernesto Stein, The welfare implications of trading blocs among countries with different endowments. In: Frankel, J.A. (Ed.), The Regionalization of the World Economy. University of Chicago Press, Chicago, pp. 149–151.
Lipsey, R.G., 1960. The theory of customs unions: a general survey. Economic Journal 70 (3), 496–513.
Linnemann, H., 1966. An Econometric Study of International Trade Flows. North-Holland, Amsterdam.
McFadden, D., 1975. The revealed preferences of a government bureaucracy: theory. Bell Journal of Economics 6 (2), 401–416.
McFadden, D., 1976. Quantal choice analysis: a survey. Annals of Economic and Social Measurement 5 (4), 363–390.
Mitchell, B.R., 1992. International Historical Statistics: Europe 1750–1988. Stockton Press, NY.
Mitchell, B.R., 1993. International Historical Statistics: The Americas 1750–1988. Stockton Press, NY.
Mitchell, B.R., 1995. International Historical Statistics: Africa, Asia and Oceania 1750–1988. Stockton Press, NY.
Nitsch, V., 1996. Do three trade blocs minimize world welfare. Review of International Economics 4 (3), 355–363.
Ornelas, E., 2001. Rent Dissipation, Political Viability, and the Strategic Adoption of Free Trade Agreements. University of Wisconsin at Madison, Mimeo.
Panagariya, A., 2000. Preferential trade liberalization: the traditional theory and new developments. Journal of Economic Literature 38 (2), 287–331.
Rivers, D., Vuong, Q.H., 1988. Limited information estimators and exogeneity tests for simultaneous probit models. Journal of Econometrics 39, 347–366.
Road Atlas of Europe, 1988. Rand McNally and Co., Chicago.

Rodrik, D., 1995. Political Economy of Trade Policy. In: Grossman, G.M., Rogoff, K. (Eds.), Handbook of International Economics, vol. 3. Elsevier Science, Amsterdam, pp. 1457–1494.

Roland-Holst, D.W., Reinhart, K.A., Shiells, C.R., 1994. A general equilibrium analysis of North American economics integration. In: Francois, J.F., Shiells, C.R. (Eds.), Modeling Trade Policy: Applied General Equilibrium Assessments of North American Free Trade. Cambridge University Press, Cambridge.

Spilimbergo, A., Stein, E., 1998. The welfare implications of trading blocs among countries with different endowments. In: Frankel, J.A. (Ed.), The Regionalization of the World Economy. University of Chicago Press, Chicago, pp. 121–145.

Srinivasan, T.N., 1998. Comment on: Jeffrey A. Frankel, Ernesto Stein, Shang-Jin Wei, continental trading blocs: are they natural or supernatural. In: Frankel, J.A. (Ed.), The Regionalization of the World Economy. University of Chicago Press, Chicago, pp. 116–120.

Trefler, D., 1993. Trade liberalization and the theory of endogenous protection: an econometric study of US import policy. Journal of Political Economy 101 (1), 138–160.

US Department of the Navy Oceanographic Office, 1965. Distance Between Ports. H.O. Publication No. 15, US Government Printing Office, Washington, DC.

Viner, J., 1950. The Customs Union Issue. Carnegie Endowment for International Peace, New York.

Wooldridge, J., 2000. Introductory Econometrics. South-Western Publishing, Cincinnati.

World Bank, 2000. World Development Indicators. World Bank, Washington, DC.

World Trade Organization, 2002. http://www.wto.org, May.

Yi, S.-S., 2000. Free-trade areas and welfare. Review of International Economics 8 (2), 336–347.

Appendix

Endogenous Equations

Consumptions of the Home Good or Service by the Home Country

$$g_{ii} = \frac{\Upsilon[w_i + r_i(K_i/L_i)]\left(\Psi_i^g\right)^{-1}}{n_i^g p_i^g\left[\Upsilon\Omega_i^g\left(\Psi_i^g\right)^{-1} + (1-\Upsilon)\,\Omega_i^s\left(\Psi_i^s\right)^{-1}\right]},$$

$$i = 1A, 1B, 2A, 2B, 3A, 3B, \qquad \text{(T1–T6)}$$

$$s_{ii} = \frac{(1-\Upsilon)[w_i + r_i(K_i/L_i)]\left(\Psi_i^s\right)^{-1}}{n_i^s p_i^s\left[\Upsilon\Omega_i^g\left(\Psi_i^g\right)^{-1} + (1-\Upsilon)\Omega_i^s\left(\Psi_i^s\right)^{-1}\right]}, \quad i = 1A, \ldots, 3B. \qquad \text{(T7–T12)}$$

Numbers of Varieties

$$n_i^g = \frac{z^g\left(K_i^g\right)^{\alpha g}\left(L_i^g\right)^{1-\alpha g}}{g + \phi^g}, \quad i = 1A, \ldots, 3B, \qquad \text{(T13–T18)}$$

$$n_i^s = \frac{z^s\left(K_i^s\right)^{\alpha s}\left(L_i^s\right)^{1-\alpha s}}{s + \phi^s}, \quad i = 1A, \ldots, 3B. \qquad \text{(T19–T24)}$$

Equality of Factor Prices and Marginal Products between Sectors within a Country

$$r_i = \frac{\alpha^g \theta^g p_i^g z_i^g \left(K_i^g\right)^{\alpha g} \left(L_i^g\right)^{1-\alpha g}}{K_i^g}$$

$$= \frac{\alpha^s \theta^s p_i^s z_i^s \left(K_i^s\right)^{\alpha s} \left(L_i^s\right)^{1-\alpha s}}{K_i^s}, \quad i = 1A, \ldots, 3B, \qquad \text{(T25–T36)}$$

$$w_i = \frac{(1-\alpha^s)\theta^s z_i^s \left(K_i^s\right)^{\alpha s} \left(L_i^s\right)^{1-\alpha s} p_i^s}{L_i^s}$$

$$= \frac{(1-\alpha^g)\theta^g z_i^g \left(K_i^g\right) \left(L_i^g\right)^{1-\alpha g} p_i^g}{L_i^g}, \quad i = 1A, \ldots, 3B. \quad \text{(T37–T48)}$$

Market-Clearing Conditions in Each Sector

$$g_i = \frac{\phi^g \theta^g}{1-\theta^g} = L_i g_{ii} + L_{i'} \left[\frac{(1-a^g)^{\theta g}}{1+(1-a^g)t_{i'i}^g} \frac{p_{i'}^g}{p_i^g} \right]^{\frac{1}{1-\theta^g}} g_{i'i'}$$

$$+ \sum_{j \neq i,i'} L_j \left[\frac{((1-a^g)(1-b^g))^{\theta g}}{1+(1-a^g)(1-b^g)t_{ji}^g} \frac{p_j^g}{p_i^g} \right]^{\frac{1}{1-\theta^g}} g_{jj}, \quad i = 1A, \ldots, 3B,$$

(T49–T54)

$$s_i = \frac{\phi^s \theta^s}{1-\theta^s} = L_i s_{ii} + L_{i'} \left[\frac{(1-a^s)^{\theta^s}}{1+(1-a^s)t_{i'i}^s} \frac{p_{i'}^s}{p_i^s} \right]^{\frac{1}{1-\theta^s}} s_{i'i'}$$

$$+ \sum_{j \neq i,i'} L_j \left[\frac{((1-a^s)(1-b^s))^{\theta^s}}{1+(1-a^s)(1-b^s)t_{ji}^s} \frac{p_j^s}{p_i^s} \right]^{\frac{1}{1-\theta^s}} s_{jj}, \quad i = 1A, \ldots, 3B.$$

(T55–T60)

Identities

$i = 1A, \ldots, 3B$

$$\Psi_i^g = 1 + \left(\frac{(1-a^g)}{1+(1-a^g)t_{ii'}^g}\frac{p_i^g}{p_{i'}^g}\right)^{\frac{\theta^g}{1-\theta^g}} \left(\frac{z_{i'}^g\left(K_{i'}^g\right)^{\alpha g}\left(L_{i'}^g\right)^{1-\alpha g}}{z_i^g\left(K_i^g\right)^{\alpha g}\left(L_i^g\right)^{1-\alpha g}}\right)$$

$$+ \sum_{J \neq i,i'} \left[\left(\frac{(1-a^g)(1-b^g)}{1+(1-a^g)(1-b^g)t_{ij}^g}\right)\left(\frac{p_i^g}{p_j^g}\right)\right]^{\frac{\theta^g}{1-\theta^g}}$$

$$\times \left(\frac{z_j^g\left(K_j^g\right)^{\alpha g}\left(L_j^g\right)^{1-\alpha g}}{z_i^g\left(K_i^g\right)^{\alpha g}\left(L_i^g\right)^{1-\alpha g}}\right),$$

$$\Psi_i^s = 1 + \left(\frac{(1-a^s)}{1+(1-a^g)t_{ii'}^s}\frac{p_i^s}{p_{i'}^s}\right)^{\frac{\theta^s}{1-\theta^s}} \left(\frac{z_{i'}^s\left(K_{i'}^s\right)^{\alpha s}\left(L_i'^s\right)^{1-\alpha s}}{z_i^s\left(K_i^s\right)^{\alpha s}\left(L_i^s\right)^{1-\alpha s}}\right)$$

$$+ \sum_{J \neq i,i'} \left[\left(\frac{(1-a^s)(1-b^s)}{1+(1-a^s)(1-b^s)t_{ij}^s}\right)\left(\frac{p_i^s}{p_j^s}\right)\right]^{\frac{\theta^s}{1-\theta^s}}$$

$$\times \left(\frac{z_j^s\left(K_j^s\right)^{\alpha s}\left(L_j^s\right)^{1-\alpha s}}{z_i^s\left(K_i^s\right)^{\alpha s}\left(L_i^s\right)^{1-\alpha s}}\right),$$

$$\Omega_i^g = 1 + \left(\frac{(1-a^g)^{\theta^g}}{1+(1-a^g)t_{ii'}^g}\left(\frac{p_i^g}{p_{i'}^g}\right)^{\theta^g}\right)^{\frac{1}{1-\theta^g}} \left(\frac{z_{i'}^g\left(K_{i'}^g\right)^{\alpha g}\left(L_{i'}^g\right)^{1-\alpha g}}{z_i^g\left(K_i^g\right)^{\alpha g}\left(L_i^g\right)^{1-\alpha g}}\right)$$

$$+ \sum\nolimits_{j \neq i,i'} \left[\left(\frac{(1-a^g)(1-b^g)^{\theta^g}}{1+(1-a^g)(1-b^g)t_{ij}^g}\right)\left(\frac{p_i^g}{p_j^g}\right)^{\theta^g}\right]^{\frac{1}{1-\theta^g}}$$

$$\times \left(\frac{z_j^g\left(K_j^g\right)^{\alpha g}\left(L_j^g\right)^{1-\alpha g}}{z_i^g\left(K_i^g\right)^{\alpha g}\left(L_i^g\right)^{1-\alpha g}}\right),$$

$$\Omega_i^s = 1 + \left(\frac{(1-a^s)^{\theta^s}}{1+(1-a^s)t_{ii'}^s}\left(\frac{p_i^s}{p_{i'}^s}\right)\right)^{\frac{1}{1-\theta^s}}\left(\frac{z_{i'}^s\left(K_{i'}^s\right)^{\alpha s}\left(L_{i'}^s\right)^{1-\alpha s}}{z_i^s\left(K_i^s\right)^{\alpha s}\left(L_i^s\right)^{1-\alpha s}}\right)$$

$$+ \sum_{j\neq i,i'}\left[\left(\frac{(1-a^s)(1-b^s)^{\theta^s}}{1+(1-a^s)(1-b^s)t_{ij}^s}\right)\left(\frac{p_i^s}{p_j^s}\right)\right]^{\frac{1}{1-\theta^s}} \qquad \text{(T61–T84)}$$

$$\times\left(\frac{z_j^s\left(K_j^s\right)^{\alpha s}\left(L_j^s\right)^{1-\alpha s}}{z_i^s\left(K_i^s\right)^{\alpha s}\left(L_i^s\right)^{1-\alpha s}}\right), \quad i = 1A, \ldots, 3B,$$

Chapter 8

Economic Determinants of Free Trade Agreements Revisited: Distinguishing Sources of Interdependence

*Scott L. Baier, Jeffrey H. Bergstrand, and Ronald Mariutto**

Abstract

One of the most notable international economic events since 1990 has been the enormous increase in the number of free trade agreements (FTAs). While Baier and Bergstrand were the first to show empirically the impact of a country-pair's economic characteristics on the likelihood of the pair having an FTA, the literature has been extended to demonstrate the importance empirically of FTA "interdependence"—the effect of other FTAs on the probability of a pair having an FTA. In the context of the Baier–Bergstrand framework, this paper delves deeper into the sources of interdependence—an "own-FTA" effect and a "cross-FTA" effect. The authors argue that the own-FTA effect (the impact on the net welfare gains of an FTA between two countries owing to either already having other FTAs) likely dwarfs the cross-FTA effect (the impact on the net welfare gains of an FTA between the pair owing to other FTAs existing in the rest of the world, or ROW). Augmenting a parsimonious logit model with simple "multilateral FTA" and "ROW FTA" terms to differentiate the own and cross effects empirically, it is shown that the marginal impact on the probability of a country-pair having an agreement of either country having one more FTA with a third country is 50 times that of one more FTA between another pair in ROW. The results suggest that "domino (own-FTA) effects" have far exceeded "competitive liberalization (cross-FTA) effects" in the proliferation of FTAs.

1. Introduction

One of the most notable economic events since 1990 has been the large increase in the number of bilateral and regional free trade agreements (FTAs) in existence from year to year.[1] In this period, international trade economists have mostly debated related normative questions—such as whether such agreements are on net welfare increasing or decreasing for member countries and/or for nonmembers—and related positive questions—such as whether preferential agreements are "stumbling" or "building" blocks toward global free trade. However, the profession has begun to provide empirical models that actually explain which pairs of countries have FTAs in a given year, starting with Baier and Bergstrand (2004).

* Bergstrand: Department of Finance, Mendoza College of Business, and Kellogg Institute for International Studies, University of Notre Dame, Notre Dame, IN 46556 USA and CESifo, Munich, Germany. E-mail: bergstrand.1@nd.edu. Baier: John E. Walker Department of Economics, Clemson University, Clemson, SC 29634 USA. Mariutto: ConAgra, 1 Conagra Drive, Omaha, NE 68102 USA. Baier and Bergstrand are grateful to the National Science Foundation for financial support under grants SES-0351018 (Baier) and SES-0351154 (Bergstrand). We are also grateful for comments from an anonymous referee and participants at presentations at the Midwest International Economics Meetings, University of Notre Dame, and ETH University in Zurich. We thank Adam Ayers, R. Ethan Braden, Francisco Briseno, Emma Buckley, Brandon Caruthers, Tom Foote, Mitch Gainer, Pedro Gimenez, Nick Goode, Drew Hill, Christine Hsieh, Tahir Imtiaz, Humberto Kravetz, Cherrica Li, Lindsey Lim, Ben O'Neill, Mo Sabet, James Schappler, Andrew Weiler, Alex Wheeler, and Chris Wittman for excellent research assistance on construction of the EIA data base.

*Originally Published in *Review of International Economics*, 22(1), pp. 31–58.

Baier and Bergstrand (2004), or BB, used a numerical version of a Krugman-type general equilibrium monopolistic competition model of international trade to show that the net economic welfare gains for two countries of having an FTA in a given year were related positively to the two countries' economic sizes (gross domestic products, or GDPs), similarity of GDPs, proximity to each other, joint remoteness from the rest of the world (ROW) and relative capital–labor ratios (up to a point). Motivated by comparative statics from this six-country theoretical model, BB employed a qualitative choice model to explain the likelihood of country-pairs having FTAs using these variables. The model explained 73% of the cross-sectional variation for 1996 among 1431 pairings of 54 countries, all RHS variables had the expected coefficient signs as suggested by theory and 85% (97%) of the country-pairs with FTAs (without FTAs) were predicted correctly.

However, BB did not address systematically the influence on the likelihood of a particular country-pair *ij* forming an FTA of *i*'s or *j*'s existing FTAs with "third countries" k ($k \neq i, j$) *or* the influence on this likelihood of existing FTAs among other "country-pairs" *kl* in the ROW (k, $l \neq i, j$).[2] The purpose of this paper is to delve deeper into the sources of FTA "interdependence" and distinguish empirically two such sources for helping to explain the proliferation of FTAs—which we will term "own-FTA" and "cross-FTA" effects—and in the context of the BB theoretical framework. The own-FTA effect refers to the impact on the net welfare gains of an FTA between two countries owing to either already having other FTAs ("third country" effects). For example, this would be the effect of an FTA between Canada and the USA on the likelihood of an FTA forming between Mexico and the USA. The cross-FTA effect refers to the impact on the net welfare gains of an FTA between the pair owing to other FTAs existing in the ROW ("third country-pair" effects). For example, this would be the effect of an agreement between France and Germany on the likelihood of an FTA forming between Canada and the USA; observers in the 1980s questioned whether the growing European Community fostered the formation of the Canadian–USA FTA in 1989. While this is not the first paper to address FTA interdependence empirically, it is the first to distinguish empirically between these two complementary sources of interdependence simultaneously—and, in particular, their relative quantitative importance. The issue is important because early arguments about "domino (own-FTA) effects" (cf. Baldwin, 1993, 1995) concerned whether an FTA formation between a pair of countries was influenced by one of the countries already having an FTA with a "third country" (e.g. Economic Community expansions), whereas early arguments about "competitive liberalization (cross-FTA effects)" (cf. Bergsten, 1996) concerned whether an FTA formation between a pair of countries was influenced by formations of FTAs between other "country-pairs" in the ROW (e.g. Economic Community's expansion influencing the formation of North Atlantic Free Trade Agreement (NAFTA)).

While the notions of FTA domino effects, competitive liberalization, contagion and interdependence have existed since 1993, only three papers have attempted to quantify its importance. However, none of the three has addressed precisely the relative quantification of third country (domino) effects from third country-pair (competitive liberalization) effects, which is our goal. The first paper to address empirically the influence of FTA interdependence on the likelihood of countries i and j having an FTA (FTA_{ij}) in a subsequent year is Egger and Larch (2008), or EL. Motivated by Baldwin's domino theory of potential trade diversion of nonmembers, EL argued that the existence of an FTA between countries k and l (a "third country-pair") would increase the likelihood of FTA_{ij} (either by joining an existing one or forming a new one), with the effect decreasing in the bilateral distance between country-pairs ij and kl. To capture interdependence empirically, EL used spatial econometrics to implement a "spatial lag" for every pair ij, a function of all third-country-pairs kl ($kl \neq ij$), but allowing $kl = il$ and $kl = kj$ to accommodate Baldwin's domino effects.[3] While EL distinguished empirically between the effects of the spatial lag on enlargements versus new FTAs, the inclusion of only a single "aggregate" spatial lag precluded distinguishing empirically own-FTA from cross-FTA effects of interdependence. The goal of this paper is to distinguish empirically these two effects as well as introduce a simpler technique.

Motivated also by the domino effect of potential trade diversion of nonmembers, Baldwin and Jaimovich (2012), or BJ, similarly employ a "spatial lag" to capture interdependence effects (termed domino or "contagion" in their paper). Unlike EL, BJ's spatial lag was constructed to capture only the effects on the likelihood of FTA_{ij} of i's and j's existing FTAs with "third countries" k, that is, domino effects. Both papers found an economically and statistically significant effect of their aggregate spatial lag on the likelihood of a country-pair ij having an FTA in a later period (5-years later in EL; 1-year later in BJ), confirming the presence of interdependence (in EL's terms) or contagion (in BJ's terms), respectively. In a related third paper, Chen and Joshi (2010), or CJ, include two dummy variables, one to capture the effects on the probability of FTA_{ij} of either i or j having an existing FTA with any "third country" k (one or more FTAs) and one to capture the effects of both i and j having an existing FTA with the same third-country k. However, in the context of a three-country model, CJ only address own-FTA effects, precluding the effects of FTAs of third-country-pairs kl (k, $l \neq i, j$) on the likelihood of FTA_{ij}. Thus, EL was the first to show empirically that FTA interdependence matters, but could not distinguish with their single aggregate spatial lag own-FTA from cross-FTA effects. By contrast, BJ and CJ found evidence of own-FTA effects, but ignored cross-FTA effects.[4]

This paper offers three potential contributions to this literature. First, we will argue that the own-FTA effect likely dwarfs quantitatively the cross-FTA effect for two reasons. Own-FTA (cross-FTA) effects reflect positive (negative) terms-of-trade effects that tend to increase (decrease) the net utility gains from FTA_{ij}. Also, own-FTA effects include additionally a role for "tariff-complementarity," which cross-FTA effects do not have, which increase the net utility gains from FTA_{ij}.[5]

Second, we formulate and estimate a simple BB logit (and, in a robustness analysis, probit) equation predicting the probability of two countries having an FTA as a function of both countries' GDP sizes, GDP similarities, bilateral distance, remoteness—factors addressed in BB—and additionally "multilateral and ROW FTA indexes" to capture the own-FTA and cross-FTA effects, respectively, without having to employ the more demanding spatial econometrics used in EL and BJ.[6] In particular, our approach can distinguish empirically the effects of the number of a country-pair's own FTAs with other countries from the number of (third-country-pair) cross-FTA effects on the likelihood of a pair forming an agreement, which the single spatial lags used in EL and BJ and the dummy variables in CJ did not. Moreover, our approach is much simpler than using spatial econometrics.[7] Our logit model generates two interesting empirical findings. We find that the marginal own effect on the probability of FTA_{ij} of either i or j having an FTA with a third country k far exceeds the marginal cross effect on the same probability of countries k and l (k, $l \neq i, j$) having an FTA—consistent with our theoretical conjecture. The own-FTA effect on the probability of FTA_{ij} is approximately 50 times that of the cross-FTA effect. Moreover, our logit model has a pseudo-R^2 of 56% compared with only 2–33% in BJ and CJ in comparable specifications (without fixed effects) and a pseudo-R^2 of 80% compared with only 24–60% in comparable specifications (with fixed effects) in EL, BJ and CJ.

Third, using our panel of pairings of 146 countries for 46 years (with over 350,000 observations), we employ a "sensitivity–specificity" analysis to establish the optimum cutoff probability for whether or not—according to the model's predictions—a country-pair should have a bilateral FTA formed in a given 5-year period. Based on this, we predict correctly 91% of the actual FTA formations (enlargements) for every 5-year-period from 1960 to 2005 and predict correctly also 91% of the time "No-FTAs" when no FTAs existed for the same periods excluding fixed effects in our model.[8] Moreover, if we raise the rate of "true negatives" (or No-FTAs) to 97% as in BB, which increases the cutoff probability, the "true positives" rate falls only to 75%, almost as high as that in BB for only a single cross-section of 1431 pairings among 53 countries in 1996 (which was 85%). Also, we find that the percentage correctly predicted tends to rise (fall) when the multilateral and ROW FTA indexes are included (excluded). The results confirm that competitive liberalization arising from other third-country-pair FTAs has been a force behind the increase from year to year in the number of FTAs, but the own-FTA effect is likely to have been a much more important force behind this increase over time.

The remainder of this paper is as follows. In section 2, we discuss theoretical considerations from BB for motivating our econometric model. In section 3, we provide the econometric specification and data. In section 4, we discuss the main empirical results and provide a robustness analysis. In section 5, we discuss the ability of the model to predict FTAs correctly. Section 6 concludes.

2. Theoretical Considerations

Our starting point is the general equilibrium Krugman-type monopolistic competition model of international trade in BB. The model featured a six-country world with three continents; inter-continental trade costs could range from 0 to infinity. Also, each country had intra-continental trade costs ranging from 0 to infinity. Consumers had Cobb–Douglas utility between the goods in two industries and constant elasticity of substitution (CES) utility for the differentiated varieties in each industry. Each good was produced using capital and labor, with some of each factor used for fixed setup costs. Firms were homogeneous in each monopolistically competitive industry and all factors in each country were full employed. The government of each country was assumed to maximize national welfare.

A numerical version of the model showed theoretically that two (of the six) countries i and j would have larger net utility gains from an FTA the larger their economic (GDP) sizes, the more similar their GDPs, the closer the two countries to each other, the more remote the two countries from ROW, the larger their relative factor endowment differences (up to a point) and the smaller their relative factor endowment differences relative to the ROW's. However, BB did not examine the effects of existing FTAs on the welfare gains of subsequent FTAs.

In the context of the model in BB, we consider here two further hypotheses. The two hypotheses are distinguished because Hypothesis 1 addresses cross-FTA effects and Hypothesis 2 addresses own-FTA effects. Figures 1 and 2 illustrate the two hypotheses, Hypothesis 1 and Hypothesis 2, respectively. Figure 1 illustrates the case of two countries, 1*A* and 1*B*—say, the USA and Canada—forming an FTA conditioned upon two other countries, 2*A* and 2*B*—say, France and Germany—already having an FTA. By contrast, Figure 2 illustrates the case of two countries, 1*A* and

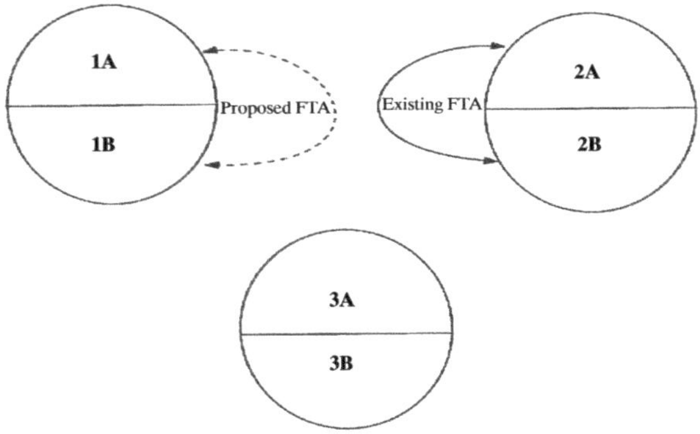

Figure 1. Hypothesis 1 (Cross-FTA Effect)

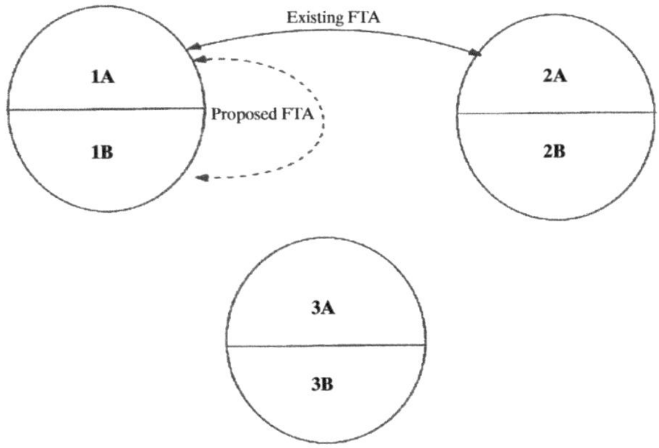

Figure 2. Hypothesis 2 (Own-FTA Effect)

1*B*—say, the USA and Mexico—forming an FTA conditioned upon one of the countries, 1*A* (say, the USA), already having an agreement with another country, 2*A* (say, Canada). It is important to note that—while countries 2*A* and 2*B* represent two countries on different continents—the BB framework allows inter- and intra-continental transport costs to vary between zero and prohibitive. Moreover, most models discussing potential trade diversion, terms-of-trade impacts and tariff-complementarity effects omit natural trade costs.

In the following, we will discuss economically the two hypotheses in the context of BB and will refer to the model and figures in that paper. We will provide also numerical comparative static effects of cross-FTAs and own-FTAs in the context of the BB model in an Online Appendix (see Supporting Information at the end of the paper). The numerical comparative statics in this Appendix are based upon the exact same theoretical and calibrated numerical model as in BB, with the exception that there is only one industry; see BB for details on the underlying theoretical model with two industries.[9]

HYPOTHESIS 1 (Cross-FTA). *The utility gain from an FTA between two countries 1A and 1B increases owing to an existing FTA between two other countries (2A, 2B)—on the same or different continents—as a result of potential trade diversion, trade creation and terms-of-trade effects.*

In the context of BB, consider the case of two countries 1*A* and 1*B* forming a bilateral FTA. Conditioned upon no other FTAs in existence, such an FTA tends to improve welfare more the higher the level of initial tariffs. With high initial tariffs, the welfare gain from creating more trade between 1*A* and 1*B* dominates the welfare loss from trade diversion with respect to nonmember countries. Moreover, terms-of-trade (real income) improvements for the members are larger the higher the initial tariffs, adding to the welfare gains. The larger the elasticity of substitution among varieties, the larger tend to be the welfare gains also for 1*A* and 1*B*; if products have low substitutability, trade diversion of valued differentiated products from nonmembers reduces on net the welfare gains.

Suppose now that countries 2*A* and 2*B* already have an FTA. Is the welfare gain from $FTA_{1A,1B}$ now larger or smaller, given the existence of $FTA_{2A,2B}$, and all else constant? Intuitively, when 2*A* and 2*B* form an FTA, each of 1*A* and 1*B* experiences trade diversion, a loss of terms of trade and erosion in real income. When a country pair (2*A*, 2*B*) is remote, there are negligible volume-of-trade and terms-of-trade (real income) effects on 1*A*'s utility from the formation of $FTA_{2A,2B}$ because there is little trade to be diverted between country 1*A* and countries 2*A* and 2*B*. However, if inter- (and intra-) continental trade costs are low, then 1*A* trades considerably with 2*A* and 2*B*. An FTA between 2*A* and 2*B* causes substantive trade diversion for 1*A*, eroding 1*A*'s volume of trade with 2*A* and 2*B* and 1*A*'s utility and real income, but improving 1*A*'s volume of trade with 1*B*. Consequently, the formation of $FTA_{1A,1B}$ has an even larger impact on 1*A*'s utility—in the presence of $FTA_{2A,2B}$ than in its absence—because the elimination of tariffs from $FTA_{1A,1B}$ on the greater volume of trade between 1*A* and 1*B* owing to $FTA_{2A,2B}$ more than offsets the terms-of-trade loss caused by trade diversion from $FTA_{2A,2B}$. $FTA_{2A,2B}$ effectively has made countries 1*A* and 1*B* more "economically remote" and this isolation has made 1*A* and 1*B* economically more natural trade partners, enhancing the gains from an FTA. Referring to either Figure 1 or Figure 2 in BB, we know that increased "remoteness" of a country-pair tends to enhance the welfare gains from an FTA.[10] Consequently, country 1*A*'s (and, by symmetry, 1*B*'s) "demand for membership" in an FTA with country 1*B* (1*A*) will tend to be higher if 2*A* and 2*B* have an existing FTA. The positive difference is the role of "third-country-pairs" creating competitive liberalization.

HYPOTHESIS 2 (Own-FTA). *The utility gain from an FTA between two countries 1A and 1B increases owing to the existence of an FTA between either of these countries with another (third) country and the gain is likely larger than in the previous case.*

Consider again the case of two countries 1*A* and 1*B* forming a bilateral FTA. Suppose now instead that 1*A* and 2*A* already have an FTA. Country 1*A*'s "demand for membership" in an FTA with country 1*B* will tend to increase if 1*A* has an existing FTA with another country (say, 2*A*). Moreover, the effect is largest when trade costs are low. Note importantly that this is not due to potential trade diversion of 1*B*; country

$1A$ is already in an agreement with $2A$, so this is different from the trade diversion arguments in EL and BJ. The economic intuition behind this is the following. At high trade costs, there is little trade between $1A$ and $2A$ so there can be little impact of $FTA_{1A,2A}$ on the gains to $1A$ from $FTA_{1A,1B}$. However, at low transport costs, $1A$ trades considerably with $2A$, and $FTA_{1A,2A}$ causes considerable trade diversion for $1A$ with $1B$, unlike the case of $FTA_{2A,2B}$ which increases $1A$'s trade with $1B$.

Two implications are worth noting. First, in contrast with Hypothesis 1, since $1A$ and $1B$ are trading less in the presence of $FTA_{1A,2A}$ than in its absence, this lower volume of trade erodes the relative gain to $1A$'s welfare of $FTA_{1A,1B}$. Second, one cannot ignore that $FTA_{1A,2A}$ increased the terms of trade and real income of country $1A$ (as well as that of $2A$). Referring to Figure 2 in BB, increased real income tends to enhance a country's welfare gain from an FTA. This improvement in terms of trade and real income has a positive benefit for improving $1A$'s utility gain from $FTA_{1A,1B}$, conditioned upon $FTA_{1A,2A}$. The combination of these effects suggests that $1A$ has an incentive to form an FTA with $1B$; this effect is analogous to the notion of "tariff-complementarity" addressed in Bagwell and Staiger (1998).[11]

We emphasize the relatively larger potential benefits from $FTA_{1A,1B}$ from the existence of $FTA_{1A,2A}$ compared with the existence of $FTA_{2A,2B}$ (as measured by the percentage change in utility). This is because $FTA_{1A,2A}$ causes a large increase in terms of trade and real income for $1A$ while $FTA_{2A,2B}$ causes a loss of terms of trade and real income for $1A$, even though $FTA_{1A,2A}$ leads to less trade volume between $1A$ and $1B$ and $FTA_{2A,2B}$ leads to more trade volume between $1A$ and $1B$. Hence, the percentage gain in utility for $1A$ from $FTA_{1A,1B}$ conditioned on $FTA_{1A,2A}$ is greater than that from $FTA_{1A,1B}$ conditioned on $FTA_{2A,2B}$ owing to the terms-of-trade effects. Moreover, while $2A$ experiences some trade diversion with respect to $1B$ as a result of $FTA_{1A,1B}$, $2A$ still has an incentive to be in an FTA with $1A$.[12]

Finally, as we would expect based upon the "domino effect" hypothesis, $1B$ suffers trade diversion and loss of real income from $FTA_{1A,2A}$. Despite the loss of real income, $1B$ on net benefits from an FTA with $1A$, raising $1B$'s demand for membership in $FTA_{1A,1B}$. Consequently, these considerations suggest that an increase in the number of FTAs that, say, country $1A$ has with other (non-$1B$) countries increases the net utility gains of $FTA_{1A,1B}$. These considerations also suggest that the marginal own-FTA effects on the probability of $FTA_{1A,1B}$ will exceed the marginal cross-FTA effects on this probability.

3. Econometric Issues and Data

Econometric Issues

The econometric framework employed is the qualitative choice model of McFadden (1975, 1976), as in BB. A qualitative choice model can be derived from an underlying latent variable model. For instance, let y^*_{ijt} denote an unobserved (or latent) variable. As in Wooldridge (2000), let y^*_{ijt} in the present context represent the percentage difference in utility levels from an action (formation of an FTA) between countries i and j in year t, where:

$$y^*_{ijt} = \alpha + x_{ijt}\beta + \varepsilon_{ijt} \qquad (1)$$

where α is a parameter, x_{ijt} is a vector of explanatory variables (i.e. economic characteristics), β is a vector of parameters and error term ε_{ijt} is assumed to be independent of x_{ijt} and to have a logistic distribution; we will also consider in the sensitivity analysis the standard normal distribution for ε_{ijt}. In the context of the BB model formally, $y^*_{ijt} = \min(\Delta U_{it}, \Delta U_{jt})$ where ΔU_{it} (ΔU_{jt}) denotes the percentage change in utility for the representative consumer in i (j) in year t. Hence, both countries' consumers need to benefit from an FTA for their governments to form one, as in BB.

Since y^*_{ijt} is unobservable, following BB we define an indicator variable, FTA_{ijt}, which assumes the value 1 if two countries have an FTA and 0 otherwise, with the response probability, Pr, for FTA:

$$\Pr(FTA_{ijt} = 1) = \Pr(y^*_{ijt} > 0) = G(\mathbf{x}_{ijt}\beta), \tag{2}$$

where $G(\bullet)$ is the logistic cumulative distribution function, ensuring that $\Pr(FTA_{ijt} = 1)$ is between 0 and 1.[13] While the statistical significance of the logit estimates can be determined using t-statistics, the coefficient estimates can only reveal the sign of the partial effects of changes in x on the probability of an FTA, owing to the nonlinear nature of $G(\bullet)$. Drawing upon analogy to the labor literature, we assume the existence of a "reservation cost" to forming an FTA (denoted y^{*R}_{ijt}). Hence, the gain in utility from forming/joining an FTA must exceed this cost (e.g. political and/or administrative cost of action) in order for an FTA "event" to occur. If $y^*_{ijt} - y^{*R}_{ijt} > 0$, then the FTA event for the pair of countries occurs at time t. Initially in our empirical specifications, we assume y^{*R}_{ijt} is exogenous and constant; however, y^{*R}_{ijt} may differ across country-pairs and also such costs may vary over time. However, in our sensitivity analysis, we can account for the possibility that the reservation costs differ across county pairs; this is easily accounted for using country-pair fixed effects (in logit specifications). Moreover, such reservation costs may be influenced by trends in policy toward "globalization." We will also be able to account for such trends over time by including a set of time dummies. All of this is explored in the empirical sensitivity analysis.

Intuition for Multilateral FTA Terms

The theoretical considerations above, alongside earlier considerations discussed in BB, suggest that x_{ijt} should be influenced not only by the distance between countries i and j, their remoteness, and the economic size and similarity of countries i and j but also by "multilateral" indexes of each of i's and j's other FTAs (for own-FTA effects) and an index of all FTAs other than those with i or j (for cross-FTA effects). While measurement of distance, economic size and economic similarity is straightforward, indexes of "multilateral FTAs" for i and j and an index of all other non-ij FTAs—henceforth, for tractability, termed ij's "ROW FTAs" index—are not readily observed.

However, intuition for the construction of our multilateral and ROW FTA indexes becomes transparent once we re-emphasize one of our main goals: to estimate the marginal impacts on the probability of FTA_{ij} of either country i or j having one more existing FTA with a third country k and of there existing one more FTA in the ROW (say, between k and l). Thus, for empirical purposes the appropriate measure of the multilateral FTA index for, say, country i is simply the count of i's FTAs with other (non-j) countries. Analogously, the appropriate measure of the multilateral FTA index for j is the count of j FTAs with other (non-i) countries. The appropriate measure of the ROW FTA index for pair ij is then simply the count of all FTAs in the world that exclude i and j.[14]

Based on these considerations, we define a multilateral index of country *i*'s FTAs with every other (non-*j*) country lagged 5 years (to avoid endogeneity bias), $MFTA_{i,t-5}$, which is an unweighted sum of country *i*'s indexes of FTAs with all other countries (excluding *j*):

$$MFTA_{i,t-5} = \sum_{k \neq j}^{N} FTA_{ik,t-5} \qquad (3)$$

where $FTA_{ik,t-5}$ is a binary variable assuming the value 1 if *i* and *k* have an FTA in year $t-5$, and 0 otherwise. Analogously, we define for *j*:

$$MFTA_{j,t-5} = \sum_{k \neq i}^{N} FTA_{jk,t-5}. \qquad (4)$$

It follows that we can define the cross-FTA index for country-pair *ij*, $ROWFTA_{ij,t-5}$, as:

$$ROWFTA_{ij,t-5} = \sum_{k \neq i,j}^{N} \sum_{l \neq i,j}^{N} FTA_{kl,t-5}. \qquad (5)$$

Hypothesis 1 ("cross-FTA" effect) suggests that the coefficient estimate for $ROWFTA_{ij,t-5}$ should be positive. Hypothesis 2 suggests that the coefficient estimates for $MFTA_{i,t-5}$ and $MFTA_{j,t-5}$ should be positive and their marginal response probabilities larger than those for $ROWFTA_{ijt}$.[15]

An alternative measure might recognize that each bilateral FTA component of these indexes should be weighted by its relative economic importance. This suggested alternative GDP-weighted multilateral and ROW indexes:

$$MFTAY_{i,t-5} = \sum_{k \neq j}^{N} Y_{k,t-5} FTA_{ik,t-5} \qquad (6)$$

where $Y_{k,t-5}$ is country *k*'s GDP in year $t-5$. We define $MFTAY_{j,t-5}$ and $ROWFTAY_{ij,t-5}$ analogously. We apply this alternative weighting method in the sensitivity analysis.[16]

Finally, alternative weights that come to mind are bilateral-trade-share weights or factors that might influence bilateral trade shares, such as inverse-bilateral-distances or GDPs divided by bilateral distances. BJ used bilateral trade shares, as did EL in a sensitivity analysis of their spatial-lag construction. However, as both studies noted, such shares may create an endogeneity bias. Consequently, EL relied upon inverse-distance weights in their construction of their primary spatial lags. Scaling by inverse distances may create problems because of the roles of inter- and intra-continental transport costs. We examine the sensitivity of the results to the roles of inter- and intra-continental transport costs later when we estimate the marginal response probabilities separately for trading partners on the same or on different continents.

Multilateral Resistance and Other Data Issues

Since Tinbergen (1962), gravity-equation analyses of bilateral trade flows have measured the presence or absence of an FTA between a country-pair using a binary variable. Following those studies and BB, variable FTA_{ijt} will have the value 1 for a pair of countries (*i*, *j*) with an FTA (specifically, FTA, customs union, common market, or economic union) in year *t*, and 0 otherwise; we exclude one-way and two-way

Table 1. Data Description[a]

Integration index	*Count*	*Percent of total*	*Percent of subtotal*
0 (None)	336,640	69.1	85.8
1 (1-way PTA)	33,821	7.0	8.6
2 (2-way PTA)	11,035	2.3	2.8
3 (FTA)	7,498	1.5	1.9
4 (Customs Union)	1,547	0.3	0.4
5 (Common Market)	1,085	0.2	0.3
6 (Economic Union)	643	0.1	0.2
Subtotal	392,269	—	100.0
Missing observations	94,641	19.5	
Total	486,910	100.0	

[a] Total observations are based upon 146 countries (146 × 145/2 = 10,585 pairings) for 46 years (1960–2005). Missing data refers to country pairs where in a given year one of two countries did not officially exist. See data source at www.nd.edu/~jbergstr.

"preferential" trade agreements (where "preferential" denotes only partial liberalization, not "free" trade). This variable was constructed using all bilateral pairings among 195 countries in the world annually from 1960 to 2005.[17] A decomposition of cells is provided in Table 1.

The only other data needed are real GDPs, bilateral distances, a dummy variable assuming the value 1 (0) if two countries are on the same continent ($CONT_{ij}$), and indexes of "remoteness." In order to employ a consistent real GDP data set for such a long period, we use real GDP data from Maddison (2009). However, the cost of a consistent real GDP panel data set for such a long time period is number of usable countries. This lowers the number of countries from 195 to 146. We construct for every country-pair the variable $SUMGDP_{ij,t-5}$, which is the natural log of the sum of *i*'s and *j*'s real GDPs 5 years prior to year *t*. We measure the dissimilarity of economic sizes using $DIFGDP_{ij,t-5}$, which is the absolute value of the difference in the log of each country's real GDP. Bilateral distances are calculated from great-circle distances using latitudes and longitudes between economic centers from the CIA's *World Factbook*, as is standard. $DIST_{ij}$ refers to the natural logarithm of the bilateral distance between the two countries *i* and *j*. However, measures of "remoteness" of a country-pair are not readily observable. We now address this issue briefly.

Recent studies by EL, BJ and CJ have followed BB and used a simple average of the logarithms of the simple averages of each of countries *i*'s and *j*'s bilateral distances to all other countries to measure a pair of countries' "remoteness," cf. BB (2004, p. 40). This variable typically has a positive coefficient estimate sign and statistical significance. However, there is no explicit theoretical foundation for its formulation. It turns out that a formulation very close to this surfaces from recent developments in the theoretical foundations for the gravity equation. These recent developments—based upon Anderson and van Wincoop (2003), as modified using a Taylor-series expansion in Baier and Bergstrand (2009)—provide guidance for measuring remoteness using "multilateral resistance" indexes that are very similar to our *MFTA* and *ROWFTA* indexes. For instance, for country *i*'s multilateral resistance index for the log of distance we use either:

$$MDIST_i = \frac{1}{N}\sum_{k}^{N} DIST_{ik} \tag{7}$$

or

$$MDISTY_{it} = \sum_{k}^{N} \theta_{kt} DIST_{ik} \tag{8}$$

where $\theta_{kt} = Y_{kt}/Y_t^W$. Analogous terms apply for $MDIST_j$ and $MDISTY_{jt}$.[18] Similarly, for country i's multilateral resistance index for the binary variable $CONT_{ij}$ we define:

$$MCONT_i = \frac{1}{N}\sum_{k}^{N} CONT_{ik} \tag{9}$$

or

$$MCONTY_{it} = \sum_{k}^{N} \theta_{kt} CONT_{ik} \tag{10}$$

and the analogous terms for $MCONT_j$ and $MCONTY_{jt}$. For parsimony, in the spirit of Baier and Bergstrand (2009), we condense these multilateral resistance terms into two variables for each country-pair. For constructing the "multilateral resistance" term for distance for the unweighted case, we have:

$$MDIST_{ij} = \frac{1}{2N}\left(\sum_{k=1}^{N} DIST_{ik} + \sum_{k=1}^{N} DIST_{jk}\right) \tag{11}$$

and analogously for the GDP-share-weighted case. For $CONT$, we use:

$$MCONT_{ij} = \frac{1}{2N}\left(\sum_{k=1}^{N} CONT_{ik} + \sum_{k=1}^{N} CONT_{jk}\right). \tag{12}$$

and analogously for the GDP-shared-weighted case (allowing for time variation in the GDP weights). See Baier and Bergstrand (2009) for details.

4. Empirical Results

Main Results

Table 2 provides the main empirical results. Specification 1 provides the results where the right-hand side variables are—in the case of unweighted averages—time-invariant variables. Specification 1 shows that $DIST_{ij}$, $CONT_{ij}$ and $MCONT_{ij}$ all have the expected signs and are statistically significant at conventional significance levels (1%). Bilateral distance has a negative effect on the probability of an FTA, while being on the same continent has a positive effect; these results are in line with the cross-sectional findings in BB and our earlier discussion for "core" economic variables. $MDIST_{ij}$ and $MCONT_{ij}$ both have negative effects on the likelihood of an FTA. While the coefficient estimate for $MCONT_{ij}$ is as expected, that for $MDIST_{ij}$ is the opposite of our expectation, since this is effectively a measure of "remoteness." However, we

Table 2. Regression Results

Variables	*Expected sign*	*(1)*	*(2)*	*(3)*	*(4)*	*(5)*	*(6)*	*(7)*	*(8)*	*(9)*	*(10)*	*(11)*	*(12)*	*(13)*
$DIST_{ij}$	–	–1.02*	–1.30*	–1.54*	–1.24*	–0.72*	–1.59*	–1.59*	–0.74*	–0.70*	–	–	–	–
		(–59.26)	(–66.97)	(71.65)	(–46.42)	(–74.67)	(–77.35)	(–35.42)	(–86.64)	(–58.87)				
$MDIST_{ij}$	+	–2.95*	–1.39*	0.25*	–0.36*	–0.03	0.36*	0.39*	–0.44*	–0.96*	–	–	–	–
		(–75.42)	(–37.37)	(5.56)	(–6.08)	(–1.40)	(8.86)	(4.32)	(–12.03)	(–18.63)				
$CONT_{ij}$	+	1.71*	1.45*	1.65*	1.43*	0.85*	1.57*	1.54*	1.87*	1.79*	–	–	–	–
		(50.78)	(41.53)	(40.72)	(27.85)	(45.68)	(40.36)	(18.74)	(59.79)	(41.36)				
$MCONT_{ij}$	–	–10.07*	–4.11*	–0.85*	–2.40*	–0.80*	–0.48	–0.90*	–2.91*	–4.12*	–	–	–	–
		(–67.73)	(–26.70)	(–5.10)	(–11.07)	(–9.79)	(–5.93)	(–2.70)	(–19.79)	(–20.77)				
$SUMGDP_{ij,t-5}$	+	–	0.80*	0.51*	0.49*	0.24*	0.48*	0.50*	0.37*	0.39*	3.20*	3.43*	2.81*	4.86*
			(79.20)	(44.79)	(34.54)	(42.96)	(32.85)	(21.51)	(39.00)	(29.69)	(14.08)	(12.32)	(6.05)	(7.34)
$DIFGDP_{ij,t-5}$	–	–	–0.56*	–0.51*	–0.42*	–0.24*	–0.47*	–0.53*	–0.44*	–0.39*	0.40	0.16	–0.10	–1.00*
			(–50.73)	(–40.67)	(–27.18)	(–40.12)	(–37.97)	(–20.72)	(–42.65)	(26.74)	(1.66)	(0.56)	(–0.33)	(–2.41)
$MFTA_{i,t-5(i\neq j)}$	+	–	–	0.09*	0.02*	0.05*	0.06*	0.09*	0.07*	0.01*	0.35*	0.84*	0.33*	0.97*
				(45.68)	(8.47)	(45.18)	(59.76)	(23.37)	(44.87)	(5.80)	(11.20)	(10.36)	(13.64)	(13.13)
$MFTA_{j,t-5(j\neq i)}$	+	–	–	0.12*	0.05*	0.06*	0.06*	0.11*	0.09*	0.04*	0.45*	0.88*	0.36*	0.84*
				(57.17)	(19.48)	(56.13)	(61.83)	(27.78)	(55.24)	(17.14)	(11.56)	(10.90)	(13.33)	(12.41)
$ROWFTA_{ij,t-5}$	+	–	–	0.0004*	0.002*	0.0002*	0.22*	0.0004*	0.00004	0.001*	0.009*	0.01*	0.01*	0.01
				(9.71)	(26.31)	(12.45)	(31.01)	(5.32)	(0.90)	(25.56)	(22.97)	(20.86)	(22.42)	(1.03)
CONSTANT		–116.17*	–50.03*	–13.69*	–33.08*	–11.27*	–6.01*	–14.90*	–41.27*	–55.69*	–	–	–	–
		(–60.61)	(–24.99)	(–6.31)	(–11.82)	(–10.67)	(–14.13)	(–3.44)	(–21.76)	(–4.83)				
Pair Fixed Ef.		No	No	No	No	No	No	No	No	No	Yes	Yes	Yes	Yes
Yr Dummies		No	No	No	No	No	No	No	No	No	No	No	Yes	Yes
No. Obs.		358,767	358,767	358,767	352,002	358,767	358,767	77,059	358,767	352,002	358,767	352,002	358,767	352,002
No. Pos. Obs.		10,478	10,478	10,478	3,811	10,478	10,478	2,490	10,478	3,811	10,478	3,811	10,478	3,811
Random Prob.		0.029	0.029	0.029	0.011	0.029	0.029	0.032	0.029	0.011	0.029	0.011	0.029	0.011
Pseudo R^2		0.39	0.46	0.56	0.34	0.57	0.56	0.56	0.54	0.32	0.80	0.73	0.87	0.85
log-likelihood		–28,953	–25,359	–20,663	–13,860	–20,587	–20,759	–4,792	–21,832	–14,260	–2,294	–2,034	–1,525	–1,142

Note: *Denotes statistical significance in one-tail t-test (or z-test) at 1% level.

will see shortly that this unexpected negative coefficient sign is reversed in a fuller specification. The pseudo-R^2 is 0.39. Recall that in logit (or probit) regressions the coefficient signs are meaningful, but the actual values of the coefficients are not directly interpretable; however, marginal response probabilities will be calculated later, as in BB, to examine the quantitative effects of one-standard-deviation changes in RHS variables (and also, for count variables, unit changes in the right-hand side variables).

Specification 2 in Table 2 augments Specification 1 to include the (5-year-lagged) logarithm of the joint economic size of countries i and j ($SUMGDP_{ij,t-5}$) and our measure of dissimilarity of economic sizes of i and j ($DIFGDP_{ij,t-5}$). We find that country-pairs are more likely to form an FTA the larger and more similar are their GDPs, in accordance with BB and earlier discussion. The results in Specification 2 confirm using a very large pooled cross-section time-series data set the results found for a single cross-section of a smaller number of countries in BB and are consistent with the pooled cross-section time-series results in EL, BJ and CJ.[19]

We now address Hypotheses 1 and 2. Specification 3 provides the results of augmenting Specification 2 with $MFTA_{i,t-5}$, $MFTA_{j,t-5}$ and $ROWFTA_{ij,t-5}$. Specification 3 is our main specification. First, all three of these variables have statistically significant positive coefficient estimates and the coefficient estimates of the other right-hand side variables retain their same signs and remain statistically significant except $MDIST_{ij}$, which reverses its sign to the expected positive one and is statistically significant. Second, the positive coefficient estimates for $MFTA_{i,t-5}$, $MFTA_{j,t-5}$ and $ROWFTA_{ij,t-5}$ all confirm Hypotheses 1 and 2. Third, the pseudo-R^2 of the logit regression is 0.56, which is substantive and very close to the pseudo-R^2 found in BB for their much smaller and select cross-section sample for the year 1996. Moreover, it is larger than the pseudo-R^2 values for comparable specifications without fixed effects in BJ and CJ of 33% and 4%, respectively; EL's specifications all included time-meaned fixed effects. We note that there are 10,478 observations with FTAs ($FTA_{ij,t} = 1$) in the sample of 358,767 observations spanning 1960–2005. Finally, we note that the coefficient estimates for $MFTA_{i,t-5}$ and $MFTA_{j,t-5}$ are substantively larger than that for $ROWFTA_{ij,t-5}$. The relatively larger coefficient estimates for the former variables are seemingly consistent with the relative quantitative predictions for the relative utility gains. However, because of the nonlinearities using logit regressions, we will delay full discussion of these relative quantitative predictions until we examine more appropriately marginal response probabilities later.

Sensitivity Analysis

Specification 3 provides the main specification for predicting later the rate of "true positives" (predicting an FTA when one exists) and the rate of "true negatives" ("No-FTA" when none exists). In this sensitivity analysis, we examine the robustness of results using Specification 3 to examining "formations" of FTAs (rather than the indicator representing "existence" of an FTA in a given year), to using probit rather than logit estimation, to using alternative weights for the various multilateral and ROW index variables, to using a panel of every 5 years (rather than annual), to using instead a duration model, to the presence of country-pair fixed effects and to inclusion of time dummies in addition to country-pair fixed effects. Finally, we report marginal response probabilities for Specification 3.

First, one concern of Specification 3 is that we are examining the "existences" of FTAs in a given year rather than their "formations." $FTA_{ij,t}$ assumes the value 1 if an

FTA exists between *i* and *j* in any year *t*, and 0 otherwise. Alternatively, we would like to consider another dummy variable for the left-hand side that assumes the value 1 in a year *t* when an FTA is formed between *i* and *j* in that year and 0 otherwise.[20] Consequently, we construct a new variable, $TFTA_{ij,t}$, which assumes the value 1 if countries *i* and *j* transitioned into an FTA in year *t*, and 0 otherwise. As a result, the number of observations with FTA formations ($TFTA_{ij,t} = 1$) is 3811, approximately one-third that for $FTA_{ij,t} = 1$. Specification 4 reports the results of replacing $FTA_{ij,t}$ with the "transition-to-FTA" binary variable $TFTA_{ij,t}$. We note that the number of total observations falls from 358,767 to 352,002 as we redefine the left-hand side dummy variable to represent the change from one year to the next in the FTA "status" of the pair. Note that the coefficient estimates in Specification 4 are qualitatively identical to those in Specification 3, with the exception of $MDIST_{ij}$ which has a negative effect now. Most importantly though, all the main results hold up; $MFTA_{i,t-5}$, $MFTA_{j,t-5}$ and $ROWFTA_{ij,t-5}$ all have positive and statistically significant coefficient estimates as expected. However, predicting transitions is more challenging than predicting the existence of FTAs; the pseudo-R^2 is lower at 0.34 compared with 0.56 for Specification 3, as expected.[21]

Second, both BB and EL used probit estimation rather than logit, the latter used here. Recall that our reason for using logit is that we will include country-pair fixed effects shortly to compare our results with EL and BJ, both of which included Chamberlain (1980) time-meaned fixed effects in their probits. As clarified in Wooldridge (2002, pp. 490–492), since the logistic transformation is a linear one standard fixed effects can be readily applied without restrictions; by contrast, fixed effects have more restrictions on their implementation because of the Chamberlain (1980) "incidental parameters" issue. However, it is useful to show that the results are robust to estimation using probit. Specification 5 provides the results of re-estimating the model of determinants of existence of an FTA ($FTA_{ij,t}$) using probit. The results in Specification 5 are qualitatively identical to the corresponding logit ones in Specification 3 with one exception; the coefficient estimate for $MDIST_{ij}$ reverses signs from positive (which is expected) to negative but statistically insignificant in the probit specification. The pseudo-R^2 is 0.57, virtually identical to the pseudo-R^2 of 0.56 in Specification 3. Quantitatively, with the exception of that for $MDIST_{ij}$, all the probit coefficient estimates are approximately a half of those in the logit equation. Thus, the results are largely robust to estimation using probit instead.[22]

Third, as discussed earlier, our theoretical model provides no clear guidance for weights for the multilateral FTA indexes. Following guidance from recent theoretical developments for the gravity equation in Anderson and van Wincoop (2003) as modified by Baier and Bergstrand (2009), the two weighting methods suggested are a simple average of components or a GDP-weighted average of bilateral components. We re-estimated our main logit specification (3) using GDP-weighted values: $MFTAY_{i,t-5}$, $MFTAY_{j,t-5}$, $ROWFTAY_{ij,t-5}$, $MDISTY_{ij}$ and $MCONTY_{ij}$. The results are provided in Specification 6 for the existence of FTAs.[23] The results in Specification 3 are robust to using the GDP-weighted (or GDP-share-weighted) alternative variables; all coefficient estimates are qualitatively identical to those in Specification 6.[24]

Fourth, in the specifications used so far, we use 5-year lagged values of $SUMGDP_{ij,t-5}$, $DIFGDP_{ij,t-5}$, $MFTA_{i,t-5}$, $MFTA_{j,t-5}$ and $ROWFTA_{ij,t-5}$ to predict the existence of (or transition to) an FTA for a country pair within the next 5 years. However, this large window for FTA predictions may introduce an endogeneity bias. Consequently, we re-estimated the main specification using only right-hand side and left-hand side variables with a sub-sample of every 5 years. This reduced our sample size for predicting existence from 358,767 to 77,059. The results are provided in Specification 7. We see in column (7) that all of the coefficient estimates are robust to this alternative specification which retains the 5-year lag for the right-hand side variables. The results for transition-to-FTA are also robust, but omitted from the table for brevity.

Fifth, Bergstrand et al. (2009) implemented instead a "duration analysis" of the likelihood of FTA events. Like logit and probit regressions, duration models fall within the class of "limited dependent variable" models, cf. Wooldridge (2002). These models estimate the "hazard rate," which is the instantaneous probability of leaving an initial state (No-FTA) in the interval $[t, t + dt)$ given survival up until time t. We also estimated a duration model using the same variables; the results are in Specification 8 (9) for existence of (transition to) FTAs. Columns (8) and (9) indicate that our main results from Specification 3 are robust qualitatively to using a duration model rather than a simple logit (or probit) model. All coefficient estimates (except, as before, that for $MDIST_{ij}$) are correctly signed and statistically significant.

Sixth, the results may be sensitive to omitted unobserved cross-sectional heterogeneity. As is often done in gravity-equation analyses of trade flows, one introduces country-pair fixed effects to account for unobserved heterogeneity to ensure unbiased coefficient estimates. Country-pair fixed effects are likely to account for variation in pair-specific political factors that may influence FTA formations. As noted earlier, one of the advantages of logit over probit estimation (or duration analysis) is the ability to use standard fixed effects; by contrast, such effects cannot be used in probit specifications owing to the normal distribution underlying probits. However, Chamberlain (1980) offers a methodology to include time-meaned fixed effects in probits; such effects were included in both EL and BJ. Of course, the introduction of country-pair fixed effects implies removing all time-invariant variables, i.e. $DIST_{ij}$, $CONT_{ij}$, $MDIST_{ij}$ and $MCONT_{ij}$. Specification 10 reports the results of introducing country-pair fixed effects into main Specification 3. We see that the remaining time-varying variables' coefficient estimates are significant, with only the estimate for our measure of size-dissimilarity having an unexpected positive sign but statistical insignificance. All the other four variables' coefficient estimates retain the same expected positive signs as in previous regressions. When we introduce the same fixed effects into the logit regressions using "transition-to-FTA" binary variable $TFTA_{ij,t}$, shown in Specification 11, the coefficient estimates remain positive and statistically significant with the exception again of insignificance for the coefficient estimate for the GDP-size-dissimilarity variable. Importantly, the pseudo-R^2 value for our fixed effect logits for existence of FTA in Specification 10 is 80%. This is substantially higher than the pseudo-R^2 values ranging from 55 to 60% for the comparable fixed effects specifications in EL and BJ and 7 to 24% in CJ.

Seventh, while the country-pair fixed effects specifications controlled for unobservable time-invariant factors, they did not control for unobservable time-varying factors. For instance, world GDP and technology change over time. More specific to the issues at hand, global liberalization of trade under the GATT/WTO may have had an influence on the likelihood of bilateralism being captured in the remaining time-varying RHS variables $SUMGDP_{ij,t-5}$, $DIFGDP_{ij,t-5}$, $MFTA_{i,t-5}$, $MFTA_{j,t-5}$ and $ROWFTA_{ij,t-5}$. Specifications 12 and 13 add to the logit fixed-effects specifications 10 and 11, respectively, time dummies. Columns (12) and (13) report the results for the existence-of-FTA and transition-to-FTA specifications, respectively. In Specification 12 the $SUMGDP_{ij,t-5}$ ($DIFGDP_{ij,t-5}$) coefficient estimate has the expected positive (negative) sign and is statistically significant (insignificant). Moreover, the coefficient estimates for $MFTA_{i,t-5}$, $MFTA_{j,t-5}$ and $ROWFTA_{ij,t-5}$ are positively signed as expected and remain statistically significant. In Specification 13, the $SUMGDP_{ij,t-5}$ and $DIFGDP_{ij,t-5}$ coefficient estimates have the expected signs and both are statistically significant. The coefficient estimates for $MFTA_{i,t-5}$ and $MFTA_{j,t-5}$ remain positively signed and statistically significant; the coefficient estimate for $ROWFTA_{ij,t-5}$ is positively signed, but statistically insignificant. These results confirm the importance of existing FTAs for enhancing the likelihood of subsequent FTAs.

Table 3 reports the marginal response probabilities, calculated at the means of the levels of all variables. Importantly, we use our main specification, Specification 3, that excludes fixed effects so as not to contaminate the predictions with pair fixed effects. We follow the approach used in BB by separating the marginal response probabilities into those calculated for "natural" trading partners (i.e. pairs on the same continent) and those for "unnatural" trading partners (i.e. pairs on different continents). There are two reasons for this here. First, as in BB, it makes little economic sense to evaluate the marginal response probabilities at the "mean" of a binary variable representing the presence or absence of being on the same continent. Second, the utility gains for a country-pair from forming an FTA are likely sensitive to the level of transportation costs. One transparent method for evaluating the influence of distance on the effects of existing FTAs on the likelihood of subsequent FTAs is to evaluate marginal response probabilities separately for natural and unnatural trading partners. The format of this table is the same as in BB.

Table 3a reports the marginal response probabilities for natural trading partners. First, for ease of reference the probability of an FTA among natural partners at the mean level of all other RHS variables is 0.1031, with a 95% confidence interval of 0.0995 to 0.1068. We now consider the effect of a one standard deviation (S.D.) increase or decrease of variables. The sixth (seventh) line of Table 3a indicates that a one S.D. increase in $MFTA_{i,t-5}$ ($MFTA_{j,t-5}$) increases the probability of $FTA_{ij,t}$ to 0.1306 (0.1381). Each of these probability changes is statistically significant at the 95% level, but not significantly different from one another.[25] By contrast, a one S.D. increase in $ROWFTA_{ij,t-5}$ increases the probability of $FTA_{ij,t}$ to only 0.1101, which is also a statistically significant change. The difference in the marginal response probabilities for $MFTA_{i,t-5}$ ($MFTA_{j,t-5}$) and $ROWFTA_{ij,t-5}$ is economically and statistically significant. Moreover, the difference in such probabilities is as expected; a one S.D. change in $MFTA_{i,t-5}$ ($MFTA_{j,t-5}$) has a quantitatively larger impact on the likelihood of $FTA_{ij,t}$ than does a one S.D. change in $ROWFTA_{ij,t-5}$. In fact, a typical (one S.D.) change in own-FTA status has approximately four times the impact on the probability of FTA_{ij} as a typical change in cross-FTA status. These results suggest that the "own-FTA" effect has an economically and statistically larger effect on the explaining FTAs than the "cross-FTA" effect.

Yet, a one S.D. change in $MFTA_{i,t-5}$ (or $MFTA_{j,t-5}$) need not be the same as a one standard deviation change in $ROWFTA_{ij,t-5}$, potentially challenging the conclusion above. Consequently, the last three rows of Table 3a report the marginal response probabilities of a one-unit increase in $MFTA_{i,t-5}$, a one-unit increase in $MFTA_{j,t-5}$ and a two-unit increase for $ROWFTA_{ij,t-5}$. Note that a one-unit—or one-*FTA*—increase in $MFTA_{i,t-5}$ ($MFTA_{j,t-5}$) increases the probability of $FTA_{ij,t}$ by 0.44 (0.54) percentage point, and the effect is economically and statistically significant. However, a two-unit increase in $ROW_{ij,t-5}$ increases the probability of $FTA_{ij,t}$ by only 0.01 percentage point, which is neither economically nor statistically significant.[26] Consequently, our conclusion above that the own-FTA effect has an economically and statistically larger effect on explaining FTAs than the cross-FTA is supported strongly.

Table 3a. Marginal Response Probabilities for Natural Trading Partners

Natural trading partners							
Existence		95% Confidence interval (C.I.)					*Difference*
		0.1031		0.0995	0.1068		
	$P(FTA\_t = 1 \mid$ CONT = 1)= $\Pr(FTA = 1 \mid X - \sigma)$	95% C.I.		$\Pr(FTA = 1 \mid X + \sigma)$	95% C.I.		$\Pr(FTA = 1 \mid X + \sigma)$ $-\Pr(FTA = 1 \mid X)$
DIFGDP	0.1494	0.1437	0.1551	0.0706	0.0678	0.0734	−0.0325
SUMGDP	0.0716	0.0688	0.0744	0.1474	0.142	0.1529	0.0443
DIST	0.1709	0.1648	0.1769	0.0612	0.0589	0.0636	−0.0419
MDIST	0.0982	0.0943	0.1021	0.1083	0.1041	0.1124	0.0051
MCONT	0.1078	0.1036	0.112	0.0986	0.0948	0.1025	−0.0045
$MFTA_i$	0.0812	0.0782	0.0841	0.1306	0.1259	0.1353	0.0275
$MFTA_j$	0.0766	0.0738	0.0794	0.1381	0.1332	0.143	0.035
ROW FTA	0.0966	0.0929	0.1002	0.1101	0.106	0.1142	0.007
$MFTA_i^*$	0.0989	0.0954	0.1024	0.1075	0.1037	0.1113	0.0044
$MFTA_j^*$	0.098	0.0945	0.1014	0.1085	0.1047	0.1124	0.0054
*ROW FTA**	0.1031	0.0994	0.1067	0.1032	0.0995	0.1068	0.0001

Notes: $\sigma = 1$ S.D. for (first nine variables); σ = count of 1 for $MFTA_i^*$ and $MFTA_j^*$, σ = count of 2 for *ROW FTA**.

Table 3b. Marginal Response Probabilities for Unnatural Trading Partners

Unnatural trading partners							
Existence				*95% Confidence interval (C.I.)*			*Difference*
		0.0066		0.0061	0.0071		
	$P(FTA\_t = 1 \mid CONT = 0) = Pr(FTA = 1 \mid X - \sigma)$	95% C.I.		$Pr(FTA = 1 \mid X + \sigma)$	95% C.I.		$Pr(FTA = 1 \mid X + \sigma) - Pr(FTA = 1 \mid X)$
DIFGDP	0.0133	0.0122	0.0143	0.0032	0.0029	0.0034	−0.0034
SUMGDP	0.0032	0.003	0.0035	0.013	0.012	0.014	0.0064
DIST	0.0171	0.0158	0.0183	0.0024	0.0022	0.0026	−0.0042
MDIST	0.006	0.0055	0.0065	0.0072	0.0066	0.0078	0.0006
MCONT	0.0072	0.0066	0.0078	0.006	0.0055	0.0065	−0.0005
$MFTA_i$	0.0041	0.0038	0.0045	0.0103	0.0095	0.0111	0.0037
$MFTA_j$	0.0037	0.0034	0.004	0.0115	0.0106	0.0123	0.0049
ROW FTA	0.0058	0.0053	0.0063	0.0075	0.0069	0.008	0.0009
$MFTA_i^*$	0.0061	0.0056	0.0065	0.0071	0.0066	0.0077	0.0005
$MFTA_j^*$	0.006	0.0055	0.0064	0.0073	0.0067	0.0078	0.0007
*ROW FTA**	0.0066	0.0061	0.0071	0.0066	0.0061	0.0071	0.0000

Notes: $\sigma = 1$ S.D. for (first nine variables); σ = count of 1 for $MFTA_i^*$ and $MFTA_j^*$, σ = count of 2 for *ROW FTA**.

In fact, the increase in the probability of FTA_{ij} of either i or j having one more FTA with another country k (approximately 0.50 percentage point) is 50 times that of the increase in the same probability of one more FTA among another pair kl (approximately 0.01 percentage point). This relative impact is consistent with the relative welfare gains to i or j of 35–60 times of the own-FTA and cross-FTA effects suggested by our numerical theoretical comparative statics.[27]

Table 3b reports the marginal response probabilities for unnatural trading partners (i.e. pairs on different continents). The probability of an FTA among unnatural trading partners at the mean level of all (other) right-hand side variables is 0.0066, with a 95% confidence interval of 0.0061 to 0.0071. The sixth (seventh) line of Table 3b indicates that a one S.D. increase in $MFTA_{i,t-5}$ ($MFTA_{j,t-5}$) increases the probability of $FTA_{ij,t}$ to 0.0103 (0.0115). Each of these probability changes is statistically significant at the 95% level, but not significantly different from one another. By contrast, a one S.D. increase in $ROWFTA_{ij,t-5}$ increases the probability of $FTA_{ij,t}$ to 0.0075, which is not a statistically significant change. The difference in the marginal response probabilities for $MFTA_{i,t-5}$ ($MFTA_{j,t-5}$) and $ROWFTA_{ij,t-5}$ is economically and statistically significant. Moreover, the difference in such probabilities is as expected; a one S.D. change in $MFTA_{i,t-5}$ ($MFTA_{j,t-5}$) has a quantitatively larger impact on the likelihood of $FTA_{ij,t}$ than does a one S.D. change in $ROWFTA_{ij,t-5}$. For brevity, we do not review the other marginal response probabilities. However, all such probabilities change in the expected directions and all such changes are statistically significant except for $MCONT_{ij}$. These results also suggest that the "own-FTA" effect has an economically and statistically larger effect on explaining FTAs than the "cross-FTA" effect.

Finally, we note that the change in the probability of FTA_{ijt} owing to an increase in $MFTA_{i,t-5}$ (or $MFTA_{j,t-5}$ or $ROWFTA_{ij,t-5}$) is much higher for natural trading partners than for unnatural trading partners. For instance, for $MFTA_{i,t-5}$ a one unit increase in this variable (that is, one more bilateral FTA for i) causes a 0.44 percentage point (0.05 percentage point) increase in the likelihood of FTA_{ij} within the next 5 years if i and j are on the same (a different) continent. This is one approach for circumventing distance-weighted measures of $MFTA$ and $ROWFTA$.

5. Predicting FTAs

An alternative measure of goodness-of-fit for logit and probit models is the "percentage correctly predicted." However, Wooldridge (2000) points out that this percentage may be misleading. For instance, in BB, the authors had a sample of 1431 country pairs for the year 1996 with 286 actual FTAs (true positives, or TPs). Hence, 20% of the observations were FTAs. The "unconditional" probability of an FTA was 20% and the unconditional probability of No-FTA was 80% (1145/1431). Consequently, even if the model had no explanatory power and failed to predict correctly even one FTA, the percentage of No-FTAs correctly predicted is almost 80%. This large percentage misrepresents the zero predictive power of the model for predicting true positives.

Wooldridge (2000) recommends examining separately the percentage correctly predicted for each of the two outcomes. That is, the percentage of "true positives" (TPs) in "all positives" (APs), or TPs/APs = TPs/(TPs + FPs) where FP denotes "false positives," is important, but so is the percentage of "true negatives" (TNs) in "all negatives" (ANs), or TNs/ANs = TNs/(TNs + FNs) where FN denotes "false negative." BB conducted this statistical summary for their cross-section analysis of year 1996 data and found that their model predicted correctly 243 of 286 FTAs, or 84.97%. They also predicted 1114 of the 1145 pairs without FTAs correctly, or 97.29%.

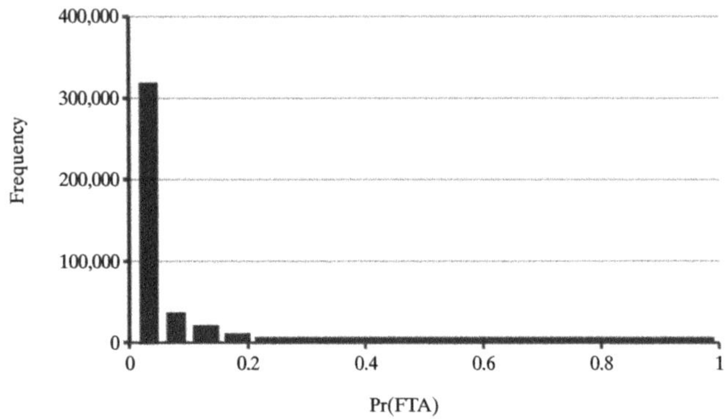

Figure 3a. Frequency of Predicted Probabilities (Existence, Logit, Simple Average Weight)

However, a critical issue in classification is the choice of the "cutoff" on the probability continuum. BB, EL and CJ followed McFadden (1975, 1976) in using a probability cutoff (p^C) of 0.5 to determine if an FTA was predicted or not. Letting p_{ij} denote the predicted probability from the probit regression in BB, if $p_{ij} > 0.5$ and the country-pair *ij* had an FTA, this would be a true positive. If $p_{ij} \leq 0.5$ and *ij* did not have an FTA, this would be a true negative.

In this part, we examine some summary statistics associated with alternative cutoff probabilities. We examine four alternative methods for assessing the overall predictive power of our main logit models for existence of and transition to FTAs, which are Specifications 3 and 4, respectively; both specifications exclude any fixed effects. The first concerns establishing a cutoff probability based upon maximizing the overall predictive power; this is determined by a "specificity–sensitivity" analysis, described shortly. The second and third concern establishing cutoff probabilities consistent with having a TN rate no lower than that in BB (97%) or EL (99%), respectively.[28] The fourth uses the arbitrary cutoff of 0.5, but it turns out that this cutoff is consistent with a true negative rate of 99% (as in the third approach).

While BB, EL and CJ used a p^C of 0.5, we believe this cutoff is not a very relevant one. The reason lies in the fact that—as noted earlier—bilateral FTA events in our panel of over 350,000 observations are rare events. First, the number of observations when an FTA exists between a country-pair in a given year is 10,478; this is only 3% of all observations. Second, the number of observations when a country-pair forms (or transitions to) an FTA is 3811; this is only 1% of all observations. Figure 3a provides a plot of the frequency of the predicted probability of an FTA (p_{ijt}) using Specification 3; this confirms visually that FTAs are rare events and that a $p_{ijt} > 0.5$ would be an extremely rare event. Consequently, we ignore this cutoff for now, although for completeness we will report the TP and TN rates for $p^C = 0.5$ later.

Cohen et al. (2003) suggests using *a priori* information about the proportion of FTA events and No-FTA events in our population. Consider first the case of FTA existences. The proportion of FTAs (No-FTAs) in our panel—which is virtually the entire population of country-pairs since 1960—is 3% (97%). Hence, the unconditional probability of an FTA existing between any country-pair in a given year is 3%. This sug-

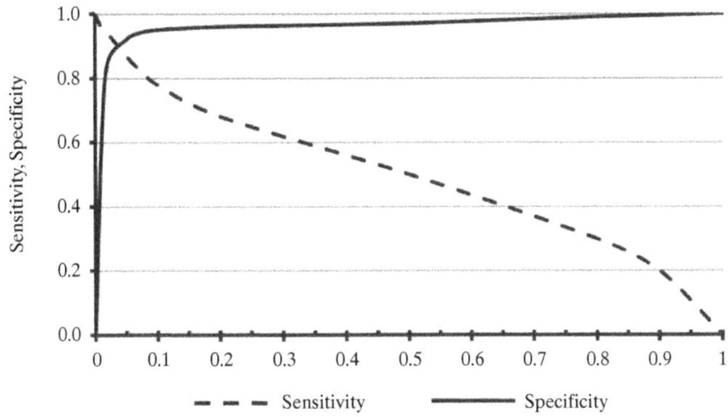

Figure 3b. Sensitivity, Specificity (Existence, Logit, Simple Average Weight)

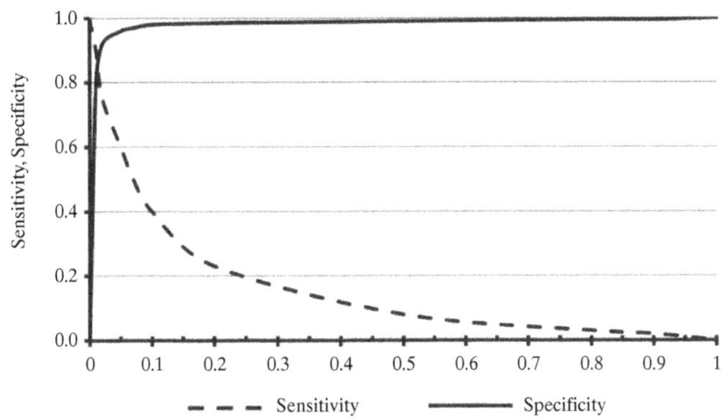

Figure 3c. Sensitivity, Specificity (Transitions, Logit, Simple Average Weight)

gests a more appropriate cutoff probability is 0.03; BJ followed this approach also. In fact, it turns out that the TP and TN rates are maximized at this cutoff, as we now show.

Naturally, one wants to maximize both the rates of true positives (TPs) and true negatives (TNs). However, there is a trade-off. Figure 3b graphs the TP and TN rates for Specification 3 (logit, FTA existence) against the entire range of possible cutoff probabilities; Figure 3c graphs the TP and TN rates against the same range of p^C for Specification 4 (logit, FTA transition). One can see from Figure 3b that at p^C of near 0, one maximizes the likelihood of predicting an FTA when one exists (sensitivity); however, the TN rate (specificity) is virtually zero, which is a severe problem since the vast bulk of observations is zero. To increase the TN rate, a higher p^C is needed. For our first approach, it turns out that at a p^C of 0.03 (specifically, 0.0328) we maximize both the TP and TN rates at 91%; this is the result from a sensitivity–specificity analysis. Thus, at a cutoff probability consistent with the unconditional probability of an

FTA existing (0.03), the model predicts correctly 91% of the cases when an FTA exists within 5 years of the agreement forming and 91% of the cases when No-FTA is correct. We have also conducted this analysis for predicting formations of FTA ($TFTA_{ijt}$ equals 1 in the year an FTA goes into force, and 0 otherwise). In this case, the model predicts correctly 89% of the true positives within 5 years of the formation and 89% of the TNs, as shown in Figure 3c.

Our second and third approaches consider two other possible cutoff probabilities. In the first approach, we obtain a success rate for predicting FTAs when FTAs exist of 91% (the TP rate). While the TN rate may seem high at 91%, we still have a false positive rate of 9%, which implies in our sample of over 350,000 observations that we incorrectly predict FTA when No-FTA exists in 9% of the cases. However, BB had a higher TN rate of 97% (owing to its $p^C = 0.5$) and EL had a TN rate of 99% (also using a $p^C = 0.5$), implying much stricter false positive rates of 3% and 1%, respectively. As Figure 3b suggests, one can raise the p^C to ensure a higher TN rate, to be consistent with these studies, which will of course lower the TP rate. We considered two alternative values of p^C. First, we considered $p^C = 0.114$, which ensured a TN rate of 97% as in BB. The associated TP rate was 75%. The latter value is only 10% less than the 85% TP rate in BB for only a cross-section of bilateral FTAs among 53 country-pairs. Our TP rate of 75% is remarkably high considering we are predicting the existence of an FTA between a country-pair within only 5 years of its formation. For a TN rate of 99% (implying $p^C = 0.307$), the TP rate for existence of an FTA between a country-pair within 5 years of its formation falls to 48%. We also considered the TP rates for predicting the actual year of formation (date of entry) of an FTA between a country-pair within 5 years of its actual formation. At a TN rate of 97%, the TP rate is 56%. At a TN rate of 99%, the TP rate is 26%. Our fourth approach simply uses the cutoff probability of 0.5.

Tables 4a and b summarize the information above and additionally provide information about the TP and TN rates by individual year as well as with and without the $MFTA_{i,t-5}$, $MFTA_{j,t-5}$ and $ROWFTA_{ij,t-5}$ terms. For economy, we provide the predictions at 5-year intervals as well as over all the years, where the logit specification in Table 4a includes the *MFTA* and *ROWFTA* terms and the specification in Table 4b excludes these terms. First, in the second and third columns, we use the cutoff that maximizes overall success rate using a sensitivity–specificity analysis, that is, maximizing both the TP and TN rates. For FTA existences including *MFTA* and *ROWFTA*, this is 91.04% in Table 4a. In Table 4b, we can see from columns (2) and (3) that the percentage correctly predicted without *MFTA* and *ROWFTA* is 88.35%. However, returning to Table 4a, this 91% still leaves 9% of the observations false negatives. The second approach considered a TN rate no lower than that in BB, 97%. With a higher TN rate, the fourth and fifth columns report a lower TP rate of 75.50% (65.34%) in the specification with (without) the *MFTA* and *ROWFTA* terms. In our third approach with a TN rate of 99% as in EL, the TP rate falls to 47.67% (32.37%) in the specification with (without) the *MFTA* and *ROWFTA* terms. Fourth, the eighth and ninth columns provide the TP rates using a cutoff of $p^C = 0.5$. The TP rate is 47.07%, which is similar to that using the 99% TN rate in the third approach. However, by contrast with the logit specification omitting the *MFTA* and *ROWFTA* terms, the predictive power of this logit is better; in Table 4b we predict only 28.31% of the FTA cells correctly using a cutoff of 0.5.[29] One more interesting result is worth noting from a comparison of Tables 4a and b. In the case of Table 4a, the presence of the *MFTA* and *ROWFTA* terms in the specification causes the percentage correctly predicted to increase as time progresses; however, in the case of Table 4b, the percentage correctly predicted falls over time. Hence,

Table 4a. *Predictions of FTAs*

	Correctly predict FTA existence in year t (FTA_t = 1) using MFTA and ROWFTA variables								
	Cutoff from Sens, Sp		*TrueNeg.Rate = 97%*		*TrueNeg.Rate = 99%*		*Prob. Cutoff at 50%*		
Year t	*%t Correct*	*Correctly predicted*	*% Correct*	*Correctly predicted*	*% Correct*	*Correctly predicted*	*% Correct*	*Correctly predicted*	*Observed*
1960	83.87	26	38.71	12	30.96	1	3.23	1	31
1965	75.44	43	56.14	32	56.98	6	10.53	6	57
1970	82.93	34	65.85	27	19.51	8	17.07	7	41
1975	86.54	90	62.50	65	22.12	23	21.15	22	104
1980	88.46	92	84.62	88	56.73	59	56.73	59	104
1985	87.22	116	75.94	101	46.62	62	45.86	61	133
1990	94.30	149	81.65	129	57.59	91	56.96	90	158
1995	93.96	280	76.85	229	45.97	137	44.30	132	298
2000	91.79	570	76.17	473	50.40	313	50.08	311	621
2005	91.94	867	76.78	724	51.64	487	51.22	483	943
Total	91.04	2267	75.50	1880	47.67	1187	47.07	1172	2490
Cutoff		0.039		0.1344		0.49		0.5	

Notes: The following predictions are from Logit, MFTA count regression, with years in multiples of 5 only. Independent variables are in t – 5.

Table 4b. Predictions of FTAs

	Correctly predict FTA existence in year t (FTA_t = 1) without MFTA and ROW FTA variables								
	Cutoff from Sens, Sp		*TrueNeg.Rate = 97%*		*TrueNeg.Rate = 99%*		*Prob. Cutoff at 50%*		
Year t	*% Correct*	*Correctly predicted*	*% Correct*	*Correctly predicted*	*% Correct*	*Correctly predicted*	*% Correct*	*Correctly predicted*	*Observed*
1960	100.00	31	90.32	28	51.61	16	41.94	13	31
1965	89.47	51	61.40	35	29.82	17	26.32	15	57
1970	97.56	40	73.17	30	48.78	20	41.46	17	41
1975	95.19	99	81.73	85	45.19	47	38.46	40	104
1980	98.08	102	82.69	86	47.12	49	43.27	45	104
1985	98.50	131	81.95	109	43.61	58	38.35	51	133
1990	98.10	155	83.54	132	44.94	71	40.51	64	158
1995	98.32	293	79.19	236	40.94	122	34.23	102	298
2000	88.24	548	63.93	397	29.95	186	25.76	160	621
2005	79.53	750	51.86	489	23.33	220	21.00	198	943
Total	88.35	2200	65.34	1627	32.37	806	28.31	705	2490
Cutoff		0.027		0.1368		0.45		0.5	

Notes: The above predictions are from Logit, (*No-MFTA*) count regression, with years in multiples of 5 only. Independent variables are in $t - 5$.

accounting for endogenous bilateralism in the logit specification contributes to a relatively more successful true positive rate over time.

6. Conclusions

One of the most notable international economic events since 1990 has been the proliferation of bilateral FTAs, argued by some to be attributable to governments having pursued a policy of "competitive liberalization." Guided by Baier and Bergstrand (2004), we have explored the relative importance for the welfare gains of an FTA between a country-pair *ij* (FTA_{ij}) of two "sources" of interdependence, own-FTA interdependence (the effect of an existing FTA of *i* or *j* with a third country *k*) and cross-FTA interdependence (the effect of an existing FTA between a third-country-pair *kl*). Theoretical considerations suggest that the own-FTA effect of one more FTA has an impact on the gains from FTA_{ij} greater than that of one more FTA among a third-country-pair. Guided by these considerations, we specified a simple logit (and probit) model to estimate the influence on the likelihood of a bilateral FTA between *i* and *j* of indexes for each country of "multilateral FTAs" and "*ROW* FTAs"—in the spirit of Anderson and van Wincoop's (2003) "multilateral resistance" terms, as linearized in Baier and Bergstrand (2009). We found that the marginal response probabilities of these indexes of "own-FTA" and "cross-FTA" effects were both statistically and economically significant, and the response probabilities suggested that one more FTA of *i* or *j* with a third country *k* (own-FTA effect) had an impact on the probability of FTA_{ij} of approximately 50 times that of one more FTA among a third-country-pair *kl* (cross-FTA effect). Moreover, using a "sensitivity–specificity" analysis, we determined the optimum cutoff probability for predicting FTAs and the results indicated that we could predict correctly an FTA ("No-FTA") when one existed (none existed) 91% of the time. The results provide economically and statistically significant evidence that own-FTA effects tend to dominate cross-FTA effects as sources of "interdependence."

References

Anderson, James E. and Eric van Wincoop, "Gravity with Gravitas: A Solution to the Border Puzzle," *American Economic Review* 93 (2003):170–92.

Bagwell, Kyle and Robert W. Staiger, "Regionalism and Multilateralism Tariff Co-operation," in John Pigott and Alan Woodland (eds), *International Trade Policy and the Pacific Rim*, New York: St. Martin's Press (1998).

Baier, Scott L. and Jeffrey H. Bergstrand, "Economic determinants of free trade agreements," *Journal of International Economics* 64 (2004):29–63.

Baier, Scott L. and Jeffrey H. Bergstrand, "*Bonus vetus* OLS: A Simple Approach for Approximating International Trade–cost Effects using the Gravity Equation," *Journal of International Economics* 77 (2009):77–85.

Baldwin, Richard E., "A Domino Theory of Regionalism," National Bureau of Economic Research working paper 4465 (1993).

Baldwin, Richard E., "A Domino Theory of Regionalism," in Richard Baldwin, Pertti Haaparanta and Jaakko Kiander (eds), *Expanding Membership of the European Union*, Cambridge: Cambridge University Press (1995).

Baldwin, Richard E. and Dany Jaimovich, "Are Free Trade Agreements Contagious?" *Journal of International Economics* 88 (2012):1–16.

Bergsten, C. Fred, "Competitive Liberalization and Global Free Trade: A Vision for the Early 21st Century," Peterson Institute for International Economics working paper 96-15 (1996).

Bergstrand, Jeffrey, Peter Egger, and Mario Larch, "Economic Determinants of the *Timing* of Preferential Trade Agreement Formations and Enlargements," unpublished manuscript, University of Notre Dame (September 2009).
Cameron, A. Colin and Pravin Trivedi, *Microeconometrics: Methods and Applications*, New York, NY: Cambridge University Press (2005).
Chamberlain, Gary, "Analysis of Covariance with Qualitative Data," *Review of Economic Studies* 47 (1980):225–38.
Chen, Maggie X. and Sumit Joshi, "Third-country Effects on the Formation of Free Trade Agreements," *Journal of International Economics* 82 (2010):238–48.
Cohen, Jacob, Patricia Cohen, Stephen G. West, and Leona S. Aiken, *Applied Multiple Regression/Correlation Analysis for the Behavioral Sciences*, 3rd Ed., Mahwah, NJ: Lawrence Erlbaum Associates (2003).
Egger, Peter and Mario Larch, "Interdependent Preferential Trade Agreement Memberships: An Empirical Analysis," *Journal of International Economics* 76 (2008):384–99.
Heydon, Kenneth and Stephen Woolcock, *The Rise of Bilateralism*, New York: United Nations Press (2009).
Maddison, Angus, "Statistics on world population, GDP and Per Capita GDP," 1-2006 AD. Available at http://www.ggdc.net/maddison/ (2009).
McFadden, Daniel, "The Revealed Preferences of a Government Bureaucracy;" Theory, *Bell Journal of Economics* 6 (1975):401–16.
McFadden, Daniel, "Quantal Choice Analysis: A Survey," *Annals of Economic and Social Measurement* 5 (1976):363–90.
Tinbergen, Jan, *Shaping the World Economy: Suggestions for an International Economic Policy*. New York: The Twentieth Century Fund (1962).
Wooldridge, Jeffrey M., *Introductory Econometrics*, Cincinnati, OH: Southwestern (2000).
Wooldridge, Jeffrey M., *Econometric Analysis of Cross Section and Panel Data*, Cambridge, MA: MIT Press (2002).

Notes

1. According to Heydon and Woolcock (2009, pp. 10–11), bilateral preferential trade agreements "account for 80% of all PTAs notified and in force; 94% of those signed and/or under negotiation; and 100% of those at the proposal stage" with the vast bulk of preferential trade agreements being FTAs. Heydon and Woolcock note that "among projected agreements" 92% are planned as FTAs, 7% as partial scope agreements and only 1% as customs unions, with customs unions differing from FTAs owing to the former having a common external tariff with nonmembers. For brevity, we refer here to FTAs and customs unions as "FTAs," as most agreements formed in the past 50 years have been FTAs. Our analysis will omit partial scope agreements.
2. The reason for this exclusion is that BB examined only a cross-section for a particular year. Evaluating that issue econometrically would have led to endogeneity issues beyond that paper's scope, necessitating the computationally demanding cross-sectional spatial econometric techniques applied in Egger and Larch (2008).
3. In their panel data estimation, the spatial lag of third-country-pairs' FTAs were time-lagged 5 years to avoid endogeneity. Also, they combined own-FTA and cross-FTA influences by allowing $kl = il$ and $kl = kj$. Moreover, to avoid possible correlation of time-varying variables with the time-invariant component of the error terms, EL employed Chamberlain (1980) time-meaned "fixed effects." We discuss implications of this later.
4. The theoretical frameworks in Baldwin and Jaimovich (2012) and Chen and Joshi (2010), to be discussed shortly, are limited to three countries and so can only address the effects of an FTA between countries k and i or k and j on the welfare gains of an FTA between i and j. Egger and Larch (2008) did not provide a formal theoretical model. The underlying theoretical framework in BB has six countries.

5. The term "tariff complementarity" was introduced in Bagwell and Staiger (1998). Tariff complementarity (static version) refers to the net welfare gain to a member of an existing FTA from lowering external tariffs on a nonmember. Neither EL nor BJ addressed tariff complementarity, focusing instead upon trade diversion of nonmembers. This will be discussed more later. Some numerical comparative statics presented in an Online Appendix based upon the BB model suggest that the own-FTA welfare effect of one more FTA exceeds the cross-FTA welfare effect by a magnitude of 35–60 times. For the Online Appendix see Supporting Information.
6. The FTA indexes are akin to (inverse) multilateral and ROW resistances in the structural gravity model in Anderson and van Wincoop (2003), as linearized using a Taylor-series expansion in Baier and Bergstrand (2009).
7. We use "count" variables. CJ does not capture the full influence of own-FTA effects as we do using count variables; instead, CJ used indicator (dummy) variables.
8. The models in EL and BJ employed fixed effects.
9. In the case of one industry, there are only two parameters in the BB model, the elasticity of substitution in consumption (σ) and the level of fixed costs in production (ϕ). We assume that the countries have identical absolute (and hence relative) factor endowments, the elasticity of substitution between varieties (σ) is 4, the level of fixed costs is set at 1 (without loss of generality), and tariff rates are initially 30% for all countries ($\tau = 0.3$), as in BB. The sensitivity of the numerical comparative statics to values of σ and τ are discussed in the Online Appendix (see Supporting Information); the results are insensitive qualitatively to the level of fixed costs, ϕ.
10. In the Online Appendix, we show explicitly in the context of the BB model that the welfare gain for $1A$ from the formation of $FTA_{1A,1B}$—conditioned upon the existence of $FTA_{2A,2B}$—is unambiguously higher than the welfare gain for $1A$ from the formation of $FTA_{1A,1B}$ in the absence of $FTA_{2A,2B}$ for $\sigma = 4$ and initial $\tau = 0.3$.
11. We refer to the incentive for $1A$ to form an FTA with $1B$, conditioned on $FTA_{1A,2A}$, as tariff complementarity; this is a "selective" form of tariff complementarity. Typically, tariff complementarity refers to MFN tariffs (cf. Bagwell and Staiger (1998)). Here, tariff complementarity does not address MFN external tariffs but rather a specific form of tariff liberalization, namely, another FTA. However, this is similar, but not identical, to using Nash equilibrium tariffs, the typical setting for discussing (static) tariff complementarity.
12. In our Online Appendix, we show explicitly in the context of the BB model that the welfare gains from $FTA_{1A,1B}$ conditioned upon $FTA_{1A,2A}$ are approximately 35–60 times the welfare gains from $FTA_{1A,1B}$ conditioned upon $FTA_{2A,2B}$ for $\sigma = 4$ and initial $\tau = 0.3$. We also show why $2A$ retains its incentive to stay in the agreement with $1A$.
13. We will also consider probit estimates for robustness. However, as will be discussed later, logit is less restrictive (and problematic) than probit for introducing fixed effects in the robustness analysis.
14. In the Online Appendix we show these measures are in accordance with our numerical comparative statics. In Appendix Figures 5a–b, we introduce one FTA between $2A$ and $2B$ to see its impact on the net welfare gains of an FTA between $1A$ and $1B$. In Appendix Figures 6a–c, we introduce one FTA between $1A$ and $2A$ to see its impact on the net welfare gains of an FTA between $1A$ and $1B$.
15. Theory cannot suggest the specific choice of the 5-year time lag. However, two considerations influenced the decision. First, the decision by a country pair to form an FTA takes considerable time, and often exceeds 5 years. Second, in many cases, interdependence may cause FTA formations to accelerate and consequently 5 years may be too short a period. We chose 5 years to balance both sets of considerations.
16. Of course, GDPs increase over time and consequently not scaling GDPs of countries by world GDP may influence the results. Consequently, we also considered weights $\theta_{k,t-5} = Y_{k,t-5}/Y^{W}_{t,t-5}$, where Y^{W}_{t-5} is world GDP. The results are robust to this alternative measure. The alternative measure only influences the absolute magnitudes of the coefficient estimates, but has no bearing on the marginal response probabilities.

17. The data base is available at www.nd.edu/ jbergstr. Documentation for its construction is provided at the website. Every positive cell entry is hyper-linked to a PDF of its original treaty (98% of cells) or a secondary source (2% of cells); not all cells are potential observations as over the period some countries formed and others dissolved, e.g. Czechoslovakia. We will use only 146 of these countries, as explained shortly.
18. In the cases of these variables, we use averages rather than "count" variables, for convenience; this has no material consequence for the results.
19. We also used $ln[(Y_{it}+Y_{jt})/Y_t^W]$ for economic size, since world GDP changes over time; the results are robust to this alternative measure. Also, as in BB and EL, we are using real GDPs as a proxy for absolute factor endowments. Consequently, the terms-of-trade (real income) effects from, say, a natural FTA relative to an unnatural FTA are captured by $DIST_{ij}$ and $CONT_{ij}$.
20. There is likely a high degree of persistence in FTAs; the effect of this persistence is mitigated by predicting instead "formations."
21. A similar fall in overall explanatory power for the same adjustment was found in EL.
22. We also ran the probit on the FTA transitions dummy ($TFTA_{ij,t}$) and the coefficient estimates are qualitatively identical to those using the corresponding logit specification, but not reported for brevity. As demonstrated in Cameron and Trivedi (2005, p. 473), probit estimates should be approximately 55% of the corresponding logit estimates ($0.55=\sqrt{3}/\pi$).
23. Since Specification 6 is the only one in Table 2 to use the GDP-weighted versions of $MFTA_{i,t-5}$, $MFTA_{j,t-5}$, $ROWFTA_{ij,t-5}$, $MDIST_{ij,t-5}$ and $MCONT_{ij,t-5}$, we do not change the names of the variables named in column (1) to keep Table 2's size manageable.
24. This conclusion also holds for the FTA transitions LHS variable ($TFTA_{ij,t}$). Using GDP weights causes $MDIST_{ij}$ and $MCONT_{ij}$ to become time-varying. Also, see note 23 regarding the effects of the alternative weights on empirical results. Coefficient estimates can change but marginal response probabilities are unaffected. Hence, the larger coefficient estimate for *ROWFTAY* in Specification 6 does not alter significantly its marginal response probability.
25. Note that each country pair enters the data set only *once*, unlike gross trade flows in gravity equations. Thus, the coefficients on $MFTA_{i,t-5}$ and $MFTA_{j,t-5}$ need not be exactly equal; if every pair entered twice, they would be exactly equal.
26. In the context of Hypothesis 1, conditioning on $FTA_{1A,2A}$ is equivalent to a one-unit increase whereas—in the context of Hypothesis 2—conditioning on $FTA_{2A,2B}$ is equivalent to a two-unit increase.
27. These numerical comparative static estimates are provided in the Online Appendix. Note, however, that our marginal response probabilities—calculated using either a one-standard-deviation or a one-unit change—are employed to evaluate empirically (as closely as feasible) our theoretical Hypotheses 1 and 2. However, one could argue that the number of third-country-pair FTAs that a typical country-pair faces combined with the $ROWFTA_{ij,t-5}$ marginal response probability should be compared with the number of own FTAs combined with the $MFTA_{i,t-5}$ marginal response probability. We leave this to future research; our theoretical model only provides predictions concerning unit increments in other FTAs.
28. However, the predicted probabilities in EL are based upon specifications using time-meaned fixed effects.
29. The near doubling in predictive TP rates is much larger than the 5 percentage point improvement in Egger and Larch (2008) from introducing their spatial lag.

Supporting Information

Additional Supporting Information may be found in the online version of this article at the publisher's web-site:

SI. Online Appendix.

Chapter 9

ECONOMIC DETERMINANTS OF THE *TIMING* OF PREFERENTIAL TRADE AGREEMENT FORMATIONS AND ENLARGEMENTS

JEFFREY H. BERGSTRAND, PETER EGGER and MARIO LARCH*

Preferential trade agreements (PTAs) have proliferated over the past 60 years. While a small number of recent studies have examined empirically the economic determinants of the likelihood of a pair of countries having a PTA, this study explains empirically the timing of all PTA formations and enlargements from 1950 through 2006 using duration analysis. Our main and novel goal is to predict (in- and out-of-sample) a substantive share of these 1,560 PTA events using a parsimonious model with mainly economic variables, taking selection dynamics into account. Our analysis reveals that we can predict correctly in-sample the actual year of entry into force for 26% of the 1,560 bilateral PTA formations/enlargements in the period 1950–2006 among 10,518 pairings of 146 countries using only a few economic and political variables. Moreover, we can predict correctly in-sample 57% of these PTA events within a 10-year window leading up to the event using this model. The model also performs well out-of-sample for the near term (82%), but not if the out-of-sample period is very long. We conclude with an evaluation of the model's ability to predict the timing of the North American Free Trade Agreement, the European Union's formation and enlargements, and the model's ten most likely post-2006 PTA events. (*JEL* F14, F15)

I. INTRODUCTION

One of the most notable economic events since World War II is the proliferation of preferential trade agreements (PTAs), including free trade agreements (FTAs) and customs unions (CUs). The study of such agreements has followed fundamentally two paths, one normative and one positive. The normative path is whether or not PTAs are welfare-improving (see Bagwell and Staiger 1997, 2005; Bond, Riezman, and Syropoulos 2004). A full survey of this literature is beyond the scope of this paper, but see Baldwin (2007) for an excellent survey.

*The authors gratefully acknowledge numerous valuable comments from the editor, Bruce Blonigen, three anonymous reviewers, Richard Baldwin, Mathias Thoenig, and several other participants at the conference "Empirical Determinants of Regionalism," The Graduate Institute of International and Development Studies, Geneva, the 25th Annual Congress of the European Economic Association, 2010, Glasgow, and the 12th Göttingen Workshop "Internationale Wirtschaftsbeziehungen", 2010, Göttingen.

Bergstrand: Professor, Department of Finance, Mendoza College of Business, University of Notre Dame, Notre Dame, IN 46556, Phone 1 574-261-1071, Fax 1 574-631-5255, E-mail bergstrand.1@nd.edu

Egger: Professor, Chair of Applied Economics, ETH Zürich, 8092 Zürich, Switzerland. Phone 41-44-632-4108, E-mail egger@kof.ethz.ch

Larch: Professor, Chair of Empirical Economics, University of Bayreuth, 95447, Bayreuth, Germany. Phone 49-921-55-6240, E-mail mario.larch@uni-bayreuth.de

ABBREVIATIONS

AFTZ: African Free Trade Zone
BB: Baier and Bergstrand (2004)
COMESA: Common Market for Eastern and Southern Africa
CUs: Customs Unions
CUSFTA: Canada–United States Free Trade Agreement
EAC: East African Community
ECCAS: Economic Community of Central African States
EEC: European Economic Community
EL: Egger and Larch (2008)
EU: European Union
FTAs: Free Trade Agreements
GATT: General Agreement on Tariffs and Trade
GDPs: Gross Domestic Products
MTN: Multilateral Trade Negotiation
NAFTA: North American Free Trade Agreement
PTAs: Preferential Trade Agreements
ROW: Rest of the World
SADC: Southern African Development Community
WTO: World Trade Organization

*Originally Published in *Economic Inquiry*, 54(1), pp. 315–341.

The second path, which is "positive," examines what factors explain and predict which pairs of countries *have* PTAs. Building on the work of Krugman (1991a, 1991b) and Frankel (1997), Baier and Bergstrand (2004), or BB, introduced asymmetric absolute and relative factor endowments into a Krugman-type increasing-returns/monopolistic-competition model to show theoretically that the net utility gains from a bilateral PTA depend on two countries' economic sizes and their economic similarity, bilateral distance, and relative factor endowments. Using a single cross-section for 1996, BB employed a probit analysis to show that these economic factors that tend to improve on net a country-pair's utility from a PTA also tend to increase the pair's probability of having a PTA. Egger and Larch (2008), Chen and Joshi (2010), and Baldwin and Jaimovich (2012) confirmed BB's findings and showed that additional variables—such as pre-existing PTAs—also tend to increase the likelihood of a pair of countries having an agreement.[1]

Despite the proliferation of PTAs over the past 60 years, there is still considerable scope for further formations or enlargements of PTAs. Governments' policy makers have long been looking for a "road map" to guide them toward selection of PTA partners for enlarging existing arrangements or forming new ones; limited resources and political obstacles have inevitably constrained governments to sequencing such formations and enlargements rather than pursuing them simultaneously. Ideally, such a road map should be consistent with improving the net economic welfare of members. This study attempts to explain and predict (in-sample) the actual *timing* of formations and enlargements of *all PTAs* among 10,518 pairings of 146 countries for 57 years from 1950 through 2006 based upon a parsimonious structure inspired by a simple economic model. Moreover, to gauge the potential usefulness of this exercise for future formations and enlargements, we also show how our approach predicts PTA events well *out-of-sample*, based primarily on economic considerations. The results suggest that most PTA formations and enlargements are influenced by factors that tend to increase pairs' economic welfare.

In econometrics, the analysis of the time elapsed until a certain event occurs is referred to as duration analysis. Duration analysis has its origin in survival analysis, which refers to the survival time of a subject in a particular state. In our context, this refers to the survival of a country-pair in the state of "No-PTA." Central to such analyses is the hazard rate, which in our context emphasizes the conditional probability of a country-pair leaving the state of No-PTA *conditional upon* having been in this state for a particular duration. The latter emphasizes the inherently dynamic nature of duration analysis, cf., Abbring and van den Berg (2002), de Ree and Nillesen (2009), and Wooldridge (2010). So, the key difference of this paper from the existing literature is predicting the *specific year* of a PTA formation/enlargement event (or a window of years leading up to the event), in-sample and out-of-sample, using a parsimonious econometric model motivated by economic and political variables.[2]

In this paper, we first address how one might interpret the decision of a pair of countries to form/enlarge a PTA in some year *conditional upon* not having had a PTA until that year. This discussion informs us about the determinants of the "hazard rate" (without economic covariates), which is the probability of a country-pair leaving the No-PTA state in a year conditional upon having been without a PTA up until that year. Classic distributions determining hazard rates include the Weibull and log-logistic distributions, which yield that such hazard rates are functions of time trends. However, a simple time trend in the absence of economic covariates can explain only 11% of the variation in the PTA events. Second, most economic duration analyses are concerned with the influence of time-invariant or time-varying economic covariates that "shift" the hazard rate in any year. Drawing upon the recent literature on economic determinants of PTAs noted above, we motivate the inclusion of several economic and political covariates that likely influence the probability of two countries forming/enlarging a PTA in any particular year, conditional upon not having a PTA until that year. These covariates include

1. Egger and Larch (2008) and Baldwin and Jaimovich (2012) examined the influence on the probabilities of PTAs of existing nearby agreements in a previous period using spatial econometrics, providing broad empirical support for potential trade diversion inducing nonmembers to either join existing PTAs (supporting Baldwin's domino theory) or form new ones. A similar analysis motivated by network formation was undertaken by Chen and Joshi (2010). However, these studies did not examine the effects of existing PTAs on the *timing* of new PTAs and enlargements, which we examine.

2. Baldwin and Jaimovich (2012) used duration analysis in one robustness analysis of their model. Liu (2008, 2010) used a duration analysis, but excluded interdependence controls. Also, neither of these studies focused on the role of time and all of them omitted in-sample and out-of-sample predictions.

three measures of *geography*, four measures of *economic size and relative factor endowments*, four measures of the influences of *other PTAs*, and six *political variables*. These covariates have an explanatory power of up to 44% when measured by the pseudo-R^2 (up to 49% including fixed effects). They predict (in-sample) up to 57% of the 1,560 bilateral PTA events in the period 1950–2006 among the 10,518 pairings of 146 countries within a 10-year window leading up to the date of entry (up to 72% when including fixed effects). The same models predict up to 26% (39% with country-pair fixed effects) of the PTA events in the very year they occurred.[3]

Third, our model also performs well out-of-sample. Taking only the periods up through 2000 for the estimation, the model predicts up to *66%* of the 284 PTAs concluded from 2001 through 2006 in the year the PTAs were concluded, and up to *82%* in a 5-year window up until the actual formation of the PTAs. The out-of-sample predictions are worse when only the years up through 1989 were used for estimation and the out-of-sample period was quite long (1990–2006), but then the regressions are informed by only 523 PTA events that happened prior to 1990. We close the study with an evaluation of the influence of multilateralism on PTA timing and of the successfulness of the model for predicting in particular the Canada–United States Free Trade Agreement (CUSFTA), the North American Free Trade Agreement (NAFTA), the formation of the original European Economic Community (EEC) and subsequent enlargements, and the model's most likely PTA events in the post-sample period of 2007–2013.

The remainder of the paper is organized as follows. Section II motivates the use of an econometric duration model to analyze the timing of PTA (formation/enlargement) "events." Section III motivates the time-invariant and time-varying economic, political, and historical determinants of the hazard rate. Section IV describes the data. Section V provides the empirical results. Section VI provides the predictive analysis. Section VII concludes.

II. MOTIVATION FOR A DURATION ANALYSIS OF TIME-TO-PTA

A. *Analyzing PTA Status versus Timing of PTAs*

Figure 1 illustrates the years in which PTA events occurred, summarizing the (cumulative) number of bilateral trade agreement "membership events" for all years from 1950 through 2006 in which some new "membership" occurred (either a new agreement or an enlargement), according to information mainly provided by the World Trade Organization (WTO).[4] The WTO categorization (labeled there regional trade agreements, or RTAs) includes two-way preferential agreements, FTAs in goods, FTAs in services, and CUs.[5] We focus on memberships at the country-pair level and avoid redundant observations by counting events such as the membership of France and (West) Germany in the original EEC as a single new membership "event" (instead of two events) and the enlargement of the original EEC to include the United Kingdom as five new membership events instead of ten events.[6] Accordingly, the events should not be interpreted as just new PTAs that have been formed, since we also count as new memberships ones that are brought about through enlargements of existing PTAs. In this study, we do not separate our empirical sample into "new

3. As will be discussed later, the potential number of observations is 599,526, given the number of country-pairs and years. However, we construct our sample such that—once a country-pair forms a PTA in a particular year—subsequent years are excluded. For instance, Germany and France entered (into force) the European Economic Community in 1958; consequently, years 1959–2006 are excluded for Germany–France. This reduces our number of observations from 599,526 to 463,289. Subsequent data constraints will reduce it further for some empirical specifications.

4. The cumulative number of all PTA events corresponds to the number of country-pairs in the sample which liberalized trade preferentially since 1950. We had to amend the data to capture agreements not included in the WTO data base. For instance, most of the members of the former communist bloc were engaged in agreements outside the WTO (or, prior to the foundation of the WTO, the General Agreement on Tariffs and Trade, GATT). Note that an event requires that explanatory variables employed in the subsequent empirical analysis are not missing for a country-pair. Accordingly, the memberships associated with this figure are the same ones used in estimation later. Figure 1 presents these cumulative events as a percentage of 10,518 country-pairs covered.

5. Higher levels of economic integration, such as common markets and economic unions, are also included; for instance, Germany and France—members of the Eurozone—are considered in the WTO listing as a customs union (CU). One-way preferential trade agreements, such as Generalized System of Preferences (GSP) agreements, are excluded.

6. For instance, the 10 events in 1958 correspond to the formation of the EEC in that year. The corresponding number of memberships is 10, because Belgium and Luxembourg are counted as a single country (as often done in economic studies), so that there are 5 founding members and the number of unique dyads is $5(5 - 1)/2$.

FIGURE 1
Years to Event for Different Groups for the Years 1950–2006

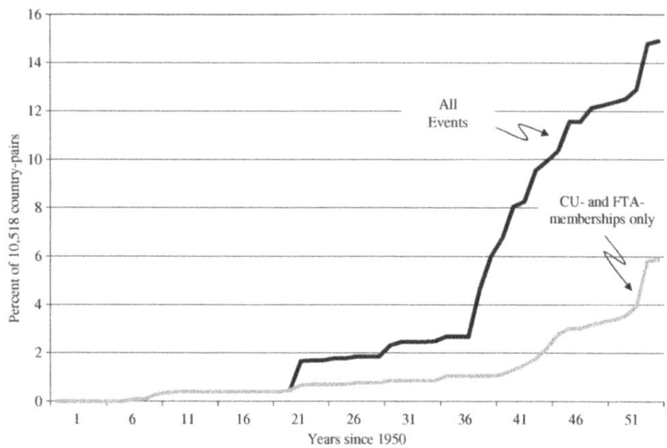

PTAs" versus "enlarged PTAs." We also show in Figure 1 the subset of PTA events that include only FTAs and CUs.

The figure suggests that there have been years with strong and weak membership activity over time. The number of all PTA membership "events" concluded since 1950 rose to 1,560 until the end of 2006, that is, 14.83% of the 10,518 country-pairs and 0.34% of the 463,289 total observations in the panel, recalling that a time-series for a country-pair ends in 2006 if no PTA is formed *or* in the year a PTA enters into force (see footnote 3). From these data, we can create a variable representing the "Time-to-PTA event," as done in duration analysis. Our focus will then be to find the economic, political, and historical determinants that explain the "Time-to-PTA event," meaning the *timing* of the formation of a new agreement or an enlargement of an existing PTA agreement.[7]

Our goal in this paper is to predict the duration (in years) before a country-pair entered a PTA (through formation or enlargement) using a duration model with a parsimonious set of time-invariant and time-varying variables. This contrasts with the goal of BB, Magee (2003), Egger and Larch (2008, henceforth EL), Chen and Joshi (2010), and Baldwin and Jaimovich (2012) who focused on explaining which country-pairs *had* a PTA in a given year. The econometric framework employed there was the qualitative choice model of McFadden (1975, 1976). In BB, the probability of a PTA was linked heuristically to an underlying latent variable, denoted ΔU_{ij} here. In that study's context, ΔU_{ij} represented the difference in utility levels from an action (formation of a PTA), where

$$\Delta U_{ij} = \mathbf{x}_{ij}\beta + e_{ij}, \quad (1)$$

and $\mathbf{x}_{ij}$ denoted a vector of explanatory variables (economic characteristics) of country-pair ij including a constant, β was a vector of parameters, and error term e_{ij} was assumed to be independent of $\mathbf{x}_{ij}$ and to have a standard normal distribution. In the context of BB's model, $\Delta U_{ij} = min(\Delta U_i, \Delta U_j)$, where ΔU_i (ΔU_j) denoted the change in utility for the representative consumer in i (j); both countries' representative consumers needed to benefit from a PTA for their governments to form one.[8] The

7. Figure 1 illustrates three apparent "waves of regionalism" since 1950. The first wave (beginning in 1958) was initiated by the formation of the European Economic Community (EEC) and then the European Free Trade Agreement (EFTA). The second wave (beginning in 1973) included several enlargements of the EEC and the introduction of several new PTAs. The third wave (beginning in 1989) included the formations of the Canada–United States FTA, NAFTA, MERCOSUR, and numerous bilateral agreements.

8. Side (or compensation) payments were ruled out.

latent variable ΔU_{ij} was assumed to generate the binary indicator variable of PTA membership, PTA_{ij}, which was unity if two countries had a PTA and zero otherwise. The response probability for a PTA, P, was then:

$$(2)\quad P\left(PTA_{ij}=1\right)=P\left(\Delta U_{ij}>0\right)=G\left(\mathbf{x}_{ij}\beta\right),$$

where $G(\cdot)$ was the standard normal cumulative distribution function, which ensured that $P(PTA_{ij}=1)$ was between 0 and 1. This literature has assumed that $P(PTA_{ij}=1)>0.5$ "indicated" $\Delta U_{ij}>0$ and $P(PTA_{ij}=1)\leq 0.5$ indicated $\Delta U_{ij}\leq 0$.

Rather than focusing on the static explanation of PTAs in a cross-section of data in a given year, this paper aims at examining the determinants of the *timing* of PTA events using duration analysis. Duration models fall within the class of limited dependent variable models in general and censored regression models in particular (cf., Wooldridge 2010). Duration analysis has been used increasingly in the economics literature since 1980. The most common application is in labor economics evaluating empirically the determinants of the length of a spell of unemployment of an individual, cf., Heckman and Singer (1984) and Kiefer (1988). There is only a small number of studies which have applied this framework in international trade.[9]

For the research question of this paper, two issues have to be addressed. First, we have to rationalize an empirical model of timing of PTAs in the *absence* of time-invariant and time-varying economic covariates. Second, we have to allude to how the hazard rate interacts with fundamental economic variables that are known to *shift* a country-pair's probability of forming an agreement at any point in time. We address these issues separately below.[10]

B. Economic Motivation for a Discrete-Time Duration Model

In this section, we discuss a simple economic motivation for a discrete-time duration model for analyzing time-to-PTA events. Suppose that, at the country-pair ij level in any year t, each of two governments choose between two states, entering a bilateral PTA or not. The decision of interest is the duration of years T_{ij} after which governments i and j will adopt a bilateral PTA. Data on elapsed time since some fixed year until the inception of a PTA are only available by year. Hence, we cannot portray time-to-PTA events by a continuous process econometrically, but need to resort to a discrete-time representation.

In the No-PTA state and year t, assume the governments of i and j receive utility $U_{ij}'(t)$ associated with bilateral trade flows. These governments may receive the possibility in any year t to form a PTA. From that, they would realize cum-PTA utility (associated with cum-PTA trade flows) drawn from a continuous distribution with density $f(U_{ij}(t))$ at a constant rate g in every year t. The probability of realizing the benefits $U_{ij}(t)$ from concluding a PTA (and the associated trade flows) after T years is gT. Suppose that the possibility to conclude PTAs is drawn independently of $f(U_{ij}(t))$, and governments know the density function $f(\cdot)$ but not the utility $U_{ij}(t)$ from a given PTA. Moreover, suppose for simplicity that reservation utility $U_{ij}'(t)$ from staying outside of a PTA is independent of the change in trade flows induced by the conclusion of the PTA, while the change in utility through PTA formation is a function of the change in trade flows but not of the functional form $f(\cdot)$. Upon receiving the possibility to conclude a PTA at random intervals, governments then decide about when to form a PTA. The decision about when to enter a PTA will depend on the comparison of the expected gains from PTA membership as captured by $U_{ij}(t)$ with

9. Joyce (2005) and Conway (2007) studied determinants of the lengths of spells of IMF programs. Besedes (2008), Besedes and Prusa (2006a,2006b), Fugazza and Molina (2009), Nitsch (2009), and Hess and Persson (2010) all have studied the determinants of bilateral trade-flow durations. Only two other studies have examined determinants of the timing of PTA events, namely Liu (2008, 2010). However, Liu (2008) focused on the marginal effects of political economy determinants of PTA timings (specifically, income-inequality's interactive effects with relative capital-labor endowment ratios) to test a "median-voter" model of PTA timing versus a "lobbying" model. That study's finding in favor of the median-voter model provides support for our economic determinants of the timing of PTA approach and our alternative focus on domino effects, competitive liberalization, and PTA interdependence. Liu (2010) extends Liu (2008) by testing competing predictions of the median voter model versus the lobbying model. However, Liu (2008, 2010) omitted controls for "interdependence," did not provide any predicted probabilities of time-to-PTA events, and did not provide any out-of-sample predictions, all of which are goals of the present paper.

10. The vast number of pairs of countries that form PTAs in our sample (1,560 events) do so permanently; our sample includes only 48 events of pairs ending agreements. By contrast, the labor economics duration literature on unemployment spells and the international economics literature on IMF program spells deal with macroeconomic policies/environments, where entering and exiting spells of unemployment or programs, respectively, is frequent. Due to the insignificant number of PTA exits, we do not address the latter events in this study.

FIGURE 2

Illustration of Hazard Rate as a Function of Time

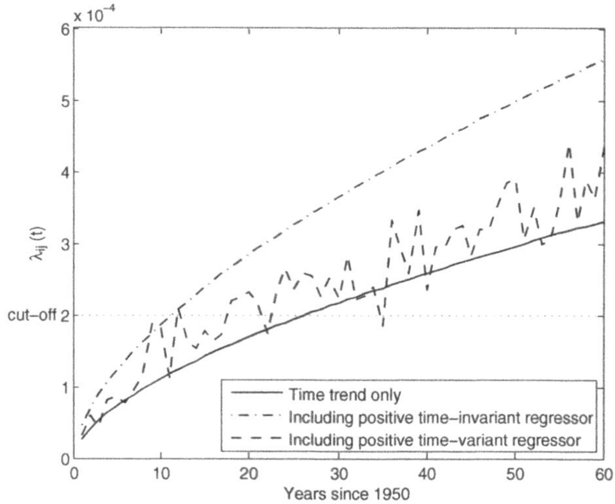

the reservation gains captured by $U_{ij}'(t)$. Accordingly, the probability that a PTA is acceptable can be written as:

$$(3) \quad P_{ij}(t) = \int_{U_{ij}'(t)}^{\infty} f\left(U_{ij}(t)\right) dU_{ij}(t).$$

Country-pair *ij*'s transition rate from No-PTA to PTA in year *t* is reflected in the product of the constant rate at which PTAs become possible in any year (g) and the probability that they are acceptable in year *t*, $P_{ij}(t)$. This transition rate is the probability of leaving the No-PTA state in *t* given that governments *i* and *j* did not conclude a PTA until then, and it may be referred to as the hazard rate for the distribution of duration until PTA formation:

$$(4) \quad \lambda_{ij}(t) = P\left(T_{ij} = t | T_{ij} \geq t\right) = gP_{ij}(t),$$

where T_{ij} is the survival time out of PTA status of country-pair *ij*.

There are several possible distributions for modeling the hazard rate, $\lambda_{ij}(t)$. For a discrete-time multivariate model as the one proposed here, the complementary log-log distribution is a common choice (see Jenkins 1995, 2005). In comparison to other distributions, this specification has the advantage of allowing for time-varying covariates—an essential element of our study discussed in the next section. Figure 1 suggests that, apart from the covariates in vector $\mathbf{x}_{ijt}$, we may want to allow for a general time trend in a specification of time-to-PTA events. The latter can be easily done with the complementary log-log distribution when specifying $\lambda_{ij}(t)$ as:

$$(5) \quad \lambda_{ij}(t) = 1 - \exp\left[-\exp\left(\mathbf{x}_{ijt}\beta + \gamma_t\right)\right],$$

where $\mathbf{x}_{ijt}\beta = \beta_0 + \beta_1 x_{1,ijt} + \beta_2 x_{2,ijt} + \ldots + \beta_K x_{K,ijt}$ and γ_t captures the general time trend.

We model the general time trend as $\gamma_t = r\ln(t)$, which implies that the shape of the hazard monotonically increases if $r > 0$, decreases if $r < 0$, or is constant if $r = 0$ (see Jenkins 2005). If concluding PTAs becomes generally easier as time marches on, we would expect $r > 0$.

Figure 2 illustrates the relationship between the hazard rate and time *t* with a complementary log-log distribution function. The slope of the hazard rate depends on the coefficient of the general time trend *r* as well as the explanatory variables. Consistent with estimates reported later on for the data underlying this study, we assume that $r = 0.61$ in Figure 2.[11] If other

11. This result is consistent with a time trend parameter of 0.61 in Specification 2 in Table 3 below.

explanatory variables do not matter and the hazard rate $\lambda_{ij}(t)$ of leaving the initial No-PTA state increases with larger t, we obtain a functional relationship as shown by the continuous concave locus labeled "Time trend only" in Figure 2 with $\lambda_{ij}(t) = 1 - \exp[-\exp(0.61\ln(t))]$. One may think of many factors underlying a rising hazard rate with time per se. For instance, falling tariffs due to multilateral trade liberalization under the General Agreement on Tariffs and Trade (GATT) or WTO may have had an influence; in fact, we examine this later empirically in Section VI. Alternatively, generally declining political costs of political and economic cooperation after World War II could be mentioned here.

Beyond a trend (and multilateralism's possible effect), the timing of PTAs is likely influenced by economic, historical, and political factors. Clearly, variables that have been found to increase the probability of concluding a PTA in previous research will lead to a reduction of the time-to-PTA events with processes as specified in Equations (3) and (5). The reason is that everything that influences the net utility gain of country-pair ij from participating in a PTA in any year t will also raise the hazard rate $\lambda_{ij}(t)$. Hence, obvious candidate variables in $\mathbf{x}_{ijt}$ to predict (in- and out-of-sample) a substantive share of the 1,560 PTA events underlying Figure 1 are the determinants of PTA memberships in a cross-section of data in BB. For instance, having a common land border (a time-invariant variable) or two countries being jointly economically larger (a time-variant variable) are strong partial predictors of PTA membership in a cross-section. Either of these factors raises the probability that a PTA is acceptable, $P_{ij}(t)$, *ceteris paribus*. Hence, either of these factors should raise the hazard rate $\lambda_{ij}(t)$. However, time-invariant and time-variant elements in $\mathbf{x}_{ijt}$ affect the hazard rate in functionally different ways. This is illustrated by the two broken loci in Figure 2. For the locus labeled "Including positive time-invariant regressor," we added 0.52 to the time trend so that $\lambda_{ij}(t) = 1 - \exp[-\exp(0.52 + 0.61\ln(t))]$.[12] For the locus labeled "Including positive time-variant regressor," we added $0.10\varepsilon_{ijt}$ to the time trend, where ε_{ijt} is drawn randomly from a normal distribution with mean and standard deviation of one. Then, $\lambda_{ij}(t) = 1 - \exp[-\exp(0.13\varepsilon_{ijt} + 0.61\ln(t))]$.[13] As can be seen from Figure 2, there is a tendency for both time-invariant and time-variant shifters of $P_{ij}(t)$ to raise the hazard rate. However, time-variant shifters of $P_{ij}(t)$ render the hazard rate a potentially *non-monotonic* function of time, which is not the case for time-invariant shifters.

III. FACTORS SHIFTING THE PROBABILITIES OF PTAs

A. *Economic Factors*

The purpose of this section is to identify economic variables that potentially "shift" the hazard rate, $\lambda_{ij}(t)$, in any year t, thus increasing or decreasing the likelihood that a PTA occurs *sooner*.[14] In the spirit of the *extant* literature, we consider determinants of the probability of PTAs suggested in recent studies by BB, EL, and Baldwin and Jaimovich (2012), as such variables are expected to alter in any period t the latent variable $U_{ij}(t)$ defined earlier.[15]

Notice that the time-to-PTA-event structure addressed in the previous section makes both the theoretical and the empirical approach in this paper fundamentally different from the ones in BB, EL, Chen and Joshi (2010), and Baldwin and Jaimovich (2012). These papers provided only a static motivation for PTA formation. Hence, conditional on observable (economic and/or political) time-specific and time-invariant determinants, PTA membership was explained in the cross-section pertaining to a specific time period. However, duration, time-to-event, or survival models as the one outlined in the previous section are inherently dynamic, since the selection into PTA membership changes conditional on the time elapsed (see Wooldridge 2010, chapter 22, Section IV.B for a discussion of the dynamic nature of duration models). However, the present approach shares with the earlier work that there are time-specific fundamental

12. A parameter on common borders of 0.52 is also consistent with Specification 2 in Table 3 below.

13. A parameter of 0.13 is, for example, consistent with the coefficient on two countries' joint economic size in Specification 2 in Table 3 below. However, we do not draw ε_{ijt} from a normal distribution with mean and variance as of two countries' joint economic size for reasons of illustration.

14. In short, period t economic variables influence $P_{ij}(t)$ in the equation $\lambda_{ij}(t) = gP_{ij}(t)$, because $P_{ij}(t)$ is a function of period t utility, $U_{ij}(t)$.

15. We provide in an online Theoretical Supplement (Appendix S1) a one-sector Krugman-type general equilibrium model to account for sequencing of PTA events to motivate all the economic factors below (except relative factor endowments).

FIGURE 3

Characteristics of RTA Insiders versus Outsiders for the Years 1950–2006

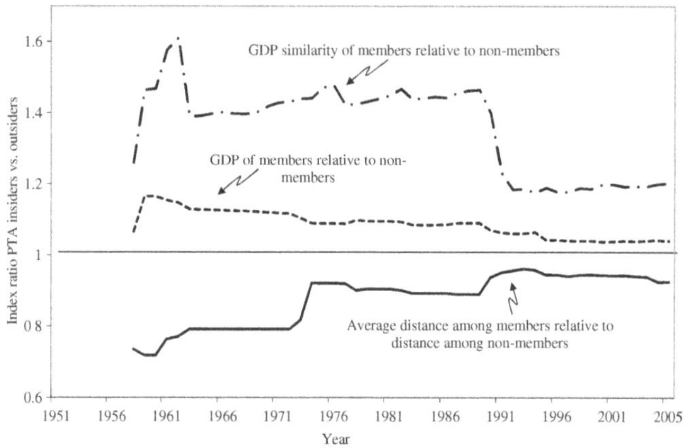

(economic, political and/or historical) drivers of PTA formation that are at play and inform the otherwise dynamic process.

Figure 3 illustrates the interplay between dynamic model aspects and shifters of the probability of becoming a PTA member. It takes the information associated with Figure 1 and combines the Time-to-PTA event data with three particular economic characteristics associated with the members of PTAs *relative to* those of nonmembers. One economic characteristic is the "proximity" of PTA members relative to nonmembers. We measure this using the average distance between the economic centers of members of PTAs relative to the average distance between economic centers of nonmembers. A second economic characteristic is the average economic size of PTA members relative to that of nonmembers; economic size is measured using countries' gross domestic products (GDPs). The third economic characteristic is the average difference between country-pairs' GDPs for PTA members relative to that of nonmembers.

Figure 3 illustrates several profoundly systematic relationships between distance, economic size, economic similarity, and the timing of PTA events.[16] The bottom line indicates two phenomena. The earliest PTA events (1958–1961) were between members whose average distance between members relative to nonmembers was the *smallest*. As time passed, the average distance between members relative to nonmembers rose systematically. This line suggests that PTAs formed or enlarged *sooner* among closer countries. The middle line indicates two phenomena related to economic size and PTA-event timing. The earliest PTA events were also between countries whose average economic size was the *largest* relative to nonmembers. Then, as time passed, the average relative economic size of members declined. This line suggests that PTAs formed or enlarged *sooner* among economically larger countries. The top line indicates two phenomena related to economic size similarity and PTA-event timing. The earliest PTA events were also among countries with very similar GDP sizes. As time passed, the degree of size similarity declined in general. This line suggests that PTAs formed or enlarged *sooner* among countries with more similar economic sizes.

BB provided theoretical motivations for the relationships between a country-pair's bilateral proximity, remoteness, economic size, economic similarity, and relative factor endowments for influencing the probability of a PTA, based upon a Krugman-type model of trade. Two countries' governments want to liberalize their bilateral

16. "Similarity" is measured (as traditionally) using the product of country *i*'s share of both countries' real GDPs with country *j*'s share.

trade through a PTA if they are less distant from each other but more distant from the rest of the world (ROW), if they are larger but more similarly sized economically, and have sufficiently different relative factor endowments.

Drawing on the domino theory in Baldwin (1995), EL enriched the BB framework by examining the role of other country-pairs' PTAs for influencing the likelihood of a PTA of a given country-pair. EL showed that, given a PTA forms, outsiders will lose in utility due to trade diversion. This creates, under some conditions, an incentive for them to join an existing PTA, or under alternative conditions form a new PTA. We introduce four new variables inspired by EL's approach to capture the influences of existing agreements on new or enlarged PTAs. First, we include the log distance of a pair of countries to the "nearest PTA" (DISTPTA). Intuitively, the closer are two countries to an existing PTA, the greater is the trade diversion they have incurred from that PTA. This implies a greater economic incentive to form/enlarge a PTA because of the potentially offsetting trade creation. Hence, DISTPTA is expected to be negatively related to the hazard rate. Second, a country-pair's utility is influenced by the "degree of regionalism" (or "competitive liberalization") in the ROW. The greater the number of PTAs in the ROW, the more trade diversion and loss of utility a country-pair experiences. We include a variable measuring the "degree of regionalism" in the ROW for every pair which is a spatially weighted average of all the PTAs that countries *i* and *j* face in ROW, denoted WPTA. WPTA is expected to be positively related to the hazard rate. Third, the variable DISTPTA influences—in the terminology of Baldwin (1995)—the "demand for membership" of outsiders into an existing PTA or a new PTA. However, in Baldwin (1995), the "supply of membership" was purposely assumed to be infinitely elastic. In reality, PTA membership is also constrained potentially by existing members; that is, supply of membership may have finite elasticity. In a theoretical model, we are able to show that the likelihood of a PTA between a country-pair may at first increase with the number of members in the "nearest PTA" but eventually may be constrained by the number of members in it, as some members of the existing agreement suffer sufficient trade diversion from other existing members as a result of a potential new entrant that these "marginally worse-off" members prevent entry. This suggests a quadratic relationship between the number of members in the nearest PTA and the hazard rate. We capture this new influence with a variable NPTA (and its squared value, SQNPTA), which is the actual number of members of the nearest existing PTA (and the square of that number). We expect NPTA (SQNPTA) to be positively (negatively) related to the hazard rate. These four variables, alongside the seven variables motivated by BB, suggest 11 economic covariates to be included in our duration analysis.[17]

B. Political and Historical Factors

In reality, political and historical factors matter. We employ several other control variables as shifters of the hazard rate as had been used in earlier work. The Polity 2 index is a well-known measure of political freedom in a country; we employ DPolity2 as a measure of the disparity in this index between country-pairs. We expect that a wider difference in two countries' degrees of political freedom will tend to reduce the likelihood of PTA formation. In an alternative specification, we also consider measures of differences of *sub-indices* of the Polity index: differences in political regimes of two countries (democracy and autocracy scores, DDEMOC and DAUTOC, respectively), differences in the party competition in the parliament (DPARCOMP) and in the political competition in government (DPOLCOMP). Earlier work has provided evidence that PTAs are less likely to form between countries with dissimilar political systems.

We also consider historical factors that have surfaced in the literature as determinants of PTAs. There are two variables related to the length and recency of wars between two countries (CUMDURAT and DIFFYEAR, respectively). The length of wars between a country-pair (CUMDURAT) is likely to have a negative effect on the hazard rate, but the number of years since the last war (DIFFYEAR) is likely to have a positive effect on the hazard rate. Earlier work

17. As noted earlier, all of these economic variables (with the exception of relative factor endowments) are shown to influence the sequencing of PTA events in our theoretical model in the Online Theoretical Supplement. Note that DISTPTA, WPTA, NPTA and SQNPTA all account for various channels through which other PTAs influence the formation of subsequent PTAs (i.e., interdependence). Other papers that have distinguished sources of interdependence include Chen and Joshi (2010), Baldwin and Jaimovich (2012), and Baier, Bergstrand, and Mariutto (2014); the latter paper details distinctions among these three papers and EL. Also, Deltas, Desmet, and Facchini (2012) provide evidence of the effects of the nature of PTA interdependencies on bilateral trade flows.

has provided evidence that PTAs are less likely to form between countries that have had long war history and recent wars (see Egger, Egger, and Greenaway 2008, and EL).

IV. DATA

A. Data on PTAs and Associated Variables

The data set for the timing-of-PTA events was compiled for the period 1950–2006 using information from notifications to the WTO, the CIA *World Fact Book*, and individual web pages of countries.

The information on the timing of PTA membership of country-pair ij at time t (the dependent variable) as well as on four explanatory variables—$WPTA_{ij,t-5}$ (the inverse-distance-weighted PTA membership of other pairs than ij at time $t-5$), $DISTPTA_{ij,t-5}$ (the minimum distance of i and j to a PTA at time $t-5$) and $NPTA_{ij,t-5}$ as well as $SQNPTA_{ij,t-5}$ (the number of members in the nearest PTA to ij at time $t-5$ and its squared value)—are based on the information on all PTAs notified to the WTO in conjunction with information on the geographic location of countries i and j (see also EL).

B. Data on Geography and Associated Variables

Geographic information is based on the CIA *World Fact Book*. Beyond $WPTA_{ij,t-5}$ and $DISTPTA_{ij,t-5}$, such information is used to construct three time-invariant, geographical variables which are supposed to capture whether two countries are "natural" trading partners or not. $DIST_{ij}$ is the (natural) logarithm of the great circle distance between the capitals of countries i and j (based on the great circle distance between their economic centers), $BORDER_{ij}$ indicates whether two countries share a common land border (=1) or not (=0), and $REMOTE_{ij}$ measures a country-pairs' remoteness from the ROW. The latter variable is the interaction of an indicator variable of 1 (0) for two countries on the same (on a different) continent, $DCONT_{ij}$, and a measure of "remoteness":

$$(6)\quad REMOTE_{ij} = DCONT_{ij} \times \frac{1}{2}\left[log\left(\sum_{k=1,k\neq j}^{N} \left(\text{Distance}_{ik}/(N-1)\right)\right) + log\left(\sum_{k=1,k\neq i}^{N} \left(\text{Distance}_{jk}/(N-1)\right)\right)\right].$$

C. Data on Country Size, Relative Factor Endowments, and Associated Variables

Countries' economic sizes are measured using real GDPs from Maddison (2003). $GDPSUM_{ij,t}$ is the log of the sum of two countries' real GDPs. $GDPSIM_{ij,t}$ is the log of the similarity of two countries' RGDPs, where "similarity" is measured (as traditionally) using the product of country i's share of both countries' real GDPs with country j's share. In order to generate variables which run up through 2006, we extrapolate the information on real GDPs from Maddison with the one on real GDPs from the World Development Indicators (2009).

Apart from GDPs, we use data from Maddison (2003) on population to construct absolute differences between two countries' log real per-capita income and its squared value, PCYDIFFA and SQPCYDIFF. As with real GDP, we extrapolate the information on population from Maddison (2003) with the one from the World Development Indicators (2009) to obtain data series that run up through 2006.

D. Data on Political and Historical Variables

We employ seven different covariates that relate to political and historical conflict factors driving PTA formation and membership. The two historical conflict variables capture the war history between two countries. DIFFYEAR measures the period elapsed since two countries i and j last saw a period of war, and CUMDURAT measures the cumulative number of days of war since 1945 (the data source is the International Institute for Strategic Studies' Armed Conflict Database, https://acd.iiss.org/). Other political variables are based on Marshall, Gurr, and Jaggers' (2013) Polity IV database, and all measure absolute differences in political characteristics between two countries i and j at time t. DPolity2 is an overall index of differences in political freedom. A higher Polity2 index means more political freedom, and a larger value of DPolity2 measures a bigger discrepancy in such freedom among two countries. As an alternative to DPolity2, we employ four sub-indices thereof which are again formulated as absolute differences in the scores of i and j at t: two countries' democracy and autocracy scores (DDEMOC, DAUTOC); the political party competition in parliament score (DPARCOMP); and the political competition in government score (DPOLCOMP).

Descriptive statistics for all variables are provided in Table 1. It is important to note that the

TABLE 1
Descriptive Statistics

Variable	Obs	Mean	SD	Minimum	Maximum
Dep. var.	463,289	0.02	0.15	0	1
TIME	463,289	2.96	0.94	0.00	4.04
PTA	463,289	0.00	0.06	0	1
YEAR	463,289	1979.04	16.65	1950	2006
Geography					
DIST	463,289	8.71	0.73	4.09	9.89
BORDER	463,289	0.02	0.13	0.00	1.00
REMOTE	463,289	1.91	3.59	0.00	9.70
Size and relative factor endowments					
GDPSUM	463,289	11.16	1.67	4.74	16.63
GDPSIM	463,289	−1.97	1.37	−9.92	−0.69
PCYDIFF	463,289	−1.25	0.89	−4.66	0.00
SQPCYDIFF	463,289	−2.36	2.90	−21.69	0.00
PTA determinants					
DISTPTA	463,289	3.44	1.81	0.17	15.21
WPTA	463,289	0.05	0.06	0.00	0.43
NPTA	463,289	10.80	3.97	7.19	18.90
SQNPTA	463,289	132.34	100.16	51.70	357.27
Historical					
DIFFYEAR	463,289	0.13	2.17	0	107
CUMDURAT	463,289	5.96	172.33	0	15,389
Political					
DPolity2	335,450	8.12	6.49	0	20
DDEMOC	340,726	10.65	21.94	0	98
DAUTOC	340,726	10.06	21.93	0	98
DPARCOMP	340,726	8.06	22.03	0	93
DPOLCOMP	340,726	10.30	22.28	0	98
Multilateralism					
WTO Members	165,962	103.98	31.02	34	147
MTN Round	172,974	0.59	0.49	0	1
Dispute 3rd	165,962	0.39	0.49	0	1
Loss 3rd	152,011	0.26	0.44	0	1

sample size falls by about 28% from 463,289 to 335,450 (or 340,726) once we include political variables. Consequently, pseudo-R^2 values will not be directly comparable for specifications due to the sample differences. Hence, we will report results with and without the political variables.[18]

Table 2 provides a list of the 146 countries included in the sample, together with each country's number of PTA partners. It is interesting to note that several countries in Latin America—notably, Chile and Mexico—have pursued a large number of bilateral PTA agreements. By contrast, the United States has only five PTA partners; however, one reason for the low number of the United States' PTAs is the cut-off of the sample in 2006.

V. EMPIRICAL RESULTS

We discuss the main empirical results as follows. First, we discuss the empirical results for a time trend only and then include the geographic controls, economic controls, and other PTA "interdependence" determinants. Next, we address the sensitivity of the results by adding the historical and political variables. We then account for unobserved heterogeneity using fixed effects for all the specifications.

Table 3 provides the results from estimating the determinants of the instantaneous probability of leaving the initial state (No-PTA) in the interval $[t, t + dt)$ given survival up until time T (i.e., the hazard rate), based upon Equation (5). Specification 1 provides the results of estimating the hazard rate on the time trend alone. We find evidence of positive duration dependence. In the absence of economic, historical, and political covariates, this result suggests that the longer a country-pair has had no PTA, the higher the probability in any period t that it will enter a PTA. This could be attributable to the trend effects of "multilateralism" (which we address later) or even trend movements in economic, political or historical variables. The very low R^2 for this variable suggests there is room to improve explanation of the

18. The last four variables in Table 1 (multilateralism variables) will be discussed later in Section VI; they are included here for convenience.

TABLE 2
Countries and Numbers of PTAs per Country, 1950–2006

Country	Number	Country	Number	Country	Number
Afghanistan	9	Guatemala	0	Paraguay	19
Albania	7	Guinea	0	People's Rep. of China	13
Algeria	38	Guinea-Bissau	44	Peru	42
Angola	16	Haiti	2	Philippines	45
Argentina	40	Honduras	0	Poland	31
Armenia	11	Hong Kong	0	Portugal	32
Australia	3	Hungary	26	Qatar	5
Austria	27	India	41	Republic of Korea	44
Azerbaijan	15	Indonesia	41	Republic of Moldova	17
Bahrain	5	Iran	46	Republic of the Congo	5
Bangladesh	45	Iraq	38	Romania	54
Belarus	10	Ireland	27	Russia	9
Belgium	23	Israel	30	Rwanda	15
Benin	44	Italy	28	São Tomé and Príncipe	0
Bolivia	40	Jamaica	2	Saudi Arabia	5
Bosnia-Herzegovina	5	Japan	2	Senegal	7
Brazil	42	Jordan	11	Sierra Leone	0
Bulgaria	28	Kazakhstan	15	Singapore	46
Burkina Faso	7	Kenya	15	Slovakia	28
Burundi	15	Kuwait	5	Slovenia	31
Cambodia	9	Kyrgyzstan	15	Somalia	0
Cameroun	43	Laos	13	South Africa	5
Canada	4	Latvia	29	Spain	26
Cape Verde	0	Lebanon	0	Sri Lanka	41
Central African Rep.	5	Liberia	0	Sudan	49
Chad	5	Libya	49	Sweden	34
Chile	68	Lithuania	29	Switzerland	35
Colombia	40	Macedonia	12	Syria	0
Comoros	15	Madagascar	15	Tadjikistan	15
Costa Rica	1	Malawi	16	Tanzania	50
Côte d'Ivoire	7	Malaysia	41	Thailand	42
Croatia	18	Mali	7	The Gambia	0
Cuba	7	Mauritania	0	Togo	7
Czech Republic	22	Mauritius	16	Trinidad and Tobago	40
Denmark	25	Mexico	53	Tunisia	44
Djibouti	15	Mongolia	7	Turkey	31
Dominican Republic	0	Morocco	46	Turkmenistan	15
Ecuador	40	Mozambique	50	Uganda	15
Egypt	70	Myanmar	41	Ukraine	9
El Salvador	2	Nepal	4	United Arab Emirates	5
Equatorial Guinea	5	Netherlands	32	United Kingdom	26
Estonia	26	New Zealand	2	United States	5
Finland	29	Nicaragua	38	Uruguay	19
France	26	Niger	7	Uzbekistan	15
Gabon	5	Nigeria	38	Venezuela	40
Georgia	11	Norway	35	Vietnam	48
Germany	25	Oman	5	Yemen	0
Ghana	38	Pakistan	50	Zambia	15
Greece	26	Panama	1		

determinants of the timing of PTA events, which we now examine.

We next turn to Specifications 2 through 4 in Table 3 including the geographic, economic, historical, and political variables. An important result to especially note in Specifications 2 through 4 is the substantive change in the coefficient estimate for "Time-to-PTA event" (i.e., the time elapsed since 1950) and its z-statistic as compared to Specification 1. This indicates that time *per se* (reflecting the dynamic mechanism behind PTA formation and enlargement) is implicitly picking up the effect of time-varying covariates in Specification 1.

Specifications 2 through 4 confirm our expectation about the relationship between geography and the hazard rate suggested by our earlier discussion (and the underlying theoretical framework). A lower distance (DIST) between two countries i and j, sharing a common land border (BORDER), and a larger distance from the ROW (REMOTE) raise the likelihood for a

TABLE 3

Economic Determinants of Hazard Rates for Country-Pairs[a]

Explanatory Variables	Theory	Spec. 1	Spec. 2	Spec. 3	Spec. 4	Spec. 5	Spec. 6	Spec. 7
Time-to-PTA event	+	2.05***	0.61***	0.53***	0.54***	1.74***	1.57***	1.71***
		(74.56)	(33.53)	(27.75)	(28.90)	(33.14)	(28.01)	(30.11)
Geography								
DIST	–		−0.15***	−0.16***	−0.16***	−0.25***	−0.25***	−0.27***
			(−8.66)	(−8.64)	(−8.79)	(−13.92)	(−13.32)	(−14.44)
BORDER	+		0.52***	0.53***	0.51***	0.49***	0.49***	0.44***
			(6.99)	(6.69)	(6.50)	(6.42)	(6.03)	(5.48)
REMOTE	+		0.01**	0.004	0.01**	12.92***	11.83***	10.42***
			(2.07)	(0.99)	(2.29)	(12.15)	(10.22)	(9.02)
Size and relative factor endowments								
GDPSUM	+		0.13***	0.15***	0.10***	2.16***	2.24***	2.31***
			(17.12)	(17.60)	(12.14)	(58.86)	(56.70)	(57.89)
GDPSIM	+		0.16***	0.18***	0.14***	0.80***	0.81***	0.77***
			(18.36)	(17.32)	(14.22)	(32.09)	(30.51)	(28.06)
PCYDIFF	+		0.26***	0.27***	0.28***	0.40***	0.38***	0.40***
			(7.44)	(7.34)	(7.92)	(8.24)	(7.43)	(7.73)
SQPCYDIFF	–		−0.08***	−0.08***	−0.08***	−0.14***	−0.12***	−0.11***
			(−7.50)	(−7.64)	(−7.40)	(−9.79)	(−8.25)	(−7.72)
PTA determinants								
DISTPTA	–		−0.17***	−0.15***	−0.17***	−0.67***	−0.65***	−0.72***
			(−13.81)	(−11.78)	(−13.84)	(−22.35)	(−20.72)	(−23.13)
WPTA	+		5.25***	5.66***	5.39***	14.68***	14.91***	14.40***
			(42.00)	(42.52)	(41.08)	(71.48)	(68.58)	(66.37)
NPTA	+		0.41***	0.27***	0.34***	−0.16***	−0.20***	−0.24***
			(10.40)	(6.55)	(8.41)	(−3.30)	(−3.85)	(−4.72)
SQNPTA	–		−0.004***	0.00	−0.002	0.003*	0.004**	0.005***
			(−2.71)	(0.26)	(−1.46)	(1.83)	(2.32)	(2.83)
Political and historical								
DPolity2	–			−0.01***			−0.03***	
				(−7.51)			(−11.90)	
DDEMOC	–				0.032***			0.07***
					(6.38)			(11.11)
DAUTOC	–				−0.03***			−0.06***
					(−6.47)			(−8.40)
DPARCOMP	–				0.05***			0.10***
					(9.25)			(14.08)
DPOLCOMP	–				−0.06***			−0.12***
					(−7.71)			(−14.73)
DIFFYEAR	+			−0.002	−0.001		0.001	0.003
				(−0.60)	(−0.33)		(0.18)	(0.46)
CUMDURAT	–			−0.00	−0.00		0.00***	0.00**
				(−0.62)	(−0.67)		(2.60)	(2.40)
Constant		−10.82***	−10.51***	−9.33***	−9.21***	−1.56	1.75	1.66
		(−106.25)	(−34.54)	(−28.55)	(−28.52)	(−1.44)	(1.54)	(1.48)
Pseudo-R^2		0.11	0.27	0.24	0.23	0.38	0.35	0.36
Number of observations		463,289	463,289	335,450	340,726	463,289	335,450	340,726
Log-likelihood (model)		−44,840	−36,521	−32,939	−34,151	−31,019	−27,978	−28,813

Notes: There are 463,289 observations, 10,518 country-pairs and 1,560 events in specifications (1), (2), and (5); 335,450 observations, 9,920 country-pairs, and 1,511 events in specifications (3) and (6); and 340,726 observations, 9,925 country-pairs, and 1,516 events in specifications (4) and (7). The likelihood value of the constant only model is −50,207. The p value of the likelihood ratio statistics on the model is 0.

[a]z-statistics in parentheses.

* $p < 0.10$, ** $p < 0.05$, *** $p < 0.01$.

pair ij to form or join the same PTA sooner. Specifications 2–4 also confirm that countries with larger and more similar economic sizes (GDPSUM and GDPSIM, respectively) appear to have larger gains from forming a PTA or joining the same PTA sooner. With regard to relative factor endowments proxied by PCYDIFF, larger relative factor endowment differences tend to enhance the likelihood of a PTA forming or enlarging sooner. Moreover, the negative coefficient estimate for SQPCYDIFF implies that this effect diminishes with the degree of per capita income differences, similar to results in BB.

Moreover, the results of Specifications 2 through 4 in Table 3 suggest that "existing PTAs," or "interdependence" in EL's terms (or "contagion" in terms of Baldwin and Jaimovich 2012), plays an influential role in the timing of PTA events. In line with expectations, the farther a country-pair is from its nearest other PTA (i.e., the larger is DISTPTA) the smaller are the potential gains from a PTA between two countries that is concluded sooner rather than later. The results also confirm that the probability of forming/enlarging a PTA earlier in time rises with the "degree of regionalism (or competitive liberalization)" in the ROW at that time, measured by WPTA. Specifications 2 through 4 also add the number of members in the nearest PTA of the pair linearly and quadratically (NPTA, SQNPTA). Consistent with our theoretical conjectures, we find a positive effect for the linear term of the number of members in the nearest PTA and a negative one for the quadratic term in the duration analysis.[19]

Specifications 3 and 4 also control for political and historical factors determining the hazard rate, beyond the geography, economic, and interdependence fundamentals. In both specifications, we control for the period elapsed since two countries *i* and *j* last saw a period of war (DIFFYEAR), and for the cumulative number of days of war since 1945 (CUMDURAT). In both specifications DIFFYEAR and CMDURAT are not significantly different from zero. However, we note, in particular, that the variable DIFFYEAR is highly collinear with the variable "Time-to-PTA event." Specification 3 includes one compact measure of the absolute difference in political freedom between two countries, captured by the difference in Polity IV scores (DPolity2). This measure is higher the larger is the average difference in two countries' political freedom. The results suggest that countries with more similar political systems and degrees of freedom tend to enter PTAs earlier than others. In contrast, Specification 4 use sub-indices behind the Polity IV index and condition on absolute differences of two countries' democracy and autocracy scores (DDEMOC, DAUTOC), as well as for the absolute differences in political party competition in parliament (DPARCOMP) and the political competition in government (DPOLCOMP). This specification suggests that the political variables are all relevant. Countries with different degrees of democracy (autocracy) tend to enter PTAs earlier (later) than ones with similar degrees. A greater similarity (dissimilarity) in party competition in parliament (political competition in government) tends to lead to an earlier entry in PTAs. In comparing pseudo-R^2 values, please note, as Table 1 suggests, that due to data constraints the sample sizes differ somewhat across specifications, with Specifications 3 and 4 having smaller sample sizes. Also, the sample size is about 5,000 observations larger when the Polity IV sub-indices are used in Specification 4, rather than the summary measure in Specification 3.

Specifications 5 through 7 add parameterized pairwise fixed effects to Specifications 2 through 4, respectively. The purpose is to see whether the results in Specifications 2 through 4 are biased by unobserved heterogeneity. The range of possible omitted variables is vast. In order to allow for a set of unobserved effects which may be correlated with $\mathbf{x}_{ij}(t)$, we consider introducing fixed country-pair effects. However, the introduction of fixed effects in a non-linear function is not a trivial endeavor, since the number of incidental parameters is increasing with sample size. Chamberlain (1980) shows that, for a fixed time dimension, maximum likelihood estimates of β will be inconsistent as the number of cross-sectional observations goes to infinity. Chamberlain (1980) provides an approach that eliminates the incidental parameters problem. Essentially, the unobserved effects can be eliminated by an appropriate differencing transformation. Chamberlain (1980) suggests including averages of all time-varying explanatory variables along with the original variables in the empirical models (see also Wooldridge 2010).

Specifications 5 through 7 report the results using the Chamberlain-Wooldridge-type model. For brevity, we do not report coefficient estimates

19. In the context of the "domino theory" in Baldwin (1995), an increase in the number of members of the nearest PTA causes a rise in demand for membership of non-members in this agreement, tending to increase the hazard rate for *ij*. However, Baldwin's domino theory assumes an infinitely elastic supply of membership by a PTA. As the number of members of a PTA increases, there are incumbent members whose utility falls when a new member is added, especially the members of the PTA most distant from the core. Every time a new member is added, the utility from the PTA of the (marginal) "worse-off" member declines. It can be shown in our simple Krugman-like model (in the Theoretical Supplement) that at some point the marginal worse-off member's utility declines from new members, dampening the average utility gain of members in the PTA. This finite-elasticity-of-membership supply implies theoretically a quadratic relationship between the number of members of the nearest PTA (*NPTA*) and the hazard rate for pair *ij*. See our Theoretical Supplement for an illustration of this argument.

for fixed effects; moreover, recall that DIST and BORDER are time-invariant (and so are not demeaned). First, unsurprisingly the pseudo-R^2's increase, from 23–27% to 35–38%. Second, Specifications 5–7 reveal that most of the coefficient estimates maintain the same qualitative effects as found in the previous specification. In particular, PTA economic determinants DIST, BORDER, REMOTE, GDPSUM, GDPSIM, PCYDIFF, SQPCYDIFF, DISTPTA, and WPTA all retain their expected coefficient signs and their coefficient estimates are statistically significant. However, NPTA and SQNPTA change signs unexpectedly; this could be attributable to multicollinearity. Third, the large change in quantitative values of the coefficient estimates should not come as a surprise. The new coefficient estimates are based upon only time variation of the variables; the coefficient estimates for DIST and BORDER are unchanged because only those two variables are not time-demeaned.[20]

In qualitative terms, virtually all of the coefficient estimates of the political and historical variables are unaffected, though most change in quantitative terms because of the time-demeaning nature of the fixed effects. Note that DIFFYEAR's coefficient estimate turns positive when including the fixed effects in Specification 7 (compare Specifications 4 and 7), but remains economically and statistically insignificant. Also, CUMDURAT turns statistically significant; however, the coefficient estimates are not economically different from zero.[21] However, we need to bear in mind that CUMDURAT is relatively time-invariant and the difference in the parameter on it from Specifications 3 and 4 to 6 and 7, respectively, may flow from multicollinearity with the pairwise fixed effects. Even though the pseudo-R^2 of the models rises if we add fixed effects, Specifications 2 through 4 appear to work reasonably well (when remembering the large amount of zeros in the dependent variable). Moreover, two advantages of Specifications 2 through 4 relative to 5 through 7 are that: (1) fixed effects cannot be estimated precisely in duration models, and (2) they are unknown whenever predictions are supposed to be made out-of-sample (i.e., high-level assumptions have to be made regarding their changes).

20. For instance, typical gravity equations of international trade have similar differences for GDP variables' coefficient estimates if variables are time-demeaned.

21. A possible reason for this positive correlation might be that countries with a higher probability of war (a longer war history) have higher opportunity costs from a war the larger are the trade gains, making PTA formation more likely (see Martin, Mayer, and Thoenig 2012).

VI. PREDICTIVE ANALYSIS

In this section, we examine the ability of the model to predict the actual *year* of the formation (or enlargement) of a PTA between each pair of countries, as well as for various "windows" leading up to PTA events. The section has four parts. The first part addresses the in-sample and out-of-sample predictive power of the model using the main specifications presented in Section V. The second part evaluates the predictive power of the model after accounting for multilateralism, but using a much smaller sample (due to data availability of multilateralism variables). The third part examines the predictive power of the model for the time-to-PTA events of the CUSFTA, the NAFTA, and the European Community's formation and subsequent enlargements. The fourth part examines whether the model's ten most likely time-to-PTA events in the post-sample period (2007–2013) have actually occurred as predicted.

A. *Predicting the Actual Years of PTA Formation or Enlargements*

In this section, we examine the predicted timings—in particular, even the predicted *year*—of *all PTA events*. Because predicting the specific year is a demanding objective, we also consider predicting an event within time "windows" of up to 10 years prior to the event. It is important to again contrast our duration analysis with previous analyses predicting the existence of a PTA in a given year. In the latter studies, predictions can occur in the years prior to the PTA's entry into force, in the year of the PTA's entry into force, or in the years following the PTA's entry into force. By contrast, our analysis can only predict the *actual year* of the PTA's entry into force, or a designated window leading up to that year. Hence, predictions from our analysis cannot be compared to previous non-duration-analysis-based predictions.

Table 4 provides a summary of the accuracy for predicting the timing of each bilateral PTA event using Specifications 1 through 7 from Table 3. It is important to note that our *preferred* specifications for predicting events are Specifications 2 through 4 for the reasons mentioned at the end of the previous subsection. In order to map the continuous linear index

TABLE 4
Predicting the Timing of the PTA Events Covered[a]

Predicted Events	Specification 1		Specification 2		Specification 3		Specification 4		Specification 5		Specification 6		Specification 7	
	Number	% of all PTA Events	Number	% of all PTA Events	Number	% of all PTA Events	Number	% of all PTA Events	Number	% of all PTA Events	Number	% of all PTA Events	Number	% of all PTA Events
Base case														
Total number PTA events	1,560	100	1,560	100	1,560	100	1,560	100	1,560	100	1,560	100	1,560	100
In the same year as the event occurred	209	13	320	21	402	26	379	24	551	35	616	39	601	39
In the same year as the event occurred or up to 1 year prior to that	353	23	384	25	468	30	434	28	651	42	713	46	690	44
In the same year as the event occurred or up to 2 years prior to that	431	28	416	27	517	33	477	31	744	48	818	52	783	50
In the same year as the event occurred or up to 3 years prior to that	531	34	541	35	635	41	600	38	840	54	901	58	868	56
In the same year as the event occurred or up to 4 years prior to that	546	35	551	35	646	41	616	39	900	58	950	61	924	59
In the same year as the event occurred or up to 5 years prior to that	678	43	640	41	710	46	679	44	971	62	991	64	968	62
In the same year as the event occurred or up to 10 years prior to that	853	55	752	48	891	57	857	55	1,121	72	1,084	69	1,076	69
Predictions using data from 1970 onwards only														
Total number PTA events	1,517	100	1,517	100	1,517	100	1,517	100	1,517	100	1,517	100	1,517	100
In the same year as the event occurred	209	14	337	22	408	27	373	25	742	49	769	51	731	48
In the same year as the event occurred or up to 1 year prior to that	353	23	394	26	477	31	435	29	855	56	883	58	843	56
In the same year as the event occurred or up to 2 years prior to that	431	28	424	28	526	35	478	32	916	60	940	62	912	60
In the same year as the event occurred or up to 3 years prior to that	531	35	550	36	643	42	607	40	995	66	1,033	68	997	66
In the same year as the event occurred or up to 4 years prior to that	546	36	569	38	655	43	625	41	1,021	67	1,067	70	1,060	70
In the same year as the event occurred or up to 5 years prior to that	678	45	647	43	731	48	692	46	1,062	70	1,111	73	1,106	73
In the same year as the event occurred or up to 10 years prior to that	853	56	762	50	918	61	871	57	1,102	73	1,156	76	1,168	77
Regression only run on data up to 2000 and out-of-sample predictions for 2001 to 2006														
Total number PTA events	284	100	284	100	284	100	284	100	284	100	284	100	284	100
In the same year as the event occurred	9	3	175	62	188	66	178	63	97	34	122	43	131	46
In the same year as the event occurred or up to 1 year prior to that	15	5	183	64	196	69	185	65	98	35	123	43	132	46

TABLE 4
Continued

Predicted Events	Specification 1 Number	Specification 1 % of all PTA Events	Specification 2 Number	Specification 2 % of all PTA Events	Specification 3 Number	Specification 3 % of all PTA Events	Specification 4 Number	Specification 4 % of all PTA Events	Specification 5 Number	Specification 5 % of all PTA Events	Specification 6 Number	Specification 6 % of all PTA Events	Specification 7 Number	Specification 7 % of all PTA Events
In the same year as the event occurred or up to 2 years prior to that	42	15	194	68	208	73	198	70	106	37	131	46	140	49
In the same year as the event occurred or up to 3 years prior to that	95	33	207	73	222	78	217	76	107	38	132	46	141	50
In the same year as the event occurred or up to 4 years prior to that	109	38	217	76	232	82	227	80	108	38	133	47	142	50
In the same year as the event occurred or up to 5 years prior to that	112	39	218	77	232	82	228	80	108	38	133	47	142	50
Regression only run on data up to 1989 and out-of-sample predictions for 1990 to 2006														
Total number PTA events	1,037	100	1,037	100	1,037	100	1,037	100	1,037	100	1,037	100	1,037	100
In the same year as the event occurred	144	14	231	22	244	24	251	24	282	27	314	30	302	29
In the same year as the event occurred or up to 1 year prior to that	222	21	263	25	277	27	274	26	317	31	343	33	331	32
In the same year as the event occurred or up to 2 years prior to that	322	31	316	30	333	32	328	32	337	32	361	35	347	33
In the same year as the event occurred or up to 3 years prior to that	337	32	331	32	349	34	342	33	338	33	361	35	347	33
In the same year as the event occurred or up to 4 years prior to that	469	45	346	33	366	35	355	34	338	33	361	35	347	33
In the same year as the event occurred or up to 5 years prior to that	474	46	346	33	366	35	355	34	338	33	361	35	347	33
In the same year as the event occurred or up to 10 years prior to that	653	63	346	33	366	35	355	34	338	33	361	35	347	33

[a]Underlying cut-off values minimize a quadratic loss function of predicting binary events by the complementary log-log model. For the base case, the cut-off for specification 1 is 0.038, for specifications 2, 3, and 4 it is 0.009, for specification 5 it is 0.023, for specifications 6 it is 0.035, and for specification 7 it is 0.033. For the predictions using data from 1970 onwards only, the cut-off for specification 1 is 0.039, the cut-off for specification 2 is 0.011, for specifications 3 and 4 it is 0.01, for specification 5 it is 0.054, for specification 6 it is 0.056, and for specification 7 it is 0.051. For the predictions using data up to 2000, the cut-off for specification 1 is 0.006, for specifications 2 and 3 it is 0.011, for specification 4 it is 0.009, for specification 5 it is 0.09, for specification 6 it is 0.08, and for specification 7 it is 0.086. For the predictions using data up to 1989, the cut-off for specification 1 is 0.002, for specifications 2 and 3 it is 0.014, for specification 4 it is 0.016, for specification 5 it is 0.041, for specification 6 it is 0.056, and for specification 7 it is 0.063.

behind the hazard rate or the hazard rate itself into discrete event predictions, we must utilize a cut-off probability. Various methods to select endogenously the cut-off exist, including Sensitivity-Specificity analysis (see Baier, Bergstrand, and Mariutto 2014) or a quadratic loss function akin to Matthew's Correlation Coefficient (see Bergstrand and Egger 2013). In the latter approach used here, the cut-off probability which distinguishes zeros from ones for the predicted PTA indicator is chosen so as to minimize the associated loss function which trades off correct and incorrect unitary and zero predictions (notice that the cut-off probability will not be at 50%, since the PTA indicator data in panel form contain numerous zeros relative to the ones).

Table 4 is organized horizontally in seven blocs (referring to Specifications 1 through 7) and vertically in four blocs. The bloc at the top represents the base case directly associated with Specifications 1–7 as reported in Table 3. The other three blocs are based on parameter estimates akin but not identical to the ones in Table 3 (we suppress presenting these parameter estimates for the sake of brevity). The results from the second bloc are based on Specifications 1–7 from Table 3 that are rerun only using data from 1970 (rather than from 1950) onwards. This set of results tells us how much of the explanatory and predictive power is due to letting the process run from a time period which is relatively distant in time from most of the PTA events in the data. The third bloc of results runs Specifications 1–7 using data from 1950 to only 2000 (rather than 2006), but predicting events *out-of-sample* for the years 2001–2006. The last bloc of results runs Specifications 1–7 using data from 1950 to only 1989 (rather than 2006), but predicting events *out-of-sample* for the years 1990 through 2006. The last two blocs are meant to assess generally the out-of-sample prediction quality of the models near-term versus long-term, respectively.

With regard to the benchmark model predictions at the top of Table 4, we see that Specifications 1–4 predict various percentages of all 1,560 events covered within the year or up to ten years prior to the event. About 13–26% of the events are predicted within the same year that they had occurred. Among the four specifications, Specification 3 performs relatively best. It predicts 26% of the events within the same year that the actual PTA membership occurred, 30% in the same year or up to 1 year prior to actual PTA membership, and 33% within the same year or up to 2 years prior to actual PTA membership, respectively. In comparison, Specification 1 only predicts 13% of the events within the same year that the actual PTA membership occurred, 23% in the same year or up to 1 year prior to actual PTA membership, and 28% within the same year or up to 2 years prior to PTA membership, respectively.

Not surprisingly, Specifications 5 to 7, which include parameterized fixed country-pair effects, perform even better in predicting PTA membership events. These specifications predict 69–72% of the events within 10 years prior to actual PTA membership. Among those, Specification 5 works best for the 10-year window and Specification 6 works best for a window of up to 3 years, explaining 39% of the events within the same year that the actual PTA membership occurred, 46% in the same year or up to 1 year prior to actual PTA membership, and 52% within the same year or up to 2 years prior to the actual event. In the subsequent discussion, we mainly focus on Specifications 2 to 4 since they will turn out to outperform Specifications 5 to 7 in terms of *out-of-sample* predictions and also exclude fixed effects (which complicates out-of-sample predicting).

In the second vertical bloc, using data from 1970 rather than from 1950 onwards leads to a better predictive performance for all specifications. This is intuitive, since the density of PTA events is relatively much higher during the more recent decades of the data than in the first ones. However, there is not a material difference in predictive power between the two blocs.

With regard to out-of-sample predictions of PTA events in the third bloc, Specification 3 tends to work best. Note that in the third bloc we only forecast events in the 6 years after the end of the estimation sample in 2000 (2001 through 2006) and we forecast the years with relatively many PTA events. We predict 66% of the events within the same year that the actual PTA membership occurred, 69% in the same year or up to 1 year prior to actual PTA membership, 73% of all 284 events within the same year or up to 2 years prior to the actual event, and 82% of all 284 actual PTA events in 2001–2006 within up to 5 years prior to their occurrence. This near-term out-of-sample performance of Specification 3 dominates the predictions of Specification 1, which uses only the time trend. No other study has provided out-of-sample predictions of PTA timings. These results suggest a strong predictive power of our model relative to the simple time trend *near term*.

However, a different outcome results for long-term forecasting of PTA events, shown in the fourth vertical bloc. Estimating the models from 1950 through 1989 and then predicting all events that had occurred between 1990 and 2006, Specification 3 predicts only 24% of the events within the same year that the actual PTA membership occurred, 27% in the same year or up to 1 year prior to actual PTA membership, and 35% within the same year or up to 10 years prior to the actual event. Not surprisingly, the previous vertical bloc in Table 4 shows a much better performance of Specification 3 to predict PTA events than in the last vertical bloc. The reasons are that, in contrast to the fourth bloc, in the third bloc we only forecast events in the 6 years after the end of the estimation sample in 2000 (2001 through 2006) and we forecast the years with relatively many PTA events. Although the predictive power is lower than previously, note that our model still outperforms out-of-sample the model with only a time trend (Specification 1) when forecasting the specific year of the event or a window up to 3 years preceding the event. Yet, for windows of up to 4, 5, or 10 years prior to the event, the model with only a time trend has better predictive power. Note, however, that the model itself is only estimated using data through 1989, and consequently includes only one-third of the events as in the entire sample (523 events for the fourth bloc versus 1,276 events for the third bloc).[22]

In sum, even relatively parsimonious specifications without fixed effects perform quite well in predicting PTA events in- *or* out-of-sample, as long as the estimates are based on data with a sufficient number of PTA events *and* if the out-of-sample forecast period is not too long.

22. Note that with out-of-sample predictions a decision has to be made with regard to the values assumed for covariates determining the time-to-PTA events. Moreover, with parameterized fixed country-pair effects, one has to decide whether to keep those effects fixed outside of the sample period and, if not, how to adjust them. In Table 4, we use the covariates as they are observed even outside of the sample period. However, it should be noted that keeping them fixed at the end of the estimation sample period does not have a substantive impact on the predictions. The reason appears to be that the covariates determine well the cross-sectional variation in hazard-rate base levels, and the time trend predicts well the cross-sectional heterogeneity in the timing-to-PTA events relative to the end of the sample period. For instance, let us compare the results for a model that is the same as Specification 3 in Table 4 for the out-of-sample predictions from 1990 to 2006 for the PTA events in those years, but keeping the covariates constant at their 1989 levels and only letting time change. In this setting, the specification predicts up to 43% (47%) of the 1,037 PTA events between 1990 and 2006 in the same year or up to 5 (10) years prior to the actual events. The corresponding number in Table 4, where the covariates change as observed in the out-of-sample period, is 35% (35%) for the same precision window.

B. Robustness to Multilateralism's Effects

As mentioned earlier, the time trend in the econometric model could likely capture overall trends in multilateral liberalization. The influence of multilateralism on PTA formation in terms of empirical work started with Mansfield and Reinhardt (2003). The focus of that study—and subsequent empirical studies—has been on four variables related to the influence of multilateralism potentially explaining PTA formations. Baldwin and Jaimovich (2012) incorporated these four variables in their predictions of PTAs. Gradeva and Jaimovich (2014) re-examined the original Mansfield and Reinhardt (2003) findings, focusing largely on the robustness of the original four Mansfield-Reinhardt multilateralism variables.

The first of the four variables is WTOMEMBERS, the number of contracting parties to the GATT/WTO (in the previous period). The argument is that an increasing number of parties reduces each party's leverage over the progress and path of multilateral liberalization, making it more difficult to conclude such rounds. Country-pairs may provide an alternative means for countries to pursue trade liberalization to avoid adverse implications of slow multilateral liberalization, that is, more PTAs. Hence, WTOMEMBERS is expected to have a positive impact on the hazard rate of PTA events.

The second variable is MTNROUND, a dummy variable indicating if a GATT or WTO multilateral trade negotiation (MTN) round is in place in the current year (1), or not (0). The expected sign on this variable is ambiguous due to two alternative views. One view is that countries' governments may believe they can increase their bargaining power in a current MTN round if they form PTAs; this suggests a positive impact of MTNROUND on the hazard rate. A second view is that PTAs and multilateral liberalizations are complements, cf., Freund (2000). Hence, if a MTN round has been completed (hence, the dummy is zero), the likelihood of a PTA is higher; this suggests a negative impact of MTNROUND on the hazard rate. Baldwin and Jaimovich (2012) found a negative but statistically insignificant effect of MTNROUND on the probability of a PTA. However, Gradeva and Jaimovich (2014) found a negative and statistically significant effect, if the sample was constrained to 1980–2007. Moreover, Fugazza and Robert-Nicoud (2011) show that the frequency in which the United States grants immediate duty-free access to PTA partners is larger for goods in which multilateral tariffs have had the largest cuts. Based on these various considerations, we expect a negative coefficient estimate.

The third variable is DISPUTE3rdPARTY, a dummy variable indicating if either *i* or *j* is a complainant or defendant in a new GATT/WTO dispute with a third party in the previous year (1), or not (0). The argument is that a country that has entered a dispute with a third party may have an incentive to form a PTA to gain leverage in the dispute. Hence, DISPUTE3rdPARTY is likely to have a positive impact on the hazard rate.

The fourth variable is LOST3rdPARTY, a dummy variable indicating if either *i* or *j* lost a GATT/WTO dispute with a third party 3 years prior (1), or not (0). The argument is that a country that recently lost a dispute is at risk for securing market access through the multilateral system. This may encourage incentives to form PTAs. Hence, LOST3rdPARTY is likely to be positively related to the hazard rate.

Consequently, we re-estimated our models above to add these four multilateralism variables to see if our results change materially, both in terms of model explanatory power as well as predictive power. However, we note one important restriction associated with this robustness analysis, and therefore present the associated results separately. Due to data availability, the overlap in data on the multilateralism variables from Gradeva and Jaimovich (2014) and our data set is narrow. As noted above, in our Specifications (3) and (4) without fixed effects ((6) and (7) with fixed effects), the sample size is either 335,450 observations (for Specifications (3) and (6)) or 340,726 observations (for Specifications (4) and (7)). Adding the multilateralism variables reduces our sample size to only 141,096 or 141,523 observations, respectively. The reason is that the data set in Gradeva and Jaimovich (2014) has considerably fewer observations than ours in the first 30 years of their sample (1948–1978). Thus, while we consider it worthwhile to see the sensitivity of the earlier regression results and predictions to including multilateralism variables, the results are *not directly comparable* due to the difference in samples.

Table 5 provides the empirical results for Specifications (3), (4), (6), and (7) now including the multilateralism variables; these are labeled accordingly Specifications (3A), (4A), (6A), and (7A), respectively. Several points are worth noting; for brevity we compare first Specification (3) in Table 3 to Specification (3A) in Table 5. First, the coefficient estimates for the four multilateralism variables are all statistically significant. Moreover, three of the four coefficient estimates' signs are as expected; only LOST3rdPARTY has a coefficient estimate sign different from the expectation. Second, we note that the coefficient estimate for the time trend now becomes trivially small, though still statistically significant. This result is consistent with our earlier conjecture that the time trend may be reflecting overall trends in multilateral trade liberalization. Third, despite the presence of the multilateralism variables causing the time trend's effect to become trivially small, their presence has little effect on the other variables' coefficient estimates in Specification (3). The coefficient estimates for the three geography and the four economic size and similarity and relative factor endowments variables are qualitatively the same. However, coefficient estimates for DISTPTA, NPTA, and SQNTA change sign. Yet, one must keep in mind that the sample is considerably different from that in the main empirical specifications, which could also explain the changes. Fourth, the changes just discussed largely carry over to the other specification comparisons, and so for brevity are not discussed.

Table 6 provides the predictions for Specifications (3A), (4A), (6A), and (7A), similar to those for comparable specifications in Table 4. The main point to note is that for Specifications (3A) and (4A) the predictive power of the model is enhanced somewhat using specifications incorporating the multilateralism variables. However, once again a caveat for any comparison is the different samples used, and hence the results are effectively not comparable. For Table 6, the results are influenced by a shorter sample for a period with a higher density of PTAs and that consequently influences the predictive power of the model.

C. Predictions of CUSFTA, NAFTA, and the European Union's Formation and Enlargements

Two of the most well-known PTAs are the NAFTA—following in the footsteps of the CUSFTA—and the European Union (EU), which began as the EEC in 1958. Since we have data going back to 1950, it would be useful to know how well our model, in retrospect, predicted the timing of these events. As apparent by now, our model explains and predicts bilateral events. So an additional evaluation of the successfulness of the model is determining the

TABLE 5

Multilateralism Determinants of Hazard Rates for Country-Pairs[a]

Explanatory variables	Theory	Spec. 3A	Spec. 4A	Spec. 6A	Spec. 7A
Time-to-PTA event	+	−0.08***	−0.09***	−1.30***	−1.26***
		(−2.70)	(−2.84)	(−9.19)	(−8.99)
Geography					
DIST	−	−0.06***	−0.07***	−0.11***	−0.11***
		(−2.60)	(−2.73)	(−4.19)	(−4.23)
BORDER	+	0.64***	0.62***	0.65***	0.60***
		(5.51)	(5.42)	(5.51)	(5.10)
REMOTE	+	0.03***	0.03***	3.38**	3.78**
		(5.30)	(5.66)	(2.21)	(2.48)
Size and relative factor endowments					
GDPSUM	+	0.06***	0.05***	0.93***	0.84***
		(4.93)	(3.79)	(13.57)	(12.05)
GDPSIM	+	0.09***	0.08***	0.64***	0.55***
		(6.34)	(5.47)	(11.28)	(9.66)
PCYDIFF	+	0.17***	0.20***	0.15**	0.18***
		(3.71)	(4.41)	(2.14)	(2.67)
SQPCYDIFF	−	−0.05***	−0.07***	−0.02	−0.04**
		(−3.41)	(−4.97)	(−0.89)	(−1.98)
PTA determinants					
DISTPTA	−	0.14***	0.15***	0.17***	0.19***
		(10.71)	(11.03)	(4.35)	(4.99)
WPTA	+	2.68***	2.64***	10.33***	10.24***
		(15.95)	(15.84)	(32.99)	(32.86)
NPTA	+	−8.00***	−8.10***	−5.85***	−5.94***
		(−56.04)	(−56.80)	(−40.03)	(−40.60)
SQNPTA	−	0.23***	0.23***	0.14***	0.15***
		(52.47)	(53.25)	(31.84)	(32.37)
Political and historical					
DPolity2	−	−0.003		−0.02***	
		(−1.11)		(−5.42)	
DDEMOC	−		−0.01*		0.003
			(−1.88)		(0.37)
DAUTOC	−		0.04***		−0.003
			(4.70)		(−0.26)
DPARCOMP	−		0.006		0.05***
			(0.78)		(5.89)
DPOLCOMP	−		−0.03***		−0.06***
			(−3.80)		(−5.69)
DIFFYEAR	+	−0.008*	−0.007*	0.002	0.003
		(−1.78)	(−1.72)	(0.15)	(0.24)
CUMDURAT	−	−0.00*	−0.00*	−0.00	−0.00
		(−1.75)	(−1.75)	(−0.11)	(−0.05)
Multilateralism					
WTO Members	+	0.43***	0.44***	0.43***	0.43***
		(70.78)	(71.38)	(65.86)	(66.27)
MTN Round	−	−1.14***	−1.17***	−0.72***	−0.75***
		(−11.75)	(−12.11)	(−7.28)	(−7.64)
Dispute 3rd Party	+	0.19***	0.21***	0.15***	0.15***
		(5.51)	(6.30)	(3.71)	(3.82)
Lost 3rd Party	+	−0.17***	−0.18***	−0.19***	−0.21***
		(−4.87)	(−5.11)	(−4.11)	(−4.70)
Constant		7.58***	8.01***	62.57***	62.45***
		(14.68)	(15.57)	(40.78)	(40.64)
Pseudo-R^2		0.44	0.44	0.49	0.49
Number of observations		141,096	141,523	141,096	141,523
Log-likelihood (model)		−14,730	−14,816	−13,427	−13,536

[a]z-statistics in parentheses. There are 141,096 observations, 6,625 country-pairs and 894 events in specification (3A) and (6A), and 141,523 observations, 6,625 country-pairs and 894 events in specifications (4A) and (7A).

* $p < 0.10$, ** $p < 0.05$, *** $p < 0.01$.

TABLE 6
Predicting the Timing of the PTA Events Covered with Multilateralism[a]

	Specification 3A		Specification 4A		Specification 6A		Specification 7A	
Predicted Events	**Number**	**% of all PTA Events**	**Number**	**% of all PTA Events**	**Number**	**% of all PTA Events**	**Number**	**% of all PTA Events**
Base case								
Total number PTA events	1,560	100	1,560	100	1,560	100	1,560	100
In the same year as the event occurred	702	45	706	45	856	55	845	54
In the same year as the event occurred or up to 1 year prior to that	715	46	720	46	880	56	870	56
In the same year as the event occurred or up to 2 years prior to that	757	49	748	48	932	60	926	59
In the same year as the event occurred or up to 3 years prior to that	802	51	800	51	953	61	965	62
In the same year as the event occurred or up to 4 years prior to that	823	53	807	52	959	61	981	63
In the same year as the event occurred or up to 5 years prior to that	901	58	902	58	975	63	999	64
In the same year as the event occurred or up to 10 years prior to that	995	64	1,022	66	999	64	1,047	67
Predictions using data from 1970 onwards only								
Total number PTA events	1,517	100	1,517	100	1,517	100	1,517	100
In the same year as the event occurred	746	49	746	49	843	56	838	55
In the same year as the event occurred or up to 1 year prior to that	761	50	759	50	872	57	865	57
In the same year as the event occurred or up to 2 years prior to that	781	51	779	51	887	58	879	58
In the same year as the event occurred or up to 3 years prior to that	825	54	823	54	948	62	937	62
In the same year as the event occurred or up to 4 years prior to that	857	56	855	56	1,068	70	1,065	70
In the same year as the event occurred or up to 5 years prior to that	905	60	903	60	1,092	72	1,086	72
In the same year as the event occurred or up to 10 years prior to that	993	65	991	65	1,129	74	1,124	74
Regression only run on data up to 2000 and out-of-sample predictions for 2001 to 2006								
Total number PTA events	284	100	284	100	284	100	284	100
In the same year as the event occurred	153	54	45	16	87	31	58	20
In the same year as the event occurred or up to 1 year prior to that	171	60	60	21	90	32	64	23
In the same year as the event occurred or up to 2 years prior to that	213	75	96	34	100	35	88	31
In the same year as the event occurred or up to 3 years prior to that	257	90	276	97	102	36	121	43
In the same year as the event occurred or up to 4 years prior to that	258	91	279	98	103	36	122	43
In the same year as the event occurred or up to 5 years prior to that	260	92	282	99	103	36	122	43
Regression only run on data up to 1989 and out-of-sample predictions for 1990 to 2006								
Total number PTA events	1,037	100	1,037	100	1,037	100	1,037	100
In the same year as the event occurred	498	48	482	46	509	49	520	50
In the same year as the event occurred or up to 1 year prior to that	512	49	504	49	526	51	554	53
In the same year as the event occurred or up to 2 years prior to that	538	52	532	51	529	51	583	56
In the same year as the event occurred or up to 3 years prior to that	539	52	573	55	531	51	624	60
In the same year as the event occurred or up to 4 years prior to that	539	52	579	56	531	51	667	64
In the same year as the event occurred or up to 5 years prior to that	539	52	628	61	531	51	716	69
In the same year as the event occurred or up to 10 years prior to that	539	52	731	70	531	51	780	75

[a]Underlying cut-off values minimize a quadratic loss function of predicting binary events by the complementary log-log model. For the base case, the cut-off value for specification 3A is 0.002, for specification 4A it is 0.001, for specification 6A it is 0.051, and for specification 7A it is 0.033. For the predictions using data from 1970 onwards only, the cut-off for specifications 3A and 4A is 0.001, and for specifications 6A and 7A it is 0.01. For the predictions using data up to 2000, the cut-off for specification 3A is 0.016, for specification 4A it is 0.001, for specification 6A it is 0.097, and for specification 7A it is 0.015. For the predictions using data up to 1989, the cut-off for specification 3A is 0.013, for specification 4A it is 0.001, for specification 6A it is 0.066, and for specification 7A it is 0.004.

clustering of the bilateral events around the plurilateral events.

We divide our analysis here into three parts. First, we examine the prediction of the original CUSFTA, which began in 1989. This constitutes the prediction of one (bilateral) event. Second, we examine the prediction of NAFTA in 1994. In this case, we are predicting two events: a Mexico-Canada event and a Mexico–U.S. event. Third, we examine the predictions associated with the formation of the EU and its subsequent enlargements. Thus, the first 10 events are the bilateral pairings among Belgium (which, for data reasons, includes Luxembourg; see earlier), the Netherlands, Germany, France, and Italy, which comprise the original EEC membership. We will then discuss the predictive power of the model for each of the seven subsequent enlargements of the EU.[23]

Table 7 will be helpful in organizing the discussion. First, we discuss CUSFTA. While CUSFTA officially began in 1989, it is important to note that the foundation for CUSFTA was in the Canadian–United States Automobile Trade Agreement, which was signed in 1965 to facilitate free Canadian–U.S. trade in autos and auto parts. Going further back historically, during the Great Depression of the 1930s following the isolationism of the world economy with rampant tariff escalation, Canada and the United States started reducing tariffs under a bilateral agreement. However, the post-World War II environment of multilateral liberalization dominated the 1950s, 1960s, and 1970s, so that little attention was given in Canada and the United States to a bilateral free trade agreement. The imbalance in macroeconomic policies of the 1980s along with expansion of the EEC provided impetus so that CUSFTA discussions began in 1985 and concluded with CUSFTA entering into force in 1989. Our model predicted CUSFTA in 1976, which we note is halfway between the start of the Canada–U.S. Auto Pact and CUSFTA's year of entry into force.

Second, we discuss NAFTA. Just as the path to NAFTA began with CUSFTA, the path to NAFTA started earlier between Mexico and the United States than between Mexico and Canada. The 1980s saw structural economic reforms beginning in Mexico. In 1985, the United States signed with Mexico the Understanding on Subsidies and Countervailing Duties, a substitute

23. For all these predictions, we used Specification 4 from Table 3; similar results were obtained using Specification 3.

TABLE 7
Prediction of CUSFTA, NAFTA, and EU Formation and Enlargements

Country	Predictions	Actual Formation
CUSFTA		
Canada–United States	1/1 from 1976 to 1989	1989
NAFTA		
Canada–United States–Mexico	1/2 from 1978 to 1993	
	2/2 in 1994	1994
EU		
EU foundation	4/10 from 1950 to 1957	
	6/10 in 1958	1958
First EU enlargement	3/15 from 1950 to 1972	
	5/15 in 1973	1973
Second EU enlargement	1/8 from 1950 to 1977	
	8/8 from 1978 onwards	1981
Third EU enlargement	2/18 from 1950 to 1960	
	4/18 from 1961 to 1972	
	5/18 from 1973 to 1977	
	18/18 from 1978 onwards	1986
Fourth EU enlargement	3/33 from 1950 to 1959	
	4/33 in 1960	
	10/33 in 1961	
	13/33 from 1962 to 1975	
	14/33 in 1976	
	15/33 in 1977	
	30/33 in 1978	
	31/33 in 1979	
	32/33 in 1980	
	31/33 in 1981	
	32/33 in 1982	
	33/33 from 1983 onwards	1995
Fifth EU enlargement	54/112 in 1990	
Note:	108/112 in 1991	
We do not have data for Cyprus and Malta and many data are missing before 1990.	103/112 in 1992 105/112 in 1993 112/112 from 1994 onwards	2004
Sixth EU enlargement	26/36 in 1990	
Note:	35/36 in 1991	
Data are missing for Czech Republic, Hungary, Poland, and Slovakia	27/36 in 1992 32/36 in 1993 36/36 from 1994 onwards	2007
Seventh EU enlargement	23/23 from 1990 onwards	2013

for Mexican participation in the subsidies code of the GATT. In 1987, Mexico and the United States signed the Framework of Principles and Procedures for Consultation Regarding Trade and Investment Relations, which established an agenda for bilateral trade and investment negotiations. In 1989, the two countries signed an Understanding Regarding Trade and Investment Facilitation Talks. Thus, while Mexican–U.S.

bilateral liberalization initiatives lagged behind Canadian-U.S. initiatives, the former started as early as 1985. In Table 7, the 1/2 (meaning "1 out of 2") refers to Mexico–United States; our model predicts the Mexican–U.S. PTA starting as early as 1978. By contrast, Canadian–Mexican agreements arose more slowly, with ten minor accords signed in 1990. Our model predicted the Canadian–Mexican PTA in 1994—the year it actually went into force. Moreover, it is interesting to note that the year that the model predicted *both* a Mexican–U.S. PTA and a Mexican–Canadian PTA was 1994 (i.e., 2/2 in 1994 in Table 7), the year NAFTA actually began.

Our third part—which is more extensive than the first two parts combined—is an analysis of the (in-sample) predictive ability of the model for the formation of the EU (termed in 1958 the EEC) and its seven subsequent enlargements.[24] Table 7 reports comprehensively the predictions of the model (in column 2) and the actual formation years (in column 3). A detailed analysis of *every row* is beyond the scope of this paper due to the eight rounds of activity; however, we will summarize the key implications using the last row of data for each of the eight rounds (the formation and seven enlargements). We begin with the formation of the EU; the Treaty of Rome went into effect in 1958. As noted above, Belgium represents Belgium and Luxembourg; hence, we have five original EEC countries and ten non-direction country-pairs (10 = [5 x 4]/2). As shown in Table 7, our model predicts *six of the ten* original EU country-pairs in 1958, the *actual* year of entry into force. Based upon economic size, proximity, political similarity, and the interdependence variables in our model, it is likely that the other four pairs would have been predicted for later years, but the data set's construction precludes that as discussed earlier. It is also possible that our historical conflict variables' influence contributed to predicting the other four country-pairs PTA events later.

We now discuss each of the seven enlargements. The first enlargement in 1973 added Denmark, Ireland, and the United Kingdom. Five of the 15 bilateral events were predicted in 1973. Likely because of (West) Germany's economic size, three of these five pairs were Germany with the three new EU partners. Once again, based upon economic size, proximity, political similarity, and the interdependence variables in our model, it is likely that the other ten pairs would have been predicted for later years, but the data set's construction precludes that. Also, it is possible again that our historical conflict variables' influence contributed to predicting the other ten country-pairs PTA events later. The second enlargement in 1981 added Greece. The model predicted all eight country-pair events for Greece with the other eight members starting in 1978, only 3 years prior to the events. The third enlargement added Spain and Portugal in 1986. Although a few of these 18 (18 = 9 x 2) bilateral events were predicted in earlier years, all 18 bilateral events were predicted beginning in 1978, 8 years prior to the event. The fourth enlargement added three new members—Austria, Finland, and Sweden—in 1995. As shown in Table 7, all 33 PTA events ($33 = 11 \times 3$) were predicted beginning in 1983 about 12 years before the events.

The fifth and sixth enlargements were all quite large in terms of numbers of new members. Actually, ten new members joined the EU in 2004. However, due to data constraints, our model was only able to make predictions for eight of these new members: Czech Republic, Estonia, Hungary, Latvia, Lithuania, Poland, Slovakia, and Slovenia. With 14 countries in our model as of the fourth enlargement in 1995, this allows 112 predictions ($112 = 14 \times 8$). Our model predicted all 112 events starting in 1994, about 10 years prior to the 2004 enlargement. Year 2007 saw the sixth enlargement by adding Bulgaria and Romania. These 36 PTA events were predicted starting in 1994 also, about 13 years prior to their inclusion. The seventh enlargement in 2013 to add Croatia was predicted in 1990.

Although the precise timing of the bilateral PTA events *by actual year* is difficult, we note two important results. First, not only the formation of the EU—but also *five of the seven* enlargements—were predicted within a 10-year window of the actual events (as summarized above). The fifth and seventh enlargements were predicted 12–13 years before the events occurred. It is feasible that politics played an influential role in the actual timing of the events. A second interesting result is the *sequencing* of the enlargements. The second enlargement was predicted no later than the third enlargement. The third enlargement was predicted before the fourth enlargement. The fourth enlargement was predicted before the fifth enlargement. The fifth enlargement was predicted no later than the six

24. The name of the EU has evolved over time. For tractability, we will use EU for the original EEC as well as for subsequent names.

TABLE 8
Ten Highest Predictions for 2007–2013

Country Pair	Probability	Predictions for Year	Actual	Details
China–Pakistan	0.840	2011	2007	China–Pakistan FTA implemented
Egypt–South Africa	0.754	2011	Proposed in 2008	Oct 2008 and June 2011 Summits; Proposed African Free Trade Zone (AFTZ) expected to be operational in 2018
Australia–Egypt	0.724	2011	None	No agreement yet under consideration
Libya–Chad	0.705	2009	Proposed in 1998	Community of Sahel-Saharan States (CEN-SAD); Founding members; Goal is to create an economic union; Not yet an effective free trade agreement
Italy–South Korea	0.701	2011	2011	EU–South Korea FTA implemented
Pakistan–Saudi Arabia	0.688	2011	None	No agreement yet under consideration
Spain–South Korea	0.673	2011	2011	EU–South Korea FTA implemented
Italy–Pakistan	0.657	2010	Proposed in 2009	EU–Pakistan 5-year Engagement Plan instituted in 2009 to develop GSP treatment into a FTA
United Arab Emirates–Pakistan	0.645	2011	None	No agreement yet under consideration
Egypt–Gabon	0.644	2011	Proposed in 2012	Proposed extension of proposed AFTZ to include Economic Community of Central African States (ECCAS)

enlargement. Thus, the model generally explains well the sequencing of the EU's enlargements.

While the discussion above has focused on in-sample predictions of particular PTA events that occurred during the sample, it would be interesting to see whether the model—based upon data from 1950 to 2006—predicts the most likely post-2006 *out-of-sample* PTA events. This is the subject of the next section.

D. Evaluating Realizations of the Model's Ten Most Likely Post-Sample Time-to-PTA Events

The main sample of the paper spanned the period 1950–2006. In this section, we consider the predictive analysis of the model for the post-2006 period—2007–2013—using actual values of right-hand-side variables. In particular, we focus on the *ten most likely* PTA events predicted post-sample by the model, comparing their predicted year of PTA formation with the *actual status* of PTA formation—either entered into force, proposed, or not yet considered.

Table 8 will be helpful in organizing the discussion. The first column of Table 8 lists the country-pairs for which a PTA was most likely to be formed in the post-sample period 2007–2013, ranked by highest to lowest probabilities.[25] The second column lists the probability associated with the PTA event. The third column lists the year predicted for the event. The fourth column specifies a year associated with an entry-into-force of an agreement, a year associated with a significant development in a proposed agreement, or the reporting of no PTA or proposed PTA.

For these ten most likely PTA events, seven of the ten pairs have PTAs entered into force or proposed; there is no reported activity for only three of the most likely events. The last column of Table 8 provides details about pairs with proposed agreements or actual PTA formations. We discuss the ten pairs in three groupings: implemented agreements, proposed agreements, and absence of agreements. First, three of the ten country-pairs with post-sample predicted PTA events formed PTAs in the post-sample period. The China–Pakistan PTA went into force in 2007, and was predicted by the model for 2011. The EU formed a PTA with South Korea in 2011. Italy and Spain were both predicted by the model to form PTAs with South Korea in 2011.

The second group of country-pairs is those with predicted PTAs but only a proposal is in place, not an actual agreement. There are four country-pairs in this group. First, Egypt and

25. Predictions were enabled by use of actual values of countries' GDPs and other time-varying right-hand-side variables for the period 2007–2013 using Specification 3; similar results were obtained using Specification 4.

South Africa had a probability of 0.705 of forming a PTA in 2011. In an October 2008 summit followed by another June 2011 summit, the African Free Trade Zone (AFTZ) was proposed. Comprised of 26 countries that span three major existing PTAs—the East African Community (EAC), the Southern African Development Community (SADC), and the Common Market for Eastern and Southern Africa (COMESA)—the AFTZ would create a free trade area that goes from Cairo to Cape Town. Interestingly, the AFTZ would actually implement the dream of Cecil Rhodes in the 1890s of free trade spanning Egypt to South Africa. The AFTZ is expected to be operational in 2018 and progress suggests this is feasible. Second, we have the special case of Libya and Chad. The model predicted a PTA in 2009. The table lists that the two countries were both founding members of the Community of Sahel-Saharan States (CEN-SAD) in 1998, which exists and has a goal of becoming an economic union. However, most observers consider that the FTA signed has not been "effective." Consequently, we consider the 1998 CES-SAD agreement as a proposed agreement. Third, our model predicted an Italy–Pakistan PTA in 2010. The EU instituted in 2009 a 5-year Engagement Plan to extend its current one-way GSP treatment to Pakistan to an FTA. Fourth, our model predicted an Egypt–Gabon PTA in 2011. There was a proposal in 2012 that the AFTZ, proposed during October 2008 and June 2011 summits, be extended from the EAC, SADC, and COMESA to include the Economic Community of Central African States (ECCAS), which would then unite Egypt and Gabon in a PTA.

The third group of country-pairs is those with no planned or existing PTA. This group includes Australia–Egypt, Pakistan–Saudi Arabia, and Pakistan–United Arab Emirates.

VII. CONCLUSION

Despite the proliferation of PTAs in the last 60 years, there have been only 1,560 bilateral formations/enlargements among 10,518 pairings of 146 countries from 1950 to 2006. We used an econometric duration analysis to determine the economic, political, and historical factors explaining the instantaneous probability at a particular year of leaving the initial state of "No-PTA" to form or enter a PTA (given survival of the state No-PTA up until that period). We found that geography, economic size and similarity, relative factor endowments, interdependence (or contagion) in PTA formation, and political and historical factors had statistically significant effects on the timing of country-pairs' PTA "events." Moreover, the coefficient estimates for the variables are consistent with relationships suggested by an underlying theoretical model, suggesting the PTA events are occurring sooner when the net welfare gains for the countries' consumers are higher.

When estimating a specification on all 1,560 PTAs over the period 1950 through 2006, the preferred parsimonious specification (without fixed effects) explains 26%, 46%, and 57% of the PTA events within 1, 5, and 10 years, respectively, up until the actual occurrence of those PTAs within the sample and estimation period. Estimating such a specification for the years 1950 through 2000, the model explains out-of-sample 66% of the events within the same year that the actual PTA membership occurred in 2001 through 2006, 69% in the same year or up to 1 year prior to actual PTA membership, and 82% within 10 years up until the actual occurrence of all 284 PTAs. The model largely explains in-sample the formations of the Canadian–U.S. FTA, NAFTA, and the EU's formation and subsequent enlargements. Moreover, for seven of the ten most likely post-2006 out-of-sample PTA events, either a PTA formed during the period 2007–2013 or one has been proposed.

The results suggest not only that the path of regionalism over time in terms of country-pairs has been one consistent with welfare-maximizing behavior of countries' governments, but that there is a feasible "road map" for policy makers for the evolution of PTAs in the world economy. While most observers might agree that overall multilateral liberalization would be the most preferred policy for the world economy in principle, in the absence of such progress the path of regionalism has likely been a beneficial one.

REFERENCES

Abbring J. H., and G. J. van den Berg. "Dynamically Assigned Treatments: Duration Models, Binary Treatment Models, and Panel Data Models." Working Paper No. 2002:20, Institute for Labour Market Policy Evaluation (IFAU), Uppsala, 2002.

Bagwell, K., and R. W. Staiger. "Multilateral Tariff Cooperation during the Formation of Customs Unions." *Journal of International Economics*, 42, 1997, 91–123.

Bagwell, K., and R. W. Staiger. "Multilateral Trade Negotiations, Bilateral Opportunism and the Rules of GATT/WTO." *Journal of International Economics*, 67, 2005, 268–94.

Baier, S. L., and J. H. Bergstrand. "Economic Determinants of Free Trade Agreements." *Journal of International Economics*, 64, 2004, 29–63.

Baier, S. L., J. H. Bergstrand, and R. Mariutto. "Economic Determinants of Free Trade Agreements Revisited: Distinguishing Sources of Interdependence." *Review of International Economics*, 22, 2014, 31–58.

Baldwin, R. E. "A Domino Theory of Regionalism," in *Expanding Membership of the European Union*, edited by R. Baldwin, P. Haaparanta, and J. Kiander. Cambridge: Cambridge University Press, 1995.

———. "The Logic of Trade Blocs as Building and Stumbling Blocks on the Road to Global Free Trade: A Survey." Unpublished manuscript, Graduate Institute for International Studies, Geneva, 2007.

Baldwin, R. E., and D. Jaimovich. "Are Free Trade Agreements Contagious?" *Journal of International Economics*, 88, 2012, 1–16.

Bergstrand, J. H., and P. H. Egger. "What Determines BITs?" *Journal of International Economics*, 90, 2013, 107–22.

Besedes, T. "A Search Cost Perspective on Formation and Duration of Trade." *Review of International Economics*, 16, 2008, 835–49.

Besedes, T., and T. J. Prusa. "Ins, Outs and the Duration of Trade." *Canadian Journal of Economics*, 39, 2006a, 266–95.

———. "Product Differentiation and Duration of US Import Trade." *Journal of International Economics*, 70, 2006b, 339–58.

Bond, E. W., R. G. Riezman, and C. Syropoulos. "A Strategic and Welfare Theoretic Analysis of Free Trade Areas." *Journal of International Economics*, 64, 2004, 1–27.

Chamberlain, G. "Analysis of Covariance with Qualitative Data." *Review of Economic Studies*, 47, 1980, 225–38.

Chen, M. X., and S. Joshi. "Third-Country Effects on the Formation of Free Trade Agreements." *Journal of International Economics*, 82, 2010, 238–48.

Conway, P. "The Revolving Door: Duration and Recidivism in IMF Programs." *Review of Economics and Statistics*, 89, 2007, 205–20.

Deltas, G., K. Desmet, and G. Facchini. "Hub-and-Spoke Free Trade Areas: Theory and Evidence from Israel." *Canadian Journal of Economics*, 45, 2012, 942–77.

Egger, H., P. H. Egger, and D. Greenaway. "Trade Liberalization with Multinational Firms: Effects on Welfare and Intra-Industry Trade." *Journal of International Economics*, 74, 2008, 278–98.

Egger, P. H., and M. Larch. "Interdependent Preferential Trade Agreement Memberships: An Empirical Analysis." *Journal of International Economics*, 76, 2008, 384–99.

Frankel, J. A. *Regional Trading Blocs*. Washington, DC: Institute for International Economics, 1997.

Freund, C. "Multilateralism and the Endogenous Formation of Preferential Trade Agreements." *Journal of International Economics*, 52, 2000, 359–76.

Fugazza, M., and A. C. Molina. "The Determinants of Trade Survival." Working Paper No. 05/2009, Graduate Institute of International and Development Studies, Geneva, 2009.

Fugazza, M., and F. Robert-Nicoud. The 'Emulator Effect' of the Uruguay Round on US Regionalism." Working Paper Series No. 11111, Institute of Economics and Econometrics, Geneva School of Economics and Management, University of Geneva, 2011.

Gradeva, K., and D. Jaimovich. "Multilateral Determinants of Regionalism Revisited." *Review of International Organizations*, 9, 2014, 163–203.

Heckman, J. J., and B. Singer. "A Method for Minimizing the Impact of Distributional Assumptions in Econometric Models for Duration Data." *Econometrica*, 52, 1984, 271–320.

Hess, W., and M. Persson. "The Duration of Trade Revisited: Continuous-Time vs. Discrete-Time Hazards." Working Paper No. 829, Research Institute of Industrial Economics (IFN), Stockholm, 2010.

Jenkins, S. P. "Easy Estimation Methods for Discrete-Time Duration Models." *Oxford Bulletin of Economics and Statistics*, 57, 1995, 129–38.

———. "Survival Analysis." Unpublished manuscript, 2005. https://www.iser.essex.ac.uk/files/teaching/stephenj/ec968/pdfs/ec968lnotesv6.pdf.

Joyce, J. P. "Time Past and Time Present: A Duration Analysis of IMF Program Spells." *Review of International Economics*, 13, 2005, 283–97.

Kiefer, N. M. "Economic Duration Data and Hazard Functions." *Journal of Economic Literature*, 26, 1988, 646–79.

Krugman, P. R. "Is Bilateralism Bad?," in *International Trade and Trade Policy*, edited by E. Helpman and A. Assaf Razin. Cambridge, MA: MIT Press, 1991a, 9–23.

———. *The Move Toward Free Trade Zones*. Jackson Hole, WY: Policy Implications of Trade and Currency Zones, Federal Reserve Bank of Kansas City, 1991b.

Liu, X. "The Political Economy of Free Trade Agreements." *Journal of Economic Integration*, 23, 2008, 237–71.

———. "Testing Conflicting Political Economy Theories: Full-fledged versus Partial-Scope Regional Trade Agreements." *Southern Economic Journal*, 77, 2010, 78–103.

Magee, C. "Endogenous Preferential Trade Agreements: An Empirical Analysis." *Contributions to Economic Analysis and Policy*, 2. Berkeley, CA: Berkeley Electronic Press, 2003.

Maddison, A. *The World Economy: Historical Statistics*. Paris, France: OECD, 2003.

Mansfield, E. D., and E. Reinhardt. "Multilateral Determinants of Regionalism: The Effects of GATT/WTO on the Formation of Preferential Trading Arrangements." *International Organization*, 57, 2003, 829–62.

Marshall, M. G., T. R. Gurr, and K. Jaggers. *Polity IV Project: Political Regime Characteristics and Transitions*, 1800–2012, Dataset Users' Manual, Center for Systemic Peace, 2013. http://www.systemicpeace.org/inscr/p4manualv2012.pdf.

Martin, P., T. Mayer, and M. Thoenig. "The Geography of Conflicts and Regional Trade Agreements." *American Economic Journal: Macroeconomics*, 4, 2012, 1–35.

McFadden, D. "The Revealed Preferences of a Government Bureaucracy: Theory." *Bell Journal of Economics*, 6, 1975, 401–16.

———. "Quantal Choice Analysis: A Survey." *Annals of Economic and Social Measurement*, 5, 1976, 363–90.

Nitsch, V. "Die Another Day: Duration in German Import Trade." *Review of World Economics*, 145, 2009, 133–54.

de Ree, J., and E. Nillesen. "Aiding Violence or Peace? The Impact of Foreign Aid on the Risk of Civil Conflict in sub-Saharan Africa." *Journal of Development Economics*, 88, 2009, 301–13.

Wooldridge, J. M. *Econometric Analysis of Cross Section and Panel Data*. 2nd ed. Cambridge, MA: MIT Press, 2010.

SUPPORTING INFORMATION

Additional Supporting Information may be found in the online version of this article:

Appendix S1. Theoretical supplement

PART 3

Estimating the Effects of Economic Integration Agreements

Chapter 10

Do free trade agreements actually increase members' international trade?

Scott L. Baier [a,b], Jeffrey H. Bergstrand [c,d,*]

[a] *John E. Walker Department of Economics, Clemson University, Clemson, SC 29634, USA*
[b] *Federal Reserve Bank of Atlanta, Atlanta, GA 30309, USA*
[c] *Department of Finance, Mendoza College of Business, and Kellogg Institute for International Studies, University of Notre Dame, Notre Dame, IN 46556, USA*
[d] *CESifo, Germany*

Received 24 April 2003; received in revised form 15 December 2005; accepted 15 February 2006

Abstract

For over 40 years, the gravity equation has been a workhorse for cross-country empirical analyses of international trade flows and — in particular — the effects of free trade agreements (FTAs) on trade flows. However, the gravity equation is subject to the same econometric critique as earlier cross-industry studies of U.S. tariff and nontariff barriers and U.S. multilateral imports: trade policy is *not* an exogenous variable. We address econometrically the endogeneity of FTAs. Although instrumental-variable and control-function approaches do not adjust for endogeneity well, a panel approach does. Accounting econometrically for the FTA variable's endogeneity yields striking empirical results: the effect of FTAs on trade flows is quintupled. We find that, on average, an FTA approximately *doubles* two members' bilateral trade after 10 years.

Keywords: Free trade agreements; International trade flows; Gravity equation

JEL classification: F1

1. Introduction

> The issue of exogeneity may also be an important problem when dummy variables are used (in a gravity equation) to estimate the effects of free trade areas (Lawrence, 1998, p. 59).

* Corresponding author. Department of Finance, Mendoza College of Business, and Kellogg Institute for International Studies, University of Notre Dame, Notre Dame, IN 46556, USA. Tel.: +1 574 631 6761; fax: +1 574 631 5255.
E-mail address: Bergstrand.1@nd.edu (J.H. Bergstrand).

*Originally Published in *Journal of International Economics*, 71(2007), pp. 72–95.

One might expect — having witnessed a virtual explosion in the number of free trade agreements (FTAs) among nations over the past decade and a half — that the answer to the question posed in this paper's title is unequivocal: *yes*! Surprisingly, international trade economists can actually claim little firm empirical support for reliable quantitative estimates of the average effect of an FTA on bilateral trade (all else constant).

Over the past 40 years, the "gravity equation" has emerged as the empirical workhorse in international trade to study the ex post effects of FTAs and customs unions on bilateral merchandise trade flows.[1] The gravity equation is typically used to explain cross-sectional variation in country pairs' trade flows in terms of the countries' incomes, bilateral distance, and dummy variables for common languages, for common land borders, and for the presence or absence of an FTA. Nobel laureate Jan Tinbergen (1962) was the first to publish an econometric study using the gravity equation for international trade flows, which included evaluating the effect of FTA dummy variables on trade. His results suggested economically insignificant "average treatment effects" of FTAs on trade flows. Tinbergen found that membership in the British Commonwealth (Benelux FTA) was associated with only 5 (4) percent higher trade flows. Since then, results have been mixed, at best. For example, Aitken (1973), Abrams (1980), and Brada and Mendez (1985) found the European Community (EC) to have an economically and statistically significant effect on trade flows among members, whereas Bergstrand (1985) and Frankel, Stein and Wei (1995) found insignificant effects. Frankel (1997) found positive significant effects from Mersosur, insignificant effects from the Andean Pact, and significant *negative* effects from membership in the EC in certain years. He noted:

> If the data from four years — 1970, 1980, 1990, 1992 — are pooled together, the estimated coefficient on the European Community is a smaller 0.15, implying a 16 percent effect" (p. 83).

Frankel (1997) concluded that several readers "have found surprising our result that intra-European trade can be mostly explained by various natural factors, with little role for the EC until the 1980s...." (p. 88). Other studies in international trade have had similar seemingly implausible results.[2]

The fragility of estimated FTA treatment effects is addressed directly in Ghosh and Yamarik (2004). These authors use extreme-bounds analysis to test the robustness of FTA dummy coefficient estimates. They find empirical evidence using cross-section data that the estimated average treatment effects of most FTAs are "fragile," supporting our claims. Thus, there still are no reliable ex post estimates of the FTA average treatment effect. This paper is aimed at addressing this puzzle.

All these studies, however, typically assume an *exogenous* right-hand-side (RHS) dummy variable to represent the FTA treatment. In reality, FTA dummies are not exogenous random variables; rather, countries likely select endogenously into FTAs, perhaps for reasons unobservable to the econometrician and possibly correlated with the level of trade.[3] This paper applies developments in the econometric analysis of treatment effects — some well-known and others more recent — to estimate the effects of FTAs on bilateral trade flows using a panel of cross-

[1] Bayoumi and Eichengreen (1997, p. 142) note that the gravity equation has "long been the workhorse for empirical studies of the pattern of trade." This study (purposefully) does not address ex ante analyses of the effects of FTAs on trade flows using computable general equilibrium models.

[2] Frankel (1997) and Oguledo and MacPhee (1994) provide summaries of FTA coefficient estimates across studies. Frankel (1997, pp. 86–90) draws considerable attention to the surprising insignificant effects (especially prior to the 1980s) of the EC and EFTA in his and others studies, such as Bergstrand (1985, 1989) and Boisso and Ferrantino (1997). However, no systematic explanation is provided.

[3] We note that, for about a decade, several researchers have acknowledged potential endogeneity bias, but only that created by GDPs as RHS variables. Several authors have instrumented for GDPs, but (with the exception of the three studies noted shortly) none have instrumented for FTAs.

section time-series data at five-year intervals from 1960 to 2000 for 96 countries. The literature on treatment effects, developed in the context of numerous labor economics studies (cf., Wooldridge, 2002), provides rich tools that have not previously been used for analyzing the effects of bilateral trade policies on international trade flows.

This is not the first paper in empirical international trade to call attention to the potential endogeneity bias in estimating the effect of trade policies on trade volumes. For instance, Trefler (1993) addressed systematically the simultaneous determination of U.S. multilateral imports and U.S. multilateral nontariff barriers in a cross-industry analysis. Trefler found using instrumental variables that, after accounting for the endogeneity of trade policies, the effect of these policies on U.S. imports increased *tenfold*. Lee and Swagel (1997) also showed using instrumental variables that previous estimates of the impact of trade liberalization on imports had been considerably underestimated.

Clearly, the literature on bilateral trade flows and bilateral FTAs using the gravity equation is subject to the same critique that Trefler raised: the presence or absence of an FTA is not exogenous. The issue is important because – if FTAs are endogenous – previous cross-section empirical estimates of the effects of FTAs on trade flows may be biased, and the effects of FTAs on trade may be seriously over- or under-estimated, as the extreme-bounds evidence in Ghosh and Yamarik (2004) suggests. To date, only three papers have attempted to address the potential bias in cross-section gravity models caused by endogenous FTAs, Baier and Bergstrand (2002, 2004b) and Magee (2003). However, all three papers — using instrumental variables with cross section data — provide at best mixed evidence of isolating the effect of FTAs on trade flows.

The empirical results in our paper suggest three important conclusions. First, several plausible reasons exist to suggest that the quantitative (long-run) effects of FTAs on trade flows using the standard cross-section gravity equation are biased; we argue that unobservable heterogeneity most likely biases estimates *downward*. Second, we find that, owing to this bias, traditional estimates of the effect of FTAs on bilateral trade flows have tended to be underestimated by as much as 75–85%. Third, we demonstrate that the most plausible estimates of the average effect of an FTA on a bilateral trade flow are obtained from a theoretically-motivated gravity equation using panel data with bilateral fixed and country-and-time effects or differenced panel data with country-and-time effects. Other methods to identify the impact, such as instrumental variables using cross-section data, are compromised by a lack of suitable instruments. We find that, on average, an FTA approximately *doubles* two members' bilateral trade after 10 years.

Section 2 presents a (traditional) atheoretical cross-section gravity equation and a (modern) theoretically-motivated cross-section gravity equation. Section 3 provides motivation for suspecting endogeneity of FTA dummy variables and suggests the likely direction of bias. Section 4 summarizes some instrumental-variable and control-function econometric studies that have tried to eliminate endogeneity bias using cross-section data. Section 5 addresses panel techniques and discusses the results from applying various fixed and time effects and first differencing to panel data. Section 6 concludes.

2. The gravity equation in international trade

The gravity equation in international trade most commonly estimated using cross-country data is:

$$PX_{ij} = \beta_0(GDP_i)^{\beta 1}(GDP_j)^{\beta 2}(DIST_{ij})^{\beta 3}e^{\beta 4(LANG_{ij})}e^{\beta 5(ADJ_{ij})}e^{\beta 6(FTA_{ij})}\varepsilon_{ij} \tag{1}$$

where PX_{ij} is the value of the merchandise trade flow from exporter i to importer j, GDP_i (GDP_j) is the level of nominal gross domestic product in country i (j), $DIST_{ij}$ is the distance between the economic centers of countries i and j, $LANG_{ij}$ is a binary variable assuming the value 1 if i and j share a common language and 0 otherwise, ADJ_{ij} is a binary variable assuming the value 1 if i and j share a common land border and 0 otherwise, FTA_{ij} is a binary variable assuming the value 1 if i and j have a free trade agreement and 0 otherwise, e is the natural logarithm base, and ϵ_{ij} is assumed to be a log-normally distributed error term.[4]

The earliest applications of the gravity equation to international trade flows were not grounded in formal theoretical foundations, cf., Tinbergen (1962), Linnemann (1966), Aitken (1973) and Sapir (1981); these earlier studies appealed either to informal economic foundations or to a physical science analogy. Since 1979, however, formal theoretical economic foundations for a gravity equation similar to Eq. (1) have surfaced, cf., Anderson (1979), Bergstrand (1985), Deardorff (1998), Baier and Bergstrand (2001), Eaton and Kortum (2002), and Anderson and van Wincoop (2003). A notable feature common to *all* these models is an explicit role for *prices*; in all six papers, price levels or some form of multilateral price indexes surface theoretically.[5] Most recently, Anderson and van Wincoop (2003) illustrated the omitted variables bias introduced by ignoring prices in the cross-section gravity equation. Their framework suggests theoretically the gravity model should be estimated as:

$$\begin{aligned}\ln[PX_{ij}/(GDP_i GDP_j)] = \beta_0 + \beta_3(\ln DIST_{ij}) + \beta_4(ADJ_{ij}) + \beta_5(LANG_{ij}) \\ + \beta_6(FTA_{ij}) - \ln P_i^{1-\sigma} - \ln P_j^{1-\sigma} + \varepsilon_{ij}\end{aligned} \tag{2}$$

subject to N equilibrium conditions:

$$P_1^{1-\sigma} = \sum_{i=1}^{N} P_i^{\sigma-1}(GDP_i/GDP^W)e^{\beta 3(\ln DIST_{i1})+\beta 4(LANG_{i1})+\beta 5(ADJ_{i1})+\beta 6(FTA_{i1})} \tag{3.1}$$

•
•
•

$$P_N^{1-\sigma} = \sum_{i=1}^{N} P_i^{\sigma-1}(GDP_N/GDP^W)e^{\beta 3(\ln DIST_{iN})+\beta 4(LANG_{iN})+\beta 5(ADJ_{iN})+\beta 6(FTA_{iN})} \tag{3.N}$$

to generate unbiased estimates of β_0, β_3, β_4, β_5 and β_6. GDP^W denotes world GDP, constant across countries. $P_i^{1-\sigma}$ and $P_j^{1-\sigma}$ are denoted "multilateral (price) resistance terms."[6] Anderson and van Wincoop then estimate this system using a custom nonlinear least squares program, treating all $P_i^{1-\sigma}$ variables (i=1,..., N countries) as endogenous. However, Anderson and van Wincoop (2003) and Feenstra (2004, Ch. 5) both suggest that an alternative — and computationally easier — method for accounting for multilateral price terms $P_i^{1-\sigma}$ and $P_j^{1-\sigma}$ in cross section — that will also generate

[4] The standard gravity equation sometimes includes the exporter and importer populations or per capita GDPs. Theoretical foundations for this alternative specification still require refinement, which is beyond the scope of this particular paper but is an issue addressed in Bergstrand (1989, 1990) and Baier and Bergstrand (2002).

[5] A seminal contribution to the theoretical foundations of the gravity equation, but in the absence of trade costs (and consequently price terms), is Helpman and Krugman (1985, Ch. 8).

[6] Assuming distance, language, adjacency and FTA are *symmetric* for ij and ji, the equilibrium multilateral resistance terms can be solved for according to Eqs. (3.1) through (3.N).

Table 1
Typical cross-section gravity equation coefficient estimates

Variable	(1) 1960	(2) 1970	(3) 1980	(4) 1990	(5) 2000
ln GDP_i	0.76 (45.79)	0.88 (57.55)	1.01 (69.37)	1.08 (85.13)	1.18 (104.13)
ln GDP_j	0.76 (48.66)	0.92 (63.95)	1.00 (72.69)	0.97 (78.08)	0.98 (87.39)
ln $DIST_{ij}$	−0.64 (−16.23)	−0.85 (−21.10)	−1.06 (−28.15)	−1.07 (−28.82)	−1.17 (−32.57)
ADJ_{ij}	0.16 (1.03)	0.14 (0.85)	0.35 (2.18)	0.59 (3.72)	0.74 (4.88)
$LANG_{ij}$	0.06 (0.65)	0.34 (3.48)	0.56 (5.84)	0.80 (8.16)	0.72 (7.71)
FTA_{ij}	0.63 (3.46)	1.37 (6.64)	−0.13 (−0.73)	−0.14 (−0.95)	0.29 (2.85)
Constant	−9.38 (−20.44)	−12.17 (−26.88)	−16.23 (−35.59)	−17.09 (−40.37)	−17.94 (−49.11)
RMSE	1.4163	1.7616	1.8900	1.9919	1.9645
R^2	0.6061	0.6334	0.6446	0.6649	0.7137
No. observations	2633	4030	5421	6474	7302

t-statistics are in parentheses. The dependent variable is the (natural log of the) nominal bilateral trade flow from *i* to *j*.

unbiased coefficient estimates of β_0, β_3, β_4, β_5 and β_6 — is estimation of Eq. (2) using country-specific fixed effects.[7]

As preliminary empirical support for our claim that FTA coefficients are biased, we estimate a typical cross-section gravity equation for multiple years: 1960, 1970, 1980, 1990, and 2000. Table 1 provides cross-section coefficient estimates for these years of a typical (log-linear version of) gravity Eq. (1), estimated using the (non-zero) nominal trade flows among 96 countries identified in the Data Appendix. The data sources are standard and are provided in Section 4.[8] The five sets of estimates in Table 1 support our claims and findings in the literature that the FTA dummy's coefficient estimates are highly unstable from year to year, are often small positive values, and in some years are even *negative*.[9]

Table 2 provides estimates for the same years of gravity Eq. (2), where — following Anderson and van Wincoop (2003, Table 6) and Feenstra (2004, Ch. 5) — we use country fixed effects to account for the multilateral price terms (rather than a custom nonlinear least squares program). The FTA dummy coefficient estimates remain unstable across years and, for several years, the FTA coefficient's estimate is negative.[10] While the country fixed effects help to account for the endogeneity bias created by prices and the influence of FTAs among other

[7] Eaton and Kortum (2002), Rose and van Wincoop (2001), and Redding and Venables (2000) similarly used country fixed effects to account for multilateral price terms.

[8] The issue of zero trade flows has been treated in other papers, such as Eichengreen and Irwin (1995) and Felbermyer and Kohler (2004). However, this issue is beyond the scope of the present paper. For instance, in 2000, we have 9120 potential trade flows among 96 countries (96×95=9120), less 1573 trade flows recorded as zero and 245 observations recorded as "missing."

[9] The basic findings in Table 1 (and Table 2) are generally unaffected when we considered fixed sample sizes for all five years. First, we restricted our sample to all trading partners who had positive trade flows in 1960; for any of these pairs that had zeros in 1970, ..., 2000, we substituted ones for zeros. Second, we restricted our sample to all trading partners who had positive trade flows in 2000; for any of these pairs that had zeros in 1960, ..., 1990, we substituted ones for zeros. The coefficient estimates were materially the same across samples.

[10] The reader may also notice the upward trend (in absolute values) in non-FTA coefficient estimates with time in Tables 1 and 2. This also is an interesting issue but is beyond the scope of this paper; the upward drift (in absolute value) of the distance coefficient estimate has been studied by other researchers, cf., Felbermyer and Kohler (2004). Our focus is instead on the instability of the FTA coefficient estimates. Indeed, the FTA coefficient estimate also had the highest coefficient of variation of all the variables' coefficient estimates. For instance, using Table 2's specification, the coefficients of variation of the coefficient estimates for the non-FTA variables ranged from 0.29 to 0.31. By contrast the coefficient of variation of the FTA coefficient estimates was 2.05, six times that of the others.

Table 2
Theory-motivated cross-section gravity equations with country fixed effects

Variable	(1) 1960	(2) 1970	(3) 1980	(4) 1990	(5) 2000
ln $DIST_{ij}$	−0.68 (−16.77)	−0.89 (−21.58)	−1.28 (−31.36)	−1.30 (−31.65)	−1.46 (−35.79)
ADJ_{ij}	0.31 (2.26)	0.35 (2.38)	0.43 (2.95)	0.58 (3.93)	0.59 (4.09)
$LANG_{ij}$	0.38 (3.99)	0.84 (8.33)	0.82 (8.06)	0.98 (9.41)	0.97 (9.78)
FTA_{ij}	0.01 (0.09)	0.61 (3.27)	−1.44 (−8.65)	−1.08 (−7.30)	−0.14 (−1.36)
Constant	−14.06 (−8.25)	−12.49 (−18.66)	−14.98 (−19.37)	−16.64 (−31.88)	−12.76 (−27.18)
RMSE	1.1826	1.5025	1.6635	1.7806	1.7851
Within R^2	0.5020	0.4300	0.3857	0.3648	0.3845
No. observations	2633	4030	5421	6474	7302

t-statistics are in parentheses. The dependent variable is the (natural log of the) nominal bilateral trade flow from country *i* to country *j* divided by the product of their nominal GDPs. Coefficient estimates of country fixed effects are not reported for brevity.

countries on the trade from *i* to *j*, they do not correct for the bias introduced if countries select into FTAs. We must turn to other methods to identify unbiased FTA treatment effects, which is the purpose of this paper.[11]

3. Endogeneity bias

A standard problem in cross-section empirical work is the potential endogeneity of RHS variables. If any of the RHS variables in Eqs. (1) or (2) are correlated with the error term, ϵ_{ij}, that variable is considered econometrically "endogenous" and ordinary least squares (OLS) may yield biased and inconsistent coefficient estimates. Potential sources of endogeneity bias of RHS variables' coefficient estimates generally fall under three categories: omitted variables, simultaneity, and measurement error (see Wooldridge, 2002, pp. 50–51). While we believe all three factors may contribute potentially to endogeneity bias caused by FTA, we will argue that the most important source is omitted variables (and selection) bias. We discuss each source in turn.

3.1. Omitted variables (and selection) bias

The gravity equation has surfaced over the past four decades as the dominant empirical framework for analyzing bilateral trade flows primarily because of its strong explanatory power. Explanatory power (R^2) generally ranges from 60 to 80%. However, as Table 1 suggests, there remains considerable unobserved heterogeneity among country pairs (leaving aside the issue of multilateral price terms, for now).

In determining the potential correlation between the gravity equation's error term, ϵ_{ij}, with FTA_{ij}, one first needs to consider what determines the likelihood of an FTA between a pair of countries. Although trade economists have examined empirically for many years the determinants of tariff rates and non-tariff barrier levels across industries and across countries, virtually no empirical work has examined the determinants of FTA_{ij}. A notable exception is Baier and Bergstrand (2004a). These authors present a theoretical and empirical model of economic determinants of FTAs. Their paper finds strong cross-section empirical evidence that pairs of

[11] We emphasize that our focus here is only on an unbiased estimate of the average *treatment* effect (β_6 in Eqs. (1) and (2)), not an estimate of the full "comparative-static" effect of an FTA, which would also account for the effects of endogenous changes in the multilateral price terms, (3.1) through (3.N), cf., Anderson and van Wincoop (2003).

countries that have FTAs *tend* to share economic characteristics that their theory suggests should enhance the net economic welfare gains from an FTA for the pairs' representative consumers. For instance, two countries tend to have an FTA the larger and more similar their GDPs, the closer they are to each other but the more remote the pair is from the rest-of-the-world (ROW), and the wider (narrower) the difference in their relative factor endowments with respect to each other (ROW). But this list includes the same factors that tend to explain large trade flows. Thus, in terms of *observable* economic characteristics, countries with FTAs have "chosen well," in the sense that most country pairs with FTAs tend to have the economic characteristics associated with considerable trade and with (in theory) welfare-enhancing net trade creation from an FTA. Yet, the estimated probit functions in Baier and Bergstrand (2004a) have pseudo-R^2 values of only 70%, still leaving considerable unobserved heterogeneity.

The important question for this paper is: How is the unobserved heterogeneity in trade flow determinants associated with the likelihood of an FTA? For instance, error term ϵ_{ij} in Eqs. (1) or (2) may be representing unobservable (to the econometrician) policy-related barriers — tending to reduce trade between two countries — that are not accounted for by standard gravity equation RHS variables but may be correlated with the decision to form an FTA. As an example, suppose two countries have extensive unmeasurable domestic regulations (e.g., internal shipping regulations) that inhibit trade (causing ϵ_{ij} to be negative). The likelihood of the two countries' governments selecting into an FTA may be high if there is a large expected welfare gain from potential bilateral trade creation if the FTA deepens liberalization beyond tariff barriers into domestic regulations (and other non-tariff barriers). Thus, FTA_{ij} and the intensity of domestic regulations may be positively correlated in a cross-section of data, but the gravity equation error term ϵ_{ij} and the intensity of domestic regulations may be negatively correlated. This reason suggests that FTA_{ij} and ϵ_{ij} are negatively correlated, and the FTA coefficient will tend to be *underestimated*.

In support of this argument, numerous authors have noted that one of the major benefits of regionalism is the potential for "deeper integration." Lawrence (1996, p. xvii) distinguishes between "international policies" that deal with border barriers, such as tariffs, and "domestic policies" that are concerned with everything "behind the nation's borders, such as competition and antitrust rules, corporate governance, product standards, worker safety, regulation and supervision of financial institutions, environmental protection, tax codes...." and other national issues. The GATT and WTO have been remarkably effective in the post-WWII era reducing border barriers such as tariffs. However, these institutions have been much less effective in liberalizing the domestic policies just named. As Lawrence states it, "Once tariffs are removed, complex problems remain because of differing regulatory policies among nations" (p. 7). He argues that in many cases, FTA "agreements are also meant to achieve deeper integration of international competition and investment" (p. 7). Gilpin (2000) echos this argument: "Yet, the inability to agree on international rules or to increase international cooperation in this area has contributed to the development of both managed trade *and regional arrangements*" (p. 108; italics added). Preeg (1998) notes:

> [Free] trade agreements over time, however, have tended to include a broader and broader scope of other trade-related policies. This trend is a reflection, in part, of the fact that as border restrictions [tariffs] are reduced or eliminated, other policies become relatively more important in influencing trade flows and thus need to be assimilated in the trade relationship (p. 50).

We believe this omitted variable (selection) bias is the major source of endogeneity facing estimation of FTA effects in gravity equations using cross-section data. Moreover, the arguments above suggest that policymakers' decisions to select into an FTA are likely related to the *level* of trade (relative to its potential level), and not to recent changes in trade levels. Thus, the determinants of FTA are likely to be cross-sectional in nature.

With cross-section data, standard econometric techniques to address omitted variables (and selection) bias include estimation using instrumental variables and Heckman control functions. Alternatively, with panel data, fixed effects and first differencing can be employed to treat endogeneity bias. We discuss these various approaches in Sections 4 and 5, respectively.

3.2. Simultaneity bias

Consider the potential endogeneity bias created by simultaneity. GDP — a function of net exports — is potentially endogenous to bilateral trade flows, as suggested by the recent literature on "trade and growth," cf., Frankel and Romer (1999). Yet, some convincing reasons exist for largely ignoring potential endogeneity of incomes here. First, GDP is a function of *net* multilateral exports. Typically, net exports tend to less than 5% of a country's GDP (in absolute terms). Moreover, while GDP is related to net exports, GDP's connection to gross exports is much less direct. Second, the gravity equation relates *bilateral* trade flows to countries' incomes. Trade between any pair of countries tends to be a very small share of any country's multilateral exports, much less its GDP. Note that the literature on "trade and growth" examines empirically the effects of multilateral — not bilateral — trade on GDP, cf., Frankel and Romer (1999). Third, Frankel (1997) and others have previously accounted for the potential endogeneity of national incomes econometrically in typical gravity equations using instrumental variables (IV) including labor forces and stocks of human and physical capital. Frankel (1997) reported that coefficient estimates in gravity equations change insignificantly using these IV techniques and concluded "Evidently, the endogeneity of income makes little difference" (p. 135). Nevertheless, we will still also account for the potential endogeneity of GDPs using a regression specification such as Eq. (2) with GDPs on the left hand side (LHS).

Of the remaining RHS variables in Eq. (1), only FTA seems potentially endogenous. It is plausible to treat DIST and ADJ as exogenous. Moreover, the presence or absence of a common language (LANG) may reasonably be treated in cross-section as exogenous also.

Yet, as discussed earlier, there exists a large empirical literature in international trade on the effects of multilateral tariff and nontariff barriers on multilateral trade volumes, and the simultaneous effects of these trade volumes on multilateral barriers using cross-industry and cross-country data for particular years, c.f. Trefler (1993) and Lee and Swagel (1997). Simultaneity may be an issue for FTA in cross-section gravity equations, motivated as in these two studies. For example, holding constant typical gravity equation RHS variables (GDPs, DIST, ADJ, LANG), two countries (say, the United States and China) that possibly trade more than their "natural" level, as predicted by a typical gravity equation, may create political pressures to avoid trade liberalization or possibly raise trade barriers. This would cause a negative simultaneity bias in the FTA coefficient estimate. On the other hand, the governments of two countries that trade more than their gravity-equation-suggested "natural" level might be induced to form an FTA because there might potentially be less "trade diversion" due to their extensive trading relationship, suggesting a positive simultaneity bias. However, since the decisions to select into FTAs are likely influenced by the levels of trade relative to "natural" levels, recent *changes* in trade levels are not likely to influence FTA formations.

To address this issue, the natural inclination is to estimate a system of simultaneous equations treating bilateral trade and FTAs as endogenous variables using instrumental variables, following in the spirit of Trefler (1993) and Lee and Swagel (1997). We will discuss some of these efforts in Section 4.

3.3. Measurement error bias

Finally, measurement error in an explanatory variable, such as an FTA dummy, is generally associated with negative bias (in absolute terms) in the variable's coefficient. For instance, with the classical "errors-in-variables" assumption, the 0–1 FTA dummy variable (FTA) would be correlated positively with the measurement error (ς) if the true trade-policy variable (say, the tariff rate, t) was assumed uncorrelated with ς ($\varsigma = \text{FTA} - t$). In Eq. (1)'s context, the correlation between FTA and the error term ($\epsilon - \beta_6 \varsigma$) would be negative, leading to the classical "attenuation bias" of FTA's coefficient estimate toward zero.[12] We believe that this may be part of the reason — but neither the entire, nor even the most important, reason — FTA coefficient estimates have been underestimated.

Of course, the best method for eliminating this bias is construction of a continuous variable that would more accurately measure the degree of trade liberalization from various FTAs. If FTAs only eliminated bilateral tariff rates, one would ideally measure this liberalization with a change in the ad valorem tariff rate (for which data is poor). However, FTAs liberalize trade well beyond the elimination of tariffs. Calculation of such measures is beyond the scope of this particular study, but is a useful direction for future research. Our goal rather is to determine reliable estimates of the *treatment effect* of an FTA, similar to the 0–1 variable representing program participation in labor econometrics. Thus, we constrain our study to estimate more accurately the ex post effect of an FTA dummy on trade flows, as has been employed in the gravity equation literature for over four decades.[13]

4. Treatment effects in cross-section models of trade flows and free trade agreements

We briefly address conventional cross-section instrumental-variables (IV) and control-function approaches to address the FTA endogeneity bias associated with omitted variables and selection. We then discuss some previous studies using these techniques and summarize their mixed findings.

4.1. Cross-section econometric techniques

Methodological issues regarding the cross-section estimation of the partial effects of an endogenous binary variable (such as FTA) on a continuous endogenous variable (such as trade flows) fall under the "treatment effect" literature in econometrics. The average treatment effect refers to the notion that the trade flow between two countries will differ depending upon whether the countries share an FTA or not. The fundamental econometric dilemma is that one can observe only one situation or the other. An excellent summary of developments in the treatment–effect

[12] Even without the classical errors-in-variable assumption, the correlation between FTA and ϵ is likely negative. Suppose the true trade policy variable is the bilateral tariff rate, t, where $t>0$. If an FTA exists, FTA=1, $t=0$, and ς consequently equals 1. If no FTA exists, FTA=0, $t>0$, and consequently $\varsigma<0$. Thus, FTA and ς are positively correlated.

[13] Another interesting direction suggested by one referee is to also examine the treatment effects by individual agreements. However, to limit the scope of this paper, this useful direction is left for future research.

literature is in Heckman (2001) and Wooldridge (2002, Ch. 18); we refer the reader to these papers for a more comprehensive discussion.

The average treatment effect (ATE) of an FTA between a country pair is defined as:

$$\text{ATE}(\boldsymbol{q}) \equiv E(x_1 - x_0 | \boldsymbol{q}, \text{FTA}) \tag{4}$$

where x_1 (x_0) denotes the logarithm of the trade flow from country i to country j with (without) the FTA, E denotes the expectation operator, and observation subscripts (ij) are omitted for simplicity. We assume that the level of trade between two countries depends upon the array of exogenous "covariates" other than the treatment — the standard set of gravity equation variables in Eq. (1) in levels or log levels as appropriate, excluding FTA — which we denote by $\boldsymbol{q}$ (GDPs, DIST, ADJ, LANG). Initially, we assume that observations of x are independently and identically distributed across country pairs; this assumption ensures that the treatment of one pair does not affect another pair's trade flow.

Consistent estimation of the average treatment effect depends upon assumptions made about relationships among the variables. Of course, in reality we do not observe both x_1 and x_0. Since one can only observe a trade flow in the presence *or* absence of an FTA, we define the observed outcome (x) for a country pair as:

$$x \equiv (\text{FTA})x_1 + (1-\text{FTA})x_0 \tag{5}$$

where FTA = 1 if an FTA exists between the pair, and 0 otherwise. If we assume trade flows x_0 and x_1 have the standard linear form as in a gravity equation, then:

$$x_0 = \mu_0 + \boldsymbol{\beta}'\boldsymbol{q} + \varepsilon_0 \tag{6}$$

$$x_1 = \mu_1 + \boldsymbol{\beta}'\boldsymbol{q} + \varepsilon_1 \tag{7}$$

Substituting Eqs. (6) and (7) in Eq. (5) yields:

$$x = \mu_0 + \boldsymbol{\beta}'\boldsymbol{q} + \alpha\text{FTA} + \varepsilon_0 + \text{FTA}(\varepsilon_1 - \varepsilon_0) \tag{8}$$

where $\alpha = \mu_1 - \mu_0$ corresponds to the average treatment effect.

Consistent estimation of the parameters in Eq. (8) depends upon correlations between the variables and the error terms. Specifically, consistent estimation of α, $\boldsymbol{\beta}$, and μ_0 depends on the correlation of: (i) FTA with error term ϵ_0, and (ii) FTA with differences in unobservables for partners with FTAs versus partners without FTAs ($\epsilon_1 - \epsilon_0$). The former is the correlation associated with omitted variables bias, and the latter with selection bias. When FTA is uncorrelated with both factors, the parameters are estimated consistently using OLS.

Consider first the case where FTA is correlated with ϵ_0, but $\epsilon_1 - \epsilon_0 = 0$ (for all country pairs). Wooldridge (2002) suggests an efficient IV estimator. First, assume the probability of FTA (P(FTA)) can be estimated by a known parametric form (such as probit) such that $P(\text{FTA}=1|\boldsymbol{q}, z) = \boldsymbol{\Phi}(\pi_0 + \boldsymbol{\pi}_1'\boldsymbol{q} + \boldsymbol{\pi}_2'z)$ where $P(\text{FTA}=1|\boldsymbol{q}, z) \neq P(\text{FTA}=1|\boldsymbol{q})$ and z is a set of exogenous variables (not in $\boldsymbol{q}$).[14] Second, assume the variance of ϵ_0 is a constant. This suggests a multi-step IV method with the following steps: (i) estimate a binary response model, such as probit, $P(\text{FTA}=1|\boldsymbol{q}, z) = \boldsymbol{\Phi}(\pi_0 + \pi_1'\boldsymbol{q} + \boldsymbol{\pi}_2'z)$ by maximum likelihood to generate predicted probabilities $\boldsymbol{\Phi}^{\text{P}}$; and (ii) estimate Eq.

[14] If a probit function, then $\boldsymbol{\Phi}(\,)$ is the standard normal cumulative distribution function.

(8) by IV, using instruments 1, $\boldsymbol{\Phi}^{P}$, $\boldsymbol{q}$ and z. The IV estimator is consistent, asymptotically efficient, and the usual 2SLS standard errors and test statistics are asymptotically valid.[15]

If FTA is correlated with ϵ_0 and $\epsilon_1 - \epsilon_0$, Heckman (1997) suggests that IV estimation only identifies the parameters consistently when economic agents' decisions to select into a program are unrelated to (or ignore) unobservable factors influencing the outcome. However, as discussed earlier, many trade-policy analysts have noted that policies tending to inhibit trade, such as nontariff barriers and domestic regulations, may be one of the main reasons governments have selected into FTAs. The intent of forming an FTA is that this agreement will lead to bilateral reductions in domestic barriers that multilateral agreements have been unable to attain. In this context, IV estimation will not yield consistent estimates in the presence of selection bias; Heckman's procedure controls for selection.

As discussed earlier, most cross-section analyses using the gravity equation including dummy variables for trade agreements have ignored the potential endogeneity bias just discussed. The introduction listed several of a myriad of gravity equation studies that have tried to infer inappropriately the average treatment effect of a trade agreement on bilateral trade ignoring this bias. The fragility of such ATEs reported in the analysis of Ghosh and Yamarik (2004) tends to confirm the likely presence of endogeneity bias.

4.2. Cross-section empirical attempts to adjust for endogeneity bias

As just established, given a cross-section the key to estimating a consistent ATE of FTAs on trade is, first, finding a probit function that predicts FTAs and, second, finding a set of suitable instruments for z that are uncorrelated with the gravity equation error term. Only three papers have attempted to adjust for the potential endogeneity of FTAs using IV or control-function techniques with cross-section data, Baier and Bergstrand (2002, 2004b) and Magee (2003). We discuss each of their findings in turn.

The starting point for all three studies is Baier and Bergstrand (2004a), which evaluated the probability of pairs of countries having FTAs using a probit function for a single year. As discussed in Section 3, Baier and Bergstrand (2004a) was the first systematic empirical analysis of economic determinants of the likelihood of FTAs between pairs of countries using a cross-section qualitative-choice model. Their empirical model correctly predicted *85%* of 286 FTAs existing in 1996 among 1431 country pairs and *97%* of the remaining 1145 pairs, based upon economic and geographic characteristics such as economic size and similarity of the country pair, differences in capital–labor ratios, and bilateral distance of the pair and their remoteness from the rest of the world (ROW).

Baier and Bergstrand (2002) followed the Wooldridge procedure described in Section 4.1, essentially augmenting the probit function in Baier and Bergstrand (2004a) to include a set of instruments that ideally would be correlated with the probability of an FTA between a country pair but uncorrelated with (unobservables causing) their bilateral trade. Critical to the methodology is the selection of instruments. The study first used relative capital–labor ratios, relative factor-endowment differences with the ROW, and an ad hoc measure of remoteness of continental FTA partners as instruments using a cross-section of bilateral trade flows among 53 countries for year

[15] Wooldridge (2002) refers to this as a two-step estimator. However, for clarity, we refer to three steps. The first stage is the estimation of the predicted probabilities, $\boldsymbol{\Phi}^{P}$. The second stage is a linear regression of FTA on a constant, $\boldsymbol{\Phi}^{P}$, $\boldsymbol{q}$ and z. The third stage is estimation of the gravity equation substituting the predicted values from the second-stage regression for FTA.

1996. While these instruments "worked" in the sense of quadrupling the average treatment effect of an FTA, two concerns arose. First, the Wooldridge estimation procedure precluded a test of over-identifying restrictions to provide empirical support that the instruments were, in fact, "exogenous" to the gravity equation error terms. More importantly, trade gravity equations have often included measures of remoteness and capital–labor ratio differences and these factors have had statistically significant effects, eroding confidence that these instruments were uncorrelated with gravity equation errors. Baier and Bergstrand (2002) also considered various "political" variables as instruments. However, the same concern arises: many of the "political" variables have been correlated in previous studies with trade flows. Despite estimating an ATE of about 90%, the instability of estimated treatment effects — ranging from increasing trade between 40 to 200% — further diminished confidence in the estimates.[16]

Baier and Bergstrand (2004b) demonstrated clearly that ATE estimates using IV or control-function techniques are quite unstable. This paper expanded the data set to trade flows and FTAs among 96 countries for multiple years. Using alternative specifications — with and without political variables, with and without fixed effects (as appropriate) — this study found that ATE estimates ranged between a decline in trade of 92% to an increase in trade of 1100%. In most specifications, the test for overidentifying restrictions rejected the null hypothesis that the instruments were exogenous. In the only two specifications where this null hypothesis could not be rejected (using a linear probability model in the first stage), the two ATE estimates were 0.41 (statistically insignificant) and −3.97 (statistically significant), varying according to the instruments included.

Magee (2003) is also one of the first papers to adjust for endogeneity of FTAs using instrumental variables. Magee (2003) viewed the relationship between trade and FTA as a simultaneous-equations system.[17] Magee uses 2SLS to estimate the effect of endogenous FTAs on trade flows, and finds similarly a range of large positive to large negative effects of FTAs on trade flows. Magee's study faces the same limitations as Baier and Bergstrand (2002, 2004b). Several of the instruments in the FTA probit equation to identify the trade-flow equation are likely correlated with the gravity equation error terms. For instance, Magee includes an index of democracies, GDP similarities, intra-industry trade indices, trade surpluses and relative-factor-endowment differences. All these variables are likely correlated in cross-section with (unobservables causing) trade flows.

We conclude from previous cross-section studies that IV estimation is not a reliable method for addressing the endogeneity bias of the FTA binary variable in a gravity equation, despite trying a wide array of economic and political instrumental variables. An alternative method for estimating the ATE of FTAs uses Heckman's control-function approach. We have estimated similar specifications using this alternative approach with qualitatively similar findings; the control-function approach does not solve the endogeneity bias issue either. The likely problem is this: the vast number of variables that are correlated cross-sectionally with the probability of having an FTA are *also* correlated cross-sectionally with trade flows, preventing elimination of the endogeneity bias using cross-section techniques.

Magee (2003) concluded that "we should be cautious in using gravity equation estimates to draw strong conclusions about the effect of PTA formation on trade." We agree with his conclusion for *cross-sectional data*. However, in the remainder of this paper, we argue that one can draw strong and reliable inferences about the ATE of FTAs using the gravity equation applied to *panel data*.

---

[16] The results using Heckman control functions were not materially different.

[17] See Baier and Bergstrand (2002, 2004b) and Maddala (1983, p. 118) for a critique of this approach in the context of a binary endogenous variable.

5. FTA treatment effects using panel data

As most standard econometrics textbooks now suggest, a ready alternative to cross-section estimation of treatment effects in the presence of unobserved time-invariant heterogeneity is the use of panel data (cf., Wooldridge, 2000). Having constructed a panel (for every five years) from 1960–2000 of the bilateral trade flows, bilateral trade agreements, and standard gravity equation covariates among 96 potential trading partners, we now pursue this approach. Three main alternative techniques exist for addressing the issue: estimating the panel with random effects, estimation with fixed effects, or differencing the data and using OLS. In Section 5.1, we describe our data set. In Section 5.2, we address the choice between random versus fixed effects, and then between fixed effects versus first differencing. In Section 5.3, we estimate the atheoretical gravity model (ignoring multilateral price terms) using fixed effects. In Section 5.4, we estimate the model again using fixed effects, but address three issues. First, we allow for the theoretically-motivated multilateral price terms and unit income elasticities. Second, we allow for the "phasing-in" of FTAs. Third, we test for "strict exogeneity." In Section 5.5, we provide the results of a robustness analysis using differenced data.

5.1. Data

We describe briefly the data used for the gravity equations. Nominal bilateral trade flows are from the International Monetary Fund's *Direction of Trade Statistics* for the years 1960, 1965,..., 2000 for 96 potential trading partners (zero trade flows are excluded); these data are scaled by exporter GDP deflators to generate real trade flows for the panel analysis. Nominal GDPs are from the World Bank's World Development Indicators (2003); these are scaled by GDP deflators to create real GDPs for the panel analysis. Bilateral distances were compiled using the *CIA Factbook* for longitudes and latitudes of economic centers to calculate the great circle distances. The language and adjacency dummy variables were compiled also from the *CIA Factbook*. The FTA dummy variable was calculated using appendices in Lawrence (1996) and Frankel (1997), various websites, and FTAs notified to the GATT/WTO under GATT Articles XXIV or the Enabling Clause for developing economies; we included only full (no partial) FTAs and customs unions. Table 3 lists the trade agreements used and sources. The Data Appendix lists the countries used.[18]

5.2. Alternative panel methodologies

5.2.1. Fixed versus random effects

Our panel estimation applies fixed effects rather than random effects for two reasons, the first on conceptual grounds and the second on empirical grounds. First, as addressed in Section 2, we believe the source of endogeneity bias in the gravity equation is unobserved time-invariant heterogeneity. In economic terms, we believe there are unobserved time-invariant bilateral variables — termed w_{ij} — influencing simultaneously the presence of an FTA and the volume of trade. Because these variables are likely correlated with FTA_{ij}, they are best controlled for using bilateral "fixed effects," as this approach allows for arbitrary correlations of w_{ij} with FTA_{ij}. By contrast, under "random effects" one assumes zero correlation between unobservables w_{ij} with FTA_{ij}, which seems less plausible.

Second, there have been recent econometric evaluations of the gravity equation with panel data using the Hausman Test to test for fixed versus random effects. For example, Egger (2000) finds

[18] The data set is available at the authors' websites (http://www.nd.edu/~jbergstr and http://people.clemson.edu/~sbaier).

Table 3
Free trade agreements

European Union, or EU (1958): Belgium–Luxembourg, France, Italy, Germany, Netherlands, Denmark (1973), Ireland (1973), United Kingdom (1973), Greece (1981), Portugal (1986), Spain (1986), Austria (1995), Finland (1995), Sweden (1995)
The Customs Union of West African States (1959): Burkina Faso, Mali, Mauritania, Niger, Senegal
European Free Trade Association, or EFTA (1960): Austria (until 1995), Denmark (until 1973), Finland (1986–1995), Norway, Portugal (until 1986), Sweden (until 1995), Switzerland, United Kingdom (until 1973)
Latin American Free Trade Agreement/Latin American Integration Agreement, or LAFTA/LAIA (1961–1979,1993–): Argentina, Bolivia, Brazil, Chile, Ecuador, Mexico, Paraguay, Peru, Uruguay, Venezuela (became inoperative during 1980–1990, but reinitiated in 1993)
African Common Market (1963): Algeria, Egypt, Ghana, Morocco
Central American Common Market (1961–1975, 1993–present): El Salvador, Guatemala, Honduras, Nicaragua, Costa Rica (1965)
Economic Customs Union of the Central African States (1966): Cameroon, Congo, Gabon
Carribean Community, or CARICOM (1968): Jamaica, Trinidad and Tobago, Guyana (1995)
EU–EFTA Agreement/European Economic Area (1973/1994)
Australia–New Zealand Closer Economic Relations (1983)
US–Israel (1985)
US–Canada (1989)
EFTA–Israel (1993)
Central Europe Free Trade Agreement, or CEFTA (1993): Hungary, Poland, Romania (1997), Bulgaria (1998)
EFTA–Bulgaria (1993)
EFTA–Hungary (1993)
EFTA–Poland (1993)
EFTA–Romania (1993)
EU–Hungary (1994)
EU–Poland (1994)
North American Free Trade Agreement, or NAFTA (1994): Canada, Mexico, United States
Bolivia–Mexico (1995)
Costa Rica–Mexico (1995)
EU–Bulgaria (1995)
EU–Romania (1995)
Group of Three (1995): Columbia, Mexico, Venezuela
Mercado Comun del Sur, or Mercosur (1991): Argentina, Brazil, Paraguay, Uruguay (formed in 1991 and a free trade area in 1995)
Andean Community (1993): Bolivia, Columbia, Ecuador, Peru, Venezuela, Peru (1997)
Mercosur–Chile (1996)
Mercosur–Bolivia (1996)
Canada–Chile (1997)
Canada–Israel (1997)
Association of Southeast Asian Nations, or ASEAN (1998): Indonesia, Philippines, Singapore, Thailand (effective on 80% of merchandise trade in 1998)
CARICOM–Dominican Republic (1998)
Hungary–Turkey (1998)
Hungary–Israel (1998)
India–Sri Lanka (1998)
Israel–Turkey (1998)
Mexico–Nicaragua (1998)
Romania–Turkey (1998)
Poland–Israel (1998)
Romania–Turkey (1998)
Mexico–Chile (1999)
Common Market for Eastern and Southern Africa (2000): Egypt, Kenya, Madagascar, Malawi, Mauritius, Sudan, Zimbabwe, Zambia

(continued on next page)

Table 3 (*continued*)

EU–Israel Agreement (2000)
EU–Mexico (2000)
Poland–Turkey (2000)
Mexico–Guatemala (2000)
Mexico–Honduras (2000)
Mexico–Israel (2000)
Mexico–El Salvador (2000)
New Zealand–Singapore (2000)

Countries listed in agreements only include those in our sample of 96 countries listed in the Data Appendix. Agreements are listed in chronological order of date of entry into force. Years in parentheses denote date of entry, except where noted otherwise.

Sources:

http://www.wto.org/english/tratop_e/region_e/summary_e.xls.

http://europa.eu.int/comm/enlargement/pas/europe_agr.htm.

http://www.comunidadandina.org/ingles/union.htm.

http://www.nafinsa.com/finsafreetrade.htm.

http://www.sice.oas.org/default.asp.

Frankel, Jeffrey A. Regional trading blocs. Institute for International Economics (1997).

Lawrence, Robert Z. Regionalism, multilateralism, and deeper integration. The Brookings Institution (1996).

overwhelming evidence for the rejection of a random-effects gravity model relative to a fixed-effects gravity model, using either bilateral-pair or country-specific fixed effects.

5.2.2. *Fixed effects versus first differencing*

Standard econometric discussions of treating endogeneity bias using panel data focus on a choice between estimation using fixed effects versus using first-differenced data, cf., Wooldridge (2002, Ch. 10). As Wooldridge notes, when the number of time periods (T) exceeds two, the fixed-effects estimator is more efficient under the assumption of serially uncorrelated error terms. The first-differencing estimator is more efficient (when $T>2$) under the assumption that the error term ϵ_{ijt} follows a random walk (i.e., that the difference in the error terms, $\epsilon_{ijt}-\epsilon_{ij,t-1}$, is white noise).[19]

First-differencing the panel data yields some potential advantages over fixed effects. First, it is quite plausible that the unobserved heterogeneity in trade flows, ϵ_{ijt}, is correlated over time. In light of discussion in Section 3, unobserved factors influencing the likelihood of an FTA (say, trade below its "natural" level) are likely slow moving and hence serially correlated. If the ϵ_{ijt} are highly serially correlated, the inefficiency of fixed effects is exacerbated as T gets large. This suggests that differencing the data will increase estimation efficiency for our large-T panel. Second, aggregate trade flow data and real GDP data are likely "close to" unit-root processes. Using fixed effects is equivalent to differencing data around the *mean* (in our sample, 1980); this may create a problem since T is large in our panel. As Wooldridge (2000, p. 447) notes, if the data follow unit-root processes and T is large, the "spurious regression problem" can arise in a panel using fixed effects. First-differencing yields data that deviates from the previous period of our panel, and thus is closer to a unit-root process. In the following, we use fixed effects in Sections 5.3 and 5.4, and for robustness use differenced data in Section 5.5.

[19] When the number of time periods is limited to two ($T=2$), estimation with fixed effects and first-differencing produce *identical* estimates and inferences; moreover, first-differencing is easier. When $T>2$, the choice depends upon the assumption the researcher makes about the error term ϵ_{ijt}.

5.3. Fixed-effects estimation of an atheoretical gravity equation ignoring multilateral price terms

In a panel context, Eq. (1) can be expressed as:

$$\ln X_{ijt} = \beta_0 + \beta_1(\ln\text{RGDP}_{jt}) + \beta_2(\ln\text{RGDP}_{jt}) + \beta_3(\ln\text{DIST}_{ij}) + \beta_4(\text{ADJ}_{ij}) + \beta_5(\text{LANG}_{ij}) + \beta_6(\text{FTA}_{ijt}) + \varepsilon_{ijt} \quad (9)$$

Table 4 provides the empirical results of estimating gravity Eq. (9) using a panel of real trade flows (X_{ijt}), real GDPs (RGDP_{it}, RGDP_{jt}) and FTA dummies (FTA_{ijt}), and using alternative specifications with and without bilateral fixed effects and time dummies. Column (1) provides the baseline gravity equation without any fixed effects or time dummies for all nine years. Exporter and importer (real) GDPs have coefficients close to unity, distance has a traditional coefficient estimate of −1, and the adjacency and language dummies have typical coefficient estimates. The ATE for FTA of 0.13 is economically small, consistent with earlier findings in cross-section. Column (2) provides the empirical results including a time dummy, where (for brevity) we omit reporting the (statistically significant) coefficient estimates for these dummy variables. The inclusion of time dummies increases the ATE for FTA slightly from 0.13 to 0.27. However, time dummies do not adjust for the endogeneity of FTAs.

Adjusting for unobserved time-invariant heterogeneity using bilateral fixed effects has a notable impact on the results. Column (3) provides results including bilateral fixed effects. The ATE for FTA (0.51) is now almost *quadruple* the coefficient estimated using OLS (0.13). Column (4) provides results using both bilateral fixed effects and year dummies. In this specification, the ATE of a free trade agreement is 0.68. This quantitative estimate suggests that the average treatment effect of the presence of a free trade agreement is to *double* trade between country pairs ($e^{0.68} = 1.97$, or 97% increase). This is seven times the effect estimated using OLS ($e^{0.13} = 1.14$, or 14% increase).[20]

Although the introduction of bilateral fixed effects and time dummies has an economically and statistically significant effect on raising the FTA average treatment effect, this specification suffers ex ante from ignoring multilateral price terms, as suggested by recent theoretical developments. In the next section, we account for such terms, as well as the potential influence of "phasing-in" agreements.

5.4. Fixed-effects estimation of a theoretically-motivated gravity equation with phased-in agreements

In this section, we consider three modifications to the previous specification. In Section 5.4.1, we include country-and-time effects to account for the theoretically-motivated multilateral price terms and consider unit income elasticities. In Section 5.4.2, we account for the fact that all FTAs are "phased-in" over time, typically over five-to-ten years, and for the possibility that the change in two members' terms of trade from formation of an FTA may have a lagged impact on their

[20] The only other published studies that have estimated the ATE of an FTA using a panel of data spanning as many years and at least 100 countries are Rose (2004) and Tomz, Goldstein and Rivers (2004). Using fixed effects, Rose found an ATE of $e^{0.94}$or 156%. However, using a classification of formal and informal GATT members, Tomz, Goldstein and Rivers (2004) estimate an ATE for FTAs (with fixed effects) of only $e^{0.76}$or 114%. Cheng and Wall (2002) used bilateral fixed effects in a four-year panel of trade among approximately only 30 high-income countries in the context of a traditional gravity equation ignoring multilateral price terms.

Table 4
Panel gravity equations in levels using various specifications

Variable	(1) No fixed or time effects	(2) With time effects	(3) With bilateral fixed effects	(4) With time and bilateral fixed effects
ln $RGDP_i$	0.95 (217.50)	0.97 (230.98)	0.71 (34.54)	1.27 (47.16)
ln $RGDP_j$	0.94 (224.99)	0.97 (235.43)	0.58 (26.57)	1.22 (41.60)
ln $DIST_{ij}$	−1.03 (−79.09)	−1.01 (−78.60)		
ADJ_{ij}	0.41 (8.23)	0.38 (7.28)		
$LANG_{ij}$	0.63 (19.06)	0.58 (17.73)		
FTA_{ij}	0.13 (3.73)	0.27 (7.19)	0.51 (10.74)	0.68 (14.27)
RMSE	1.9270	1.8601		
Overall R^2	0.6575	0.6809		
Within R^2			0.2036	0.2268
No. observations	47,081	47,081	47,081	47,081

t-statistics are in parentheses. The dependent variable is the (natural log of the) real bilateral trade flow from *i* to *j*. Coefficient estimates for various fixed/time effects are not reported for brevity.

bilateral trade. In Section 5.4.3, we address "strict exogeneity" issues; we test for the possibility of reverse causality by addressing the effect of *future* FTA dummies on current trade flows.

5.4.1. Accounting for multilateral price terms and unit income elasticities

While the results in the previous section are encouraging, the gravity equation suggested by recent formal theoretical developments — summarized in the system of Eqs. (2), (3.1), ..., (3.N) in Section 2 — suggests that one needs to account for the multilateral price variables and to scale the LHS trade flow variable by real GDPs. None of the four specifications in Table 4 accounts for these two elements. First, accounting for the multilateral price variables in a panel context suggests estimating:

$$\begin{aligned}\ln X_{ijt} = {} & \beta_0 + \beta_1(\ln \mathrm{RGDP}_{it}) + \beta_2(\ln \mathrm{RGDP}_{jt}) + \beta_3(\ln \mathrm{DIST}_{ij}) + \beta_4(\mathrm{ADJ}_{ij}) \\ & + \beta_5(\mathrm{LANG}_{ij}) + \beta_6(\mathrm{FTA}_{ijt}) - \ln P_{it}^{1-\sigma} - \ln P_{jt}^{1-\sigma} + \varepsilon_{ijt}\end{aligned} \tag{10}$$

Furthermore, scaling the LHS variable by the product of real GDPs suggests estimating:

$$\begin{aligned}\ln[X_{ijt}/(\mathrm{RGDP}_{it}\mathrm{RGDP}_{jt})] = {} & \beta_0 + \beta_3(\ln \mathrm{DIST}_{ij}) + \beta_4(\mathrm{ADJ}_{ij}) + \beta_5(\mathrm{LANG}_{ij}) \\ & + \beta_6(\mathrm{FTA}_{ijt}) - \ln P_{it}^{1-\sigma} - \ln P_{jt}^{1-\sigma} + \varepsilon_{ijt}\end{aligned} \tag{11}$$

In a panel setting, the multilateral price variables would be *time varying*, and consequently the results in specifications (1)–(4) in Table 4 may suffer from an omitted variables bias as a result of ignoring these time-varying terms — a dilemma that cannot be resolved by the use of bilateral fixed effects using the panel data in its current form.[21] Moreover, the theoretical model in Eqs. (2), (3.1),..., (3.N) suggests that the coefficient estimates for the real GDP variables should be unity, even though using bilateral fixed effects in specifications (3) and (4) suggests income elasticities are significantly different from unity.

[21] Random effects estimation would not be of any use either, as theory suggests that the multilateral price terms and the FTA variable would be correlated.

We first estimate Eq. (10) using bilateral (*ij*) fixed effects to account for variation in DIST, ADJ, and LANG along with country-and-time (*it*, *jt*) effects to account for variation in real GDPs and the multilateral price terms. In the context of the theory (though ignoring the restriction of unitary income elasticities), this should generate an unbiased estimate of β_6. Column (1) in Table 5 provides the results of estimating this equation using bilateral fixed effects and the country-and-time effects. As indicated, the FTA coefficient estimate of 0.46 suggests that an FTA increases trade by about 58% on average.

We can impose the restriction of unitary income elasticities implied by theoretical Eq. (2) and estimate Eq. (11) using bilateral-pair (*ij*) fixed effects along with the country-and-time (*it*, *jt*) effects. Here, the country-and-time (*it*, *jt*) effects account explicitly for the time-varying multilateral price terms. However, on net, scaling or not scaling real trade flows by real GDPs will not matter for estimating the ATE. In log-linear form, the variation in the logs of real GDPs is captured by the country-and-time effects, and only the estimates of the intercept and the country-and-time effects' coefficients change; the FTA coefficient estimate is unaffected. Column (2) in Table 5 provides the results of estimating this equation. The results using "trade shares" (real trade flows scaled by the product of real GDPs) are virtually identical to those for Eq. (10). Thus, imposing the unitary income elasticities restrictions has no impact on the FTA coefficient estimate. The FTA coefficient estimate of 0.46 implies again that an FTA increases trade by a cumulative amount of about 58%. In the remainder of the results, we use the real trade flow for the LHS variable; the FTA coefficient estimates are identical using trade shares instead (and are available on request).

The average treatment effect of an FTA accounting for the theoretically-motivated country-and-time effects, 0.46, is considerably smaller than the effect estimated in column (4) of Table 4, 0.68. However, although the estimated FTA effects in columns (1) and (2) of Table 5 are smaller, they may not reflect fully the cumulative effects on trade of an FTA.

5.4.2. Accounting for "phased-in" FTAs and lagged terms-of-trade effects

In this section, we introduce lagged effects of FTA on trade. The economic motivation for including lagged changes stems partly from the institutional nature of virtually all FTAs. The 0–1 FTA_{ijt} variable was constructed using the "Date of Entry into Force" of the agreement, as best surmised by scrutinizing multiple data sources provided earlier. However, virtually every FTA is

Table 5
Panel gravity equations with bilateral fixed and country-and-time effects[a]

Variable	(1)	(2)	(3)	(4)	(5)
$FTA_{ij,t}$	0.46** (9.07)	0.46** (9.06)	0.29** (4.95)	0.28** (4.66)	0.35** (4.20)
$FTA_{ij,t-1}$			0.38** (5.62)	0.27** (3.30)	0.16* (1.64)
$FTA_{ij,t-2}$				0.21** (2.60)	0.17* (1.87)
$FTA_{ij,t+1}$					−0.04 (−0.62)
Constant	8.85** (151.71)	−24.59** (−429.81)	9.70** (147.93)	10.06** (124.57)	9.98**(93.20)
Total ATE[a]	0.46	0.46	0.67	0.76	0.68
Within R^2	0.3102	0.1891	0.3044	0.2750	0.2516
No. observations	47,081	47,081	36,563	34,105	27,575

t-statistics are in parentheses. The dependent variable for specifications (1), (3), (4), and (5) is the (natural log of the) real bilateral trade flow; the dependent variable for specification (2) is the (natural log of the) real bilateral trade flow divided by the product of the real GDPs. * (**) denotes statistical significance at 5 (1) percent level in one-tailed *t*-test. Coefficient estimates for bilateral fixed and country-and-time effects are not reported for brevity.

[a] Total ATE is the sum of the statistically-significant FTA coefficient estimates.

"phased-in," typically over 10 years. For instance, the original EEC agreement of 1958 had a 10-year phase-in period. NAFTA had a similar 10-year provision. Thus, the entire economic (treatment) effect cannot be captured fully in the concurrent year only. It is reasonable to expect an FTA entered into "legally" in 1990 to not come into economic effect fully until 2000. Thus, it is reasonable to include one or two lagged levels of the FTA dummy ($FTA_{ij,t-1}$ and/or $FTA_{ij,t-2}$).

Moreover, economic effects of an FTA include altering the terms of trade. However, as is well known from a large literature in international economics, terms-of-trade changes tend to have lagged effects on trade volumes. Thus, it is reasonable to assume that an FTA which enters into force in 1960, and which is even fully "phased-in" by 1965, might still have an effect on trade flows in 1970.

The results in columns (3) and (4) in Table 5 reveal that FTA has statistically significant lagged effects on trade flows. Moreover, the coefficient estimates have economically plausible values, balanced across periods. The cumulative ATE with one lag is 0.65; with two lags, the total ATE is 0.76. We also experimented with adding a third lag; however, estimated coefficients of the third lag were statistically insignificant. The economic interpretation of the ATE of 0.76 is that — after 10 years — formation of an FTA increases the level of trade by *114%*.

5.4.3. Strict exogeneity

The introductory quote in this paper suggests questioning whether traditional cross-section estimates of FTA on trade can be interpreted as FTAs causing trade *or* trade causing FTAs. The results of previous sections suggest that — after accounting for endogeneity using panel data — one can find economically significant ATEs for FTA. However, to confirm that there are no "feedback effects" from trade changes to FTA changes, we run one more regression using the fixed-effects specification.[22] Wooldridge (2002, p. 285) suggests that it is easy to test for the "strict exogeneity" of FTAs in our context. To do this, we add a *future* level of FTA to the regression model. In the panel context here, if FTA changes are strictly exogenous to trade flow changes, $FTA_{ij,t+1}$ should be uncorrelated with the concurrent trade flow. The results in column (5) of Table 5 confirm this. The effect of $FTA_{ij,t+1}$ on the trade flow is economically small and not significantly different from zero. Moreover, the coefficient estimate of −0.04 suggests — if anything — that firms delay trade temporarily in anticipation of an impending agreement.

5.5. First-differenced panel gravity equation estimates

As discussed in Section 5.2, for two econometric reasons we may expect first-differenced data to provide better estimates of the average treatment effect; at worst, differenced data provide an evaluation of the robustness of previous estimates. In the context of differenced panel data, the potential omitted variables bias created by time-varying multilateral price terms for each country would require again country-and-time effects to obtain consistent estimates of FTA's ATE. As before, with country-and-time effects the coefficient estimates of the FTA treatment effects are insensitive to the real bilateral trade flow being scaled or not scaled by real GDPs; for consistency to earlier results, we present those for the flows (the virtually identical results are available on

[22] An empirical finding that trade leads an FTA need not even imply that trade "causes" an FTA. Trade may increase in anticipation of an FTA as infrastructure and delivery systems involving sunk costs are redirected, cf., McLaren (1997). Alternatively, trade may decrease — be delayed — in anticipation of the benefits of an FTA.

Table 6
First-differenced panel gravity equations with country-and-time effects[a]

Variable	(1)	(2)	(3)	(4)
$dFTA_{ij,t-(t-1)}$	0.31** (8.03)	0.30** (7.70)	0.28** (7.54)	0.29** (6.77)
$dFTA_{ij,(t-1)-(t-2)}$		0.22** (4.80)	0.19** (4.24)	0.16** (2.62)
$dFTA_{ij,(t-2)-(t-3)}$			0.14** (2.34)	0.09 (1.12)
$dFTA_{ij,(t+1)-t}$				−0.06 (−1.02)
Constant	0.00 (0.00)	0.00 (0.00)	0.00 (0.00)	0.00 (0.00)
Total ATE[a]	0.31	0.52	0.61	0.45
Overall R^2	0.0007	0.0009	0.0008	0.0006
No. observations	36,563	34,105	31,172	24,642

t-statistics in parentheses. The dependent variable is the (natural log of the) real bilateral trade flow. * (**) denotes statistical significance at 5 (1) percent level in one-tailed t-test. Coefficient estimates for country-and-time effects are not reported for brevity.

[a] Total ATE is the sum of the statistically-significant FTA coefficient estimates.

request using trade flows scaled by the product of real GDPs). We start by first-differencing the natural logarithm of X_{ijt}, creating $d\ln X_{ij,t-(t-1)}$. Second, we regress $d\ln X_{ij,t-(t-1)}$ on 768 country-and-time effects ($Dum_{i,t-(t-1)}$, where i denotes a country and $t-(t-1)$ a 5-year period, e.g., 1995–2000) and retain the residuals. Third, we difference FTA_{ijt}, creating $dFTA_{ij,t-(t-1)}$, and regress $dFTA_{ij,t-(t-1)}$ on the same 768 country-and-time fixed effects and retain these residuals. Fourth, a regression of the residuals from the first ($d\ln X$) regression on the residuals from the second (dFTA) regression will yield unbiased estimates of the ATE effect of an FTA holding constant time-varying multilateral price terms.

The procedure described above is equivalent to estimating:

$$d\ln X_{ij,t-(t-1)} = \beta_6 dFTA_{ij,t-(t-1)} + \beta_{i,t-(t-1)} Dum_{i,t-(t-1)} + \beta_{j,t-(t-1)} Dum_{j,t-(t-1)} + v_{ij,t-(t-1)} \quad (12)$$

where $v_{ij,t-(t-1)} = \varepsilon_{ijt} - \varepsilon_{ij,t-1}$ is white noise. With nine years in the panel, we have 8 time periods $t-(t-1)$. Since there are 96 countries that can potentially trade, our procedure above effectively introduces 768 (=8×96) country-and-time fixed effects ($Dum_{i,t-(t-1)}$ and $Dum_{j,t-(t-1)}$) to account for the changes in the unobservable theoretical multilateral resistance terms, $d\ln P^{1-\sigma}_{i,t-(t-1)}$ and $d\ln P^{1-\sigma}_{j,t-(t-1)}$, to obtain an unbiased estimate of β_6. In the context of the theoretical model, the 768 estimates of $\beta_{i,t-(t-1)}$ and $\beta_{j,t-(t-1)}$ can be interpreted as changes in the countries' multilateral resistance terms.

Table 6 reports the coefficient estimates for the effects of concurrent, lagged and future changes in FTA (dFTA) on trade flow changes. Column (1) reports the ATE without any lagged effects; the ATE is 0.30. Including one lagged change in FTA increases the cumulative ATE to 0.52. With two lagged values of dFTA, the cumulative ATE of an FTA is 0.61. This estimate implies that an unbiased ATE of an FTA on the trade between a pair of countries is *84%*.[23] This

[23] Additional lags of FTA were also evaluated. None of these extra lags were economically or statistically significant. The results suggest that FTAs have a *level* effect on trade, but do not influence the long-run growth rate of trade. Bayoumi and Eichengreen (1997) used first-differenced data to estimate the effects on member trade of the six-member EEC and seven-member EFTA, but did not account for theoretically-motivated time-varying multilateral price resistance terms and only examined one 15-year period for these two agreements (1957–1972).Yet, the implied cumulative ATE for the EEC was 0.60, very similar to our estimated ATE of 0.61.

result is only slightly smaller than the comparable fixed-effects estimate in column (4) of Table 5 (0.76). For completeness, column (4) of Table 6 provides the results of adding a future change in FTA. Analogous to the fixed-effects results, future changes in FTA have no significant effect on trade flow changes. Thus, our estimates using differenced panel data suggest that — after 10 years — an FTA essentially *doubles* the level of members' international trade, confirming the previous section's results.

6. Conclusions

The purpose of this paper was to answer the question posed in the title: Do free trade agreements actually increase members' international trade? A motivation for this paper was that — after forty years of gravity equation estimates of the (treatment) effect of FTAs on trade flows — there seems no clear and convincing empirical evidence using the workhorse for empirical international trade studies that the answer is "yes." This seems surprising in light of the proliferation of FTAs in the last 15 years and widespread expectations that such agreements should increase trade. Our goal has been to provide a thorough empirical analysis of the average treatment effect of FTAs on trade, in light of prevailing knowledge on the theoretical foundations for the trade gravity equation and on modern econometric techniques to estimate "average treatment effects."

Our answer to the question: *yes!* Standard cross-section techniques using instrumental variables and control functions do not provide stable estimates of these ATEs in the presence of endogeneity and tests of overidentifying restrictions generally fail. However, we find convincing empirical evidence using panel data of unbiased estimates of ATEs ranging from 0.61 to 0.76. These estimates are five to six times those using OLS. The average of these two ATE estimates is 0.685. Stated succinctly, this estimate suggests that an FTA will on average increase two member countries' trade about *100%* after 10 years (using $e^{0.685}=1.98$). This is seven times the effect estimated using OLS ($e^{0.13}=1.14$, or 14% increase).

Some caveats are necessarily in order. While we have addressed multilateral price (resistance) terms of a country pair, we have not addressed the general equilibrium "comparative static" effects of an FTA on two members' trade. Nor have we addressed the impact of such agreements on trade with nonmembers, nor trade among nonmembers. Moreover, we have not addressed the welfare implications of FTAs. These are topics left for other research; our focus has been solely on trying to provide policymakers with more resolution on an unbiased estimate of the average treatment effect of an FTA on two members' trade. A second caveat is that the effect of an FTA is likely to differ depending upon the agreement. We consider this a useful extension for future research. A related caveat to the previous one is that the effect of an FTA on two members' trade may be influenced by the economic size, per capita incomes, and even distance between the two countries. That is, there may be interactive effects not addressed in this study, to limit its scope. This topic is left for future research.

Nevertheless, in light of the wide range of previous estimates of the average treatment effect of FTAs on trade, we hope that future research will acknowledge the importance of the endogeneity of FTAs, as the international trade literature recognized years ago for multilateral trade volumes and countries' tariff and nontariff barrier policies. Researchers using the gravity equation have already started to account for the endogeneity of multilateral price terms. We hope that future research will also come to appreciate the need to adjust also for endogeneity of FTAs when estimating the effects of such agreements on trade flows.

Acknowledgements

The authors are grateful to Jonathan Eaton, Judith Dean, Rob Feenstra, Scott Kastner, Mika Saito, Curtis Simon, Jeff Wooldridge, Eduardo Zambrano, two anonymous referees and participants at presentations at the American Economic Association annual meetings, Midwest International Economics meetings, U.S. International Trade Commission, and ISNIE meetings for excellent comments on earlier drafts. We thank Doru Cojuc, Katie Martin, Kushlani Rajapakse, Duncan Stewart, Li Zhang and Mike Jaszkowiak for excellent research assistance. The authors are very grateful for financial support to the National Science Foundation under grant numbers SES-0351018 (Baier) and SES-0351154 (Bergstrand), the Center for International Trade at Clemson University, and the Mendoza College of Business and the Kellogg Institute for International Studies at the University of Notre Dame.

Data appendix

The following is a list of the 96 countries potentially used in the regressions, depending upon availability of non-zero and non-missing trade flows:

Austria	Belgium–Luxembourg	Denmark
Finland	France	Germany
Greece	Ireland	Italy
Netherlands	Norway	Portugal
Spain	Sweden	Switzerland
United Kingdom	Canada	Costa Rica
Dominican Republic	El Salvador	Guatemala
Haiti	Honduras	Jamaica
Mexico	Nicaragua	Panama
Trinidad and Tobago	United States	Argentina
Bolivia	Brazil	Chile
Colombia	Ecuador	Guyana
Paraguay	Peru	Uruguay
Venezuela	Australia	New Zealand
Bulgaria	Hungary	Poland
Romania	Egypt	India
Japan	Philippines	Thailand
Turkey	Korea	Algeria
Angola	Ghana	Kenya
Morocco	Mozambique	Nigeria
Tunisia	Uganda	Zambia
Zimbabwe	China (Hong Kong)	Indonesia
Iran	Israel	Pakistan
Singapore	Sri Lanka	Syrian Arab Republic
China,P.R.: Mainland	Albania	Bangladesh
Burkina Faso	Cameroon	Cyprus
Côte d'Ivoire	Ethiopia	Gabon
Gambia, The	Guinea–Bissau	Madagascar
Malawi	Malaysia	Mali
Mauritania	Mauritius	Niger
Saudi Arabia	Senegal	Sierra Leone
Sudan	Congo, Dem. Rep. of	Congo, Republic of

References

Abrams, R.K., 1980. International trade flows under flexible exchange rates. Federal Reserve Bank of Kansas City. Economic Review 65 (3), 3–10.

Aitken, Norman D., 1973. The effect of the EEC and EFTA on European trade: a temporal cross-section analysis. American Economic Review 5, 881–892 (December).

Anderson, James E., 1979. A theoretical foundation for the gravity equation. American Economic Review 69 (1), 106–116 (March).

Anderson, James E., van Wincoop, Eric, 2003. Gravity with gravitas: a solution to the border puzzle. American Economic Review 93 (1), 170–192 (March).

Baier, Scott L., Bergstrand, Jeffrey H., 2001. The growth of world trade: tariffs, transport costs, and income similarity. Journal of International Economics 53 (1), 1–27 (February).

Baier, Scott L., Bergstrand, Jeffrey H. "On the endogeneity of international trade flows and free trade agreements." Manuscript, August 2002, http://www.nd.edu/~jbergstr/Working_Papers/EndogeneityAug2002.pdf.

Baier, Scott L., Bergstrand, Jeffrey H., 2004a. Economic determinants of free trade agreements. Journal of International Economics 64 (1), 29–63 (October).

Baier, S.L., Bergstrand, J.H. "Do free trade agreements actually increase members' international trade?" Manuscript, October 2004b, http://www.nd.edu/~jbergstr/Working_Papers/BaierBergstrandFTA2Oct2004.pdf.

Bayoumi, Tamim, Eichengreen, Barry, 1997. Is regionalism simply a diversion? Evidence from the evolution of the EC and EFTA. In: Ito, Takatoshi, Krueger, Anne O. (Eds.), Regionalism vs. Multilateral Arrangements. The University of Chicago Press, Chicago.

Bergstrand, Jeffrey H., 1985. The gravity equation in international trade: some microeconomic foundations and empirical evidence. Review of Economics and Statistics 67 (3), 474–481 (August).

Bergstrand, Jeffrey H., 1989. The generalized gravity equation, monopolistic competition, and the factor-proportions theory in international trade. Review of Economics and Statistics 71 (1), 143–153 (February).

Bergstrand, Jeffrey H., 1990. The Heckscher–Ohlin–Samuelson model, the Linder hypothesis, and the determinants of bilateral intra-industry trade. Economic Journal 100 (4), 1216–1229 (December).

Boisso, Dale, Ferrantino, Michael, 1997. Economic distance, cultural distance, and openness in international trade: empirical puzzles. Journal of Economic Integration 12 (4), 456–484 (December).

Brada, Josef C., Mendez, Jose A., 1985. Economic integration among developed, developing and centrally planned economies: a comparative analysis. Review of Economics and Statistics 67 (4), 549–556 (November).

Cheng, I.-Hui, Wall, Howard J., 2002. Controlling for heterogeneity in gravity models of trade. Federal Reserve Bank of St. Louis Working Paper, vol. 1999-010C.

Deardorff, Alan, 1998. Does gravity work in a neoclassical world? In: Frankel, Jeffrey A. (Ed.), The Regionalization of the World Economy. The University of Chicago Press, Chicago.

Eaton, Jonathan, Kortum, Samuel, 2002. Technology, geography, and trade. Econometrica 70 (5), 1741–1779 (September).

Egger, Peter, 2000. A note on the proper econometric specification of the gravity equation. Economics Letters 66, 25–31.

Eichengreen, Barry, Irwin, Douglas, 1995. Trade blocs, currency blocs and the reorientation of world trade in the 1930. Journal of International Economics 38 (1/2), 1–24 (February).

Feenstra, Robert, 2004. Advanced International Trade: Theory and Evidence. Princeton University Press, Princeton, NJ.

Felbermyer, Gabriel J., Kohler, Wilhelm. "Exploring the intensive and extensive margins in world trade." Manuscript, August 2004.

Frankel, J.A., 1997. Regional Trading Blocs. Institute for International Economics, Washington, DC.

Frankel, Jeffrey A., Romer, David, 1999. Does trade cause growth? American Economic Review 89 (3), 379–399 (June).

Frankel, Jeffrey A., Stein, Ernesto, Wei, Shang-Jin, 1995. Trading blocs and the Americas: the natural, the unnatural, and the super-natural. Journal of Development Economics 47 (1), 61–95 (June).

Ghosh, Sucharita, Yamarik, Steven, 2004. Are regional trading arrangements trade creating? An application of extreme bounds analysis. Journal of International Economics 63 (2), 369–395 (July).

Gilpin, Robert, 2000. The Challenge of Global Capitalism. Princeton University Press, Princeton, NJ.

Heckman, James J., 1997. Instrumental variables: A study of implicit behavioral assumptions used in making program evaluations. Journal of Human Resources 32 (3), 441–462 (Summer).

Heckman, James J., 2001. Micro data, heterogeneity, and the evaluation of public policy: Nobel lecture. Journal of Political Economy 109 (4), 673–748 (August).

Helpman, Elhanan, Krugman, Paul, 1985. Market Structure and Foreign Trade. MIT Press, Cambridge, MA.

Lawrence, Robert Z., 1996. Regionalism, Multilateralism, and Deeper Integration. The Brookings Institution, Washington, DC.

Lawrence, Robert Z., 1998. Comment on 'The role of history in bilateral trade flows'. In: Frankel, Jeffrey A. (Ed.), The Regionalization of the World Economy. The University of Chicago Press, Chicago, pp. 57–59.
Lee, Jong-Wha, Swagel, Phillip, 1997. Trade barriers and trade flows across countries and industries. Review of Economics and Statistics 79, 372–382.
Linnemann, Hans, 1966. An Econometric Study of International Trade Flows. North-Holland, Amsterdam.
Maddala, G.S., 1983. Limited-Dependent and Qualitative Variables in Econometrics. Cambridge University Press, Cambridge, MA.
Magee, Chris, 2003. Endogenous preferential trade agreements: an empirical analysis. Contributions to Economic Analysis and Policy, vol. 2, no. 1. Berkeley Electronic Press.
McLaren, John E., 1997. Size, sunk costs, and Judge Bowker's objection to free trade. American Economic Review 87 (3), 400–420 (June).
Oguledo, Victor I., MacPhee, Craig R., 1994. Gravity models: a reformulation and an application to discriminatory arrangements. Applied Economics 26, 107–120.
Preeg, Ernest H., 1998. From Here to Free Trade. The University of Chicago Press, Chicago.
Redding, Stephen, Venables, Anthony J., 2000. Economic geography and international inequality. Centre for Economic Policy Research Discussion Paper, vol. 2568.
Rose, Andrew, 2004. Do we really know that the WTO increases trade? American Economic Review 94 (1), 98–114 (March).
Rose, Andrew, van Wincoop, Eric, 2001. National money as a barrier to international trade: the real case for currency union. American Economics Review 91 (2), 386–390 (May).
Sapir, Andre, 1981. Trade benefits under the eec generalized system of preferences. European Economic Review 15, 339–355.
Tinbergen, Jan, 1962. Shaping the World Economy. The Twentieth Century Fund, New York.
Tomz, Michael, Judith Goldstein, Douglas Rivers, June 2004. "Membership has its privileges: the impact of GATT on international trade," Stanford University, Dept. of Political Science Working Paper.
Trefler, Daniel, 1993. Trade liberalization and the theory of endogenous protection: an econometric study of U.S. import policy. Journal of Political Economy 101 (1), 138–160 (February).
Wooldridge, Jeffrey M., 2000. Introductory Econometrics. South-Western College Publishing, Cincinnati, OH.
Wooldridge, Jeffrey M., 2002. Econometric Analysis of Cross-Section and Panel Data. MIT Press, Cambridge, MA.
World Bank. *World development indicators*, CD-ROMs. Washington, DC: World Bank, 2003.

Chapter 11

Estimating the effects of free trade agreements on international trade flows using matching econometrics

Scott L. Baier [a,b], Jeffrey H. Bergstrand [c,d,*]

[a] The John E. Walter Department of Economics, Clemson University, Clemson, SC 29634 USA
[b] Federal Reserve Bank of Atlanta, Atlanta, GA 30309 USA
[c] Department of Finance, Mendoza College of Business, and Kellogg Institute for International Studies, University of Notre Dame, Notre Dame, IN 46556 USA
[d] CESifo, Munich, Germany

ARTICLE INFO

Article history:
Received 5 December 2006
Received in revised form 16 July 2008
Accepted 9 September 2008

Keywords:
International trade flows
Free trade agreements
Matching econometrics
Treatment effects

JEL classification:
F10
F13
F15

ABSTRACT

This paper provides the first cross-section estimates of long-run treatment effects of free trade agreements on members' bilateral international trade flows using (nonparametric) matching econometrics. Our nonparametric cross-section estimates of *ex post* long-run treatment effects are much more stable across years and have more economically plausible values than corresponding OLS cross-section estimates from typical gravity equations. We provide plausible estimates of the long-run effects of membership in the original European Economic Community (EEC) and the Central American Common Market (CACM) between 1960 and 2000 and the estimates confirm anecdotal reports of these agreements' effectiveness.

1. Introduction

For the past half century, quantitative evaluation of the effect of a trade policy change on the bilateral international trade of a pair of countries has been addressed traditionally in two ways, one *ex ante* and one *ex post*. *Ex ante* quantitative analysis of the effects of a policy change – such as formation of a free trade agreement (FTA) – on bilateral trade flows has been conducted using computable general equilibrium (CGE) models of trade, such as GTAP and the Michigan Model.[1] While pros and cons of these techniques have been discussed extensively, CGE models remain a standard tool to evaluate quantitatively *ex ante* trade effects of FTAs.

For decades, most *ex post* analyses of the (partial) effects of FTAs on trade flows have been conducted using "gravity equations," a log-linear ordinary least squares (OLS) regression specification that typically is interpreted theoretically as the reduced-form from a formal general equilibrium model, cf., Anderson (1979), Bergstrand (1985), Anderson and van Wincoop (2003, 2004), Baier and Bergstrand (2001, 2002, 2007a,b), Eaton and Kortum (2002), Evenett and Keller (2002), Feenstra (2004), and Bergstrand et al. (2007). Up until a few years ago, empirical researchers typically employed cross-sectional data for a particular year or for multiple years and used the coefficient estimates associated with a dummy variable representing the presence or absence of an FTA to estimate the "average (partial) treatment effect" (ATE) of an FTA on members' bilateral trade, cf., Linnemann (1966), Aitken (1973), Sapir (1981, 2001), Baldwin (1994), Frankel (1997), and Schott (2005). However, such dummy variables' coefficient estimates often display extreme instability across years, and in many cases seemingly successful economic integration agreements – such as the European Union (formerly, European Economic Community) – have *negative* estimated treatment effects, cf., Frankel (1997). The "fragility" of these estimates has been documented using extreme-bounds analysis, cf., Ghosh and Yamarik (2004).[2]

* Corresponding author. Department of Finance, Mendoza College of Business, and Kellogg Institute for International Studies, University of Notre Dame, Notre Dame, IN 46556 USA. Tel.: +1 574 631 6761; fax: +1 574 631 5255.
E-mail address: Bergstrand.1@nd.edu (J.H. Bergstrand).

[1] In reality, there are numerous types of international economic integration agreements: free trade agreements, customs unions, common markets, and economic unions. For ease of reference, we use the term "free trade agreements" generically, as most economic integration agreements are FTAs or customs unions. The European Economic Community and Central American Common Market were customs unions initially.

[2] Widely varying estimates have also been found in empirical analyses of the effects of currency unions on trade, cf., Alesina et al. (2002, Table 8).

*Originally Published in *Journal of International Economics*, 77(2009), pp. 63–76.

Yet, a fundamental question that remains to be addressed as the world continues to pursue economic integration agreements is simply this: What is the *ex post* long-run effect of a particular economic integration agreement between a pair of countries on the level of trade between those members? This is the central question addressed here.[3]

This paper is the first to evaluate *cross-sectionally* the (*ex post*) long-run treatment effects of FTAs on trade flow volumes using nonparametric estimation.[4] Several reasons exist to employ a matching estimator as a nonparametric benchmark for the empirical analysis of FTA treatment effects. First, while the log-linear gravity equation has worked well for decades to explain fundamental determinants of bilateral trade flows (such as GDPs and bilateral distance), the effects of FTAs on trade flows may be related to the levels of trade flows and other covariates (i.e., nonlinearities may exist), cf., Brada and Mendez (1985), Frankel (1997), Baier and Bergstrand (2002), Anderson and van Wincoop (2003), Santos Silva and Tenreyro (2006), Bergstrand et al. (2007), and Henderson and Millimet (2008). Matching provides an alternative approach to log-linear gravity equations to estimate treatment effects without knowing a precise functional relationship. Since it is not yet clear that there is any *well-accepted* methodology for estimating *ex post* the effects of an FTA on trade between a country pair in a given year, it is important to consider alternative methodologies, which may or may not confirm previous estimates using gravity equations, such as those in Baier and Bergstrand (2007a), Baier et al. (2007), and Baier et al. (2008). Second, matching estimators allow ready estimation of average treatment effects when FTA treatments are subject to self-selection and the relationships between FTA treatments and other trade-flow covariates are nonlinear. As Baier and Bergstrand (2004a) show, selection into FTAs is not random. In fact, country pairs that select into FTAs tend to share similar economic characteristics that gravity equations use to explain their trade flows. The combination of non-random selection into FTAs and omitted non-linearities can bias OLS estimates of FTA treatment effects, cf., Persson (2001) for similar concerns in estimating the effects on trade of currency unions. Matching econometrics provide a simple method to form treatment and control groups by selecting on observable covariates and comparing observations drawn from the "same" distribution. For each country pair with an FTA, we construct a control group of country pairs with nearly identical economic characteristics but having no FTA; the average difference in trade flows between the pairs with FTAs and their control groups provides an estimate of "treatment." Third, if the relationships between the FTA treatments and other trade-flow determinants are nonlinear, then the OLS average treatment effect (ATE) on a randomly selected pair will differ from the average treatment effect on the *treated* (ATT), and the latter may be of relevance for the policymaker.

We focus on two sets of potential contributions, one methodological and the other empirical. Methodologically, matching econometrics have been employed in economics predominantly in the labor economics literature, in particular in the evaluation of either job training or benefits programs in large cross-sections of individuals. The key consideration for matching econometrics is the formulation of a credible counterfactual, cf., Diamond (2006a,b). First, international trade provides an excellent context (outside of labor economics) for evaluating treatment effects because the theoretical foundations for the gravity equation in international trade offer a convincing method for constructing a credible counterfactual. Well-established theoretical foundations for the gravity equation provide an excellent framework for selecting "control groups" (i.e., matched pairs without FTAs). Second, we are able to match treatments with their nearest neighbor controls and ensure that there are no statistically significant observable differences between the treatment and control groups for *all* conditioning characteristics common to the two groups. Successful identification of the control group requires acknowledging empirically the multilateral (price) resistance terms influencing trade identified in Anderson and van Wincoop (2003). By employing a simple Taylor-series expansion of the theoretically motivated Anderson–van Wincoop multilateral resistance terms, we are able to construct theoretically appropriate bilateral *and* multilateral "trade cost" covariates for selection. The theory and structure of the gravity model of trade is very useful to help determine the "selection on observables."[5]

Empirically, we provide the first cross-sectional nonparametric matching estimates of long-run FTA treatment effects on levels of the volume of trade. First, we find across many settings and years that the matching estimates of treatment effects are much more stable and economically plausible than average treatment effect (ATE) estimates using typical cross-section OLS (or OLS with country fixed effects) gravity equations. The three main findings are: our ATT estimates indicate that FTAs increased members' trade by an economically and statistically significant amount in each of the nine years of our sample; the average treatment effects on the treated (ATTs) are lower than the ATEs for a randomly selected country pair; and the ATTs have less variance across years than ATEs calculated using matching techniques or using OLS. Second, we use matching econometrics to assess the effects of two historically prominent economic integration agreements on trade in a given year; specific treaties help to ensure an important assumption in matching estimation is met. Using nine cross-sections of annual trade flows from 1960 to 2000 (every 5 years), we find interesting results for two (still active) regional economic integration agreements that were formed between 1957 and 1960. First, the average treatment effect for a typical pair of members (ATT) of the *original* European Economic Community (EEC) was positive and economically significant from 1960 to 1970; by 1970, the EEC's Treaty of Rome had more than *doubled* on average the six members' bilateral trade. However, the enlargements of the Community in the early 1970s, the EC–EFTA free trade agreements, and the economic liberalization of Central and Eastern European countries and their subsequent FTAs with EC and EFTA members in the early 1990s reduced the original six members' bilateral trade significantly (i.e., trade diversion).[6] Second, we find that the treatment effect for a typical pair of countries in the original Central American Common Market (CACM) was positive and rose monotonically until 1970. However, in the early 1970s and early 1980s, the treatment effect was considerably lower, rebounding in the 1990s. These estimates support anecdotal evidence that the CACM flourished in the 1960s, but as some member countries faced considerable political instability and cross-border armed conflicts beginning in 1969 and then again in 1979, CACM became less effective between 1970 and 1990, reinvigorated by the nations' presidents in the 1990s.

[3] Evidence for long-run effects of other trade policies and their importance has been addressed in the literature, cf., Trefler (1993). Moreover, Anderson and van Wincoop (2003) and Bergstrand et al. (2007) remind us that there are both long-run partial- and general-equilibrium effects. In this paper, we focus only on the long-run partial (or "treatment") effects. However, the partial effects estimated here could be combined with a nonlinear system of structural equations to generate general-equilibrium comparative statics, as done in the two papers just noted.

[4] We know of one other study that has used matching estimation for FTA effects on trade flows, cf., Egger et al. (2008). However, that study focused on the effects of FTAs on intra-industry trade-share indexes, rather than trade volumes, and focused on *short-run* changes requiring a panel to do difference-in-differences estimation. As a tangent, that study did provide panel estimates of short-run (2-year) new FTA effects on trade flows using difference-in-differences matching. In international trade, a few nonparametric studies have addressed the long-run effects of *currency unions* on trade flow volumes using propensity-score estimates in cross-section, cf., Persson (2001), Kenen (2002), and Chintrakarn (2008), but not long-run effects of FTAs.

[5] Note that instrumental variables (IV) is not appropriate for addressing the bias raised by selection on observables. IV can address potentially the issue of selection bias on unobservables, cf., Baier and Bergstrand (2002). However, two points are worth noting. First, many have argued that the selection bias on observables may well dominate that on unobservables. Second, it is difficult to find instruments for FTAs that are not also correlated with trade flows, making IV techniques' usefulness limited, cf., Baier and Bergstrand (2007a), discussed more later.

[6] The EEC began to be called the EC (European Community) in the 1970s. EFTA denotes the European Free Trade Association), which was formed in 1960.

S.L. Baier, J.H. Bergstrand / Journal of International Economics 77 (2009) 63–76

The structure of the paper is as follows. Section 2 motivates the matching estimator as an alternative to gravity equations in the empirical trade literature to estimate *ex post* the effects of FTAs on members' trade flows. Section 3 addresses the matching estimator approach. Section 4 presents the empirical findings for average treatment effects across all FTAs and a sensitivity analysis. Section 5 presents the estimated average treatment effects for two particular treatments: EEC and CACM. Noting some caveats, Section 6 concludes that FTAs have had considerably larger effects on members' trade (*ex post*) than previous gravity models have suggested and that the coefficient estimates have economically plausible values and are much less fragile.

2. Motivation for nonparametric estimation of FTA effects on trade

Conventional wisdom leads one to argue that the trade between a pair of countries should increase when two countries enter into an FTA. First, trade could increase due to (gross) trade "creation" as the pair benefits from lower trade costs between them. Second, trade between a pair could result from the "diversion" of imports from (previously) lower cost suppliers. For both reasons, trade (on the extensive and intensive margins) between the pair should increase. As Table 1 verifies, country pairs with FTAs trade more on average than those without FTAs. However, such statistics do not imply that FTAs necessarily *cause* more trade.

2.1. Traditional (atheoretical) gravity equations

Ex post econometric analysis of the effects of FTAs on (bilateral) trade has been dominated over the past 45 years by the gravity equation. A typical specification estimated by OLS is:

$$\ln TF_{ijt} = \beta_0 + \beta_1(\ln GDP_{it}GDP_{jt}) + \beta_2(\ln DIST_{ij}) + \beta_3\left(ADJ_{ij}\right) + \beta_4(LANG_{ij}) + \beta_5(FTA_{ijt}) + \varepsilon_{ijt} \quad (1)$$

where TF_{ijt} denotes the sum of the values of the nominal bilateral trade flows between countries i and j in year t, GDP_{it} (GDP_{jt}) denotes the nominal gross domestic product in country i (j) in year t, $DIST_{ij}$ denotes the bilateral distance between the economic centers of countries i and j, ADJ_{ij} is a dummy variable assuming the value 1 if both countries are adjacent (i.e., share a land border) and 0 otherwise, $LANG_{ij}$ is a dummy variable assuming the value 1 if both countries share a common language and 0 otherwise, FTA_{ijt} is a dummy variable assuming the value 1 if both countries are members of a free trade agreement (or deeper economic integration agreement) in t and 0 otherwise, and ε_{ijt} is a normally-distributed error term.[7]

Formulations in Frankel (1997, Table 4.2) provide representative and highly cited *ex post* estimates of average treatment effects (ATEs) of several FTAs for several years.[8] As is common, the effects of such agreements – say, the EEC – on trade vary considerably across years, even though the coefficients of the other RHS variables are fairly stable. One even finds *negative* effects of the EEC on trade – other things constant – in some years. The instability of these estimates across years – and even some negative values – raised concerns in Frankel (1997), but were not addressed. Moreover, Ghosh and Yamarik (2004) conducted an extreme-bounds analysis of the estimated effects of several FTAs on trade using cross-section data in typical gravity equations and found the estimates to be quite "fragile."

[7] Some studies have shown recently that zero trade flows can be accounted for by estimating a multiplicative version of the gravity equation using a Poisson Quasi Maximum Likelihood estimator, cf., Santos Silva and Tenreyro (2006). However, this issue is beyond the scope of our paper, but a useful direction for future research.

[8] OLS estimates of the coefficient for the *FTA* dummy variable provide an average treatment effect (ATE) on a randomly selected country pair. By contrast, policymakers may be interested in the average treatment effect on a country pair with an FTA – that is, the treated (ATT). Generally, the ATE is an average of the ATT and the average treatment effect on an untreated pair (ATU).

Table 1
Sum of bilateral trade flows in countries with FTAs and without FTAs (in logs)

	Log sum of trade (with an FTA)	Log sum of trade (without an FTA)	Difference in logs
1960	11.33	9.21	2.11
1965	11.55	9.32	2.23
1970	12.21	7.68	4.53
1975	12.55	9.30	3.25
1980	13.22	9.94	3.28
1985	14.33	10.57	3.76
1990	14.14	10.43	3.71
1995	14.92	10.41	4.51
2000	14.57	10.50	4.07

Nominal bilateral trade flows are from the International Monetary Fund's *Direction of Trade Statistics* for 96 countries, which are listed in Baier and Bergstrand (2007a, Data Appendix). There are potentially 96×95/2=4560 bilateral trade sums (e.g., aggregate trade flow from France to Germany plus that from Germany to France); however, zero trade flows and missing values are excluded. For later analysis for real trade flows, nominal flows are divided first by the exporter's GDP deflator.

Table 2 provides some representative ATE estimates of FTAs for several years for 96 countries using OLS estimation of Eq. (1). We note first that in some years (e.g., 1970) an FTA had a large positive effect on trade. However, in other years (e.g., 1980, 1990, 1995) an FTA had a *negative* effect on trade (though statistically insignificant); these results are quite similar to those in Frankel (1997). Frankel (1997, p. 62) showed that, for some years, membership in the European Community *reduced* trade. Second, the ATEs are very unstable across years.[9] Although we would expect different agreements to have different economic effects, even allowing for differing economic impacts, one might not expect the average effect of an FTA to vary from an *increase* in trade of 274% in 1970 to a *decrease* of 10% in 1980. Such empirical results seem implausible.

2.2. Methodological problems

Several methodological reasons can potentially explain the fragility of these ATE estimates. First, the FTA dummy is likely representing other factors – unobserved by the researcher – that influence trade but are omitted. These omitted variables may bias the coefficient estimates up or down. Considerable work has been done over the past four decades to address conventional omitted variables bias in gravity equations. Rose (2004), for example, provides one of the most extensive treatments of omitted variables bias by including a range of "trade cost" proxies.

Perhaps the most influential recent theoretical and empirical paper addressing omitted variables bias in the gravity equation is Anderson and van Wincoop (2003). These authors demonstrate that traditional gravity Eq. (1) is mis-specified and coefficient estimates of RHS variables are likely biased owing to omission of nonlinear "multilateral (price) resistance" terms of countries i and j in each year (or including inappropriately atheoretical "remoteness" indexes). Anderson and van Wincoop show that estimation of unbiased coefficients ($\alpha_0, \ldots, \alpha_4$) requires minimizing the sum-of-squared residuals of (with time-subscript t now omitted):

$$\ln\left[TF_{ij}/(GDP_iGDP_j)\right] = \alpha_0 + \alpha_1 \ln DIST_{ij} + \alpha_2 ADJ_{ij} + \alpha_3 LANG_{ij} + \alpha_4 FTA_{ij} - \ln P_i^{1-\sigma} - \ln P_j^{1-\sigma} + \varepsilon_{ij} \quad (2)$$

subject to the N nonlinear market-equilibrium conditions:

$$P_i^{1-\sigma} = \sum_{k=1}^{N} P_k^{\sigma-1}\left(GDP_k/GDP^T\right)e^{\alpha_1 \ln DIST_{ki} + \alpha_2 ADJ_{ki} + \alpha_3 LANG_{ki} + \alpha_4 FTA_{ki}} \quad i = 1, \ldots, N \quad (3)$$

[9] As evidence, the coefficient of variation of the coefficient estimates for *FTA* across the nine years was six times that of the next highest coefficient estimate's coefficient of variation.

Table 2
Typical gravity equation coefficient estimates

Variable	(1) 1960	(2) 1965	(3) 1970	(4) 1975	(5) 1980	(6) 1985	(7) 1990	(8) 1995	(9) 2000
ln (GDP_i GDP_j)	0.75 (43.53)	0.76 (53.07)	0.81 (57.18)	0.84 (63.64)	0.90 (71.01)	0.87 (73.25)	0.90 (79.62)	0.95 (93.88)	0.99 (100.11)
ln $DIST_{ij}$	−0.56 (−1.33)	−0.65 (−14.40)	−0.65 (−14.10)	−0.75 (−16.29)	−0.88 (−21.19)	−0.88 (−22.48)	−0.98 (−24.24)	−1.01 (−26.15)	−1.08 (−27.39)
ADJ_{ij}	0.31 (1.64)	0.06 (0.37)	0.10 (0.54)	0.33 (1.93)	0.45 (2.77)	0.43 (2.80)	0.40 (2.40)	0.63 (3.99)	0.84 (5.17)
$LANG_{ij}$	0.03 (0.25)	0.24 (2.33)	0.36 (3.29)	0.48 (4.57)	0.47 (4.72)	0.39 (3.98)	0.68 (6.57)	0.76 (7.62)	0.63 (6.35)
FTA_{ij}	0.43 (2.02)	0.80 (4.24)	1.32 (6.08)	0.42 (2.47)	−0.11 (−0.62)	0.32 (1.98)	−0.04 (−0.27)	−0.04 (−0.27)	0.15 (1.37)
Constant	−9.66 (−15.28)	−9.45 (−17.45)	−11.58 (−20.89)	−12.17 (−23.04)	−13.40 (−26.11)	−12.66 (−26.76)	−13.49 (−28.83)	−14.97 (−35.52)	−15.87 (−37.12)
RMSE	1.1504	1.1089	1.2715	1.3218	1.3342	1.3227	1.4315	1.4029	1.4717
R^2	0.6649	0.6985	0.6969	0.7038	0.7250	0.7171	0.7308	0.7684	0.7741
No. observ.	1059	1325	1570	1947	2189	2433	2802	3073	3342

t-statistics are in parentheses. The dependent variable is natural log of the sum of nominal bilateral trade flows between *i* and *j*. The gravity equation was also estimated using the log of the bilateral trade flow from *i* to *j*; the results are not materially different. The data are the same as used in Baier and Bergstrand (2007a). The binary variable for an FTA (which also includes customs unions, common markets, and economic unions) was constructed by the authors, is described in Section 5 and Table 3 (a listing of all the agreements used) of Baier and Bergstrand (2007a), and is available at http://www.nd.edu/~jbergstr and http://people.clemson.edu/~sbaier. See Section 4.1, Data Description for sources for other variables.

where, in the model's context, $\alpha_0 = -\ln GDP^T$, where GDP^T is world GDP (a constant). One insight from Eqs. (2) and (3) is that the potential effect of FTA_{ij} on TF_{ij} is nonlinear. This obviously requires a custom nonlinear least squares (NLS) program to estimate unbiased coefficients.

Estimation of this system of nonlinear equations using NLS for the non-zero trade flows among the 96 countries in our study is beyond the scope of this paper. However, as Anderson and van Wincoop (2003) and Feenstra (2004) note, unbiased estimates of α_0 through α_4 can be obtained also using country fixed effects for $P_i^{1-\sigma}$ and $P_j^{1-\sigma}$. Table 3 reports the results of estimating Eq. (2) using fixed effects to account for the multilateral resistance terms $P_i^{1-\sigma}$ and $P_j^{1-\sigma}$. A comparison of Table 2 with Table 3 indicates that omission of the multilateral resistance terms in the traditional gravity specification tends to bias the FTA coefficient estimates. However, considerable instability of the ATEs for FTAs from year to year remains, several estimates are statistically insignificant, and – perhaps most importantly – some negative estimates seem implausible. For example, the effect of an FTA in 1970 was to more than *double* members' trade. However, by 1980, an FTA on average *reduced* trade by 54%. In fact, the results imply that by 2000 an FTA had *no* economically or statistically significant effect on members' trade! Thus, the issues raised in Anderson and van Wincoop (2003) are important, but do not fully address our concerns. Proper estimation of the gravity equation does require recognizing theoretically-motivated multilateral price terms. However, the Anderson–van Wincoop procedure cannot fully ensure unbiased estimation of the effect of an FTA on two members' trade for reasons detailed below. Still, these recent advances in the theoretical foundations of the gravity equation will be quite important for our matching estimation technique's "selection on observables."

Even after accounting for multilateral price terms, (log-) linear regressions may not provide accurate estimates of the average treatment effect of an FTA if (nonlinear) interactions of FTA_{ij} and typical gravity-equation trade-flow determinants are significant *and* selection into FTAs is non-random (i.e., FTA_{ij} is systematically correlated with these standard gravity-equation covariates). First, there is now significant evidence that FTAs are not determined randomly. For instance, Baier and Bergstrand (2004a) provide empirical evidence that pairs of countries that are larger in economic (GDP) size, more similar in GDPs, closer in distance, and more remote from other countries tend to have FTAs and they provide a theoretical rationale for each relationship. Of course such variables are typical gravity equation regressors. Indeed, Table 4 reveals that the means of traditional gravity equation covariates differ significantly between country pairs with FTAs (i.e., treated) versus those without FTAs (i.e., untreated) for 1990. Moreover, Figs. 1 and 2 show quite dramatically that for two typical gravity equation covariates – (log) bilateral distance and (the sum of the logs of) GDPs – the distributions of treated pairs differ substantively from those of untreated pairs for all nine years of our sample. In Fig. 1, the kernel density function of (log) bilateral distances for non-FTA country pairs (dashed line) is centered considerably to the right of that for FTA country pairs (solid line); country pairs with FTAs tend to be closer. In Fig. 2, the kernel density function of GDPs of pairs with FTAs (solid line) is centered to the right of that for pairs without FTAs (dashed line); country pairs with FTAs tend to be economically larger. Similar results hold for other covariates (not shown, for brevity).

Second, it is possible that the effects of an FTA on trade *are dependent* on levels of typical gravity-equation covariates. For instance, Brada and Mendiz (1985) and Frankel (1997) found economically and statistically significant interaction effects between FTA dummies and log bilateral distance in gravity equations. Baier and Bergstrand (2002) provide empirical evidence that interaction terms of FTA_{ij} with log GDPs and FTA_{ij} with log populations are economically and statistically significant in gravity equations. Moreover, in the parallel gravity-equation literature on the effects of currency unions on trade flows, Rose (2000) and Persson (2001) provide evidence of significant nonlinear terms interacting currency union dummies with typical gravity-equation covariates, such as log GDPs and log distance. As noted in Persson (2001), if selection into FTAs is non-random and if nonlinearities exist between the FTA variable and other covariates in the gravity equation, then parametric estimates of treatment effects will be biased and the average

Table 3
Theoretically-motivated gravity equation coefficient estimates (using country fixed effects)

Variable	(1) 1960	(2) 1965	(3) 1970	(4) 1975	(5) 1980	(6) 1985	(7) 1990	(8) 1995	(9) 2000
ln (GDP_i GDP_j)	0.32 (1.68)	0.79 (11.55)	1.00 (18.17)	0.97 (24.72)	0.98 (71.01)	0.89 (26.75)	0.90 (79.62)	1.06 (38.09)	1.16 (39.47)
ln $DIST_{ij}$	−0.70 (−13.47)	−0.79 (−17.25)	−0.74 (−16.15)	−0.88 (−18.53)	−1.06 (−24.40)	−1.05 (−25.39)	−0.98 (−24.24)	−1.20 (−29.00)	−1.35 (−32.26)
ADJ_{ij}	0.28 (1.68)	−0.05 (−0.31)	0.12 (0.77)	0.45 (2.90)	0.39 (2.60)	0.33 (2.34)	0.40 (2.40)	0.48 (3.34)	0.61 (4.19)
$LANG_{ij}$	0.22 (1.80)	0.42 (3.92)	0.76 (6.70)	0.60 (5.43)	0.69 (6.68)	0.62 (6.11)	0.68 (6.57)	0.88 (8.57)	0.80 (7.81)
FTA_{ij}	−0.01 (−0.06)	0.33 (2.00)	0.74 (3.86)	−0.10 (−0.62)	−0.78 (−4.60)	−0.42 (−2.74)	−0.41 (−2.72)	−0.23 (−1.79)	−0.08 (−0.75)
Constant	−14.94 (−29.22)	−9.19 (−4.79)	−16.16 (−10.15)	−14.72 (−11.92)	−14.50 (−12.54)	−11.59 (−10.82)	−14.40 (−13.72)	−16.48 (−18.21)	−18.65 (−19.88)
RMSE	0.9369	0.9144	1.0497	1.1262	1.1395	1.1317	1.2325	1.2222	1.2679
R^2	0.7919	0.8056	0.8024	0.7930	0.8064	0.7999	0.8063	0.8289	0.8365
No. observ.	1059	1325	1570	1947	2189	2433	2802	3073	3342

t-statistics are in parentheses. The dependent variable is natural log of the sum of nominal bilateral trade flows between *i* and *j*. Coefficient estimates and *t*-statistics for country fixed effects are not presented (for brevity).

Table 4
Summary of 1990 covariate means

	Country pairs with an FTA	Country pairs without an FTA	Difference
Log of distance	6.66	8.28	−1.62 (−23.80)
Sum of the logs of GDPs	38.55	34.69	3.87 (15.98)
Adjacency dummy	0.18	0.07	0.11 (10.46)
Language dummy	0.07	0.02	0.05 (−0.11)

t-statistics are in parentheses.

treatment effects on the *treated* (ATTs) will differ from the average treatment effects on randomly selected pairs (ATEs).

This paper employs nonparametric matching techniques to provide unbiased estimates of the long-run treatment effects of FTAs on trade flows using cross-section data. First, the key to successful matching estimates is to generate a credible counterfactual trade flow for an "untreated" matched country pair. Theoretical foundations for the gravity equation provide an excellent context for the selection of observables that can be used to generate matched untreated country pairs that are statistically indistinguishable from treated pairs, except for treatment. Matching estimation can avoid the bias introduced by non-random selection on observables and by non-linearities.

Second, while parametric techniques exist that can adjust for selection on observables bias and nonlinearities can be introduced in regressions, the virtually unlimited potential specifications suggest that matching estimates of treatment effects provide "benchmark" nonparametric estimates of long-run treatment effects. Consequently, they provide a useful "check" upon ATE and ATT estimates computed using regression analysis with alternative nonlinear structures used on nonexperimental data.

Third, there has been no study that has attempted to estimate *long-run* effects of FTAs on trade based upon cross-section data using nonparametric techniques. In international trade, several papers have used nonparametric techniques, such as propensity-score estimators, to evaluate the long-run effects of currency unions on trade. For instance, Persson (2001) found strikingly different treatment-effect estimates for currency unions using a propensity-score matching estimator in comparison to Rose (2000) using cross-section gravity equations. Rose found a treatment effect for currency unions of over 200%; Persson found treatment effects that were not (statistically) significantly different from zero.[10] However, while Persson's currency union ATEs were statistically insignificant, the specifications of his propensity-score functions lacked theoretical foundations, and many of the "balancing properties" were violated. Our study differs from Persson (2001) by examining FTA – not currency union – treatment effects, focusing on a matching technique,[11] and selecting covariates based upon recent theoretical developments for the trade gravity equation, cf., Anderson and van Wincoop (2003) and Baier and Bergstrand (2006, 2007b).[12]

One recent study in international trade has investigated the effects of FTAs on trade volumes and intra-industry trade indexes. Egger et al. (2008) used a difference-in-differences panel matching estimator to examine primarily the effect of FTA formations on *changes* in shares of intra-industry trade. However, with a two-year window on either side of the "events," this study could only determine *short-run* effects of FTAs on changes in the trade volumes and degrees of intra-industry trade among countries. Difference-in-differences techniques for 5-year windows might not nearly capture the trade-enhancing effects of FTAs. First, the vast bulk of FTAs have phase-in periods of 5 to 10 years. Second, even once the agreements are fully phased in, changed terms-of-trade have lagged effects on trade flows. Using first-differenced data and parametric techniques, Baier and Bergstrand (2007a) showed that FTAs affected trade *15 years after* their first year of implementation. Thus, our study differs from Egger et al. (2008) by examining "long-run" volume of trade treatment effects of FTAs rather than short-run effects, focusing on volume-of-trade rather than intra-industry-index effects of FTAs, and selecting covariates based upon the recent theoretical developments for the trade gravity equation.[13]

3. A matching-estimator approach

The literature on matching econometrics is now well established, cf., Moffitt (2004), Cameron and Trivedi (2005), Lee (2005), and Abadie and Imbens (2006). In our context, the key is finding a (control) group of country pairs without FTAs that are virtually identical in all other respects as trade partners to a pair with an FTA. The two groups of country pairs are selected to be identical in all respects but treatment by selecting on observables for the pairs; members of the two groups are assigned based upon a set of common economic characteristics. The key is to simulate random assignment into treatment and control. The average treatment effect for the entire sample (ATE) and the average treatment effect for treated groups (ATT) are obtained by comparing the trade flows between two groups, the treated and untreated (or control group), and taking the average difference.

Interestingly, large-sample properties of such estimators have not been established until just recently, cf., Abadie and Imbens (2006). That study notes that matching estimators are highly "nonsmooth functionals" of the distribution of data, which are not readily addressed using standard asymptotic distribution theory. They find that matching estimators include a conditional bias, the stochastic order of which increases with the number of continuous matching variables. In this paper, we use nearest neighbor matching as suggested by Abadie–Imbens (nearest three neighbors) and adjust for the conditional bias using the Abadie–Imbens (A–I) technique in a robustness analysis, which does not require consistent nonparametric estimation of unknown functions. For robustness, we also estimate propensity scores, to be discussed later.

We determine the ATTs for various years and treated groups; for brevity, we ignore the *ij* variable subscripts in the following. Let TF_1 (TF_0) denote the value of trade between two countries with (without) an FTA and let *FTA* be a dummy variable assuming the value 1 (0) if the two countries have (do not have) an FTA. Let $\mathbf{x}$ denote a set of characteristics (covariates) that influence the trade flow between pairs of countries, and $\mathbf{X}$ be a random vector of dimension k of continuous covariates distributed on $\mathbb{R}^k$ with compact and convex support X.

We follow Abadie and Imbens (2006) and make three conventional assumptions. First, for almost every $\mathbf{x} \in X$, assume *FTA* is independent of TF_1 and TF_0 – conditional upon the set of covariates $\mathbf{X}=\mathbf{x}$, which is the assumption of "conditional mean independence" or "ignorability of treatment" according to Rosenbaum and Rubin (1983); this is

[10] Tenreyro also found smaller effects of currency unions on trade, taking into account self-selection of country pairs into currency unions, building upon the work of Alesina and Barro (2002) and Alesina et al. (2002).

[11] A limited number of covariates determining trade flows implies we do not face the "curse of dimensionality," necessitating a propensity-score approach.

[12] As discussed in footnote 3, we focus only on estimating long-run "partial," or treatment, effects; we do not address general equilibrium comparative statics in this analysis, an issue for future research.

[13] As in Persson (2001), our focus is on addressing potential selection bias on observables and nonlinearities. We do not address selection on unobservables. In nonparametric estimation, the standard approach to address selection bias on unobservables is to construct difference-in-difference estimators for pre- and post-treatments over short and balanced periods, as in Egger et al., 2008; such a method would preclude estimating the long-run effects of FTAs (which can be up to 15 years), which is the focus of this paper. The standard cross-section parametric technique to adjust for selection bias on unobservables ("endogeneity" bias) is to use instrumental variables. However, parametric estimation requires specifying functional form and it is very difficult to find an instrument to predict FTAs that is not also correlated with trade flows, cf., Baier and Bergstrand (2004b, 2007a).

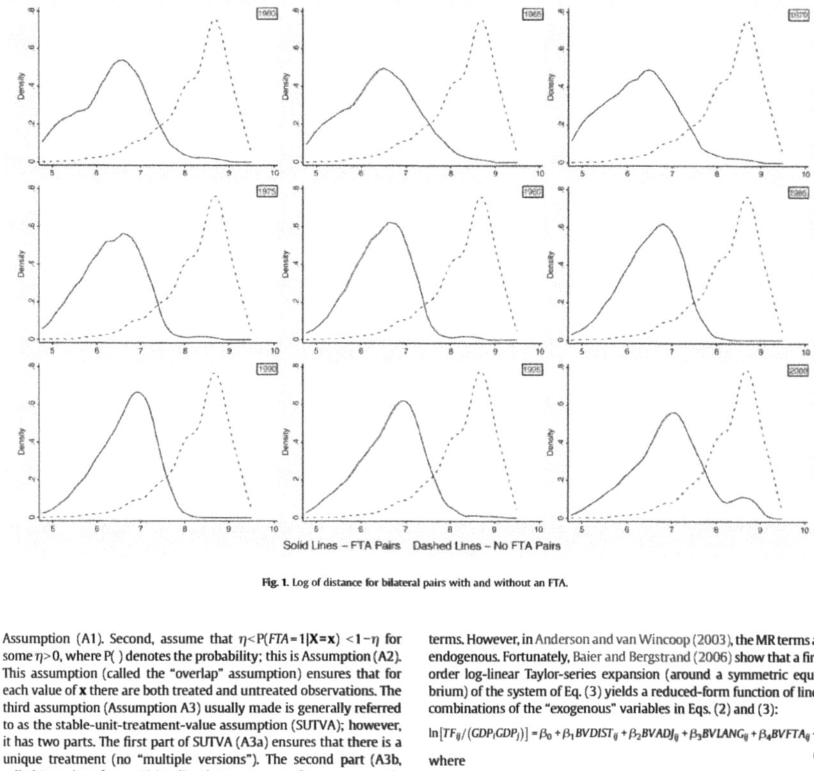

Fig. 1. Log of distance for bilateral pairs with and without an FTA.

Assumption (A1). Second, assume that $\eta < P(FTA=1|\mathbf{X}=\mathbf{x}) < 1-\eta$ for some $\eta > 0$, where P( ) denotes the probability; this is Assumption (A2). This assumption (called the "overlap" assumption) ensures that for each value of **x** there are both treated and untreated observations. The third assumption (Assumption A3) usually made is generally referred to as the stable-unit-treatment-value assumption (SUTVA); however, it has two parts. The first part of SUTVA (A3a) ensures that there is a unique treatment (no "multiple versions"). The second part (A3b, called "non-interference") implies that treatment of any country pair does not influence the trade of other (untreated) pairs; that is, *TF*, **x**, and *FTA* are independent draws from their distributions. We now discuss the feasibility of all three assumptions in the context of international trade flows and their determinants.

3.1. Ignorability Assumption (A1)

The ignorability (also called "unconfoundedness") assumption states that, conditioned on covariates **x**, *FTA* is independent of TF_0 and TF_1 (omitting observational subscripts for country pairs). The purpose of this assumption is to try to ensure that treatment assignment is "random." This assumption is assured by choosing a control group for each treated pair that is matched closely to the treated pair in terms of all relevant covariates influencing trade (other than *FTA*). Hence, this assumption is also known as "selection on observables."

Fortunately, theoretical foundations for the gravity equation of trade flows provide guidance for selecting observables. As Eqs. (2) and (3) above suggest, relevant covariates to use for selection on observables include the sum of logs of GDPs, log of bilateral distance, adjacency and language dummies, and measures of the "multilateral resistance" (MR) terms. However, in Anderson and van Wincoop (2003), the MR terms are endogenous. Fortunately, Baier and Bergstrand (2006) show that a first-order log-linear Taylor-series expansion (around a symmetric equilibrium) of the system of Eq. (3) yields a reduced-form function of linear combinations of the "exogenous" variables in Eqs. (2) and (3):

$$\ln[TF_{ij}/(GDP_iGDP_j)] = \beta_0 + \beta_1 BVDIST_{ij} + \beta_2 BVADJ_{ij} + \beta_3 BVLANG_{ij} + \beta_4 BVFTA_{ij} + \varepsilon_{ij} \quad (4)$$

where

$$BVDIST_{ij} = \ln DIST_{ij} - (1/N)\sum_{j=1}^{N} \ln DIST_{ij} - (1/N)\sum_{i=1}^{N} \ln DIST_{ij} + (1/N^2)\sum_{i=1}^{N}\sum_{j=1}^{N} \ln DIST_{ij}$$

$$BVADJ_{ij} = ADJ_{ij} - (1/N)\sum_{j=1}^{N} ADJ_{ij} - (1/N)\sum_{i=1}^{N} ADJ_{ij} + (1/N^2)\sum_{i=1}^{N}\sum_{j=1}^{N} ADJ_{ij}$$

$$BVLANG_{ij} = LANG_{ij} - (1/N)\sum_{j=1}^{N} LANG_{ij} - (1/N)\sum_{i=1}^{N} LANG_{ij}(1/N^2)\sum_{i=1}^{N}\sum_{j=1}^{N} LANG_{ij}$$

$$BVFTA_{ij} = FTA_{ij} - (1/N)\sum_{j=1}^{N} FTA_{ij} - (1/N)\sum_{i=1}^{N} FTA_{ij} + (1/N^2)\sum_{i=1}^{N}\sum_{j=1}^{N} FTA_{ij}$$

and the βs have theoretically interpretable values, cf., Baier and Bergstrand (2006, 2007b).[14] This framework suggests exogenous

[14] In the case of centering at a symmetric equilibrium, each of the "*BV*" variables is quite simple. For instance, for $BVDIST_{ij}$ the second (third) component is the mean distance of *i* (*j*) from all its trading partners and the fourth term is simply a constant. Baier and Bergstrand (2006) also show that a first-order log-linear Taylor-series expansion of Eq. (3) around alternatively a frictionless equilibrium yields terms similar to *BVDIST*, etc., except that the second, third, and fourth components are *GDP-share-weighted* (rather than simple) averages. See Baier and Bergstrand (2006, 2007b) for the economic intuition.

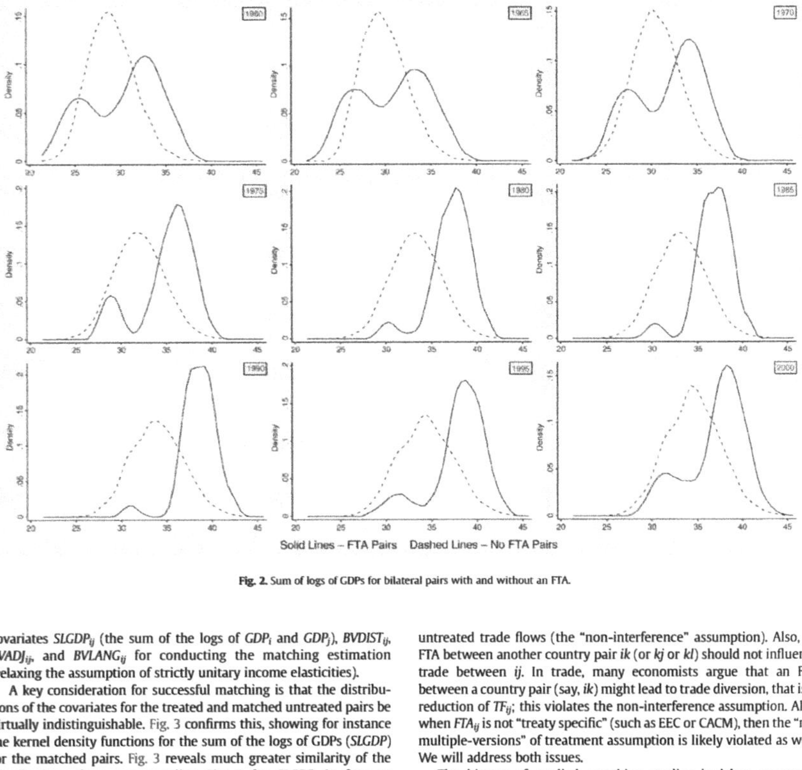

Fig. 2. Sum of logs of GDPs for bilateral pairs with and without an FTA.

covariates $SLGDP_{ij}$ (the sum of the logs of GDP_i and GDP_j), $BVDIST_{ij}$, $BVADJ_{ij}$, and $BVLANG_{ij}$ for conducting the matching estimation (relaxing the assumption of strictly unitary income elasticities).

A key consideration for successful matching is that the distributions of the covariates for the treated and matched untreated pairs be virtually indistinguishable. Fig. 3 confirms this, showing for instance the kernel density functions for the sum of the logs of GDPs (*SLGDP*) for the matched pairs. Fig. 3 reveals much greater similarity of the distributions than corresponding Fig. 2 for *SLGDP*. In fact, as conventional we estimated the differences of the means for treated and matched untreated pairs for all four exogenous covariates for all nine years. Among the 36 two-tailed *t*-tests for the four variables, we could reject at the 5% significance level the null of identical means in only two cases (*SLGDP* in 1990 and *BVDIST* in 2000). For brevity, we do not report all 36 statistics (but these are available on request).

3.2. Overlap Assumption (A2)

The second assumption ("overlap") ensures that for each value of **x** there are both treated and untreated observations. In our trade context, the very large number of country pairs with FTAs and without FTAs ensures that the overlap assumption is not violated.

3.3. SUTVA (A3)

In matching estimation, SUTVA is used to ensure (*a*) that the "treatment" (here, the FTA) is identical for each treated observation (i.e., no "multiple versions" of the treatment) and (*b*) that the formation of an FTA between a country pair *ij* does not influence untreated trade flows (the "non-interference" assumption). Also, an FTA between another country pair *ik* (or *kj* or *kl*) should not influence trade between *ij*. In trade, many economists argue that an FTA between a country pair (say, *ik*) might lead to trade diversion, that is, a reduction of TF_{ij}; this violates the non-interference assumption. Also, when FTA_{ij} is not "treaty specific" (such as EEC or CACM), then the "no-multiple-versions" of treatment assumption is likely violated as well. We will address both issues.

The history of applied matching studies in labor economics regarding job training programs suggests that researchers have justified their use of this assumption on the notion that the program is identical for treated individuals and that no single treated individual's income gains influence materially others' incomes (nor do others' treatments influence materially their incomes). Given the growing interest in matching estimators in the social sciences – and in economics, in particular – we use the theoretical foundations for the gravity equation to offer some clarity regarding this assumption in our context of international trade, in the spirit of Diamond (2006a,b). First, suppose world trade flows are determined according the Anderson and van Wincoop (2003) structural model represented by Eqs. (2) and (3) in Section 2. By convention, the "treatment effect" might be measured by the value of α_4. However, these equations show clearly the potential "general-equilibrium" effects that the non-interference assumption attempts to preclude. For instance, suppose the gravity-equation specification ignored $P_i^{1-\sigma}$ and $P_j^{1-\sigma}$. A change in any FTA_{ik} would alter the multilateral price term $P_i^{1-\sigma}$, confounding measurement of α_4.

One solution, of course, for estimating the parameters is to follow the path of estimating the entire system of structural equations using,

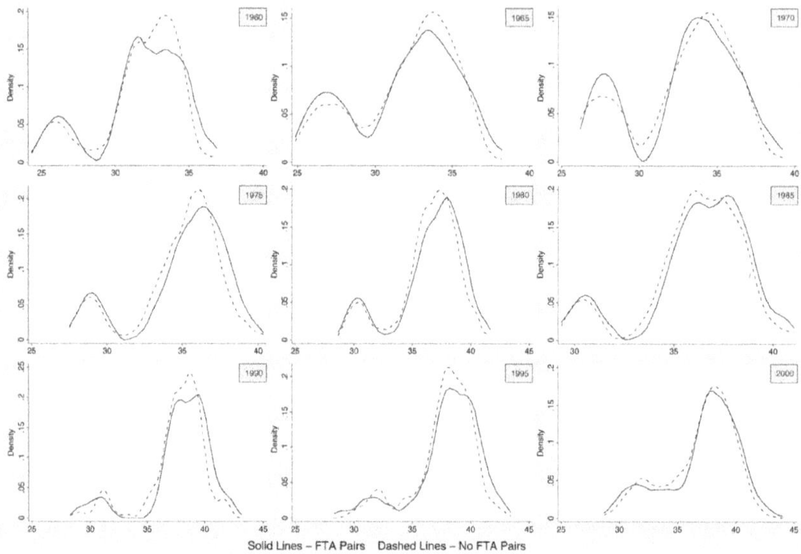

Fig. 3. Sum of logs of GDPs for matched bilateral pairs with and without an FTA.

say, nonlinear least squares, cf., Anderson and van Wincoop (2003) and Heckman et al. (1998). However, this approach imposes even more structure on the estimates of α_4, which is exactly what nonparametric estimation is trying to avoid. Is there a theoretically feasible way to account for the variation in variables $P_i^{1-\sigma}$ and $P_j^{1-\sigma}$ given the system of nonlinear Eqs. (2) and (3) – in the context of matching econometrics – which must also address the "curse of dimensionality"?

This issue is addressed by again appealing to the Baier and Bergstrand (2006, 2007b) framework discussed above. By selecting on observables such as $BVDIST_{ij}$, $BVADJ_{ij}$, and $BVLANG_{ij}$, we account for the general equilibrium aspects other than FTAs among other pairs for estimating treatment effects. However, in the context of the theory, the "treatment" is $BVFTA_{ij}$. That is, the difference in the trade flows between the observed and the counterfactual for country pair *ij* is driven by FTAs between the country pair *ij* – but also between country *i* with *any* of its trading partners, between country *j* with any of its trading partners, and between any country pair *kl*, which some may argue violates the "non-interference" assumption.

However, the researcher knows *when* policies were implemented. This identifies more precisely the actual "treatment" and potentially eliminates interference from the second, third and fourth terms in $BVFTA_{ij}$. For example, later in Section 5 we will consider the Treaty of Managua signed in 1960 to create the Central American Common Market (CACM). In this case, SUTVA is more likely to hold as the "treaty" and degree of integration was well-defined for every CACM member (no "multiple versions" is ensured by the common treatment of internal tariff elimination and imposition of identical external tariff rates) *and* – because the Central American nations were both economically small and remote from the only other effective FTAs in the 1960s, 1970s, and 1980s (EEC and EFTA) – there was likely little interference (no "general equilibrium effects"). That is, the small economic size and trade of CACM countries likely ensured no perceptible influence on untreated pairs' trade (similar to job-retrained individuals likely not having any perceptible impact on untreated individuals' incomes), and the remoteness of the CACM countries from Europe likely ensured that the formation of EEC and EFTA had no perceptible influence on CACM members' trade. Hence, for CACM in particular, $BVFTA_{ij}$ equals FTA_{ij} (implying no interferences) and members shared a common treatment (Treaty of Managua).

3.4. *Abadie and Imbens (2006) matching estimator*

Under these assumptions, the sample ATE with $\mathbf{X}=\mathbf{x}$ is given by:

$$ATE(\mathbf{x}) = E[TF|FTA=1, \mathbf{X}=\mathbf{x}] - E[TF|FTA=0, \mathbf{X}=\mathbf{x}] = E[TF_1 - TF_0|\mathbf{X}=\mathbf{x}] \quad (5)$$

which is the *ATE* conditional on **x**. By iterated expectations, averaging across the distribution of **X** gives $ATE=E[TF_1-TF_0]$. Similarly, the average treatment effect on the treated (ATT) is $ATT=E[TF_1-TF_0 \mid FTA=1]$.

The problem, of course, is that only one of TF_1 and TF_0 is observable. The Abadie–Imbens (A–I) matching estimator imputes the missing potential values using average outcomes for individuals with similar values for the covariates. Using notation from Abadie and Imbens (2006), let $||\mathbf{x}||_V=(\mathbf{x}'\mathbf{V}\mathbf{x})^{0.5}$ be a vector norm with **V** a positive definite weight matrix. Let $j_m(i)$ be an index ($j=1,\ldots, N$), where N

denotes the number of country pairs, which solves $FTA_j = 1 - FTA_i$, ensuring that when j has an FTA then i does not, and:

$$\sum_{l:FTA_l = 1-FTA_i} 1\{\|X_l - X_i\| \leq \|X_j - X_i\|\} = m \qquad (6)$$

where 1{ } is an indicator function; the function assumes the value 1 if the bracketed expression holds and equals 0 otherwise. Then $j_m(i)$ is an index of the unit that is the mth closest unit to unit i among the covariates (among units with opposite treatment to unit i). Let $J_M(i)$ denote the set of indices for the first M matches for unit i; in our empirical work, we will use the three nearest neighbors. Let $K_M(i)$ denote the number of times unit i is used as a match given that M matches are used per unit:

$$K_M(i) = \sum_{l=1}^{N} 1\{i \in J_M(l)\} \qquad (7)$$

The matching estimator imputes the missing potential outcomes as:

$$TF_i^*(0) = \begin{cases} TF_i, & \text{if } FTA_i = 0 \\ \frac{1}{M}\sum_{j \in J_M(i)} TF_j, & \text{if } FTA_i = 1 \end{cases} \qquad (8)$$

and

$$TF_i^*(1) = \begin{cases} \frac{1}{M}\sum_{j \in J_M(i)} TF_j, & \text{if } FTA_i = 0 \\ TF_i, & \text{if } FTA_i = 1 \end{cases} \qquad (9)$$

As noted in Abadie and Imbens (2006), the estimator for the average treatment effect (*ATE*) is:

$$ATE_M = \frac{1}{N}\sum_{i=1}^{N} \left[TF_i^*(1) - TF_i^*(0)\right] \qquad (10)$$

The estimator for the average treatment effect on the treated (*ATT*) is:

$$ATT_M = \frac{1}{N}\sum_{FTA_i = 1} \left[TF_i - TF_i^*(0)\right] \qquad (11)$$

If the variables in **x** are discrete (i.e., matching is "exact"), then ATE_M and ATT_M will be unbiased estimates of the population average treatment effects. However, in our context **x** will include some continuous variables. Consequently, both estimators will have a conditional bias in finite samples. Abadie and Imbens (2006) show that, with k continuous covariates, a term corresponding to the matching "discrepancies" will be of order $O_P(N^{-1/k})$. Abadie and Imbens (2006) propose a "bias-adjusted" estimator that adjusts for differences in covariate values within the matches, which we will provide in a sensitivity analysis.[15]

4. An application of matching econometrics to international trade flows and FTAs

4.1. Data description

Nominal bilateral trade flows are from the International Monetary Fund's *Direction of Trade Statistics* for the years 1960, 1965, ..., 2000 for 96 potential trading partners (zero trade flows are excluded); we will allow for zero trade flows in the sensitivity analysis. These data are scaled by exporter GDP deflators to generate real trade flows, which are also used. Nominal GDPs are from the World Bank's *World Development Indicators* (2003); these are scaled by GDP deflators to create real GDPs. Bilateral distances were compiled using the CIA *World Factbook* for longitudes and latitudes of economic centers to calculate the great circle distances. The language and adjacency dummy variables were compiled also from the CIA *World Factbook*. The FTA dummy variable was calculated using appendices in Lawrence (1996) and Frankel (1997), various websites, and FTAs notified to the GATT/WTO under GATT Articles XXIV or the Enabling Clause for developing economies; we included only full (no partial) FTAs and customs unions. A list of the trade agreements and countries used and sources is in Baier and Bergstrand (2007a).

4.2. Empirical results: average treatment effects of FTAs

Using the four covariates and the A–I matching estimator for the three nearest neighbors, we calculated the ATEs and ATTs for a sample of 96 countries for 9 years: 1960, 1965, ..., 2000. The average difference between the trade flows of the treated pairs and of their three nearest matched neighbors is an estimate of the average treatment effect on the treated. Table 5 provides the results. Columns (3)–(8) provide the baseline results. Columns (9)–(11) in Table 5 provide some sensitivity analysis to methods of estimation. Columns (12) and (13) will be addressed in detail in Section 5.

4.2.1. Baseline results for all FTAs

For convenience, columns (3) and (4) in Table 5 report the same ATE estimates reported earlier in Tables 2 and 3 using OLS and OLS with fixed effects for the traditional and theory-motivated gravity equations, respectively, for nominal bilateral trade flows for the nine years; we provide these for comparison. As noted, OLS and fixed-effects estimates vary widely across years, are often insignificant, and are significantly negative in several years.

Column (5) in Table 5 reports the ATEs estimated using the A–I matching estimator described above for nominal trade flows. Several interesting results are worth noting. First, unlike the previous numbers, for every year the ATE is positive and economically significant. This suggests our *first main result*: FTAs increase bilateral trade in every year. Second, considerable variance remains; in fact, the range of estimates is even wider than that using OLS or fixed effects. The standard deviation of OLS ATEs across the nine years is 0.46 whereas the standard deviation for the A–I ATEs is 0.62. Third, the values of some of the years' ATE estimates seem excessively "large," i.e., even larger than the currency-union effects motivating Persson's comment on Rose (2000). For instance, in 1990, the estimated average effect of an FTA was to increase trade by *tenfold*, or 900% ($e^{2.36} = 10.59$). Fourth, the large drop in the ATE from 1995 to 2000 raises concern.

One reason the ATEs in column (5) may be excessively large is the extrapolation problem raised in Imbens (2004). ATEs provide estimates of treatment on a randomly selected pair. A second reason the ATEs in column (5) may be large is that they require two imputed values, whereas ATTs require only one imputed value, cf., Section 3.4. Column (6) provides the ATT estimates. This leads to our *second main result*: The effects of an FTA on the treated are smaller than the corresponding ATEs (although in some years the ATE and ATT estimate differences are not statistically significant). As in column (5), the ATTs are all positive, economically significant, and statistically significant from zero. The ATT estimates yield more plausible effects of an FTA on a member pair. For instance, in 1995, the A–I ATE was 2.27, implying an 867% increase in trade. By contrast, in 1995, the A–I ATT was 0.84, implying only a 132% increase in trade. The lower ATT is quite plausible economically because the ATE reflects the trade increase of a randomly selected pair and is an average of ATTs and ATUs (average

[15] Abadie and Imbens (2006) show that simple matching estimators have biases related to the number of observations (*N*) under standard normalizations with continuous covariates. The bias is driven by "matching discrepancies" on the continuous covariates; matching on continuous variables can never be "exact." For instance, for ATE_M in Eq. (10), the bias-adjusted estimator replaces the TF_j in Eq. (8) with $TF_j + \mu(X_i, FTA = 0) - \mu(X_j, FTA = 0)$ and the TF_j in Eq. (9) with $TF_j + \mu(X_i, FTA = 1) - \mu(X_j, FTA = 1)$ where $\mu(\ )$ is a consistent (regression) estimator. In our case, the number of continuous covariates is small so the bias is minimal.

72 S.L. Baier, J.H. Bergstrand / Journal of International Economics 77 (2009) 63–76

Table 5
FTA treatment effects for bilateral trade flows

(1) Year	(2) # of observations (# of FTAs)	(3) Nominal level OLS ATEs	(4) Nominal level fixed effects ATEs	(5) Nominal level A–I ATEs	(6) Nominal level A–I ATTs	(7) Real level A–I ATTs	(8) Real share A–I ATTs	(9) Real share bias-adj. A–I ATTs	(10) Real share P-S ATTs	(11) Real share bias-adj. P-S ATTs	(12) EEC real share A–I ATTs	(13) CACM real share A–I ATTs
1960	1059 (37)	0.43*	−0.01	0.71*	0.48**	0.28	0.35**	0.23	0.36	0.02	0.24	0.82
		(2.02)	(−0.06)	(1.90)	(2.16)	(1.48)	(2.11)	(1.55)	(1.23)	(0.05)	(1.03)	(1.40)
1965	1325 (42)	0.80**	0.33**	1.13**	0.54**	0.57**	0.61**	0.48**	1.04**	0.60	0.47*	1.36**
		(4.24)	(2.00)	(2.68)	(2.92)	(3.27)	(3.24)	(2.99)	(2.89)	(1.12)	(1.80)	(2.38)
1970	1570 (41)	1.32**	0.74**	1.86**	1.35**	1.30**	1.30**	1.03**	1.31**	1.23**	1.04**	2.94**
		(6.08)	(3.86)	(3.92)	(6.16)	(6.10)	(5.75)	(5.39)	(4.08)	(2.85)	(2.71)	(2.70)
1975	1947 (86)	0.42**	−0.10	1.83**	0.90**	0.79**	0.46**	0.40**	0.56**	0.99**	0.52**	2.18**
		(2.47)	(−0.62)	(4.18)	(4.84)	(4.29)	(2.88)	(2.73)	(2.31)	(3.20)	(1.97)	(2.32)
1980	2189 (84)	−0.11	−0.78**	1.32**	0.83**	0.75**	0.49**	0.39**	0.52**	0.83**	0.59**	2.24**
		(−0.62)	(−4.60)	(2.51)	(5.08)	(4.77)	(3.27)	(2.94)	(2.32)	(2.90)	(2.18)	(2.54)
1985	2433 (98)	0.32*	−0.42**	1.60**	1.13**	0.72**	0.51**	0.37**	0.55**	0.61**	0.84**	0.74*
		(1.98)	(−2.74)	(3.93)	(6.88)	(5.20)	(4.20)	(3.23)	(2.78)	(2.43)	(2.43)	(1.72)
1990	2802 (129)	−0.04	−0.41**	2.36**	1.00**	0.94**	0.61**	0.51**	0.55**	0.51**	0.90**	1.05**
		(−0.27)	(−2.72)	(4.43)	(6.85)	(6.76)	(5.47)	(5.01)	(3.27)	(2.72)	(2.20)	(2.38)
1995	3073 (163)	−0.03	−0.23*	2.27**	0.84**	0.84**	0.55**	0.46**	0.39**	0.39**	0.78**	1.25**
		(−0.27)	(−1.79)	(5.03)	(6.67)	(6.67)	(5.20)	(4.77)	(2.49)	(2.07)	(2.09)	(2.09)
2000	3342 (263)	0.15	−0.08	0.68**	0.59**	0.61**	0.38**	0.29**	0.26*	0.28	0.77**	1.08**
		(1.37)	(−0.75)	(2.34)	(5.08)	(5.20)	(3.59)	(2.88)	(1.93)	(1.38)	(2.16)	(2.18)

z-statistics are in parentheses. * (**) denotes statistical significance at the 10 (5) percent level in two-tailed tests. For 1960, 1965 and 1980, the number of (non-zero-trade) observations for real trade are 1010, 1291, and 2163, respectively. Column (3) refers to OLS results using typical gravity Eq. (1). Column (4) refers to OLS results including country fixed effects for multilateral price terms in gravity Eq. (2). Column (5) refers to ATEs using Eq. (10) for nominal trade flows. Column (6) refers to ATTs using Eq. (11) for nominal trade flows. Column (7) refers to ATTs using real trade flows. Column (8) refers to ATTs using real trade flow shares (real trade flows scaled by the product of the two countries' real GDPs). Column (9) refers to "bias-adjusted" ATTs using real trade flow shares. Column (10) refers to propensity scores using real trade flow shares. Column (11) refers to propensity scores using real trade flow shares. Columns (12) and (13) refer to ATTs for only the EEC and CACM, respectively, using real trade shares.

treatment effect on the untreated). Most country pairs without FTAs (untreated) are smaller, developing economies with much higher tariff rates, likely to have more trade created from an FTA. Consequently, the ATEs are likely to be higher, reflecting potentially large ATUs.

Our *third main result* is that the A–I ATTs have less variance across years than the A–I ATEs. The standard deviation of A–I ATTs is only 0.3, half that of A–I ATEs and two-thirds that of OLS ATEs. There is also more of a potentially explainable pattern to the average treatment effects over time, in contrast to the seemingly random pattern in the OLS and fixed-effects estimates. Although considerable variance remains, there is an economic explanation that we will discuss shortly.

Up to now, we have focused on *nominal* (bilateral) trade flows, rather than real trade flows. The reason is that most cross-sectional gravity equation analyses traditionally have used nominal trade flow and nominal GDP data. However, two reasons suggest that real trade flows and real GDPs should be examined. First, policymakers are likely to be interested more in the trade *volume* effect of an FTA, rather than the trade value effect. Second, future analyses may examine changes in trade flows, and price changes should likely be removed from the analysis. Column (7) reports the A–I ATTs using real trade flows and real GDPs. As expected, the average ATT is lower for real than nominal trade flows; inflation has been removed.[16] The average ATT across all nine years for real (nominal) trade flows is 0.75 (0.85); the standard deviation of the ATTs for real (nominal) flows across the nine years are 0.29 (0.30). Thus, across all years of our sample, on average an FTA approximately *doubles* two members' real trade (i.e., $e^{0.75}=2.12$, implying a 112% increase).

Even though one of the conditioning covariates is real GDP, policymakers may be interested in the effect on the volume of trade *relative* to national outputs, denoted henceforth the *real trade share*. Here, the log of real trade share is defined as the log of the sum of the real trade flows of the two countries less the sum of the logs of their real GDPs; this is a standard scaling in the gravity equation literature (the results were robust to alternative GDP scalings). We would expect the ATTs for real trade shares to be smaller than those for real trade levels. Column (8) confirms they are, in general. In some years, the real trade share ATTs are approximately the same as those for real trade levels; only in 1960 and 1965 were the real trade share ATTs marginally higher. The average real trade share ATT across all nine years was 0.58, implying that the real trade share was on average 79% higher with an FTA than without an FTA. There remains variance across years; the standard deviation for the ATTs in column (8) is 0.29. We have also run specifications for nominal trade shares and the results are similar (omitted for brevity).

Using the ATTs in column (8), we can now provide some explanation for the pattern of change across the nine years, taking into account phase-ins of agreements, lagged terms-of-trade effects, and the growth of regionalism. First, with the exception of 1960, 1970, and 2000, the ATT for *FTA* in any year is between 0.46 and 0.61. We now explain the three outliers. From 1960 to 1970, the main agreements in place were the EEC, EFTA, and CACM, which all began between 1958 and 1961. However, all of the agreements were phased-in, which partly explains that the effects of these agreements likely phased-in also over the 1960s. Moreover, terms-of-trade changes from agreements likely have a lagged effect on trade flows, contributing further to the delay in the full treatment effects from these agreements. As Table 5's column (2) shows, in 1960, 1965, and 1970, there were only 37, 42, and 41 pairs of countries with FTAs, respectively. Thus, the ATT in 1960 was lower than average because only the EEC had been in effect for more than 1 year (in fact, for only 2 years). This interpretation is confirmed in columns (12) and (13) which show that the ATTs for the EEC and for CACM were both statistically insignificant in 1960.[17]

The next outlier to explain is the large ATT for 1970, followed by a much lower value in 1975. While we delay a detailed explanation of the effects of the EEC and CACM until Section 5, by 1970 both agreements had been fully phased in. Moreover, note the

[16] Note that in 1995 (the base year for real variables) the nominal and real ATTs are identical, as expected.

[17] The economically large and marginally statistically significant (at 20%) ATT for the CACM in 1960 may seem surprising, since the treaty was only signed on December 15, 1960. However, it must be noted that after World War II, there was a wave of *bilateral* FTAs signed among Costa Rica, El Salvador, Guatemala, Honduras, and Nicaragua between 1950 and 1956, which preceded our data set, cf., U.S. Library of Congress (1993, p.2).

exceptionally large value for CACM in 1970 in column (13). While this value may seem implausible to the reader, we will discuss in Section 5 that – by historical accounts – the CACM "flourished" in the 1960s (on the heels of the Central American bilateral FTAs formed between 1950 and 1956), followed by political and civil ruptures in the subsequent two decades. The large value for the ATT for *FTA* in 1970 in column (8) is plausible.

But the ATT in 1975 is sharply lower than that in 1970. The addition of Denmark, Ireland, and the United Kingdom to the EEC in 1973 likely led to trade diversion from the original EEC. Moreover, the new agreements with these countries *and* the creation and phasing-in of FTAs between EC countries and EFTA countries between 1970 and 1975 contributed to a large expansion in the number of *new* agreements. From 1970 to 1975, the number of FTAs more than doubled from 41 to 86. As we saw in 1960 and 1965, the role of phase-ins and lagged terms-of-trade effects will cause the ATT to be much lower for new agreements. The doubling of the number of FTAs from 1970 to 1975 – and the consequent presence of brand new FTAs – had the effect of causing the ATT to decrease from its 1970 level of 1.30 to 0.46 in 1975.[18]

While plausible explanations such as subsequent FTA formations and the introduction of the European Monetary System can explain minor fluctuations in the level of the ATT from 1975 to 1995, the last notable change in column (8) is the decline from 0.55 to 0.38 in the ATT from 1995 to 2000. Although the number of FTAs increased from 1980 to 2000, the largest absolute and percentage increase in treated pairs in our sample in these two decades occurred between 1995 and 2000, when the number of treated pairs increased by 100 from 163 (in 1995) to 263 (in 2000). This 61% increase in the number of FTAs introduced a large number of *new* FTAs – likely all phased-in over 5-to-10 years – that probably caused the treatment effect to decline from 0.55 to 0.38.

4.2.2. Sensitivity analysis

There are three dimensions in which we examine the robustness of the estimates. First, Abadie and Imbens (2006) show that the matching estimator above will be biased in finite samples when matching is not "exact," that is, if covariate values are not identical within matches. They show that, with k continuous covariates, a term corresponding to the matching "discrepancies" will be of order $O_P(N^{-1/k})$. Abadie and Imbens (2006) propose a "bias-adjusted" estimator that adjusts for differences in covariate values within the matches. Column (9) provides the bias-adjusted ATTs for the real trade shares. Except for one year's estimate (1970), the bias-adjusted ATTs are within 0.15 of the unadjusted ATTs in column (8). Thus, the results are largely robust to adjustment for the bias.

Second, a common alternative nonparametric estimator is the propensity-score estimator. The advantage of the propensity-score estimator is that matching is done on only one characteristic, which is a probit or logit function of several observables; this technique avoids the "curse of (high) dimensionality." However, the reduction in dimension is at a cost of being a less precise matching procedure. Nevertheless, a useful check is to determine if the results above are largely robust to this estimator. In the propensity-score approach, one controls for all the observables by controlling for a particular function of the covariates, the conditional probability of treatment, $P[FTA=1|\mathbf{x}]$. If selection bias is absent in controlling for $\mathbf{x}$, it will be absent in the propensity scores (P-S). We then match on the propensity scores for the country pairs with and without FTAs. The covariates used are the same ones used for matching earlier. See Dehejia and Wahba (2002) or Cameron and Trivedi (2005) for further details. Columns (10) and (11) provide the results for real trade shares for the unadjusted and bias-adjusted P-S ATTs, respectively. The results for columns (8) and (10) are largely similar; the results for columns (9) and (11) are largely similar. The only substantive difference between the A-I and P-S estimates are that the A-I estimates are estimated more precisely, either for the unadjusted or bias-adjusted values. In fact, every A-I estimate has a lower standard error than its corresponding P-S estimate, as expected.

Third, note that the potential sample size varies across years; this is because we only allowed non-zero trade flows for potential matched pairs. The reason is – by allowing matched pairs with zero trade – this may introduce an unobservable factor influencing potential trade that could bias results (i.e., an inappropriate extrapolation). We re-estimated the A-I results for columns (7) and (8) – real trade levels and real trade shares – allowing all 4560 pairs in each year. We summarize the results. First, the alternative ATTs were less precisely estimated; the standard errors of the estimates (z-statistics) were higher (lower) than the corresponding ATTs using the original samples. Second, the ATTs for the full sample are much more unstable across years than the original ones. Third, typically the ATTs with the full sample are considerably higher (in some cases, implausibly higher) than the baseline results.

5. Estimating the treatment effects of the Treaty of Rome and the Treaty of Managua

The main conclusion of the previous section is that the overall long-run average treatment effect of an FTA on trade between a pair of member countries is to roughly double their trade. However, as noted above, the variation across ATT estimates in Table 5 tends to display a trend that is notably absent from typical OLS estimates (Table 5, column 3). We also note that the results suggested that the average effect of an FTA tended to occur over 10–15 years, to account for lagged effects of FTAs on their terms of trade and for "phasing-in" of agreements, cf., Baier and Bergstrand (2007a) for more on such effects.

In this section, we address two issues. First, we provide *ex post* estimates of the average treatment effect of an FTA (or customs union) on the treated focusing on two specific "treaties." By examining two particular long-standing agreements, we can explain readily most of the variation in ATTs across the nine years reported in Table 5. The only long-standing effective agreements since 1960 are the (EEC) Treaty of Rome, the (CACM) Managua Treaty, and the (EFTA) Treaty of Stockholm, so these are relevant agreements to examine and exploit our data set. In the interest of methodology and brevity, we focus on only two of the trade agreements over the period 1960–2000, the original six-member European Economic Community (treaty signed in 1957) and the original five-member Central American Common Market (treaty signed in 1960; Costa Rica joined in 1962 and Panama was excluded).[19]

The second issue we address is that an examination of specific treaties more likely ensures that the stable-unit-value-treatment assumption (SUTVA) is not violated. In the cases of the original six-member EEC and the original five-member CACM, the "no-multiple-versions" assumption is more likely to hold; the membership of these groups never changed and the Treaties of Rome and Managua are well defined.[20] Section 5.1 reports and explains the results for the EEC. However, the "non-interference" assumption may be violated in the case of the original EEC members, since EFTA was formed at approximately the same time and the EEC had subsequent enlargements to include former EFTA countries. In this case, the general equilibrium effects are consistent with standard trade diversion

[18] Moreover, as will be detailed in Section 5, 1969 witnessed the first political rupture in CACM with an El Salvador–Honduras war.

[19] Results for EFTA are in accord with those for the EEC, but omitted for brevity (available on request).

[20] Although EFTA was signed in 1960, its membership has fluctuated considerably, such that only two of the four small economies currently comprising EFTA (Norway and Switzerland) were even in the original group of seven EFTA countries. If we were to focus only on this pair, we would risk violating the overlap assumption (A2).

arguments. By contrast, the non-interference assumption is less likely to be violated for CACM. Since the CACM countries are economically small (akin to individuals in the labor economics job-training matching studies), CACM members' trade is likely to have an imperceptible impact on untreated pairs' trade. Also, since the Central American countries in CACM are remote from Europe, the EEC and EFTA agreements are unlikely to have a perceptible impact on CACM members' trade.[21] The results for CACM are reported and explained in Section 5.2.

5.1. The original six-member European Economic Community

The EEC was formed upon the signing of the Treaty of Rome in 1957. The original six members were Belgium, Luxembourg, the Netherlands, France, (West) Germany, and Italy; the first three countries were, at the signing of the treaty, already in a free trade agreement (BENELUX). All six original members have stayed members of the European Community since its inception a half-century ago; we will address the deepening of the agreement to an economic union in the 1990s later. The EEC went into force in 1958 with a ten-year phase-in period. By 1967, tariffs on virtually all manufactured products were eliminated. Thus, taking into account the phased-in liberalizations, likely lagged effects on terms of trade of the agreement, and the absence of any expansions of the community until 1973, the likely largest effect of the EEC on members' trade should have been around 1970, as suggested in Baier and Bergstrand (2004b, 2007a).

Table 5, columns (12) and (13), provide the ATT estimates using the (bias-unadjusted) A–I real trade share matching estimator technique for EEC and for CACM, respectively. Recall, the real trade share is measured as the sum of the real trade flows between a country pair divided by the product of their real GDPs; we then logged the variable. Column (12) reports the real trade share ATTs for treated relative to untreated pairs for the original six EEC members' trade. Column (12) shows that, only 3 years into the EEC, members' trade was 27% higher ($e^{0.24}$) than their matched control pairs, suggesting a plausible 8 percent average annual increase. By 1965, EEC trade was 60% higher. By 1970, such trade was 183% higher because of phase-ins of liberalization and lagged effects on trade volume of terms-of-trade changes; 183% higher trade suggests once again an 8% average annual increase.

The European Community (or EC, as it began to be called in the 1970s) has both enlarged and deepened in degree of economic integration over time. In 1973, after 15 years of existence, the EC enlarged to include three more countries: Denmark, Ireland, and the United Kingdom. In the same year, the members of the EC and EFTA formed free trade agreements. Thus, in the period from 1973 to 1980 (and perhaps longer), the original six members of the EC (or EEC-6) should have experienced a *diversion* of trade among themselves as $BVFTA_{ijt}$ fell, and trade between the original EC members with the new EC members and with EFTA members likely expanded.

From 1970 to 1975, the ATT for the EEC-6 fell by half or 0.52, from 1.04 to 0.52, and only increased slightly to 0.59 by 1980. This result is consistent with the likely trade-diverting effects on original EEC members' trade of these expansions of free trade between the EEC-6 members with eight new countries (3 new EC members and the remaining 5 EFTA members). Using these values, the average annual decrease in EEC-6 members' trade was 4.4%.

The period 1980–1985 witnessed two policy changes within the EC. First, the EC had its second enlargement. Yet, adding Greece to the EC is not likely to have had an economically significant trade-diversion effect on the original EC members' common trade. However, the second major policy change was the entry into the European Monetary System (EMS) of all six of the original EC members. The introduction of much smaller exchange rate variability, and consequent reduced relative price variability, is likely to have had a significant effect on increasing trade among members, as the economic literature on exchange rate variability and trade suggests, cf., Alesina et al. (2002). This effect may have dwarfed any Greece-enlargement effect. Column (12) reports that the ATT level effect rose 0.59 to 0.84.

Between 1985 and 1990, the third enlargement of the EC occurred, with the addition of Portugal and Spain in 1986. The addition of these two countries to the EC is likely to have caused little trade diversion among the original EEC-6 members, as all these countries already had free trade with Portugal. The EEC-6 level ATT actually rose slightly from 0.84 to 0.90, perhaps reflecting the lagged trade-creating effects of the EMS dominating small trade-diverting effects for EEC-6 countries of adding Spain.

The major economic policy change facing Europe between 1990 and 1995 was the political and economic liberalization of Central and Eastern Europe and the creation of free trade agreements between the EC members and Bulgaria, the Czech Republic, Hungary, Poland, Romania, and the Slovak Republic, which caused a dramatic and rapid reduction in trade barriers in these countries and fostered trade diversion from the original EEC-6 countries. In many goods, full liberalization was immediate. This liberalization of Central and Eastern European countries' trade had a material impact on the EEC level ATT in column (12), reducing it from 0.90 to 0.78.

In 1995, a fourth and even larger expansion of the EC occurred, creating the EC-15. This enlargement to include Austria, Sweden and Finland would again likely have caused a reduction in trade among the original six EEC countries. However, by 1995 the EEC-6 already had FTAs in place with these three countries. The other most notable policy development in the 1990s was the creation of the European Union (EU). The formation of the EU in 1992 deepened the degree of economic integration considerably, phased in over several years. The likely trade impact on the original EEC countries was positive, most likely not occurring until the late 1990s (1995–2000); most aspects of the EU did not take effect until January 1, 1994 or January 1, 1995. The level ATT estimate had no material change, falling slightly from 0.78 to 0.77.

The stability of the EEC ATT from 1995 to 2000 also helps to explain the fall in the ATTs in Table 5, columns (3)–(11), from 1995 to 2000. The period 1995–2000 saw an enormous increase (from 163 to 263) in the number of "treated" pairs, i.e., country pairs adopting FTAs. However, such FTAs were likely phased in (such as NAFTA and MERCOSUR) and much of their impact would have been minimal, as it was for the EEC, EFTA, and CACM in 1960. Consequently, with many country pairs having "brand new" FTAs, trade flows would not yet have adjusted substantively, and we would then expect the overall FTA ATTs in 2000 in columns (3)–(11) to be lower than those in 1995. However, we should find no such diminution in the ATT for the EEC-6, and we do not; any potential trade diversion for the EEC-6 would also not have had much effect yet.

According to our level ATT estimates, the formation of the EEC-6 and subsequent policy changes in the European Community that caused either trade diversion or more trade creation among these members left the original EEC-6 members' international trade relative to GDP on average about 116% higher by 2000 ($e^{0.77}=2.16$), or 1.9% higher per year.

5.2. The Central American Common Market

The other agreement we address in detail is the Central American Common Market (CACM), formed in 1960. Entered into force in 1961, the agreement was novel among such agreements by providing *immediate free trade* on 95% of all goods traded among El Salvador, Guatemala, Honduras, and Nicaragua; Costa Rica joined in 1962 (Panama has had only an association agreement with CACM

[21] In last 5 years of our analysis, however, CACM members' trade may have been influenced by the formation of AFTA and MERCOSUR.

members). As for the EEC-6, the no-multiple-versions assumption is likely to hold. Yet, unlike for the EEC, the non-interference assumption is more likely to hold. First, CACM's membership was constant (*de jure*) from 1962 to 2000, so there were no enlargements and consequently potential trade diversions. The small size of trade among CACM members ensures imperceptible impact on untreated pairs' trade. CACM countries' remoteness – from Europe – ensures imperceptible impact on CACM trade of the major regional FTAs formed and altered between 1960 and 1990 (EEC and EFTA).

According to SICE (2006), CACM "flourished as the most advanced and successful regional integration scheme of Latin America in the 1960s." Intra-regional (CACM) trade grew from $33 million in 1960 to $1000 million in 1980; that is, intra-regional trade grew by a *factor of 30*. Unfortunately, in 1969 a war between El Salvador and Honduras led to Honduras' (*de facto*) withdrawal and re-imposition of tariffs on imports from the other Central American countries. From 1970 to 1990, political unrest in the region left CACM moribund according to most observers. Nicaragua instituted the Marxist Sandanista region in 1979, which continued until 1990; during the 1980s, anti-Sandanistas were prevalent in Honduras, leading to armed cross-border conflicts in the region. In June 1990, a summit of the Central American countries' presidents called for the revival of the CACM.

The ATT estimates in column (13) of Table 5 confirm the rapid success of the CACM in the 1960s (as well as bilateral FTAs among these countries between 1950 and 1956), followed by much lower effects in the 1970s and 1980s, and finally a resurgence of effectiveness in 1990. In column (13), the real trade share ATT estimates indicate that by 1970 the CACM increased members trade by 1800% ($e^{2.94} = 18.92$). While such a figure may appear unrealistically high, one should be reminded that tariffs in Latin American economies were considerably higher than those in Northern Hemisphere countries (typically, 200% higher) in 1960; estimates put them at approximately 40%. Thus immediate and nearly full trade liberalization from high tariff levels under CACM could conceivably have had such a substantial effect, especially on the heels of the countries' bilateral FTAs formed between 1950 and 1956 (a period for which bilateral trade data are unavailable).

From 1970 to 1990, political instability, war, and the resurgence of protectionism in the region explains why CACM was less effective in that period. From 1970 to 1980 (following the 1969 El Salvador–Honduras war and the withdrawal of Honduras from CACM), the real trade share level ATT fell from 2.94 to 2.24, or a 50% decline in the effect of CACM. From 1980 to 1985 (following the 1979 ascendancy of the Marxist Sandanista regime and the Honduras–Nicaraguan border war), the CACM level ATT declined again from 2.24 to 0.74, a further 78% decline in the trade effect. Following a June 1990 summit of Central American presidents to revive the Treaty of Managua, a reversal in the trade impact of CACM occurred. By 2000, the CACM ATT on the level of the real trade share was higher at 1.08; thus, by 2000, the effect of CACM had been to roughly triple members' trade.

On net, the estimated ATTs for CACM provide economically plausible measures of the effects on trade of this agreement. The direction of changes in the effects are consistent with anecdotal evidence of its initial success, followed by a rapid dissolution of its effectiveness due to political and military conflict, and finally a resuscitation in the 1990s.

6. Conclusions

This paper has provided the first nonparametric empirical estimates using matching econometrics of the long-run effects of FTAs (and customs unions) on members' trade for a wide range of such agreements, as well as for two specific agreements that were formed in the period 1957–1960. Matching estimators provide plausible estimates of the average treatment effect of an FTA on the trade of members that actually form one (ATTs), avoiding selection bias on observables in the presence of potential nonlinearities between the FTA variable and other covariates. We find a narrower range (across years) and more economically plausible values of the long-run effects of FTAs on members' trade using nonparametric estimates than parametric ones in cross-section. Interestingly, our results using nonparametric techniques suggest an average long-run effect of an FTA of 100%. Such an estimate is not far from those found using panel data and parametric techniques, such as the gravity equation, cf., Baier and Bergstrand (2007a) and references therein. Thus, our nonparametric estimates suggest that the gravity equation may still provide a baseline parametric framework for evaluating the effects of the FTAs on trade flows, but continued investigation is warranted.

We note that our matching estimates do not address explicitly selection bias on unobservables. Alternative nonparametric methods exist, such as "difference-in-differences" techniques, to eliminate such bias. But the construction and computation of these effects using pre- and post-treatments for 15-year balanced periods for treated and control pairs is a large endeavor beyond the scope of this particular paper, and is left for future research. Nevertheless, the results here provide a further step toward providing more precise and credible *ex post* estimates of *long-run* effects of FTAs on trade flows. We hope future work will continue to develop better matching estimates of FTAs and other trade policies.

Acknowledgements

The authors are grateful for excellent comments from Dan Trefler, Peter Egger, Daniel Millimet, and two anonymous referees and for financial support from the National Science Foundation under grants SES 0351018 (Baier) and SES 0351154 (Bergstrand).

References

Abadie, Alberto, Imbens, Guido W., 2006. Large sample properties of matching estimators for average treatment effects. Econometrica 74 (1), 235–267 January.
Aitken, Norman D., 1973. The effect of the EEC and EFTA on European Trade: a temporal cross-section analysis. American Economic Review 63 (5), 881–892 December.
Alesina, Alberto, Barro, Robert, 2002. Currency unions. Quarterly Journal of Economics 117 (2), 409–436 May.
Alesina, Alberto, Barro, Robert, Tenreyro, Silvana, 2002. Optimal currency areas. In: Gertler, Mark, Rogoff, Kenneth (Eds.), NBER Macroeconomics Annual 2002. MIT Press, Cambridge, MA.
Anderson, James E., 1979. A theoretical foundation for the gravity equation. American Economic Review 69 (1), 106–116 March.
Anderson, James E., van Wincoop, Eric, 2003. Gravity with gravitas: a solution to the border puzzle. American Economic Review 93 (1), 170–192 March.
Anderson, James E., van Wincoop, Eric, 2004. Trade costs. Journal of Economic Literature 62 (3), 691–751 September.
Baier, Scott L., Bergstrand, Jeffrey H., 2001. the growth of world trade: tariffs, transport costs, and income similarity. Journal of International Economics 53 (1), 1–27 February.
Baier, Scott L., Bergstrand, Jeffrey H., 2002. On the Endogeneity of International Trade Flows and Free Trade Agreements. manuscript, http://www.nd.edu/~jbergstr/Working_Papers/EndogeneityAug2002.pdf.
Baier, Scott L., Bergstrand, Jeffrey H., 2004a. Economic determinants of free trade agreements. Journal of International Economics 64 (1), 29–63 October.
Baier, Scott L., Bergstrand, Jeffrey H., 2004b. Do Free Trade Agreements Actually Increase Members' International Trade?manuscript.
Baier, Scott L., Bergstrand, Jeffrey H., 2006. Bonus Vetus OLS: A Simple Method for Addressing the 'Border Puzzle' and Other Gravity-Equation Issues. manuscript, http://www.nd.edu/~jbergstr/Working_Papers/BVOLSMarch2006.pdf.
Baier, Scott L., Bergstrand, Jeffrey H., 2007a. Do free trade agreements actually increase members' international trade? Journal of International Economics 71 (1), 72–95 March.
Baier, Scott L., Bergstrand, Jeffrey H., 2007b. Bonus Vetus OLS: A Simple Method for Approximating International Trade-Cost Effects using the Gravity Equation. manuscript, http://www.nd.edu/~jbergstr/Working_Papers/BVOLSOctober2007.pdf.
Baier, Scott L., Bergstrand, Jeffrey H., Vidal, Erika, 2007. Free trade agreements *in* the Americas: are the trade effects larger than anticipated? The World Economy 30 (9), 1347–1377 September.
Baier, Scott L., Bergstrand, Jeffrey H., Egger, Peter, McLaughlin, Patrick A., 2008. Do economic integration agreements actually work? Issues in understanding the causes and consequences of the growth of regionalism. The World Economy 31 (4), 461–497 April.
Baldwin, Richard E., 1994. Towards an Integrated Europe. CEPR, London.
Bergstrand, Jeffrey H., 1985. The gravity equation in international trade: some microeconomic foundations and empirical evidence. Review of Economics and Statistics 67 (3), 474–481 August.

Bergstrand, Jeffrey H., Egger, Peter, Larch, Mario, 2007. Gravity *Redux*: Structural Estimation of Gravity Equations with Asymmetric Bilateral Trade Costs. manuscript, http://www.nd.edu/~jbergstr/Working_Papers/GravityReduxOctober2007.pdf.

Brada, Josef, Mendez, Jose, 1985. Economic integration among developed, developing, and centrally planned economies: a comparative analysis. Review of Economics and Statistics 67 (4), 549–556.

Cameron, A. Colin, Trivedi, Pravin K., 2005. Microeconometrics: Methods and Applications. Cambridge University Press, Cambridge, UK.

Chintrakarn, Pandej, 2008. Estimating the Euro effects on trade with propensity score matching. Review of International Economics 16 (1), 196–198 February.

Dehejia, Rajeev H., Wahba, Sadek, 2002. Propensity score-matching methods for nonexperiental causal studies. Review of Economics and Statistics 84 (1), 151–161 February.

Diamond, Alexis, 2006a. Thoughts on SUTVA, Part I. http://www.iq.harvard.edu/blog/sss/archives/2006/02/thoughts_on_sut.shtml.

Diamond, Alexis, 2006b. Thoughts on SUTVA, Part II. http://www.iq.harvard.edu/blog/sss/archives/2006/03/thoughts_on_sut_1.shtml.

Eaton, Jonathan, Kortum, Samuel, 2002. Technology, geography, and trade. Econometrica 70 (5), 1741–1779 September.

Egger, Hartmut, Egger, Peter, Greenaway, David, 2008. The trade structure effects of endogenous regional trade agreements. Journal of International Economics 74, 278–298.

Evenett, Simon, Keller, Wolfgang, 2002. AOn theories explaining the success of the gravity equation. Journal of Political Economy 110 (2), 281–316 April.

Feenstra, Robert, 2004. Advanced International Trade: Theory and Evidence. Princeton University Press, Princeton, NJ.

Frankel, Jeffrey A., 1997. Regional Trading Blocs. Institute for International Economics, Washington, DC.

Ghosh, Sucharita, Yamarik, Steven, 2004. Are regional trading arrangements trade creating?: an application of extreme bounds analysis. Journal of International Economics 63 (2), 369–395 July.

Heckman, James, Lochner, Lance, Taber, Christopher, 1998. General-equilibrium treatment effects: a study of tuition policy. American Economic Review 88 (2), 381–386 May.

Henderson, Daniel J., Millimet, Daniel M., 2008. Is gravity linear? Journal of Applied Econometrics 23 (2), 137–172.

Imbens, Guido W., 2004. Nonparametric estimation of average treatment effects under exogeneity: a review. Review of Economics and Statistics 86 (1), 4–29 February.

Lawrence, Robert Z., 1996. Regionalism, Multilateralism, and Deeper Integration. The Brookings Institution, Washington, DC.

Kenen, Peter B., 2002. Currency unions and trade: variations on themes by Rose and Persson. Reserve Bank of New Zealand Discussion Paper DP/2002/08, December.

Lee, Myoung Jae, 2005. Micro-econometrics for Policy, Program, and Treatment Effects. Oxford University Press, Oxford, UK.

Linnemann, Hans, 1966. An Econometric Study of International Trade Flows. North-Holland, Amsterdam.

Moffitt, Robert A., 2004. Introduction to the symposium on the econometrics of matching. Review of Economics and Statistics 86 (1), 1–3 February.

Persson, Torsten, 2001. Currency unions and trade: how large is the treatment effect? Economic Policy 435–448 October.

Rose, Andrew K., 2000. One money, one market: the effect of common currencies on trade. Economic Policy 9–45 April.

Rose, Andrew K., 2004. Do we really know that the WTO increases trade? American Economic Review 94 (1), 98–114 March.

Rosenbaum, Paul R., Rubin, Donald B., 1983. The central role of the propensity score in observational studies for causal effects. Biometrika 70 (1), 41–55.

Santos Silva, J.M.C., Tenreyro, Silvana, 2006. The log of gravity. Review of Economics and Statistics 88 (4), 641–658 November.

Sapir, Andre, 1981. Trade benefits under the EEC generalized system of preferences. European Economic Review 15, 339–355.

Sapir, Andre, 2001. Domino effects in Western European regional trade. European Journal of Political Economy 17, 377–388.

Schott, Jeffrey, 2005. Free Trade Agreements: U.S. Strategies and Priorities. Institute for International Economics, Washington, DC.

SICE, 2006. http://www.sice.oas.org.

Tenreyro, Silvana, in press. "On the Causes and Consequences of Currency Unions." Harvard University unpublished working paper.

Trefler, Daniel, 1993. Trade liberalization and the theory of endogenous protection: an econometric study of U.S. import policy. Journal of Political Economy 101, 138–160 February.

The World Bank, 2003. World Development Indicators 2003. The World Bank, Washington, DC.

Chapter 12

Economic integration agreements and the margins of international trade

Scott L. Baier [a,b], Jeffrey H. Bergstrand [c,d,e,*], Michael Feng [a]

[a] John E. Walker Department of Economics, Clemson University, Clemson, SC 29634, USA
[b] Federal Reserve Bank of Atlanta, Atlanta, GA, USA
[c] Department of Finance, Kellogg Institute for International Studies, University of Notre Dame, Notre Dame, IN 46556, USA
[d] Department of Economics, Kellogg Institute for International Studies, University of Notre Dame, Notre Dame, IN 46556, USA
[e] CESifo, Munich, Germany

ARTICLE INFO

Article history:
Received 23 November 2011
Received in revised form 18 March 2014
Accepted 19 March 2014
Available online 1 April 2014

JEL classification:
F1
F15

Keywords:
Free trade agreements
International trade
Extensive margins
Intensive margins

ABSTRACT

One of the main policy sources of trade-cost changes is the formation of an economic integration agreement (EIA), which potentially affects an importing country's welfare. This paper: (i) provides the first evidence using gravity equations of *both* intensive and extensive (goods) margins being affected by EIAs employing a panel data set with a large number of country pairs, product categories, and EIAs from 1962 to 2000; (ii) provides the first evidence of the differential (partial) effects of various "types" of EIAs on these intensive and extensive margins of trade; and (iii) finds a novel differential "timing" of the two margins' (partial) effects with intensive-margin effects occurring sooner than extensive-margin effects, consistent with recent theoretical predictions. The results are robust to correcting for potential sample-selection, firm-heterogeneity, and reverse causality biases.

1. Introduction

The gravity equation has long dominated the international trade literature as the main econometric approach toward estimating ex post the "partial" (or direct) effects of economic integration agreements and other natural and policy-based bilateral trade costs on aggregate bilateral trade flows.[1] Economic integration agreements (EIAs) refer broadly to preferential trade agreements, free trade agreements, customs unions, common markets, and economic unions.[2] Recently, Baier and Bergstrand (2007) demonstrated that estimation (ex post) of the (partial) effects of EIAs suffered from endogeneity bias, mainly due to self-selection of country-pairs' governments into agreements. They showed that – after accounting for such bias using panel techniques – EIAs had much larger effects on trade flows than revealed in the earlier gravity equation literature and these estimates were more precise. Anderson and Yotov (2011) confirmed these findings using panel data also. Such results followed in the footsteps of empirical trade studies such as Trefler (1993) and Lee and Swagel (1997) that showed that previous estimates of trade-policy liberalizations on imports were underestimated considerably due to endogeneity bias.

While such positive estimates for EIA dummy variables were interpreted in the context of either Armington or Krugman models as EIAs increasing trade volumes of existing homogeneous firms (i.e., the "intensive margin"), consideration of zeros in bilateral trade, fixed export costs, and firm heterogeneity have led researchers more recently to examine various "extensive margins" of trade. Such extensive margins fall under three general categories: country, goods (or products), and firm. The existence of zeros in aggregate bilateral trade flows among many country pairs has led some researchers to explore the probability that a pair of countries trades at all; to the extent that an EIA affects this probability, this changes the *country* extensive margin of trade and potentially economic welfare.

A second margin is known as the "goods" margin of trade. Hummels and Klenow (2005), or HK, introduced this notion by examining zeros in bilateral trade flows at *highly disaggregated product-category levels*. The motivation for HK was to explore in a cross section of a large number of products and among a large number of U.S. trading partners a fundamental question: Do large economies export more because they export

* Corresponding author at: Department of Finance, Mendoza College of Business, University of Notre Dame, Notre Dame, IN 46556, USA.
E-mail addresses: sbaier@clemson.edu (S.L. Baier), bergstrand.1@nd.edu (J.H. Bergstrand), fdayu@clemson.edu (M. Feng).

[1] Partial (or direct) effects refer to the absence of general-equilibrium (or indirect) effects; see Anderson and van Wincoop (2003) and Baier and Bergstrand (2009) on partial versus general equilibrium trade effects of trade-cost changes. "Aggregate" refers to all "goods" (or industries or product categories).

[2] In this study, we use the term "preferential trade agreement" to denote one with only partial liberalization (not free trade).

*Originally Published in *Journal of International Economics*, 93(2014), pp. 339–350.

larger quantities of a given good (i.e., intensive goods margin) *or* a wider set of goods (extensive goods margin)?[3] They found in their cross section that about 60% of larger exports of large economies was attributable to the extensive goods margin; specifically, as the exporter country's economic size grew, it exported a larger number of product categories (or "goods") to more markets. However, HK did not investigate the relationship between trade liberalizations and the intensive and extensive goods margins of trade. The purpose of this paper is to address this shortcoming.

In this paper, we explore the impact of EIAs on aggregate trade flows, intensive (goods) margins, and extensive (goods) margins for a large number of goods, country pairs, and years.[4] This is important for at least three reasons. First, the relative impacts on intensive versus extensive margins of trade liberalizations may matter for estimating the welfare gains from trade. Traditionally, the welfare gains from trade liberalizations in models such as Armington and Krugman arise due to terms-of-trade changes; this is summarized succinctly in Arkolakis et al. (2012). In Eaton and Kortum (2002), trade liberalizations increase welfare due to an increase in economic efficiency a la the Dornbusch–Fisher–Samuelson model. In the Melitz (2003) model, trade liberalizations lead to gains due to firm heterogeneity and resulting increases in aggregate productivity. Second, while Arkolakis et al. (2012) recently argued that the welfare gains are iso-morphic across many modern quantitative trade models, they note that the gains can vary across models allowing heterogenous firms depending upon the type of Melitz model; hence, the distinction between intensive margin effects and extensive margin effects is important for ultimately quantifying with more precision the "gains from trade."[5] Third, the HK analysis limited itself to a cross section. In a panel, however, intensive margin and extensive margin effects of EIAs may have differential "timings." For instance, Arkolakis et al. (2012) recently introduced staggered "Calvo pricing" into their Ricardian model of trade and showed that the intensive margin likely reacts sooner to trade liberalizations than does the extensive margin. Moreover, since the two margins have different "trade elasticities," the quantitative path of the welfare gains is time sensitive.

Our paper extends the literature by offering three potential empirical contributions. First, we extend the Baier and Bergstrand (2007) panel econometric methodology for the (partial) effects of EIAs on aggregate trade flows using a gravity equation to examine in a setting with a large number of country pairs the effects of virtually all EIAs on the extensive and intensive goods margins, using the HK trade-margin-decomposition methodology. In the context of an econometric analysis, we are the first to find economically and statistically significant EIA effects on both the intensive *and* extensive (goods) margins in the context of a large number of country pairs, EIAs, and years.

Second, we examine the effects of various *types* of EIAs – one-way preferential trade agreements (OWPTAs), two-way preferential trade agreements (TWPTAs), free trade agreements (FTAs), and a variable for customs unions, common markets and economic unions (CUCMECUs) – on trade flows, extensive margins, and intensive margins.[6] While two recent studies have adapted the Baier–Bergstrand methodology for estimating the effect of differing "types" of EIAs on bilateral aggregate trade flows, *no* econometric study has examined the effect of various types of EIAs on the (goods) extensive and intensive margins of trade using a large number of country pairs and EIAs.[7] Neither Helpman et al. (2008) nor Egger et al. (2011) distinguished among various types of EIAs in their analyses of country intensive and extensive margins. We find not only that deeper EIAs have larger trade effects than FTAs, and the latter have larger effects than (partial) two-way and one-way PTAs, but we distinguish between these various trade effects at the extensive and intensive margins using a panel of (disaggregate) bilateral trade flows from 1962 to 2000 covering 98% of world exports.

Third, Bernard et al. (2009) is likely the only empirical study to date to explore the "timing" of extensive and intensive margin responses to shocks. Using cross-sectional variation to examine long-run aspects, Bernard et al. (2009) find that variation in trade flows across country pairs is explained largely by the extensive margin, using firm-level data (the "firm" margin); this result is consistent with HK using their "goods" margin. But using *time-series* variation, Bernard et al. (2009) find that a larger proportion of trade variation can be explained by the intensive margin at short (five-year) time intervals. They show that, following the Asian financial crisis of 1997, virtually all of the variation in trade flows within 2–3 years could be explained by the *intensive* margin. This finding is consistent with two recent theoretical studies arguing that the low trade-cost elasticity found in macroeconomic analyses of business cycles should be associated with the intensive margin of trade compared with the relatively higher trade-cost elasticity found in international trade, which reflects the intensive and extensive margin effects.[8] In this paper, we allow for differential "timing" of EIA effects using panel data. We find the first comprehensive empirical evidence that the shorter-term effects of EIAs on trade flows are more at the (goods) intensive margin and longer-term effects are more at the extensive margin (the latter entailing either fixed export costs or staggered "Calvo pricing" by consumers), consistent with intuition and results in Bernard et al. (2009). Moreover, our results shed empirical light on theoretical conjectures for the *relative* quantitative effects on intensive and extensive margins of variable trade cost changes in a Melitz-type model. Finally, we show our results are robust to potential country-selection, firm-heterogeneity, and reverse causality biases.

The remainder of this paper is as follows. Section 2 discusses our methodology, based on the HK linear trade-margins-decomposition method and the Baier and Bergstrand (2007) approach for estimating partial effects of EIAs on trade flows in gravity frameworks. Section 3 discusses data and measurement issues. Section 4 provides the main empirical results and findings from three sensitivity analyses. Section 5 concludes.

2. Methodology

Only three empirical studies have explored the effects of trade liberalizations – and, in particular, EIAs – on the intensive and extensive goods margins of trade using the HK methodology. The earliest study using the HK decomposition to explore this issue is Hillberry and McDaniel (2002), focusing solely on the North American Free Trade Agreement (NAFTA). Although they do not attempt to establish causal effects from NAFTA to trade increases, they provide a decomposition of post-NAFTA trade among the three partners into goods intensive and extensive margins using 4-digit Standard International Trade Classification (SITC) data. They find evidence of both margins changing between 1993 and 2001. Kehoe and Ruhl (2009) examined NAFTA, the earlier Canada–U.S. FTA trade liberalization, and some structural

[3] Each "good" was a 6-digit SITC category. They also explored the effects of country size and per capita GDP on the quality of goods exported, as well as the two margins.

[4] Because firm-level data is not available for a large number of country-pairs for a large number of years, we are constrained to investigating EIAs impacts on products defined at the 4-digit SITC category level, as in Hillberry and McDaniel (2002), Kehoe and Ruhl (2009), and Foster et al. (2011) discussed below.

[5] For instance, welfare estimates could be sensitive to the presence or absence of intermediates or multiple sectors. See also Melitz and Redding (2013) and Feenstra and Weinstein (2013).

[6] The HK methodology is based on Feenstra (1994). Due to few observations on common markets and economic unions, we combine these two types of "deeper" EIAs with customs unions to form the variable CUCMECU, representing "deep" EIAs.

[7] The two studies that extended the Baier–Bergstrand framework to differing types of EIAs are Magee (2008) and Roy (2010); both found that customs unions had larger aggregate trade flow effects than FTAs. However, neither study examined extensive versus intensive margin issues.

[8] Ruhl (2008) explains the delayed effect of the extensive-margin effects to fixed export costs on the supply side, while Arkolakis et al. (2011) explain the delayed effect of the extensive-margin effects to "Calvo pricing" by consumers on the demand side.

transformations using a modified version of the HK decomposition methodology and applied to a series of cross sections. Similar to Hillberry and McDaniel (2002), they do not conduct an econometric analysis trying to explain the effect of NAFTA (or the Canada–U.S. FTA) on trade flows conditional on other variables. They decompose actual goods extensive and intensive margin changes post-agreement also using 4-digit SITC data for goods categories from Feenstra et al. (2005). They find significant evidence of both extensive and intensive margin changes using their modified HK decomposition methodology. Both studies' evidence of goods intensive and extensive margins of trade expanding following the signing of NAFTA suggests the need for a comprehensive *econometric* analysis (conditional on other covariates) of the effects of EIAs in general on the goods intensive and extensive margins of trade, in the spirit of HK's original analysis of the effect of country size and per capita GDP on the two goods' margins.

The only study to our knowledge that like us uses a data set for a large number of country pairs and years, a large number of EIAs, and the HK methodology is Foster et al. (2011). However, the partial effect they found of an EIA on the goods extensive margin was an economically insignificant 10%, and they found virtually no effect of EIAs on the intensive margin. The latter result is a puzzle because it is existing exporters and importers that seek EIAs and the theoretical studies noted above suggest that the shorter-term effect of EIAs should be on the intensive margin. Yet, there are several differences between our study and theirs. First, their estimation was based upon a traditional gravity-equation specification ignoring recent theoretical developments that emphasize the importance of relative price or "multilateral resistance" terms. Our paper is based upon state-of-the-art gravity-equation specifications, such as discussed in Arkolakis et al. (2012). Second, Foster et al. (2011) use a short three-year window on both sides of the EIA formation, and consequently can only capture *short-term* EIA effects; this likely explains their economically small partial effects but does not explain finding only an extensive margin effect. As shown in Baier and Bergstrand (2007), EIAs can take 10–15 years to have their full impact on aggregate bilateral trade flows. Moreover, by allowing longer lags, we can distinguish between short-term vs. longer-term effects. Third, Foster et al. (2011) examine the impact of EIAs using a single dummy variable; we use multiple EIA variables to distinguish the effects of one-way PTAs, two-way PTAs, FTAs, and deeper EIAs on aggregate trade flows, extensive margins, and intensive margins. Even disregarding the potential endogeneity biases introduced by their ignoring relative prices, their study did not distinguish between various "types" of EIAs and did not distinguish between the "timing" of intensive and extensive margin effects. Indeed, Foster et al. (2011) suggest in their concluding paragraph that examination of the shorter-run versus longer-run effects and accounting for the differing "depth and breadth" of EIAs would be useful extensions.

2.1. The gravity equation

As Arkolakis et al. (2012) and others have noted, there is a number of models commonly considered in the trade literature (such as Armington, Krugman, Ricardian, Melitz) that yield iso-morphic gravity equations. Following Arkolakis et al. (2012), using a Melitz model one can generate a standard gravity equation:

$$X_{ijt}^{m} = N_{it}^{m} Y_{jt}^{m} \left(\frac{(a_{Lit}^{m})^{-\gamma^m} w_{it}^{-\gamma^m} \tau_{ijt}^{-\gamma^m} f_{ijt}^{-[\gamma^m/(\sigma^m-1)-1]}}{\sum_{k=1}^{K} N_{kt}^{m} (a_{Lkt}^{m})^{-\gamma^m} w_{kt}^{-\gamma^m} \tau_{kjt}^{-\gamma^m} f_{kjt}^{-[\gamma^m/(\sigma^m-1)-1]}} \right) \tag{1}$$

where X_{ijt}^{m} is the trade flow from i to j in year t in "good" m, N_{it}^{m} is the number of firms in i (exporting and non-exporting) that produce output in good m, Y_{jt}^{m} is the expenditure in j on good m, a_{Lit}^{m} (defined as unit input requirements of labor) is the lower bound of the Pareto distribution of productivities in m in i, γ^m is an index of productivity heterogeneity among firms in good m, w_{it} is the wage rate in i, τ_{ijt} is variable trade costs of exporting i's products into j, f_{ijt} is fixed export costs from i to j, and σ^m is the elasticity of substitution in consumption.[9] Note that the relative price term in large parentheses is a standard representation of relative prices in the gravity equation, but now also reflecting productivity heterogeneity (through a_{Lit}^{m} and γ^m) and fixed exporting costs (f_{ijt}), cf., Melitz (2003), Chaney (2008), Redding (2011), and Arkolakis et al. (2012).

In the context of these models, variable trade costs, τ_{ijt}, affect X_{ijt}^{m} via both the intensive and extensive margins. As Chaney (2008) demonstrates in his Melitz-type model, $\gamma^m = (\sigma^m - 1) + [\gamma^m - (\sigma^m - 1)]$. $\sigma^m - 1$ represents the intensive margin elasticity of variable trade costs whereas $\gamma^m - (\sigma^m - 1)$ is the extensive margin elasticity of variable trade costs. For finite means in the theory, $\gamma^m/(\sigma^m - 1)$ must exceed 1. Empirically, Chaney (2008) notes empirical estimates of $\gamma^m/(\sigma^m - 1)$ range between 1.5 and 2. Hence, these models suggest that the intensive margin variable-trade-cost elasticity *should be larger* than the extensive margin variable-trade-cost elasticity. For instance, if $\gamma = 1.5(\sigma - 1)$, then the intensive margin elasticity is twice as large as the extensive margin elasticity; if $\gamma = 2(\sigma - 1)$, then the intensive margin elasticity is equal to the extensive margin elasticity.[10]

Interestingly, the theoretical result that the (variable-trade-cost) intensive margin elasticity should be at least as large as the extensive margin elasticity *conflicts* with the empirical results for the EIA partial effects in Foster et al. (2011) discussed earlier. We evaluate empirically this implication later, a potential contribution of this paper.

2.2. Accounting for endogenous EIAs: the Baier–Bergstrand methodology

Baier and Bergstrand (2007), or BB, re-evaluated usage of the gravity equation econometrically for estimating partial effects of EIAs on pairs of countries' trade flows.[11] The first of two main contributions was that self-selection of country-pairs into EIAs (cf., Baier and Bergstrand, 2004) likely created a significant endogeneity bias in previous gravity-equation estimates of the (partial) effects of EIAs on trade flows. This is precisely the concern raised in Arkolakis et al. (2012, section V) for gravity-equation estimates of trade elasticities; the observed variable trade cost measure may be correlated with unobservable trade costs hidden in the gravity equation's error term. The second main contribution of BB was that – given the slow-moving nature of EIAs' determinations – gravity equation estimation could use panel techniques and data to avoid endogeneity bias and also capture lagged influences, incorporating either bilateral fixed effects (in a log-levels specification) or first-differencing to account for time-invariant bilateral unobservable RHS variables, as well as incorporating exporter-time and importer-time effects to capture time-varying unobservable "multilateral price/resistance" terms of the exporter and importer. BB showed that EIAs on average increased two members' bilateral trade by approximately 100% after 10–15 years. Such a panel approach allows estimates of the "timing" of EIAs' effects on trade flows between short run and long

[9] We refer here to Eq. (23) in Arkolakis et al. (2012), under the assumption that fixed export costs are paid in the importing country (i.e., $\mu = 0$).

[10] However, f_{ijt} works entirely through the extensive margin, so that there is no clear theoretical hypothesis for the relative sizes of intensive and extensive margin effects of a given EIA formation. Yet, in light of estimates of $\gamma/(\sigma - 1)$ between 1.5 and 2, this additional fixed-trade-cost elasticity can range feasibly between only 0.5 and 1. Such an effect is dwarfed by the intensive margin elasticity $(\sigma - 1)$ with likely values between 4 and 9 (if σ ranges between 5 and 10), under certain assumptions. The key assumption pertains to the effect of an EIA on fixed costs versus variable costs. Suppose $ln\tau_{ijt} = \rho_0 - \rho_1 lnDIST_{ij} - \rho_2 EIA_{ijt} + \mu_{ijt}$, as is conventional ($\mu_{ijt}$ denoting a random error term). Suppose also $lnf_{ijt} = \delta_0 - \delta_1 lnDIST_{ij} - \delta_2 EIA_{ijt} + \phi_{ijt}$ (ϕ_{ijt} denoting a random error term). If $\delta_2 > \rho_2$ by a large amount, the effect of f_{ijt} changes on the extensive margin may be sufficient to cause the extensive margin trade elasticity to exceed the intensive margin trade elasticity. To date, to our knowledge, there are no firm estimates of δ_2 because there is no data on lnf_{ijt}.

[11] Partial (or direct) effects ignore general-equilibrium (or indirect) effects. While techniques exist for estimating the indirect effects, such estimation is beyond this paper's scope, cf., Anderson (2011), Bergstrand and Egger (2011), and Egger et al. (2011) on these issues.

run, as well as offers an alternative approach to instrumental variables using cross-sectional data (and potentially avoids possible shortcomings of the latter approach).[12]

Given the problems associated with accounting for endogeneity of EIAs using instrumental variables and cross-section data, BB argued that a better approach to eliminate endogeneity bias of EIAs is to use panel techniques. In the context of the theory and endogenous self-selection of country pairs into EIAs, BB argued that one method to obtain consistent estimates of the partial effect of EIAs is by fixed effects estimation of:

$$\ln X_{ijt} = \beta_0 + \beta_1\left(EIA_{ijt}\right) + \eta_{ij} + \delta_{it} + \psi_{jt} + \epsilon_{ijt} \qquad (2)$$

where η_{ij} is a country-pair fixed effect to capture all time-invariant unobservable bilateral factors influencing nominal trade flows and δ_{it} and ψ_{jt} are exporter-time and importer-time fixed effects, respectively, to capture time-varying exporter and importer GDPs as well as all other time-varying country-specific unobservables in i and j influencing trade, *including* the exporter's and importers' "multilateral price/resistance" terms (cf., Anderson and van Wincoop, 2003). We refer to this as the fixed-effects (FE) specification. It is important to note that, in most gravity-equation applications using a comprehensive set of RHS variables, the vast bulk of "bilateral" trade-cost variables are time-invariant, such as bilateral distance, common border, common language, etc. BB showed that the partial effect of the typical EIA on nominal trade flows was about 0.76, implying that the typical EIA increased bilateral trade by about114% after 10–15 years.

BB also employed an alternative specification using first-differencing:

$$\Delta_5 \ln X_{ijt} = \beta_0 + \beta_1\left(\Delta_5 EIA_{ijt}\right) + \delta_{5,it} + \psi_{5,jt} + \upsilon_{5,ijt} \qquad (3)$$

where Δ_5 refers to first-differencing over 5 years. We refer to this as the first-difference (FD) specification. Note that the bilateral country-pair fixed effects are eliminated; however, the exporter-time ($\delta_{5,it}$) and importer-time ($\psi_{5,jt}$) fixed effects are retained to capture *changes* in the time-varying exporter and importer GDPs and multilateral price terms over the same 5-year period. The latter effects were ignored in Foster et al. (2011), creating potential omitted variables bias.

First-differencing the panel data yields some potential advantages over fixed effects.[13] First, it is quite plausible that the unobserved factors influencing the likelihood of an EIA (say, trade below its "natural" level) are likely slow moving and hence serially correlated. If the ϵ_{ijt} are highly serially correlated, the inefficiency of FE is exacerbated as T gets large. This suggests that differencing the data will increase estimation efficiency for our large-T panel. Second, aggregate trade flow data and real GDP data are likely "close to" unit-root processes. Using FE is equivalent to differencing data around the mean (in our sample, year 1980); this may create a problem since T is large in our panel. As Wooldridge (2000, p. 447) notes, if the data follow unit-root processes and T is large, the "spurious regression problem" can arise in a panel using FE. FD yields data that deviates from the previous period of our panel, and thus is closer to a unit-root process. In the following, we focus on a first-difference approach; however, the FE estimates are provided in the online appendix to this paper.[14]

In this paper, we introduce one further innovation relative to BB.[15] While changes over time in exporter-specific and importer-specific unobservable variables are captured with δ_5 and ψ_5, changes over time in *pair-specific* unobservables, such as falling variable and fixed export costs unrelated to EIAs, are not accounted for. Wooldridge (2000) suggests a "random growth" (also called, random trend) first-difference model, henceforth, RGFD model. Unobservable pair-specific changes over time can be partially accounted for by including pair-specific ij fixed effects in Eq. (3), suggesting specification:

$$\Delta_5 \ln X_{ijt} = \beta_0 + \beta_1\left(\Delta_5 EIA_{ijt}\right) + \delta_{5,it} + \psi_{5,jt} + \eta_{ij} + \upsilon_{5,ijt}. \qquad (4)$$

Consequently, if unobservable declines in bilateral variable and fixed trade costs (say, due to technological improvements) evolve smoothly over time, the η_{ij}s in Eq. (4) will account for these influences. The incorporation of such fixed effects (η_{ij}s) in a first-difference specification was used in Trefler (2004), with such effects referred to there as "secular growth" controls.

One of the other potential contributions of BB's panel methodology was to show that the full impact of EIAs on trade flows took 10–15 years. One reason is that most EIAs are "phased-in" over 5–10 years. The second reason is the lagged effect of the trade-cost changes (such as terms-of-trade changes) on trade flows. As in BB, using a panel allows for differentiating the shorter-term effects (5 years) from the longer-term effects (5–10 years). In the context of the recent developments in the trade literature emphasizing intensive versus extensive margin effects, our panel approach allows for differential timing of these effects. In reality, one would expect that the intensive margin would be affected by a trade-cost change sooner than the extensive margin, because intensive margin changes in volumes do not require any startup costs. Such costs – critical to the extensive margin – may delay the entry of new firms into exporting, and thus we should expect the intensive margin to be influenced in the shorter term and the extensive margin in the longer term, as the results in Bernard et al. (2009) show. Our panel data approach allows for evaluating this hypothesis.[16]

It will be useful now to rationalize the use of 5-year differencing of data as in BB, rather than, say, annual differencing. Cheng and Wall (2005) and Wooldridge (2000) both argue in favor of using data differenced over a longer period than annually. Cheng and Wall (2005, p. 8) note that "Fixed-effects estimations are sometimes criticized when applied to data pooled over consecutive years on the grounds that dependent and independent variables cannot fully adjust in a single year's time." Wooldridge (2000, p. 423) confirms the reduction in standard errors of coefficient estimates using changes over longer periods of time than using "year-to-year" changes. Based upon these considerations, we chose as in BB 5-year differences; similar considerations led to the use of 4-year differences in Anderson and Yotov (2011).

[12] As argued in BB, the problem with using cross-section data and consequently having to employ IV techniques to account for EIA selection bias is the inability practically of satisfying the "exclusion restriction" with confidence. Most variables that influence trade flows also explain selection into EIAs, and it is difficult to find a variable that explains EIAs that does not also explain trade flows. Egger et al. (2011) used the IV approach to account for the endogeneity of EIAs in their single cross-section, also allowing for selection into zeros trade (i.e., a bivariate probit model). They found using an approach similar to Helpman et al. (2008), except also allowing for endogenous EIAs, that EIAs predominantly affected trade at the (country) intensive margin.

[13] As Wooldridge (2010, Ch. 10) notes, when the number of time periods (T) exceeds two, the FE estimator is more efficient under the assumption of serially uncorrelated error terms ϵ_{ijt}. The FD estimator is more efficient (when $T > 2$) under the assumption that the error term ϵ_{ijt} follows a random walk (i.e., that the error term $\upsilon_{5,ijt} = \epsilon_{ijt} - \epsilon_{ij,t-5}$ is white noise). When the number of time periods is exactly two ($T = 2$), estimation with FE and FD produce identical estimates and inferences; then, FD is easier to estimate. When $T > 2$, the choice depends upon the assumption one wants to make about the distribution of the error term ϵ_{ijt}.

[14] It turns out that, for FTAs and deeper EIAs, the results using FE and FD are quite similar. As a practical matter, the choice is more important for TWPTAs and OWPTAs; we discuss this later.

[15] We thank a referee and the editor for motivating this innovation.

[16] These differential timing effects were ignored in Foster et al. (2011). As discussed earlier, two recent theoretical papers suggest a reason for the low trade-cost elasticity of trade flows in macroeconomic analyses using time-series data and the relatively higher trade-cost elasticities of trade in cross-sectional trade analyses. Ruhl (2008) explains this puzzle by noting that the macroeconomic time-series approach is estimating the intensive margin effect of trade, whereas the trade literature's cross-sectional approach is capturing the intensive and extensive margin effects, due to export fixed costs for new producers delaying trade effects and entry. In a complementary approach, Arkolakis et al. (2011) present a demand-oriented staggered-adjustment "Calvo-pricing" approach to explain the lower time-series elasticity in terms of solely an intensive margin effect, and the higher long-run cross-section trade–cost elasticity capturing the longer-term extensive margin elasticity also.

Nevertheless, in a sensitivity analysis later, we will confirm our findings using annual data.

BB did not estimate differential effects of various types of EIAs (in terms of depth of integration) on trade flows. Magee (2008) and Roy (2010) using the methodology of BB found that trade flows were impacted by larger amounts for customs unions relative to FTAs. However, no empirical study has examined the differential impact of FTAs relative to deeper EIAs on the extensive versus intensive margins – much less the differential timing of such effects; these are goals of this paper.[17] The next section discusses how we decompose data into the two margins.

2.3. The Hummels–Klenow margin-decomposition methodology

Hummels and Klenow (2005), or HK, was the first paper to highlight a tractable method for decomposing transparently the extensive and intensive *goods* margins of trade for a large set of countries' bilateral trade flows using publicly available disaggregate trade data.[18]

Let X_{ijt} denote the value of country i's exports to country j in year t. Following HK, the extensive margin of goods exported from i to j in any year t is defined as:

$$EM_{ijt} = \frac{\sum_{m \in M_{ijt}} X^m_{Wjt}}{\sum_{m \in M_{Wjt}} X^m_{Wjt}} \tag{5}$$

where X^m_{Wjt} is the value of country j's imports from the world in product m in year t, M_{Wjt} is the set of all products exported by the world to j in year t, and M_{ijt} is the subset of all products exported from i to j in year t. Hence, EM_{ijt} is a measure of the fraction of all products that are exported from i to j in year t, where each product is weighted by the importance of that product in world exports to j in year t.[19]

HK define the intensive margin of goods exported from i to j as:

$$IM_{ijt} = \frac{\sum_{m \in M_{ijt}} X^m_{ijt}}{\sum_{m \in M_{ijt}} X^m_{Wjt}} \tag{6}$$

where X^m_{ijt} is the value of exports from i to j in product m in year t. Thus, IM_{ijt} represents the market share of country i in country j's imports from the world within the set of products that i exports to j in year t.

One of the notable properties of the HK decomposition methodology is that the product of the two margins equals the ratio of exports from i to j relative to country j total imports:

$$EM_{ijt} IM_{ijt} = \frac{\sum_{m \in M_{ijt}} X_{ijmt}}{\sum_{m \in M_{Wjt}} X_{Wjmt}} = X_{ijt}/X_{jt} \tag{7}$$

where X_{jt} denotes j's imports from the world. Taking the natural logs of Eq. (7) and some algebra yields:

$$\ln X_{ijt} = \ln EM_{ijt} + lnIM_{ijt} + \ln X_{jt}. \tag{8}$$

Consequently, the HK decomposition methodology yields that the log of the value of the trade flow from i to j in any year t can be decomposed *linearly* into (logs of) an extensive margin, an intensive margin, and the value of j's imports from the world. We note three issues regarding the HK methodology. First, since we will focus empirically on the RGFD specification similar to Eq. (4), the term $\Delta_5 lnX_{jt}$ will be subsumed in the importer-time fixed effect $\psi_{5,jt}$. Second, HK applied their methodology to only a cross section. By contrast, we are applying it to a time series of cross sections. Consequently, the trade weights used in constructing EM_{ijt} and IM_{ijt} will likely vary from year to year. To address this, we will also consider later in a sensitivity analysis fixed-year trade-share weights and also a chain-weighting technique. Third, there are numerous zeros in the variables in Eq. (8) and the results may be biased by ignoring the existence of firm heterogeneity. Hence, we will address later why our panel approach largely alleviates sample-selection bias and firm-heterogeneity bias, as raised in Helpman et al. (2008).[20]

Finally, we are distinguishing between various types of EIAs and allow for lagged effects. Hence, the actual specification for the RGFD versions of our model with no lags is:

$$\begin{aligned} \Delta_5 \ln X_{ijt} = {} & \beta_0 + \beta_1 \left(\Delta_5 CUCMECU_{ijt}\right) + \beta_2 \left(\Delta_5 FTA_{ijt}\right) + \beta_3 \left(\Delta_5 TWPTA_{ijt}\right) \\ & + \beta_4 \left(\Delta_5 OWPTA_{ijt}\right) + \delta_{5,it} + \psi_{5,jt} + \eta_{ij} + \upsilon_{5,ijt} \end{aligned} \tag{9}$$

$$\begin{aligned} \Delta_5 \ln EM_{ijt} = {} & \theta_0 + \theta_1 \left(\Delta_5 CUCMECU_{ijt}\right) + \theta_2 \left(\Delta_5 FTA_{ijt}\right) + \theta_3 \left(\Delta_5 TWPTA_{ijt}\right) \\ & + \theta_4 \left(\Delta_5 OWPTA_{ijt}\right) + \delta_{5,it} + \psi_{5,jt} + \eta_{ij} + \upsilon_{5,ijt} \end{aligned} \tag{10}$$

$$\begin{aligned} \Delta_5 \ln IM_{ijt} = {} & \lambda_0 + \lambda_1 \left(\Delta_5 CUCMECU_{ijt}\right) + \lambda_2 \left(\Delta_5 FTA_{ijt}\right) + \lambda_3 \left(\Delta_5 TWPTA_{ijt}\right) \\ & + \lambda_4 \left(\Delta_5 OWPTA_{ijt}\right) + \delta_{5,it} + \psi_{5,jt} + \eta_{ij} + \upsilon_{5,ijt}. \end{aligned} \tag{11}$$

In specifications including lagged EIA variables, we will use, for instance, the notation $Lag\Delta_5 EIA_{ijt}$ to denote an EIA formed 5 to 10 years prior to the trade-flow change and $Lead\Delta_5 EIA_{ijt}$ to denote an EIA formed in the 5 years prior to the trade-flow change. Recall that *OWPTA* denotes a one-way preferential trade agreement, *TWPTA* denotes a two-way preferential trade agreement, *FTA* denotes a free trade agreement, and *CUCMECU* denotes "deeper" EIAs, defined just below.

Consequently, the literature to date suggests that the endogeneity of EIAs in typical gravity equations may bias the estimation of partial effects of EIAs on trade flows and trade margins. We augment the panel approach in BB to account for random growth in bilateral trade flows and the margins of trade due to unobservable changes in bilateral

---

[17] It is useful to note here a parallel literature examining the effect of GATT and/or WTO membership on trade flows. For brevity, we note that there now appears little convincing evidence of substantive GATT/WTO effects on trade, once one accounts for EIA dummies, multilateral resistance, and unobserved country-pair fixed effects (as we do here). This is the conclusion of Eicher and Henn (2011) (though they found a non-trivial WTO "terms-of-trade" effect) and of Felbermayr and Kohler (2010) who examined possible extensive margin effects; Eicher and Henn (2011) ignored extensive versus intensive margin effects. We also note an issue raised in Martin and Ng (2004), which is the role of multilateral tariff reductions under the GATT/WTO. Most-Favored-Nation (MFN) tariff cuts could also be affecting results. However, such MFN tariff cuts by country would be accounted for by the exporter-time and importer-time fixed effects.

[18] Studies have also used country-specific data on individual plants (or firms) to study the extensive and intensive *firm* margins of trade liberalization, but such studies have necessarily been confined to particular countries because such data is widely known to be much more costly to access and such data sets have not been concorded for international comparisons, as noted in Helpman et al. (2008). See Eaton et al. (2008) for a study of French firms, Trefler (2004) for a study of Canada and the United States, and Pavcnik (2002) for a study of Indian firms. Another relevant theoretical and empirical piece with similar overtones is Arkolakis et al. (2008).

[19] Alternatively, one could use an unweighted average, which would then be simply the fraction of all products exported from i to j. However, HK – as well as researchers since then – use the weighted average. A weighted average seems more appropriate since cars and pencils do not have the same values in trade. Also, since we will use a time series of cross sections, we will consider later two alternative methods for fixing the trade-share weights over time.

[20] Besedes and Prusa (2011) emphasize that extensive margin (intensive margin) effects may be overstated (understated) in examining effects of liberalizations using panel data, due to "survival" issues. Addressing this issue is beyond the scope of this particular paper. However, our results may not be biased excessively by this issue since we find material intensive margin effects from EIAs, unlike Foster et al. (2011).

variable and fixed export costs that evolve smoothly over time. We follow the methodology established in HK to decompose trade flows (log-) linearly into extensive and intensive margins. In the next section, we estimate equations such as Eqs. (9)–(11) above to determine if both intensive and extensive (goods) margins are affected by EIAs, the differential effects of various "types" of EIAs on these extensive and intensive margins of trade, and the differential "timing" of the partial effects of EIAs on the two margins.

3. Data

The two key variables for our empirical analysis are disaggregate bilateral trade flows and a multichotomous index of the level of economic integration agreement (EIA) between a large number of country pairs for a large number of years.

First, while several earlier gravity-equation analyses have used dummy variables indicating the presence or absence of an EIA between country pairs for numerous years, such as Rose (2004), there are few publicly available systematic data sets that have multichotomous indexes of EIAs for a large number of country pairs and number of years (a panel). We use the data set constructed by Scott Baier and Jeffrey Bergstrand and provided at Jeffrey Bergstrand's website, www.nd.edu/jbergstr/.[21] The index is defined as: no EIA (0), one-way preferential trade agreement, or *OWPTA* (1), two-way preferential trade agreement *TWPTA* (2), free trade agreement, or *FTA* (3), customs union (4), common market (5), and economic union (6). The definitions are conventional, based upon Frankel (1997), and are defined explicitly in the data set. Because of the small number of "deeper EIAs," we combined customs unions (4), common markets (5), and economic unions (6) into one variable, *CUCMECU*. One of the strengths of the Baier–Bergstrand EIA panel is, for 98.6% of the cells where the EIA status of the country pair changes (from 0 to 1, 0 to 3, 2 to 3, etc.), there exists a hyperlink to a copy (PDF format) of the original treaty. Because of the extensive number of bilateral and plurilateral EIAs of differing degrees of depth, the difficulty of listing all such agreements precludes a table; we recommend downloading the zip file from the web site.

Second, annual bilateral trade flows for 1962–2000 are from the NBER-United Nations trade data set at www.nber.org/data and documented in Feenstra et al. (2005). The data are organized by 4-digit SITC, Revision 2. It covers trade flows reported by 149 countries and covers 98% of world exports. This is the most disaggregated publicly available data set for bilateral trade flows for a large number of years and a large number of country pairs, constructed on a consistent basis, necessary for the analysis at hand. This 4-digit SITC data was also used in Hillberry and McDaniel (2002), Kehoe and Ruhl (2009), and Foster et al. (2011). In 1962, this resulted in 969 categories of "goods"; in 2000, this resulted in 1,289 categories of goods. One concern is that the level of disaggregation is not high enough, biasing results toward the intensive margin, as discussed transparently in HK; as one aggregates up, there become fewer categories in which a country does not export. Other studies have used higher levels of disaggregation to calculate trade flows in a good to avoid this (intensive margin) aggregation bias. For instance, Broda and Weinstein (2006) used 7-digit data for the years 1972–1988 and then 10-digit data for the years 1990–2001. However, this was *U.S.* import data only, and for two short panels. Constraining ourselves to U.S. import trade flows only is problematic because the United States has only a small number of FTAs and has no deep EIAs, precluding evaluating our hypotheses. Since our decomposition of the extensive and intensive margins is based upon HK, we compare our data set to theirs. First, HK used only a cross section of UNCTAD TRAINS data for the year 1995, but for a large number of country pairs like here.[22] Using a cross section is problematic because we are relying upon panel techniques to avoid endogeneity bias. Second, HK used data at the Harmonized System 6-digit classification code; this yielded 5017 goods categories, five times our number of categories. However, HK examined the levels of extensive margins and the correlations between the extensive margin and factors influencing the extensive margin in cross-sectional data – GDP, employment (L), GDP/L – at various levels of aggregation (1-digit, 2-digit, ..., 6-digit) and found two interesting results. As expected, extensive margins were much lower, and the correlation between the extensive margin of trade and determinants of it (such as GDP) were lower, as data became more aggregated. For example, at the 6-digit level, 62% of the GDP elasticity of exports could be explained by the extensive margin, whereas at the 1-digit level only 11% of the elasticity could be explained by the extensive margin. However, interestingly, at the 4-digit level, a sizable 54% of this elasticity could *still* be explained by the extensive margin. For the per capita GDP elasticity of exports, 66 (62) percent of this elasticity was explained by the extensive margin at the 6-digit (4-digit) level. These results suggest that the (intensive margin) aggregation bias may not be that severe in using 4-digit categories, rather than the 6-digit categories in HK.

In a previous section, we provided an econometric justification for using 5-year differencing of the data (beginning in 1970 and ending in 2000, i.e., the first 5-year period is 1965–1970). Nevertheless, in a sensitivity analysis later, we will confirm our empirical findings using annual data. Due to space constraints of the journal, we focus in this paper on the random growth first-difference (RGFD) results. However, FD results (without random-growth trends) and fixed effects results in levels are reported in an online appendix.

4. Empirical results

The main empirical results for Eqs. (9)–(11) are presented in Table 1 in Section 4.1. In Section 4.2, Table 2 reports another set of RGFD results using an alternative chain-weighted technique for weights, due to the estimation of a time series of cross sections. In Section 4.3, we discuss the role of potential endogeneity bias due to country selection and firm heterogeneity. We address how our panel techniques largely alleviate these biases, raised in Helpman et al. (2008). In Section 4.4, we address the sensitivity of the findings to using instead annual data and show why the results are largely insensitive to reverse causality bias.

Within each set are the results of running the same specification for three alternative LHS variables. TRADE refers to the aggregate bilateral trade flow from i to j (or X_{ijt} in Eq. (8)). EM refers to the extensive margin (or EM_{ijt} in Eq. (8)). IM refers to the intensive margin (or IM_{ijt} in Eq. (8)). From Eq. (8), once changes in lnX_{jt} are controlled for with importer-year fixed effect ψ, the sum of variations in the extensive and intensive margins must equal the variation in the aggregate trade flow. This allows us to use the empirical results to infer the relative extensive and intensive margin elasticities to a trade liberalization.

4.1. Main results

Table 1 reports the results using RGFD Eqs. (9)–(11) with no lag in Set 1 and with one lag in Set 2.[23] Our first set of results in Set 1 is promising; we highlight the key issues. First, we note in column (1a) that deeper EIAs have larger effects on aggregate trade flows than FTAs, and the latter have larger effects on trade than two-way or one-way PTAs, as expected. The coefficient estimates for $\Delta_5 CUCMECU_{ijt}$ and for $\Delta_5 FTA_{ijt}$ are economically and statistically significant. Second, for deep EIAs, FTAs, and one-way PTAs, the intensive-margin effects in

[21] This data set was constructed under National Science Foundation grants SES-0351018 and SES-0351154 and includes annually from 1960 to 2005 for the pairings of 195 countries an index ranging from 0 to 6 of the level of any EIA between the pair.

[22] For robustness, HK also examined a cross section of U.S. imports only at a higher level of disaggregation. But this raises the same problem as in Broda and Weinstein (2006) of U.S. data only.

[23] FD and FE results are in the online appendix.

Table 1
5-Year differenced data.

Variables	Set 1 (RGFD)			Set 2 (RGFD)		
	(1a)	(1b)	(1c)	(2a)	(2b)	(2c)
	Δ_5 ln $TRADE_{ijt}$	Δ_5 ln EM_{ijt}	Δ_5 ln IM_{ijt}	Δ_5 ln $TRADE_{ijt}$	Δ_5 ln EM_{ijt}	Δ_5 ln IM_{ijt}
$\Delta_5 CUCMECU_{ijt}$	0.329***	0.100*	0.229***	0.387***	0.106*	0.281***
	(0.072)	(0.062)	(0.065)	(0.077)	(0.067)	(0.069)
Lag $\Delta_5 CUCMECU_{ijt}$				0.309***	0.131**	0.179***
				(0.076)	(0.065)	(0.072)
$\Delta_5 FTA_{ijt}$	0.192***	0.074*	0.118***	0.242***	0.085**	0.157***
	(0.053)	(0.043)	(0.046)	(0.056)	(0.10046)	(0.049)
Lag ΔFTA_{ijt}				0.228***	0.084**	0.145***
				(0.055)	(0.047)	(0.049)
$\Delta_5 TWPTA_{ijt}$	−0.001	0.012	−0.013	0.069	0.023	0.046
	(0.072)	(0.055)	(0.063)	(0.079)	(0.063)	(0.068)
Lag $\Delta_5 TWPTA_{ijt}$				0.111*	0.071	0.041
				(0.071)	(0.063)	(0.068)
$\Delta_5 OWPTA_{ijt}$	0.072	−0.064	0.135**	0.116**	−0.043	0.159***
	(0.065)	(0.053)	(0.062)	(0.067)	(0.055)	(0.063)
Lag $\Delta_5 OWPTA_{ijt}$				0.285***	0.171***	0.114**
				(0.069)	(0.055)	(0.067)
Constant	0.413***	0.167*	0.247*	0.608***	−0.089	0.697**
	(0.120)	(0.130)	(0.182)	(0.247)	(0.274)	(0.342)
Fixed effects						
Exporter-year $(i,t-(t-5))$	Yes	Yes	Yes	Yes	Yes	Yes
Importer-year $(j,t-(t-5))$	Yes	Yes	Yes	Yes	Yes	Yes
Country-pair (ij)	Yes	Yes	Yes	Yes	Yes	Yes
R^2	0.294	0.365	0.357	0.330	0.402	0.403
No. of observations	48,619	48,619	48,619	41,767	41,767	41,767

Notes: Robust standard errors in parentheses. *, **, and *** denote statistical significance at the 10, 5, and 1% levels, respectively, in two-tailed t-tests.

column (1c) are economically and statistically significant. The effect is largest for $\Delta_5 CUCMECU_{ijt}$, next largest for $\Delta_5 OWPTA_{ijt}$, and slightly smaller for $\Delta_5 FTA_{ijt}$; the $\Delta_5 TWPTA_{ijt}$ effect is trivially small. The extensive margin effects in column (1b) are statistically significant for deep EIAs and FTAs; moreover, the extensive margin effect for $\Delta_5 CUCMECU_{ijt}$ is larger than that for $\Delta_5 FTA_{ijt}$, as expected. Third, we note that – in the absence of lagged effects – for deep EIAs, FTAs, and OWPTAs the intensive margin effect is *always larger* than its corresponding extensive margin effect, consistent with our interpretation of the Melitz model in Chaney (2008). Thus, the Set 1 results using specifications (9)–(11) provide substantive support for three major hypotheses. However, by adding a lagged change in the EIAs, we can even provide evidence for a fourth hypothesis, extensive (intensive) margin effects should become relatively more (less) important with time.

Even more interesting are the results in Set 2 where we allow current and lagged changes, consequently capturing the effects on trade and the margins of 10 years of EIA changes. As discussed earlier and in BB, EIAs are likely to have delayed impacts on trade flows. One reason is that EIAs are typically "phased-in" over 5 to 10 years, delaying the full implementation of liberalization. Second, the impact on trade flows of EIAs works largely through terms-of-trade effects. It is well known that terms-of-trade changes can also have a delayed impact on trade flows. BB found that most of the impact of EIAs on aggregate trade flows was captured using panel techniques in a period of 10 years. Consider deep EIAs in columns (2a)–(2c). First, for aggregate trade, consistent with earlier results, common membership in a deep EIA increases two members' bilateral trade flow by a plausible 101% after 10 years ($e^{0.387+0.309}=2.01$). Second, we find that in the short term, the effect on trade comes primarily through the intensive margin, as expected. The intensive-margin effect (0.281) dominates the extensive-margin effect (0.106) for $\Delta_5 CUCMECU_{ijt}$, with both effects statistically significant. However, for the lagged change the extensive margin effect (0.131) is statistically significant and larger than the current-period extensive margin effect. Also, while the lagged intensive margin effect (0.179) is statistically significant, it is smaller than the current-period intensive margin effect (0.281). Third, when we sum the current period and lagged effects for each margin, we find an extensive margin effect of 0.237 and an intensive margin effect of 0.460, consistent with our theoretical conjecture on the relative size of intensive margin and extensive margin elasticities.

Consider now FTAs. First, for aggregate trade, common membership in an FTA increases two members' bilateral trade flow by 60% after 10 years ($e^{0.242+0.228}=1.60$). The intensive margin effect dominates the extensive margin effect in both current period and lagged period. The extensive margin effect does not increase over time; however, in a robustness analysis later for the FD specification, we find the relative size of the extensive margin effect increasing in the lag. Second, when we sum the current-period and lagged effects for each margin, we find an extensive margin effect of 0.169 and an intensive margin effect of 0.302. Hence, the ratio of these effects is similar to that for *CUCMECU*, with the intensive margin elasticity larger than the extensive margin elasticity as expected.

For two-way PTAs, we found in Set 2 only a statistically significant effect of the lagged $\Delta_5 TWPTA$ change on Δ_5 ln $TRADE_{ijt}$. We found only small positive but not statistically significant effects on the two margins. Nevertheless, the relative effects for $\Delta_5 TWPTA_{ijt}$ conformed to earlier results. For the short term, the relatively larger effect was at the intensive margin (0.046 for intensive relative to 0.023 for extensive). For the lagged change, the relatively larger effect was at the extensive margin (0.071 for extensive relative to 0.041 for intensive).

For one-way PTAs, we found in the current period the intensive margin effect (0.159) was economically and statistically significant and dominated the statistically insignificant extensive-margin effect (−0.043). For the lagged effect, the extensive margin effect dominated the intensive margin effect as expected. In fact, the extensive margin effect of 0.171 was statistically significant and the intensive margin effect of 0.114 was also statistically significant.

Our evidence indicates that the four hypotheses posed earlier generally hold. Both extensive and intensive margins are affected by EIAs, deeper EIAs tend to have larger impacts on trade, the extensive margin, and the intensive margin than shallower agreements, and intensive margin effects tend to occur sooner than extensive margin effects. Moreover, total intensive margin elasticities tend to be larger than total extensive margin elasticities, consistent with our fourth hypothesis suggested by the Melitz model in Chaney (2008) and empirical estimates of $\gamma/(\sigma - 1)$. In the next sections, we evaluate the robustness of these results.

4.2. Sensitivity analysis 1: chain-weighting

The original HK analysis of extensive and intensive margins was conducted using a cross section for a particular year (using two alternative data sets). Our analysis uses a time series of cross sections. Consequently, the variables EM_{ijt} and IM_{ijt} defined in Eqs. (5) and (6), respectively, include trade "weights" that change over time. Consequently, we consider two alternative methods for holding constant the trade weights, X_{Wjmt}, over time.

The first alternative measure of the extensive margin, denoted EM^{*}_{ijt}, uses values for X_{Wjmt} set to a "base year"; we chose 1995. Hence, EM^{*}_{ijt} is defined as:

$$EM^{*}_{ijt} = \frac{\sum_{m \in M_{ijt}} X_{Wjm1995}}{\sum_{m \in M_{Wjt}} X_{Wjm1995}} \tag{12}$$

where $X_{Wjm1995}$ is the value of country j's imports from the world in product m in year 1995. M_{Wjt} and M_{ijt} are defined as before. In order to ensure that the log-linear decomposition holds analogous to Eqs. (7) and (8), we define the intensive margin of goods exported from i to j as:

$$IM^{*}_{ijt} = \frac{\sum_{m \in M_{ijt}} X_{ijmt}}{\sum_{m \in M_{ijt}} X_{Wjm1995}}. \tag{13}$$

Consequently, the product of EM^{*}_{ijt} and IM^{*}_{ijt} results in:

$$\ln X_{ijt} = \ln EM^{*}_{ijt} + ln IM^{*}_{ijt} + \ln X_{j1995}. \tag{14}$$

In estimation (using log-levels), the last term on the RHS is subsumed in a fixed effect.

One problem with the fixed-year trade weights is that the particular year chosen may bias the results, especially given that our data set spans 1965–2000. To address this, we considered another trade-weight approach. The second alternative measure for our RGFD specification uses a "chain-weighted" approach. Since the LHS variables are 5-year differences, we used the same chain-weighting technique as used in National Income Accounts. For the X_{Wjmt}s, we used for t the geometric average of the trade flows for the corresponding years.

Table 2 presents in Set 3 the results of using the chain-weighted trade weights; consequently, the results for Set 3 can be compared readily to the previous identical Set 2 specifications (which use the time-varying weights).[24] For brevity, we report only the result for the RGFD specification including one lag. Of course, the alternative weighting approach has no bearing on the aggregate trade flow regressions. It is readily seen that there is no material difference between Set 2 and Set 3 results for the extensive and intensive margins.

4.3. Sensitivity analysis 2: accounting for country-selection and firm-heterogeneity biases

First, as is well known, most bilateral trade flows among a large number of country pairs include numerous observations with "zeros." As noted in both Helpman et al. (2008), or HMR, and Egger et al. (2011), such zeros can be associated with selection bias (often referred to as "selection into exporting"); this can arise from the existence of fixed exporting costs and may be associated with firm heterogeneity in productivities (but does not require it). Second, even in the absence of zero trade flows, the existence of firm heterogeneity may bias our results. Hence, our results may be sensitive to absence of controls for sample-selection and firm-heterogeneity biases. While one option is to adapt the cross-sectional approach of HMR to our panel setting (which we actually do and present in the online appendix), it is unnecessary due to the random-growth first-difference (RGFD) approach we use. We explain in the context of a representative gravity equation generated from a Melitz model, such as Eq. (1). In this case, there are fixed export costs and firm heterogeneity. The key issue is the existence of these two factors allows selection of firms in country i as exporters into destination market j. In our context, let Z^{m}_{ijt} be a latent variable reflecting the ratio of variable export profits to fixed export costs for the most productive firm in country i in year t (a^{m}_{Lit}); positive exports from i to j occur if $Z^{m}_{ijt} > 1$. As discussed in HMR, coefficient estimates in an (aggregate) trade flow gravity equation need to control for variation in Z^{m}_{ijt}; HMR show that accounting for Z^{m}_{ijt} controls both for Heckman selection bias (because the inverse Mills' ratio is a monotonic function of Z^{m}_{ijt}) and for firm-heterogeneity bias (with a control that is a function of both Z^{m}_{ijt} and the inverse Mills' ratio (which is a function of Z^{m}_{ijt})). Hence, for our purposes, we need to account for fluctuations in Z^{m}_{ijt} across country pairs and over time. However, this is the purpose of using the *random-growth* first-difference model. If the factors influencing selection and firm heterogeneity evolve smoothly over time, the RGFD model will account for the controls used in HMR. Unlike the cross-sectional context of HMR and Egger et al. (2011), we use first-differences to eliminate any unobservable differences between country pairs in the time-invariant components of τ^{m}_{ijt}, f^{m}_{ijt}, and Z_{ijt}, and we use the RGFD model to capture any pair-specific time-varying trends in τ^{m}_{ijt}, f^{m}_{ijt}, and Z_{ijt}. Thus, the RGFD model accounts for (unobserved) changes

Table 2
5-Year differenced data (chained).

Variables	Set 3 (RGFD-Chained)		
	(3a)	(3b)	(3c)
	Δ_5 ln $TRADE_{ijt}$	Δ_5 ln EM_{ijt}	Δ_5 ln IM_{ijt}
$\Delta_5 CUCMECU_{ijt}$	0.387***	0.113**	0.274***
	(0.077)	(0.068)	(0.070)
Lag $\Delta_5 CUCMECU_{ijt}$	0.309***	0.124**	0.185***
	(0.076)	(0.067)	(0.073)
$\Delta_5 FTA_{ijt}$	0.242***	0.090**	0.152***
	(0.056)	(0.047)	(0.050)
Lag ΔFTA_{ijt}	0.228***	0.076*	0.153***
	(0.055)	(0.048)	(0.050)
$\Delta_5 TWPTA_{ijt}$	0.069	0.025	0.044
	(0.079)	(0.064)	(0.069)
Lag $\Delta_5 TWPTA_{ijt}$	0.111*	0.053	0.058
	(0.071)	(0.064)	(0.069)
$\Delta_5 OWPTA_{ijt}$	0.116**	−0.051	0.168***
	(0.067)	(0.055)	(0.064)
Lag $\Delta_5 OWPTA_{ijt}$	0.285***	0.168***	0.117**
	(0.069)	(0.060)	(0.068)
Constant	0.608***	−0.066	0.679**
	(0.247)	(0.278)	(0.348)
Fixed effects			
Exporter-year $(i,t-(t-5))$	Yes	Yes	Yes
Importer-year $(j,t-(t-5))$	Yes	Yes	Yes
Country-pair (ij)	Yes	Yes	Yes
R^2	0.330	0.407	0.407
No. of observations	41,767	41,767	41,767

Notes: Robust standard errors in parentheses. *, **, and *** denote statistical significance at the 10, 5, and 1% levels, respectively, in two-tailed t-tests.

[24] The 1995 base-period approach yielded results not materially different.

across pairs and over time in Z_{ijt}^{m}.[25] Nevertheless, for robustness, we also consider an alternative two-stage approach to control for selection bias and firm heterogeneity in the spirit of HMR to capture changes in the controls that might not be fully accounted for using the RGFD model. Due to space constraints, we can only summarize the results of this sensitivity analysis; the actual results are presented in the online appendix. Importantly, as anticipated based upon the discussion above, the main finding is that there is no material difference in the results after correcting for sample-selection bias and firm heterogeneity using a panel adaptation of the HMR cross-sectional approach. To emphasize, this does not imply that selection bias and firm heterogeneity are absent in the data; our results imply that such biases are largely eliminated due to the first-differencing and pair fixed effects in our RGFD regressions.[26]

4.4. Sensitivity analysis 3: annual data and reverse causality

Our preferred methodology has been to use 5-year differences of annual data to estimate the partial effects of various types of EIAs on bilateral trade flows, extensive margins, and intensive margins, although estimates using fixed effects are in the online appendix. Based upon Wooldridge (2000, p. 423) and Cheng and Wall (2005, p. 8), we have argued that 5-year differences are more appropriate than annual differences, due to the likelihood that trade flows cannot adjust *within one year* to EIA formations and that time is needed to capture full effects. This is supported by the result that it can take 10–15 years for an EIA to have its full effect. Nevertheless, we have annual data on EIAs, trade flows, and extensive and intensive margins. For robustness, we examine annual data also because we may be able to find even more evidence of the time path of adjustment of trade flows, extensive margins, and intensive margins to EIAs.

In particular, examination of annual data may be useful to better identify the potential role of "reverse causality." Do EIAs "cause" trade, or does trade "cause" EIAs? This question is relevant because Baier and Bergstrand (2004) showed that the factors that tend to explain bilateral aggregate trade flows also tend to explain the selection of country-pair governments into EIAs. Thus, one might well expect that trade "leads" EIA formations because of this selection effect. However, the key issue here is to try to make sure that these selection effects do not bias our estimates of the partial contemporaneous and lagged effects of EIAs on trade. That is, any leading of trade before EIAs needs to be well in advance of our estimates of EIAs' effects on trade, needs to be economically small, and needs to diminish as the date of entry into the agreement approaches.

Before proceeding to the annual data, we conducted a simple exogeneity test using the 5-year differenced data as used in Baier and Bergstrand (2007), as suggested in Wooldridge (2010, p. 325). We re-estimated the RGFD specifications in Set 2 to also include either the level of the EIA variables five years forward (e.g., $CUCMECU_{ij,t+5}$) or the change in the EIA variables 5 years before the trade-flow or margin changes (e.g., $CUCMECU_{ij,t+5} - CUCMECU_{ijt}$). We found evidence of positive, statistically significant coefficient estimates of 5-year lead levels of *CUCMECU* on aggregate trade flows, extensive margins, and intensive margins, of *FTA* on aggregate trade flows and extensive margins, and of *TWPTA* on aggregate trade flows and intensive margins.[27] Unfortunately, adding further "leads" would further reduce the size of our sample, providing motivation for examining annual data.

As with the 5-year data, we considered both RGFD, FD and FE specifications using annual data. We first examined the relationships using annual first-differenced data and both the FD and RGFD models. One of the inherent problems with differencing annual data is that the resulting trade-flow, extensive margin, and intensive margin changes are "noisy." The main result from re-estimating Eqs. (3) and (4) with annual data is that – in general – neither current, lagged, nor lead formations of EIAs had any *systematic* statistically significant effects on annual log-differences in aggregate trade flows, extensive margins, and intensive margins (using up to 7 annual lead and lag changes). The results are presented in the online appendix.

To avoid multicollinearity and the consequent reduced sample size of adding more lead and lag changes, we turned to another approach.[28] We introduced linear trends of the lead and lag changes in the EIA variables alongside the concurrent EIA variable. This methodology proved useful, yielding two important insights. Consider the RGFD specification. First, while there were few statistically significant coefficient estimates, the key findings from Set 2 and Set 3 held up. For concurrent $\Delta CUCMECU_{ijt}$ and ΔFTA_{ijt}, their coefficient estimates for the intensive margin were positive (0.115 and 0.075, respectively) and statistically significant at 1%; however, the extensive margin concurrent effects were insignificant. For the lagged trends of $\Delta CUCMECU$ and ΔFTA, their coefficient estimates for the extensive margin were positive (0.034 and 0.033, respectively) and statistically significant; however, the intensive margin effects were insignificant for the lagged trends. The two trends' annual estimates implied total lagged extensive margin effects of 65% and 63% for CUCMECU and FTA, respectively. All these results made sense. However, the second important finding was that the *lead* trend for $\Delta CUCMECU$ on the extensive margin was an unexpectedly *positive* and statistically significant 0.047.[29]

Yet, two findings of economically and statistically significant lead effects for *CUCMECU* on the extensive margin using (5-year and 1-year) first-differenced data suggested further analysis of the annual data using log-levels was warranted. Applying FE specification (2) to annual data with analogous 15-year linear lead and lag annual trends yielded informative results, provided in Table 3.[30] We note that Table 3 reports results only for *CUCMECU* and *FTA*. The reason is that the FE specifications – whether using all annual data from 1962 to 2000 or only 8 cross-sections five years apart – yielded several negative coefficients for *TWPTA* and *OWPTA*, whereas the coefficient estimates for *CUCMECU* and *FTA* yielded qualitatively and quantitatively similar coefficient estimates using the FE, FD, and RGFD specifications.[31]

Table 3 provides coefficient estimates for *CUCMECU* and *FTA* for the linear trend model. The first column of Table 3 lists the two EIAs of interest. *CUCMECU* refers to coefficient estimates for the concurrent year for

[25] This issue was ignored in Foster et al. (2011) and Eicher and Henn (2011). Also, variation in a_{Lit}^{m} is accounted for by the time-varying exporter fixed effect.

[26] In the online appendix, we address that, even though the Religion variable (the first-stage variable providing identification in the second stage) has little variation over time, separate probit cross-section regression coefficient estimates allow identification in the second stage. A possible preferred approach would be a dynamic selection equation, but this approach (as one referee noted) is beyond the scope of the present paper.

[27] Using forward changes in EIAs yielded similar results.

[28] Even with only 7 leads and lags, sample size declined from 313,189 to 102,059 observations.

[29] The only other statistically significant effects were a positive lag trend effect for aggregate trade flows for ΔFTA and statistically significant negative lead trends for trade flows and extensive margin for $\Delta OWPTA$, which make sense. The full set of results for the RGFD and FD specifications are reported in the online appendix.

[30] Note the large number of observations using annual data. Because of the large number of fixed effects in this estimation, we employed the "high dimensional" fixed effects (HD-FE) approach of Abowd and Kramarz (1999). In particular, we extended the two-way high HD-FE iterative approach of Carneiro et al. (2012) to our three-way FE context, clustering the standard errors on the bilateral fixed effects. The procedure employs the notion that the FEs are simple averages. The iterative procedure runs a partitioned regression on the EIAs, the means for each FE are computed, and the regression is re-run using the means as controls, updating at each iteration the mean values until convergence is achieved (with a convergence criteria that the residual sum of squares between the $(n-1)^{th}$ and n^{th} regressions is less than 2.0e−16.) The approach yields exact least squares solutions for coefficients and standard errors.

[31] The reason is that the growth of intra-industry trade over this period dominated inter-industry trade growth, and this trend over time caused the coefficient estimates for *TWPTA* and *OWPTA* to be *biased downward*; TWPTAs and especially OWPTAs are typically between developed and developing countries. In fact, it was specifically for this reason we focused on the RGFD specification, because the pair fixed effects in the 5-year differenced data accounted for this bias, resulting in positive and some statistically significant coefficients in Sets 1, 2, and 3 in Tables 1 and 2 for *TWPTA* and *OWPTA*. Nevertheless, the full set of FE coefficient estimates using annual data for 1962–2000 are available in the online appendix.

Table 3
Annual data in log-levels, 15-year linear trends.

Variables	Set 4		
	(4a)	(4b)	(4c)
	ln $TRADE_{ijt}$	ln EM_{ijt}	ln IM_{ijt}
$CUCMECU_{ijt}$	0.450***	0.057**	0.393***
	(0.029)	(0.025)	(0.026)
$CUCMECU_{Lag\ Trend}$	0.025***	0.010***	0.015***
	(0.003)	(0.003)	(0.003)
$CUCMECU_{Lead\ Trend}$	−0.006***	−0.001	−0.005***
	(0.001)	(0.001)	(0.001)
FTA_{ijt}	0.262***	0.080***	0.182***
	(0.019)	(0.016)	(0.018)
$FTA_{Lag\ Trend}$	0.028***	0.025***	0.004**
	(0.002)	(0.002)	(0.002)
$FTA_{Lead\ Trend}$	−0.020***	−0.007***	−0.013***
	(0.001)	(0.001)	(0.001)
Constant	−3.829***	−3.126***	−3.830***
	(0.002)	(0.002)	(0.002)
Fixed effects			
Exporter-year (i,t)	Yes	Yes	Yes
Importer-year (j,t)	Yes	Yes	Yes
Country-pair (ij)	Yes	Yes	Yes
R^2	0.838	0.780	0.686
No. of observations	313,189	313,189	313,189

Notes: Robust standard errors in parentheses. *, **, and *** denote statistical significance at the 10, 5, and 1% levels, respectively, in two-tailed t-tests.

CUCMECU, $CUCMECU_{LagTrend}$ refers to coefficient estimates on the linear trend for the 15 years of lagged values, and $CUCMECU_{LeadTrend}$ refers to coefficient estimates on the linear trend for the 15 years of *lead* values. Analogous interpretations hold for *FTA*. The second, third, and fourth columns of numbers report the coefficient estimates for aggregate trade flows, extensive margin, and intensive margin, respectively.

Consider first *CUCMECU*. The partial effect for *CUCMECU* (0.450) for aggregate trade flows implies that a CUCMECU increases trade in the current quarter by 57%. The lagged trend for *CUCMECU* increases trade 2.5% annually, or 45% over 15 years; the combined effect is 102%, which is quite close to the 101% estimated using the 5-year differenced RGFD results in Table 2. Yet the 15-year lead trend for *CUCMECU decreases* trade by only 0.6% annually, or 8.6% over 15 years.

For the extensive margin, the partial effect of *CUCMECU* (0.057) implies that a CUCMECU increases the extensive margin in the current quarter a trivial 6%. However, the lagged trend for *CUCMECU* is 1% annually, or 16% over 15 years; the combined effect is 22%, which is quite close to the 27% estimated using the 5-year differenced RGFD results in Table 2. The 15-year lead trend for *CUCMECU decreases* the extensive margin by only 0.1% annually, or 1.5% over 15 years.

For the intensive margin, the partial effect of *CUCMECU* (0.393) implies a CUCMECU increases the intensive margin in the current quarter by 48%. This effect is larger than the respective one for the extensive margin, consistent with our hypothesis. The lagged trend for *CUCMECU* is 1.5% annually, or 25% over 15 years; the combined effect is 73%, which is slightly higher than the 58% estimated using the 5-year differenced RGFD results in Table 2. The 15-year lead trend for *CUCMECU decreases* the intensive margin by 0.5% annually, or 7% over 15 years.

Similar results are found for *FTA* and are reported in Table 3.

Finally, how do we reconcile the *declining* 15-year trend effect for annual leads on trade flows using annual data with the earlier 5-year differenced RGFD specifications that found *positive* 5-year lead effects? These are reconciled readily by examining Figs. 1 and 2. Fig. 1 reports the annual estimated effects of a CUCMECU using the 15-year lead and lag linear trends. 15–20 years before date of entry, country pairs that form a CUCMECU tend to trade *more* than country pairs that do not form an agreement; this is the selection effect. However, over the 15 years prior to date of entry, this selection effect declines; this causes the lead trend effect – which is small relative to current and lagged effects – to virtually disappear. Following date of entry, the CUCMECU increases trade, and the effect grows over time. Importantly, note that upon the date of entry the intensive margin effect (0.393) dominates the extensive margin effect (0.06). Yet, after 15 years, the intensive margin effect is a much smaller share of the total trade flow effect. After 15 years, the extensive margin effect is three times the current-period extensive margin effect. Fig. 2 provides similar results using the 15-year lead and lag linear trends for FTAs. The notable difference is that the lagged effects on the extensive margin are relatively larger for FTAs than for CUCMECUs. Thus, the annual data provide evidence that there is a material selection effect 15 years prior to formation of CUCMECUs and FTAs. However, the effect dissipates and the annual data provide convincing supporting evidence of robust partial effects

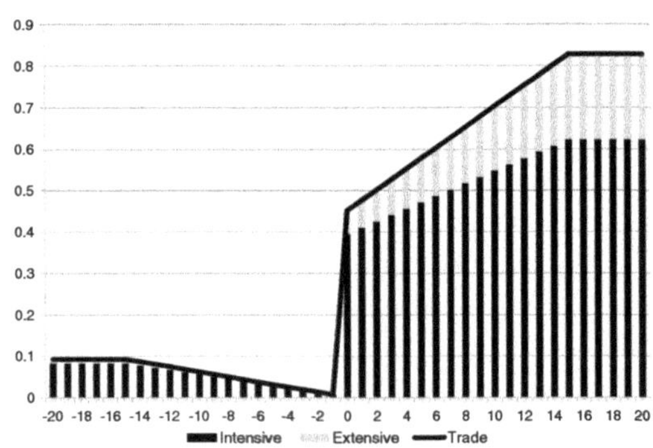

Fig. 1. CUCMECUs.

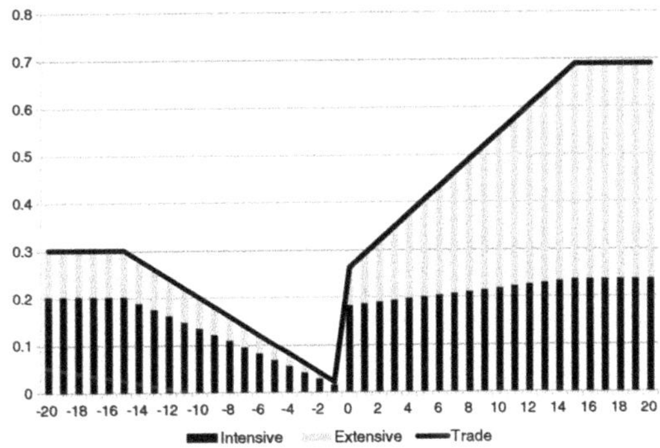

Fig. 2. FTAs.

of CUCMECUs and FTAs on aggregate trade flows, extensive margins, and intensive margins that take 10–15 years following date of entry.[32]

5. Conclusions

Recent developments in estimating ex post the average treatment effects (ATEs) of economic integration agreements (EIAs) on international trade flows to account for the endogeneity of such agreements have led to larger and more precise estimates than found earlier in the gravity-equation literature. Separately, recent developments in international trade theory allowing for firm heterogeneity and fixed export costs have allowed researchers to explore the effects of trade-policy liberalizations on various extensive and intensive "margins of trade," but most have used simulations. Only one study has explored econometrically the effect of EIAs on the intensive and extensive goods margin of trade with a large number of country-pairs' trade flows, product categories, years, and EIAs, and no study has explored the relative effects on the margins of trade of alternative *types* of EIAs – partial trade agreements, free trade agreements, customs unions, etc. – much less the relative *timing* of such effects.

Extending methodology established in Hummels and Klenow (2005) and Baier and Bergstrand (2007), this paper provided the first evidence using gravity equations of *both* the intensive and extensive (goods) margins being affected by economic integration agreements (EIAs) employing a panel data set with a large number of country pairs, product categories, and EIAs from 1962 to 2000. We found the first evidence of the differential partial effects of various "types" of EIAs on these intensive and extensive margins of trade with deeper integration agreements having larger impacts on aggregate trade flows, extensive margins, and intensive margins than shallower agreements. We found the first evidence of a novel differential "timing" of the two margins' ATEs, with intensive margin effects occurring sooner than extensive margin effects for deep EIAs, FTAs, and one-way PTAs, consistent with two recent theoretical studies. Finally, we found relative sizes of (cumulative) intensive margin and extensive margin effects consistent with implications of a gravity equation based upon a standard Melitz model. These results were robust to correcting for potential biases from sample selection, firm heterogeneity, and reverse causality.

[32] Similar findings were obtained using quadratic trends.

Acknowledgments

The authors are grateful to co-editor Dan Trefler and two anonymous referees for their excellent comments that have improved this paper substantively, and to Matthew Clance for his excellent research assistance. We are also grateful for the comments from the presentations at the 2011 Aarhus University conference on "Globalization: Strategies and Effects" in Koldingfjord (Denmark), ETH University in Zurich, Florida International University, Drexel University, Georgia Tech, and the University of Notre Dame. We thank Adam Ayers, R. Ethan Braden, Francisco Briseno, Emma Buckley, Brandon Caruthers, Stephen Cray, Tom Foote, Mitch Gainer, Pedro Gimenez, Nick Goode, Drew Hill, Christine Hsieh, Tahir Imtiaz, Humberto Kravetz, Cherrica Li, Lindsey Lim, Ron Mariutto, Ben O'Neill, Clare Robinson, Mo Sabet, James Schappler, Andrew Weiler, Alex Wheeler, and Chris Wittman for their excellent research assistance on the construction of the EIA data base.

Appendix A. Supplementary data

Supplementary data to this article can be found online at http://dx.doi.org/10.1016/j.jinteco.2014.03.005.

References

Abowd, John, Kramarz, Francis, 1999. Econometric analysis of linked employer–employee data. Labor Econ. 6, 53–74 (March).
Anderson, James E., 2011. The gravity model. Ann. Econ. Res. 3, 133–160.
Anderson, James E., van Wincoop, Eric, 2003. Gravity with gravitas: a solution to the border puzzle. Am. Econ. Rev. 93 (1), 170–192.
Anderson, James E., Yotov, Yoto, 2011. Terms of trade and global efficiency effects of free trade agreements, 1990–2000. NBER Research Working Paper No. 17003.
Arkolakis, Costas, Demidova, Svetlana, Klenow, Peter J., Rodriguez-Clare, Andres, 2008. Endogenous variety and the gains from trade. Am. Econ. Rev. 98 (2), 444–450 (May).
Arkolakis, Costas, Eaton, Jonathan, Kortum, Samuel, 2011. Staggered adjustment and trade dynamics. Working Paper.
Arkolakis, Costas, Costinot, Arnaud, Rodriguez-Clare, Andres, 2012. New trade models, same old gains? Am. Econ. Rev. 102 (1), 94–130.
Baier, Scott L., Bergstrand, Jeffrey H., 2004. Economic determinants of free trade agreements. J. Int. Econ. 64, 29–63.
Baier, Scott L., Bergstrand, Jeffrey H., 2007. Do free trade agreements actually increase members' international trade? J. Int. Econ. 71, 72–95.
Baier, Scott L., Bergstrand, Jeffrey H., 2009. *Bonus vetus* OLS: a simple method for approximating international trade–cost effects using the gravity equation. J. Int. Econ. 77 (1), 77–85.
Bergstrand, Jeffrey H., Egger, Peter, 2011. Gravity equations and economic frictions in the world economy. In: Bernhofen, D., Falvey, R., Greenaway, D., Kreickemeier, U. (Eds.), Palgrave Handbook of International Trade (forthcoming).

Bernard, Andrew B., Jensen, J. Bradford, Redding, Stephen J., Schott, Peter K., 2009. The margins of U.S. trade. Am. Econ. Rev. 99 (2), 487–493 (May).

Besedes, Tibor, Prusa, Thomas J., 2011. The role of extensive and intensive margins and export growth. J. Dev. Econ. 96 (2), 371–379.

Broda, Christian, Weinstein, David E., 2006. Globalization and the gains from variety. Q. J. Econ. 121 (2), 541–585.

Carneiro, Anabela, Guimaraes, Paulo, Portugal, Pedro, 2012. Real wages and the business cycle: accounting for worker, firm, and job title heterogeneity. Am. Econ. J. Macroecon. 4 (2), 133–152 (April).

Chaney, Thomas, 2008. Distorted gravity: the intensive and extensive margins of international trade. Am. Econ. Rev. 98 (4), 1707–1721 (September).

Cheng, I.-Hui, Wall, Howard J., 2005. Controlling for heterogeneity in gravity models of trade and integration. Fed. Reserv. Bank St. Louis Rev. 49–63 (January/February).

Eaton, Jonathan, Kortum, Samuel, 2002. Technology, geography, and trade. Econometrica 70 (5), 1741–1779.

Eaton, Jonathan, Kortum, Samuel, Kramarz, Francis, 2008. An anatomy of international trade: evidence from French firms. National Bureau of Economic Research Working Paper No. 14610 (December).

Egger, Peter, Larch, Mario, Staub, Kevin E., Winkelmann, Rainer, 2011. The trade effects of endogenous preferential trade agreements. Am. Econ. J. Econ. Policy 3 (3), 113–143 (August).

Eicher, Theo, Henn, Christian, 2011. In search of WTO trade effects: preferential trade agreements promote trade strongly, but unevenly. J. Int. Econ. 83, 137–153.

Feenstra, Robert C., 1994. New product varieties and the measurement of international prices. Am. Econ. Rev. 84 (1), 157–177.

Feenstra, Robert C., Weinstein, David E., 2013. Globalization, markups and U.S. welfare. working paper (February).

Feenstra, Robert C., Lipsey, Robert E., Deng, Haiyan, Ma, Alyson C., Mo, Hengyong, 2005. World trade flows: 1962-2000. NBER Paper No. 11040 (January).

Felbermayr, Gabriel, Kohler, Wilhelm, 2010. Modelling the extensive margin of world trade: new evidence on GATT and WTO membership. World Econ. 33 (11), 1430–1469 (November).

Foster, Neil, Poeschl, Johannes, Stehrer, Robert, 2011. The impact of preferential trade agreements on the margins of international trade. Econ. Syst. 35, 84–97.

Frankel, Jeffrey, 1997. Regional Trading Blocs. Institute for International Economics, Washington, DC.

Helpman, Elhanan, Melitz, Marc, Rubinstein, Yona, 2008. Estimating trade flows: trading partners and trading volumes. Q. J. Econ. 123 (2), 441–487 (May).

Hillberry, Russell, McDaniel, Christine, 2002. A decomposition of North American trade growth ince NAFTA. U.S. International Trade Commission Working Paper 2002-12-A (July).

Hummels, David, Klenow, Peter J., 2005. The variety and quality of a nation's exports. Am. Econ. Rev. 95 (3), 704–723.

Kehoe, Timothy J., Ruhl, Kim J., 2009. How important is the new goods margin in international trade? Federal Reserve Bank of Minneapolis Staff Report 324 (June).

Lee, Jong-Wha, Swagel, Philip, 1997. Trade barriers and trade flows across countries and industries. Rev. Econ. Stat. 79, 372–382.

Magee, Christopher S.P., 2008. New measures of trade creation and trade diversion. J. Int. Econ. 75, 349–362.

Martin, Will, Ng, Francis, 2004. A Note on Sources of Tariff Reductions in Developing Countries, 1983-2003. World Bank (October).

Melitz, Marc J., 2003. The impact of trade on intra-industry reallocations and aggregate industry profitability. Econometrica 71 (6), 1695–1725 (November).

Melitz, Marc J., Redding, Stephen J., 2013. Firm heterogeneity and aggregate welfare. National Bureau of Economic Research Working Paper No. 18919 (March).

Pavcnik, Nina, 2002. Trade liberalization, exit, and productivity improvements: evidence from Chilean plants. Rev. Econ. Stud. 69, 245–276.

Redding, Stephen J., 2011. Theories of heterogeneous firms and trade. Ann. Econ. Res. 3, 77–105.

Rose, Andrew, 2004. Do we really know that the WTO increases trade? Am. Econ. Rev. 94 (1), 98–114 (March).

Roy, Jayjit, 2010. Do customs union members engage in more bilateral trade than free-trade agreement members? Rev. Int. Econ. 18 (4), 663–681.

Ruhl, Kim, 2008. The international elasticity puzzle. Working Paper.

Trefler, Daniel, 1993. Trade liberalization and the theory of endogenous protection: an econometric study of U.S. import policy. J. Polit. Econ. 101 (1), 138–160 (February).

Trefler, Daniel, 2004. The long and short of the Canada-U.S. free trade agreement. Am. Econ. Rev. 94 (4), 870–895.

Wooldridge, Jeffrey M., 2000. Introductory Econometrics. South-Western, Chicago, IL.

Wooldridge, Jeffrey M., 2010. Econometric Analysis of Cross Section and Panel Data, Second edition. MIT Press, Cambridge, MA.

Chapter 13

Economic integration agreements, border effects, and distance elasticities in the gravity equation

Jeffrey H. Bergstrand[a,b,*], Mario Larch[c], Yoto V. Yotov[d,e]

[a] Department of Finance, Department of Economics, Kellogg Institute for International Studies, University of Notre Dame, Notre Dame, IN 46556, USA
[b] CESifo, Munich, Germany
[c] Chair of Empirical Economics, University of Bayreuth, CESifo, ifo Institute, and GEP at University of Nottingham, Universitätsstraße 30, 95440 Bayreuth, Germany
[d] School of Economics, LeBow College of Business, Drexel University, Philadelphia, PA 19104, USA
[e] Economic Research Institute, Bulgarian Academy of Sciences, Sofia, Bulgaria

ARTICLE INFO

Article history:
Received 14 February 2014
Accepted 5 June 2015
Available online 24 June 2015

JEL classification:
F13
F14
F15

Keywords:
International trade
Economic integration agreements
Gravity equations

ABSTRACT

Using a novel common econometric specification, we examine the measurement of three important effects in international trade that historically have been addressed largely separately: the (partial) effects on trade of economic integration agreements, international borders, and bilateral distance. First, recent studies focusing on precise and unbiased estimates of effects of economic integration agreements (EIAs) on members' trade may be biased upward owing to inadequate control for time-varying exogenous unobservable country-pair-specific changes in bilateral export costs (possibly decreasing the costs of international relative to intranational trade); we find evidence of this bias using a properly specified gravity equation. Second, our novel methodology yields statistically significant estimates of the declining effect of "international borders" on world trade, now accounting for endogenous EIA formations and unobserved country-pair heterogeneity in initial levels. Third, we confirm recent evidence providing a solution to the "distance-elasticity puzzle," but show that these estimates of the declining effect of distance on international trade are biased upward by not accounting for endogenous EIA formations and unobserved country-pair heterogeneity. We conclude our study with numerical general equilibrium comparative statics illustrating a substantive difference on trade effects of EIAs with and without allowance for the declining effects of international borders on world trade.

1. Introduction

It's a Small World After All.... (Walt Disney, New York World's Fair, 1964)

Using a novel common econometric specification, we examine the measurement of three important effects on international trade flows that have historically been addressed largely separately: the (partial) effects on trade of economic integration agreements (EIAs), international borders, and bilateral distance.[1] First, one of the most prominent aspects of the global economy over the past 20 years has been the proliferation of economic integration agreements (EIAs) – notably free

* Corresponding author at: Department of Finance, Mendoza College of Business, USA. Tel.: +1 574 631 6761; fax: +1 574 631 5255
E-mail addresses: Bergstrand.1@nd.edu (J.H. Bergstrand), mario.larch@uni-bayreuth.de (M. Larch), yotov@drexel.edu (Y.V. Yotov).

[1] We are concerned primarily in this study with estimating partial (or direct) effects, not general equilibrium effects as in Anderson and van Wincoop (2003); Baier and Bergstrand (2009); Anderson and Yotov (2011), and Bergstrand et al. (2013). Nevertheless, general equilibrium effects hinge upon partial

*Originally Published in *European Economic Review*, 78(2015), pp. 307–327.

trade agreements but also some customs unions. Policy makers at national and supra-national government levels increasingly rely on *ex post* estimates of the (partial) effects of EIAs on trade flows based upon gravity equations to evaluate subsequently the welfare effects of EIAs.[2] Only recently have economists been able to provide more precise and unbiased *ex post* estimates of the effects of EIAs on members' international trade flows, in contrast to the highly variable and often economically implausible estimates generated over 45 years from 1962 to 2007.[3] Using panel data and accounting for the endogeneity of EIAs and prices and for unobserved country-pair heterogeneity, Baier and Bergstrand (2007), or BB, found using a sample spanning 1960–2000 and ordinary least squares (OLS) that a typical EIA increases two members' aggregate goods bilateral trade about 100 percent after 10–15years – five times the effect estimated using atheoretical gravity equations. Anderson and Yotov (2011) found similar results using the same BB specification (but using a Poisson quasi maximum likelihood (PQML) estimator) and showed the method also generated plausible, precise, and statistically significant effects for disaggregate trade flows. Eicher et al. (2012) use Bayesian Model Averaging (BMA) techniques to confirm the trade-creating effects of EIAs under model uncertainty. The key in BB, Anderson and Yotov (2011), and Eicher et al. (2012) was accounting for unobserved heterogeneity in exporters' and importers' time-varying multilateral influences (such as countries' prices and GDPs) and for unobserved heterogeneity in time-invariant bilateral influences. However, all of these studies failed to account for possible unobservable exogenous *time-varying* country-pair-specific changes in bilateral export costs (possibly decreasing the costs of international relative to intranational trade) that may have resulted in estimates of EIAs' effects being biased upward. The potential bias introduced by time-varying bilateral fixed export costs is especially important in light of their prominence in the "New New" trade theory, cf., Redding (2011) and Melitz and Redding (2014), and their empirical relevance, cf., Roberts and Tybout (1997) and Das et al. (2007). In this paper, we address this potentially important shortcoming using a properly specified gravity equation motivated by formal theoretical foundations. In doing so, we also contribute to two related literatures: the "(international) border puzzle" and the "distance-elasticity puzzle."

The "border puzzle" refers to the seminal estimate using traditional atheoretical gravity equations in McCallum (1995) that the Canada–U.S. international border caused Canadian inter-province trade to be 22 times – or 2100 percent – greater than province-state international trade in 1988, other things equal. This result implied that international borders imposed dramatic costs on international relative to intranational trade. This finding inspired an entire literature, including Anderson and van Wincoop's seminal (2003) paper formulating a new theoretical foundation for the gravity equation, building upon formal foundations in Anderson (1979) and Bergstrand (1985). While Anderson and van Wincoop (2003) addressed the importance of accounting properly for endogenous prices (in their terms, "multilateral resistances") in estimation and in general equilibrium comparative statics, to date estimates of the border effect are still very large. For instance, de Sousa et al. (2012) report that on average a country traded 493 times more intranationally than internationally in 1990 (cf., their Figure 1 for 1990 ($e^{6.2} = 493$)), even dwarfing the McCallum estimate. Moreover, they estimate that on average this effect fell 63 percent to 181 in 2002 ($e^{5.2} = 181$), that is, in only 12 years. However, using a time-series of cross-sections, they did not control for unobserved country-pair heterogeneity in border effects, did not account for endogenous EIAs as in BB, and, while recognizing multilateral prices in their estimation, did not account for the endogeneity of prices as addressed in Anderson and van Wincoop (2003). In this paper, we use an enhanced version of the BB panel-data methodology (and also an expansion of the data to include intranational trade flows) to provide consistent and precise estimates of the average declining effects of international borders on international trade, using a properly specified gravity equation accounting also for the effects of endogenous EIA formations, endogenous prices, and unobserved country-pair heterogeneity in initial border effects.

The "distance-elasticity puzzle" refers to the issue that – despite widespread anecdotal evidence that the effect of distance on international trade is declining over time, as suggested by Thomas Friedman's "flatter world" – systematic academic empirical evidence suggests that the distance elasticity of bilateral international trade has *not* declined, as established in the Disdier and Head (2008) meta analysis of the distance elasticity.[4] While some authors have offered alternative explanations, they have met mixed success (cf., footnote 1 in Yotov (2012) and our discussion later). However, Yotov (2012) recently provided a persuasive solution to the distance-elasticity puzzle by recognizing the importance of including *intranational*, alongside international, trade flows and bilateral distances in estimation (using OLS and PQML), a feature actually common to the "border effects" literature, cf., Wei (1996). By typically excluding intranational trade flows and intranational distances, gravity-equation estimates cannot identify the impact on international trade of international trade costs *relative to* intranational trade costs; previous studies of the distance-elasticity puzzle ignored this. However, Yotov (2012) suffered from two shortcomings. The study did not account for unobserved heterogeneity across country pairs and omitted controls for EIAs, potentially biasing upward his estimates of the declining effect of distance. Recently, Bosquet

(*footnote continued*)
effects, and we provide general equilibrium comparative statics of trade effects of EIAs with and without allowance for the declining effects of international borders on world trade at the end of the paper.

[2] See, for example, Berden et al. (2010) or, more recently, Head and Mayer (2014) and Costinot et al. (2014).

[3] In a meta-analysis of 1827 earlier studies (including several using flawed specifications), Cipollina and Salvatici (2010) find a range of estimates between 12 percent and 285 percent. Their mean effect is 80 percent and median effect is 46 percent.

[4] The international border puzzle differs from the distance-elasticity puzzle in the following respect. Typically, the border puzzle is associated with arguably economically implausible estimates of the *level* effect of an international border on international trade flows. By contrast, the distance-elasticity puzzle is only concerned with an absence of declines in the distance elasticity of international trade, not the average *level* of the distance elasticity *per se*.

and Boulhol (2015) using PQML included country-pair fixed effects to account for country-pair heterogeneity and exporter-time and importer-time fixed effects, but could not find declining distance elasticities; however, they did not include intranational trade and distances. In this paper, we address all these shortcomings and find statistically significant *declining* distance elasticities that indicate the upward bias in estimates in Yotov (2012).

This is the first paper to address all three related – but historically often disjointed – issues using a common econometric framework.[5] Using a state-of-the-art gravity equation with international and intranational trade flows, we reconcile methodologically and empirically all three issues. We provide three potential contributions. First, some bilateral fixed and variable export costs are unobservable. If some bilateral fixed and variable export costs are declining over time – as anecdotal evidence suggests – the Melitz (2003) model suggests that aggregate bilateral trade of existing exporters should expand (i.e., intensive margin response to lower variable trade costs), some previously domestic firms should select into exporting (i.e., extensive margin response to lower fixed and variable trade costs), and the number of domestic firms should decrease (due to market competition). Hence, omission of variables that account for some of the increase in international relative to intranational trade – other than an EIA – could bias upward EIA coefficient estimates under the approach in BB. Thus, the resounding "yes" claimed in BB in response to their question, "Do free trade agreements actually increase members' international trade?", may have been premature, as the issue of declining bilateral fixed and variable export costs was ignored.[6] In this paper, we use three alternative methods to account more fully for *time-varying* unobserved heterogeneity in bilateral international trade costs relative to intranational trade costs.[7] We find that previous estimates of EIAs' partial effects have been biased upward. When using the PQML estimator, the effects of an EIA fall by 30 percent.

Second, we draw upon the notion used in Anderson and van Wincoop (2003), or AvW, that international border dummies imbed international trade costs relative to intranational trade costs in gravity equations with international and intranational trade flows. In the cross-sectional context of AvW, their international border dummy variable measured 1 if two sub-national regions (Canadian province or U.S. state) were from different countries, and 0 otherwise (and hence from the same country). Thus, their international border dummy was an exogenous index of whether the trade flow was an international versus intranational flow. Here, we use a panel data set of international and intranational trade flows for a large number of country pairs for a large number of years. Since intranational trade is a nation's gross output less exports, we focus our analysis on manufactures trade, since exports are measured on a gross basis and data on manufactures gross output is available.[8] We then construct an exogenous dummy variable $INTERNATIONAL_{ij}$ that assumes the value 1 if the source (i) and destination (j) countries are different ($i \neq j$) and the value 0 if i and j are the same ($i=j$). By incorporating this variable interacted with a set of year dummies – creating $INTER_{ij,t}$, $INTER_{ij,t+1}$, etc. – and then using the BB panel approach, we can isolate the effect of EIAs on bilateral trade to determine how much an EIA actually increases two members' trade, but now accounting for any possibly declining trends in unobservable bilateral fixed and variable trade costs that may have increased international relative to intranational trade. Moreover, the coefficient estimates for the multiple $INTER_{ij,t}$ dummies also provide direct estimates of the changing (partial) effect of an international border on a pair's trade flow. A novel aspect of our approach – accounting for unobserved country-pair heterogeneity in a panel – is to allow the *level* of the international border effect to vary across every country pair using pair fixed effects (or pair fixed effects interacted with a trend); by contrast, previous studies constrain the level border effect to be identical across all country pairs or certain groups of country pairs using cross-sectional data (excluding country-pair fixed effects).[9] We find direct estimates of the (average) falling partial effect of an international border (after accounting for EIAs) using a specification motivated by a formal theoretical foundation for the gravity equation and avoiding the endogeneity bias (attributable to endogenous prices and endogenous EIA formations) present in several studies.[10] One of our estimates suggests that the cost of an international border (in terms of trade flows) has declined on average by 25.3 percent from 1990 to 2002, or about 2.4 percent per year.

Third, we will provide a battery of sensitivity analyses to determine the robustness of the results to phase-ins of agreements, lagged terms-of-trade effects, reverse causality, various estimation techniques, disaggregation, and accounting for firm-heterogeneity and country-selection biases introduced potentially by using aggregated data. In one sensitivity analysis, our alternative measure to our international border dummies to control for declining trade costs is an interaction of bilateral distance with year dummies. These results confirm the findings in Yotov (2012) that the effect of bilateral distance – owing to

[5] As we will clarify later, we note that studies of the border puzzle typically do not address the distance-elasticity puzzle, and vice versa. Also, some studies of the border puzzle and some of the distance-elasticity puzzle include dummy variables for economic integration agreements, but typically do not examine in detail how EIAs' effects are sensitive to the specifications. This paper addresses all three issues using a unified framework.

[6] Unfortunately, there is little systematic evidence of *observed* declines in bilateral fixed and variable export costs. A few studies have explored the issue of declining information technology (IT) costs, cf., Freund and Weinhold (2004), Tang (2006), and Berthelon and Freund (2008). However, all these studies include time-varying *multilateral*, not bilateral, indexes of IT factors. Such multilateral factors will be accounted for in our estimation using exporter-year and importer-year fixed effects. No study has yet accounted for time-varying declines in *bilateral* trade costs, except those associated with EIAs or currency unions.

[7] As will be discussed shortly, the three methods are interacting time-invariant pair fixed effects with a time trend, interacting a bilateral "international border" dummy with year effects, and interacting bilateral distance (and other standard gravity covariates) with year effects.

[8] We will address aggregate and disaggregate manufactures trade. In one robustness analysis, we will look at aggregate merchandise trade allowing GDP (a value added measure) to be an imperfect proxy for gross output. As we will discuss later, studies in the border-effects literature, starting with McCallum (1995) and Wei (1996), have incorporated intranational along with international trade flows.

[9] The level of a country-pair's border effect is imbedded in our fixed effect estimate.

[10] For instance, Head and Mayer (2000) and de Sousa et al. (2012) accounted for relative prices using measured national prices, but not for the endogeneity of prices as raised by Anderson and van Wincoop (2003).

likely falling bilateral variable and fixed export costs – *is* declining over time. Like Yotov (2012), we use a more appropriate measurement of intranational trade (using manufactures gross output and (gross) exports rather than aggregate trade and GDPs). However, unlike Yotov (2012) our specification accounts for unobserved time-varying bilateral heterogeneity and for the effects of EIA formations, which potentially biased upward Yotov's estimates of the declining effect of distance. We find evidence of this upward bias and estimate that the effect of distance on international trade has fallen by 1.2 percent per year.[11] Our results also suggest that the declining effect of international borders on trade and of distance on trade are two sides of the same coin; international trade costs have likely been declining relative to intranational trade costs.

The remainder of the paper is as follows. Section 2 provides theoretical background for the estimating equation that will be used. Section 3 addresses econometric issues and provides a data description. Section 4 discusses the empirical results for EIAs' partial effects on total bilateral manufactures trade flows, including the results of a series of sensitivity analyses, and provides estimates of the declining effect of international borders on trade. Section 5 discusses the results for disaggregate manufactures trade flows. Section 6 evaluates the sensitivity of the results to using aggregate *goods* trade flows, a broader sample of countries, and a longer time series. Section 7 uses an alternative method to account for declining bilateral export costs (other than EIAs), and provides estimates of the declining effect of distance on international relative to intranational trade. In Section 8, we distinguish quantitatively between the general equilibrium trade impacts of EIAs with *and* without allowance for declining effects of international borders on world trade. As for the case of partial effects, general equilibrium world trade impacts are significantly larger when the declining effects of distance are also accounted for. In Section 9, we conclude that the specifications suggested several years ago in Baier and Bergstrand (2007) to account for endogenous EIAs can be substantively improved by including international border dummies (or distances interacted with year dummies) in panel specifications to account for systematic declines over time in unobserved time-varying bilateral export costs (while *simultaneously* accounting for the heteroskedasticity bias in OLS estimates), including intranational trade and distance in samples, and accounting for unobserved time-invariant heterogeneity in country-pair international border level effects. In short, just as BB showed several years ago that panel techniques along with a properly specified gravity equation were critical to finding unbiased and precise EIA estimates, this paper is designed to show that an enhanced version of BB using panel techniques are critical to finding unbiased and precise estimates of EIA effects on international trade, of the declining effect of international borders on trade, and of the declining distance-elasticity of international trade.

2. Motivating the gravity-equation specification

The gravity equation has become the empirical workhorse for estimating partial effects of EIAs on members' trade flows. Arkolakis et al. (2012) demonstrated that a gravity equation surfaces for a large class of "quantitative trade models" that feature four main assumptions: (1) Dixit–Stiglitz preferences; (2) one factor of production (typically, labor); (3) linear cost functions; and (4) perfect or monopolistic competition.[12] Trade models satisfying these four assumptions are Armington (cf., Anderson and van Wincoop, 2003), Ricardian (cf., Eaton and Kortum, 2002), Krugman (1980), and Melitz (2003). Arkolakis et al. (2012) concluded that the gravity equation provides a common method for estimating the trade elasticity across these different approaches.

Arkolakis et al. (2012) show that a gravity equation consistent with all four theoretical frameworks in a *K*-country world can be described by

$$X_{ij,t} = \frac{\chi_{ij,t} N_{i,t} (w_{i,t}\tau_{ij,t})^{\epsilon} Y_{j,t}}{\sum_{k=1}^{K} \chi_{kj,t} N_{k,t} (w_{k,t}\tau_{kj,t})^{\epsilon}} \tag{1}$$

where $X_{ij,t}$ is the trade flow from exporter i to importer j in year t, $N_{i,t}$ is the measure of goods in country i that can be produced in year t, $w_{i,t}$ is the wage rate in country i, $\tau_{ij,t}$ is (gross) variable trade costs of country i's products into j, ϵ is the elasticity of imports with respect to variable trade costs ($\epsilon < 0$), $Y_{j,t}$ is aggregate expenditure in j, and $\chi_{ij,t}$ captures all "structural parameters" other than $\tau_{ij,t}$ (for example, fixed export costs from i to j, or $f_{ij,t}$).

For the purposes of this paper, the variables of interest are $\tau_{ij,t}$, $f_{ij,t}$, and $\chi_{ij,t}$. Typically, researchers have assumed that the formation of an EIA (such as a free trade agreement) between i and j lowers $\tau_{ij,t}$. However, EIAs are broad agreements reaching beyond elimination of tariff rates and variable trade costs; they likely also lower fixed export costs, $f_{ij,t}$. Yet, in reality, all types of "structural parameters" may alter $\chi_{ij,t}$ over time, such as informational considerations, historical factors, nontariff barriers unrelated to EIAs, and bilateral preferences, cf., Head and Mayer (2000). Thus, the use of ***time-invariant*** pair-specific fixed effects, as in BB, may be insufficient to isolate an unbiased partial effect of an EIA's formation on trade, via lowering $\tau_{ij,t}$, because trade flows may also be influenced by falling (rising) values of $f_{ij,t}$ ($\chi_{ij,t}$).

Moreover, every theoretical quantitative trade model yielding a gravity equation embodies "intranational trade" ($X_{ii,t}$), i.e., a country's domestic spending on its own products. Our novel approach in this paper – using international *and* intranational trade flows – is to introduce a variable $INTER_{ij,t}$ to account for average (across all pairs of different countries) declines in unobservable bilateral (fixed and variable) export costs (unassociated with EIAs), but in the context of a properly

[11] This contrasts with the stable estimates of the distance elasticity over time using PQML in Bosquet and Boulhol (2015), likely due to their omission of intranational trade and distances in their sample.

[12] Arkolakis et al. (2012) also note three macro-level restrictions: (1) trade is balanced; (2) aggregate profits are a constant share of aggregate revenues; and (3) the import demand system is constant elasticity of substitution (CES).

J.H. Bergstrand et al. / European Economic Review 78 (2015) 307–327 311

specified gravity equation motivated by a formal theoretical foundation. $INTER_{ij,t}$ is defined as the product of a year dummy, D_t, and a time-invariant binary variable, $INTERNATIONAL_{ij}$, which assumes the value 1 if the source and destination countries, i and j, respectively, are different countries ($i \neq j$) and the value 0 if i and j are the same country ($i=j$).

The economic motivation is explained most easily by reviewing first AvW.[13] Consider AvW's cross-sectional context of trade flows between and among Canadian provinces and U.S. states in 1993. In the context of AvW's Armington framework, trade costs were determined by two variables, bilateral distance ($DISTANCE_{ij}$) and a dummy for whether the two regions were in different countries ($=1$, if $i \neq j$) or the same country ($=0$, if $i=j$). In their paper, they used non-linear least squares to estimate their gravity equation to account for endogenous non-linear multilateral price terms. However, most researchers, such as Feenstra (2004), have focused since then on consistent estimation of the bilateral border dummy and bilateral distance coefficient estimates using a specification such as

$$\ln X_{ij} = \beta_0 + \beta_1 \ln DISTANCE_{ij} + \beta_2 INTERNATIONAL_{ij} + \eta_i + \theta_j + \upsilon_{ij}. \tag{2}$$

where η_i is an exporter fixed effect, θ_j is an importer fixed effect, and υ_{ij} is an error term. In AvW's cross-sectional context, $INTERNATIONAL_{ij}$ captures any factor influencing international relative to intranational trade. An international border imposes considerable costs. Thus, $INTERNATIONAL_{ij}$ would capture any cross-sectional variation in *bilateral* trade costs, beyond the role of bilateral distance which is also present in Eq. (2); $INTERNATIONAL_{ij}$ should have a negative effect on trade flows.[14] Of course, many other factors influence bilateral flows (international or intranational), so it is feasible to replace $INTERNATIONAL_{ij}$ and $\ln DISTANCE_{ij}$ with a country-pair fixed effect (in a panel). This is a novel aspect of our panel approach as previous border-effect studies have *not* used country-pair fixed effects to allow for variation across pairs in the *level* border effect.[15]

Our approach is to estimate each of the following equations using a panel of international and intranational trade flows:

$$X_{ij,t} = \exp\,[\beta_0 + \beta_1 EIA_{ij,t} + \beta_2 INTER_{ij,t} + \beta_3 DIST_{ij,t} + \eta_{i,t} + \theta_{j,t} + \phi_{ij}] + \zeta_{ij,t}, \tag{3}$$

and alternatively

$$X_{ij,t} = \exp\,[\beta_0 + \beta_1 EIA_{ij,t} + \beta_2 INTER_{ij,t} + \beta_3 DIST_{ij,t} + \eta_{i,t} + \theta_{j,t} + (\phi_{ij} \times Trend)] + \zeta_{ij,t}, \tag{4}$$

where $EIA_{ij,t}$ is a dummy assuming the value 1 (0) if an EIA exists (does not exist) in year t between countries i and j. Let *exp* denote the exponentiated value of the term in brackets and, for now, we allow the error term, $\zeta_{ij,t}$, to enter additively. This specification allows for estimation in levels using Poisson estimators and allows for zeros in trade.[16] In Eqs. (3) and (4), $\eta_{i,t}$ captures all time-varying multilateral factors of exporting country i, such as – in the context of Eq. (1) above – $N_{i,t}$ and $w_{i,t}$. $\theta_{j,t}$ captures all time-varying multilateral factors of importing country j, such as $Y_{j,t}$ and the denominator of the relative price term in Eq. (1).[17] Accordingly, our paper addresses the issue raised in AvW that direct inclusion of price variables creates potential endogeneity bias.[18] The inclusion of time-invariant country-pair fixed effects ϕ_{ij} captures all time-invariant factors that might otherwise be picked up by $EIA_{ij,t}$. However, there may exist trends over time in the effects of unobserved bilateral heterogeneity. Consequently, in Eq. (4) we interact the bilateral fixed effects (ϕ_{ij}) with a time trend (*Trend*).[19]

Yet, as Eq. (1) reveals, $\tau_{ij,t}$ and $\chi_{ij,t}$ are time-varying and reflect both policy-based and "natural" trade costs influencing international relative to intranational trade. However, there is a way to account for time-varying changes in these bilateral export costs, separate from policy-based trade liberalizations such as EIA formations. Recall that the variable $INTER_{ij,t}$ is defined as $INTER_{ij,t} = D_t \times INTERNATIONAL_{ij}$, where D_t is a year dummy. The variable $DIST_{ij,t}$ is defined analogously as the product of $\ln DISTANCE_{ij}$ and a year dummy.[20] In the presence of time-invariant pair fixed effects ϕ_{ij}, variation in $INTER_{ij,t}$ will capture all bilateral factors influencing international relative to intranational trade over time *on average* relative to the base period (hence, deviations over time relative to the pair fixed effect). Thus, any time-varying pair-specific variable such as $EIA_{ij,t}$ will capture only the effects on trade over time associated with the EIA's formation and not other factors causing $\tau_{ij,t}$ and $\chi_{ij,t}$ to change over time.

---

[13] An excellent treatment of this model and these issues is in chapter 5 of Feenstra (2004).

[14] Typically, gravity equations include other variables, such as dummies for sharing a common language, a common colonial history, or a common land border. Our empirical specifications below will account for these as well; we ignore them in Eqs. (2)–(4) to avoid clutter and abbreviate the equations in the text.

[15] It is important to note that some previous border-effect studies appropriately accounted for intranational as well international trade flows, such as Wei (1996), Head and Mayer (2000), Fontagne et al. (2005), and de Sousa et al. (2012). However, all such studies used a cross-sectional approach (for multiple years), including typical bilateral variables such as distance but constraining all country-pairs to have the same border-effect level. Our panel approach using country-pair fixed effects (and alternatively such effects interacted with a time trend) accounts for unobserved heterogeneity across country-pairs in initial border-effect levels. Moreover, by using our panel approach, we also account for the endogeneity of EIAs. Finally, all four studies noted above included variables representing prices, but did not account for the endogeneity of prices, i.e., the AvW critique. Wei (1996) included a linear approximation of the two countries' multilateral prices, but the approximation was not complete because it used only bilateral distances, cf., Baier and Bergstrand (2009).

[16] We address these econometric issues later.

[17] It is important to note that reductions in MFN tariff rates in importer j would be accounted for by $\theta_{j,t}$ as well.

[18] See footnote 15.

[19] Note that inclusion of an ij fixed effect *for each year* is infeasible; it would perfectly predict trade flows.

[20] As shown below, we will construct isomorphic dummies for common language, common colonial history, and common land border (i.e., contiguity). For brevity, we ignore these additional dummies in Eqs. (3) and (4).

Consequently, the addition of $INTER_{ij,t}$ alongside incorporating *intranational* trade flows and distances – consistent with theoretical foundations for the gravity equation explaining intranational as well as international flows – to the otherwise similar specifications in BB will essentially "purge" the partial EIA effects estimated in BB of omitted variables bias caused by changes in $\tau_{ij,t}$ and $\chi_{ij,t}$ unassociated with EIAs.[21] Moreover, the country-pair fixed effect ϕ_{ij} will capture the average trade-depressing effect of an international border, allowed to vary across all pairs. If trade costs unassociated with EIAs are falling over time, raising international relative to intranational trade, $INTER_{ij,t}$ will have a positive coefficient estimate. Also, the inclusion of $DIST_{ij,t}$ will account for any possible *additional* changing influence of distance over time on trade flows, not already captured by $INTER_{ij,t}$. As Yotov (2012) suggests, one of the factors most likely to explain increasing international relative to intranational trade is the declining effect of distance. However, that effect is likely to be absorbed by $INTER_{ij,t}$. In the absence of $INTER_{ij,t}$, $DIST_{ij,t}$ is likely to play a prominent role; we address this issue separately in a later section of the paper.

3. Econometric issues and data description

3.1. Econometric issues

The previous section dealt with many specification issues. However, one issue omitted above was the estimation approach. Historically, gravity equations have been estimated using OLS. The original analysis of the Canadian–U.S. "border puzzle" in McCallum (1995) used OLS. Baier and Bergstrand (2007) used OLS. Because of the introduction of a two-equation "structural" gravity model in AvW where one of the equations was non-linear, AvW used non-linear least squares. But with most of the literature focusing first on estimating the partial (or direct) effect of a border, most cross-section estimates have used OLS employing exporter and importer fixed effects (cf., Feenstra, 2004) and recently panel estimates have used OLS employing exporter-year, importer-year, and country-pair fixed effects, cf., Baier et al. (2014).

However, a large sub-literature of the gravity equation, starting with Haveman and Hummels (2004), Felbermayr and Kohler (2006), and Helpman et al. (2008), has addressed the importance of zeros in international trade flows, cf., Head and Mayer (2014). Santos Silva and Tenreyro (2006) showed using empirical specifications and a Monte Carlo analysis that, even in the absence of zeros, log-linear estimates of gravity equations suffered from heteroskedasticity bias (owing to Jensen's inequality). They showed that the PQML estimator could eliminate this heteroskedasticity bias as well as allow for inclusion of zeros. Consequently, as in many recent studies, we prefer the PQML estimator for Eqs. (3) and (4) above. However, we will show that our results are qualitatively the same using OLS.[22]

Summarizing, the key features of our specifications, for which previous analyses have excluded at least one dimension, are

1. Exporter-year and importer-year fixed effects to account for endogenous prices and unobserved time-varying exporter and importer multilateral heterogeneity;
2. Country-pair fixed effects or country-pair fixed effects interacted with a time trend to account for unobserved time-invariant or time-varying, respectively, bilateral effects, including pair-specific initial border effect levels;
3. Intranational as well as international trade flows and bilateral distances, so that the international border dummies can account for average declining international *relative to* intranational bilateral trade costs; and
4. PQML estimation to account for heteroskedasticity bias (owing to Jensen's inequality) and to account for zero trade flows.

3.2. Data description

Unlike the original estimates in BB, which examined aggregate bilateral goods trade flows, our analysis here focuses on manufactures trade flows. The reason is that a key right-hand-side (RHS) variable, $INTER_{ij,t}$, captures the effect *over time* of the (likely declining) average cost of international relative to intranational trade. Hence, as in McCallum (1995) and AvW, the left-hand-side (LHS) variable needs to include observations on *intranational* trade. Since exports are measured on a "gross" (not value added) basis, national output needs to be measured on a comparable basis to estimate intranational trade. The data used are the sectoral manufacturing data from Anderson and Yotov (2011). These data cover 41 trading partners (40 separate countries and a Rest-of-World (*ROW*) aggregate, consisting of 24 additional nations).[23] The eight manufacturing

[21] BB actually used country-and-year dummies (rather than exporter-and-year and importer-and-year dummies) along with pair fixed effects. The specifications here are akin to Baier et al. (2014), which used exporter-and-year, importer-and-year, and pair fixed effects.

[22] See the recent survey of the gravity equation literature in Head and Mayer (2014) for a useful discussion of new directions on these estimation issues. See also SantosSilva and Tenreyro (2011) on the robustness of PQML.

[23] Results will be provided with and without the *ROW* aggregate. The 40 main countries are Argentina, Australia, Austria, Belgium-Luxembourg, Bolivia, Brazil, Bulgaria, Canada, Chile, China, Colombia, Costa Rica, Denmark, Ecuador, Finland, France, Germany, Greece, Hungary, Iceland, Ireland, Israel, Italy, Japan, Korea (South), Mexico, Morocco, The Netherlands, Norway, Poland, Portugal, Romania, Spain, Sweden, Switzerland, Tunisia, Turkey, United Kingdom, United States, and Uruguay. The 24 countries in the *ROW* aggregate are Cameroon, Cyprus, Egypt, Hong Kong, Indonesia, India, Iran, Jordan, Kenya, Kuwait, Sri Lanka, Macao, Malta, Myanmar, Malawi, Malaysia, Niger, Nepal, Philippines, Senegal, Singapore, Trinidad and Tobago, Tanzania, and South Africa.

sectors are classified according to the United Nations' 2-digit International Standard Industrial Classification (ISIC) Revision 2.[24] The period of investigation is 1990–2002. For our analysis, we use only the years 1990, 1994, 1998, and 2002, akin to BB's use of data for every five years. We use a shorter four-year interval than BB's five-year interval due to the shorter time-series for our data. However, the use of every four years (or five years in BB) addresses the concern raised in Cheng and Wall (2005) that "Fixed-effects estimations are sometimes criticized when applied to data pooled over consecutive years on the grounds that dependent and independent variables cannot fully adjust in a single year's time" (p. 8). Also, Wooldridge, 2009 confirms the reduction in standard errors of coefficient estimates using changes over longer periods of time than using "year-to-year" changes (p. 459).[25]

Bilateral international trade flows are defined as the value of exports from exporter i to importer j. We use the CEPII *Trade, Production and Bilateral Protection Database*[26] (TradeProd) as the main trade data source because it implements a consistent procedure for mapping the CIF (cost, insurance and freight) values reported by the importing countries in COMTRADE to the FOB (free on board) values reported by the exporters in COMTRADE.[27] This decreases the number of missing observations in the sample.[28] To further decrease the number of missing trade flows, we add export values from the United Nations Statistical Division (UNSD) Commodity Trade Statistics Database (COMTRADE).[29] Internal commodity-level (intranational) trade for each country is constructed as the difference between total manufactures output and aggregate manufactures exports to all trading partners, which come from the same data sources. The number of zero trade flows in the sample is very small and we will document this later. This suggests that the consequences of throwing information away by using the standard log-linear OLS estimator should not be severe. Nonetheless, the PQML estimator is still preferable because, in addition to accounting for the zero trade flows, it also controls for heteroskedasticity bias introduced due to Jensen's inequality.

Industrial gross output value data come from two sources. The primary source is the United Nations' UNIDO Industrial Statistics database, which reports industry-level output data at the 3-digit and 4-digit level of ISIC Code (Revisions 2 and 3). We use the CEPII TradeProd database as a secondary source of product-level output data.[30] We interpolate some of the missing output values for the sample countries, which account for 15.6% of the observations; however, results are robust to inclusion or exclusion of observations using interpolated output values.

Data on EIA dummies come from the Database on Economic Integration Agreements on Jeffrey Bergstrand's website (http://www.nd.edu/ jbergstr). Baier and Bergstrand's EIA database categorizes bilateral EIA relationships from 1950–2005 for pairings of 195 countries using a multichotomous index. In this study, $EIA_{ij,t}=1$ denotes a free trade agreement between a pair of countries ij in year t or deeper integration (such as a customs union, common market, or economic union), or 0 otherwise, as in BB. Table 1 lists the agreements. In our *ROW* aggregate, there are no countries with EIAs with the main 40 countries. Initially, our results will include observations for $ROW_{ij,t}$; however, in a sensitivity analysis, we show the results are insensitive to the inclusion or exclusion of observations for $ROW_{ij,t}$ or for those with interpolated output values.[31]

Following Mayer and Zignago (2006), bilateral distance (between countries and internally within countries) is calculated as $DISTANCE_{ij}=(\sum_{k\in i}Pop_k/Pop_i)\,(\sum_{l\in j}Pop_l/Pop_j)D_{kl}$, where Pop_k is the population of agglomeration k in country i in year 2004, Pop_l is the population of agglomeration l in country j, and D_{kl} is the bilateral distance in kilometers between agglomeration k and agglomeration l (using Great Circle Distance formula). All data on latitudes, longitudes, and population are from the World Gazetteer web page. An important feature of this variable is that the same procedure is used to construct (consistently) international as well as intranational distances. The other dummy variables in our analysis are from CEPII.

4. Empirical results for total manufacturing trade flows

Table 2 presents our main results using aggregate international and intranational manufactures bilateral trade flows and some alternative specifications for robustness. Table 2 is partitioned into two panels, 2A and 2B. Panel 2A provides estimates omitting our key variable $INTER_{ij,t}$, as well as $DIST_{ij,t}$ and the analogous dummies for sharing a common language ($LANG_{ij,t}$), a

[24] The nine 2-digit ISIC manufacturing categories are (short labels, used for convenience throughout the paper, are noted in parentheses): 31. Food, Beverages, and Tobacco Products (Food); 32. Textile, Apparel, and Leather Products (Textile); 33. Wood and Wood Products (Wood); 34. Paper and Paper Products (Paper); 35. Chemicals, Petroleum, Coal, Rubber, and Plastic Products (Chemicals); 36. Other Non-metallic Products (Minerals); 37. Basic Metal Industries (Metals); 38. Fabricated Metal Products, Machinery, Equipment (Machinery); 39. Other manufacturing. Inspection of the output data at the 3-digit and 4-digit ISIC level of aggregation reveals that many countries report Equipment production, and especially Scientific Equipment production, under the category Other Manufacturing. Therefore, to avoid inconsistencies, we combine the last two 2-digit categories into one, which we label Machinery.

[25] For robustness, we will also examine later the sensitivity of our findings to aggregate goods trade flows and GDPs, using a broader sample of countries representing 98 percent of world output and for a longer time period.

[26] For details regarding this database see Mayer et al. (2008).

[27] The TradeProd database is based on the CEPII *Base pour l'Analyse du Commerce International* (BACI) data. For details regarding BACI see Gaulier and Zignago (2008).

[28] As noted in Anderson and Yotov (2010), in principle, gravity theory calls for valuation of exports at delivered prices. In practice, valuation of exports FOB avoids measurement error arising from poor quality transport cost data.

[29] We access COMTRADE through the World Integrated Trade Solution (WITS) software, http://wits.worldbank.org/witsweb/ The software reports trade data in three different concordances including Harmonized System (HS) Revisions 1989/92 and 1996, and the Standard International Trade Classification (SITC), which are automatically converted to ISIC Rev. 2. To obtain maximum number of observations, we combine the data from the different concordances.

[30] TradeProd uses the OECD STAN Industrial Database in addition to UNIDO's Industrial Statistics Database.

[31] An online appendix reports results excluding observations using the *ROW* aggregate region and observations using interpolated output values.

314 J.H. Bergstrand et al. / European Economic Review 78 (2015) 307–327

Table 1
Economic Integration Agreements in the Data Set.

European Union, or EU (1958): Belgium–Luxembourg, France, Italy, Germany, The Netherlands, Denmark (1973), Ireland (1973), United Kingdom (1973), Greece (1981), Portugal (1986), Spain (1986), Iceland (1994) Austria (1995), Finland (1995), Sweden (1995)
European Free Trade Association, or EFTA (1960): Austria (until 1995), Denmark (until 1973), Iceland (1970), Finland (1986–1995), Norway, Portugal (until 1986), Sweden (until 1995), Switzerland, United Kingdom (until 1973)
Latin American Free Trade Agreement/Latin American Integration Agreement, or LAFTA/LAIA (1993–): Argentina, Bolivia, Brazil, Chile, Ecuador, Mexico, Uruguay
EU–EFTA Agreement/European Economic Area (1973/1994)
US–Israel (1985)
US–Canada (1989)
EFTA–Israel (1993)
Central Europe Free Trade Agreement, or CEFTA (1993): Hungary, Poland, Romania (1997), Bulgaria (1998)
EFTA–Turkey (1992)
EFTA–Bulgaria (1993)
EFTA–Hungary (1993)
EFTA–Poland (1993)
EFTA–Romania (1993)
Andean Community (1993): Bolivia, Columbia, Ecuador
EU–Hungary (1994)
EU–Poland (1994)
North American Free Trade Agreement, or NAFTA (1994): Canada, Mexico, United States
Bolivia–Mexico (1995)
Costa Rica–Mexico (1995)
EU–Bulgaria (1995)
EU–Romania (1995)
Columbia–Mexico (1995). As part of the Group of Three. The third country, Venezuela, is not in the sample.
Mercosur (1991): Argentina, Brazil, Uruguay (formed in 1991 FTA in 1995)
Mercosur–Chile (1996)
Mercosur–Bolivia (1996)
EU–Turkey (1996)
Canada–Chile (1997)
Canada–Israel (1997)
Hungary–Turkey (1998)
Hungary–Israel (1998)
Israel–Turkey (1998)
Romania–Turkey (1998)
Poland–Israel (1998)
EU–Tunisia (1998)
Mexico–Chile (1999)
EU–Israel Agreement (2000)
EU–Mexico (2000)
EU–Morocco (2000)
EFTA–Morocco (2000)
Poland–Turkey (2000)
Mexico–Israel (2000)
Chile–Costa Rica (2002)

Notes: This table lists, in chronological order, all economic integration agreements (EIAs) used in estimation. Only agreements involving the countries in our sample are included. EIAs that entered into force before 1990 are used, as needed, to construct the lagged variables of the EIA dummy variable; the EIA data set includes EIA dummies from 1950 to 2011. For all estimates, EIAs include free trade agreements and deeper integration agreements based upon the Baier–Bergstrand data set.

common colonial history ($CLNY_{ij,t}$), and a common land border or contiguity ($CNTG_{ij,t}$). Panel 2B includes $INTER_{ij,1994}$, $INTER_{ij,1998}$, and $INTER_{ij,2002}$; $INTER_{ij,1990}$ is omitted due to the inclusion of a constant.[32]

The first specification for column (1) in panel 2A is based upon Eq. (3) using PQML. We include lagged values of $EIA_{ij,t}$ along with the current value, based upon numerous previous studies that have found effects lasting up to 10–15 years. Typically, most EIAs are phased in over 5–10 years. Moreover, EIAs likely have lagged effects on trade as flows respond slowly to terms-of-trade changes. Lagged values of EIAs capture these influences. As discussed above, our preferred econometric estimator is PQML; however, later in Table 2 we present results using OLS. To show that the zeros issue is not a problem, our first specification is on positive trade flows only. Consistent with previous findings, column (1) in panel 2A indicates that the partial effects of EIAs are economically and statistically significant, both for current and most lagged values of $EIA_{ij,t}$. The total (partial) effect of an EIA is 157 percent ($= 100 \times [e^{0.945} - 1]$). Compared to earlier studies using OLS and aggregate goods trade flows this estimate is large; however, our study uses PQML and manufactures trade flows. As first

[32] However, due to the inclusion of the other fixed effects, the constant cannot be interpreted as an estimate of $INTER_{ij,1990}$.

Table 2
Estimates for manufactures trade flows.

2A. EIAs	(1) PQML(+)	(2) PQML	(3) PQML Lead	(4) PQML Trend	(5) PQML sub-sample	(6) OLS
$EIA_{ij,t}$	0.241	0.241	0.239	0.251	0.237	0.132
	(0.038)**	(0.038)**	(0.048)**	(0.039)**	(0.037)**	(0.055)*
$EIA_{ij,t-4}$	0.294	0.294	0.294	0.299	0.292	0.123
	(0.050)**	(0.050)**	(0.049)**	(0.050)**	(0.053)**	(0.051)*
$EIA_{ij,t-8}$	0.248	0.248	0.248	0.253	0.258	0.025
	(0.033)**	(0.033)**	(0.034)**	(0.034)**	(0.032)**	(0.051)
$EIA_{ij,t-12}$	0.069	0.069	0.069	0.074	0.066	0.027
	(0.045)	(0.045)	(0.045)	(0.046)	(0.045)	(0.063)
$EIA_{ij,t-16}$	0.093	0.093	0.093	0.100	0.094	0.014
	(0.030)**	(0.030)**	(0.030)**	(0.030)**	(0.031)**	(0.068)
$EIA_{ij,t+4}$			0.005			
			(0.048)			
Total EIA	0.945	0.944	0.944	0.977	0.948	0.321
	(0.085)**	(0.085)**	(0.095)**	(0.088)**	(0.084)**	(0.141)*
N	6639	6724	6724	6724	6116	6639
2B. EIAs and INTER						
$EIA_{ij,t}$	0.111	0.110	0.144	0.111	0.114	0.110
	(0.043)*	(0.043)*	(0.047)**	(0.043)**	(0.045)*	(0.051)*
$EIA_{ij,t-4}$	0.218	0.218	0.215	0.216	0.222	0.114
	(0.041)**	(0.041)**	(0.039)**	(0.041)**	(0.044)**	(0.050)*
$EIA_{ij,t-8}$	0.159	0.159	0.155	0.157	0.178	0.017
	(0.029)**	(0.029)**	(0.029)**	(0.029)**	(0.032)**	(0.050)
$EIA_{ij,t-12}$	−0.024	−0.024	−0.023	−0.026	−0.023	0.010
	(0.027)	(0.027)	(0.027)	(0.028)	(0.026)	(0.066)
$EIA_{ij,t-16}$	0.044	0.044	0.043	0.045	0.057	0.002
	(0.030)	(0.030)	(0.030)	(0.031)	(0.031)+	(0.068)
$EIA_{ij,t+4}$			−0.089			
			(0.052)+			
$INTER_{ij,1994}$	0.099	0.099	0.104	0.107	0.061	0.387
	(0.021)**	(0.021)**	(0.022)**	(0.021)**	(0.021)**	(0.028)**
$INTER_{ij,1998}$	0.282	0.282	0.286	0.298	0.259	0.654
	(0.028)**	(0.028)**	(0.030)**	(0.029)**	(0.033)**	(0.036)**
$INTER_{ij,2002}$	0.292	0.292	0.296	0.316	0.250	0.689
	(0.043)**	(0.043)**	(0.044)**	(0.044)**	(0.055)**	(0.044)**
Total EIA	0.507	0.506	0.534	0.504	0.550	0.252
	(0.099)**	(0.099)**	(0.102)**	(0.100)**	(0.114)**	(0.135)+
N	6639	6724	6724	6724	6116	6639

Notes: This table reports panel gravity estimates with data on total manufacturing, 1990–2002. All specifications include exporter-time, importer-time and country-pair fixed effects. Fixed effects estimates are not reported for brevity. Robust standard errors, clustered by country pair, are in parentheses. Panel 2A offers different variations of the main specification from Baier and Bergstrand (2007). In Panel 2B, we account for declining international border effects using time-varying border variables $INTER_{ij,t}$. Column 1, PQML(+), presents PQML estimates using only positive trade flows. The estimates in column (2), PQML, use all observations in the sample. In column (3), PQML Lead, we test for reverse causality by introducing a lead EIA effect. The estimates in column (4), PQML Trend, are obtained with pair-fixed effects interacted with a time trend. In column (5), PQML sub-sample, we drop the observations for the Rest-of-World (*ROW*) region and the observations that rely on interpolated output data. Finally, column (6) reports OLS estimates. See text for further details.
+ $p < 0.10$
* $p < .05$
** $p < .01$

seen in Santos Silva and Tenreyro (2006), PQML estimates tend to be systematically larger than OLS estimates for EIAs' coefficients. Also, highly tradable manufactures tend to be impacted much more by EIAs than most non-manufactured goods; evidence will be provided later by contrasting results for manufactures trade with those for aggregate goods trade.

The first specification in column (1) in panel 2B, also based on Eq. (3), includes $INTER_{ij,t}$. The first notable finding is a substantive decline in column (1) from panel 2A to panel 2B in the total (partial) EIA effect from 0.945 (157 percent) to 0.507 (66 percent). The impact of a typical EIA is *halved*. The second notable finding is that the effect of an international border has been declining over time, and this effect is economically and statistically significant. The coefficient estimate of 0.292 for $INTER_{ij,2002}$ implies that the declining effect of the international border has increased international relative to intranational trade by 34 percent over 12 years ($=100 \times [e^{0.292} - 1]$), or approximately 2.5 percent per year.[33] Hence, the costs of

[33] de Sousa et al. (2012) only report declining border effects using OLS. Bosquet and Boulhol (2015) estimate the changing effects of distance and common land borders using PQML; however, as discussed later, they do not find falling distance elasticities, likely due to omitting intranational trade. Note

international borders on international relative to intranational trade have been declining over time about 2.4 percent per year ($=100 \times [1-(1/e^{0.292})^{1/12}]$) and the absence of accounting for international border effects biases upwards EIA effects.

The second specification in panels 2A and 2B is identical to that in column (1) except that zeros are added to the sample. The addition of zeros to the sample has no material bearing on our results, partly due to the small number of zeros. However, for completeness we include them in our remaining specifications.

The specification in column (3) considers the potential bias created by "reverse causality." Wooldridge (2010, p. 325) suggests that it is easy to test for the "strict exogeneity" of EIAs in our context. To do this, we add a future level of EIA to the model. In the panel context here, if EIA is exogenous to trade flows, $EIA_{ij,t+4}$ should be uncorrelated with the current trade flow. Column (3) in panels 2A and 2B reports the results. In panel 2A, the future level of EIA has no economically or statistically significant effect on current trade. In Panel 2B, the effect is only marginally economically and statistically significant. Consequently, we do not consider reverse causality to be a serious problem.

The specification in column (4) is based upon Eq. (4). This specification allows for a trend change in the effect of the pair fixed effects, cf., (Wooldridge, 2010). Note that inclusion of ij fixed effects interacted with year dummies is infeasible; it would perfectly predict trade flows. Column (4) reports the results using Eq. (4), which are directly comparable to those in column (2). It is evident that there is not much difference in the results using equation specifications (3) or (4). Consequently, for the remainder of the analysis we focus on Eq. (3) specifications, which are computationally less demanding.

The specification in column (5) is based upon Eq. (3), but excludes observations for *ROW* and for any observations using interpolated output values. The specification in (5) is identical to that in column (2). Importantly, in both panels the EIA coefficient estimates are essentially the same; there are neither economically nor statistically significant differences. The only noticeable difference in panel 2B between columns (2) and (5) is that the coefficient estimates for the $INTER_{ij,t}$ dummies are larger in column (2) relative to (5). However, even by 2002, the declining effect of the international border on raising international relative to intranational trade is only 6 percent more in column (2) relative to column (5) ($[e^{0.292}-e^{0.250}] \times 100$). Moreover, none of these differences is statistically significant. Hence, for the remainder of the analysis we include observations for *ROW* and the observations using interpolated output values; however, the results excluding those are available in an online appendix.

While PQML has desired econometric properties as discussed above, the literature has not accepted completely a preference for PQML, cf., Head and Mayer (2000). Much earlier work in this literature has used OLS. For completeness, we also run the specification based upon Eq. (3) using OLS for positive trade flows only. Two results, reported in column (6) and comparing to columns (1) or (2), are worth noting. First, as found in most other studies, EIA effects are smaller using OLS compared to those using PQML, cf., Santos Silva and Tenreyro (2006). The total EIA effect in panel 2B using OLS is 0.252 relative to the PQML estimate of 0.507. Second, using OLS the coefficient estimates for $INTER_{ij,t}$ are higher.[34]

We provide one more sensitivity analysis using total manufactures trade flows. Reflecting upon Eq. (3), this specification suggests that – in principle – there is no reason not to include also variables analogous to $INTER_{ij,1994}$, $INTER_{ij,1998}$, and $INTER_{ij,2002}$, such as for bilateral distance and dummies for common language, common colonial history, and contiguity. Practically, a potential concern is that – since variables such as bilateral distance are highly correlated with a dummy for international relative to intranational trade – their additional presence may cause a multicollinearity problem. Nevertheless, we expanded the main specification in column (2) in panel 2B to also include $DIST_{ij,1994}$, $DIST_{ij,1998}$, $DIST_{ij,2002}$ (defined above) and analogous variables for common language ($LANG_{ij,t}$), common colonial history ($CLNY_{ij,t}$), and contiguity ($CNTG_{ij,t}$). These results are reported in column (3) of Table 3. For comparison, Table 3 first provides in column (1) a specification identical to that in Table 2, column (2), panel A. The total EIA (partial) effect is 0.944. In column (2) of Table 3, we add the $INTER_{ij,t}$ variables; as in the identical specification in Table 2, column (2), panel B, the total EIA effect falls significantly as expected. In column (3) of Table 3, we add $DIST_{ij,1994}$, $DIST_{ij,1998}$, $DIST_{ij,2002}$ and the analogous variables for common language ($LANG_{ij,t}$), common colonial history ($CLNY_{ij,t}$), and contiguity ($CNTG_{ij,t}$). Two main conclusions result. First, these additional variables – with two exceptions – have no significant effects on trade flows; the two exceptions are $CNTG_{ij,1994}$ and $CNTG_{ij,2002}$. Second, the EIA effects are higher in column (3) relative to column (2); there is some muting of the decline in EIA effects due to the additional variables.

The explanation for the limited explanatory power of the standard gravity covariates is straightforward. The bilateral variables that most influence $INTER_{ij,t}$ – a dummy for international relative to intranational bilateral trade – are likely $DIST_{ij,t}$, $LANG_{ij,t}$, $CLNY_{ij,t}$, and $CNTG_{ij,t}$. The presence of $INTER_{ij,t}$ subsumes the effects of those other variables; this leads to low coefficient estimates for the additional variables. Nevertheless, in a later sensitivity analysis that will help resolve the "distance-elasticity puzzle," we will demonstrate that – in the *absence* of the $INTER_{ij,t}$ dummies – these additional variables (notably, $DIST_{ij,t}$) have significant roles. Finally, Table 3, column (4) reports the results for the Eq. (4) version of column (3)'s specification; there is no material difference between the results in columns (3) and (4). Since Eq. (3) is computationally less demanding, we will use Table 3's column (3) specification for the baseline rather than column (4)'s specification.

(*footnote continued*)
that the initial international border effect levels for each country pair in our study are allowed to differ across pairs, and are subsumed in the pair fixed effects.

[34] The OLS total partial EIA estimate of 0.321 in panel 2A is within the range of partial EIA effect estimates reported earlier, where the median is about 0.46. The lower estimate here reflects estimation over a more recent time period (1990–2002) than used in most studies, such as BB which used 1960–2000. As found in recent research related to Baier et al. (2015), EIA partial effects have declined over the decades since 1960 because the (likely) most welfare-improving EIAs formed earlier and had larger partial effects.

Table 3
Estimates for manufactures trade flows.

	(1) PQML	(2) PQML	(3) PQML	(4) PQML Trend
$EIA_{ij,t}$	0.241	0.110	0.117	0.117
	(0.038)**	(0.043)*	(0.044)**	(0.044)**
$EIA_{ij,t-4}$	0.294	0.218	0.243	0.244
	(0.050)**	(0.041)**	(0.043)**	(0.043)**
$EIA_{ij,t-8}$	0.248	0.159	0.225	0.226
	(0.033)**	(0.029)**	(0.035)**	(0.036)**
$EIA_{ij,t-12}$	0.069	−0.024	0.020	0.021
	(0.045)	(0.027)	(0.037)	(0.036)
$EIA_{ij,t-16}$	0.093	0.044	0.022	0.023
	(0.030)**	(0.030)	(0.035)	(0.035)
$INTER_{ij,1994}$		0.099	0.171	0.175
		(0.021)**	(0.074)*	(0.074)*
$INTER_{ij,1998}$		0.282	0.231	0.241
		(0.028)**	(0.093)*	(0.094)*
$INTER_{ij,2002}$		0.292	0.294	0.309
		(0.043)**	(0.145)*	(0.146)*
$DIST_{ij,1994}$			−0.024	−0.022
			(0.029)	(0.029)
$DIST_{ij,1998}$			0.035	0.039
			(0.037)	(0.038)
$DIST_{ij,2002}$			0.021	0.026
			(0.055)	(0.056)
$LANG_{ij,1994}$			0.032	0.032
			(0.048)	(0.048)
$LANG_{ij,1998}$			0.005	0.004
			(0.073)	(0.073)
$LANG_{ij,2002}$			0.026	0.025
			(0.075)	(0.075)
$CNTG_{ij,1994}$			−0.144	−0.145
			(0.065)*	(0.066)*
$CNTG_{ij,1998}$			−0.078	−0.080
			(0.094)	(0.095)
$CNTG_{ij,2002}$			−0.226	−0.229
			(0.112)*	(0.112)*
$CLNY_{ij,1994}$			−0.034	−0.034
			(0.045)	(0.045)
$CLNY_{ij,1998}$			−0.030	−0.030
			(0.071)	(0.071)
$CLNY_{ij,2002}$			−0.057	−0.057
			(0.070)	(0.070)
Total EIA	0.944	0.506	0.626	0.630
	(0.085)**	(0.099)**	(0.111)**	(0.111)**
N	6724	6724	6724	6724

Notes: This table reports panel gravity estimates with data on total manufacturing, 1990–2002. All specifications include exporter-time, importer-time and country-pair fixed effects. Fixed effects estimates are not reported for brevity. Robust standard errors, clustered by country pair, are in parentheses. Columns (1) and (2) reproduce the results from column (2) of panel 2A and from column (2) of panel 2B, respectively. Column (3) introduces the standard gravity covariates as described in the text. Finally, the results in column (4) are obtained with pair-fixed effects scaled up by a time trend. See text for further details.

+ $p < 0.10$.
* $p < .05$
** $p < .01$

One potential bias we have not accounted for is firm-heterogeneity bias. As discussed in Helpman et al. (2008), or HMR, and Egger et al. (2011), the existence of firm heterogeneity may bias coefficient estimates in gravity equations using aggregate data. One of the advantages of HMR's two-stage approach is that it accounts for zeros, but also for firm heterogeneity, when using aggregate trade flows. HMR concluded that firm-heterogeneity bias mattered even more than country-selection bias in their cross-section estimates.[35] However, accounting also for endogeneity (self-selection) bias of EIAs, Egger et al. (2011) found that firm-heterogeneity bias hardly mattered at all. We argue here that – for our panel

[35] HMR also estimated their model pooling several cross-sections over time. However, their estimation never included bilateral country-pair fixed effects in their second stage, which is critical to our discussion below.

specification shown in Eq. (3) – the results are not likely influenced materially by firm-heterogeneity bias, due to the inclusion of the bilateral country-pair fixed effects. This is an issue explored only recently in Baier et al. (2014).

To understand why, we first review briefly the HMR approach, which was used in a cross section (1986 trade flows). The two-stage methodology entails estimating first a probit equation to determine the probability of a positive observation between a country pair. The probit estimates are then used to construct inverse Mills' ratios (denoted $IMR_{ij,t}$) to capture selection bias and variables $Z_{ij,t}$, $Z^2_{ij,t}$, and $Z^3_{ij,t}$ to control for heterogeneous productivities of firms. $IMR_{ij,t}$, $Z_{ij,t}$, $Z^2_{ij,t}$, and $Z^3_{ij,t}$ are then used as additional regressors in the second-stage gravity-equation specification to control for country-selection and firm-heterogeneity biases.[36] Both stages of estimation in HMR used exporter and importer fixed effects to account for multilateral variables, but did not use bilateral country-pair fixed effects (as HMR used a cross-section).

In our panel specification of Eq. (3), we have time-invariant bilateral country-pair fixed effects. If most of the variation in the predicted probit probabilities of trading (i.e., selection of country-pairs into positive trade) is cross-sectional in nature, then time-invariant country-pair bilateral fixed effects in the second stage will account for most of the variation in $IMR_{ij,t}$, $Z_{ij,t}$, $Z^2_{ij,t}$, and $Z^3_{ij,t}$. The only possible bias in gravity equation coefficient estimates using our panel attributable to selection and firm-heterogeneity would be time variation in $IMR_{ij,t}$, $Z_{ij,t}$, $Z^2_{ij,t}$, and $Z^3_{ij,t}$. It becomes an empirical issue then to determine if such bias is material.

Baier et al. (2014), or BBF, recently addressed the HMR two-stage estimation procedure in a panel with bilateral fixed effects (and alternatively first-differencing) in the second stage. Akin to HMR, BBF first estimated eight individual cross-section probits for the years 1965, 1970,..., 2000 to generate predicted probabilities of positive aggregate goods trade flows for a large number of country pairs. They then used these predicted probabilities to construct for each year $IMR_{ij,t}$, $Z_{ij,t}$, $Z^2_{ij,t}$, and $Z^3_{ij,t}$. In the second stage, they estimated a specification similar to Eq. (3), but excluding $INTER_{ij,t}$ and using OLS. Their results from the second stage regressions were reported in BBF's Appendix Table A4, which can be readily compared to the results from omitting $IMR_{ij,t}$, $Z_{ij,t}$, $Z^2_{ij,t}$, and $Z^3_{ij,t}$ which were presented in Table 1 of BBF. A comparison of the results from the two tables reveals clearly that there is very little quantitative and *no* qualitative differences between the respective coefficient estimates. The reason is the presence in the second stage of the bilateral fixed effects (or first-differencing). Put simply, most of the variation in the predicted probabilities of positive trade flows is cross-sectional, not time-varying; bilateral fixed effects (or first-differencing) accounts largely for the influences of country-selection and firm-heterogeneity. Based upon those results, we argue our results are likely robust to firm-heterogeneity bias. Moreover, one feature of our data is that there are very few zero trade flows that are not perfectly explained by our fixed effects (country-pair, exporter-time, and importer-time). This implies that there are few country-pairs that start or stop trading in our data set.[37]

5. Empirical results for disaggregate manufactures trade

One dimension which BB ignored entirely is the sensitivity of the findings to disaggregation of trade flows. The empirical literature on partial effects of EIAs using disaggregate data is actually quite small. Anderson and Yotov (2011) is one of the few studies using the BB approach to analyze disaggregate trade flow effects, and our study allows us to explore disaggregation since it is based upon the same data. Table 4 provides the results of estimating the partial EIA effects using Eq. (3) for the eight 2-digit ISIC categories of manufactures. Table 4 is divided into two panels, 4A and 4B. Panels 4A and 4B provide the main PQML specification results using each of eight manufactures industries. In Table 4, *DIST*, *LANG*, *CLNY*, and *CNTG* are included for the reasons discussed above.

Panel 4A provides the results of EIA effects in the analysis of disaggregate trade flows using PQML and excluding $INTER_{ij,t}$, $DIST_{ij,t}$ and the analogous variables. The results are largely consistent with those in the previous section for total manufactures trade flows. First, compare the results in Panel 4A of Table 4 with those in column (1) of Table 3. Using the total EIA estimates, we find positive and economically and statistically significant partial effects of EIAs on trade flows in seven out of the eight sectors, with the total partial effects of these seven sectors ranging from 0.175 (Wood) to 1.641 (Textile). Only in the Wood sector we do not find significant total effects of EIAs.

Panel 4B provides the results including the international border dummies and associated gravity variables. As in previous estimates, the EIA effects tend to diminish, but many remain economically and statistically significant. Using the total EIA estimates again, the partial effect for Machinery Products falls from 1.145 to 0.640. Yet, this still implies that an EIA increases trade by 90 percent (absent any general equilibrium effects). Estimates of the sums of current and lagged significant effects range from 0.291 to 1.045. Moreover, we find that the coefficient estimates for the $INTER_{ij,t}$ dummies are positive (except for Wood, Paper, and Chemicals for some years) and, in many cases, statistically different from zero. We do not present the results for PQML with positive flows only, as these results were very close to those including zeros, as we established in Table 2. Also, in an online appendix we provide the results for PQML excluding observations for *ROW* and for interpolated output values, as these results also are very close to those in Table 4 (as we established earlier in Table 2).

[36] When exporting fixed costs are present and productivities are bounded from above (as, for example, in HMR), the gravity equations stated in Eqs. (1), (3), and (4) apply only for the positive trade flows. In Eq. (1), besides representing structural parameters $\chi_{ij,t}$ would also capture the corrections for country selection (the inverse Mills ratio) and firm heterogeneity, and those correction terms would have to be included as additional regressors in Eqs. (3) and (4).

[37] For this issue, it is critical to note that identification of the HMR terms $IMR_{ij,t}$, $Z_{ij,t}$, $Z^2_{ij,t}$, and $Z^3_{ij,t}$ relies on the variation of the export-status (positive or zero). The HMR approach was explored using our data set; however, convergence could not be achieved precisely because of the very small number of zeros.

Table 4
Estimates for sectoral manufactures trade flows.

4A. EIAs	(1) Food	(2) Textile	(3) Wood	(4) Paper	(5) Chemicals	(6) Minerals	(7) Metals	(8) Machinery
$EIA_{ij,t}$	0.366	0.569	−0.151	−0.109	0.099	−0.038	0.355	0.313
	(0.104)**	(0.108)**	(0.069)*	(0.048)*	(0.038)**	(0.070)	(0.048)**	(0.072)**
$EIA_{ij,t-4}$	0.253	0.459	0.203	0.121	0.221	0.390	0.202	0.351
	(0.048)**	(0.085)**	(0.039)**	(0.040)**	(0.051)**	(0.089)**	(0.049)**	(0.064)**
$EIA_{ij,t-8}$	0.202	0.323	0.010	0.332	0.187	0.145	0.280	0.297
	(0.034)**	(0.069)**	(0.081)	(0.068)**	(0.036)**	(0.026)**	(0.049)**	(0.057)**
$EIA_{ij,t-12}$	0.268	0.175	−0.152	−0.089	0.049	−0.011	0.067	0.098
	(0.028)**	(0.049)**	(0.050)**	(0.048)**	(0.063)	(0.055)	(0.042)	(0.041)*
$EIA_{ij,t-16}$	0.126	0.116	0.263	0.093	0.096	−0.062	0.095	0.087
	(0.047)**	(0.039)**	(0.054)**	(0.049)$^{+}$	(0.055)$^{+}$	(0.052)	(0.062)	(0.048)$^{+}$
Total EIA	1.215	1.641	0.175	0.348	0.652	0.422	0.998	1.145
	(0.123)**	(0.207)**	(0.114)	(0.096)**	(0.065)**	(0.095)**	(0.109)**	(0.173)**
N	6692	6708	6596	6540	6724	6628	6564	6724
4B. EIAs, INTER, and other variables								
$EIA_{ij,t}$	0.320	0.349	−0.099	−0.160	0.021	−0.066	0.247	0.149
	(0.090)**	(0.067)**	(0.069)	(0.054)**	(0.047)	(0.080)	(0.049)**	(0.062)*
$EIA_{ij,t-4}$	0.205	0.324	0.256	0.131	0.255	0.368	0.109	0.290
	(0.032)**	(0.061)**	(0.038)**	(0.043)**	(0.047)**	(0.093)**	(0.050)*	(0.054)**
$EIA_{ij,t-8}$	0.151	0.130	0.138	0.297	0.279	0.181	0.214	0.210
	(0.036)**	(0.053)*	(0.058)*	(0.053)**	(0.046)**	(0.040)**	(0.055)**	(0.056)**
$EIA_{ij,t-12}$	0.202	−0.050	−0.032	−0.052	0.070	−0.036	−0.020	0.026
	(0.036)**	(0.058)	(0.059)	(0.046)	(0.047)	(0.056)	(0.063)	(0.052)
$EIA_{ij,t-16}$	0.167	0.083	0.246	0.075	0.093	−0.088	−0.007	−0.035
	(0.054)**	(0.047)$^{+}$	(0.052)**	(0.062)	(0.065)	(0.070)	(0.063)	(0.044)
$INTER_{ij,1994}$	0.151	0.554	0.218	−0.024	−0.065	0.021	0.343	0.192
	(0.062)*	(0.118)**	(0.113)$^{+}$	(0.064)	(0.068)	(0.102)	(0.088)**	(0.083)*
$INTER_{ij,1998}$	0.160	0.810	−0.106	0.071	−0.024	0.009	0.101	0.347
	(0.075)*	(0.161)**	(0.131)	(0.109)	(0.084)	(0.165)	(0.184)	(0.116)**
$INTER_{ij,2002}$	0.021	0.742	−0.184	0.034	−0.179	0.017	0.517	0.585
	(0.087)	(0.216)**	(0.169)	(0.163)	(0.119)	(0.284)	(0.106)**	(0.178)**
$DIST_{ij,1994}$	−0.039	−0.100	−0.101	0.041	0.046	−0.029	−0.092	−0.021
	(0.029)	(0.052)$^{+}$	(0.048)*	(0.031)	(0.027)$^{+}$	(0.046)	(0.047)*	(0.034)
$DIST_{ij,1998}$	−0.027	−0.106	0.063	0.035	0.107	0.046	0.137	0.028
	(0.035)	(0.069)	(0.061)	(0.046)	(0.034)**	(0.065)	(0.103)	(0.047)
$DIST_{ij,2002}$	0.021	−0.081	0.091	0.041	0.161	0.046	−0.093	−0.027
	(0.043)	(0.087)	(0.079)	(0.068)	(0.047)**	(0.104)	(0.062)	(0.069)
$LANG_{ij,1994}$	0.074	0.082	0.020	0.043	0.064	0.110	0.134	−0.021
	(0.049)	(0.096)	(0.097)	(0.049)	(0.062)	(0.115)	(0.081)$^{+}$	(0.061)
$LANG_{ij,1998}$	0.153	0.089	−0.033	0.064	0.026	0.073	0.054	0.006
	(0.063)*	(0.153)	(0.109)	(0.080)	(0.066)	(0.109)	(0.108)	(0.083)
$LANG_{ij,2002}$	0.240	0.134	−0.055	0.053	0.213	0.076	−0.092	−0.029
	(0.060)**	(0.147)	(0.124)	(0.089)	(0.147)	(0.106)	(0.116)	(0.089)
$CNTG_{ij,1994}$	−0.053	−0.142	−0.214	−0.026	−0.029	−0.113	−0.232	−0.153
	(0.055)	(0.091)	(0.103)*	(0.056)	(0.069)	(0.083)	(0.071)**	(0.076)*
$CNTG_{ij,1998}$	−0.025	0.027	−0.108	−0.048	−0.024	−0.077	0.041	−0.133
	(0.067)	(0.151)	(0.128)	(0.099)	(0.082)	(0.112)	(0.127)	(0.111)
$CNTG_{ij,2002}$	0.049	0.045	−0.136	−0.112	−0.273	−0.149	−0.106	−0.341
	(0.067)	(0.161)	(0.148)	(0.128)	(0.138)*	(0.182)	(0.091)	(0.136)*
$CLNY_{ij,1994}$	−0.072	−0.048	−0.141	−0.073	−0.054	−0.058	−0.029	0.002
	(0.047)	(0.161)	(0.120)	(0.061)	(0.051)	(0.081)	(0.102)	(0.039)
$CLNY_{ij,1998}$	−0.051	−0.145	0.008	−0.105	−0.017	−0.058	0.007	−0.052
	(0.085)	(0.227)	(0.144)	(0.092)	(0.068)	(0.124)	(0.136)	(0.071)
$CLNY_{ij,2002}$	−0.087	−0.267	0.012	−0.045	−0.014	−0.148	0.076	−0.079
	(0.076)	(0.249)	(0.147)	(0.102)	(0.141)	(0.115)	(0.161)	(0.115)
Total EIA	1.045	0.836	0.509	0.291	0.718	0.358	0.544	0.640
	(0.115)**	(0.160)**	(0.146)*	(0.139)*	(0.122)**	(0.191)**	(0.117)**	(0.146)**
N	6692	6708	6596	6540	6724	6628	6564	6724

Notes: This table reports panel gravity estimates for the eight 2-digit ISIC categories of manufactures, 1990–2002. All specifications are estimated with PQML, pair (*ij*), exporter-year (*it*), and importer-year (*jt*) fixed effects and allow for phasing-in of the EIA effects. Fixed effects estimates are not reported for brevity. Robust standard errors, clustered by country pair, are reported in parentheses. See text for further details.

$^{+}$ $p < 0.10$

* $p < .05$

** $p < .01$

In sum, the main PQML results shown in column (3) of Table 3 for total manufactures are robust to using disaggregate trade flows. These results suggest that – after accounting for likely declining bilateral variable and fixed trade costs using a novel set of time-varying international border dummies capturing relative international-to-intranational trade-flow changes – EIAs still have economically and statistically significant partial effects on trade flows, but that ignoring the international border dummies tends to bias upward EIA estimates. Moreover, the novel time-varying international border dummies reveal the average cost of international relative to intranational trade has declined for several sectors.

6. Empirical results for aggregate trade flows

One of the limitations of the manufactures data set employed is the short time series; we are able to explain the effect of declining bilateral trade costs over a period of only 12 years.[38] However, data is available for a longer time series for bilateral aggregate goods trade flows. The drawback of using aggregate goods trade flows is that the only available (imperfect) proxy of gross output, from which to construct intranational trade flows, is Gross Domestic Product (GDP) – a "value-added" (not gross output) measure. Nevertheless, we thought it worthwhile in this section to evaluate the sensitivity of the earlier results for total manufactures trade flows using a shorter time series to use of aggregate goods trade flows for a longer period, keeping in mind the shortcoming in our measure of intranational trade.

The aggregate goods trade flow data are from COMTRADE. We nearly doubled the time period relative to earlier; it is 1991–2011. We have also more than doubled the number of countries covered from 40 to 89; the 89 countries included represent 98 percent of world output.[39] The GDP data come from the latest edition of the Penn World Tables 8.0.[40]

Table 5 provides the results. In the first column of results using PQML, we show that as before the current and lagged EIA dummies have economically and statistically significant positive effects. The introduction in the next specification of the international border dummies (and other gravity covariates) causes as expected the coefficient estimates of $EIA_{ij,t}$ and its lags to decline. The total EIA partial effect in column (2) of 0.496 is smaller than the comparable estimate in column (3) of Table 3 of 0.626; however, EIA effects tend to be lower for aggregate goods trade than for manufactures trade. It is worth noting the pattern of coefficient estimates for the five border dummies. All of the *INTER* coefficient estimates are positive and statistically significant.

The third and fourth columns report the results using OLS instead. As found earlier, EIAs' coefficient estimates are smaller using OLS relative to PQML and international border effects are larger. Consequently, the results for manufactures trade using a smaller number of countries and years are essentially comparable to the results using aggregate goods trade flows for a larger number of countries and years.

7. The "distance-elasticity" puzzle

One of the potential key contributions of this paper is the introduction of a variable $INTER_{ij,t}$ to account for likely declining trends in bilateral fixed and variable trade costs that are potentially increasing international relative to intranational trade. Moreover, as seen in Tables 3, 4B and 5, the further introduction of typical gravity-equation variables that likely explain international trade relative to intranational trade – *DIST*, *LANG*, *CNTG*, and *CLNY* – add virtually no further explanatory power once *INTER* is included.

However, what happens once *INTER* is excluded? Our expectation is that many of the typical gravity-equation variables matter. Table 6 provides the results from excluding *INTER*. Not surprisingly, $DIST_{ij,t}$ – the logarithm of bilateral distance interacted with the year dummies – replaces the influence of $INTER_{ij,t}$, and as before the other variables play a limited role. Yet, these results raise the possibility of addressing another important issue. One of the well-known puzzles in the empirical international trade literature is the "distance-elasticity puzzle." This puzzle is that – in spite of likely falling bilateral fixed and variable trade costs – a time series of cross-sectional estimates of a properly-specified gravity equation yield *rising* distance elasticities (in absolute values). That is, international trade in such cross sections declines more in response to distance in recent years relative to earlier years, cf., Disdier and Head (2008).

While several researchers have made attempts to solve the puzzle, Yotov, 2012 addressed the issue by including observations for *intranational* trade, along with including on the right-hand-side a variable measuring intranational distances. Such intranational trade flows and distances have actually been a common feature of several border-effect studies, but had not yet permeated the distance-elasticity literature. Yotov (2012) "solved" the distance-elasticity puzzle by

[38] The effective constraint is available production data.

[39] The 89 countries (with their respective labels in parentheses) include: Angola (AGO), Argentina (ARG), Australia (AUS), Austria (AUT), Azerbaijan (AZE), Bangladesh (BGD), Belarus (BLR), Belgium (BEL), Brazil (BRA), Bulgaria (BGR), Canada (CAN), Chile (CHL), China (CHN), Colombia (COL), Croatia (HRV), Czech Republic (CZE), Cyprus (CYP), Denmark (DNK), Dominican Republic (DOM), Ecuador (ECU), Egypt (EGY), Estonia (EST), Ethiopia (ETH), Finland (FIN), France (FRA), Germany (DEU), Ghana (GHA), Greece (GRC), Guatemala (GTM), Hong Kong (HKG), Hungary (HUN), India (IND), Indonesia (IDN), Iran (IRN), Iraq (IRQ), Ireland (IRL), Israel (ISR), Italy (ITA), Japan (JPN), Kazakhstan (KAZ), Kenya (KEN), Korea, Republic of (KOR), Kuwait (KWT), Lebanon (LBN), Lithuania (LTU), Latvia (LVA), Luxembourg (LUX), Macedonia (MKD), Malaysia (MYS), Malta (MLT), Mexico (MEX), Morocco (MAR), Netherlands (NLD), New Zealand (NZL), Nigeria (NGA), Norway (NOR), Oman (OMN), Pakistan (PAK), Peru (PER), Philippines (PHL), Poland (POL), Portugal (PRT), Qatar (QAT), Romania (ROU), Russia (RUS), Saudi Arabia (SAU), Serbia (SRB), Singapore (SGP), Slovak Republic (SVK), Slovenia (SVN), South Africa (ZAF), Spain (ESP), Sri Lanka (LKA), Sudan (SDN), Sweden (SWE), Switzerland (CHE), Syria (SYR), Tanzania (TZA), Thailand (THA), Tunisia (TUN), Turkey (TUR), Turkmenistan (TKM), Ukraine (UKR), United Kingdom (GBR), United States (USA), Uzbekistan (UZB), Venezuela (VEN), Vietnam (VNM), Zimbabwe (ZWE).

[40] These series are now maintained by the Groningen Growth and Development Centre and reside at http://www.rug.nl/research/ggdc/data/penn-world-table

Table 5
Estimates for aggregate goods trade flows, 1991–2011.

	(1) PQML	(2) PQML	(3) OLS	(4) OLS
$EIA_{ij,t}$	0.511	0.085	0.172	0.158
	(0.070)**	(0.058)	(0.039)**	(0.039)**
$EIA_{ij,t-4}$	0.351	0.228	0.132	0.136
	(0.045)**	(0.035)**	(0.034)**	(0.035)**
$EIA_{ij,t-8}$	0.295	0.186	−0.016	−0.020
	(0.044)**	(0.040)**	(0.036)	(0.037)
$EIA_{ij,t-12}$	0.276	0.016	0.070	0.075
	(0.060)**	(0.050)	(0.037)+	(0.038)*
$EIA_{ij,t-16}$	0.279	−0.019	0.007	0.007
	(0.022)**	(0.041)	(0.041)	(0.043)
$INTER_{ij,1995}$		0.176		0.311
		(0.056)**		(0.161)+
$INTER_{ij,1999}$		0.192		0.252
		(0.075)*		(0.164)
$INTER_{ij,2003}$		0.460		0.549
		(0.106)**		(0.180)**
$INTER_{ij,2007}$		1.055		1.165
		(0.114)**		(0.196)**
$INTER_{ij,2011}$		1.206		1.478
		(0.126)**		(0.227)**
$DIST_{ij,1995}$		−0.002		−0.008
		(0.020)		(0.035)
$DIST_{ij,1999}$		−0.024		0.031
		(0.026)		(0.035)
$DIST_{ij,2003}$		−0.062		0.002
		(0.035)+		(0.038)
$DIST_{ij,2007}$		−0.078		0.033
		(0.040)+		(0.039)
$DIST_{ij,2011}$		−0.021		0.045
		(0.044)		(0.041)
$LANG_{ij,1995}$		0.040		0.002
		(0.044)		(0.080)
$LANG_{ij,1999}$		0.004		0.128
		(0.072)		(0.085)
$LANG_{ij,2003}$		−0.040		0.070
		(0.060)		(0.092)
$LANG_{ij,2007}$		−0.096		0.098
		(0.078)		(0.091)
$LANG_{ij,2011}$		−0.213		−0.018
		(0.094)*		(0.093)
$CNTG_{ij,1995}$		−0.069		0.197
		(0.066)		(0.119)
$CNTG_{ij,1999}$		−0.134		0.058
		(0.107)		(0.112)
$CNTG_{ij,2003}$		−0.211		0.128
		(0.093)*		(0.121)
$CNTG_{ij,2007}$		−0.239		−0.005
		(0.087)**		(0.134)
$CNTG_{ij,2011}$		−0.184		0.078
		(0.102)+		(0.125)
$CLNY_{ij,1995}$		−0.060		−0.011
		(0.050)		(0.095)
$CLNY_{ij,1999}$		0.027		−0.126
		(0.058)		(0.084)
$CLNY_{ij,2003}$		−0.073		−0.159
		(0.074)		(0.099)
$CLNY_{ij,2007}$		−0.165		−0.207
		(0.092)+		(0.103)*
$CLNY_{ij,2011}$		−0.201		−0.178
		(0.103)+		(0.104)+
Total EIA	1.713	0.496	0.364	0.356
	(0.124)**	(0.096)**	(0.064)**	(0.068)**
N	44,078	44,078	41,726	41,726

Notes: This table reports panel gravity estimates with aggregate data of the effects of all EIAs that entered into force during the period 1991–2011. Columns (1) and (2) use the PQML estimator, while columns (3) and (4) use the OLS estimator. All specifications allow for phasing-in of the EIA effects. All specifications are estimated with pair (*ij*), exporter-year (*it*), and importer-year (*jt*) fixed effects. Fixed effects estimate are not reported for brevity. Robust standard errors, clustered by country pair, are in parentheses.

+ $p < 0.10$
* $p < .05$
** $p < .01$

noting the importance of measuring international distances *relative to* intranational distances, as theoretical foundations for gravity equations actually suggest.

However, a shortcoming of Yotov (2012) is that – by using a time-series of cross-sections – the author does not control for unobserved bilateral heterogeneity and consequently the results suffer from omitted variables bias. Moreover, the results did not account for endogenous EIA effects. In order to estimate the distance elasticity, country-pair fixed effects cannot be used, as they would subsume the cross-country variation in bilateral distance. Consequently, researchers typically include bilateral distance and many other pair-specific variables to explain trade cross-sectionally. This leads to potentially biased results.

To obtain unbiased estimates, our approach uses a panel with pair fixed effects. The pair fixed effects capture the cross-sectional negative impact of bilateral distance on trade flows. By then introducing a set of year dummies interacted with bilateral distance – $DIST_{ij,1994}$, $DIST_{ij,1998}$, and $DIST_{ij,2002}$ – we capture the changing effects of bilateral distance on trade flows *relative to the initial year*. Another way to look at this variable is that it is a time-varying measure of the changing costs of international trade relative to intranational trade, but using a continuous measure rather than the earlier employed international border dummies. Note that the variables $DIST_{ij,t}$ in Table 6B have economically and statistically significant positive effects. Moreover, the size of the coefficient estimates tends to increase from 1994 to 2002. For total manufactures in column (9), the sizes of the positive coefficients increase monotonically.

What do these coefficient estimates suggest? The country-pair fixed effects (whose coefficient estimates are not shown due to the very large number) pickup that bilateral distance has a negative effect on trade. However, the *positive* and typically increasing over time coefficient estimates for $DIST_{ij,1994}$, $DIST_{ij,1998}$, and $DIST_{ij,2002}$ indicate that the negative effect of bilateral distance is *declining* over time. In the context of the discussion above and gravity Eq. (1), these results are consistent with the costs of international trade falling over time relative to intranational trade, likely attributable to decreasing – but unobservable – bilateral fixed and variable trade costs, that are increasing international relative to intranational trade. In fact, the coefficient estimate in panel 6B for $DIST_{ij,2002}$ of 0.141 for total manufactures trade suggests that the average effect of distance on international relative to intranational trade has diminished by 13 percent over 12 years ($[(1/e^{0.141})-1] \times 100$ percent), or 1.2 percent per year. A comparison of our results with those in Yotov (2012, Table 2) also reveals lower estimates using our approach. For instance, in Yotov (2012) the distance elasticity for textiles fell 57 percent over 10 years. By contrast, our results in Panel 6B imply that the distance elasticity for textiles fell only 20 percent ($[(1/e^{0.229})-1] \times 100$ percent) over a similar 12-year period, and this was the largest estimated distance-elasticity decrease. In fact, the smaller declines in the distance elasticities in our study relative to Yotov (2012) suggest that the estimates in the latter study were biased upward by ignoring the effects of EIAs.

This result is novel because it is generated allowing the country-pair fixed effects to subsume the level effect of distance on trade flows, and allows this effect to differ across country pairs in the initial year.[41] Only two previous studies have included bilateral country-pair fixed effects to address the distance-elasticity puzzle. Carrere et al. (2009) account for unobserved bilateral heterogeneity in their OLS estimates as well as linear approximations of the multilateral price terms. They find rising distance elasticities; however, they do not account for EIAs or intranational trade and distances. Bosquet and Boulhol (2015) could not find declining distance elasticities using PQML including bilateral fixed effects, but that is likely attributable to their exclusion of intranational trade and distances. However, unlike Carrere et al. (2009) and Bosquet and Boulhol (2015), we include as in Yotov (2012) intranational trade and distances; this feature is important to find declining distance effects on international trade, because we identify the effects of the (change in) the distance elasticity using variation in international and intranational trade flows.

Finally, it is useful to compare the results in, say, the last column in Table 6B (for Total Manufactures) with those in column (3) of Table 3 (for Total Manufactures). The total EIA (partial) effect from Table 6B is 0.728, whereas the total EIA effect from Table 3 is 0.626; these differ by 0.104 and the difference is not statistically significant. Moreover, when we ignore the statistically insignificant EIA coefficient estimates, the total EIA effects differ by only 0.063 (0.648–0.585), which is also statistically insignificant. The importance of this is that the EIA coefficient estimates are apparently not biased much by the choice of specification. $DIST_{ij,t}$ and $INTER_{ij,t}$ are – as noted earlier – "two sides of the same coin." Consequently, it is reasonable to conclude that the $DIST_{ij,t}$ coefficient estimates are also unbiased estimates of the declining effect of distance on international relative to intranational trade.

8. General equilibrium comparative statics

The paper so far has focused solely on partial, or direct, EIA effects. However, as Anderson and van Wincoop (2003) and (Head and Mayer, 2000) suggest, general equilibrium effects are also important for quantitative evaluation of trade-policy changes. Consequently, it is potentially interesting to determine how much the general equilibrium (GE) trade effects of EIAs are influenced by the different partial effect estimates with *and* without accounting for the declining effect of international borders on trade. In this section, we consider two quantitative general equilibrium (GE) comparative static exercises. First, we provide the GE trade effects of all observed EIAs that formed between 1990 and 2002 using the partial effect coefficient estimates ignoring $INTER_{ij,t}$ (and the other gravity covariates); these estimates are from column (1) of Table 3. We provide these GE effect estimates for all (bilateral) trade flows of each of our 40 countries and the *ROW* aggregate, the trade flows

[41] Coe et al. (2007) found evidence of declining distance elasticities by employing non-linear estimation (including PQML), although the declines ended between 1990 and 2000, but could not find declining distance elasticities using OLS. Berthelon and Freund (2008) found rising distance elasticities since 1985 using OLS. Larch etal (2015) found a declining distance effect using non-linear estimators, but not using OLS. However, Coe et al. (2007), Berthelon and Freund (2008), and Larch etal (2015) did not account for unobserved bilateral heterogeneity or for the endogeneity of EIAs, and did not include intranational trade flows and distances.

Table 6
Estimates to address the distance-elasticity puzzle.

	(1) Food	(2) Textile	(3) Wood	(4) Paper	(5) Chemicals	(6) Minerals	(7) Metals	(8) Machinery	(9) Total
6A. EIAs									
$EIA_{ij,t}$	0.366	0.569	−0.151	−0.109	0.099	−0.038	0.355	0.313	0.241
	(0.104)	(0.108)	(0.069)	(0.048)	(0.038)	(0.070)	(0.048)	(0.072)	(0.038)
$EIA_{ij,t-4}$	0.253	0.459	0.203	0.121	0.221	0.390	0.202	0.351	0.294
	(0.048)	(0.085)	(0.039)	(0.040)	(0.051)	(0.089)	(0.049)	(0.064)	(0.050)
$EIA_{ij,t-8}$	0.202	0.323	0.010	0.332	0.187	0.145	0.280	0.297	0.248
	(0.034)	(0.069)	(0.081)	(0.068)	(0.036)	(0.026)	(0.049)	(0.057)	(0.033)
$EIA_{ij,t-12}$	0.268	0.175	−0.152	−0.089	0.049	−0.011	0.067	0.098	0.069
	(0.028)	(0.049)	(0.050)	(0.048)	(0.063)	(0.055)	(0.042)	(0.041)	(0.045)
$EIA_{ij,t-16}$	0.126	0.116	0.263	0.093	0.096	−0.062	0.095	0.087	0.093
	(0.047)	(0.039)	(0.054)	(0.049)	(0.055)	(0.052)	(0.062)	(0.048)	(0.030)
Total EIA	1.215	1.641	0.175	0.348	0.652	0.422	0.998	1.145	0.944
	(0.123)	(0.207)	(0.114)	(0.096)	(0.065)	(0.095)	(0.109)	(0.173)	(0.085)
N	6692	6708	6596	6540	6724	6628	6564	6724	6724
6B. EIAs and other variables									
$EIA_{ij,t}$	0.329	0.409	−0.122	−0.151	0.024	−0.066	0.242	0.181	0.133
	(0.089)	(0.061)	(0.074)	(0.052)	(0.046)	(0.077)	(0.051)	(0.058)	(0.042)
$EIA_{ij,t-4}$	0.201	0.356	0.238	0.131	0.232	0.369	0.171	0.356	0.268
	(0.035)	(0.059)	(0.041)	(0.038)	(0.047)	(0.087)	(0.045)	(0.044)	(0.039)
$EIA_{ij,t-8}$	0.158	0.193	0.106	0.309	0.274	0.182	0.230	0.262	0.247
	(0.035)	(0.049)	(0.061)	(0.055)	(0.045)	(0.035)	(0.052)	(0.045)	(0.030)
$EIA_{ij,t-12}$	0.191	0.005	−0.071	−0.050	0.050	−0.036	0.031	0.095	0.047
	(0.037)	(0.055)	(0.056)	(0.042)	(0.046)	(0.044)	(0.056)	(0.048)	(0.034)
$EIA_{ij,t-16}$	0.160	0.091	0.233	0.075	0.078	−0.087	0.031	0.007	0.033
	(0.051)	(0.040)	(0.053)	(0.062)	(0.065)	(0.062)	(0.057)	(0.041)	(0.031)
$DIST_{ij,1994}$	0.029	0.140	−0.004	0.030	0.018	−0.020	0.053	0.056	0.047
	(0.009)	(0.027)	(0.016)	(0.013)	(0.009)	(0.013)	(0.027)	(0.014)	(0.010)
$DIST_{ij,1998}$	0.046	0.239	0.019	0.066	0.097	0.050	0.182	0.165	0.130
	(0.012)	(0.039)	(0.025)	(0.016)	(0.013)	(0.019)	(0.041)	(0.023)	(0.013)
$DIST_{ij,2002}$	0.031	0.229	0.015	0.056	0.087	0.053	0.121	0.203	0.141
	(0.015)	(0.036)	(0.033)	(0.026)	(0.020)	(0.028)	(0.038)	(0.027)	(0.017)
$LANG_{ij,1994}$	0.079	0.073	0.041	0.043	0.069	0.110	0.123	−0.032	0.032
	(0.052)	(0.088)	(0.103)	(0.049)	(0.062)	(0.116)	(0.077)	(0.059)	(0.047)
$LANG_{ij,1998}$	0.156	0.076	−0.037	0.067	0.028	0.073	0.045	−0.004	0.005
	(0.064)	(0.144)	(0.111)	(0.080)	(0.067)	(0.108)	(0.107)	(0.075)	(0.070)
$LANG_{ij,2002}$	0.241	0.122	−0.059	0.054	0.218	0.077	−0.099	−0.047	0.024
	(0.060)	(0.138)	(0.126)	(0.088)	(0.149)	(0.106)	(0.109)	(0.082)	(0.071)
$CNTG_{ij,1994}$	0.040	0.177	−0.077	−0.044	−0.069	−0.100	−0.021	−0.040	−0.039
	(0.040)	(0.049)	(0.086)	(0.037)	(0.055)	(0.069)	(0.045)	(0.053)	(0.043)
$CNTG_{ij,1998}$	0.076	0.483	−0.158	−0.005	−0.032	−0.071	0.082	0.057	0.056
	(0.050)	(0.124)	(0.110)	(0.073)	(0.067)	(0.062)	(0.060)	(0.079)	(0.072)
$CNTG_{ij,2002}$	0.061	0.440	−0.222	−0.096	−0.377	−0.139	0.185	−0.018	−0.060
	(0.047)	(0.108)	(0.127)	(0.085)	(0.125)	(0.083)	(0.062)	(0.079)	(0.068)
$CLNY_{ij,1994}$	−0.083	0.012	−0.157	−0.071	−0.059	−0.057	−0.007	0.019	−0.025
	(0.048)	(0.139)	(0.123)	(0.061)	(0.051)	(0.079)	(0.090)	(0.033)	(0.037)
$CLNY_{ij,1998}$	−0.062	−0.071	0.012	−0.111	−0.021	−0.057	0.016	−0.018	−0.017
	(0.086)	(0.189)	(0.146)	(0.093)	(0.068)	(0.122)	(0.132)	(0.065)	(0.061)
$CLNY_{ij,2002}$	−0.088	−0.198	0.015	−0.047	−0.024	−0.147	0.116	−0.021	−0.038
	(0.077)	(0.211)	(0.151)	(0.102)	(0.141)	(0.110)	(0.142)	(0.112)	(0.060)
Total EIA	1.039	1.052	0.383	0.313	0.657	0.362	0.705	0.901	0.728
	(0.113)	(0.124)	(0.143)	(0.117)	(0.110)	(0.131)	(0.109)	(0.102)	(0.085)
N	6692	6708	6596	6540	6724	6628	6564	6724	6724

Notes: This table reproduces the results from Table 5 but without the *INTER* variable. All specifications are estimated with PQML, pair (*ij*), exporter-year (*it*), and importer-year (*jt*) fixed effects and allow for phasing-in of the EIA effects. Fixed effects estimates are not reported for brevity. Robust standard errors, clustered by country pair, are reported in parentheses. See text for further details.

+ $p < 0.10$

* $p < .05$

** $p < .01$

among all countries in the world (denoted World), the trade flows among countries where EIAs formed, and the trade flows among countries where EIAs did *not* form. In the spirit of Head and Mayer (2000), we provide three GE comparative static estimates: a "Partial Trade Impact" (PTI) estimate that ignores (endogenous) changes in multilateral resistance (MR) terms and GDPs, a "Multilateral Trade Impact" (MTI) estimate that accounts for changes in multilateral resistance terms but

Table 7
General equilibrium trade effects of globalization.

	EIAs			EIAs and Borders		
	(1) PTI	(2) MTI	(3) GETI	(4) PTI	(5) MTI	(6) GETI
ARG	30.286	25.718	26.173	83.446	65.587	67.330
AUS	0.000	−0.962	−0.859	64.078	47.315	48.924
AUT	55.157	32.435	34.741	83.461	42.766	46.537
BGR	62.978	54.326	55.159	110.020	85.872	88.154
BLX	5.131	1.524	1.872	41.793	13.331	16.084
BOL	45.598	32.906	34.170	95.865	62.975	66.076
BRA	13.280	10.444	10.736	72.969	57.948	59.437
CAN	56.880	42.363	43.795	97.162	66.135	69.073
CHE	2.973	0.638	0.851	41.867	23.980	25.628
CHL	17.045	12.637	13.081	80.715	57.715	59.899
CHN	0.000	−0.847	−0.753	60.512	43.799	45.407
COL	6.427	3.611	3.904	65.115	49.207	50.770
CRI	1.878	−0.040	0.126	62.528	34.251	37.011
DEU	11.504	7.138	7.563	53.179	32.038	33.997
DNK	12.674	6.041	6.694	59.460	26.979	29.982
ECU	27.982	21.954	22.554	87.145	63.838	66.060
ESP	41.676	32.248	33.164	84.665	58.209	60.650
FIN	49.619	34.853	36.289	98.718	60.719	64.155
FRA	7.823	4.741	5.035	45.201	27.596	29.228
GBR	6.480	3.690	3.956	61.102	38.218	40.346
GRC	20.390	14.377	14.969	69.085	43.146	45.535
HUN	92.769	55.076	58.712	148.591	77.108	83.434
IRL	3.135	0.826	1.037	48.466	17.363	20.413
ISL	2.624	0.425	0.620	60.613	35.755	38.025
ISR	30.825	22.766	23.563	87.760	57.427	60.229
ITA	8.736	5.379	5.702	57.376	36.998	38.886
JPN	0.000	−1.241	−1.106	60.981	48.016	49.308
KOR	0.000	−0.918	−0.820	58.040	41.402	43.005
MAR	22.205	15.624	16.272	72.223	46.202	48.603
MEX	95.290	45.032	50.115	120.119	50.214	56.916
NLD	5.694	1.905	2.274	46.404	16.215	19.119
NOR	3.957	0.256	0.584	53.405	28.797	31.013
POL	98.102	72.814	75.198	132.552	87.433	91.486
PRT	45.379	31.282	32.659	91.281	55.687	58.930
ROM	62.123	53.850	54.654	116.898	92.058	94.416
ROW	0.000	−0.935	−0.847	62.238	39.466	41.638
SWE	45.178	27.937	29.681	95.432	50.403	54.502
TUN	59.379	41.008	42.821	112.449	68.369	72.375
TUR	53.335	42.794	43.807	111.234	79.769	82.659
URY	51.072	38.388	39.636	95.920	65.776	68.614
USA	19.055	13.605	14.190	74.464	53.666	55.743
World	14.365	9.583	10.079	63.852	40.389	42.650
EIA	73.174	53.587	55.603	108.855	68.449	72.295
No EIA	0.000	−2.262	−2.044	51.413	32.006	33.868

Notes: This table reports the general equilibrium trade effects of introducing all EIAs that entered into force during the period of investigation from 1990 to 2002. Manufacturing output values are taken from 1990. The first scenario, labeled "EIAs," is based on estimates from column (1) in Table 3. The second scenario, labeled "EIAs and Borders" is based on estimates from column (3) in Table 3. For both scenarios, we report three different trade impacts: the Partial Trade Impact (PTI), which only takes the partial, direct effect into account; the Multilateral Trade Impact (MTI), which takes changes in the multilateral resistances (MR) into account, but holds GDPs constant; and the General Equilibrium Trade Impact (GETI), where MRs and GDPs adjust. The row "World" gives results for the average change in total world trade flows, the row "EIA" reports the average change in total trade flows where EIAs are formed, and the row "No EIA" gives the average change in total trade flows where no EIAs are formed.

ignores changes in GDPs, and a "General Equilibrium Trade Impact" (GETI) estimate that accounts for changes in MR terms and GDPs. Second, we provide the GE trade effects allowing for $INTER_{ij,t}$; these are based on coefficient estimates from column (3) of Table 3. Hence, the latter estimates account for GE effects of both formations of EIAs and the declining effects of international borders. We then compare the results.

Table 7 provides the results from the two comparative static exercises. Vertically, the results are reported first for the trade flows of each of the 40 countries and *ROW* aggregate, then the trade flows of the world, then the trade flows among countries where EIAs formed, and then the trade flows among countries where EIAs did not form. Columns (1)–(3) report the results for each of PTI, MTI, and GETI for the first exercise, ignoring the effects of $INTER_{ij,t}$. Columns (4)–(6) report the results for the second exercise, formations of EIAs and declining effects of borders (denoted "EIAs and Borders"). We discuss first the results in columns (1)–(3).

Several results from columns (1) to (3). First, the PTIs differ across countries even though the "partial effect" (or EIA coefficient estimate) is the same. The reason is that the PTI for each country reflects the total trade (partial) effect for that country. Countries that formed more agreements (like Hungary, Mexico, and Poland) had larger total trade changes, and thus larger PTIs. For the world on average, trade increased only about 14 percent, due to the fact that EIAs are rare events; note that the PTI for *ROW* was 0. Trade increases about 73 percent among countries where EIAs formed. For trade among countries where no EIAs formed, the PTI was 0.

Second, as expected, the MTIs are smaller than the PTIs. As the countries' multilateral resistance terms decline with the EIAs, the PTIs are offset, cf., Head and Mayer (2014). Typically for our comparative statics, the MR effects reduce the trade impacts by about one-third. For trade among countries where EIAs did not form, MTIs expectedly fell.

Third, the positive GDP effects from the EIAs did raise trade. But as found in previous like estimates, such effects are quantitatively small. Hence, the GETIs are quite similar to the MTIs.

We now consider a comparison of the trade effects from just EIAs versus those from EIAs *alongside* declining effects of international borders. First, as expected the PTIs are larger in columns (4)–(6) vis-á-vis their respective counterparts. These PTIs reflect both EIA effects as well as falling international border effects.

Second, note that, for trade among countries where EIAs did not form, the trade effect of declining borders is about 51 percent. Comparing this PTI with that for trade among countries where EIAs formed, the marginal trade gain from having EIAs is only about 57 percent (108.9–51.4). This reflects that the PTI for trade among countries where EIAs formed is less in the second exercise, as expected; the PTI from EIAs is smaller once declining border effects are accounted for, consistent with our earlier empirical findings.

Third, as before, the MTIs are smaller than the PTIs in columns (4)–(6) as expected. The decline is again about one-third. Also, the GETIs are slightly larger than the MTIs in columns (4)–(6), as expected.

In summary, the basic insights from the earlier analysis hold up in a GE comparative static analysis. Not surprisingly, the differential effect across countries is largely driven by differences in the PTIs, which by construction capture the extent of EIA liberalizations that countries pursued during the 1990–2002 period. These results support the notion that consistent and unbiased estimates of partial EIA effects are important for subsequent GE analysis. Moreover, the GETI for the world accounting for EIAs and the declining effect of international borders of 43 percent, compared to only 10 percent for EIAs alone, suggests that the declining GE effects of distance are non-trivial.

9. Conclusions

Using a common gravity-equation specification, we have attempted to provide consistent and precise estimates of the (partial) effects of three important factors in international trade that typically have been addressed in three somewhat separate literatures. First, we have improved upon the specification in BB for estimating the effects of EIAs on international trade flows by controlling now for unobservable exogenous *time-varying* bilateral fixed and variable export costs that may have increased international relative to intranational trade; our results suggest that previous estimates of EIAs' effects were biased upward. Using our econometrically preferred estimator (PQML), the partial effect of an EIA falls by 30 percent; using OLS (as in BB and BBF), the partial EIA effect falls by much less.

Second, our novel approach allows us to estimate precisely the declining effect of international borders on international relative to intranational trade, allowing for unobserved bilateral country-pair heterogeneity and endogenous EIAs. While previous authors have found evidence of declining border effects (also, as typical, using data sets including intranational along with international trade flows), one of the shortcomings of these previous studies is omitted variables bias due to not accounting for differences in initial border-effect levels nor for endogenous EIAs. Our results suggest that previous estimates of the declining effect of international borders were biased upward, and we find the depressing effects of international borders on international trade have declined by 2.4 percent per year from 1990 to 2002.

Third, in an extensive sensitivity analysis, we introduce another method for accounting for unobserved time-varying declines in the costs of bilateral international relative to intranational trade. Accounting for endogenous EIAs and unobserved country-pair heterogeneity, we provide plausible estimates of the declining effect of distance on international trade, providing empirical support for the elusive declining "distance elasticity" of international trade. While our approach recognizes as in Yotov (2012) the importance of including intranational trade flows and using PQML in estimation in order to find declining distance elasticities, our novel contribution here is to account for unobserved country-pair heterogeneity and endogenous EIAs. We find that the estimates in Yotov (2012) of the declining effects of distance on international relative to intranational trade have been biased upward by not accounting for endogenous EIAs and unobserved bilateral heterogeneity. Our results suggest that the effect of distance on international trade has declined by 1.2 percent annually.

Just as BB contributed to the literature by emphasizing the importance of accounting for exporter-year, importer-year, and country-pair fixed effects in estimating the (partial) effects of EIAs, our hope is that – going forward – subsequent analyses account for all of the following using panel techniques:

1. Exporter-year and importer-year fixed effects to account for endogenous prices and unobserved time-varying exporter and importer multilateral heterogeneity;

2. Country-pair fixed effects or country-pair fixed effects interacted with a time trend to account for unobserved time-invariant or time-varying, respectively, bilateral effects (that subsume pair-specific border effect levels);
3. Intranational as well as international trade flows and bilateral distances, so that international border dummies can be introduced to account for declining international *relative to* intranational bilateral trade costs other than EIAs; and
4. PQML estimation to account for heteroskedasticity bias (owing to Jensen's inequality) and to account for zero trade flows.

Finally, it is important to note that estimates of general equilibrium effects of trade-cost changes are very sensitive to partial effect estimates. Anderson and van Wincoop (2003) and Bergstrand et al. (2013) provide extensive analyses of the sensitivity of general equilibrium estimates of trade-flow changes to underlying partial effects. Our final robustness analysis confirmed that general equilibrium estimates of EIA formations are also sensitive to accounting properly for declining effects of international borders.

Acknowledgements

The authors are grateful for excellent comments from editor Theo Eicher, two anonymous referees, Peter Egger, Anson Soderbery, as well as from participants at the CESifo/ETH University conference "Estimation of Gravity Models of Bilateral Trade" in Munich, SIRE workshop "Country Size and Border Effects in a Globalised World" in Edinburgh, Spring 2014 meeting of the Midwest International Economics Group in Indianapolis, 68th European meeting of the Econometric Society in Toulouse, the Economics Department seminar at University of Missouri at Columbia, and the 2014 Southern Economics Association meeting. Bergstrand gratefully acknowledges research support from the Kellogg Institute at Notre Dame and Larch gratefully acknowledges research support from the German Research Foundation (DFG). We thank Ryan Bernet, Stephen Cray, Stephen Gilcrest, Sree Kancherla, and Andrew Weiler for excellent work on the Economic Integration Agreement database.

Appendix A. Supplementary data

Supplementary data associated with this article can be found in the online version at http://dx.doi.org/10.1016/j.euroecorev.2015.06.003.

References

Anderson, J., 1979. A theoretical foundation for the gravity equation. Am. Econ. Rev. 69 (1), 106–116.
Anderson, J., van Wincoop, E., 2003. Gravity with gravitas: a solution to the border puzzle. Am. Econ. Rev. 93 (1), 170–192.
Anderson, J., Yotov, Y., 2010. The Chang. Incid. Geogr. Am. Econ. Rev. 100 (5), 2157–2186.
Anderson, J., Yotov, Y., 2011. Terms of trade and global efficiency effects of free trade agreements, NBER Working Paper No. 17003.
Arkolakis, C., Costinot, A., Rodriguez-Clare, A., 2012. New trade models, same old gains? Am. Econ. Rev. 102 (1), 94–130.
Baier, S., Bergstrand, J., 2007. Do free trade agreements actually increase members' international trade? J. Int. Econ. 71 (1), 72–95.
Baier, S., Bergstrand, J., 2009. Bonus VetusOLS: a simple method for approximating international trade-cost effects using the gravity equation. J. Int. Econ. 77 (1), 77–85.
Baier, S., Bergstrand , J., Clance, M., 2015. Preliminary examination of heterogeneous effects on international trade of economic integration agreements. In: Dur, A., Elsig, M. (Eds.), Trade Cooperation. Cambridge University Press, Cambridge, UK, pp. 355–373.
Baier, S., Bergstrand, J., Feng, M., 2014. Economic integration agreements and the margins of international trade. J. Int. Econ. 93 (2), 339–350.
Berden, K., Francois, J., Tamminen, S., Thelle, M., Wymenga, P., 2010. ECORYS, The Netherlands, Non-Tariff Measures in EU-US Trade and Investment.
Bergstrand, J., 1985. The gravity equation in international trade some microeconomic foundations and empirical evidence. Rev. Econ. Stat. 67 (3), 474–481.
Bergstrand, J.H., Egger, P., Larch, M., 2013. Gravity redux estimation of gravity-equation coefficients, elasticities of substitution and general equilibrium comparative statics under asymmetric bilateral trade costs. J. Int. Econ. 89 (1), 110–121.
Berthelon, M., Freund, C., 2008. On the conservation of distance in international trade. J. Int. Econ. 75 (2), 310–320.
Bosquet, C., Boulhol, H., 2015. What Is really puzzling about the "Distance Puzzle". Rev. World Econ. 151 (1), 1–21.
Carrere, C., de Melo, J., Wilson, J. 2009. The Distance Effect and the Regionalization of the Trade of Low-Income Countries, CEPR Working Paper.
Cheng, I., Wall, H., 2005. Controlling for heterogeneity in gravity models of trade and integration. Fed. Reserv. Bank St. Louis Rev. 87 (1), 49–63.
Cipollina, M., Salvatici, L., 2010. Reciprocal trade agreements in gravity models: a meta-analysis. Rev. Econ. Lit. 18 (1), 63–80.
Coe, D., Subramanian, A., Tamirisa, N., 2007. The missing globalization puzzle: evidence of declining importance of distance. IMF Staff Pap. 54 (1), 34–58.
Costinot, A., Rodriguez-Clare, A., 2014. Trade theory with numbers. In: Gopinath, G., Helpman, E., Rogoff, K. (Eds.) Handbook of Interantional Economics, vol. 4. Elsevier, Amsterdam.
Das, S., Roberts, M.J., Tybout, J.R., 2007. Market entry costs, producer heterogeneity, and export dynamics. Econometrica 75 (3), 837–873.
de Sousa, J., Mayer, T., Zignago, S., 2012. Market access in global and regional trade. Reg. Sci. Urban Econ. 42 (6), 1037–1052.
Disdier, A., Head, K., 2008. The puzzling persistence of the distance effect on bilateral trade. Rev. Econ. Stat. 90 (1), 37–48.
Eaton, J., Kortum, S., 2002. Technology, geography and trade. Econometrica 70 (5), 1741–1779.
Egger, P., Larch, M., Staub, K., Winkelmann, R., 2011. The trade effects of endogenous preferential trade agreements. Am. Econ. J., Econ. Policy 3 (3), 113–143.
Eicher, T., Henn, C., Papageorgiou, C., 2012. Trade creation and diversion revisited: accounting for model uncertainty and natural trading partner effects. J. Appl. Econom. 27 (2), 296–321.
Feenstra, R., 2004. Advanced International Trade: Theory and Evidence. Princeton University Press, Princeton, New Jersey.
Felbermayr, G., Kohler, W., 2006. Exploring the intensive and extensive margins of world trade. Rev. World Econ. 142 (4), 642–674.
Fontagne, L., Mayer, T., Zignago, S., 2005. Trade in the triad: how easy is the access to large markets?. Can. J. Econ. 38 (4), 1401–1430.
Freund, C., Weinhold, D., 2004. The effect of the internet on international trade. J. Int. Econ. 62 (1), 171–189.
Gaulier, G., Zignago, S., 2008. BACI: A World Database of International Trade Analysis at the Product Level, CEPII Working Paper.
Haveman, J., Hummels, D., 2004. Alternative hypotheses and the volume of trade: the gravity equation and the extent of specialization. Can. J. Econ. 37 (1), 199–218.
Head, K., Mayer, T., 2000. Non-Europe: the magnitude and causes of market fragmentation in the EU. Weltwirtschaftliches Arch. 136 (2), 284–314.

Head, K., Mayer, T., 2014. Gravity equations: workhorse, toolkit, and cookbook. In: Gopinath, G., Helpman, E., Rogoff, K. (Eds.) Handbook of Interantional Economics, vol. 4. Elsevier, Amsterdam.
Helpman, E., Melitz, M., Rubinstein, Y., 2008. Trading partners and trading volumes. Q. J. Econ. 123 (2), 441–487.
Krugman, P., 1980. Scale economies, product differentiation, and the pattern of trade. Am. Econ. Rev. 70 (5), 950–959.
Larch, M., Norbäck, P., Sirries, S., Urban, D. 2015. Heterogeneous Firms, Globalization, and the Distance Puzzle, Research Institute of Industrial Economics Working Paper.
Mayer, T., Paillacar, R., Zignago, S., 2008. TradeProd. The CEPII Trade, Production and Bilateral Protection Database: Explanatory Notes, CEPII.
Mayer, T., Zignago, S., 2006. Notes on CEPII's Distance Measures, CEPII.
McCallum, J., 1995. National Borders Matter. Am. Econ. Rev. 85(3), 615–623.
Melitz, M., 2003. The Impact of trade on intra-industry reallocations and aggregate industry productivity. Econometrica 71 (6), 1695–1725.
Melitz, M., Redding, S., 2014. Heterogeneous firms and trade. In: Gopinath, G., Helpman, E., Rogoff, K. (Eds.) Handbook of Interantional Economics, vol. 4. Elsevier, Amsterdam.
Redding, S., 2011. Theories of heterogeneous firms. Annu. Rev. Econ. 3, 77–105.
Roberts, M., Tybout, J., 1997. The decision to export in Colombia: an empirical model of entry with sunk costs. Am. Econ. Rev. 87 (4), 545–564.
Santos Silva, J., Tenreyro, S., 2006. The log of gravity. Rev. Econ. Stat. 88 (4), 641–658.
Santos Silva, J., Tenreyro, S., 2011. Further simulation evidence on the Poisson-PML estimator. Econ. Lett. 112 (2), 220–222.
Tang, L., 2006. Communication costs and trade of differentiated goods. Rev. Int. Econ. 14 (1), 54–68.
Wei, S., 1996. Intra-National versus International Trade: How Stubborn are Nations in Global Interactions? National Bureau of Economic Research Working Paper 5531.
Wooldridge, J., 2009. Introductory Econometrics: A Modern Approach, fourth ed. Cengage Learning Services, Florence, KY.
Wooldridge, J., 2010. Econometric Analysis of Cross Section and Panel Data, second ed. The MIT Press, Cambridge, Massachusetts.
Yotov, Y.V., 2012. A simple solution to the distance puzzle in international trade. Econ. Lett. 117 (3), 794–798.

PART 4

Foreign Direct Investment, Foreign Affiliate Sales, and Multinational Enterprises

Chapter 14

A knowledge-and-physical-capital model of international trade flows, foreign direct investment, and multinational enterprises

Jeffrey H. Bergstrand [a,b,*], Peter Egger [c,d,e]

[a] *Department of Finance, Mendoza College of Business, and Kellogg Institute for International Studies, University of Notre Dame, Notre Dame, IN 46556, USA*
[b] *CESifo, Munich, Germany*
[c] *Department of Economics, University of Munich, Munich, Germany*
[d] *IFO Institute, Munich, Germany*
[e] *CESifo, Munich, Germany*

Received 8 March 2006; received in revised form 25 October 2006; accepted 22 March 2007

Abstract

This paper addresses two important issues at the nexus of the literatures on international trade, foreign direct investment (FDI), foreign affiliate sales (FAS), and multinational enterprises (MNEs). First, the introduction of a third internationally-mobile factor (physical capital) to the standard $2 \times 2 \times 2$ "knowledge-capital" model of MNEs with skilled and unskilled labor allows us to resolve fairly readily the puzzle in the modern MNE literature that foreign affiliate sales among two identical economies completely displace their international trade. Intra-industry trade *and* intra-industry FDI (and FAS) can coexist for national and multinational firms (with identical productivities) in identical countries. Second, the introduction also of a third country to the model suggests a formal N-country theoretical rationale for estimating gravity equations of bilateral FDI flows and FAS, in a manner consistent with estimating gravity equations for bilateral trade flows.

Keywords: Foreign direct investment; International trade; Multinational firms; Gravity equation

JEL classification: F11; F12; F21; F23

* Corresponding author. Department of Finance, Mendoza College of Business, and Kellogg Institute for International Studies, University of Notre Dame, IN 46556, USA. Tel.: +1 574 631 6761; fax: +1 574 631 5255.
E-mail address: Bergstrand.1@nd.edu (J.H. Bergstrand).

*Originally Published in *Journal of International Economics*, 73(2007), pp. 278–308.

1. Introduction

"Multinationals displace trade...." (Markusen, 1995, p. 180).

"The cross-country pattern of FDI is quite well approximated by the 'gravity' relationship." (Barba Navaretti and Venables, 2004, p. 32).

This paper addresses two important issues at the nexus of the literatures on international trade, foreign direct investment (FDI), foreign affiliate sales (FAS), and multinational enterprises (MNEs). First, the modern $2 \times 2 \times 2$ general equilibrium theory of MNEs synthesized in Markusen (2002) implies that – in two countries with identical absolute and relative factor-endowments (other things equal) – horizontal MNEs' foreign affiliate sales displace *completely* national firms (with identical productivities) and trade between the two countries. However, the European Union and the United States, for instance, have both the largest intra-industry bilateral foreign direct investment flows (and FAS) *and* intra-industry trade flows. This is a puzzle. Second, while multi-country theoretical foundations for the trade gravity equation are now well established (cf., Anderson and van Wincoop, 2004, and Feenstra, 2004, ch. 5, for overviews), there have been virtually no formal N-country ($N>2$) theoretical frameworks provided in international economics for estimating gravity equations of aggregate bilateral FDI, despite numerous empirical studies over the past decade using the gravity equation to explain such flows.[1] Blonigen et al. (in press) note that the "gravity model is arguably the most widely used empirical specification for FDI" (p. 8). Yet the typical rationale for applying the gravity equation to bilateral FDI is by analogy to the trade gravity equation, cf., Mutti and Grubert (2004, p. 339) and Blonigen (2005, p. 21). This suggests a puzzle similar to one posed 30 years ago for trade: The gravity equation explains bilateral FDI empirically quite well... *but why*?

We suggest a simple, integrated solution to both puzzles. First, the introduction of a third factor – physical capital – to Markusen's two-factor "knowledge-capital" model with only skilled and unskilled labor, combined with the assumption that headquarters (plant) setups require human (physical) capital, implies that national exporting enterprises (NEs) can coexist with horizontal MNEs (HMNEs) in pairs of countries with identical relative *and* absolute factor-endowments (and all firms sharing identical technologies). With skilled labor not being the only factor used to setup both plants and firms, skilled labor is not completely displaced from plant setups to firm setups as two countries' GDPs converge in size. In the $2 \times 2 \times 2$ model of Markusen and Venables (2000), there is only a (highly unlikely) unique combination of trade costs, investment costs and ratio of

[1] Martin and Rey (2004) have advanced a theory of the gravity equation for bilateral *portfolio* investment flows. However, no studies have developed a theory for the gravity equation for bilateral FDI stocks/flows. Recently, a few studies have offered theoretical rationales for estimating bilateral FAS gravity equations, cf., Grazalian and Furtan (2005), Kleinert and Toubal (2005), and Lai and Zhu (2006); however, these studies assume exogenously heterogeneous productivities to generate coexistence of multinational and national firms, in the spirit of the model in Helpman et al. (2004), and only explain FAS. By contrast, we motivate the endogenous coexistence of country pairs' horizontal MNEs and national firms sharing identical productivities, even for identical economies. Moreover, by incorporating capital flows, we provide simultaneously theoretical rationales for trade, FAS, *and* FDI gravity equations, distinguishing explicitly between FDI (a measure of MNE capital flow) and FAS (a measure of MNE production). Consequently, our analysis is in the spirit of the "new trade theory" where, as noted in Helpman (2006, p. 592), within-industry heterogeneity results from product differentiation and monopolistic competition, and heterogeneous productivities among firms are unnecessary to explain large volumes of intra-industry trade. Since our theoretical model will be static, conventional to the trade and knowledge–capital MNE literatures (cf., Markusen, 2002), bilateral "flows" and "stocks" are conceptually identical. In empirical work, however, flows and stocks will be distinguished. Traditionally, gravity equations have used bilateral FDI stock data, cf., Blonigen et al. (in press).

plant-to-firm setup costs where NEs and HMNEs can coexist. By contrast, with three factors, NEs and HMNEs with identical productivities can coexist over a wide range of combinations of trade costs, investment costs, and plant-to-firm setup costs due to the endogenous adjustment of the relative price of human-to-physical capital. Intra-industry trade *and* FDI can coexist for two *identical* countries.[2] Moreover, the existence of human and physical capital allows distinguishing MNEs' foreign affiliate production from MNEs' capital flows, two different "concepts of FDI."[3]

Second, while introducing a third factor implies coexistence of NEs and HMNEs for identically-sized economies, this extension cannot explain empirically the "complementarity" of bilateral trade and FDI flows to GDP similarity. Typical empirical gravity equations of international trade and FDI tend to suggest that both trade and FDI from country *i* to country *j* should be positively related to the size *and* similarity of their GDPs. However, the introduction of a third country – rest-of-world (ROW) – to our "knowledge-and-physical-capital" model can explain readily the complementarity of bilateral trade, FDI, and FAS to changes in a pair of countries' economic size and similarity as typical to gravity equations. In a two-country world, gross multilateral and bilateral trades (or FAS) are identical; NEs and HMNEs must substitute for one another when the two countries are identically sized in the face of trade and investment costs. However, introducing a third country along with capital mobility allows two countries' trade, FDI, and FAS to covary positively with increases in these two countries' GDP similarity because the "substitution effect" associated with exogenous trade-to-investment costs is potentially offset by a "complementarity effect" generated by endogenous relative prices of physical-to-human capital interacting with the three countries' economic sizes. With three countries, both bilateral trade *and* FAS are maximized when a pair of countries' GDPs is identical, unlike a two-country world. Moreover, the presence of the third country can explain why FDI from one country to another is *not* maximized when GDPs are identical — which is observed empirically!

The complexity of the nonlinear relationships between trade, foreign affiliate sales, FDI, GDP sizes and similarities, trade costs, and investment costs precludes closed-form solutions, such as the trade gravity equations derived in Helpman and Krugman (1985) or Anderson and van Wincoop (2003). As in Markusen (2002), we must employ a numerical version of the general equilibrium (GE) model to motivate the gravity-like relationships among these variables. However, the theoretical relationships between the bilateral flows – trade, foreign affiliate sales, and FDI – and GDP sizes and similarities demonstrated graphically are similar, but not identical. Consequently, to avoid "ocular-metrics" and in the presence of approximation errors associated with the nonlinear relationships, we employ regressions of "theoretical" flows on pairs of countries' GDPs, trade and investment costs, and ROW GDP to motivate theoretically *and*

[2] We are not the first to try to address this puzzle. Blonigen (2001) and Head and Ries (2001a,b) introduce intermediate goods to address the issue. However, the nature of trade in these models is "vertical," nor horizontal; Baldwin and Ottaviano (2001) argue that the "intermediates augmented proximity-versus-scale model still has trade and FDI as substitutes" (p. 432). As an alternative, Baldwin and Ottaviano argue that obstacles to trade generate an incentive for multiproduct firms to simultaneously engage in FDI and trade, in the spirit of the Brander–Krugman "reciprocal-dumping" model for goods trade. Our focus on a third factor and third country is an alternative to this.

[3] See Lipsey (2002) for more on the distinction between FAS and FDI. The modern $2\times2\times2$ MNE model explains trade and FAS simultaneously, but not FDI. As Markusen (2002) notes, "the models in this book are addressed more closely to affiliate output and sales than to investment stocks" (p. 8). Similarly, the heterogeneous productivities models cited in Footnote 1 cannot explain FDI as these models have only one factor, immobile labor.

quantitatively that bilateral trade, FAS, and FDI flows' economic determinants should be "well-approximated" by gravity equations — yet not precisely the *same* gravity relationships.[4]

The remainder of the paper is as follows. Section 2 presents some typical empirical regression results for trade and FDI gravity equations to motivate our analysis. Section 3 presents our $3\times3\times2$ GE model of FDI, MNEs and trade. Section 4 discusses the calibration of the numerical version of the GE model. Section 5 shows how introduction of the third factor generates "coexistence" of NEs (bilateral intra-industry trade) and HMNEs (bilateral intra-industry investment) for two identical countries. Section 6 demonstrates how the further introduction of a third country generates "complementarity" of bilateral FAS, FDI, and trade flows with respect to the country pair's economic size and similarity. Section 7 addresses the regressions of "theoretical flows" on GDP sizes and similarities, trade and investment costs, and ROW GDP to show that bilateral trade, FAS, and FDI flows' determinants should be "well-approximated" by gravity equations — though not quantitatively identical gravity relationships. Section 8 concludes.

2. Typical empirical gravity equations for trade and FDI flows

In a simple theoretical world of N (>2) countries, one final differentiated good, no trade costs, but internationally-immobile factors (e.g., labor and/or capital), we know from the trade gravity–equation literature that the trade flow from country i to country j in year t (Flow_{ijt}) will be determined by:

$$\text{Flow}_{ijt} = \text{GDP}_{it}\text{GDP}_{jt}/\text{GDP}_t^W \tag{1}$$

where GDP^W is world GDP, or in log-linear form:

$$\ln \text{Flow}_{ijt} = -\ln(\text{GDP}_t^W) + \ln(\text{GDP}_{it}) + \ln(\text{GDP}_{jt}). \tag{2}$$

Of course, the real world is not so generous as to allow international trade to be "frictionless." Hence, specification (2) is augmented typically to include various empirical proxies for bilateral trade costs, such as time-invariant bilateral distance (DIST_{ij}), a dummy variable for common language (LANG_{ij}), a (potentially time-varying) dummy variable for common membership in a regional trade agreement (RTA_{ijt}), and a time trend. Table 1 provides representative gravity equations using pooled cross-section time-series empirical data for bilateral trade and FDI flows among the 17 most developed OECD countries for 11 years (1990–2000) in columns (1)–(4).[5]

[4] We will not provide a theoretical framework that is the perfect complement to the Anderson and van Wincoop (2003) theoretical foundation using a "conditional" general equilibrium (GE) model, which enabled them to derive a closed-form, analytic solution for the trade gravity equation with unit GDP elasticities. Instead, we use an "unconditional" GE approach, where the allocation of bilateral flows across countries is non-separable from production and consumption allocations within countries, whereas a "conditional" GE approach assumes separability of bilateral flows from production and consumption allocations, cf., Anderson and van Wincoop (2004). Our model is in the spirit of Markusen (2002). The benefit of our approach is illuminating the endogenous determination of representative firms' outputs, countries' numbers of NEs vs. MNEs, allocation of MNEs' capital between countries, etc. The cost is we forego a closed-form solution for the gravity equation, relying instead on regressions of "theoretical" flows (from a numerical GE model) on GDPs, etc. to motivate theoretically estimation of log-linear gravity equations for trade flows, FAS, and FDI flows. Shim (2005) extends the Anderson and van Wincoop conditional GE model to include FAS to further explain the "border puzzle"; however, Shim assumes exogenously the (unlikely) unique equilibrium in Markusen and Venables (2000) that generates coexistence of NEs and MNEs.

[5] For our sample, RTA has cross-sectional but no time variation, as the Canadian–U.S. FTA and the EC, EFTA, and EC-EFTA FTAs were in place over the entire period. The limitation on number of countries and years in the sample was dictated by measures of bilateral trade and investment costs to be addressed later.

While numerous studies separately have estimated gravity equations for trade flows and for FDI flows, few studies have estimated such equations for both flows using the same specification and years.[6] Specification (1) provides empirical results for trade using the specification analogous to Eq. (2) including typical RHS covariates. Coefficient estimates have plausible values, consistent with the literature.

Of course, the standard frictionless gravity equation can be altered algebraically to separate economic size ($\mathrm{GDP}_i+\mathrm{GDP}_j$) and similarity ($s_is_j$), where $s_i=\mathrm{GDP}_i/(\mathrm{GDP}_i+\mathrm{GDP}_j)$ and analogously for j:

$$\mathrm{Flow}_{ijt} = \mathrm{GDP}_{it}\mathrm{GDP}_{jt}/\mathrm{GDP}_t^W = (\mathrm{GDP}_{it} + \mathrm{GDP}_{jt})^2(s_{it}s_{jt})/\mathrm{GDP}_t^W. \quad (3)$$

When countries i and j are identical in size ($s_i=s_j=1/2$), s_is_j is at a maximum. In log-linear form, (3) is:

$$\ln\mathrm{Flow}_{ij} = -\ln(\mathrm{GDP}^W) + 2\ln(\mathrm{GDP}_i + \mathrm{GDP}_j) + \ln(s_is_j). \quad (4)$$

Specification (2) in Table 1 for trade flows provides results using the formulation in Eq. (4). Specifications (3) and (4) in Table 1 provide coefficient estimates for representative FDI gravity equations for the same OECD countries and years. We note three interesting results.

First, the gravity equation works almost as well for bilateral FDI as for bilateral trade (using R^2 values), as typically found. Bilateral trade and FDI both increase in economic size *and* similarity. These results suggest that NEs and HMNEs coexist when pairs of (similar per capita income) countries have identical GDPs, and that trade and FDI are complements with respect to GDP similarity. This conflicts with the modern $2\times2\times2$ theory of MNEs.

Second, we observe a notable asymmetry from comparing specification (1) with (3). For trade, the exporter's GDP elasticity is similar to the importer's. However, for FDI the exporter's GDP elasticity is significantly greater than the importer's. Alternatively, a comparison of specification (2) with (4) reveals notably different elasticities of trade and FDI with respect to GDP similarity.[7] These results suggest that bilateral trade and FDI are "well-approximated by the gravity relationship" — but not precisely the *same* gravity equation. This is a puzzle.

Third, following Egger (2000) and others, in the presence of panel data, it has become common to include bilateral-pair fixed effects to eliminate any omitted variables bias associated with unobserved time-invariant pair-specific heterogeneity (not captured by bilateral distance and the language and RTA dummies). Columns (5)–(8) report the results for estimating the trade and FDI gravity equations using pair-specific fixed effects. Since only GDPs have time variation, their coefficient estimates are presented using within variation (Within-R^2 values reported). Specifications (5)–(8) provide even *more striking* asymmetries in GDP coefficient estimates. The notable difference between specifications (5) and (7) is that the exporting (home FDI) country's GDP elasticity is much smaller (larger) than the importing (host FDI) country's GDP elasticity. For specifications (6) and (8), as before for specifications (2) and (4), the GDP

[6] Bilateral FAS data is currently available only for a few developed countries and so omitted. By contrast, trade and FDI data is available for many countries. A time trend is included. Data are described in a Data Appendix.

[7] Bilateral distance and language-dummy coefficient estimates are also quantitatively different; however, this issue is outside our scope. The different coefficient estimates for the RTA dummy variable are addressed later.

Table 1
Coefficient estimates from gravity equations*

RHS variables	Empirical (LHS) flows, pooled cross-section, time-series data				Empirical (LHS) flows, bilateral fixed effects				"Theoretical" flows for LHS variables				Empirical (LHS) flows, bilateral fixed effects			
	(1)	(2)	(3)	(4)	(5)	(6)	(7)	(8)	(9)	(10)	(11)	(12)	(13)	(14)	(15)	(16)
	ln $Trade_{ijt}$	ln $Trade_{ijt}$	ln FDI_{ijt}	ln FDI_{ijt}	ln $Trade_{ijt}$	ln $Trade_{ijt}$	ln FDI_{ijt}	ln FDI_{ijt}	ln $Trade_{ijt}$	ln $Trade_{ijt}$	ln FDI_{ijt}	ln FDI_{ijt}	ln $Trade_{ijt}$	ln $Trade_{ijt}$	ln FDI_{ijt}	ln FDI_{ijt}
ln GDP_{it}	0.82		0.93		0.52		2.01		0.35		0.59		0.29		1.47	
	(86.77)		(39.62)		(5.44)		(5.74)		(89.13)		(36.00)		(2.19)		(12.85)	
ln GDP_{jt}	0.80		0.78		1.51		1.39		0.58		0.21		1.04		0.73	
	(85.62)		(33.83)		(15.71)		(4.02)		(146.80)		(146.80)		(7.80)		(1.38)	
ln $GDPT_{ijt}$		1.62		1.78		2.07		3.45		0.99		0.95		1.36		2.11
		(111.93)		(50.45)		(14.58)		(6.75)		(138.25)		(61.99)		(5.85)		(2.17)
ln $GDPSim_{ijt}$		0.81		1.28		0.64		1.31		0.74		1.53		0.61		1.18
		(38.02)		(25.86)		(5.07)		(2.95)		(83.50)		(75.13)		(4.13)		(2.09)
ln $DIST_{ij}$	−0.62	−0.62	−0.84	−0.75												
	(−42.43)	(−41.09)	(−24.24)	(−21.11)												
ln $LANG_{ij}$	0.67	0.67	1.32	1.36												
	(19.69)	(19.65)	(16.70)	(17.42)												
RTA_{ijt}	0.57	0.57	−0.53	−0.47												
	(14.52)	(14.48)	(−5.79)	(−5.17)												
ln $ROWGDP_{ijt}$													−4.10	−3.80	−9.18	−9.75
													(−4.86)	(−3.42)	(−2.90)	(2.20)
ln transport $costs_{ijt}$													−0.02	−0.02	−0.003	−0.003
													(−5.78)	(−5.73)	(−0.21)	(−0.21)
ln investment $costs_{ijt}$													−0.004	−0.005	−0.01	−0.01
													(−2.73)	(−3.66)	(−1.94)	(−1.72)
ln $[(S/U)_{it}/(S/U)_{jt}]$													1.81	1.49	5.48	5.73
													(5.35)	(4.47)	(4.18)	(4.43)
ln $[(K/U)_{it}/(K/U)_{jt}]$													−0.07	−0.20	0.56	0.67
													(−0.09)	(−2.65)	(1.73)	(2.21)
R^2	0.87	0.87	0.57	0.58	0.49	0.49	0.33	0.33	0.89	0.86	0.37	0.71	0.51	0.49	0.28	0.27
No. of pairs	272	272	266	266	272	272	266	266	272	272	266	266	263	263	254	254
No. of observations	2983	2983	2683	2683	2983	2983	2683	2683	2983	2983	2683	2683	2069	2069	1828	1828

*T–statistics are in parentheses. In empirical regressions, time dummies are included, but coefficient estimates omitted. Bilateral fixed effects' coefficient estimates are also not reported for brevity. In bilateral fixed effects (empirical) regressions, R^2 denotes "Within-R^2." All RHS variables use empirical data.

similarity elasticity is notably smaller for trade than for FDI flows. We address this puzzle as well.[8]

3. Theoretical framework

The model we use is a straightforward extension of the $2 \times 2 \times 2$ knowledge-capital model in Markusen (2002) with NEs, HMNEs, and vertical MNEs (VMNEs). The demand side is modeled analogously to that model. However, we extend that model in two ways. The first distinction is to use *three* primary factors of production: unskilled labor, skilled labor (or human/knowledge capital), and physical capital. We assume unskilled and skilled labor are immobile internationally, but physical capital is mobile in the sense that MNEs will endogenously choose the optimal allocation of domestic physical capital between home and foreign locations to maximize profits, consistent with the BEA definition of foreign "direct investment positions" using domestic and foreign-affiliate shares of real fixed investment.[9] The introduction of a third factor – combined with an assumption that the setup of a headquarters requires home skilled labor (to represent, say, research and development) while the setup of a plant in any country requires the home country's physical capital (to represent, say, equipment) – helps explain "coexistence" of HMNEs and NEs for two identically-sized developed-countries for a wide range of parameter values. Differentiated final goods are produced from physical capital, skilled labor, and unskilled labor.[10]

The second distinction of our model is to introduce a third country. The presence of the third country helps to explain the "complementarity" of bilateral FAS and trade with respect to a country pair's economic size and similarity and that bilateral FDI empirically tends to be maximized when the home country's GDP is larger than the host country's. One implication of a third country is that (in equilibrium) both two-country HMNEs and three-country HMNEs may surface. As a first venture into the 3-factor, 3-country setting, we limit our scope in this paper to the 3-country HMNE equilibrium and to studying inter-developed-country bilateral interactions, but where ROW can be either a developed or developing economy.[11] Due to space constraints, we leave study of other interactions for future work.

[8] See Egger (2000) for more on the appropriateness of bilateral-pair-specific fixed effects. As noted in Anderson and van Wincoop (2003), an important potential source of omitted variables bias in gravity equations is the role of "multilateral resistance" terms. In the context of a panel, this suggests including also country-specific dummies for each time period; these "country-and-time" effects are addressed in Baier and Bergstrand (2007). For our sample of 17 OECD countries for 1990–2000, we assume here that the MR terms are slow moving, so bilateral pair "fixed" effects should capture the (most important) cross-sectional influence of these terms and time-invariant pair-specific unobserved heterogeneity. This allows estimating coefficients of the GDP terms using time variation.

[9] In the typical $2 \times 2 \times 2$ model, headquarters use home skilled labor exclusively for setups; home (foreign) plants use home (foreign) skilled labor for setups (cf., Markusen, 2002, p. 80). With only immobile skilled and unskilled labor, the 2-factor models preclude home physical capital being utilized to setup foreign plants. We often refer to the transfer of physical capital by MNEs as capital "mobility," in the tradition of the pre-1960 literature, cf., Mundell (1957, pp. 321–323) and Lipsey (2002); practically speaking, it is easiest to think of FDI as "greenfield" investment. Consistent with Markusen (2002) and the modern MNE literature, the model is real; there are no paper assets. Moreover, while physical capital can be utilized in different countries, ownership of any country's endowment of such capital is immobile, again following Mundell (1957). In reality, the presence of (paper) claims to physical capital allows much easier transfer of resources and is *one* way of measuring FDI. However, the "current-cost" method of measuring FDI is related to the shares of an MNE's *real* fixed investment in plant and equipment that is allocated to the home country relative to foreign affiliate(s); this effectively measures physical capital mobility, cf., Borga and Yorgason (2002, p. 27).

[10] As in Markusen (2002), internationally-immobile skilled labor still creates firm-specific intangible assets that are costlessly shared internationally by MNEs with their plants. This aspect is maintained.

[11] In earlier versions (cf., Bergstrand and Egger, 2004, 2006), we included notation explicitly for possible 2-country HMNEs. However, space constraints limit discussion here to only the 3-country HMNEs, noting that all the results generalize to allowing 2-country HMNEs.

3.1. Consumers

Consumers are assumed to have a Cobb–Douglas utility function between final differentiated goods (X) and homogeneous goods (Y). Consumers' tastes for differentiated products (e.g., manufactures) are assumed to be of the Dixit–Stiglitz constant elasticity of substitution (CES) type, as typical in trade. We let V_i denote the utility of the representative consumer in country i ($i=1$, 2, 3). Let η be the Cobb–Douglas parameter reflecting the relative importance of manufactures in utility and ε be the parameter determining the constant elasticity of substitution, σ, among these manufactured products ($\sigma \equiv 1-\varepsilon$, $\varepsilon<0$). Manufactures can be produced by three different firm types: national firms (n), horizontal multinational firms (h), and vertical multinational firms (v). In equilibrium, some of these firms may not exist (depending upon absolute and relative factor-endowments and parameter values). These will be reflected in three sets of components in the first of two RHS bracketed terms in Eq. (5) below:

$$V_i = \left[\sum_{j=1}^{3} n_j \left(\frac{x_{ji}^{n}}{t_{Xji}}\right)^{\frac{\varepsilon}{\varepsilon-1}} + \sum_{j=1}^{3} h_j (x_{ii}^{h})^{\frac{\varepsilon}{\varepsilon-1}} + \sum_{k \neq j} \sum_{j=1}^{3} v_{kj} \left(\frac{x_{ji}^{v}}{t_{Xji}}\right)^{\frac{\varepsilon}{\varepsilon-1}}\right]^{\frac{\varepsilon-1}{\varepsilon}\eta} \left[\sum_{j=1}^{3} Y_{ji}\right]^{1-\eta}. \tag{5}$$

The first component reflects *national* (non-MNE) firms that can produce differentiated goods for the home market or export to foreign markets from a single plant in the country with its headquarters, where x_{ji}^{n} denotes the (endogenous) output of country j's national firm in industry X sold to country i, n_j is the (endogenous) number of these national firms in j, and t_{Xji} is the gross trade cost of exporting X from j to i.

The second component reflects *horizontal* MNEs that have plants in foreign countries to be "proximate" to markets to avoid trade costs; horizontal MNEs cannot export goods. In a three-country HMNE equilibrium, every HMNE has a plant in its headquarters country and two foreign plants. Let x_{ii}^{h} denote the output of a representative (three-country) HMNE producing in i and selling in i and h_j denote the number of multinationals that produce in all (three) countries and are headquartered in j.

The third component reflects *vertical* MNEs. VMNEs have a headquarters in one country and a plant in one of the other countries, just not in the headquarters country. The primary motivation for a VMNE is "cost differences"; different relative factor intensities and relative factor abundances motivate separating headquarters and production into different countries. Let v_{kj} denote the number of VMNEs with headquarters in k and a plant in j ($j \neq k$) with the plant's output potentially sold to any country (including k); such VMNEs include global "export-platform" MNEs, such as discussed in Ekholm, Forslid, and Markusen (in press) and Blonigen et al. (in press). Let x_{ji}^{v} denote the output of the representative VMNE with production in j and consumption in i.

In the second bracketed RHS term, let Y_{ji} denote the output of the homogenous (e.g., agriculture) good produced in country j under constant returns to scale using unskilled labor and consumed in i.

We let t_{Xji} (t_{Yji}) denote the gross trade cost for shipping differentiated (homogeneous) good X (Y) from j to i.[12] Let $t_{Xji}=1$ for $i=j$, and analogously for t_{Yji}. It will be useful to define:

$$t_{Xji} = (1+b_{Xji})(1+\tau_{Xji})$$
$$t_{Yji} = (1+b_{Yji})(1+\tau_{Yji})$$

[12] For modeling convenience, we define Y_{ji} net of trade costs; t_{Yji} surface explicitly in the factor-endowment constraints.

where τ denotes a "natural" trade cost of physical shipment (cif/fob − 1) of the "iceberg" type, while b represents a "policy" trade cost (i.e., tariff rate) which generates potential revenue. For instance, b_{Xji} denotes the tariff rate (e.g., 0.05 = 5%) on imports from j to i in differentiated final good X.

The budget constraint of the representative consumer in country i is assumed to be:

$$\begin{aligned}&\sum_{j=1}^{3} n_j p_{Xj}^n x_{ji}^n + \sum_{j=1}^{3} h_j p_{Xi}^h x_{ii}^h + \sum_{k\neq j}\sum_{j\neq i} v_{kj} p_{Xj}^v x_{ji}^v + \sum_{j=1}^{3} p_{Yj} Y_{ji}\\ &\quad = r_i K_i + w_{Si} S_i + w_{Ui} Ui + \sum_{j\neq i} n_j b_{Xji} p_{Xj}^n x_{ji}^n + \sum_{k\neq j}\sum_{j\neq i} v_{kj} b_{Xji} p_{Xj}^v x_{ji}^v + \sum_{j\neq i} b_{Yji} p_{Yj} Y_{ji}\end{aligned} \tag{6}$$

where p_{Xi}^h denotes the price charged by the representative HMNE with a plant in i. Let p_{Xj}^n, p_{Xj}^v, and p_{Yj} denote the prices charged by producers in j for goods X (NEs and VMNEs, respectively) and Y, respectively. In the second line of Eq. (6), the first three RHS terms denote factor income; the last three RHS terms denote tariff revenue redistributed lump-sum by the government in i back to the representative consumer. Let r_i denote the rental rate for physical capital in i, K_i is the physical capital stock in i (used at home or transferred abroad at a cost in units of capital of γ), w_{Si} (w_{Ui}) is the wage rate for skilled (unskilled) workers in i, and S_i (U_i) is the stock of skilled (unskilled) workers in i.

Maximizing (5) subject to (6) yields the domestic demand functions:

$$x_{ii}^{\ell} \geq (p_{Xi}^{\ell})^{\varepsilon-1} P_{Xi}^{-\varepsilon} \eta E_i; \quad \ell = \{n, h, v\} \tag{7}$$

where E_i is the income (and expenditure) of the representative consumer in country i from Eq. (6), and

$$P_{Xi} = \left[\sum_{j=1}^{3} n_j (t_{Xji} p_{Xj}^n)^{\varepsilon} + \sum_{j=1}^{3} h_j (p_{Xi}^h)^{\varepsilon} + \sum_{k\neq j}\sum_{j=1}^{3} v_{kj} (t_{Xji} p_{xj}^v)^{\varepsilon}\right]^{\frac{1}{\varepsilon}} \tag{8}$$

is the corresponding CES price index. Following the literature, we assume all firms producing in the same country face the same technology and marginal costs and we assume complementary-slackness conditions (cf., Markusen, 2002). Hence, mill (or ex-manufacturer) prices of all varieties in a specific country are equal in equilibrium. Then, the relationship between differentiated goods produced in j and at home in i is:

$$\frac{x_{ji}}{x_{ii}} = \left(\frac{p_{Xj}}{p_{Xi}}\right)^{\varepsilon-1} t_{Xji}^{\varepsilon} (1 + b_{Xji})^{-1}. \tag{9}$$

Hence, from now on we can omit superscripts for both prices and quantities of differentiated products for the ease of presentation. It follows that homogeneous goods demand is:

$$\sum_{j=1}^{3} Y_{ji} \geq \frac{1-\eta}{p_{Yi}} E_i. \tag{10}$$

3.2. Differentiated goods producers

We assume that manufactures can be produced in all three countries using skilled labor, unskilled labor, and physical capital. Each country is assumed to be endowed with exogenous amounts of internationally immobile skilled and unskilled labor. Each country is also endowed with an exogenous amount of physical capital; however, physical capital can be transferred endogenously across countries by MNEs to maximize their profits, thus making endogenous determination of bilateral FDI flows, cf., Footnote 9. Differentiated goods producers operate in monopolistically competitive markets, similar to Markusen (2002, Ch. 6). Two assumptions used for our theoretical results that follow are the existence of a third, internationally-mobile factor – physical capital – *and* that any headquarters setup (fixed cost) requires home skilled labor – to represent R&D – and any plant setup requires the home country's physical capital — to represent the resources needed for a domestic or foreign direct investment.[13]

Assume the production of differentiated good X is given by a nested Cobb–Douglas-CES technology where F_{Xi} denotes production of these goods for both the domestic and foreign markets; we assume MNEs and NEs have access to the same technology. Let K_{Xi}, S_{Xi}, and U_{Xi} denote the quantities used of physical capital, skilled labor, and unskilled labor, respectively, in country i to produce X:

$$F_{Xi} = B(K_{Xi}^{\chi} + S_{Xi}^{\chi})^{\frac{\alpha}{\chi}} U_{Xi}^{1-\alpha}. \tag{11}$$

The specific form of the production function is motivated by two literatures. First, the Cobb–Douglas function provides a standard, tractable, and empirically relevant method of combining capital and labor; α denotes the share of "capital" in production. Second, early work by Griliches (1969) indicates that physical capital and human capital tend to be complements in production; recent evidence for this in the domestic literature is in Goldin and Katz (1998) and in the MNE literature is in Slaughter (2000). We nest a CES production function within the Cobb–Douglas function to allow for potential complementarity of physical and human capital; χ determines the degree of complementarity or substitutability.

NEs and MNEs differ in fixed costs. Each NE incurs only one firm (or headquarters) setup and one plant setup; each MNE incurs one firm setup (the cost of which is assumed larger than that of an NE, as in Markusen, 2002) and a plant setup for its home market and for each foreign market it enters endogenously. A horizontal MNE has headquarters at home and plants in three markets to serve them; it has no exports. A vertical MNE has headquarters at home and one plant abroad, which can export to any market. Maximizing profits subject to the above technology yields a set of conditional factor demands reported in a technical supplement (available from the authors).

3.3. Homogeneous goods producers

We assume homogeneous good (Y) is produced under constant returns to scale in perfectly competitive markets using only unskilled labor; assume the technology $Y_i = Ui$ (i=1,2,3). In the presence of positive trade costs, we assume country 1 is the numeraire; hence, $p_{Y1} = w_{U1} = 1$.

[13] Note it is not necessary that plants (firms) require only physical (human) capital to setup plants (firms); what is necessary is that setups of plants (firms) are *relatively* more physical (human) capital intensive, which we conjecture is true empirically. Also, the model is robust to assuming instead that plants (firms) require human (physical) capital for setups. The key is that two factors are used in setups, and that the two setups (firms and plants) have different relative factor intensities.

3.4. Profit functions, pricing equations, and the definition of FDI

Firms are assumed to maximize profits given the technologies and the demand relationships suggested above. The profit functions are:

$$\pi_i^n = (p_{Xi} - c_{Xi}) \sum_{j=1}^{3} x_{ij} - a_{Sni} w_{Si} - a_{Kni} r_i \tag{12a}$$

$$\pi_i^h = \sum_{j=1}^{3} (p_{Xj} - c_{Xj}) x_{jj} - a_{Shi} w_{Si} - a_{Khi} [3 + \sum_{j \neq i} \gamma_{ij}] r_i \tag{12b}$$

$$\pi_{ij}^v = (p_{Xj} - c_{Xj}) \sum_{k=1}^{3} x_{jk} - a_{Svi} w_{Si} - a_{Kvi} [1 + \gamma_{ij}] r_i. \tag{12c}$$

Eq. (12a) is the profit function for each NE in i. Let c_{Xi} denote marginal production costs of differentiated good X in country i and the last two RHS terms represent, respectively, fixed human and physical capital costs for the NE producer. Eq. (12b) is the profit function for each HMNE in country i with three plants. The last two terms in (12b) represent fixed costs of each 3-country HMNE, a single fixed cost of home skilled labor to setup a firm and a fixed cost of home physical capital for each plant. Each foreign investment incurs an additional investment cost γ (say, policy or natural foreign direct investment barrier). Consequently, in the context of our model, the flow (and stock) of FDI of country i's representative three-country MNE in country j (if profitable) would be $a_{Khi} r_i (1 + \gamma_{ij})$; in our model, international capital "mobility" is defined as country i's physical capital being used abroad (say, in j), but the factor rewards are earned in i, cf., Footnote 9. Eq. (12c) is the profit function for a vertical MNE with a headquarters in i and a plant in j; FDI from i to j is analogously $a_{Kvi} r_i (1 + \gamma_{ij})$.

A key element of our model is that – in each country – the numbers of NEs (type n), HMNEs (type h), and VMNEs (type v) are *endogenous* to the model. Two conditions characterize models in this class. First, profit maximization ensures markup pricing equations:

$$p_{Xi} \leq \frac{c_{Xi}(\varepsilon - 1)}{\varepsilon}. \tag{13}$$

Second, free entry and exit ensure:

$$a_{Sni} w_{Si} + a_{Kni} r_i \geq \frac{c_{Xi}(\varepsilon - 1)}{\varepsilon} \sum_{j=1}^{3} x_{ij} \tag{14a}$$

$$a_{Shi} w_{Si} + a_{Khi} [3 + \sum_{i \neq j} \gamma_{ij}] r_i \geq \sum_{j=1}^{3} \frac{c_{Xj}(\varepsilon - 1)}{\varepsilon} x_{jj} \tag{14b}$$

$$a_{Svi} w_{Si} + a_{Kvi} [1 + \gamma_{ij}] r_i \geq \frac{c_{Xj}(\varepsilon - 1)}{\varepsilon} \sum_{k=1}^{3} x_{jk}. \tag{14c}$$

3.5. Factor-endowment and current-account-balance constraints

We assume that, in equilibrium, all factors are fully employed and that every country maintains multilateral (though not bilateral) current-account-balance; endogenous bilateral current-account imbalances allow for endogenous bilateral FDI of physical capital. Following the established literature, this is a static model. The formal factor-endowment and multilateral current-account-balance constraints are provided in a technical supplement (available from the authors).

4. Calibration of the model

The complexity of the model (including the complementary-slackness conditions) introduces a high degree of nonlinearity, and it cannot be solved analytically. As in Markusen (2002), we provide numerical solutions to the model. As common, results may be sensitive to choice of parameters. Hence, we go to some effort to choose parameters and exogenous variables' values closely related to econometric evidence and empirical data. With three countries, we have several potential types of asymmetries, e.g., large vs. small GDPs, developed (DC) vs. developing (LDC) economies. To limit the scope, we focus here on bilateral flows between two developed economies, initially assuming the third economy (ROW) is also developed. However, in a robustness analysis later, we compare the results to those with a developing ROW. We use *GAMS* for our numerical analysis.

4.1. Values of (exogenous) factor-endowment, trade cost, and investment cost variables

We assume a world endowment of physical capital (K) of 240 units, skilled labor (S) of 90 units, and unskilled labor (U) of 100 units. Initially, each of the three-country's shares of the world endowments is 1/3; hence, all three countries have identical absolute and relative factor-endowments initially.

We appealed to actual trade data to choose initial values for transport costs (rather than choosing values arbitrarily, as typical). Using the bilateral final goods trade data from the United Nations' (UN's) COMTRADE data for weights, we calculated the mean final goods bilateral transport cost factors [(cif − fob)/fob] for intra-DC trade (7.6%) and trade between DCs and LDCs (20.2%).

We constructed initial values for tariff rates using Jon Haveman's TRAINS data for the 1990s. Tariff rates are available at the Harmonized System 8-digit level. Using the UN's COMTRADE data again, we classified tariff rates by final goods 5-digit SITC categories. We then weighted each country's 5-digit SITC final goods tariff to generate average tariffs at the country level for each year 1990–2000. Tariff rates were then weighted by aggregate bilateral final goods imports to obtain mean regional tariff rates, accounting for free trade agreements and customs unions. For final goods, the tariff rate was 1.1% for intra-DC trade and 9.7 (4.0) percent for trade from DCs to LDCs (LDCs to DCs).

Data on bilateral costs of investment and on policy barriers to FDI are not available. Carr et al. (2001) used a time-varying country "rating" score from the World Economic Forum's *World Competitiveness Report* that ranges from 0 to 100 (used in Section 7). However, *ad valorem* measures are not available across countries, much less over time. Consequently, we assumed values to represent informational costs and policy barriers to FDI between countries. We assumed initially a "tax-rate" equivalent (for γ) of 40% for intra-DC FDI and 90% for FDI flows between LDCs and DCs.

4.2. Utility and technology parameter values

Consider first the utility function. In Eq. (5), the only two parameters are the Cobb–Douglas share of income spent on differentiated products from various producers (η) and the CES parameter (ε) influencing the elasticity of substitution between differentiated products ($\sigma \equiv 1-\varepsilon$). Initially, we use 0.71 for the value of η, based upon an estimated share of manufactures trade in overall world trade averaged between 1990 and 2000 using 5-digit SITC data from the UNs' COMTRADE data set, which is a plausible estimate. The initial value of ε is set at -5, implying an elasticity of substitution of 6 among differentiated final goods, consistent with a wide range of recent empirical studies estimating the elasticity between 2 and 10, cf., Baier and Bergstrand (2001) and Head and Ries (2001a,b).

Consider next production function (11) for differentiated goods. Labor's share of differentiated goods gross output is assumed to be 0.8; the Cobb–Douglas formulation implies the elasticity of substitution between capital and labor is unity. As discussed earlier, Griliches (1969) found convincing econometric evidence that physical capital and skilled labor were relatively more complementary in production than physical capital and unskilled labor. Most evidence to date suggests that skills and physical capital are relatively complementary in production, cf., Goldin and Katz (1998) and Slaughter (2000). Initially, we assume $\chi=-0.25$, implying a technical rate (elasticity) of substitution of 0.8 [$=1/(1-\chi)$] and complementarity between physical and human capital.

As in Markusen (2002, ch. 5), a firm (or headquarters) setup uses only skilled labor. For national final goods producers, we assume a headquarters setup requires a unit of skilled labor per unit of output ($a_{Sn,1}=a_{Sn,2}=a_{Sn,3}=1$). As in Markusen, we assume "jointness" for MNEs; that is, services of knowledge-based assets are joint inputs into multiple plants. Markusen suggests that the ratio of fixed headquarters setup requirements for a horizontal or vertical MNE relative to a domestic firm ranges from 1 to 2 (for a 2-country model). We assume initially a ratio of 1.01 ($a_{Sh,1}=a_{Sh,2}=a_{Sh,3}=a_{Sv,1}=a_{Sv,2}=a_{Sv,3}=1.01$). Hence, to bias the theoretical results initially *in favor of multinational activity* (that is, in favor of MNEs completely displacing trade), we assume the additional firm setup cost of an MNE over a national firm is quite small. We assume that every plant (national or MNE) requires one unit of home physical capital ($a_K=1$); MNEs setting up plants abroad face additional fixed investment costs (γ), values for which were specified above.

5. Coexistence: the two-country, three-factor case

In this section, we show theoretically that bilateral intra-industry FAS and intra-industry trade can coexist when two countries have identical GDPs; HMNEs need not displace NEs completely. The third country is unnecessary to address coexistence, so we assume for now ROW has zero factor-endowments.

In the $2\times2\times2$ model of Markusen (2002) where the two countries have identical absolute as well as relative factor-endowments, the reason HMNEs displace final goods trade completely lies in "setups" of plants and firms *both* requiring human capital. The intuition is straightforward: if transport costs between two countries are sufficiently high and the ratio of headquarters scale economies (fixed costs) relative to plant scale economies (fixed costs) is large (small), then the relative cost for country *i* of supplying a foreign market *j* with goods from foreign affiliates of *i*'s HMNEs is low relative to exporting from *i*. While in some (asymmetric) combinations of the two countries' GDPs, HMNEs and NEs can coexist, a redistribution of the world's factor-endowments (with no relative factor-endowment change) *always* causes trade and FAS to move in opposite directions (due to scarcity of human capital).

Fig. 1a and b illustrate the issue for the $2\times2\times2$ case with no physical capital. First, we explain the figures' axes and labeling. Given the nonlinear, non-monotonic relationships in this class of GE models, we must rely on numerical solutions to the model to obtain "theoretical" relationships, using figures generated by the numerical model. In these figures, we focus on the bilateral relationships between two economies with identical relative factor-endowments and transaction cost levels. Fig. 1a and b illustrate the relationships between country economic size (referred to as the sum of GDPs of *i* and *j*) on the *y*-axis, similarity of economic size on the *x*-axis, and final good exports of NEs from *i* to *j* (the values of foreign affiliate sales of country *i*'s HMNEs in country *j*) on the *z*-axis in Fig. 1a (b).[14] The lines on the *y*-axis in the bottom plane range from 1 to 21. The *y*-axis indexes the joint absolute factor-endowments of countries *i* and *j*; line 1 denotes the smallest combination and line 21 denotes the largest combination. The *x*-axis is indexed from 0 to 1. Each line represents *i*'s share of both countries' absolute factor-endowments; the center line represents 50%, or *identical GDP shares for i and j*.[15]

These figures are three-dimensional analogues to a two-dimensional figure in Markusen (2002, p. 99, Fig. 5.5, bottom). Our figures allow a range of total economic sizes for the two countries, whereas Markusen's corresponding figure was for a (single) given total economic size for the two countries.[16] Suppose initially that country *j* has the smallest possible GDP (i.e., virtually no factor-endowments) and country *i* has virtually all of the two countries' endowments; this is the first point on the far RHS of Fig. 1a and b. When country *j* is very small, it is most profitably served by the only other country, *i*, by national firms exporting from *i*; hence, HMNEs based in *i* will not serve *j* with foreign affiliate sales ($FAS_{ij}=0$). Even a slightly larger GDP in country *j* (the point to the left of the initial one) is not enough to make human capital sufficiently scarce to warrant FAS. However, at higher levels (moving to the left), country *j* is a large enough market to warrant foreign affiliate production by country *i* given investment barriers, and exports by national firms in *i* are partially "displaced" by the scarcity of human capital. At equal GDPs, HMNEs displace trade *completely* ($FAS_{ij}>0$ and trade is zero).

The complete displacement of trade in the $2\times2\times2$ model was formalized in Markusen and Venables (2000, section 4). More accurately, in their model there exists only a (highly unlikely) *unique* combination of trade costs (t) and ratio of national-to-multinational-firm setup costs (f/g) where HMNEs and NEs can coexist when the two countries are symmetric and the equilibrium is in the factor-price-equalization set (where mill prices and marginal production costs are equal). In the two-factor case, only if f/g is chosen to equal precisely $(1+t^{1-\varepsilon})/2$ can NEs and HMNEs coexist, where ε is the elasticity of substitution between varieties in their model.[17]

[14] Gross bilateral FAS from *i* to *j* is for HMNEs in industry *X*. Exports from *i* to *j* denote the aggregate gross bilateral trade flow of good *X* and good *Y* products from *i* to *j*.

[15] The theoretical flows are generated using *GAMS* and the figures are generated using *MATLAB*. As with all such programs, *MATLAB* requires the *y* (*x*) axis to be indexed by the sum of exogenous absolute factor-endowments (*i*'s share of the two countries' absolute factor-endowments), not endogenous GDPs. As in Markusen (2002), we often use the terms GDPs, economic sizes, and absolute factor-endowments interchangeably; for brevity, the figures' axes are labeled using GDPs. Of course, in empirical work, instrumenting GDPs by absolute factor-endowments in gravity equations generates virtually identical GDP coefficient estimates, cf., Frankel (1997).

[16] Of course, in the two-country case, the sum of GDPs of *i* to *j* is world GDP. However, to maintain consistent labeling of axes with the three-country case later, we label the *y*-axis with sum of GDPs of *i* to *j*.

[17] Shim (2005) used this assumption to motivate exogenously coexistence of MNEs and NEs.

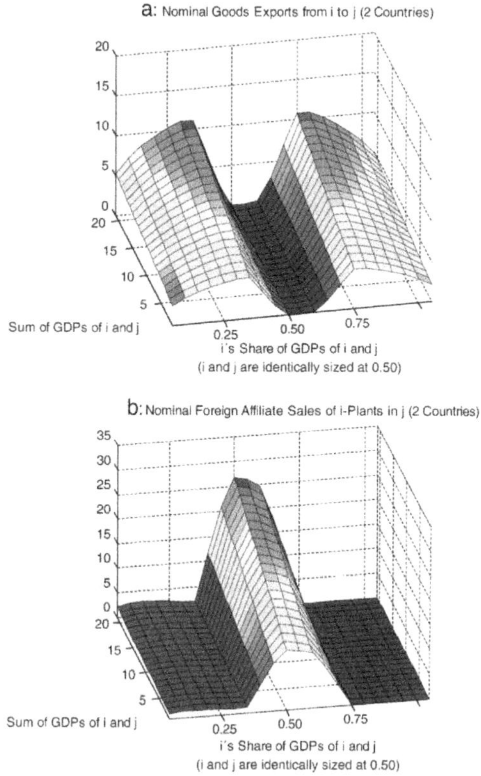

Fig. 1. a. Nominal goods exports from 1 to *j* (2 countries). b. Nominal foreign affiliate sales of *i*-plants in *j* (2 countries).

A resolution to this puzzle lies readily in introducing a third internationally-mobile factor and an assumption that home physical (human) capital is used to setup a plant (firm). The introduction of physical capital and the setup requirements can explain the observed *coexistence* of final goods trade (NEs) and FAS (HMNEs) when the two countries' GDPs are identical for a wide range of parameters. In simulations below, ROW has zero factor-endowments; conclusions result solely from introducing physical capital and the setup requirements.

Fig. 2a–c illustrate the implications for foreign affiliate sales, trade, and horizontal foreign direct investment, respectively, between a pair of developed-countries (i,j) with identical relative factor-endowments in our *three-factor*, two-country, two-good world. The most important point worth noting is, when the two countries have identical GDPs, NEs and HMNEs can *coexist*. However, similar to the $2 \times 2 \times 2$ world, once HMNEs arise, FAS tends to *partially* displace trade and national exporters *no matter how large* are the GDPs of countries *i* and *j*, cf., middle columns in Fig. 2a and b. The intuition can be seen by starting at the far right side of Fig. 2b, when *j*'s GDP is small relative to *i*'s. When *j*'s GDP share becomes positive (via an exogenous reallocation of

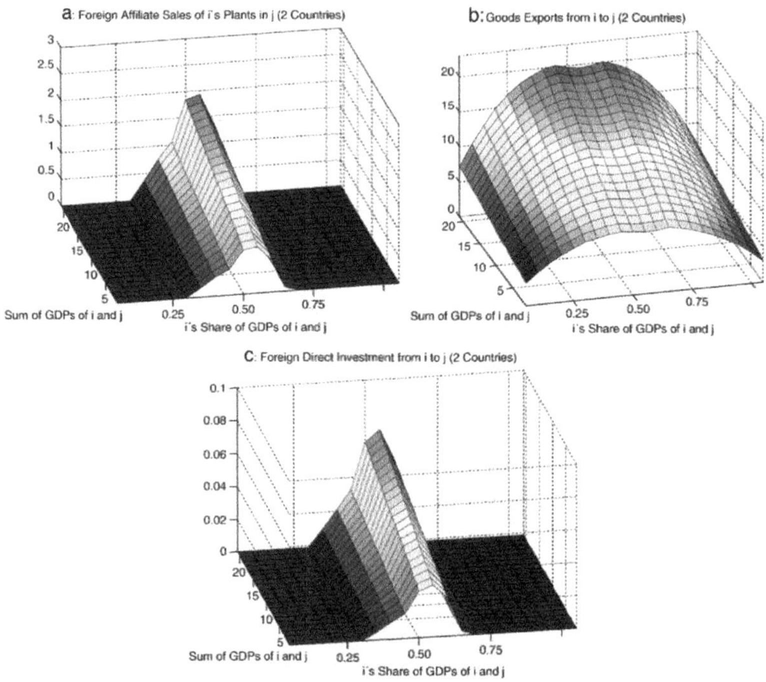

Fig. 2. a. Foreign affiliate sales of i's plants in j (2 countries). b. Goods exports from i to j (2 countries). c. Foreign direct investment from i to j (2 countries).

initial factor-endowments from i to j), j's relatively small market is most profitably served by exports from national firms in i and domestic production in j, identical to the $2 \times 2 \times 2$ case. Thus, i exports extensively to j.

As j's (i's) share of their combined GDPs gets larger (smaller), the number of exporters and varieties in i (n_i) contracts, cf., Fig. 3a. However, output per firm in j (x_{jj}, not shown), production, and overall demand expands proportionately more, such that exports from i to j increase, cf., Fig. 2b.

At some point (around 0.7 on the x-axis), as i's (j's) share gets even smaller (larger), it becomes more profitable for i to serve j's market using HMNEs (h_{2ij}) to avoid trade costs, cf., Fig. 3b. So FDI – physical capital – flows from i to j, so that both countries' markets can be more efficiently served by HMNEs based in i, cf., Fig. 2c. In the two-factor case with only human capital used to setup plants and firms, this would unambiguously increase the price of skilled (relative to unskilled) labor, displacing completely national firms in i. This need not occur here. While the replacement of NEs by MNEs requires more human capital for firm setups (as in the $2 \times 2 \times 2$ model), the net demand for human capital in i goes down because in our model plant setups require only physical capital. Since single-plant NEs are being increasingly replaced by multi-plant HMNEs as i and j become more similar in size (note the "dip" in the center columns of Fig. 3a when i's and j's shares are very similar), the relative demand for human capital falls and that for physical capital rises, lowering (raising) the price of human (physical) capital, cf., Fig. 3c and d.[18] This has two important implications for NEs not being *completely* displaced, and thus coexistence of NEs and HMNEs when i and j are identical. First, a higher price of physical capital in i (as i and j converge in size) raises the relative price of multi-plant HMNE firm setups, *reducing* the displacement of single-plant national firms (which serve markets via exports instead) and helping secure their coexistence with HMNEs. Second, a lower price of human capital in i lowers the price of HMNE and NE firm setups, also securing coexistence of both types of firms. As j's share approaches that of i, HMNEs continue to partially displace national firms. However, even with identical GDPs, HMNEs and national firms can *coexist* — a result precluded in the 2 × 2 × 2 model.

With physical capital, coexistence of HMNEs and NEs occurs over a wide range of economic sizes, GDP similarities, plant-to-firm setup costs, and trade costs, because of variable relative prices of human-to-physical capital, cf., Fig. 3c and d. We now demonstrate formally such coexistence for a wide parameter range. Consider the case of two symmetric economies where mill prices of the countries' differentiated products are identical ($p_{Xi}=p_{Xj}$), as in Markusen and Venables (2000, section 4). Begin with profit functions (12) from Section 3.4. With only two countries, there are no three-country HMNEs; we will have two-country HMNEs in equilibrium (h_2). With two symmetric economies in size and relative factor-endowments, there are no vertical MNEs (v). Hence, in equilibrium, zero profits ensure for the representative firm in i (and symmetrically in j):

$$\pi_n = (p_X - c_X)(x_{ii} + x_{ij}) - a_{Sn}w_S - a_{Kn}r = 0 \tag{15a}$$

$$\pi_{h2} = (p_{Xi} - c_{Xi})x_{ii} + (p_X - c_X)x_{jj} - a_{Sh2}w_S - a_{Kh2}[2 + \gamma]r = 0. \tag{15b}$$

Since mill prices are the same in i and j, we can use Eq. (9) to note:

$$\frac{x_{ij}}{x} = t_X^{1-\sigma}(1 + b_X)^{-1} \tag{16}$$

where, due to symmetry, $x=x_{ii}=x_{jj}$.

We can now solve for the necessary condition that ensures coexistence of NEs and HMNEs. Substituting Eq. (16) into Eq. (15a) and solving for $(p_X-c_X)x$ yields:

$$(p_X - c_X)x = (a_{Sn}w_S + a_{Kn}r)/[1 + t_X^{1-\sigma}(1 + b_X)^{-1}].$$

However, we know from Eq. (15b) that:

$$2(p_X - c_X)x = (a_{Sh2}w_S + a_{Kh2}[2 + \gamma]r).$$

Hence, after some algebra, the necessary condition for coexistence is:

$$[(a_{Sh2}(w_S/r) + a_{Kh2}(2 + \gamma)]/2 = [a_{Sn}(w_S/r) + a_{Kn}]/[1 + t_x^{1-\sigma}(1 + b_X)^{-1}].$$

Thus, unlike in Markusen and Venables (2000), NEs and HMNEs can coexist for two *identically-sized* economies across a wide variety of values of trade costs, investment costs, and plant-to-firm setup costs due to the endogeneity of the relative price of human-to-physical capital.[19]

[18] Recall, human and physical capitals are complements in *production* of differentiated goods, not in setups.

[19] We can also show that the addition of the third factor alone is not sufficient to ensure coexistence. Eliminating the physical capital requirement in plant setup costs (replacing it with human capital) leads to a unique solution result, as in Markusen and Venables (2000). However, it is not critical that physical (human) capital is used for plant (firm) setups; this assumption can be reversed, as long as the world endowment of skilled labor is increased (to ensure positive FDI and FAS).

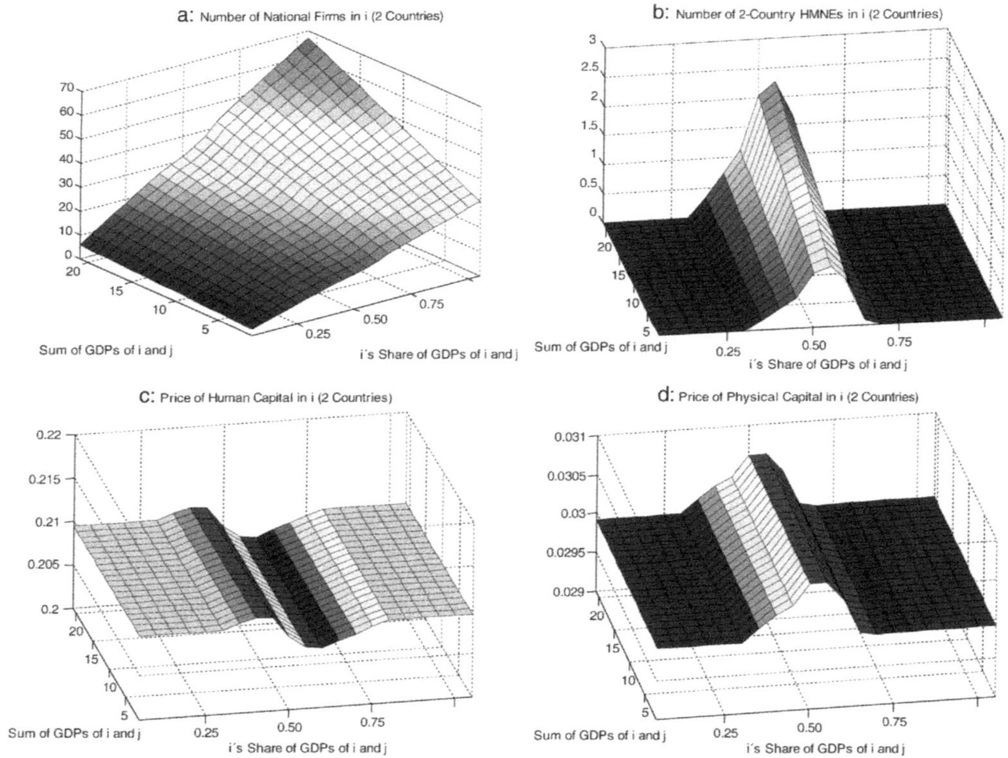

Fig. 3. a. Number of national firms in *i* (2 countries). b. Number of 2-country HMNEs in *i* (2 countries). c. Price of human capital in *i* (2 countries). d. Price of physical capital in *i* (2 countries).

As in this class of models, the results are, of course, sensitive quantitatively to levels of transport costs, investment costs, firm fixed costs, and plant fixed costs. However, these results hold for a wide range of values. Although the presence of physical capital and the assumption that plant setups use only physical capital generate the result that horizontal MNEs need not displace trade completely, the degree of substitutability or complementarity of bilateral trade and FDI with respect to economic size and similarity depends upon the presence of a "third country."

6. Complementarity: the three-country, three-factor case

While the gravity equation is familiar in algebraic form, it will be useful to *visualize* the frictionless "gravity" relationship. Fig. 4a illustrates the gravity–equation relationship between bilateral trade flows, GDP size, and GDP similarity summarized in Eq. (3) for an arbitrary hypothetical set of country GDPs ($N>2$). Of course, one notes a qualitative similarity of Fig. 4a to Fig. 2a–c.

However, there are (at least) three notable shortcomings that the *two-country* model cannot address. First, Fig. 2a–c represent bilateral *and* multilateral international flows; these figures depict a two-country world. With only two countries one cannot identify the effect of ROW on the bilateral flow from *i* to *j*; a theoretical foundation for the bilateral gravity equation needs at least three countries.

Second, with two countries the trade flow from *i* to *j* is *non-monotonic* in GDP similarity, cf., Fig. 2b. In a gravity equation, the trade flow is monotonic in economic similarity, cf., Fig. 4a. This conflicts with empirical results of trade and FDI gravity equations that imply bilateral trade and FDI are *complements* with respect to GDP size and similarity.

Third, in contrast to trade gravity equations, typical FDI gravity equation estimates find home country GDP elasticities *significantly larger* than host country GDP elasticities, cf., Table 1. This asymmetry cannot be explained using the two-country, three-factor model, cf., Fig. 2c.

In part 6.1, we address these three shortcomings. First, we explain why the introduction of a third country is necessary to generate "complementary" relationships between two countries' bilateral trade, FDI, and FAS flows with the two countries' GDP size and similarity. We address why the numbers of NEs and HMNEs also change in a complementary way with respect to changes in the two countries' economic size and similarity — even though NEs and HMNEs remain "overall" substitutes. Moreover, by introducing the third country, we can explain readily why typical empirical FDI gravity equations find home country (*i*) GDP elasticities significantly larger than host country (*j*) GDP elasticities. In part 6.2, we show the explicit relationship between size of the third country's (ROW's) GDP and trade, FDI and FAS of countries *i* and *j*, and suggest some "testable" hypotheses about the relationships between trade from *i* to *j* and FDI from *i* to *j* with GDP_{ROW}.

6.1. A theoretical rationale for estimating gravity equations of trade, FAS, and FDI

In this section, we introduce a third country – ROW – which initially is *identical* to the other two countries; the three countries are referred to as *i*, *j*, and ROW. Figs. 4b–d (5a–d) are the analogous "three-country" figures to two-country Figs. 2a–c (3a–d).[20] First, we note unsurprisingly in Fig. 4b–d that bilateral FAS, trade, and FDI from *i* to *j*, respectively (henceforth, FAS_{ij}, $Trade_{ij}$, and FDI_{ij}) are all positive monotonic functions of the *size* of the two countries' GDPs for any given share of *i* in *i*'s and *j*'s total GDP, as the gravity equation suggests (cf., Fig. 4a) for a given GDP_{ROW}. Note in Fig. 5a

[20] In the center cell of the *x*- and *y*-axes of Figs. 4 and 5, all three countries' GDPs are identical.

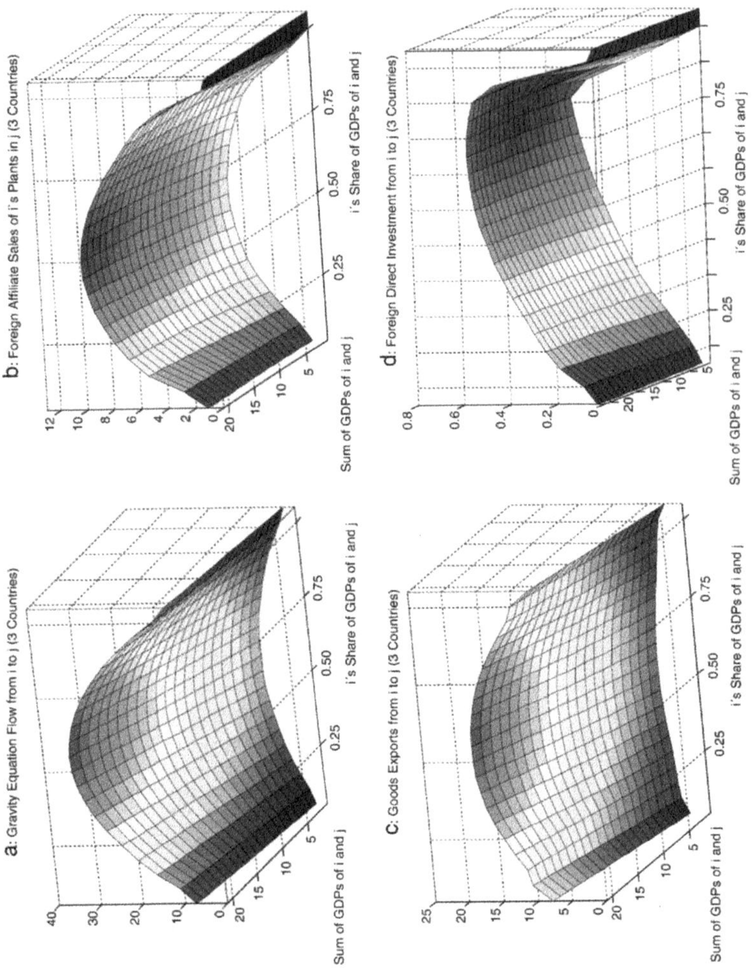

Fig. 4. a. Gravity equation flow from *i* to *j* (3 countries). b. Foreign affiliate sales of *i*'s plants in *j* (3 countries). c. Goods exports from *i* to *j* (3 countries). d. Foreign direct investment from *i* to *j* (3 countries).

and b that the numbers of both NEs and HMNEs increase with a larger joint economic size. More resources cover more setup costs of NEs and HMNEs; economies of scale and love of variety expand the number of total varieties produced for all three countries by both types of firms in *i*.

Second, and more interesting, even though NEs and HMNEs remain substitutes *overall*, the presence of the third country allows *both* bilateral FAS and trade from *i* to *j* to reach maximums as these two countries converge in GDP size, as a gravity equation would suggest; unlike the two-country case, FAS_{ij} and $Trade_{ij}$ are "complements" with respect to similarity in *i*'s and *j*'s GDPs. Note first that Figs. 4b and c (5a and b) illustrate that FAS_{ij} and $Trade_{ij}$ (NEs and HMNEs in *i*) remain substitutes overall. For any given size and similarity, the number of HMNEs (NEs) is larger (smaller) in the 3-country world than in the 2-country world; compare any cell in Fig. 5b (5a) with the corresponding cell in Fig. 3b (3a). Enlarging the world's economic size shifts the structure of all three economies toward relatively more HMNEs and fewer NEs; in this dimension, NEs and HMNEs are "overall" substitutes. With three countries, HMNEs surface more readily to avoid expensive trade costs; *i* can more profitably serve *j* and ROW by avoiding trade costs and investing in plants abroad. Note in Fig. 5b (4d) that *i*'s number of three-country HMNEs (*i*'s bilateral FDI from *i* to *j*) is positive even when *j*'s GDP is quite small relative to *i*'s. FAS_{ij} and FDI_{ij} ($Trade_{ij}$) is larger (smaller) in the 3-country relative to 2-country world. The overall substitution of FAS and FDI for trade also explains the "flattening" of the FAS (FDI) theoretical surface in Fig. 4b (d) relative to that in Fig. 2a (c); with more HMNEs in the 3-country world, FAS spreads out over a wider range of GDPs sizes and similarities since FDI occurs even when *j*'s GDP is small.

Yet, if the presence of a third country causes FAS_{ij} to tend to substitute more for $Trade_{ij}$ for any given level of GDP size and similarity, why do both increase as the country pair's GDPs become more identical with three countries but not with two? As the GDPs of countries *i* and *j* become more identical, Fig. 5c and d illustrate that the price of human (physical) capital tends to fall (rise). However, the larger percentage fall (rise) in the price of human (physical) capital with three countries than with two dampens the increase in HMNEs and the decrease in NEs more with three countries.[21] The dampening of the increase in the number of HMNEs contributes to "flattening" the FAS and FDI surfaces with three countries compared with two. The dampening of the decrease in the number of NEs is sufficient to cause $Trade_{ij}$ to be *monotonic* in size and similarity of the GDPs of countries *i* and *j* in the three-country case. The combined effect is to cause FAS_{ij} *and* $Trade_{ij}$ to – on net – covary positively and monotonically with respect to country *i*'s and *j*'s GDP size and similarity in the three-country world. This is the main economic reason behind the gravity equation working for FAS, FDI, and trade flows *simultaneously*!

Consequently, *i*'s FAS in *j and* trade from *i* to *j* are maximized when these two countries have identical GDPs (Fig. 4b and c), as a result of a third country and third factor. Thus, the theoretical relationships between bilateral trade, FDI, and FAS flows and GDPs in Fig. 4b–d are "well approximated" by the gravity relationship. However, note that the theoretical surface for FDI in Fig. 4d is distinctly asymmetric relative to the other surfaces. FDI from *i* to *j* is maximized when *i*'s share of the two countries' GDPs is larger than *j*'s share. It can be shown mathematically that such a surface implies the home country GDP elasticity of FDI *has to be larger* than the host country GDP elasticity. Thus, with three countries one should expect the empirical result found in specification (3) in Table 1, that is, a larger home country (*i*) GDP elasticity than host country (*j*) GDP elasticity for FDI_{ij}.

[21] For instance, as *j*'s share of *i*'s and *j*'s GDPs goes from 0 to 1/2 (for the smallest sum of GDPs of *i* and *j*), the fall in the price of *i*'s human capital is 7.8 (1.2) percent for the three-(two-) country case and the rise in the price of *i*'s physical capital is 16.7 (2.0) percent for the three-(two-) country case.

J.H. Bergstrand, P. Egger / Journal of International Economics 73 (2007) 278–308 299

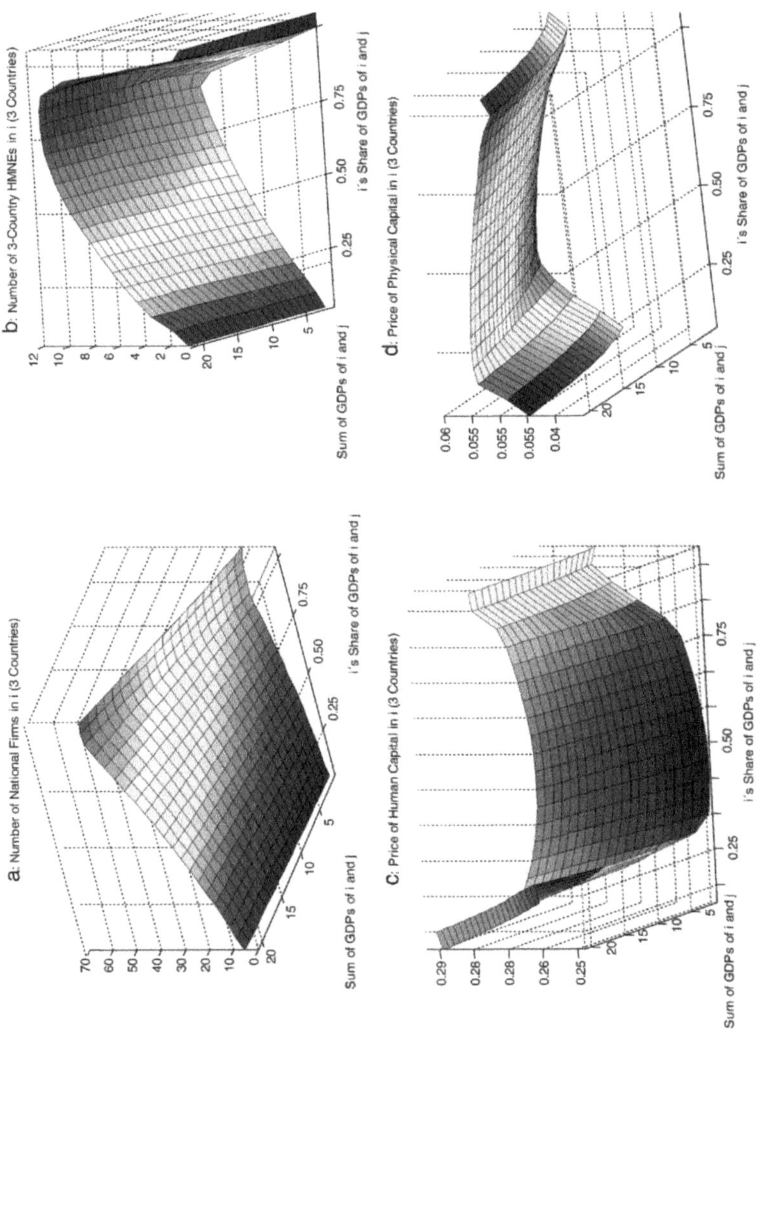

Fig. 5. a. Number of national firms in *i* (3 countries). b. Number of 3-country HMNEs in *i* (3 countries). c. Price of human capital in *i* (3 countries). d. Price of physical capital in *i* (3 countries).

However, "eyeballing" surfaces 4c and 4d *cannot* explain the empirical results using (the more econometrically appropriate) fixed-effects results in specifications (5)–(8) in Table 1. In Section 7 we move beyond "ocular-metrics" to provide a quantitative theoretical rationale for GDP elasticities estimated using fixed effects.

6.2. The effect of ROW on bilateral trade

In this part, we motivate potentially "testable" propositions about the empirical correlations between FDI_{ij} and GDP_{ROW} and between $Trade_{ij}$ and GDP_{ROW}. Fig. 6a–c show the relationships between the ROW's GDP (x-axis), the combined GDPs of i and j (y-axis), and $Trade_{ij}$, FAS_{ij}, and FDI_{ij}, respectively (z-axis). Here, the GDPs of countries i and j are set to be identical to each other, but their combined GDPs can vary. The cell in the middle row of the first column is defined to be identical absolute (and relative) factor-endowments for countries i, j and ROW. Suppose all three countries have identical absolute factor-endowments; when countries i and j have two-thirds of the world's GDP (for which there is no empirical counterpart, as will be shown), an increase in ROW's GDP makes FDI_{ij} relatively more attractive and $Trade_{ij}$ less attractive. As ROW's size initially increases, the profitability in country i from having more three-country HMNEs rises to avoid expensive transport costs to either j or ROW; hence, FDI from i to j (as well as i to ROW)

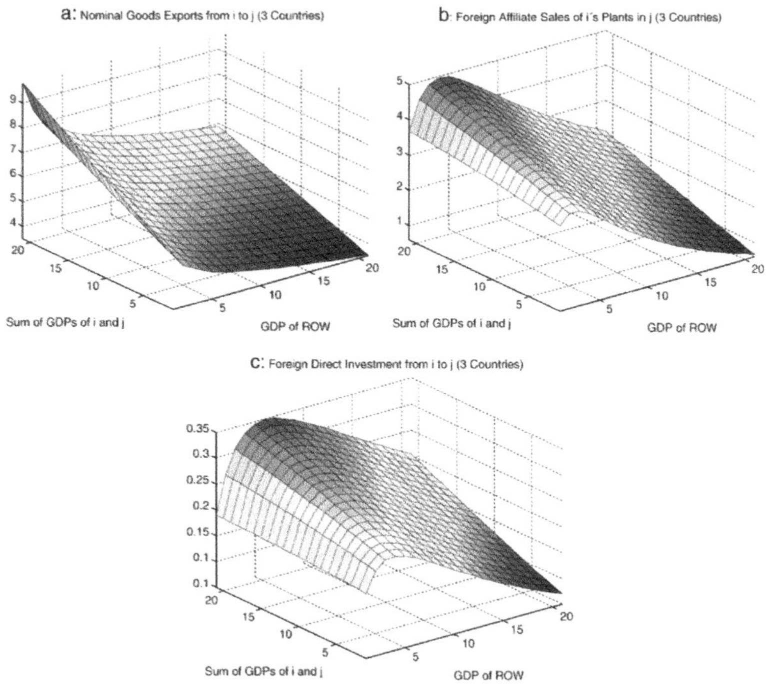

Fig. 6. a. Nominal goods exports from i to j (3 countries). b. Foreign affiliate sales of i's plants in j (3 countries). c. Foreign direct investment from i to j (3 countries).

increases, substituting for exports from i to j (Trade$_{ij}$ falls). However, as ROW continues to increase in economic size (moving to the right along the middle row of the x–y plane), the relative market sizes of i and j shrink, attracting less exports from i to j by NEs and countries i and j become less attractive markets in size to be served efficiently by HMNEs in i and j.

The model suggests two potentially "testable" hypotheses. First, Trade$_{ij}$ should decrease monotonically as ROW's GDP increases, consistent with previous formal theoretical models for the trade gravity equation ignoring MNEs and FDI. Second, the model suggests a *quadratic* relationship between FDI$_{ij}$ and GDP$_{ROW}$; this hypothesis is novel. Clearly, a positive or negative relationship depends on relative GDPs of i, j, and ROW.

However, examination of actual GDPs suggests the likely relationship to dominate empirically for the second hypothesis is negative. Recall first that the x-axis has 21 columns. In Fig. 6c, GDP$_{ROW}$ ranges from the same size as i (or j) in column 1 to 10 times GDP$_i$ (or GDP$_j$) in column 21. Thus, column 2 represents $GDP_{ROW}=1.5*GDP_i$ and column 3 represents $GDP_{ROW}=2*GDP_i$, or $GDP_{ROW}=GDP_i+GDP_j$. Thus, the model hypothesizes that FDI$_{ij}$ and GDP$_{ROW}$ should be negatively (positively) correlated for observations where $GDP_i+GDP_j<GDP_{ROW}$ ($GDP_i+GDP_j>GDP_{ROW}$).

Does GDP data provide any guidance on the relevant hypothesis? For the last year of our sample (2000), the combined nominal GDP of the two largest economies in the world – the United States and Japan – was US$14.52 trillion; this was less than *half* of world GDP ($31.43 trillion, using the 160 largest economies) and hence less than GDP$_{ROW}$ (US$16.91 trillion). Consequently, *all* empirical observations lie in the negatively-sloped region of Fig. 6c. Thus, the model implies two "testable" propositions: Trade$_{ij}$ and FDI$_{ij}$ should *both* be negatively related to ROW GDP. We evaluate these later empirically.

7. A quantitative description of the theoretical gravity equations of trade and FDI

The diversity of gravity-like relationships in specifications (5)–(8) in Table 1 suggests a need for a more quantitative "description" of the theoretical relationships in Fig. 4c and d.[22] To move beyond "ocular-metrics," in part 7.1 we describe a new methodology to describe *quantitatively* the relationship between each of the "theoretical flows" and the exogenous RHS variables, similar to how a regression describes empirical relationships. In part 7.2, we present the results of these exercises for describing the theoretical relationships between GDP size, GDP similarity, and the various flows, and compare these to the empirical results in Table 1. In part 7.3, we use the numerical GE model to illustrate theoretical relationships between trade costs, investment costs, RTAs, trade flows, and FDI. In part 7.4, we use data on ROW GDP and bilateral trade and investment costs to extend empirical results to determine if the "testable" propositions regarding ROW GDP, trade costs, investment costs, and trade and FDI flows hold. In part 7.5, we discuss some sensitivity analyses that were conducted.

7.1. Methodology

The key notion behind the methodology that follows is to describe quantitatively using a single regression equation a nonlinear theoretical surface relating bilateral flows to GDP size and

[22] The diversity of quantitative gravity relationships reflects the model's "unconditional" GE structure, i.e., non-separability of production, consumption, trade and FDI allocations. This differs from a standard gravity equation, such as Eq. (1), which is consistent with the "conditional" GE structure emphasized in Anderson and van Wincoop (2004, pp. 706–707), which employs a critical "trade-separability" assumption, resulting in unit GDP elasticities. See also Footnote 4.

similarity generated by a numerical GE model. We have empirical data on GDP sizes and similarities. Our surfaces map certain "theoretical" levels of bilateral (trade, FDI, or FAS) flows to various GDP sizes and similarities. However, since it is a nonlinear surface, there is an "approximation error" relating the level of the flow to GDP sizes and similarities. We treat this error term as normally distributed (and can confirm that assumption) so that a regression of the "theoretical" flow on GDP sizes and similarities describes the surface quantitatively.

Our methodology using regressions on "theoretical" flows is described most transparently using several steps. First, consider the bottom plane in Fig. 4c. The x-axis indexes country i's share of i's and j's total GDP, ranging from 0 to 1. The y-axis represents the sum of GDPs of countries i and j (GDPT).[23] The x-(y-) axis actually consists of 99 columns (600 rows); however, if we had used 99 columns (600 rows) in Fig. 4c, the entire figure would be black due to too many lines on the grid. For readability, the figures shown aggregate the 99 columns (600 rows) into 21 columns and rows so each cell's color content is visible. On the y-axis, the initial level of the country pair's GDP sum is set to one. The next line's GDP sum is six percent larger than the first line's GDP, the third line's GDP sum is six percent larger than the second line's GDP, and so on for 600 entries. Thus, GDP sums vary from 1 to (approximately) 37. This generates 59,400 (=99 × 600) cells with "theoretical" observations on (i's and j's) GDP sums, GDP shares, and the level of trade flow, FDI, or FAS implied by the model.

We could run a regression of the numerical GE model's estimates of the (log) levels of the theoretical trade flows from i to j on (logs of) i's and j's GDP sum and similarity ($E_i + E_j$ and $s_i s_j$, respectively) using each "cell" once as an observation, similar to Fig. 4a. The "error terms" would be the approximation (or rounding) errors generated from the nonlinearity of the surface and behave as if randomly distributed.[24] However, running such a regression would have limited economic meaning since each cell has the same weight in the distribution. Some of the cells (in terms of GDP totals and similarity) might not even be observed empirically!

Consequently, we create a more relevant distribution for the cells by benchmarking the (bottom) plane to empirical data on GDPs from *World Development Indicators*. We then fill each cell based upon observations of GDP sums and i's share of their GDP for that cell; that is, we "match" theoretical values of GDP size and similarity to their empirical observations for each country pair. Using our sample of the 17 most developed OECD countries' annual GDPs for 1990–2000, we fill the cells with the observations corresponding to each country pair with a certain GDP sum and GDP share (i's share of the GDP of i and j). For example, along the x-axis the first column includes all observations in the panel for which i's GDP share is between 0 and (approximately) 1% of a country pair's total GDP (recall, there are actually 99 columns). Along the y-axis, the first row (of actually 600 rows) includes all observations in the panel for which the GDP sum is smallest and up to 6% higher than that. The largest GDP sum in the sample (i.e., U.S.–Japan GDP sum for year 2000) amounts to about 37 times that of the smallest country pair. Thus, we have created a distribution of frequencies of cells based upon GDP sums and similarities using cross-section and time-series data. We then estimate the regression relationship between the *theoretical* value for a country pair's flow from i to j (using separately each of the three flows) based upon the model with the values for the GDP sums and i's GDP shares based on actual GDP data.[25]

[23] GDPs are, of course, an endogenous variable. The exogenous variables are the absolute endowments of unskilled labor, skilled labor, and physical capital. Simulations using these variables yield similar outcomes.

[24] We could have even added a stochastic error term explicitly; this would not have changed our results.

[25] Not every one of the 59,400 theoretical cells will be used. Also, we exclude all zero theoretical flows. The only difference between our regressions and typical regression analysis using empirical data on both sides of the regression is that the LHS variable is from the theoretical surface; RHS variables are random variables and the error term is normally distributed. Note, we are *not testing* the theory; we are simply describing the theory quantitatively.

7.2. Regression results using theoretical flows

Specifications (9)–(12) in Table 1 are the results of running the regressions using "theoretical" flows from i to j. Specification (9) reveals that theoretical trade flows from i to j are positively related to the countries' GDPs. The results are qualitatively identical to those in fixed-effects specification (5) in Table 1 using *actual* trade flows. The exporter GDP elasticity is smaller than the importer GDP elasticity in both specifications. A comparison of specification (10) using theoretical flows with fixed-effects specification (6) using actual trade flows shows that the results are qualitatively similar for GDP size and similarity. GDP similarity elasticities are nearly the same.

Specifications (11) and (12) in Table 1 report the coefficient estimates using the analogous specifications for "theoretical" FDI flows. Notably, the home country GDP elasticity is larger than the host country GDP elasticity in specification (11), consistent with fixed-effects specification (7) using actual FDI flows. Moreover, the GDP similarity elasticity in specification (12) is comparable to that in specification (8) using actual FDI flows. However, the GDP size elasticities are much larger in specifications (6) and (8) using empirical trade and FDI flows than in corresponding specifications (10) and (12) using theoretical flows. The relatively high GDP size elasticities may be sensitive to omitted variables or the particular period used for empirics (1990–2000); our time series was constrained by bilateral trade and investment cost data availability. We address potential omitted variables bias in part 7.4.

7.3. Effects of trade and investment costs, regional trade agreements, and relative factor-endowments

Of course, one of the most important variables in any trade or FDI gravity equation is bilateral distance, typically included as a proxy for trade or investment costs, respectively. Both trade and investment costs are included explicitly in our theoretical model (as in Markusen, 2002). Fig. 7a (b) shows the relationship between bilateral trade (FDI) flows, trade costs, and investments costs in our model. As expected, Trade_{ij} (FDI_{ij}) is negatively related to trade (investment) costs between i and j. Moreover, the model suggests, as common in this literature, that Trade_{ij} (FDI_{ij}) is *positively* related to investment (trade) costs between i and j. These "testable" propositions are evaluated empirically later.[26]

Fig. 7c and d illustrate the effect of introducing a bilateral regional free trade agreement (RTA) between countries i and j in our three-country model. The theory suggests that a reduction in bilateral trade costs is associated with a higher level of bilateral trade, cf., Fig. 7c. However, a reduction in trade costs makes bilateral investment less economical, and should tend to reduce bilateral FDI, cf., McCulloch (1985, 1993). Fig. 7d confirms that the model suggests that a free *trade* agreement between i and j should be associated with a lower level of bilateral investment from i to j. (Fig. 7c–d also provide a theoretical rationale for the multiplicative relationships between measures of trade and investment costs, GDPs, and trade and FDI flows in typical gravity equations.) In Section 7.4, we evaluate empirically whether trade (investment) is positively (negatively) related to RTA.

[26] The relationships shown in Fig. 7a and b are for the case of three countries that are identical in absolute and relative factor-endowments, as in Markusen (2002, sections 5.5). If relative factor-endowments were allowed to differ, such as in Markusen (2002, sections 8.5 and 8.6), we would obtain non-monotonic relationships. However, our purpose in Fig. 7a and b is to motivate expected empirical relationships for trade and FDI flows with trade and investment costs in the context of an empirical gravity equation where the interaction of such costs and relative factor-endowments is assumed to be minimized by the logarithmic transformation.

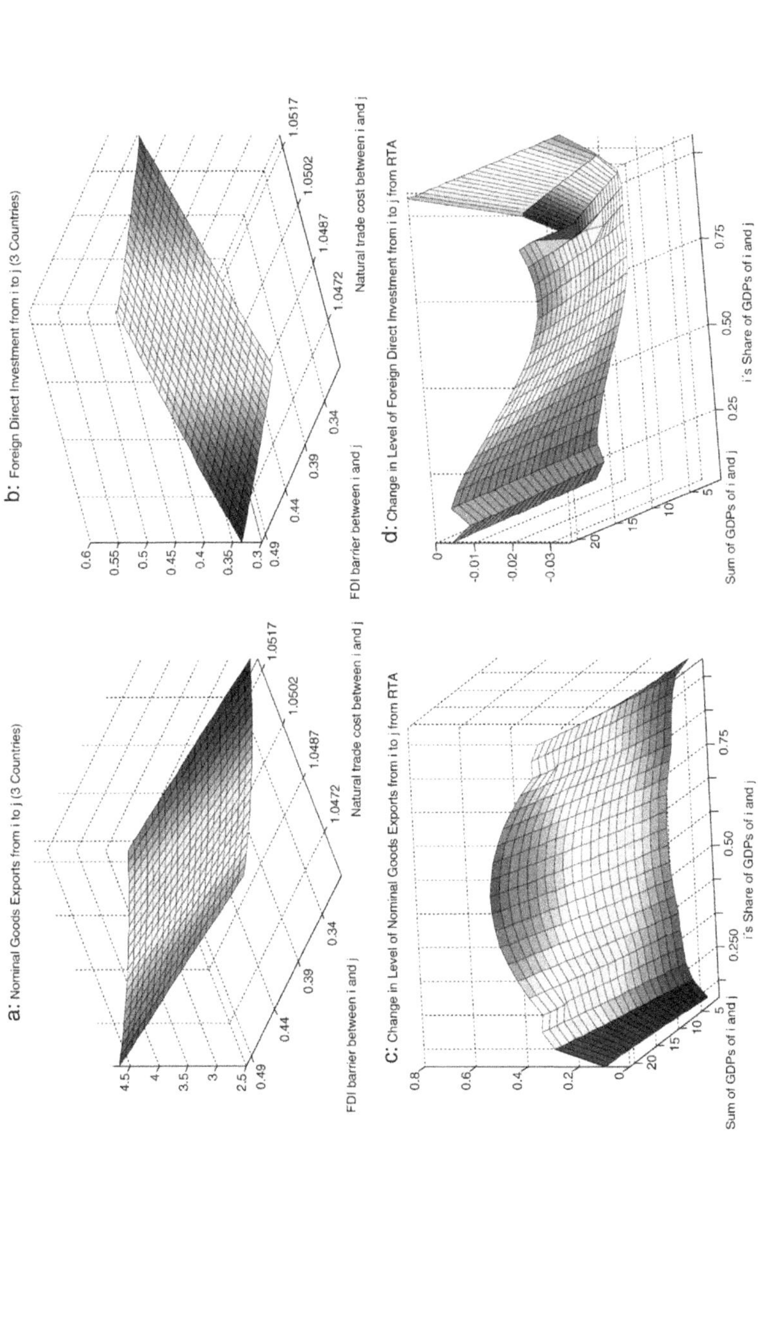

Fig. 7. a. Nominal goods exports from *i* to *j* (3 countries). b. Foreign direct investment from *i* to *j* (3 countries). c. Change in level of nominal goods exports from *i* to *j* from RTA. d. Change in level of foreign direct investment from *i* to *j* from RTA.

Up to now, countries have had identical relative factor-endowments. In the interest of robustness, we allowed ROW to be a developing country by having a larger (smaller) initial share of the world's unskilled labor (human and physical capital). With this change, vertical MNEs surface. However, the results are largely robust to this change. The surfaces examined in Figs. 4–7 are qualitatively (not quantitatively) identical with a developed or developing ROW; figures are omitted due to space constraints.

Also, our theoretical surfaces assume countries i and j have identical relative factor-endowments. As discussed in Carr et al. (2001), Blonigen et al. (2003), and Braconier et al. (2005), theoretical relationships between relative factor-endowments of countries i and j and trade, FAS, and FDI flows from i to j are interesting as well. However, examining those theoretical relationships for our three-factor model is well beyond the scope of this paper and the subject of future research. Nevertheless, even developed-country pairs are likely to have different relative factor-endowments. To ensure the empirical results that follow account for variation in relative factor-endowments between i and j, we include relative factor-endowments of country pairs.

7.4. Final empirical results

The previous sections suggest three potentially "testable" propositions that can be investigated empirically using time-series (within) variation. First, Section 6.2 suggested $Trade_{ijt}$ should be negatively related to GDP_{ROW} and – based upon the actual size distribution of the world's GDPs – FDI_{ijt} should also be related negatively to GDP_{ROW}. Second, Section 7.3 suggested $Trade_{ijt}$ (FDI_{ijt}) should be negatively related to bilateral trade (investment) costs and positively related to bilateral investment (trade) costs. Third, Section 6.3 suggested $Trade_{ijt}$ (FDI_{ijt}) should be positively (negatively) related to an RTA dummy.

Specifications (13)–(16) in Table 1 report the results using bilateral fixed effects of estimating the same specifications similar to (5)–(8) but now adding ROW GDP, bilateral trade (cif−fob) and investment costs, and relative factor-endowments of countries i and j. Trade and investment costs data were described in Section 4; factor-endowment data are from Baier et al. (2004). First, we find that $Trade_{ij}$ and FDI_{ij} are both statistically significantly negatively related to GDP_{ROW} as expected. Second, we find that $Trade_{ij}$ (FDI_{ij}) is negatively related to bilateral trade (investment) costs as expected and the coefficient estimate is statistically significant at the 10% level (two-tailed t-tests). The relationship between $Trade_{ij}$ (FDI_{ij}) and bilateral investment (trade) costs is not correctly signed, but these cross-price elasticities are much smaller than the own-price elasticities. Third, due to our data set (which was limited by investment cost data), we have no time-series variation in the free trade agreement dummy variable. However, we do have cross-section variation. A reexamination of Table 1's empirical gravity equation coefficient estimates for the dummy variable representing a free trade agreement (=1 if RTA present, =0 otherwise) using panel data in specifications (1)–(4) shows that a reduction in "trade costs" (in the form of the presence of a free trade agreement) is correlated with a higher level of bilateral trade – but a lower level of bilateral investment – between a pair of countries, consistent with our theory. Finally, while theoretical predictions for the relationships between relative factor-endowments of country i relative to j on flows are beyond the scope of this paper, we find that FDI_{ij} is positively and statistically significantly related to the (log) physical–capital-to-unskilled-labor (K/U) ratios (in i relative to j) and the (log) human-capital-to-unskilled-labor (S/U) ratios. $Trade_{ij}$ is negatively related to the relative K/U ratios, but is positively and statistically significantly related to the relative S/U ratios.

7.5. Sensitivity of results to parameter selections and exogenous variables

Of course, the potential number of alternative calibrations of our numerical GE model is virtually unlimited. Paper space constraints prevent an exhaustive analysis of permutations from our base calibration. Nevertheless, we evaluated the sensitivity of the model's theoretical surfaces to assuming setups of headquarters (plants) require human (physical) capital and to varying trade-relative-to-investment costs, MNE/NE ratio firm setup costs, the capital–skill elasticity of technical substitution, and the elasticity of substitution of differentiated goods in utility. A complete discussion of these findings is in a technical supplement (at http://www.nd.edu/~jbergstr).

8. Conclusions and directions for future research

The introduction of a third internationally-mobile factor to the standard $2\times2\times2$ model allows us to resolve fairly readily a puzzle in the modern knowledge–capital literature on MNEs (without heterogeneous productivities among firms) that foreign affiliate sales among two identical economies completely displace their intra-industry trade. The introduction of a third country suggests a formal N-country theoretical rationale for estimating gravity equations of FDI flows and foreign affiliate sales, in a manner consistent with estimating trade gravity equations.

Our future research agenda is quite large. We intend to extend our methodological framework to examine theoretically the economic determinants of trade, FDI, and FAS flows *between* developed and developing countries, and *among* developing countries. We plan to incorporate intermediate goods to better understand the role of "outsourcing" for NEs and MNEs. We intend to investigate further the role of physical capital for better understanding the empirical relationships between relative factor-endowments and the pattern of MNE behavior as raised in Carr et al. (2001) and Blonigen et al. (2003).

Acknowledgements

We deeply appreciate extensive and insightful comments on earlier drafts by Eric van Wincoop, Bruce Blonigen, Ron Davies, Kishore Gawande, Amy Glass, David Hummels, Keith Maskus, Jim Markusen, Howard Schatz, Deborah Swenson, Chong Xiang, two anonymous referees, and participants at presentations at Purdue University, Syracuse University, Texas A&M University, the European Economic Association meetings (2005), and the Empirical Investigations in International Trade conference at UC-Santa Cruz (2004). Bergstrand acknowledges research funding from the Mendoza College of Business and Kellogg Institute for International Studies at Notre Dame and Egger acknowledges research funding from the Austrian Science Fund through grant P17713-G05.

Appendix A. Data appendix

Bilateral trade flow data are from the UN World Trade Database for 1990–2000. Bilateral (outbound) FDI stock data are from UNCTAD (country profiles) for same years. GDPs are from *World Development Indicators* (2004). Bilateral distance was computed using "great circle" distances. Dummy variables for adjacency and common language are from CEPII (Centre d'Etudes Prospectives et d'Informations Internationales). The 17 OECD countries include Australia, Austria, Belgium, Canada, Denmark, Finland, France, Germany, Italy, Netherlands, New Zealand, Norway, Sweden, Switzerland, United Kingdom, and United States.

References

Anderson, James E., van Wincoop, Eric, 2003. Gravity with gravitas: a solution to the border puzzle. American Economic Review 93 (1), 170–192 (March).

Anderson, James E., van Wincoop, Eric, 2004. Trade costs. Journal of Economic Literature 42 (3), 691–751 (September).

Baier, Scott L., Bergstrand, Jeffrey H., 2001. The growth of world trade: tariffs, transport costs, and income similarity. Journal of International Economics 53 (1), 1–27 (February).

Baier, Scott L., Bergstrand, Jeffrey H., 2007. Do free trade agreements actually increase members' international trade? Journal of International Economics 71 (1), 72–95 (February).

Baier, Scott L., Dwyer, Gerald, Tamura, Robert, 2004. How important are capital and total factor productivity for economic growth? Economic Inquiry 44 (1), 23–49 (January).

Baldwin, Richard E., Ottaviano, Gianmarco, 2001. Multiproduct multinationals and reciprocal FDI dumping. Journal of International Economics 54, 429–448.

Barba Navaretti, G., Venables, Anthony J., 2004. Multinational Firms in the World Economy. Princeton University Press, Princeton, NJ.

Bergstrand, Jeffrey H., Egger, Peter, 2004. A theoretical and empirical model of international trade and foreign direct investment with outsourcing: part I, developed countries. Working Paper. April.

Bergstrand, Jeffrey H., Egger, Peter, 2006. A knowledge-and-physical–capital model of international trade, foreign direct investment, and foreign affiliate sales: developed countries. Working Paper. Jan.

Blonigen, Bruce A., 2001. In search of substitution between foreign production and exports. Journal of International Economics 53 (1), 81–104 (February).

Blonigen, Bruce A., 2005. A review of the empirical literature on FDI determinants. Atlantic Economic Journal 33 (4), 383–403 (December).

Blonigen, Bruce A., Davies, Ronald B., Head, Keith, 2003. Estimating the knowledge–capital model of the multinational enterprise: comment. American Economic Review 93 (3), 980–994.

Blonigen, Bruce A., Davies, Ronald B.,Waddell, Glen R., Naughton, H., in press. FDI in space: spatial autoregressive relationships in foreign direct investment. European Economic Review.

Borga, Maria, Yorgason, Daniel R., 2002. Direct investment positions for 2001: country and industry detail. Survey of Current Business. U.S. Department of Commerce, pp. 25–35. July.

Braconier, Henrik, Norback, Pehr-Johan, Urban, Dieter, 2005. Reconciling the evidence on the knowledge–capital model. Review of International Economics 13 (4), 770–786 (September).

Carr, David, Markusen, James R., Maskus, Keith E., 2001. Estimating the knowledge–capital model of the multinational enterprise. American Economic Review 91 (3), 693–708 (June).

Egger, Peter, 2000. A note on the proper econometric specification of the gravity equation. Economics Letters 66 (1), 25–31.

Ekholm, Karolina, Forslid, Rikard, Markusen, James R., in press. Export-platform foreign direct investment. Journal of the European Economic Association.

Feenstra, Robert C., 2004. Advanced International Trade: Theory and Evidence. Princeton U. Press, Princeton, NJ.

Frankel, Jeffrey A., 1997. Regional Trading Blocs in the World Economic System. Institute for International Economics, Washington, DC.

Goldin, Claudia, Katz, Lawrence F., 1998. The origins of technology-skill complementarity. Quarterly Journal of Economics 113 (3), 693–732.

Grazalian, Pascal L., Furtan, W. Hartley, 2005. The border effects: recognizing the role of FDI. Working Paper. University of Saskatchewan.

Griliches, Z., 1969. Capital–skill complementarity. Review of Economics and Statistics 51 (4), 465–468 (Nov.).

Head, Keith, Ries, John, 2001a. Overseas investment and firm exports. Review of International Economics 9 (1), 108–122 (February).

Head, Keith, Ries, John, 2001b. Increasing returns versus national product differentiation as an explanation for the pattern of U.S–Canada Trade. American Economic Review 91 (4), 858–876 (September).

Helpman, Elhanan, 2006. Trade, FDI, and the organization of firms. Journal of Economic Literature 44 (3), 589–630 (September).

Helpman, Elhanan, Krugman, Paul, 1985. Market Structure and Foreign Trade. MIT Press, Cambridge, MA.

Helpman, Elhanan, Melitz, Marc, Yeaple, Stephen, 2004. Export versus FDI with heterogeneous firms. American Economic Review 94 (1), 300–316 (March).

Kleinert, Jorn, Toubal, Farid, 2005. Gravity for FDI. Working Paper. Georg-August-Universitat Gottingen.

Lai, Huiwen, Zhu, Susan Chun, 2006. U.S. exports and multinational production. Review of Economics and Statistics 88 (3), 531–548 (August).

Lipsey, Robert E., 2002. Home and host country effects of FDI. NBER Working Paper, vol. 9293. October.

Markusen, James R., 1995. The boundaries of multinational enterprises and the theory of international trade. Journal of Economic Perspectives 9 (2), 169–189 (Spring).

Markusen, James R., 2002. Multinational Firms and the Theory of International Trade. MIT Press, Cambridge, MA.

Markusen, James R., Venables, Anthony J., 2000. The theory of endowment, intra-industry, and multi-national trade. Journal of International Economics 52, 209–234 (December).

Martin, Philippe, Rey, Helene, 2004. Financial supermarkets: size matters for asset trade. Journal of International Economics 64 (2), 335–361 (December).

McCulloch, Rachel, 1985. US direct foreign investment and trade. In: Erdilek, Asim (Ed.), Multinationals as Mutual Invaders: Intra-Industry Direct Foreign Investment. St. Martin's Press, New York, pp. 129–151.

McCulloch, Rachel, 1993. New perspectives on foreign direct investment. In: Froot, Kenneth (Ed.), Foreign Direct Investment. University of Chicago Press, Chicago, pp. 37–53.

Mundell, Robert, 1957. International trade and factor mobility. American Economic Review 47 (3), 321–335.

John, Mutti, Grubert, Harry, 2004. Empirical asymmetries in foreign direct investment and taxation. Journal of International Economics 62 (2), 337–358 (March).

Shim, Kieun, 2005. Border effects and FDI: can FDI explain the border puzzle? Working Paper. U. of Virginia.

Slaughter, Matthew J., 2000. Production transfer within multinational enterprises and American wages. Journal of International Economics 50 (2), 449–472 (April).

Technical Supplement

I note a typo in equations (14a)–(14c) in the text of Chapter 14. The term $(\varepsilon - 1)$ should be replaced by (-1).

Appendix A

The conditional factor demands for final goods production are given by:

$$K^*_{Xi} = F_{Xi}\underbrace{\frac{1}{B}\left(\frac{w_{Ui}}{r_i}\frac{\alpha}{1-\alpha}\right)^{1-\alpha} T_{1i}^{\frac{\alpha(\chi-1)-\chi}{\chi}}}_{a_{KXi}},$$

$$S^*_{Xi} = F_{Xi}\underbrace{\frac{1}{B}\left(\frac{w_{Ui}}{w_{Si}}\frac{\alpha}{1-\alpha}\right)^{1-\alpha} T_{2i}^{\frac{\alpha(\chi-1)-\chi}{\chi}}}_{a_{SXi}}, \tag{A.1}$$

$$U^*_{Xi} = F_{Xi}\underbrace{\frac{1}{B}\left(\frac{r_i}{w_{Ui}}\frac{1-\alpha}{\alpha}\right)^{\alpha}\left(T_{1i}^{-\chi} + T_{2i}^{-\chi}\right)^{\frac{-\alpha}{\chi}}}_{a_{UXi_i}},$$

where B is a constant and we introduce the definitions:

$$T_{1i} = 1 + \left(\frac{r_i}{w_{Si}}\right)^{\frac{\chi}{1-\chi}}; \quad T_{2i} = 1 + \left(\frac{w_{Si}}{r_i}\right)^{\frac{\chi}{1-\chi}}. \tag{A.2}$$

We assume that, in equilibrium, all factors are fully employed for each country i ($i = 1, 2, 3$), so that:

$$K_i \geq a_{KXi}\left[n_i \sum_{j=1}^{3} x_{ij} + x_{ii}\left(\sum_{j=1}^{3} h_{3,j}\right) + \sum_{j \neq i} v_{ji}\left(\sum_{j=1}^{3} x_{ij}\right)\right]$$
$$+ a_{Kni}n_i + a_{Kmi}\left\{\left[3 + \sum_{j \neq i} \gamma_{ij}\right] h_{3,i} + [1 + \gamma_{ij}]v_{ij}\right\},$$
$$S_i \geq a_{SXi}\left[n_i \sum_{j=1}^{3} x_{ij} + x_{ii}\left(\sum_{j=1}^{3} h_{3,j}\right) + \sum_{j \neq i} v_{ji}\left(\sum_{j=1}^{3} x_{ij}\right)\right] \tag{A.3}$$
$$+ a_{Sni}n_i + a_{Smi}\left(h_{3,i} + \sum_{j \neq 1} v_{ij}\right),$$
$$U_i \geq a_{UXi}\left[n_i \sum_{j=1}^{3} x_{ij} + x_{ii}\left(\sum_{j=1}^{3} h_{3,j}\right) + \sum_{j \neq 1} v_{ji}\left(\sum_{j=1}^{3} x_{ij}\right)\right]$$
$$+ a_{UYi} \sum_{j=1}^{3} t_{Yij}Y_{ij}.$$

Multilateral current account balance for each country i ($i = 1, 2, 3$; $i \neq j \neq k$) requires the following to hold:

$$(n_i + v_{ji} + v_{ki})p_{Xi}(x_{ij} + x_{ik}) + p_{Yj}Y_{ij} + p_{Yk}Y_{ik}$$
$$+ \frac{1}{1-\varepsilon}(h_{3,i}p_{Xj}x_{jj} + h_{3,i}p_{Xk}x_{kk})$$
$$+ \frac{1}{1-\varepsilon}(v_{ij}p_{Xj}[x_{jj} + x_{ji} + x_{jk}] + v_{ik}p_{Xk}[x_{kk} + x_{ki} + x_{kj}])$$
$$= (n_j + v_{ij} + v_{kj})p_{Xj}x_{ji} + (n_k + v_{ik} + v_{jk})p_{Xk}x_{ki} + p_{Yi}(Y_{ji} + Y_{ki})$$
$$+ \frac{1}{1-\varepsilon}(h_{3,j} + h_{3,k})p_{Xi}x_{ii}$$
$$+ \frac{1}{1-\varepsilon}(v_{ji} + v_{ki})p_{Xi}(x_{ii} + x_{ij} + x_{ik}). \tag{A.4}$$

The first line in equation (A4) represents the exports of goods of country i. The second and third lines represent income earned on capital invested by country i in horizontal and vertical affiliates, respectively, in countries j and k (k denoting the ROW for country i). The fourth line represents country i's imports of goods from j and k. The fifth and sixth lines represent i's repatriation of income on capital of countries j and k invested in country i in horizontal and vertical affiliates, respectively.

Appendix B

This appendix is intended to report the results of some sensitivity analysis of our findings. Of course, the potential number of alternative calibrations is virtually unlimited; resource constraints prevent us from exploring an exhaustive analysis of permutations from our base calibration. Nevertheless, we believe it is important to show that our results are relatively robust to empirically relevant parameter selections.

B.1. *Robustness of simulation results to assuming headquarters (plant) setups use physical (human) capital*

Two critical assumptions used to generate coexistence in Section 5 are the existence of physical capital and the assumption that headquarters (plant) setups require human (physical) capital. We proved in Section 5 analytically the importance of the third factor for coexistence of FAS, FDI and bilateral trade across a wide range of parameter values for firm and plant setup costs, trade costs, and investment costs. However, the results in Sections 5 and 6 may be sensitive to assuming headquarters (plant) setups require human (physical) capital. To illustrate the results are robust to an alternative assumption, we ran the model assuming plant (headquarters) setups require human (physical) capital. At the initial world endowments, FDI and FAS went to zero because of the scarcity of human capital. After increasing the world endowment of human capital (with again three symmetric economies), qualitatively identical results obtained for Figs. 4b–4d. See, for example, Figs. B1a–B1c.

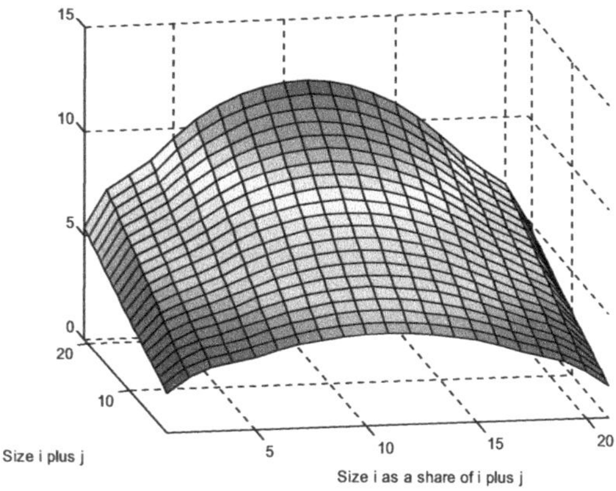

Figure B1a: Final Goods Exports from i to j (3 Countries)

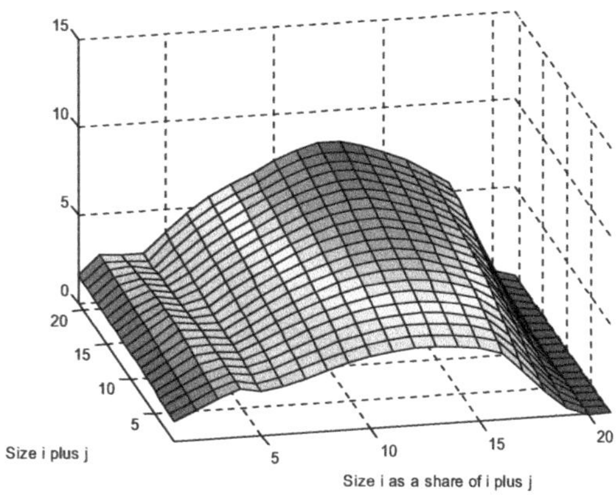

Figure B1b: Foreign Affiliate Sales of i's Plants in j (3 Countries)

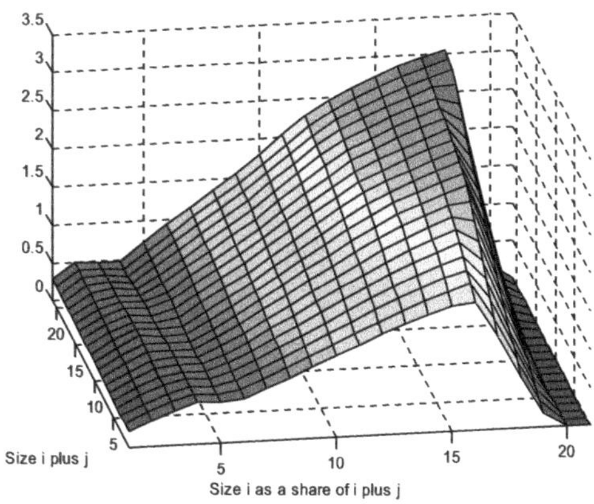

Figure B1c: Foreign Direct Investment from i to j (3 Countries)

Robustness: Plant set-up uses skilled labor S whereas firm set-up uses capital K.

B.2. *Robustness of simulation results to variation in capital–skill elasticity-of-substitution parameter*

The theoretical model has only four "parameters" (in the utility and production functions). On the technology side, there are two parameters in the differentiated goods production function: the elasticity of substitution between knowledge and physical capital and the share of capital (versus labor) in gross output. While empirical data guided the selection of the last parameter (0.2), the selection of the first parameter — the elasticity of substitution between knowledge and physical capital — was based upon econometric studies. As discussed in the text, there is wide-ranging evidence — not just from the production literature, but also the MNE literature (cf., Slaughter, 2000) — that physical capital and skills are complements (in a relative sense). However, physical capital and skills may be substitutes.

For an alternative calibration, we made capital and skills substitutes, choosing a value for χ of 0.167 which implied an elasticity of substitution of 1.2 (instead of a value for χ of -0.25, implying an elasticity of 0.8, in the baseline case). The results corresponding to Figs. 4b–4d are presented in Figs. B2a–B2c. We found that the overall GDP size and similarity relationships were qualitatively the same.

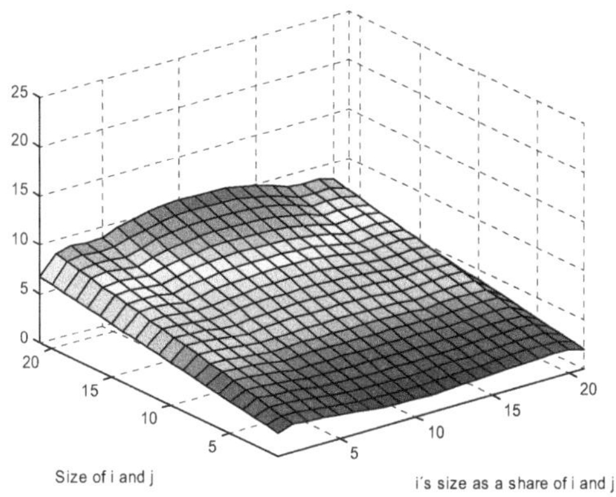

Figure B2a: Nominal Goods Exports from i to j (3 Countries)

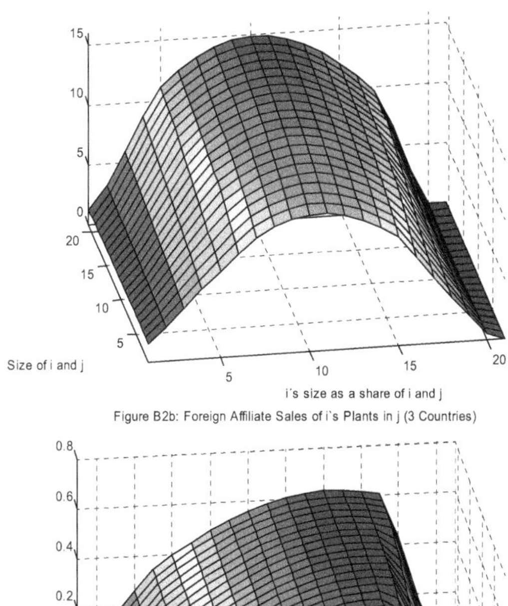

Figure B2b: Foreign Affiliate Sales of i's Plants in j (3 Countries)

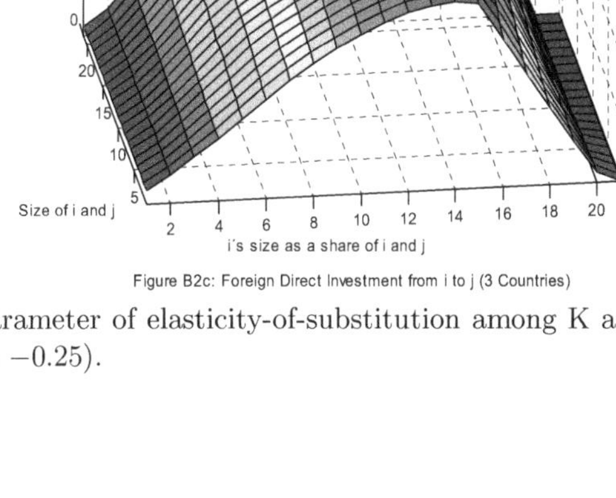

Figure B2c: Foreign Direct Investment from i to j (3 Countries)

Robustness: Parameter of elasticity-of-substitution among K and S is $\chi = 0.167$ (instead of $\chi = -0.25$).

B.3. *Robustness of simulation results to variation in elasticity of substitution of differentiated goods*

On the preferences side, there are only two parameters in the utility function: the elasticity of substitution among differentiated goods and the share of expenditure on differentiated goods (versus the homogenous good). The expenditure share was determined by empirical data. Evidence from econometric studies usually suggests an elasticity of substitution among differentiated goods ranging from 5 to 10 (cf., Anderson and van Wincoop, 2004, p. 716). Our base case of an elasticity of substitution of 6 ($\varepsilon = -5$) was premised upon this.

Consequently, we considered alternative calibrations with two different elasticities of substitution for differentiated goods, 5 and 10. The results are provided in Figs. B3a–B3c and B4a–B4c, respectively. The relationships between economic size, economic similarity, and the bilateral interactions were qualitatively identical to the base case when the elasticity of substitution was lowered to 5 (which assumes a value for $\varepsilon = -4$). When the elasticity of substitution among differentiated goods was raised to 10 ($\varepsilon = -9$), the FAS and FDI relationships were qualitatively identical as well. However, while trade flows were still positively related to economic size of i and j, trade flows were negatively related to their similarity when GDPs of i and j were small, which would be inconsistent with typical trade gravity equations. At such a high elasticity of substitution, the net effect of "complementarity" becomes diminished. Of course, a small decrease in trade costs can be shown to reverse this readily and ensure that complementarity still obtains over a wide range of parameter values.

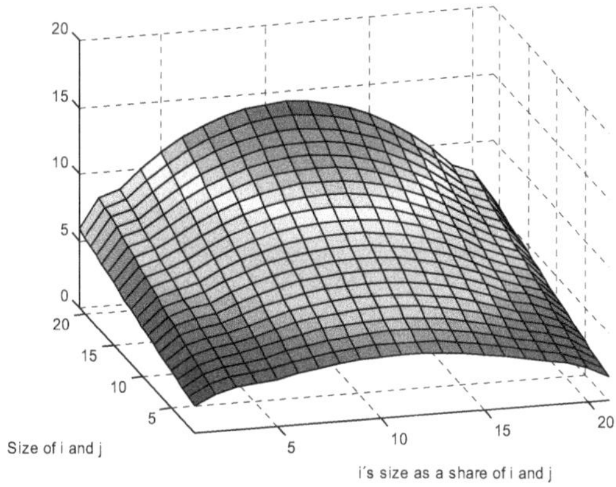

Figure B3a: Nominal Goods Exports from i to j (3 Countries)

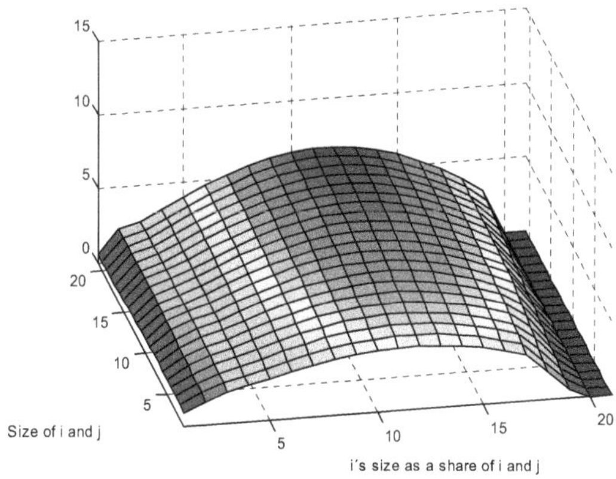

Figure B3b: Foreign Affiliate Sales of i's Plants in j (3 Countries)

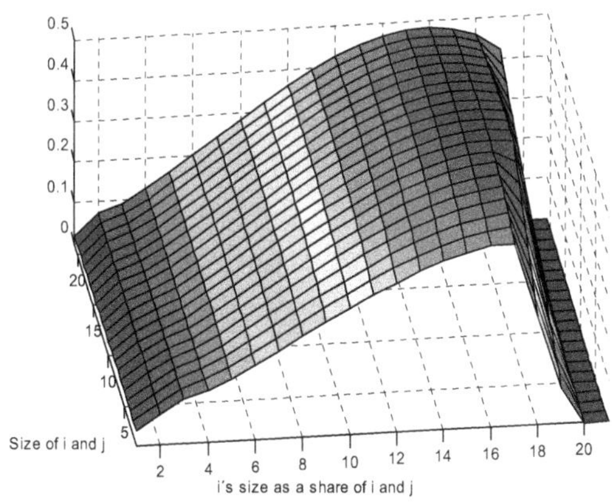

Figure B3c: Foreign Direct Investment from i to j (3 Countries)

Robustness: Parameter of elasticity of substitution among manufacturing is $\varepsilon = -4$ (instead of $\varepsilon = -5$).

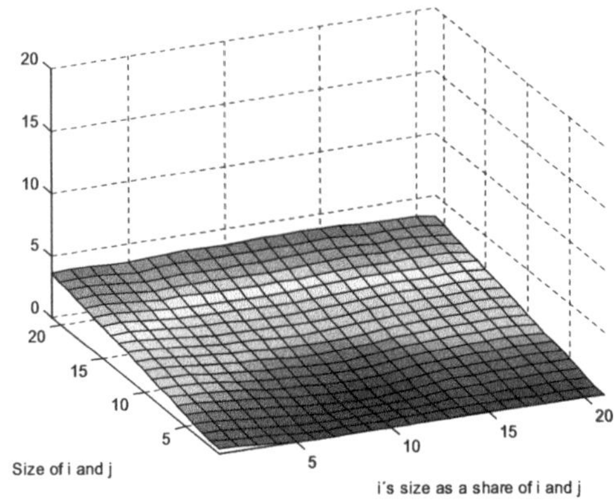

Figure B4a: Nominal Goods Exports from i to j (3 Countries)

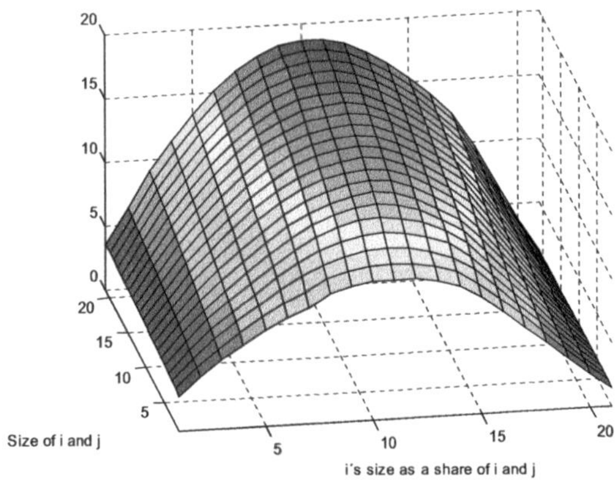

Figure B4b: Foreign Affiliate Sales of i's Plants in j (3 Countries)

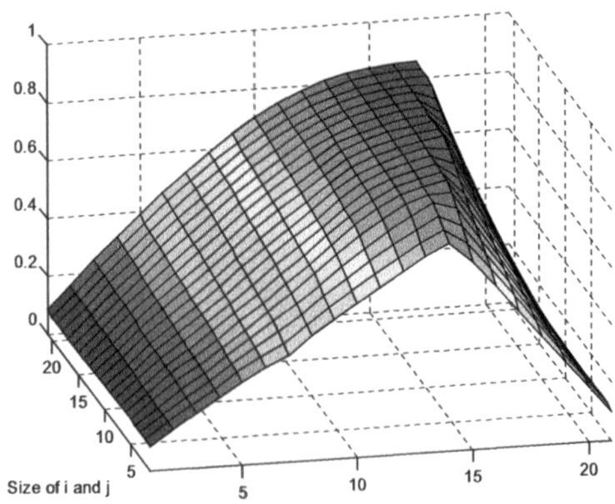

Figure B4c: Foreign Direct Investment from i to j (3 Countries)

Robustness: Parameter of elasticity of substitution among manufacturing is $\varepsilon = -9$ (instead of $\varepsilon = -5$).

B.4. *Robustness of simulation results to varying investment costs and MNE/NE ratio firm setup costs*

The relationships depicted in figures are, of course, sensitive to values chosen for "exogenous" variables as discussed in Section 4. In almost all cases, we tried to use empirical data to guide choices. For instance, levels of transport costs and tariff rates were selected based upon averages of actual data. In some cases, it is difficult to choose parameter values due to the absence of empirical evidence; two difficult choices were the selection of exogenous investment costs (γ) and the ratio of headquarters setup costs for an MNE relative to an NE. In the base simulations, we chose a "tax rate" (i.e., the "tax" on home capital to invest in a plant in another country) of 40 percent for capital investments by a developed country (DC) MNE is another DC; we assumed these investment barriers do not generate revenue. In order to bias our results against finding "complementarity" of trade and FAS (in particular, zero trade for identical economies), we assumed the minimum feasible ratio of setting up an MNE headquarters relative to an NE headquarters suggested in Markusen (2002). — 1.01 — indicating that an MNE consumed only 1 percent more skilled labor for firm setup relative to an NE.

In a sensitivity analysis, we experimented with lower investment costs. We found that trade was still complementary to FAS when investment costs were half of the base values; when lowered by 60 percent of their base value, final goods trade went to zero when counties i and j had identical GDPs. However, we also found that — even with investment costs at 40 percent of base values — small, and plausible, increases in MNE/NE headquarters setup costs offset investment costs, yielding complementarity of trade, FDI and FAS to economic size and similarity. As one example, Figs. B5a–B5c illustrate that the complementarity relationships are maintained when investment costs are 50 percent of the initial base levels.

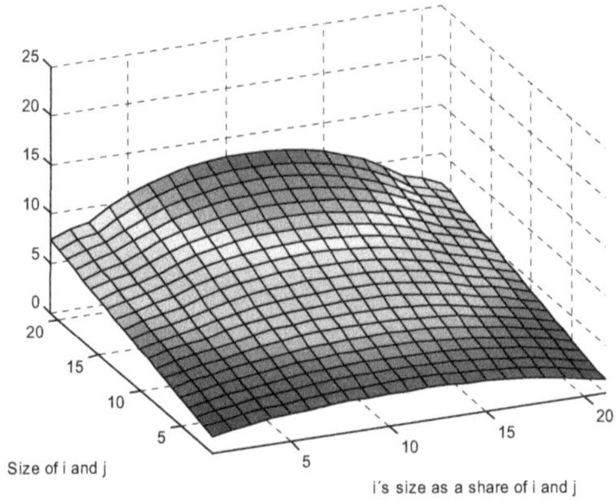

Figure B5a: Nominal Goods Exports from i to j (3 Countries)

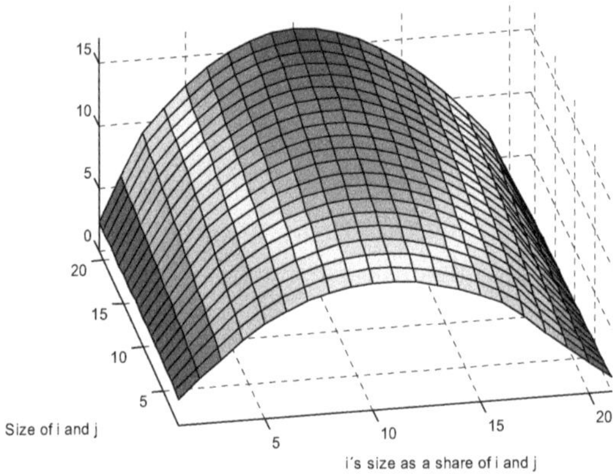

Figure B5b: Foreign Affiliate Sales of i's Plants in j (3 Countries)

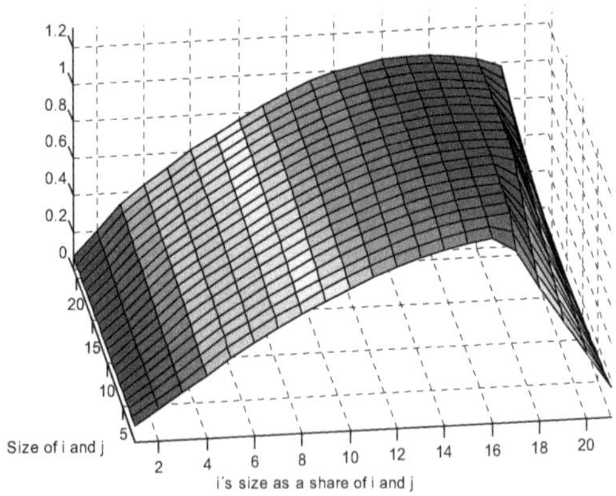

Figure B5c: Foreign Direct Investment from i to j (3 Countries)

Robustness: Parameter of additional foreign plant set-up costs (γ) is half its original size.

Chapter 15

Shouldn't Physical Capital *Also* Matter for Multinational Enterprise Activity?

*Jeffrey H. Bergstrand and Peter Egger**

Abstract

The foreign direct investment (FDI) literature has generally failed to find strong systematic evidence of "vertical" motivations in bilateral aggregate FDI and foreign affiliate sales (FAS) data, despite recent evidence of vertical FDI in firm-level data. Moreover, a Bayesian analysis of the empirical determinants of FDI (and FAS) flows reveals that the parent country's *physical capital* per worker has a strong positive effect on FDI alongside typical gravity-equation variables; however, this variable is ignored in the knowledge-capital (KC) model and most empirical work. We address these two puzzles by introducing relative factor endowment differences into the three-factor, three-country knowledge and physical capital extension of the $2 \times 2 \times 2$ KC model. Using a numerical version of our model, we show that horizontal and vertical multinational enterprises' (MNEs') headquarters surface in different parts of the Edgeworth box relating the parent country's skilled labor share relative to its physical capital share (of the parent's and host's endowments). The key economic insight is that horizontal MNE headquarters will be relatively more abundant than vertical MNE headquarters in countries that are abundant in physical capital relative to skilled labor, because of the multi-plant (single-plant) structure of horizontal (vertical) MNEs—assuming plants (headquarters) use physical capital (skilled labor) relatively intensively in their setups. The theoretical relationships suggest augmenting empirical FAS gravity equations with (polynomials of) the parent's skilled labor share alongside the parent's physical capital share to explain in aggregate bilateral data the coexistence of horizontal and vertical FAS. The theoretical and empirical results shed light on the positive effect of parent's physical capital share on FAS flows, but also suggest that MNE headquarters may be prominent in parent countries with relatively high and low skilled labor shares—once physical capital is accounted for—a result not suggested by the two-factor KC model.

> *It seems clear that vertical motivations are not prevalent in the general FDI patterns.* (Bruce Blonigen, 2005)

1. Introduction

This paper addresses the issue of finding evidence of vertical multinational enterprise (MNE) activity alongside horizontal MNE activity in aggregate bilateral data by examining the seemingly "schizophrenic treatment" of physical capital in modern analyses of foreign direct investment (FDI) and foreign affiliate sales (FAS). On the one hand, the modern general equilibrium theory of MNE activity focuses upon the role of intangible assets of firms—such as knowledge capital—for explaining MNEs' existence, cf. Markusen (2002). Using the knowledge capital model, most empirical analyses have focused upon the roles of relative economic sizes to explain "horizontal" MNE activity and relative skilled-to-unskilled labor ratios to explain "vertical"

---

* Bergstrand: Department of Finance, Mendoza College of Business and Kellogg Institute for International Studies, University of Notre Dame and CESifo, Notre Dame, IN 46556, USA. Email: Bergstrand.1@nd.edu. Egger: Department of Economics, ETH University, CESifo, and Ifo Institute, Weinbergstrasse 35, 8092 Zurich, Switzerland. The authors are grateful for very useful comments from the editor, an anonymous referee, and participants at presentations at the University of Oxford, London School of Economics and Political Science, Drexel University, European Trade Study Group annual conference, and Southern Economics Association annual conference.

---

*Originally Published in *Review of International Economics*, 21(5), pp. 945–965.

MNE activity, cf. Carr et al. (2001, 2003), Blonigen et al. (2003), Markusen and Maskus (2001, 2002), Braconier et al. (2005), and Davies (2008). Motivated by a two-factor model with only skilled and unskilled labor, physical capital plays no role theoretically or empirically in these analyses.

On the other hand, Blonigen and Piger (2011) found evidence that bilateral aggregate FDI outflows are strongly and positively influenced by parent countries' physical capital per worker. Moreover, the extension of the international economics literature to recognize "heterogenous productivities" among national, exporting, and multinational enterprises reveals that MNEs tend to be very physical-capital intensive (as well as skilled labor intensive) firms and MNEs tend to be headquartered in relatively physical-capital abundant (as well as skilled-labor abundant) countries, cf. Bernard et al. (2005), Helpman et al. (2004), and Helpman (2006). Even one of the measures of FDI in the US Bureau of Economic Analysis (BEA) data uses the share of a MNE's real investment in physical plant and equipment in a foreign affiliate. This schizophrenic treatment of physical capital in the MNE literature and the apparent absence of "vertical motivations" for FDI in the bilateral aggregate data suggests re-considering a role for physical capital.

In reality, of course, *both* relative physical capital to unskilled labor (K/U) and skilled labor to unskilled labor (S/U) ratios are likely to influence aggregate bilateral FDI/FAS flows in general equilibrium, alongside economic size and similarity as well as investment costs. This paper addresses physical capital's role theoretically and empirically, and offers two potential contributions. First, we introduce differences in relative physical capital endowments—alongside differences in relative skilled and unskilled labor endowments—into the three-factor, three-country, two-good "Knowledge and Physical Capital" model of Bergstrand and Egger (2007) and provide some testable hypotheses for predicted vertical and horizontal FAS that are different than those suggested by the workhorse $2 \times 2 \times 2$ "Knowledge Capital" (KC) model. Bergstrand and Egger (2007) presented a three-country, three-factor, two-good extension of Markusen's two-country, two-factor, two-good KC model, but assumed identical relative factor endowments to focus only on the roles of gross domestic product (GDP) size and similarity for explaining the coexistence of horizontal bilateral FAS/FDI flows and intra-industry trade flows for countries with identical absolute and relative factor endowments and for motivating a theoretical rationale for estimating "gravity equations" of bilateral FAS and FDI flows alongside bilateral trade flows. Vertical MNEs played no role in Bergstrand and Egger (2007). We find here that general equilibrium relationships between relative skilled-to-unskilled labor ratios and bilateral FAS are sensitive to relative endowments of physical capital. A key theoretical economic insight is that horizontal MNE headquarters will be relatively more abundant than vertical MNE headquarters in countries that are abundant in physical capital relative to skilled labor, because of the multi-plant (single-plant) structure of horizontal (vertical) MNEs—assuming plants (headquarters) use physical capital (skilled labor) relatively intensively in their setups. An implication of this is that physical capital rich economies will tend to have high levels of bilateral horizontal FAS when skilled labor is scarce relative to physical capital and such economies will tend to have high levels of bilateral vertical FAS when skilled labor is abundant relative to physical capital (for given levels of unskilled labor). This suggests that the relationship between a parent country's skilled labor share (of two countries' joint skilled labor endowment) and the FAS of the parent country may be a fourth-order polynomial.[1]

Second, empirical explanations for determinants of bilateral international trade flows have long used the "gravity equation," the workhorse of international trade.

Moreover, the gravity equation is also the workhorse for empirical analysis of determinants of bilateral FAS and FDI flows.[2] Using a Bayesian moving average (BMA) analysis, Blonigen and Piger (2011) found inclusion probabilities of 100% for standard gravity variables such as parent and host countries' GDPs and the bilateral distance between two countries. Moreover, they also found an inclusion probability for the parent's capital stock per worker of 94%, but an inclusion probability of only 54% for the parent's education level. Our theoretical analysis suggests a rationale for the inclusion of parent's physical-capital share (of parent and host countries' physical capital). Moreover, our theoretical analysis suggests a rationale for including fourth-order polynomials of the parent's skilled labor share and of the parent's physical capital share in an augmented gravity equation. We find that the inclusion in a FAS gravity equation of fourth-order polynomials of the parent country's shares of (two countries *i* and *j*) skilled labor and physical capital helps to explain the patterns of aggregate bilateral FAS. Three empirical findings are notable. First, the parent's skilled labor share has the expected fourth-order polynomial relationship with bilateral FAS. In fact, the empirically predicted bilateral FAS flows reveal two "peaks" in the empirical Edgeworth-box space, one where horizontal MNE activity should be maximized and one where vertical MNE activity should be maximized—consistent with the corresponding theoretical Edgeworth-box predictions. Second, the parent's physical capital share also has a significant effect on bilateral FAS, and the fourth-order polynomial empirical relationship corresponds also with the model's theoretical predictions. Third, the parent's unskilled labor share has the expected negative, monotonic relationship with FAS. In the context of our model, our empirical results provide evidence for vertical motivations for FAS in the bilateral aggregate data, alongside horizontal motivations.[3] In fact, we find evidence suggesting—consistent with firm-level categorizations in Alfaro and Charlton (2009) of horizontal and vertical MNEs—that vertical MNE (VMNE) motivations are as important as horizontal MNE (HMNE) motivations.

The remainder of the paper is as follows. In section 2, we discuss the limitations of the two-factor KC model for identifying vertical MNE activity separately from horizontal MNE activity in aggregate bilateral FAS data. In section 3, we summarize the three-factor, three-country, two-good Knowledge and Physical Capital (KAPC) model in Bergstrand and Egger (2007), allowing now asymmetric relative factor endowments. In section 4, we use the numerical version of our model to postulate theoretical hypotheses about relationships between relative factor endowments and FAS. In section 5, we examine empirically the determinants of bilateral aggregate FAS flows. Section 6 concludes.

2. Limitations of the 2 × 2 × 2 Knowledge-Capital for Finding Vertical MNEs

We argue here that the evidence against the KC model in favor of just HMNEs explaining bilateral aggregate FAS flows should actually come as no surprise if one examines closely the theoretical predictions of the KC model—limited to a 2-factor, 2-country world. In the following, reference to the "KC model" necessarily implies a 2-factor, 2-country world. Figures 1a and 1b from Markusen (2002) and Figure 1c from BNU help to illustrate this point, based upon the KC model. Figure 1a presents the Edgeworth box (figure 7.1 from Markusen, 2002, p. 143) relating country *i*'s (*j*'s) share of the two countries' skilled labor stocks along the vertical axis, country *i*'s (*j*'s) share of the two countries unskilled labor stocks (also called by Markusen the "composite factor") along the horizontal axis, and the equilibrium "regimes" of types of firms (see

(a)

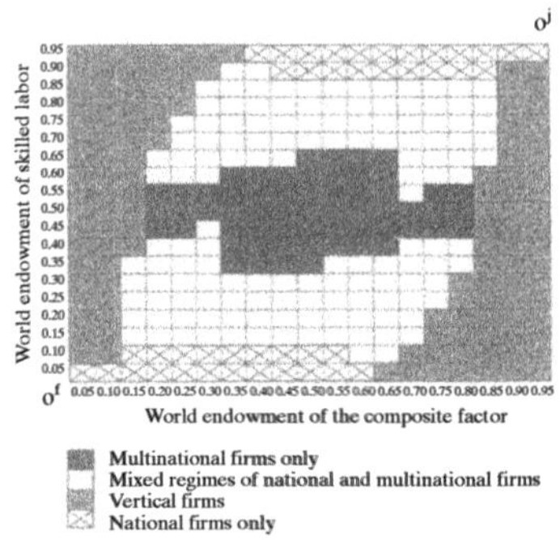

(b)

Types of firms active in equilibrium: Regime (the number in the cell) = $I_i^d + I_j^d + I_i^v + I_j^v + I_i^h + I_j^h$ (I is for indicator ")

102.000	102.000	102.000	102.000	102.000	102.000	102.000	100.000	100.000	100.000	100.000	100.000	100.000	100.000	100.000	100.000	100.000	100.000	100.000	100.000
102.000	102.000	102.000	102.000	102.010	102.010	100.010	100.010	100.000	100.000	100.000	100.000	100.000	100.000	100.000	100.000	100.000	100.000	100.200	100.200
102.000	102.000	102.000	102.010	102.010	100.010	100.010	100.010	100.010	100.010	100.010	100.010	100.010	100.010	100.010	100.011	100.001	100.001	100.200	100.200
102.000	102.000	102.010	102.010	102.010	100.010	100.010	100.010	100.010	100.010	100.010	100.010	100.010	100.010	100.010	100.011	100.001	100.001	100.201	100.200
102.000	102.010	102.010	102.010	100.010	100.010	100.010	100.010	100.010	100.010	100.010	100.010	100.010	100.010	100.010	100.001	100.001	100.001	100.201	100.200
102.000	102.010	102.010	102.010	100.010	100.010	100.010	100.010	100.010	100.010	100.010	100.010	100.010	100.010	100.011	100.001	100.001	100.001	0.201	0.200
102.000	102.010	102.010	100.010	100.010	100.010	100.010	100.010	100.010	0.010	0.010	0.010	0.010	0.011	100.011	100.001	100.001	100.001	0.201	0.200
102.010	102.010	102.010	100.010	100.010	100.010	0.010	0.010	0.010	0. 010	0. 010	0.011	0.011	0.011	100.011	100.001	100.001	0.201	0.201	0.201
2.010	2.010	102.010	0.010	0.010	0.010	0.010	0.010	0.011	0.011	0.011	0.011	0.011	0.011	100.001	0.001	0.001	0.201	0.201	0.201
2.010	2.010	2.010	0.010	0.010	0.010	0.010	0.011	0.011	0.011	0.011	0.011	0.011	0.001	0.001	0.001	0.001	0.201	0.201	0.201
2.010	2.010	2.010	0.010	0.010	10.010	0.011	0.011	0.011	0.011	0.011	0.011	0.001	0.001	0.001	0.001	0.001	10.201	0.201	0.201
2.010	2.010	2.010	10.010	10.010	10.011	0.011	0.011	0.011	0.001	0.001	0.001	0.001	0.001	10.001	10.001	10.001	10.201	10.201	10.201
2.000	2.010	10.010	10.010	10.010	10.011	0.011	0.001	0.001	0.001	0.001	10.001	10.001	10.001	10.001	10.001	10.001	10.201	10.201	10.200
2.000	12.010	10.010	10.010	10.010	10.011	10.001	10.001	10.001	10.001	10.001	10.001	10.001	10.001	10.001	10. 001	10.201	10.201	10.201	10.200
12.000	12.010	10.010	10.010	10.010	10.001	10.001	10.001	10.001	10.001	10.001	10.001	10.001	10.001	10.001	10.001	10.201	10.201	10.201	10.200
12.000	12.010	10.010	10.010	10.011	10.001	10.001	10.001	10.001	10.001	10.001	10.001	10.001	10.001	10.001	10.201	10.201	10.201	10.200	10.200
12.000	12.000	10.010	10.010	10.011	10.001	10.001	10.001	10.001	10.001	10.001	10.001	10.001	10.001	10.001	10.201	10.201	10.200	10.200	10.200
12.000	12.000	10.000	10.000	10.000	10.000	10.000	10.000	10.000	10.000	10.000	10.000	10.001	10.001	10.201	10.201	10.200	10.200	10.200	10.200
10.000	10.000	10.000	10.000	10.000	10.000	10.000	10.000	10.000	10.000	10.000	10.000	10.000	10.200	10.200	10.200	10.200	10.200	10.200	10.200

I_i^d = 100 if type-d_i firms active, 0 otherwise I_i^v = 2.0 if type-v_i firms active, 0 otherwise I_i^h = 0.01 if type-h_i firms active, 0 otherwise

I_j^d = 10 if type-d_j firms active, 0 otherwise I_j^v = 0.2 if type-v_j firms active, 0 otherwise I_j^h = 0.001 if type-h_j firms active, 0 otherwise

(c)

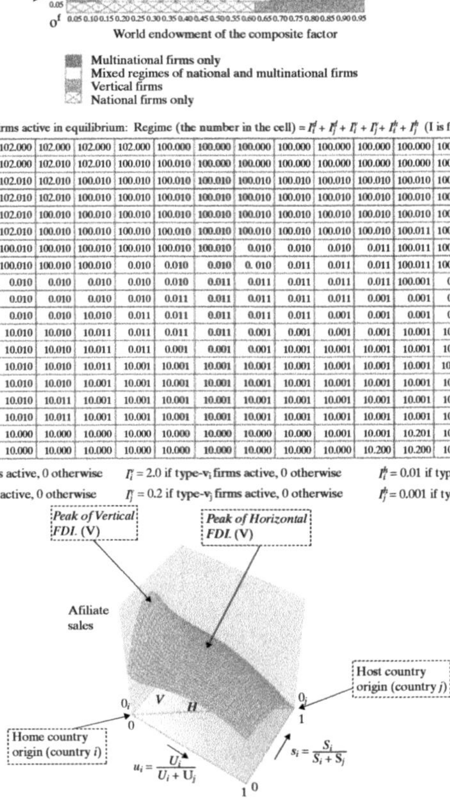

Figure 1(a–c). Equilibrium Regimes of Types of Firms and Empirically Predicted Foreign Affiliate Sales (a) Types of Firms Active in Equilibrium (b) Types of Firms Active in Equilibrium: Regime (the Number in the Cell) = $I_i^d + I_j^d + I_i^v + I_j^v + I_i^h + I_j^h$ (I is for "Indicator") (c) Empirically Predicted Foreign Affiliate Sales

Figure 1a's index). Depending upon relative skilled to unskilled labor ratios, HMNEs ("Multinational firms only"), VMNEs ("Vertical firms"), NEs ("National firms only"), or "Mixed regimes of national and multinational firms" may be found in equilibrium. Cursory examination of this figure suggests two main propositions evaluated in the KC literature. First, when two countries are identical in economic size and relative factor endowments, both countries will have only HMNEs in equilibrium; there will be no VMNEs (nor NEs or international trade, for that matter) in equilibrium. Second, however, when country *i* is moderately relatively skill abundant (moving left from the center cell, or towards the left vertical axis), HMNEs based in *i* will still exist in equilibrium (because HMNEs' headquarters setups use relatively more skilled labor than NEs' headquarters setups). Yet when country *i* becomes even more relatively skill abundant (further left), Figure 1a suggests that HMNEs cease to exist in *i*. However, HMNEs are actually joined by VMNEs (because it becomes profitable for *i* to "outsource" final goods production to *j* and ship output anywhere in the world), as explained below.

Initial empirical estimation of the KC model to find both HMNEs and VMNEs in *i* was virtually doomed to fail for the following reason. Figure 1b (actually table 7.2 from Markusen, 2002) reports the sum of different types of operations in existence in equilibrium, which is the data underlying Figure 1a. Consider three results. First, at the center cell (when the two countries are identical in absolute and relative factor endowments), both countries have HMNEs headquartered in their own countries, with plants in their home and foreign markets; no VMNEs or NEs are profitable (0.011 = 0.010 + 0.001), consistent with Figure 1a. Second, moving leftward, country *i* eventually becomes relatively smaller and more skilled-labor abundant, making HMNEs based in *i* the only profitable firms (0.010), consistent with Figure 1a. Third, continuing leftward, the three columns on the far left indicate that relatively skilled-labor abundant *i* will headquarter both HMNEs and VMNEs (2.010 = 2.0 + 0.010), as explained in Markusen (2002, p. 145). That is, for the ratio of skilled-to-unskilled labor in *i* shown in the far left column and middle row, FAS for home country *i* in host country *j* is motivated by both horizontal and vertical activity! In fact, careful examination of the entire first (left-hand side) column of Figure 1b reveals that HMNEs exist in equilibrium for moderate levels of skill abundance, but VMNEs exist also for high, moderate, and low levels of skill abundance. The fundamental problem with using the $2 \times 2 \times 2$ KC model to distinguish VMNE from HMNE activity is this: overlap of vertical and horizontal MNEs (cells in Figure 1b with values of either 2.01, 12.01, or 102.01) comprise 18% of the 190 cells in the upper-left quadrant of Figure 1b, making it very difficult to distinguish VMNE from HMNE activity using only relative factor endowments of skilled to unskilled labor.

Thus, Carr, Markusen, and Maskus (2001), or CMM (2001), econometric estimation of the KC model to find both HMNEs and VMNEs was compromised from the start because the Edgeworth surface described bilateral FAS motivated by both HMNEs and VMNEs at the same skilled to unskilled labor ratio—even if the central regression "specification" was mapped *directly* from the theory as in Braconier et al. (2005), or BNU, i.e. factor shares of the Edgeworth box.[4] BNU made a useful contribution to this literature by generating a regression specification that mapped "directly" from the theoretical framework, taking into account properly the geometric considerations of Edgeworth boxes. Motivated by this important analytical consideration alongside employing a broader data set (in terms of country pair coverage) of FAS bilateral flows, BNU argued that—when properly specified—VMNEs could be found in the data, alongside HMNEs. Figure 1c (from Braconier et al., 2005) illustrates their "empirically predicted" FAS_{ij}. However, while their empirically predicted FAS surface is visually similar to the theoretically predicted FAS surface in Markusen (2002, figure 10.1, p. 221), the problem still remains. Where BNU predict the "peak of vertical FDI_{ij}" in Figure 1c—when i is economically smaller and skilled-labor abundant relative to j—the data cells in Figure 1b inform us that both vertical and horizontal MNEs can be headquartered in i (note the cell entry 2.010 in the far left column in rows 9, 10, 11, and 12). Thus, BNU does not resolve the issue empirically because the problem lies in finding—in Edgeworth-box space—relative factor endowment configurations where VMNE headquarters can be clearly distinguished from HMNE headquarters.

3. Theoretical Framework: A Summary of the Knowledge and Physical Capital Model

The model we use is a more general version of the three-country, three-factor, two-good KAPC model in Bergstrand and Egger (2007) by allowing differences in relative skilled to unskilled labor (S/U) ratios and relative physical capital to unskilled labor (K/U) ratios, consequently generating horizontal and vertical MNEs as well as national exporting enterprises (NEs) in equilibrium. Bergstrand and Egger (2007) is an extension of the $2 \times 2 \times 2$ KC model in Markusen (2002) with national exporters (NEs), horizontal MNEs (HMNEs), and vertical MNEs (VMNEs). However, Bergstrand and Egger (2007) assumed identical relative factor endowments to focus on the roles of economic size and similarity and provide a theoretical foundation for gravity equations of trade, FAS, and FDI simultaneously; consequently, no VMNEs surfaced in that paper, except in one sensitivity analysis. The demand side in the model is analogous to that in the KC model.

The key difference between our KAPC model and Markusen's KC model is that we add a third factor, physical capital (K), the services of which can be used at home or transferred abroad (via FDI) either as a "greenfield" investment or an acquisition (and not necessarily a costless transfer). We assume that all three internationally immobile primary factors are used in the production of the differentiated good: unskilled labor (U), skilled labor (S), and private physical capital (K). Moreover, following evidence from Griliches (1969), Goldin and Katz (1998), and Slaughter (2000), we assume that skilled labor and physical capital are complements in production, which is also consistent with evidence in Bernard et al. (2005) that MNEs tend to be relatively abundant in countries that are relatively abundant in both skilled labor and physical capital. However, for the setups of headquarters and plants, we assume that the services of only skilled labor are used to setup headquarters and the services of only physical capital are used to setup plants. HMNEs headquartered in any country i, for example, arise endogenously, and the services of home physical capital are "used up" (owing to their "rival" nature) to setup a plant in the home country or abroad to maximize firm profits (with an implied no-arbitrage incentive for rates of return on physical capital; no profits are left "on the table"), but physical capital need not actually move internationally. In the presence of imperfect international (financial) capital mobility, firms may choose to have financial claims to physical capital at home or—via FDI—abroad. The key distinction from knowledge capital is that claims to physical capital are rival, and FDI—owing to foreign government restrictions—may not move costlessly between countries. The second distinction of our model from the KC model is to introduce a "third country," Rest-of-World (ROW). The presence of the third country helps explain the observed complementarity of bilateral FAS and trade flows with respect to a country pair's economic size and similarity and that bilateral FDI and FAS tend empirically to be as well explained by a gravity equation as bilateral trade flows are. Since the structure and calibration of the model is described explicitly in Bergstrand and Egger (2007), to conserve space we present the model in Appendix A and a description of the calibration of the model in Appendix B of this paper (both available online at www.nd.edu/~jbergstr).

4. Theoretical Hypotheses

The numerical version of our general equilibrium model can be used to generate (at least) three "testable propositions" relating pairs of countries' relative factor endowments to aggregate bilateral FAS activity. We focus first on predicting theoretically the numbers of HMNEs based in home country *i* with plants in *i*, *j*, and/or ROW, the numbers of VMNEs based in home country *i* with plants in *j* or ROW, and the aggregate bilateral FAS of parent country *i* in host country *j*—contingent upon different configurations of relative factor endowments. We use these predictions to suggest three testable hypotheses about the relationship between a country pair *ij*'s relative factor endowments and the FAS of headquarters country *i* with a foreign affiliate in country *j*.

Owing to the presence of three factors, three countries, and highly nonlinear relationships, there are potentially an enormous number of relationships to explain. To make the testable hypotheses tractable in a world with three factors, three countries, and two goods, we use the "workhorse" tool of international trade—the Edgeworth box—for studying relationships between relative factor endowments and FAS, as used in Markusen (2002) and BNU. However, all the papers just noted assumed two-factor worlds; we have a three-factor world.

In a three-factor world, Edgeworth boxes actually are slices from an Edgeworth "cube," showing the relationship between a flow and two countries' shares of two factors—for any given shares of the two countries of the third factor (and for any given level of ROW's endowments). To focus initially on the relationships between physical capital, skilled labor, unskilled labor, and horizontal and vertical MNEs, we consider first the Edgeworth box relationship between country *i*'s share of countries *i*'s and *j*'s physical capital stocks (k_i) for a given physical capital stock in ROW, country *i*'s share of *i*'s and *j*'s skilled labor stocks (s_i) for a given skilled labor stock in ROW, and the numbers of HMNEs and VMNEs headquartered in *i*—at the mean of u_i, which is *i*'s share of *i*'s and *j*'s unskilled labor endowments (for a given unskilled labor endowment in ROW). Henceforth, FAS_{ij} denotes the theoretically predicted bilateral FAS of parent/home country *i* in host country *j*; later in the empirical work, FAS_{ij} (without italics) denotes the empirically predicted bilateral FAS of MNEs with headquarters in *i* and plants in *j*.

Since we are examining the relationships among k_i, s_i, and determinants of FAS_{ij}, our relationships are conditional upon the level of u_i (a third factor) as well as the economic size of ROW (a third country). Because we will pursue a regression analysis later, it will be useful to show slices of the Edgeworth cube at the empirical mean of the implicit third factor, say u_i. The reason is that—in a regression of bilateral FAS on numerous variables—the interpretation of, say, the coefficient estimate for k_i would be holding constant s_i and u_i at their "means"; thus, the theoretical predictions relating, say, the numbers of HMNEs in *i* with plants in *j* with k_i and s_i are being made at the mean of u_i. However, it will be convenient now to note that the *empirical* means for k_i, s_i, and u_i all range between 0.53 and 0.56. Hence, for convenience, the mean of each factor share is effectively 0.50.[5]

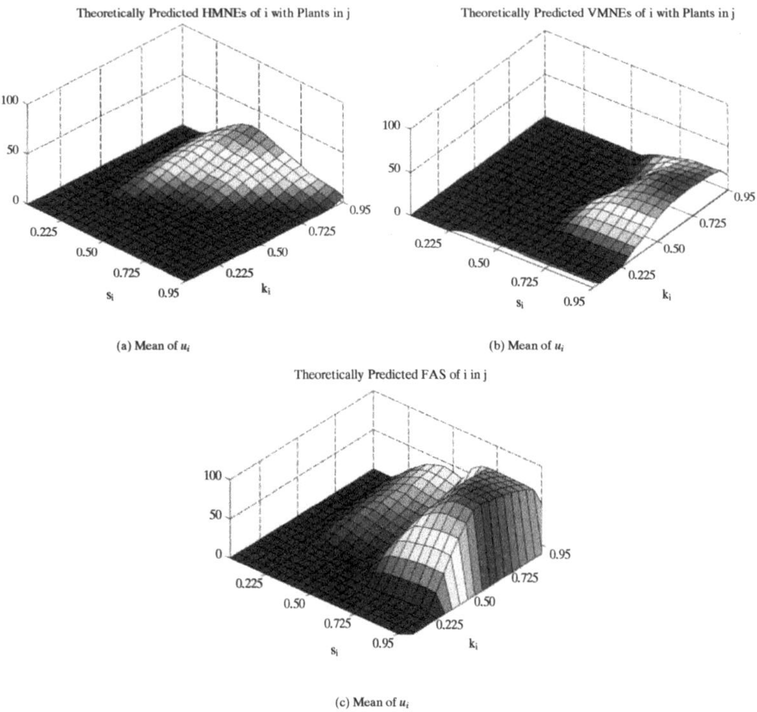

Figure 2(a–c). Theoretically Predicted Numbers of HMNEs, Numbers of VMNEs, and Foreign Affiliate Sales (a) Mean of u_i (b) Mean of u_i (c) Mean of u_i

Our first testable hypothesis (Hypothesis 1) builds on two theoretical results:

Result 1: The number of HMNEs based in *i* with plants in *j* will be maximized when *i* is abundant in physical capital relative to skilled labor relative to *j*, owing to the multi-plant structure of HMNEs and plant (headquarters) setups being physical capital (skilled labor) intensive; and
Result 2: The number of VMNEs based in *i* with a plant in country *j* will be maximized when *i* is abundant in skilled labor relative to physical capital relative to *j*, owing to the single-plant structure of VMNEs alongside the assumed physical capital intensity of plant setups relative to headquarters setups.

Figures 2a and b illustrate the relationships between k_i, s_i, and the numbers of HMNEs based in *i* with plants in *j* (and ROW) and VMNEs based in *i* with plants in *j*, respectively, evaluated at the empirical mean of u_i (effectively, 0.5). Consider Figure 2a first. HMNEs are multi-plant structures, whose plant setups are physical capital intensive (specifically, such setups are intensive in the internationally-mobile "services" of physical capital via FDI). Consequently, HMNEs will be abundant in country *i* if *i* is abundant in physical capital relative to skilled labor (and also to unskilled labor), as shown in Figure 2a (i.e. $k_i > s_i$). By contrast, VMNEs require only one plant (located abroad) along with its headquarters (located at home). Since headquarters setups use skilled labor services and plant setups use physical capital services, VMNEs will be prominent in *i* when skilled labor and physical capital are both abundant relative to *j* (and assuming $u_i = 0.5$) and skilled labor is only slightly more abundant in *i* than physical capital (as all MNE headquarters setups require more skilled labor than NE setups). Figure 2b illustrates the theoretical relationships between k_i, s_i, and the number of VMNEs headquartered in *i* with a plant in *j* at the mean of u_i. Figure 2b suggests that VMNEs will be prominent in *i* when skilled labor is slightly more abundant than physical capital, as a result of the single-plant, single-headquarters structure of VMNEs. The key economic insight is that—assuming plants (headquarters) are physical capital (skilled labor) services intensive in setups—countries that are physical capital abundant (scarce) relative to skilled labor should tend to headquarter HMNEs (VMNEs), for given u_i and given endowments in ROW.

Figures 2a and b together suggest that empirical FAS_{ij} may in a regression be fourth-order polynomial function of s_i, as illustrated in Figure 2c. Figure 2c provides the model's depiction of theoretical FAS_{ij}. Consider first s_i. If we are interested in the relationship between variation in s_i and FAS_{ij}, then we must hold constant k_i and u_i at their means (about 0.5). Figure 2c represents the relationships between s_i, k_i, and FAS_{ij}—evaluated at the mean of u_i ($u_i = 0.5$). In Figure 2c, we see from varying s_i from 0 to 1 at the mean of k_i ($k_i = 0.5$), and knowing that this Edgeworth "slice" is at $u_i = 0.5$, that there are three inflection points. This implies that FAS_{ij} is a fourth-order polynomial function of s_i, as horizontal FAS_{ij} is generated by HMNEs of country *i* with plants in *j* and vertical FAS_{ij} is generated by VMNEs of country *i* with plants in *j*. Specifically, at $k_i = u_i = 0.5$, assume $s_i = 0$ initially. There will be no HMNEs or VMNEs headquartered in *i*. As s_i increases from 0, the relative abundance of physical capital (since $k_i = 0.5$) causes HMNEs in *i* to become profitable first and the number of HMNEs increases (Figure 2a) and FAS_{ij} rises above 0. However, as s_i continues to rise past 0.5, physical capital becomes scarce relative to skilled labor (as $k_i = 0.5$), reducing the profitability of HMNEs in *i*, but increasing the profitability of VMNEs in *i* since VMNEs have only one plant to setup abroad, requiring less physical capital than an HMNE. This suggests testable Hypothesis 1:

> *Hypothesis 1*: Empirical FAS_{ij} in a regression should be a fourth-order polynomial function of s_i at the means of k_i and u_i ($k_i = u_i = 0.5$).

For robustness, we generated the theoretical *k–s* surfaces for the numbers of VMNEs and HMNEs in *i* also for u_i at the 30th and 70th percentiles. The shapes of the theoretical surfaces are qualitatively the same; figures omitted for brevity, but available on request.[6]

We now consider the theoretical relationship between k_i and FAS_{ij}. If we are interested in the relationship between variation in k_i and FAS_{ij}, then we must hold constant s_i and u_i at their means (0.5). Figures 3a and b present the theoretical Edgeworth boxes relating k_i, u_i, and the numbers of HMNEs and VMNEs headquartered in *i* with affiliates in *j*, respectively, at $s_i = 0.5$. Figure 3a shows that HMNE headquarters will be prominent in *i* when physical capital is abundant; this makes intuitive sense since multi-plant HMNEs require physical capital for setups. However, at $s_i = u_i = 0.5$, as k_i falls from 1, the number of HMNEs headquartered in *i* declines. But as shown in Figure 3b, as k_i falls closer to 0.5, skilled labor becomes abundant in *i* relative to physi-

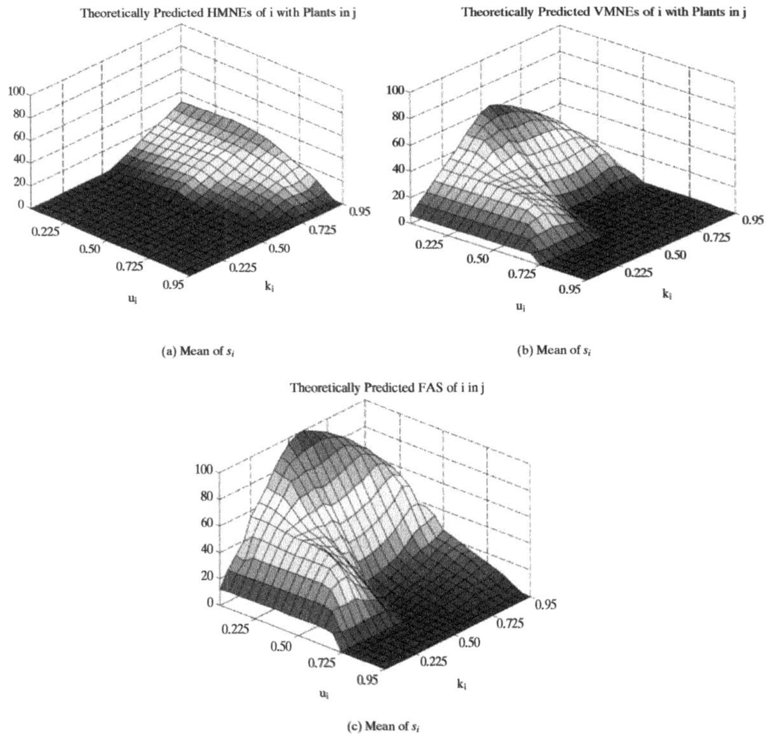

Figure 3(a–c). Theoretically Predicted Numbers of HMNEs, Numbers of VMNEs, and Foreign Affiliate Sales (a) Mean of s_i (b) Mean of s_i (c) Mean of s_i

cal capital, making it profitable for VMNEs to surface in *i*. This suggests that the relationship between k_i and FAS_{ij} is also a fourth-order polynomial. This suggests testable Hypothesis 2:

> *Hypothesis 2*: Empirical FAS_{ij} in a regression should be a fourth-order polynomial function of k_i at the means of s_i and u_i ($s_i = u_i = 0.5$).

For completeness, Figure 3c shows the relationships between k_i, u_i and FAS_{ij}. Figure 3c requires careful inspection; it is both quantitatively and qualitatively different from Figure 3b at $u_i = 0.5$. In Figure 3b, at $u_i = 0.5$ when *i* is very physical capital abundant ($k_i = 1.0$), there are no VMNEs headquarted in *i*. However, Figure 3c shows that at $u_i = 0.5$ and $k_i = 1.0$ there is positive FAS_{ij}; this FAS_{ij} is entirely *horizontal* FAS_{ij} (see Figure 3a). As k_i decreases from $k_i = 1.0$ along $u_i = 0.5$, horizontal MNEs decline in Figure 3c owing to the fall in physical capital abundance relative to skilled labor, but vertical MNEs increase. However, as k_i continues to decline toward 0, even VMNEs headquarted in *i* become unprofitable. Thus, we expect empirical FAS_{ij} to be a fourth-order polynomial function of k_i at the means of s_i and u_i (0.5).

In anticipation of our empirical results, we offer one note of clarification. Note that the z-axes in all figures (measuring FAS_{ij}) are indexed to 100. Hence, the more limited effect of HMNEs FAS in Figure 3c relative to vertical FAS reflects the calibration of the model. In the numerical simulations, at the peaks vertical MNE FAS activity is larger than HMNE FAS activity. This is apparent also in Figure 2c. It should be noted that our hypotheses are only qualitative predictions, not quantitative ones; we do not necessarily expect vertical FAS_{ij} to exceed horizontal FAS_{ij}. Indeed, earlier empirical evaluations suggest that, if anything, horizontal FAS activity should dominate vertical FAS activity. Our goal here is to introduce physical capital in such a manner as to suggest an empirical regression specification to better distinguish vertical FAS from horizontal FAS. We leave it to the data to reveal the relative quantitative importance of the two sources of FAS activity.

Finally, Figures 3a, 3b, and 3c all suggest Hypothesis 3, which is also potentially testable:

> *Hypothesis 3*: Empirical FAS_{ij} should be a negative monotonic function of u_i.

The reason is that at $k_i = 0.5$ and $s_i = 0.5$ an increase in u_i is associated with an unambiguous decline in FAS_{ij}. The economic rationale is straightforward. If country i's share of unskilled labor increases, i's comparative advantage in production—of either differentiated good X or homogeneous good Y—increases, and consequently it loses a comparative advantage in hosting multinational headquarters, either horizontal or vertical ones.

This expected relationship is confirmed for FAS_{ij} in s_i–u_i space; again, FAS_{ij} is decreasing in u_i monotonically.[7] For robustness Figures 4a–b depict the relationships in s_i–u_i space, which correspond to the axes in BNU. Figure 4a shows the theoretical relationship between numbers of HMNEs with headquarters in i and plants in j (as well as in i and ROW), s_i, and u_i at $k_i = 0.5$. Figure 4b shows the theoretical relationship between numbers of VMNEs with headquarters in i and plants in j, s_i, and u_i at $k_i = 0.5$. As expected, when u_i is low and s_i is low, more HMNEs are headquartered in i. When u_i is low and s_i is high, more VMNEs are headquartered in i.

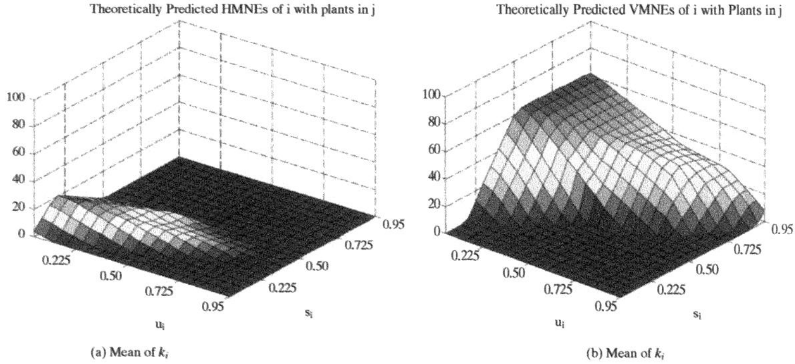

Figure 4(a,b). Theoretically Predicted Numbers of HMNEs and VMNEs (a) Mean of k_i (b) Mean of k_i

5. Empirical Framework and Results

Empirical Framework

The three-factor, three-country, two-good theoretical framework and empirical evidence in Bergstrand and Egger (2007) provides the starting point for a central regression specification—that is, a gravity equation—to capture economic size and similarity and bilateral trade and investment costs in determining bilateral horizontal FAS and bilateral intra-industry trade, consistent with Blonigen and Piger's (2011) Bayesian Moving Average analysis that confirmed the empirical importance of gravity-equation variables.[8] However, Bergstrand and Egger (2007) provided no conceptual guidance on the specification of relative factor endowments.

BNU provided three important contributions to empirical investigation of the roles of relative factor endowments for explaining FAS flows in the two-factor, two-country KC model. One contribution was to extend empirical analysis from just US inward and outward FAS flows to a broad sample of countries. We follow this suggestion using bilateral FAS data from the United Nations Conference on Trade and Development (UNCTAD) country profiles for 1986–2000 among 36 countries listed in the Data Appendix; unfortunately, a consistent bilateral FAS data set among a larger number of countries is unavailable. Second, BNU measured relative factor endowments of skilled and unskilled labor using factor endowment share measures implied directly by Edgeworth-box (geometric) considerations (i.e. s_i and u_i). We follow this suggestion as well, and detail in the next paragraph how we adapt it to our three-factor, three-country setting. Third, BNU summarized the empirically predicted FAS values (based upon their final regression specification) using an Edgeworth box to confirm visually the "goodness of fit," alongside conventional R^2 measures; we adopt this later.

The second BNU methodological innovation just noted reminds us that a country's factor shares measure precisely the "location" of a pair of countries in an Edgeworth box. First, we know from the $2 \times 2 \times 2$ KC literature that a traditional two-dimensional Edgeworth box can be used theoretically to reflect the relationship between s_i, u_i, and bilateral FAS of headquarters country i in affiliate country j (FAS_{ij}). Hence, a regression equation trying to capture the theoretical surfaces relating vertical FAS and horizontal FAS to relative factor endowments implied by the Edgeworth box should include s_i and u_i explicitly. Moreover, in a three-factor setting, we are in an Edgeworth "cube." Hence, to evaluate a slice of the cube—say, for a given k_i—the regression must include k_i to hold it constant (at its mean). For given absolute endowments, a regression specification for capturing the relationships between FAS_{ij}, s_i, u_i, and k_i should include—on the right-hand side—s_i, u_i, and k_i explicitly in some functional form suggested by theory.

Second, a critical assumption of an Edgeworth box is that absolute factor endowments are held constant. In the two-country case, this is accounted for by including the two countries' GDPs, as the gravity equation would suggest; in cross-section, as is well established, the correlation between GDP and absolute factor endowments is very high (so that inclusion of GDP for economic size is sufficient). However, the three-country methodology of Bergstrand and Egger (2007) suggests that the GDPs of countries i, j, and ROW need to be accounted for. In a large cross-section, ROW GDP variation is virtually zero, and so need not be included. In a panel, changes in ROW GDP are easily accounted for using time dummies.

Consequently, our regression specifications to explain bilateral FAS flows basically "wed" the methodological contributions of Bergstrand and Egger (2007)—suggesting a standard gravity equation to account for economic size (or absolute factor endowments), trade costs, and investment costs—and of BNU—suggesting the use of factor shares s_i, u_i, and k_i to account for relative factor endowments. Typical gravity equation specifications include several variables to capture bilateral trade and/or investment costs. In this regard, we include standard time-invariant bilateral "cost" variables: the log of bilateral distance, a dummy variable for common land border (1 if adjacent, and 0 otherwise), and a dummy variable for common official language (1 if the same, and 0 otherwise). Following Markusen (2002), we also include cross-sectional and time-varying logarithms of multilateral measures of country trade resistance and investment resistance indexes from CMM (2001): $\log(Tc_i)$, $\log(Tc_j)$, and $\log(\text{Invc}_j)$. Unfortunately, data constraints preclude bilateral measures, which would be preferable. Third, in the specifications below, we include a time "dummy" for each year (except one, becouse of the constant) to capture potentially time-varying ROW GDP; however, for brevity we do not report the coefficient estimates for the intercept and time dummies.[9]

For estimation, we use a Poisson quasi-maximum likelihood (PQML) approach, which has become widely accepted. The reason for the PQML estimation method is the following. First, because of the multiplicative relationship between levels of flows and their economic determinants and owing to Jensen's inequality, in the presence of heteroskedasticity ordinary least squares (OLS) estimation of log-linearized equations may lead to biased coefficient estimates for right-hand side variables. The PQML estimation method can address this concern, cf. Santos Silva and Tenreyro (2006). Second, PQML can be applied with dependent variables that include zero and positively valued observations, such as FAS flows. PQML exploits variation from both zero and non-zero observations, and our theoretical model predicts a large number of zeros and our empirical FAS data set has a large number of zeros. Data sources are listed in the Data Appendix.

Empirical Results

Regression results Table 1 reports various specifications for PQML regressions for bilateral FAS flows. The first two columns in Table 1 provide, respectively, a list of the right-hand side variables and their expected coefficient signs. The third through ninth columns report coefficient estimates and z-statistics (in parentheses) for specifications 1–7 for explaining bilateral FAS.

Specification 1 provides the results of estimating a traditional gravity equation for FAS_{ij}, where right-hand side variables capture economic size (a proxy for absolute factor endowments) and similarity and various factors that either impede or enhance flows. Since $\text{GDP}_i\text{GDP}_j = (\text{GDP}_i + \text{GDP}_j)^2\{[\text{GDP}_i/(\text{GDP}_i + \text{GDP}_j)][\text{GDP}_j/(\text{GDP}_i + \text{GDP}_j)]\}$, we include separately $\log(\text{GDP}_i + \text{GDP}_j)$ and $\log(\text{Similarity}_{ij})$ where $\text{Similarity}_{ij} = [\text{GDP}_i/(\text{GDP}_i + \text{GDP}_j)][\text{GDP}_j/(\text{GDP}_i + \text{GDP}_j)]$. Economic size and similarity have the expected positive and statistically significant relationships with FAS_{ij}.The two coefficient estimates suggest a clear "horizontal motivation" for MNE activity, as in Bergstrand and Egger (2007).

We now discuss the other "traditional" gravity-equation variables included in specification 1. As often found, the log of bilateral distance has a negative and statistically significant coefficient estimate and a conventional value throughout all the specifications (and so we will provide no further discussion of it). Of course, as in the KC

Table 1. Bilateral FAS PQML Regressions

Variables	*Expected sign*	*FAS (1)*	*FAS (2)*	*FAS (3)*	*FAS (4)*	*FAS (5)*	*FAS (6)*	*FAS (7)*
$\log(\text{GDP}_i + \text{GDP}_j)$	+	2.08*	2.07*	2.06*	2.19*	2.10*	2.33*	2.36*
		(20.21)	(19.71)	(19.69)	(22.76)	(20.03)	(19.86)	(18.35)
$\log(\text{Similarity}_{ij})$	+	0.13*	0.17*	0.16*				
		(2.36)	(2.72)	(2.46)				
$\log(\text{Distance}_{ij})$	—	–0.70*	–0.67*	–0.67*	–0.69*	–0.66*	–0.64*	–0.61*
		(–15.41)	(–15.41)	(–14.27)	(–14.88)	(–15.30)	(–14.94)	(–13.98)
Contiguity	?	0.25*	0.27*	0.35*	0.36*	0.33*	0.27*	0.25*
		(2.61)	(2.84)	(3.11)	(3.08)	(2.97)	(2.40)	(2.23)
Language	+	0.02	0.03	–0.00	–0.03	0.11	–0.07	–0.06
		(0.13)	(0.21)	(–0.00)	(–0.21)	(1.01)	(–0.68)	(–0.55)
$\log(\text{Invc}_j)$	—	–0.69*	–0.69*	–0.92*	–0.84*	–0.86*	–0.85*	–0.79*
		(–5.37)	(–5.35)	(–6.85)	(–6.12)	(–6.78)	(–6.56)	(–6.01)
$\log(Tc_j)$	?	–0.03	–0.14	–0.10	–0.11	–0.19*	–0.14	–0.12
		(–0.31)	(–1.57)	(–1.20)	(–1.35)	(–2.24)	(–1.62)	(–1.31)
$\log(Tc_i)$	—	0.59*	0.74*	0.67*	0.54*	0.62*	0.56*	0.57*
		(6.23)	(7.42)	(6.46)	(5.40)	(6.71)	(6.15)	(6.42)
s_i	+		0.93*	0.32	0.02	26.63*	11.83*	9.90*
			(2.89)	(0.88)	(0.06)	(7.69)	(2.92)	(2.26)
s_i^2	—					–89.37*	–55.65*	–43.90*
						(–6.40)	(–3.64)	(–2.87)
s_i^3	+					113.89*	80.86*	52.07*
						(5.56)	(3.55)	(2.13)
s_i^4	—					–49.23*	–36.61*	–21.74
						(–4.93)	(–3.27)	(–1.79)
k_i	+			2.39*	2.48*	3.06*	24.93*	29.25*
				(5.77)	(5.68)	(6.95)	(6.77)	(7.36)
k_i^2	—						–67.71*	–93.09*
							(–4.86)	(–5.26)
k_i^3	+						85.72*	118.67*
							(4.21)	(5.04)
k_i^4	—						–38.34*	–54.87*
							(–3.96)	(–4.80)
u_i	—		–0.97*	–2.98*	–2.87*	–3.79*	–3.73*	–5.19*
			(–3.18)	(–7.30)	(–6.63)	(–8.95)	(–9.00)	(–6.07)
s_ik_i	?							7.95
								(1.22)
s_iu_i	?							0.41
								(0.08)
k_iu_i	?							1.92
								(0.43)
No. of Obs.		1370	1370	1370	1370	1370	1370	1370
Pseudo R^2		0.61	0.61	0.63	0.63	0.66	0.67	0.67

Notes: * Denotes statistically significant at 5% in two-tailed z-test. Numbers in parentheses are z-statistics. Coefficient estimates for the constant and time dummies are not presented for brevity.

literature, actual "distance" has no theoretical role, but is often interpreted as an investment "friction" and typically included. We specify the expected sign on contiguity as ambiguous for FAS_{ij}. The reason is that—if FAS has a horizontal motivation—then FAS is a substitute for trade, and contiguity may have a negative effect (lower trade costs cause more trade and less FAS). If contiguity reduces information costs, then it may have a positive effect on FAS_{ij}. In all the FAS specifications, Contiguity has a positive and statistically significant effect. A common language is likely to enhance information flows, and the expected effect is positive; in all the FAS specifications, the coefficient estimate is effectively zero and statistically insignificant. The log of the investment cost index in j ($\log(\mathrm{Invc}_j)$) is expected to have a negative effect on FAS_{ij}, representing a barrier to either vertical or horizontal investment in j. Throughout the FAS specifications, this variable has the expected negative sign and is statistically significant. Finally, we include two indexes of "trade costs," one multilateral trade-cost index for j ($\log(Tc_j)$) and one such index for i ($\log(Tc_i)$). For $\log(Tc_j)$, we have no unambiguous sign expectation. The reason is that, if FAS has a horizontal motivation, we would expect a positive coefficient, as FAS and trade are substitutes. However, in reality, even HMNEs based in i with plants in j require some intermediate inputs from i, for which trade costs in j would impede FAS_{ij}. It turns out that the coefficient estimates for $\log(Tc_j)$ tend to be effectively zero for most FAS specifications. Distance may be effectively capturing much of this variable's cross-sectional effect. Finally, the expected coefficient sign for $\log(Tc_i)$ is negative. If FAS_{ij} has a vertical motivation, then we would expect goods to flow from j to i; trade costs in i would diminish these flows. Hence, FAS_{ij} may indirectly be reduced because of trade costs in i; this creates a negative expected effect. However, the coefficient estimates for $\log(Tc_i)$ are positive and statistically significant for all the FAS specifications, which is unexpected. The overall pseudo-R^2 value for specification 1 is 0.61, which is about the same (0.58) as that for a similar gravity specification for FDI flows in Bergstrand and Egger (2007).

We now turn to the focus of this paper, the effect of relative factor endowments on FAS flows. Specification 2 enhances the FAS gravity equation, adding just s_i and u_i to the previous specification. The reason for reporting this specification—even though our theoretical model suggests that s_i should be included as a fourth-order polynomial—is to determine if we can find a similar (positive) effect as for the variables $SKILL_{ij}$ ($= s_i/u_i$) in BNU and $SKDIFF_{ij}$ (measured as the difference in i's and j's skilled labor stocks as shares of total labor force) in CMM (2001). We confirm this.[10] Holding u_i constant, s_i has a positive and statistically significant coefficient estimate and—holding s_i constant—u_i has a negative and statistically significant coefficient estimate; this suggests that there is some "vertical motivation" for FAS. Of course, this specification is not motivated by our theoretical Edgeworth boxes and is subject to the same potential specification concern as raised in Blonigen et al. (2003). However, it is useful to ascertain that this simple specification "accords" with earlier results of CMM and BNU motivated by the two-factor, two-country KC model. Finally, we note that none of the other (gravity equation motivated) variables' coefficient estimates change materially, and so there remains evidence of "horizontal motivation" for FAS as well.

In specification 3, we consider for the first time the role of physical capital endowments by adding k_i to the previous specification. Interestingly, the only variable whose coefficient estimate changes materially is i's skilled labor share, s_i. This is interesting because it suggests that measures of relative skilled labor endowments in previous studies may have been effectively a proxy for relative physical capital endowments in explaining FAS. Only physical capital (k_i) and unskilled labor (u_i) factor endowment shares—of the three relative endowment variables s_i, k_i, and u_i—are statistically significant.

As noted earlier, the inclusion of variables s_i, k_i, and u_i maps relative factor shares *directly* from the theory. However, also noted earlier, variation in any one variable—such as s_i—for given values of k_i and u_i—necessarily (in an Edgeworth box) changes relative economic sizes of i and j. Thus, one can argue that the change in any one factor share (vertically or horizontally in the box) changes relative factor endowments and economic size, so that the inclusion of log(Similarity$_{ij}$) is inappropriate. By these considerations, we ran specification 4 which differs from previous specification 3 only by the exclusion of log(Similarity$_{ij}$). The important outcome is that the exclusion of log(Similarity$_{ij}$) does not create any significant omitted variables bias; none of the other variables' coefficient estimates changes materially. Consequently, in the remaining specifications we exclude log(Similarity$_{ij}$); however, for robustness all subsequent specifications' results are largely insensitive to its absence (and available on request).

Theoretical discussion in section 4, theoretical Figures 2a–c, and Hypothesis 1 imply that—for given k_i and u_i—FAS$_{ij}$ should be a fourth-order polynomial function of s_i. Specification 5 modifies the previous specification by including s_i, s_i^2, s_i^3, and s_i^4. The expected signs for these four variables' coefficients in specification 5 for a fourth-order polynomial function to follow the shape suggested by theoretical Figure 2c at the means of k_i and u_i (about 0.5) are listed in the second column of Table 1. Specification 5 shows that the coefficient estimates have the expected signs and all are statistically significant. Hence, in a comparison of specifications 4 and 5, s_i in specification 4 (without the fourth-order polynomial function) is economically and statistically insignificant, but using a fourth-order polynomial s_i has the expected theoretical relationship with FAS$_{ij}$. Moreover, none of the other variables' coefficient estimates changes materially between specifications 4 and 5. Thus, Hypothesis 1 is confirmed empirically.

Section 4, theoretical Figures 3a–c, and Hypothesis 2 imply that—for given s_i and u_i—FAS$_{ij}$ should be a fourth-order polynomial function of k_i. Specification 6 modifies the previous specification by including k_i, k_i^2, k_i^3, and k_i^4. The expected signs for these four variables' coefficients in specification 6 for a fourth-order polynomial function to follow the shape suggested by theoretical Figures 3a–c at the means of s_i and u_i (0.5) are listed in the second column of Table 1. Specification 6 shows that the coefficient estimates follow a fourth-order polynomial function with coefficient estimate signs corresponding precisely to the expected ones, and all coefficient estimates for these four variables are statistically significant. Moreover, none of the other variables' coefficient estimates changes materially between specification 5 and 6. Thus, Hypothesis 2 is confirmed empirically.

We note across all six FAS specifications that u_i has the expected negative coefficient sign with statistical significance, confirming Hypothesis 3. This accords with the intuition that FAS of MNEs based in i will be lower the relatively more unskilled labor abundant i is, because unskilled labor raises its comparative advantage in production over forming MNE headquarters. Theoretical Figure 3c suggests a monotonic negative relationship between FAS_{ij} and u_i. Indeed, FAS$_{ij}$ and u_i are negatively correlated with a statistically significant coefficient estimate.

Even though the fourth-order polynomial functions for s_i and k_i captured the theoretical relationships in Edgeworth-box space, as a robustness check we were curious to see if specification 6's results were sensitive to interaction terms, commonly used in the KC literature. While many interaction terms are possible, we considered adding only the interaction terms s_ik_i, s_iu_i, and k_iu_i—that is, interactions among the key factor-share variables. Specification 7 reports the results of adding these interaction terms. Interestingly, none of the coefficient estimates of the interaction terms was statistically significantly different from zero. Moreover, their inclusion had no material impact on the other coefficient estimates.

Empirically-predicted FAS flows In this section, we draw upon one of the innovations in BNU—which employed the empirically-predicted bilateral FAS flows using its central regression equation—to examine the similarity of the Edgeworth boxes using the theoretically predicted FAS_{ij} and those using empirically predicted FAS_{ij}. Moreover, we must extend this approach in our three-factor setting to slices of an Edgeworth "cube," evaluating the Edgeworth slices at the empirical means of the third factor.

Figure 5a provides the Edgeworth box relating empirically predicted FAS_{ij} from Specification 6 to k_i and s_i at the empirical mean of u_i (about 0.5) and provides empirical support for one of the main economic insights of this paper. This figure corresponds to theoretical Figure 2c (except for the relative quantitative importance of HMNE vs VMNE activity). Predicted (empirical) FAS_{ij} reaches a maximum when

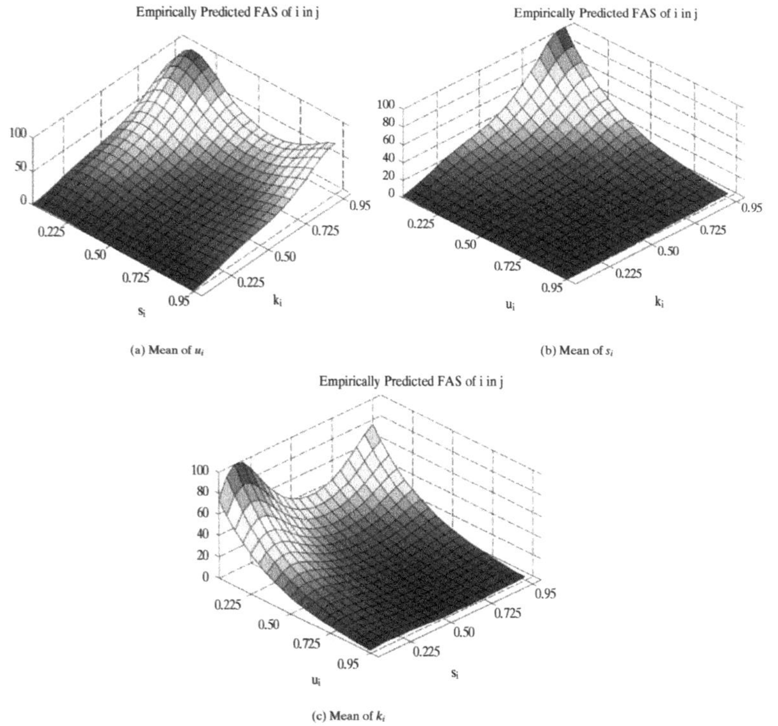

Figure 5(a–c). Empirically Predicted Foreign Affiliate Sales (a) Mean of u_i (b) Mean of s_i (c) Mean of k_i

either country *i* is abundant in skilled labor and physical capital (relative to unskilled labor)—which favors VMNE activity (see theoretical Figure 2b)—or country *i* is abundant in physical capital relative to skilled labor—which favors HMNE activity (see theoretical Figure 2a). Figure 5a confirms empirically that both horizontal and vertical FAS are important—but with HMNE activity more important empirically in the aggregate bilateral data—and each type of FAS attains its maximum in the Edgeworth box approximately where Figures 2a–c predict. Figure 5a is consistent with Hypothesis 1; FAS_{ij} is a fourth-order polynomial of s_i at the means of k_i and u_i.

Figure 5b confirms Hypotheses 2 and 3, but only upon careful examination. Figure 5b provides the Edgeworth box relating empirically-predicted FAS_{ij} to k_i and u_i at the empirical mean of s_i and provides empirical support for two other main economic insights of this paper: FAS_{ij} is a fourth-order polynomial function of k_i and a monotonic negative function of u_i. The figure is the empirical analogue to theoretical Figure 3c (except for the relative quantitative importance of HMNE vs VMNE activity). It is clear—when comparing Figure 5b with Figures 3a and b—that HMNE activity tends to dominate FAS activity in the bilateral aggregate data. However, vertical MNE activity is not trivial; it is important to recall that the predicted (empirical) FAS_{ij} surface in Figure 5b is generated by the statistically significant fourth-order polynomials in k_i and s_i. Indeed, careful examination of Figure 5b reveals that empirically predicted FAS_{ij}'s are a fourth-order polynomial of k_i for any given value of u_i (and recalling that $s_i = 0.5$). Moroever, at $u_i = s_i = 0.5$, the peak of vertical FAS empirical activity in Figure 5b is at k_i equal to approximately 0.225, which corresponds precisely to that in Figures 3b and c (at $u_i = s_i = 0.5$).

Finally, Figure 5c shows the empirical relationship between predicted FAS_{ij} with s_i and u_i at $k_i = 0.5$. Consistent with the results above, vertical FAS co-exists with horizontal FAS, but horizontal MNE activity is more prevalent.

6. Conclusions

Finding vertical MNE activity has remained relatively elusive in econometric analyses of bilateral aggregate FAS data. This paper has offered an approach to try to better understand empirically and theoretically the relationships between horizontal and vertical MNEs' bilateral aggregate foreign affiliate sales (FAS) and countries' relative factor endowments. By extending the KC model with only skilled and unskilled labor to include a third factor (physical capital) and a third country (ROW) as in Bergstrand and Egger (2007), we could explain theoretically the complex, nonlinear, nonmonotonic empirical relationships between bilateral FAS flows of two countries and their relative endowments of skilled labor, unskilled labor, and physical capital. Our empirical evidence suggests that both horizontal and vertical motivations for FAS exist in the bilateral aggregate FAS data—and physical capital matters in the explanation.

Data Appendix

Bilateral foreign affiliate sales data are from UNCTAD (country profiles) for 1986–2000. GDPs are from the World Bank's *World Development Indicators* (2004). We followed Carr et al. (2001) by deflating nominal foreign affiliate sales in US dollars by host country producer price indices (base year 2000) taken from the *World Development Indicators*. Physical capital stocks are computed by using the perpetual inventory method following Leamer (1984), using gross fixed capital formation and investment deflator data from the *World Development Indicators* and assuming a depreciation rate of 13.3%. Data on human capital endowments were kindly provided by Scott Baier and are based on information in the *World Development Indicators* on school enrollment (see Baier et al., 2006). Remaining workers are classified as unskilled. Bilateral distance was computed using "great circle" distances. The country trade resistance and investment resistance indexes are from Carr et al. (2001), kindly provided by Keith Maskus. The exporting (FAS parent) and importing (host) countries include the following: Argentina, Australia, Austria, Belgium, Brazil, Canada, Chile, Colombia, Denmark, Egypt (imports/FAS host only), Finland, France, Germany, Greece, Hong Kong, Ireland, Israel, Italy, Japan, Korea, Mexico, Netherlands, New Zealand, Norway, Philippines, Portugal, Singapore, South Africa, Spain, Sweden, Switzerland, Turkey, UK, USA, and Venezuela.

References

Alfaro, Laura and Andrew Charlton, "Intra-industry Foreign Direct Investment," *American Economic Review* 99 (2009):2096–119.

Anderson, James E. and Eric van Wincoop, "Gravity with Gravitas: A Solution to the Border Puzzle," *American Economic Review* 93 (2003):170–92.

Baier, Scott L., Gerald P. Dwyer, Jr., and Robert Tamura, "How Important are Capital and Total Factor Productivity for Economic Growth?" *Economic Inquiry* 44 (2006):23–49.

Baier, Scott L. and Jeffrey H. Bergstrand, "Do Free Trade Agreements Actually Increase Members' International Trade?" *Journal of International Economics* 71 (2007):72–95.

———, "*Bonus Vetus* OLS: A Simple Method for Approximating International Trade-cost Effects using the Gravity Equation," *Journal of International Economics* 77 (2009):77–85.

Bergstrand, Jeffrey H. and Peter Egger, "A Knowledge-and-physical-capital Model of International Trade Flows, Foreign Direct Investment, and Multinational Enterprises," *Journal of International Economics* 73 (2007): 278–308.

———, "Gravity Equations and Frictions in the World Economy," in Daniel Bernhofen, Rod Falvey, David Greenaway, and Udo Kreickemeier (eds), *Palgrave Handbook of International Trade*, New York, NY: Palgrave Macmillan (2011).

Bernard, Andrew B., J. Bradford Jensen, and Peter K. Schott, "Importers, Exporters, and Multinationals: A Portrait of Firms in the U.S. that Trade Goods," Tuck School of Business at Dartmouth working paper 2005–17 (2005).

Blonigen, Bruce A., "A Review of the Empirical Literature on FDI Determinants," *Atlantic Economic Journal* 33 (2005):383–403.

Blonigen, Bruce A. and Jeremy Piger, "Determinants of Foreign Direct Investment," National Bureau of Economic Research working paper 16704 (2011).

Blonigen, Bruce A., Ronald B. Davies, and Keith Head, "Estimating the Knowledge-capital Model of the Multinational Enterprise: Comment," *American Economic Review* 93 (2003):980–94.

Braconier, Henrik, Pehr-Johan Norbäck, and Dieter Urban, "Reconciling the Evidence on the Knowledge-capital Model," *Review of International Economics* 13 (2005):770–86.

Carr, David, James R. Markusen, and Keith E. Maskus, "Estimating the Knowledge-capital Model of the Multinational Enterprise," *American Economic Review* 91 (2001):693–708.

———, "Estimating the Knowledge-capital Model of the Multinational Enterprise: Reply," *American Economic Review* 93 (2003):995–1001.

Davies, Ronald B., "Hunting High and Low for Vertical FDI," *Review of International Economics* 16 (2008):250–67.

Goldin, Claudia and Lawrence Katz, "The Origins of Technology–Skill Complementarity," *Quarterly Journal of Economics* 113 (1998):693–732.

Griliches, Z., "Capital-Skill Complementarity," *Review of Economics and Statistics* 51 (1969):465–68.
Helpman, Elhanan, "Trade, FDI, and the Organization of Firms." *Journal of Economic Literature* 46 (2006):589–630.
Helpman, Elhanan, Marc J. Melitz, and Stephen R. Yeaple, "Export Versus FDI with Heterogeneous Firms," *American Economic Review* 94 (2004):300–16.
Leamer, Edward E., *Sources of International Comparative Advantage: Theory and Evidence*, Cambridge, MA: MIT Press (1984).
Markusen, James R., *Multinational Firms and the Theory of International Trade*. Cambridge, MA: MIT Press (2002).
Markusen, James R. and Keith E. Maskus, "Multinational Firms: Reconciling Theory and Evidence," in Magnus Blomstrom and Linda Goldberg (eds), *Topics in Empirical International Economics: A Festschrift in Honor of Robert E. Lipsey,* Chicago: University of Chicago Press (2001).
———, "Discriminating Among Alternative Theories of the Multinational Enterprise," *Review of International Economics* 10 (2002):694–707.
Santos Silva, J.M.C. and Silvana Tenreyro, "The Log of Gravity," *Review of Economics and Statistics* 88 (2006):641–58.
Slaughter, Matthew J., "Production Transfer withing Multinational Enterprises and American Wages," *Journal of International Economics* 50 (2000):449–72.

Notes

1. This is implied by two peaks in the Edgeworth box relating the parent country's skilled labor share to FDI/FAS, one for horizontal FDI/FAS flows and one for vertical FDI/FAS flows.
2. Most FDI studies using the gravity equation simply justify using it by analogy to the theoretical foundations for the trade gravity equation. However, see Bergstrand and Egger (2007) for a theoretical foundation for gravity equations of bilateral FDI and FAS flows, simultaneously with one for trade flows, in the presence of national and multinational firms. See Bergstrand and Egger (2011) for a survey of the literature.
3. Braconier et al. (2005) find some evidence of vertical FAS. However, their $2 \times 2 \times 2$ approach has a limitation because there may exist HMNEs in the factor-endowment space where VMNEs are supposed to be uniquely identified, as discussed in the next section.
4. In fairness, Carr et al. (2003) candidly indicated that finding a "central regression specification" is a very difficult task.
5. We note now that the discussion above has important implications for hypotheses about the relationship between GDP similarity and FAS_{ij}. In our three-factor, three-country world, when u_i is at its mean the cell in the middle of the Edgeworth box relating k_i and s_i may not be where i and j are identically sized in absolute factor endowments (for some given endowments for ROW), because u_i may not be precisely 0.5 (but as noted above, it will be close). Moreover, a proportionate reduction in k_i and s_i—such that k_i/s_i is unchanged—but holding u_i at its mean—changes i's and j's relative economic sizes and also their relative factor endowments. This differs from the two-factor KC world examined in all the previous studies (also with only two countries) where a movement along the Southwest–Northeast (SW–NE) diagonal implies a change in relative economic sizes (absolute factor endowments) of the two countries without a change in relative factor endowments. In our three-factor world, a movement along this diagonal also changes relative factor endowments.
6. We have done extensive sensitivity analyses for various alternative values of the parameters, and the results are qualitatively robust and available on request.
7. Note that all figures are indexed between 0 and 100. Hence, the theoretical figures are not designed to predict effects quantitatively, just qualitatively.
8. Recall that formal theoretical foundations for the gravity equation are based upon N-country worlds, so the ROW is taken into account.

9. Regarding other "third-country" effects such as ROW trade and investment barriers, these effects are more difficult to capture because any country-specific dummies would preclude cross-section variation in s_i, k_i, and u_i, cf. Anderson and van Wincoop (2003) or Baier and Bergstrand (2009). Moreover, in a panel, such effects would require country and time dummies, which would also preclude variation in s_{it},k_{it}, and u_{it}, cf. Baier and Bergstrand (2007). We leave this issue for researchers to address in the future.

10. Variables s_i, k_i, and u_i are not expressed in logs, so their coefficients are not reflecting "elasticities."

Appendix: Calibration of Model

The underlying theoretical model is described in Bergstrand and Egger (2007), or Chapter 14. The complexity of the model (including the complementary-slackness conditions) introduces a high degree of nonlinearity, and it cannot be solved analytically. Consequently, as in Markusen (2002) we provide numerical solutions to the model. With three countries, we have several potential types of asymmetries, e.g., large vs. small GDPs, developed vs. developing economies. We focus initially on bilateral flows between three identical economies (in absolute and relative factor endowments). We then introduce absolute and relative factor endowment asymmetries. We use *GAMS* for our numerical analysis. The calibration of the model is very similar to that in Bergstrand and Egger (2007).

1. *Values of (Exogenous) Factor Endowment, Trade Cost, and Investment Cost Variables*

We assume a world endowment of capital (K) of 500 units, skilled labor (S) of 200 units, and unskilled labor (U) of 2000 units. Initially, countries i and j together have half of the world's endowments of each factor, and i's and j's factor endowments are identical.

"Trade costs" include both the costs of shipping and distributing goods. Initially, we set the former costs for good X and good Y at (*ad valorem* equivalents of) 30 percent and 45 percent, respectively. This reflects recent estimates that homogeneous goods' transport costs are higher than those of differentiated goods, cf., Bergstrand and Egger (2006). Both values exceed estimated (c.i.f.-f.o.b.)/f.o.b. factors in that paper of 15 and 20 percent, respectively. However, values used are in the range of levels discussed in Anderson and van Wincoop (2004) on trade costs. For simplicity, we set tariff rates initially at *ad valorem* equivalents of 2 percent.

In reality, of course, informational costs and policy barriers to FDI exist between countries. We assumed initially a "tax-rate" equivalent (for γ) of 60 percent for FDI.

2. *Utility and Technology Parameter Values*

Consider first the utility function (see Appendix A equation (1) for details). The only two parameters are the Cobb-Douglas share of income spent on differentiated products from various producers (η) and the CES parameter (ε) influencing the elasticity of substitution between differentiated products ($\sigma \equiv 1 - \varepsilon$). Initially, we use 0.71 for the value of η, based upon an estimated share of manufactures trade in overall world trade averaged between 1990 and 2000 using 5-digit SITC data from the UNs' COMTRADE data set, which is a plausible estimate. The initial value of ε is set at -5, implying an elasticity of substitution of 6 among differentiated final goods, consistent with a wide range of recent empirical studies estimating the elasticity between 2 and 10, cf., Feenstra (1994).

Consider next the production function for differentiated goods. Labor's share of differentiated goods gross output is assumed to be 0.8; the Cobb-Douglas formulation implies the elasticity of substitution between capital and labor is unity. Griliches (1969) proposed — in a three-factor world with unskilled labor, skilled labor, and physical capital — that skills were more complementary with physical capital than with unskilled labor in production. Griliches found convincing econometric evidence that physical capital and skilled labor were relatively more complementary in production than physical capital and unskilled labor. Most evidence to date suggests that human and physical capital are relatively complementary in production, cf., Goldin and Katz (1998). In the only empirical study of MNE behavior considering this issue, Slaughter (2000) finds statistically significant evidence in favor of capital-skill complementarity. Initially, we assume $\chi = -0.25$, implying a technical rate (elasticity) of substitution of 0.8 [$= 1/(1 - \chi)$] and complementarity between physical and human capital.

As in the 2x2x2 KC model in CMM (2001), a firm (or headquarters) setup uses only skilled labor. For national final goods producers, we assume a headquarters setup requires one unit of skilled labor per unit of output ($a_{\mathrm{Sn},1} = a_{\mathrm{Sn},2} = a_{\mathrm{Sn},3} = 1$). As in the knowledge-capital model, we assume "jointness" for MNEs; that is, services of knowledge-based assets are joint inputs into multiple plants. Markusen suggests that the *ratio* of fixed headquarters setup requirements for a horizontal or vertical MNE relative to a domestic firm ranges from 1 to 2 (for a 2-country model). We assume initially a headquarters cost for MNEs of 1.01 ($a_{\text{Sh},1} = a_{\text{Sh},2} = a_{\text{Sh},3} = a_{\text{Sv},1} = a_{\text{Sv},2} = a_{\text{Sv},3} = 1.01$); hence, we assume the additional firm setup cost of an MNE over a national firm is quite small. We assume that every plant (national or MNE) requires two units of home physical capital ($a_K = 2$); however, MNEs setting up plants abroad face additional fixed investment costs (γ), for which we assumed a value of 0.60 (60 percent).

Chapter 16

What determines BITs?

Jeffrey H. Bergstrand [a,b,c,d,*], Peter Egger [d,e,f,g,h,i,j,k,1]

[a] Department of Finance, Mendoza College of Business, University of Notre Dame, USA
[b] Department of Economics, University of Notre Dame, USA
[c] Kellogg Institute for International Studies, University of Notre Dame, USA
[d] CESifo Munich, Germany
[e] ETH Zürich, Switzerland
[f] CEPR, United Kingdom
[g] WIFO, Austria
[h] Ifo, Germany
[i] AAU, Czech Republic
[j] GEP at University of Nottingham, United Kingdom
[k] OUCBT at Oxford University, United Kingdom

ARTICLE INFO

Article history:
Received 4 February 2011
Received in revised form 15 October 2012
Accepted 7 November 2012
Available online 15 November 2012

JEL classification:
F1
F2

Keywords:
Bilateral investment treaties
Foreign direct investment
Multinational firms
Free trade agreements
International trade

ABSTRACT

Similar to bilateral or regional preferential trade agreements (PTAs), bilateral investment treaties (BITs) have proliferated over the past 50 years. The purpose of this study is to provide the first systematic empirical analysis of the economic determinants of BITs and of the likelihood of BITs between pairs of countries using a qualitative choice model, in a manner consistent with explaining PTAs. We develop the econometric specification for explaining the two based upon a general equilibrium model of world trade and foreign direct investment with three factors, two products, and trade and investment costs among multiple countries in the presence of national and multinational firms. The empirical model for BITs and PTAs is bivariate in nature and supports a set of hypotheses drawn from the general equilibrium model. Using the preferred empirical model for a sample of 12,880 country-pairs in the year 2000, we predict correctly 88% of all pairs with a BIT and a PTA, 81% with a BIT but no PTA, and 84% with a PTA but no BIT.

1. Introduction

> "*The primary problem for researchers wishing to assess the impacts of policies to promote FDI is that policy adoption is endogenously determined.*" (Aisbett, 2009, p. 396)

> "*The literature on BITs is limited, making it difficult to truly understand the determinants for signing.*" (Tobin and Rose-Ackerman, 2005, p. 15)

One of the most notable economic events since World War II is the proliferation of preferential trade agreements (PTAs), including predominantly free trade agreements (FTAs) and some customs unions (CUs). However, the proliferation of bilateral investment treaties (BITs) has been significant as well. For instance, in 2010 the U.S. government had 40 BITs in force while it had only 17 PTAs in force. Fig. 1 presents the numbers of BITs in existence in the world in every year from 1980 to 2007. Moreover, Table 1 indicates the numbers of country-pairs with BITs and with PTAs (including those with both) in the year 2000 for 161 countries. Table 1 shows, for this sample of 12,880 country-pairs, 923 pairs with a BIT but no PTA, 1478 pairs with a PTA but no BIT, and 556 pairs with both.[2]

Yet in contrast to the vast international trade literatures on the theoretical net benefits and costs of FTAs and CUs and on the empirically-estimated effects of FTAs and CUs on trade flows, the literature on BITs is not only considerably smaller but dominated by legal and political science scholars rather than economists (cf., Salacuse, 1990;

* Corresponding author at: Department of Finance, Mendoza College of Business, University of Notre Dame, Notre Dame, IN 46556, USA.
E-mail addresses: bergstrand.1@nd.edu (J.H. Bergstrand), egger@kof.ethz.ch (P. Egger).
[1] ETH Zürich, WEH E6, Weinbergstrasse 35, 8092 Zürich, Switzerland.

[2] We note that, since 1990, many PTAs have introduced substantive investment provisions; such agreements are more accurately "preferential trade *and investment* agreements" (or PTIAs). However, the number of PTIAs still is fewer than 10% of the number of BITs (cf., Sauvant and Sachs, 2009) and this issue will be discussed later in a sensitivity analysis.

*Originally Published in *Journal of International Economics*, 90(2013), pp. 107–122.

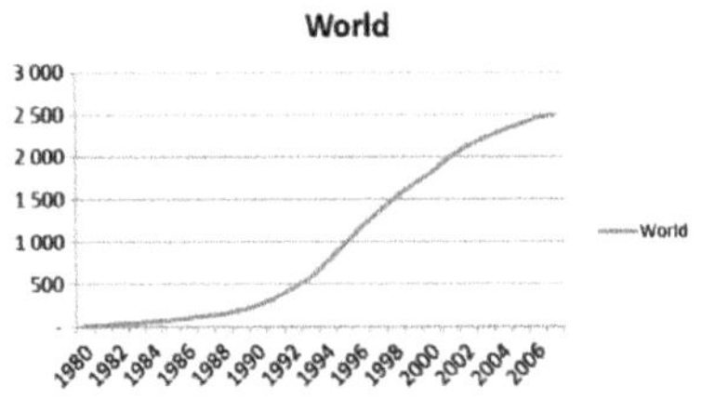

Fig. 1. Number of BITs in the world by year, 1980–2007.

Vandevelde, 1998, 2000; Tobin and Rose-Ackerman, 2005; Buthe and Milner, 2009).[3] Consequently, none of these papers address factors explaining BITs' formations using formal theoretical economic models, and few provide econometric empirical analyses. Also, relative to the trade and PTA literature, there are very few papers – some by economists and some by legal/political scholars – that have looked systematically and econometrically at the impact of BITs on foreign direct investment (FDI). Hallward-Driemeier (2003), Tobin and Rose-Ackerman (2005), Gallagher and Birch (2006), and Aisbett (2009) find little economically and statistically significant effect of BITs on FDI flows. By contrast, Egger and Pfaffermayr (2004a), Salacuse and Sullivan (2005), Neumayer and Spess (2005), and Buthe and Milner (2009) find economically and statistically significant effects.[4] Furthermore, there is *no study* trying to systematically explain empirically the economic determinants of BITs — much less one motivated by a formal general equilibrium model. This paper addresses this shortcoming.[5]

In this paper, we examine theoretically and econometrically the economic determinants of BITs — in a manner consistent with understanding the economic determinants of PTAs. While BITs have been examined much less in the international economics literature, the motivation for such agreements for FDI is actually quite similar to that for PTAs for trade. While "Friendship, Commerce and Navigation" treaties surfaced as early as the 18th century, modern BITs were effectively created in the late 1950s in response to numerous expropriations of FDIs as well as the limitation of the General Agreement on Tariffs and Trade (GATT) to trade only; (West) Germany concluded the first modern (post-World War II) BIT with Pakistan in 1959. The first modern BITs were intended to reduce for home countries the relative cost of FDI outflows by reducing the risk of "expropriation" by host countries' governments. Hence, the likelihood of a BIT should be positively related to the degree of expropriation risk, other things equal. More recently, BITs have addressed FDI-related issues beyond expropriation risk to promote investment liberalization. UNCTAD (2007) notes that many of the existing BITs guarantee foreign investors fair-and-equitable, non-discriminatory, and "national" treatment. Consequently, more recently BITs have been spurred by host countries as "instruments" of investment liberalization to encourage capital exporting countries to

Table 1
Bilateral investment treaties (BITs) and preferential trade agreements (PTAs) across 12,880 country-pairs in the year 2000.
Sources: WTO and UNCTAD.

		PTAs		Sum
		Yes (1)	No (0)	
BITs	Yes (1)	556	923	1479
	No (0)	1478	9923	11,401
	Sum	2034	10,846	12,880

Notes: There are 161 countries (12,880 pairs) in the sample.

provide FDI inflows to developing and developed capital importing countries, much as PTAs have proliferated as instruments of trade liberalization among and between developed and developing countries.

Since the fundamental purpose of a BIT is to encourage FDI flows between country-pairs by reducing the relative cost of FDI and that of a PTA is to encourage trade between country-pairs by reducing the relative cost of trade, economic determinants of BITs may well share many similarities to those of PTAs. Since there has been no previous formal theoretical or econometric model of the determinants of BITs, our starting point is the new literature on the economic determinants of PTAs. This literature, surveyed in Freund and Ornelas (2009), starts with Baier and Bergstrand (2004), or BB, who developed a qualitative choice econometric model of the likelihood of a pair of countries having a PTA in a given year.[6] Motivated by a general equilibrium model of world trade with two factors, two monopolistically-competitive markets with national exporting firms, and explicit intercontinental and intracontinental trade costs among multiple countries on multiple continents, the BB model suggests that country-pairs are more likely to have a PTA: (1) the closer together they are; (2) the more remote they are from other markets; (3) the larger their joint economic size; (4) the more similar their economic sizes; and (5) the larger the difference in the pairs' relative factor endowments (up to a point). BB showed that all these economic factors were economically and statistically significant (with expected signs) in explaining cross-sectional variation in country-pairs' probabilities of having PTAs with a pseudo-R^2 of 73%. Using a larger sample of 10,585 pairs in the year 2000, Egger and Larch (2008) predicted correctly about 781 of the 1263 pairs with PTAs (or 62%). Their pseudo-R^2 was considerably lower at 27% (as expected) due to their much larger and less selective sample.

However, the economic determinants of BITs are not likely to be explained by the same econometric model, due to several considerations. First, BITs potentially influence FDI flows. Consequently, while economic size and similarity help to predict PTAs, they may not simultaneously predict BITs; as mentioned, most BITs are between developed and developing countries (and the latter tend also to be economically smaller than the former). Other factors – such as bilateral trade and investment costs and relative factor endowments – are likely to have differing effects on explaining BITs relative to PTAs.[7] Since FDI is generated by multinational enterprises (MNEs), a theoretical framework should incorporate MNEs' behavior; consequently, a simple Helpman–Krugman–Heckscher–Ohlin general equilibrium model of trade as in BB is insufficient. An extension of the BB framework to include MNEs, FDI flows, and foreign affiliate sales (FAS), in the spirit of the "Knowledge–Capital" (KC) models of Markusen (2002) and Markusen and Maskus (2001, 2002), is a natural direction. Fortunately, Bergstrand and Egger (2007), or BE, extended the $2 \times 2 \times 2$ KC model

[3] An excellent edited volume of recent studies on the effect of BITs (and double taxation treaties) on foreign direct investment, including many of the papers noted in this paragraph, is Sauvant and Sachs (2009).

[4] Moreover, only one paper – Aisbett (2009) – provides a formal game-theoretic model of BIT formation based upon expropriation risk. We refer to this model later for motivating the inclusion of a measure of expropriation risk in our empirical analysis. However, that model does not address how factors such as economic size and similarity, trade and investment costs, relative factor endowments, and their interactions can help explain the likelihood of a BIT between a country-pair, which is our focus.

[5] The only empirical study close to ours is Swenson (2005), who provides an econometric analysis that explains the number of BITs across countries in terms of per capita incomes, expropriation risk, and pre-existing levels of FDI stocks. However, the study is not motivated by a formal economic model and does not address the economic determinants emphasized in our study.

[6] Recent extensions of the model include, for example, Egger and Larch (2008), Chen and Joshi (2010), and Baldwin and Jaimovich (2012), who examined the role of "third-country PTAs" for explaining subsequent PTA formations and enlargements, and Bergstrand et al. (2011), who examined the role of several economic variables for the "timing" of PTA formations and enlargements.

[7] For instance, a dummy variable for common land border can – and does – have differential effects, since this variable tends to be positively correlated with trade flows but negatively correlated with FDI flows.

to three factors and three countries, and provide a ready framework to address the economic determinants of BITs and PTAs. BE is especially relevant because it is the first general equilibrium model to demonstrate that bilateral FDI *and* trade are maximized between countries with *identical* relative *and absolute* factor endowments, consistent with the large literature on gravity equations that explain very well both bilateral trade and FDI flows.[8] Thus, the first potential contribution of this paper is to use the theoretical framework in BE to generate new comparative statics to show (initially, in the absence of any relative factor endowment differences): (1) how economic size and size similarity of two countries influence their net utility gains (or losses) from a BIT and from a PTA; (2) how bilateral investment and trade costs between two countries influence such gains; and (3) how interactions among these factors influence these gains. Note that, in general equilibrium, the net utility gains from BITs and PTAs are influenced by the behavior of multinational enterprises as well as national (exporting) firms. In the presence of MNEs and general equilibrium, the influences of these economic variables on the net utility gains from a PTA are not *necessarily* the same as those found in BB, where MNEs and FDI were absent.

Second, in reality relative factor endowments are not identical across countries, and such differences matter for economic determinants of BITs because many BITs (not to mention PTAs) are "North–South" in nature, that is, between countries with quite different relative factor endowments.[9] The second potential contribution of this paper is to show the relationship using the BE model between relative factor endowment differences between two countries and the net utility gains from BITs and from PTAs. With three factors – skilled labor, unskilled labor, and physical capital – the relationships are complex. However, using traditional Edgeworth boxes and recent developments in specifying properly the relationships between relative factor endowments and bilateral FAS flows in Braconier et al. (2005), our theoretical relationships suggest easily specified empirical counterparts to capture some of the influences of relative factor endowment differences on the net utility gains from BITs and PTAs in the presence of national exporting firms, horizontal MNEs, and vertical MNEs.[10] Moreover, we examine the interactive effects of relative factor endowments and investment costs on utility gains from such agreements.

Third, guided by the theoretical comparative statics, we specify a bivariate probit model of the probabilities of BITs and PTAs existing between country pairs in the year 2000. We choose to estimate a bivariate probit model because the error terms may be correlated across probabilities, and this provides more efficient coefficient estimates. To anticipate some of the results, we find the following empirical conclusions. First, as much of trade is "intra-industry" and much of FDI is "horizontal," one would expect that the net utility gains from a BIT and from a PTA are positively related to economic size and similarity. Such results are confirmed here. Second, our theoretical model suggests that a higher initial level of expropriation risk should increase the gains from a BIT, and higher natural investment costs (such as political instability) should decrease the gains from a BIT. Our theoretical model also suggests that a higher initial level of expropriation risk should decrease the gains from a PTA, and higher natural investment costs should increase the gains from a PTA. Using measures of investment costs that should influence FDI and trade oppositely, we find evidence of these "substitution effects." Moreover, due to the non-linear probit model, we can estimate the sensitivity of the effects of investment costs on the probability of a BIT for a country-pair to their economic size. Third, in the presence of three factors of production, the relationships between relative factor endowments and net utility gains of a pair of countries from a BIT or a PTA are complex, non-linear, and non-monotonic. However, we draw upon the geometric features of an Edgeworth box to introduce a measure of dissimilarity of factor shares that helps explain the importance of relative abundance of skilled labor for increasing the net utility gains from a BIT for a country-pair.[11] Alongside another (more standard) measure of deviations of capital–unskilled-labor ratios from the Edgeworth box diagonal, we show empirically how relative factor endowments affect the probabilities of a BIT and of a PTA, and estimate the sensitivity of the effects of investment costs to relative factor endowments. Finally, the bivariate empirical model has a relatively high explanatory power that holds up to an extensive sensitivity analysis, including extensions to "third-country-pair" effects and lagged effects. Moreover, the inclusion of different relative factor endowment variables for the BIT and PTA equations allows for potential identification in a (recursive) simultaneous equations system, which we explore. Using our sample of 12,880 country-pairs in the year 2000, we predict correctly 88% of the 556 country-pairs with a BIT and a PTA, 81% of the 923 country-pairs with a BIT but no PTA, and 84% of the 1478 country-pairs with a PTA but no BIT. The overall pseudo-R^2 of 28% for our bivariate probit model is comparable to the 27% pseudo-R^2 found in Egger and Larch (2008) for PTAs using a univariate probit model and a similar large sample. The results provide quantitative guidance as to the determinants of BITs and PTAs simultaneously (and also sequentially) and to addressing potentially the endogeneity bias inherent in many previous empirical analyses of the effects of BITs on FDI flows.

The remainder of the paper is as follows. In Section 2, we summarize the theoretical BE model and the parameter values chosen for the numerical version of the general equilibrium model. In Section 3, we discuss the general equilibrium comparative static results for the relationships between the net utility gains from a BIT and from a PTA with economic size and similarity, investment costs, and trade costs, assuming identical relative factor endowments across countries. In Section 4, we relax the assumption of identical relative factor endowments and, using conventional Edgeworth boxes and their geometric properties, provide general equilibrium comparative statics to motivate two relative-factor-endowment variables for the empirical analysis. In Section 5, we describe our econometric methodology and data set. Section 6 provides the results from the bivariate probit empirical analysis, including the robustness analysis, marginal response probability estimates, and predicted probabilities. Section 7 concludes.

2. Theoretical framework: a summary of the Bergstrand and Egger (2007) Knowledge-and-Physical-Capital model

The model we use is the 3-country, 3-factor, 2-good Knowledge-and-Physical-Capital (KAPC) model in BE, an extension of the $2 \times 2 \times 2$ Knowledge–Capital (KC) model in Markusen et al. (1996), Carr et al. (2001), and Markusen (2002) to allow for a third factor (imperfectly mobile physical capital) and a third country (*ROW*). Since the theoretical model is identical to that in BE except for the introduction of a bilateral investment cost representing expropriation risk (g), we need not reproduce the model here. We summarize it briefly.[12]

[8] Blonigen and Piger (2011), using a Bayesian moving average statistical technique, have recently shown that the most important factors for explaining FDI flows are basic gravity equation variables, parent-country and host-country real GDPs and bilateral distance.

[9] The KC model first introduced relative endowments of skilled and unskilled labor into a model with only HMNEs to illustrate the simultaneous presence of vertical and horizontal FAS (cf., Markusen et al., 1996; Carr et al., 2001; Markusen and Maskus, 2002; Markusen, 2002).

[10] Blonigen and Piger (2011) show that – beyond parent- and host-country real GDPs and bilateral distance – the most important variables explaining FDI flows are parent real GDP per capita, parent *physical capital per worker*, relative skilled-labor endowments, common official language, urban concentration of the host country, and remoteness of the host country from *ROW*.

[11] Also, our model allows us to see how the effects of investment costs on utility gains from a BIT are sensitive to levels of relative factor endowments.

[12] See Bergstrand and Egger (2007) or the online supplement to this article for the theoretical model (Appendix A), the description of the calibration of the numerical version of the model (Appendix B), and supplementary figures (Appendix C).

110 J.H. Bergstrand, P. Egger / Journal of International Economics 90 (2013) 107–122

The demand side of the KAPC model is analogous to that in the KC model. Consumers have Cobb–Douglas preferences between a differentiated good and a homogeneous (numeraire) good and constant-elasticity-of-substitution preferences among differentiated goods. Differentiated products can be produced under monopolistic competition by national exporting firms potentially located in all countries, horizontal multinational enterprises (HMNEs) with headquarters and a plant in the home country and plants potentially in either of the other two countries to serve markets directly through foreign affiliate sales (FAS), and vertical multinational enterprises (VMNEs) with headquarters in the home country and a plant abroad which can produce for the local market and/or export to the other two markets.[13] Differentiated goods are produced using physical capital, skilled labor, and unskilled labor under increasing returns to scale with skilled labor used to set up headquarters and physical capital used to set up plants. Trade costs – both natural factors and government tariffs – are of the iceberg type. Investment costs are implied by ad valorem cost-of-capital markups on foreign plant setups. The KAPC model is distinguished from the KC model in two ways. First, there is no factor in the KC model to represent the *tangible* assets of firms; physical capital has been omitted from the KC model.[14] In reality, of course, national firms and MNEs use both (rival) private capital — often measured by financial claims to tangible assets such as physical capital at home or abroad, as well as (non-rival) knowledge capital — often associated with skilled labor. Hence, the KAPC model has private physical capital, the services of which can be used at home or transferred abroad (via FDI, and not necessarily costlessly) either as a "greenfield" investment or an acquisition (though only home capital is used in *production* alongside home skilled and unskilled labor).[15] The second distinction of the KAPC model from the KC model is a third country, *ROW*. The presence of *ROW* helps explain the observed complementarity of bilateral FAS and trade flows with respect to a country pair's economic size and similarity and that bilateral FDI and FAS tend empirically to be as well explained by gravity as are bilateral trade flows.

The complexity of the model (including the complementary-slackness conditions) introduces a high degree of nonlinearity, and the model cannot be solved analytically. As in BE, we provide numerical solutions to the model, requiring parameter choices. Utility and production function parameter values are identical to those in BE, as are the skilled labor costs to setup national firms' and MNEs' headquarters (MNE headquarter setups use 1% more skilled labor than national firms). Each home plant setup requires two units of capital, with foreign plants requiring an additional "natural" bilateral investment cost of 40% (representing, say, political instability, which a BIT cannot insure against) and a bilateral investment cost of 10% representing expropriation risk (which a BIT can insure against).[16] The ad valorem rate for natural international trade costs is 30 (45) percent for differentiated (homogeneous) products, following evidence in Bergstrand and Egger (2006), and ad valorem tariff rates are initially 20% (which are then removed by a PTA). The world endowment of physical capital is 500 units, of skilled labor is 200 units, and of unskilled labor is 2000 units; initially, country *i* has one-quarter of the world's endowment, country *j* has one-quarter, and *ROW* has one-half.[17] In Section 3, we assume no relative factor endowment differences (as in BE); in Section 4, we introduce relative factor endowment differences into the BE model (as present in the KC model). Distinct from BE (which assumed no relative factor endowment differences), the existence of relative factor endowment differences in the present paper creates VMNE activity as well as HMNE activity; Bergstrand and Egger (in press) show that both HMNEs and VMNEs are important in explaining bilateral foreign affiliate sales in the presence of relative factor endowment differences.[18]

3. Economic determinants of BITs and PTAs

In this section, we focus on eight theoretical results (summarized in four hypotheses), assuming that countries are identical in *relative* factor endowments. First, we address the relationship between economic (GDP) size and similarity for influencing the net utility gains from PTAs and BITs (four results). Second, we discuss the relationship between bilateral trade and investment costs for influencing such gains (four results). Finally, we discuss some interactive effects on these gains.

3.1. Economic size, economic similarity, and welfare gains from BITs and PTAs

We simulated the model under alternative scenarios of absolute factor endowments among three countries *i*, *j*, and *ROW*. The effect of a PTA was introduced between *i* and *j* by reducing the ad valorem tariff rate (b_{ij}) from 20% to 0%. It is standard in the PTA literature to consider theoretically the introduction of a PTA by reducing the tariff rate. Since BITs have not been analyzed yet in the context of the KC or KAPC models, we follow BE which assumed that an FDI barrier increased by some proportion the cost of capital needed for the FDI. In the KAPC model in BE, this barrier was γ; we have simply augmented that model's FDI barriers to include an additional ad valorem barrier g, representing expropriation risk, which the BIT removes. The effect of a BIT was introduced by reducing the ad valorem FDI barrier representing expropriation risk between *i* and *j* (g_{ij}) from 10% to 0%.[19]

---

[13] See Alfaro and Charlton (2009) for firm-level evidence on the co-existence of HMNEs and VMNEs.

[14] As noted earlier in footnote 8, Blonigen and Piger have found empirically that parent country physical capital per worker is an important determinant of bilateral FDI flows.

[15] Hence, in the KC model, skilled labor is immobile internationally, but the services of (non-rival) "knowledge capital" are (costlessly) mobile. In our model, this still holds, but additionally physical capital is immobile internationally, but the services of (rival) "financial capital" are internationally mobile for plant setups (with potential investment costs such as expropriation risk or political instability risk). Physical capital (*K*) in our model can just as easily be interpreted as financial equity claims on any tangible assets (other than knowledge). The key issue for our model is that there is another factor (*K*) that complements skilled labor (*S*) in production and that (rival) *K* is "used up" in the fixed costs of setting up a plant at home or abroad. One can also interpret physical capital as "putty" capital, with the fraction of home capital used in domestic production and the fraction that is used up in setting up plants at home and abroad as endogenously determined by the MNE's profit maximization decision.

[16] As noted in Salacuse and Sullivan (2005, pp. 86–87), "One of the primary functions of any BIT is to protect foreign investments against nationalization, expropriation, or other forms of interference with property rights by *host country governmental authorities*.... Many BITs also deal with losses to an investment due to armed conflict or internal disorder. However, they do *not normally establish a right to compensation*" (italics added). In the context of simulations conducted in BE, the introduction of the expropriation risk factor, g, of 10% would increase trade levels and reduce FDI and FAS levels, all else constant.

[17] For more details, see our online theoretical supplement.

[18] Recently, Ramondo and Rodriguez-Clare (in press) have introduced firm heterogeneity in a one-factor model of international trade and foreign affiliate sales with three countries using Eaton-Kortum (2002) type productivity distributions. They explore welfare gains using a numerical version of their theoretical model. Akin to Arkolakis et al. (2012) for (modern) "quantitative trade models," the welfare gains from trade-cost changes are a function of openness (import or FAS penetration) and the "trade-cost" elasticity. An important implication of Arkolakis et al. (2012) is that the welfare gains from trade-cost changes are insensitive to the presence or absence of firm heterogeneity (i.e., welfare gains are identical if the underlying model is Krugman, Eaton–Kortum, or Melitz, if the trade-cost elasticity value is identical). The Ramondo–Rodriguez-Clare model shares common elements to the KAPC model here, including: (i) existence of national firms; (ii) existence of HMNE activity; (iii) existence of VMNE activity; (iv) a third-country allowing "export-platform" FDI; and (v) a modification of the effects of trade costs on trade and FAS flows and welfare due to the existence of HMNEs and VMNEs. Thus, the theoretical welfare analyses of trade-cost changes in Arkolakis et al. (2012) for "quantitative trade models" and that in Ramondo and Rodriguez-Clare (in press) suggest that the welfare gains from BITs or PTAs implied by our model might be insensitive to the presence or absence of firm-heterogeneity.

[19] The original motivation for BITs is the insurance for the capital exporter against expropriation "risk" in the capital importing country. "Risk," of course, raises the relative cost of capital for investing abroad. In the context of the model, our ad valorem factor g raises the cost of capital, $r_i(1+\gamma_{ij}+g_{ij})$, of the capital exporting country in the host country. A BIT, by insuring the capital exporter against this risk, eliminates g; see our online theoretical supplement Appendix A equations (8b)–(8d). A recent paper by Moser and Rose (2011) provides event-study evidence on "excess returns to capital" created by announcements of PTAs; by analogy, such a methodology could also be applied to BITs.

Fig. 2A and B presents the results of the utility change for countries i and j from their forming alternatively a PTA and a BIT, respectively, depending upon their joint economic size (y-axis) and their similarity of economic size (x-axis). The z-axis represents the utility change for *both* i and j from their forming the agreement.[20] The y-axis is the sum of the GDPs of countries i and j, i.e., their "joint economic size." The lines on the y-axis are indexed from 1 to 1.7. The y-axis indexes country-pairs' GDPs from the smallest joint GDP (line 1) to the largest joint GDP (line 1.7).[21] The x-axis is indexed from 0.45 to 0.55. Each line represents i's share of both countries' GDPs, where the center line represents 50% or identical GDP shares for i and j, i.e., "similarity in economic size."

Hypothesis 1. The net utility gain from (and likelihood of) a PTA and of a BIT between i and j is a positive function of their joint economic sizes.

Consider Fig. 2A first. When i and j have identical relative factor endowments, all bilateral trade is intra-industry exports of national enterprises (NEs). Consequently, when two countries are larger, there will be a larger volume of intra-industry trade of NEs (and associated larger number of varieties produced and consumed), since there are no VMNEs. The formation of a PTA will then reduce bilateral trade costs on a larger volume of trade for two larger countries, and consequently increase the utility gains more for both countries relative to two smaller countries, similar to that in BB in the absence of MNEs. As established in BE, national firms can *coexist* with HMNEs when both countries are identical in absolute (and relative) factor endowments and trade costs. In the qualitative choice framework used later, this result suggests that the probability of a PTA between i and j increases with their economic size (for a given *ROW* GDP).

Fig. 2B shows the relationship between the economic size of i and j and the utility gain from a BIT. When i and j have identical relative factor endowments as currently assumed, there are HMNEs in equilibrium, but no VMNEs, consistent with BE. All FDIs (and FAS) are intra-industry. Consequently, when two countries are larger, there will be a larger volume of horizontal FDI. The formation of a BIT will then reduce bilateral investment costs on a larger volume of FDI for two larger countries (and associated larger number of varieties produced and consumed), and consequently increase the utility gains more for both countries relative to two smaller countries. This increases the probability of a BIT between i and j (for given *ROW* GDP).[22]

Hypothesis 2. The net utility gain from (and likelihood of) a BIT and of a PTA between i and j is a positive function of the similarity in their economic sizes.

The economic rationale is based upon similar intra-industry reasoning. Consider Fig. 2A first. We know from BE that – for a given total economic size of i and j – bilateral trade (and the numbers of varieties traded) will be maximized when the two countries have identical absolute factor endowments. All trade will be intra-industry. Hence, the gains from a PTA are larger the more similar their GDPs are, as in BB in the absence of MNEs.

A similar though not identical economic rationale holds for BITs (cf., Fig. 2B). Intuitively, suppose i had all of the two countries' (is and js) GDP. Then there would be no reason for i to set up an affiliated plant in j, and consequently there would be no economic gain from forming

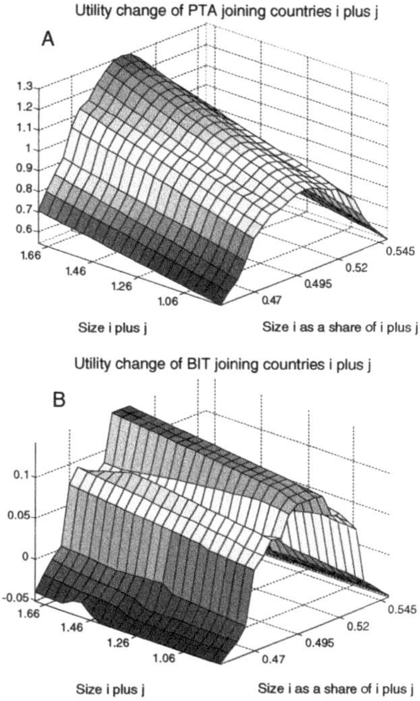

Fig. 2. A. Utility change of PTA joining countries i plus j. B. Utility change of BIT joining countries i plus j.

a BIT. However, as shown in BE, the bilateral volume of FDI from i to j is not maximized when both countries have the same economic size. Yet, because of the symmetry of horizontal FDI flows from i to j and from j to i, the total number of HMNEs (and consequently varieties available) to consumers in i and j will be maximized when the two countries have identical absolute factor endowments. Consequently, the gains from a BIT will be maximized when the two countries have identical sizes. However, we note that because gross bilateral trade flows are maximized at identical GDP sizes but bilateral FDI flows are not, the theoretical relationship between similarity and gains from a BIT is not as strong as that for a PTA. Consequently, we expect the estimated marginal effect (in our probit analysis) of GDP similarity on the probability of a BIT to be *smaller* than that of a PTA.

3.2. Investment costs, trade costs, and welfare gains from BITs and PTAs

Fig. 3A and B presents the results of the utility change for two identical countries (i, j) from introducing alternatively a PTA between i and j and a BIT between i and j, respectively, at various values of natural trade (τ_{ij}) and natural investment (γ_{ij}) costs. First, we provide a brief explanation of the axes for these two figures. The "vertical" axis (or z-axis) represents the net utility gain (or, if negative, loss) for countries i and j from introducing either a PTA (cf., Fig. 3A) or a BIT between i and j (cf., Fig. 3B). The y-axis is labeled from 1 to 1.13

[20] We assume the existence of transfers between the two countries' governments so that the relevant consideration is the sum of the two countries' representative consumers' utilities for the social planner.

[21] See Bergstrand and Egger (2007) on determination of relative GDP sizes; the dispersion is based upon empirical GDP data.

[22] Note that the simultaneous gains in utility from a BIT and a PTA for two countries with identical absolute and relative factor endowments are not possible in the $2\times2\times2$ KC model because intra-industry trade is zero, as shown in BE.

112 J.H. Bergstrand, P. Egger / Journal of International Economics 90 (2013) 107–122

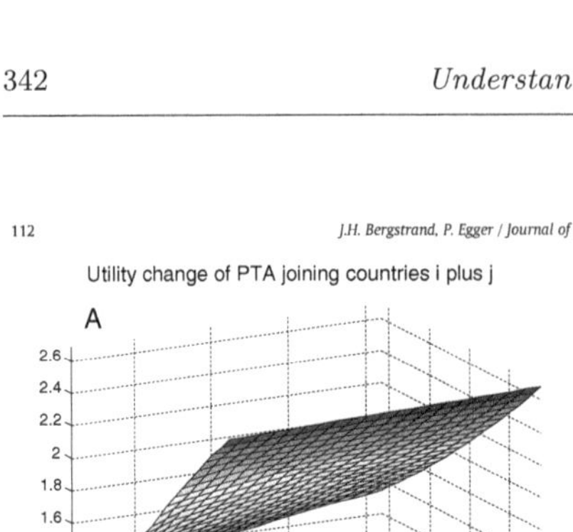

Fig. 3. A. Utility change of PTA joining countries *i* plus *j*. B. Utility change of BIT joining countries *i* plus *j*.

and represents the gross bilateral natural trade cost from *i* to *j*, τ_{ij}; $\tau = 1$ implies zero natural trade cost. The *x*-axis is labeled from 0.4 to 0.8 and represents a bilateral natural FDI investment cost, γ_{ij}, such as "political instability." A higher value of γ_{ij} represents a higher risk premium (added to the cost of capital) in ad valorem terms for an MNE with a headquarters in *i* to invest in *j*.[23] As above, the BIT between *i* and *j*, or BIT_{ij}, is captured by a reduction of the investment cost representing expropriation risk between *i* and *j* (g_{ij}) from 10% to zero.[24] The PTA between *i* and *j*, or PTA_{ij}, is captured by a reduction of the tariff rate between *i* and *j* (b_{ij}) from 20% to zero.

Hypothesis 3. The net utility gain from (and likelihood of) a PTA between *i* and *j* is a negative function of their natural bilateral trade costs and a positive function of their natural bilateral investment costs.

[23] The selection of "political instability" as an important foreign direct investment cost is motivated partly by evidence of a strong empirical negative (positive) relationship between political instability and FDI (trade) flows established in Berden et al. (2011).

[24] The higher the level of expropriation risk, the larger the net utility gains from a BIT, other things constant.

Consider first the negative relationship between the gains to countries *i* and *j* of PTA_{ij} and "natural" trade costs between *i* and *j* (τ_{ij}) established in BB, and shown here in Fig. 3A. Common examples of "natural" bilateral trade costs (from the large trade gravity equation literature) are the absence of a common land border and absence of a common language. As shown in BB, a low value of natural trade costs (such as the presence of a common land border) between *i* and *j* – other things the same – implies a high value of bilateral trade. Consequently, a given reduction in the bilateral tariff rate between *i* and *j* will lead to a large increase in bilateral trade and a large gain in utility for *i* and *j*. Hence, larger natural bilateral trade costs reduce the net utility gains from and likelihood of PTA_{ij}.

Consider now the "cross-price" effect. A higher natural bilateral investment cost between *i* and *j* will tend to reduce bilateral FDI between *i* and *j*, but increase bilateral trade between *i* and *j*.[25] Thus, a PTA between *i* and *j* will liberalize a larger volume of trade the higher the natural bilateral investment costs, leading to a larger net utility gain for *i* and *j*, and increasing the likelihood of PTA_{ij} (cf., Fig. 3A). Hence, the likelihood of PTA_{ij} is higher the larger the natural bilateral investment costs (such as political instability).[26]

Hypothesis 4. The net utility gain from (and likelihood of) a BIT between *i* and *j* is a negative function of their natural bilateral investment costs and a positive function of their natural bilateral trade costs.

Consider now the relationship between the gains for *i* and *j* from BIT_{ij} and natural bilateral investment costs (γ_{ij}), shown in Fig. 3B. Using political instability again as a "natural" bilateral investment cost, a higher degree of political instability in host country *j* leads to a lower level of bilateral FDI from *i* to *j*. Since FDI is lower, the gains to FDI_{ij} from BIT_{ij} are lower. Hence, the net utility gains from and likelihood of BIT_{ij} are lower the higher the degree of political instability in *j*.

Consider now the "cross-price" effect. A higher natural bilateral trade cost between *i* and *j* will tend to reduce bilateral trade between *i* and *j*, but increase bilateral FDI between *i* to *j*.[27] While for most country pairs, bilateral FDI flows in reality tend to be large when the countries' bilateral trade flows are large as in BE, FDI and trade are substitutes with respect to relative price effects. Thus, a BIT between *i* and *j* will liberalize a larger volume of FDI the higher are the countries' bilateral trade costs, leading to a larger net utility gain for *i* and *j*, and increasing the likelihood of BIT_{ij} (cf., Fig. 3B). Hence, the net utility gains from and likelihood of BIT_{ij} are larger the higher the natural bilateral trade costs.

3.3. Interactions

The effects of natural investment costs (γ_{ij}) and the initial level of expropriation risk (g_{ij}) on the utility gains from a BIT (or PTA) are likely to be sensitive to country-pairs' economic characteristics, such as their GDP size, GDP similarity, or natural trade costs (τ_{ij}). Our theoretical model allows for such interactions. For instance, suppose a pair of countries *ij* are larger in absolute factor endowments than pair *kl*; pair *ij* will have more bilateral FDI (and FAS) than pair *kl*. Suppose pair *ij* also faces lower natural investment costs γ (or higher initial level of expropriation risk, *g*) than pair *kl*. Then a BIT between pair *ij* is likely to lead to larger utility gains than that between pair *kl* not just due to lower γ (or higher *g*) but that effect interacted with pair *ij*'s larger economic size. This theoretical conclusion is confirmed using the numerical model (figure not

[25] Recall that, in this section, all FDI is horizontal. Since relative factor endowments are assumed identical between *i* and *j*, there are no VMNEs (and consequently no VMNE exports from foreign plants). If relative factor endowment differences existed (as in Section 4 later), then the increase in bilateral trade may be diminished by less VMNE activity.

[26] PTAs are assumed here to be trade agreements only, with no FDI provisions. We address this issue later in the empirical analysis.

[27] As for Hypothesis 3, we are assuming only horizontal FDI.

shown).[28] We will evaluate this and other interactions later in the non-linear bivariate probit empirical analysis based upon estimated marginal effects.

4. Relative factor endowments and determinants of BITS and PTAs

4.1. Relative factor endowments hypotheses

As noted in the BIT literature, most BITs are between developed and developing countries, motivated initially (in the late 1950s) by the risk of expropriation. Consequently, relative factor endowment differences may well be influential in the likelihood of a BIT between a country-pair. We now allow relative factor endowments to vary between countries and consider the net utility gains (or losses) from either a PTA or a BIT. For tractability, we use the traditional Edgeworth box to illustrate our results. However, an Edgeworth box is designed to illustrate the impacts in a world with two countries and two factors. In our three-factor setting, we are taking a "slice" of an Edgeworth cube for the two countries. For instance, if we consider two factors, physical capital (K) and unskilled labor (U), there is a continuum of such slices for the various values of s_i – the share of i's and j's skilled labor (S) in country i. Let k_i (u_i) denote country i's share of i's and j's physical capital (unskilled labor) endowment. For illustration below, we will examine the relationship between the utility gains for i and j from PTA_{ij} with k_i and u_i at $s_i=0.5$; similarly, we will examine the relationship between the utility gains for i and j from BIT_{ij} with k_i and u_i at $s_i=0.5$.[29] Also, since we are operating in a three-country world, we are examining these relationships for a *given* endowment of factors K, S and U in the *ROW*. Of course, the Edgeworth box relationships are quantitatively sensitive to the economic size of and relative factor endowments in *ROW*.[30]

Hypothesis 5. The net utility gain from (and likelihood of) a PTA between i and j is decreasing in the difference of the two countries' ratios of physical capital to unskilled labor.

It is well established that a PTA between a pair of countries should increase trade between them. However, it *may not* be the case that the welfare of the country-pair is enhanced from this PTA – especially if the pair has large differences in physical capital–unskilled labor endowment ratios. Baier and Bergstrand (2004) showed in a world excluding MNEs that the welfare benefits from PTA_{ij} were positive in relative factor endowment differences, up to a point, based upon traditional comparative advantage interacted with trade costs.[31] While that study's empirical results supported that result, Egger and Larch (2008) found in a much larger sample that wider relative capital–unskilled labor ratios had a negative marginal effect on the likelihood of a PTA. The model here can help to explain this latter result.

Fig. 4A illustrates the utility gain to i and j from PTA_{ij}. The prominent aspect of this figure is that the two countries' utility gains are decreasing in larger differences in their K/U ratios. Our model can explain this, drawing once again on changes in the activities of NEs, HMNEs, and VMNEs. Note initially that when i and j have identical shares of all three factors, pure intra-industry trade of NEs will be maximized (cf., Fig. 4B; middle of the diagram). With a large amount of bilateral intra-industry trade, a PTA causes a large increase in trade between them, consistent with net utility gains at the center of Fig. 4A. Moreover, the increase in the volume of trade due to a PTA is also very large if countries i and j have very *different* K/U ratios (cf., Fig. 4B), consistent with a PTA benefiting traditional Heckscher–Ohlin trade, as in Baier and Bergstrand (2004).[32]

However, in our context with MNEs also, the utility gains on net from PTA_{ij} may in fact be a *negative* function of relative K/U ratios for i and j because of a large loss of HMNEs' varieties (and consequently utility) when K/U ratios of i and j are vastly different. The number of HMNEs is maximized when countries i and j are identical. With wider relative K/U ratios, there will be fewer HMNEs in i and j (and demand will be met more by NEs). The loss in volume of the relatively few varieties produced by HMNEs with PTA_{ij} – see Fig. 4C – causes a greater loss of utility for i or j when K/U ratios are very large than the gain in utility for trading large volumes of the varieties of goods produced by NEs (see Fig. 4B).

Moreover, VMNE activity cannot offset these welfare losses. There is little change in the volume of VMNE activity from PTA_{ij}.[33] Consequently, the large utility loss from the decline in production of the few HMNEs in i or j in the presence of large K/U ratio differences offsets the utility gains from trading more of NEs' outputs following a PTA, suggesting that the probability of a PTA between i and j – in the context of MNEs – may fall the greater the K/U endowment ratio differences between the two countries, as stated in Hypothesis 5.

Hypothesis 6. The net utility gain from (and likelihood of) a BIT between i and j is increasing in the abundance of skilled labor relative to physical capital and unskilled labor in i or j.

Fig. 5A presents the relationships between the utility gains for i and j from BIT_{ij} with k_i and u_i, at $s_i=0.5$. Fig. 5A suggests that the net utility gains for i and j from BIT_{ij} are maximized when either i or j has a very small amount of the two countries' K and U, given $s_i=0.5$ (that is, i or j is very skilled labor abundant). Intuitively, the benefits of BIT_{ij} will be greater the larger the FDI/FAS created by the BIT. FAS will be larger with greater numbers of vertical MNEs (VMNEs) and horizontal MNEs (HMNEs). VMNEs and HMNEs will be prominent when skilled labor is abundant relative to physical capital and to unskilled labor, because such a country would have a comparative advantage in setting up headquarters (which are S intensive) and a comparative disadvantage in production at home (low K and U for plant setups and production). Hence, the benefits from a BIT between i and j should be maximized when either i or j is abundant in S relative to K and U (note that the utility gains are maximized near the two countries' origins, given $s_i=s_j=0.5$).[34]

---

[28] Due to page constraints, we can only present here some of the numerical simulations; others are available from the authors. Yet, later we show explicitly theoretical interaction effects between relative factor endowments, γ_{ij}, and g_{ij}.

[29] Empirically, for the data set used later the actual means of s_i, u_i, and k_i all range between 0.53 and 0.56, so using $s_i=0.5$ is a feasible choice.

[30] In the simulations below, we assume for *ROW* that its endowments of K, S and U are exactly one-half of the world's endowments and that trade and investment costs in the benchmark equilibrium are the same between i and j as they are between either of these countries and the *ROW*.

[31] Baier and Bergstrand (2004) showed a quadratic relationship, both theoretically and empirically.

[32] Hence, bilateral trade of NEs is very large when countries i and j are identical in absolute and relative factor endowments (i.e., intra-industry trade) *or* when the two countries have very different K/U ratios (i.e., inter-industry trade).

[33] Omitted figure for VMNE activity confirms this.

[34] We can confirm using additional figures of the numbers of VMNEs and HMNEs headquartered in i and j that both countries benefit the most from a BIT when i or j is very skilled labor abundant. It is important to note that when k_i and u_i are small, k_j and u_j are large by construction ($k_i=1-k_j$). Also, when k_i and u_i are small, they are small relative to s_i (since $s_i=s_j=0.5$ in Fig. 4A), implying that i is relatively abundant in skilled labor, and consequently has a comparative advantage in setting up an MNE and benefitting from a BIT. Alternatively, when k_j and u_j are small, they are small relative to s_j, implying that j is relatively abundant in skilled labor, and consequently has a comparative advantage in setting up an MNE and benefitting from a BIT. Thus, the potential gains from a BIT are maximized when either i or j is abundant in skilled labor relative to physical capital and unskilled labor. Economically, consider initially the center of Fig. 5A when $k_i=u_i=s_i=0.5$. As k_i and u_i decrease (and we move toward the near origin), the relative abundance of skilled labor makes multi-plant HMNEs headquartered in i profitable (because HMNE headquarters (plants) setups require skilled labor (physical capital)), increasing the utility gain from BIT_{ij}. However, as k_i and u_i decrease further, multi-plant HMNEs based in i become less profitable (because of relative physical capital scarcity), but single-plant VMNEs based in i become profitable. The omitted Appendix C figures C1 and C2, available in an online supplement, confirm this.

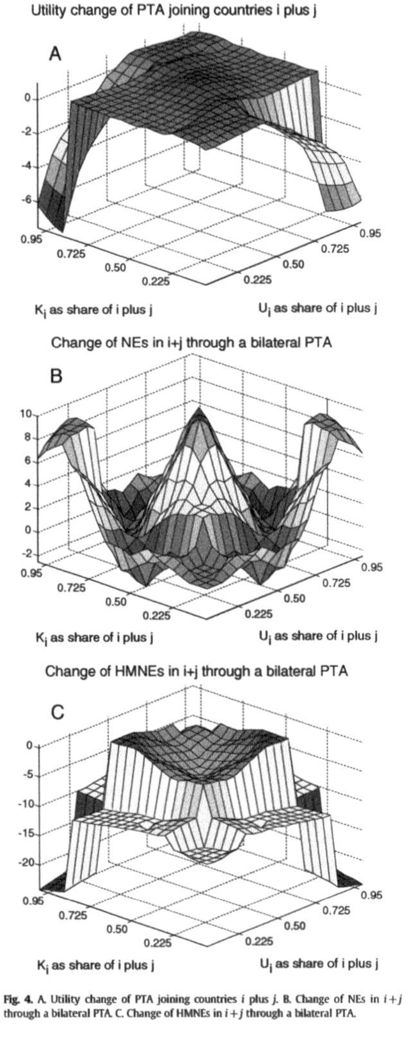

Fig. 4. A. Utility change of PTA joining countries i plus j. B. Change of NEs in $i+j$ through a bilateral PTA. C. Change of HMNEs in $i+j$ through a bilateral PTA.

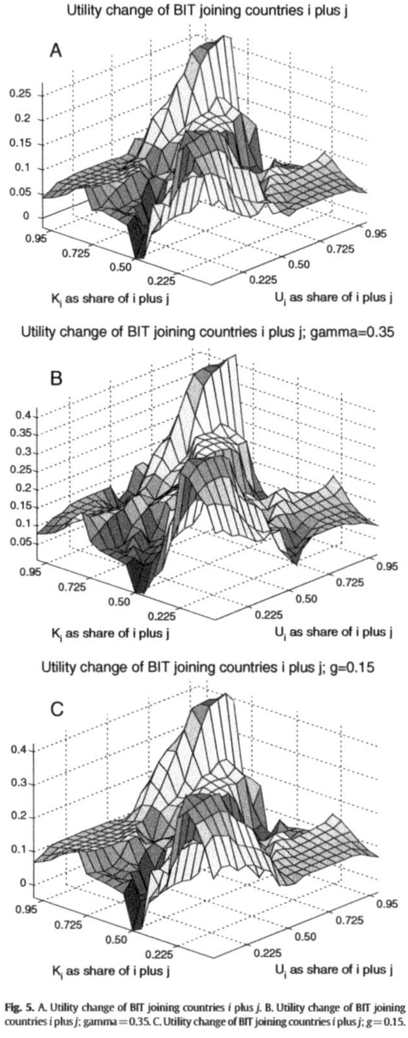

Fig. 5. A. Utility change of BIT joining countries i plus j. B. Utility change of BIT joining countries i plus j; gamma = 0.35. C. Utility change of BIT joining countries i plus j; $g = 0.15$.

4.2. Interactions

In anticipation of our empirical analysis later which examines – among other things – the *sensitivity* of some variables' effects on the probability of a BIT (or PTA) to countries' economic characteristics (i.e., interactions), we provide two more numerical theoretical results. First, the effect of relative skilled abundance in i (or j) on the gains from a BIT between i and j is sensitive to the level of natural bilateral investment costs (γ_{ij}). If natural investment costs are lower (say, $\gamma_{ij}=0.35$, rather than 0.40), FDI from i to j and j to i, and the gains from a BIT, will not only be larger, but are disproportionately larger for skilled labor abundant countries. Fig. 5B confirms this by showing the relationship between k_i, u_i, and the gains from BIT_{ij}, at $s_i=0.5$, at a *lower* value of $\gamma_{ij}=0.35$ than in Fig. 5A (where $\gamma_{ij}=0.40$). A comparison of Fig. 5B with Fig. 5A shows that the gains from BIT_{ij} increase disproportionately more when either i is very skilled labor abundant or j is (at either of the countries' origins). Economically, the benefits of BIT_{ij} should be larger, when there are lower natural investment costs, the more skilled labor abundant is i (or j) because i (or j) would headquarter more MNEs.

Second, the effect of relative skill abundance of i or j on the gains from BIT_{ij} should be larger the higher the initial level of expropriation risk (g_{ij}). If expropriation risk is higher, the gains from a BIT between i and j are higher, but should be disproportionately higher if i (or j) is relatively skilled abundant, since i (or j) would be headquartering more MNEs. Fig. 5C confirms this, showing that the gains from BIT_{ij} are disproportionately larger if one country is very skilled labor abundant when g_{ij} is 0.15 initially (examining at either origin), rather than 0.10 (see Fig. 5A).

4.3. Measuring influences of relative factor endowments

Since the Edgeworth surfaces are handy, we address briefly the method for which we will capture empirically the influence of relative K/U ratios of i and j on the likelihood of PTA_{ij}, in the context of our theoretical model. First, as in Braconier et al. (2005), we want this measure of relative factor endowment differences to capture as precisely as possible the relationships between relative factor endowment shares as shown in the figures. Consequently, the absolute difference in the natural logs of k_i/u_i and k_j/u_j captures deviations of relative factor endowments from the NW–SE diagonal in Fig. 4A (where i's origin is the SW corner); in the regressions later, we use specifically $KURatio_{ij}\equiv|\ln(k_i/u_i)-\ln(k_j/u_j)|$.

By contrast, measuring the difference in economic size *along* the SW–NE diagonal in Fig. 5A (from i's origin to j's origin) has not been done traditionally in the international trade literature using factor-endowment shares. Typically, similarity in economic size is captured by variables such as $sh_i sh_j$, discussed in BE, where sh_i is the share of country i's GDP in the sum of countries' i's and j's GDPs. However, one cannot just use $sh_i sh_j$ to capture the difference in endowments of both K and U along the SW–NE diagonal in Fig. 5A. The reason is that – when k_i and u_i are very small – s_i in Fig. 5A is *still* 0.5; hence in an Edgeworth box, variation in k_i and u_i along the diagonal changes *relative* factor endowments as well. However, there is a way to capture variation along the SW–NE diagonal in Fig. 5A (for a given s_i). Using the geometric properties of the Edgeworth box, variation in the diagonal is captured by a variable, $KUDiff_{ij}$:

$$KUDiff_{ij}\equiv\ln\left|\left(k_i^2+u_i^2\right)^{1/2}\mu-\left(k_j^2+u_j^2\right)^{1/2}\mu\right|, \tag{1}$$

where

$$\mu\equiv\frac{1}{\left(k_i^2+u_i^2\right)^{1/2}+\left(k_j^2+u_j^2\right)^{1/2}}.$$

A rise in $KUDiff_{ij}$ reflects a wider difference in k_i *and* u_i relative to k_j *and* u_j, for given s_i. We expect $KUDiff_{ij}$ to be positively related to the probability of a BIT.

We provide no other hypotheses regarding the effects of relative factor endowments. Examination of the analogous comparative statics in S–U space and in K–S space yielded no clear empirically "testable" relationships between relative factor endowments and the utility gains or losses from a BIT or PTA.[35] Moreover, it will be important later for econometric purposes that BIT is likely related to $KUDiff_{ij}$ but not to $KURatio_{ij}$, and vice-versa for PTA. This satisfies the necessary *exclusion restriction* for estimating a simultaneous equation system in the robustness analysis later. Finally, in order to evaluate Hypotheses 5 and 6 holding constant s_i and $s_j=(1-s_i)$, we include the variable $Ssim_{ij}$ defined as:

$$Ssim_{ij}\equiv\ln s_i+\ln(1-s_i) \tag{2}$$

as a control variable.

5. Econometric specification and data description

5.1. Econometric specification

Similar to Baier and Bergstrand (2004), the econometric framework employed is a qualitative choice model. A qualitative choice model can be derived from an underlying latent variable model. In this paper, we consider a bivariate probit model because of possible correlation among the error terms. Let the underlying latent variable for BIT be denoted y_1^* and for PTA be denoted y_2^*. Let y_1^* (y_2^*) represent the difference in utility levels from having a BIT (PTA), where

$$y_{1ij}^*=\mathbf{x}_{1ij}\beta_1+e_{1ij} \tag{3}$$

$$y_{2ij}^*=\mathbf{x}_{2ij}\beta_2+e_{2ij}, \tag{4}$$

where $\mathbf{x}_{1ij}$ ($\mathbf{x}_{2ij}$) denotes a vector of explanatory variables (i.e., economic characteristics) of country-pair ij including a constant, β_1 (β_2) is a vector of parameters, and error terms e_{1ij} and e_{2ij} are assumed to be independent of $\mathbf{x}_{1ij}$ and $\mathbf{x}_{2ij}$, but possibly correlated with each other, and to have a bivariate normal distribution. In the context of the model formally, $y_{1ij}^*=\Delta U_{1i}+\Delta U_{1j}$ where ΔU_{1i} (ΔU_{1j}) denotes the change in utility for the representative consumer in i (j) from a BIT, and analogously for PTA. We are assuming implicitly the existence of transfers between the two countries' governments so that the relevant consideration is that the sum of the utility changes of the two countries' representative consumers needs to be positive for their governments to form a BIT or PTA.

Since y_{1ij}^* and y_{2ij}^* are unobservable, we define an indicator variable BIT_{ij}, which assumes the value 1 if the two countries have a BIT and 0 otherwise, and an indicator variable PTA_{ij}, which assumes the value 1 if the two countries have a PTA and 0 otherwise, with the response probabilities:

$$Pr\left(BIT_{ij}=1,PTA_{ij}=1\right)=\Phi_B\left(\mathbf{x}_{1ij}\beta_1,\mathbf{x}_{2ij}\beta_2,\rho\right), \tag{5}$$

where $\Phi_B(\cdot)$ denotes the bivariate normal distribution and ρ captures the covariance between the vectors of disturbances $\mathbf{e}_1$ and $\mathbf{e}_2$, $Cov(\mathbf{e}_1,\mathbf{e}_2)$ (see Greene, 1997, ch. 19).[36] In this study, we are concerned with the determination of four probabilities, $Pr(BIT_{ij}=1, PTA_{ij}=1)$, $Pr(BIT_{ij}=1, PTA_{ij}=0)$, $Pr(BIT_{ij}=0, PTA_{ij}=1)$, and $Pr(BIT_{ij}=0, PTA_{ij}=0)$, depending on economic (and some political) fundamentals.

Notice that the model in Eq. (5) is nonlinear. Hence, none of the covariates included in $\mathbf{x}_{1ij}$ will display a linear effect on the response probabilities (see Greene, 1997). This feature means that there is no explicit need to include interactive terms or other nonlinear terms in the model per se (see Greene, 2010). Inclusion of interactive terms or powers of variables actually renders the interpretation of coefficients difficult (see Ai and Norton, 2003; Greene, 2010). However,

[35] See online supplement Appendix C, figures C3–C6.

[36] In a sensitivity analysis later, we consider a 3SLS estimation of two linear probability models with endogenous explanatory variables as well as a (recursive) simultaneous equations probit model as possible alternatives to the bivariate probit model.

we can and do calculate marginal response probabilities later to quantify interactive effects of variables.

5.2. Data description

A general equilibrium model such as the one outlined earlier is mainly informative about long-run economic relationships. Therefore, as in BB we use cross-section data to infer the aforementioned hypotheses. These data capture the state of BITs and PTAs as of the year 2000 and use explanatory variables which are averages of the five years prior to the year 2000. With regard to the dependent and independent variables, we use data from the following sources.

First, information on BITs in force as of 2000 was collected from the United Nations Conference on Trade and Development (UNCTAD). We use this information to define a binary variable BIT_{ij}, which is unity if countries i and j had a BIT in force by the end of the year 2000 and zero otherwise. Second, we collected data on preferential trade agreements (customs unions, free trade areas, and other preferential trade agreements) from the World Trade Organization (WTO) and individual countries' sources. On the basis of that data, we defined an indicator variable PTA_{ij}, which is unity whenever two countries i and j had a preferential trade agreement in force (either under or outside of the auspices of the WTO) and zero otherwise. It is the case that some of the PTAs in our sample are actually preferential trade *and investment* agreements (PTIAs), such as the European Union (EU) and NAFTA. Since our dependent variable for BITs is actual bilateral investment treaties, investment liberalizations covered under "trade" agreements are not included in our BITs' dependent variable. For instance, for Germany and France – members of the European Union – PTA_{ij} is recorded as a 1 whereas BIT_{ij} is recorded as a 0. To use in a robustness check later, we also constructed an alternative measure of BIT_{ij} termed $AdjBIT_{ij}$. This alternative "adjusted" variable includes also any country-pairs with bilateral investment provisions "akin to a BIT" that are within any country-pairs' PTIAs. In this regard, we modified 108 "0s" to "1s" of the BIT variable to capture the influence of investment agreements in the EU and in NAFTA as representing BITs. We compare the empirical results using the alternative BIT variables later; essentially, the results are materially the same using the alternative variables.[37]

Third, data on a number of economic fundamentals such as real GDP in US dollars (GDP_i), labor force (L_i), and gross fixed capital formation at constant US dollars of 2000 (K_i) were taken from the World Bank's World Development Indicators (2005). These variables were used to construct the following determinants for our analysis: (i) a measure of bilateral economic size, $GDPSum_{ij} = \ln(GDP_i + GDP_j)$; (ii) a measure of similarity in bilateral economic size, $GDPSim_{ij} = \ln[sh_i(1 - sh_i)]$; and (iii) capital endowments of country i, K_i, and, in turn, the variable $k_i = K_i/(K_i + K_j)$.[38]

Fourth, data on skilled workers (S) come from a new database constructed by researchers at the World Population Program of the International Institute for Applied Systems Analysis (IIASA) which establishes panel data on attained education of the average workers in a comparable way for 120 countries (see Lutz et al., 2008). These data serve to distinguish between high-skilled workers (S) and low-skilled workers (U) in four education categories. We classify workers in education categories 3 and 4 (corresponding to upper secondary and tertiary education) as highly-skilled ones and workers with lower levels of attained education (categories 1 and 2) as unskilled workers. This obtains s_i and u_i as measures of i's share of skilled and unskilled workers, respectively, between i and j. Furthermore, we use s_i to construct $Ssim_{ij}$ to hold constant relative endowments of skilled workers between two countries i and j in some of the empirical specifications later (see above for theoretical rationale).

Fifth, we use data from CEPII on the distance between economic centers of countries ($Distance_{ij}$), a common land border indicator ($Adjacency_{ij}$), and a common language indicator ($Language_{ij}$). We use bilateral distance not only to measure $Distance_{ij}$ but also to construct a measure of remoteness ($REMOTE_{ij}$) of country-pair ij from the rest of the world. The latter is constructed as an average distance of i and j from all other countries, as in Baier and Bergstrand (2004) and Egger and Larch (2008). The variables $Adjacency_{ij}$ and $Language_{ij}$ are typically found in trade gravity equations, as measures of *inverse* bilateral trade costs, e.g., two adjacent countries have lower trade costs. Hence, we expect both of these to be negatively related to τ_{ij} (natural bilateral trade costs).

Sixth, we also need proxies for natural bilateral investment costs (γ_{ij}) – which cannot be removed by a BIT – and for the bilateral investment cost representing expropriation risk (g_{ij}). The literature on FDI determinants suggests that political instability in a host country is associated with lower FDI; we use this as a proxy for natural bilateral investment costs γ_{ij}. BERI publishes data on countries' political risk. We define $PolStab_{ij}$ such that a higher level measures greater political *stability* in the less stable of the two countries i and j; hence, like for our trade-cost variables, we are proxying for the *inverse* of γ_{ij}. BERI also provides data on expropriation risk. We define $IExpRisk_{ij}$ such that a higher level measures *less* expropriation risk in the riskier one of two countries i and j for investments between them. Hence, like above, we are proxying for the *inverse* of g_{ij}. Hence, our investment-cost variables $PolStab_{ij}$ and $IExpRisk_{ij}$ are negatively related to γ_{ij} and g_{ij}, respectively.[39]

Seventh, as addressed in Egger and Larch (2008), the probability of a country-pair having a PTA in the year 2000 may be influenced by the degree of "PTA interdependence." That is, Baldwin's "domino effects" (Baldwin, 1993) may cause the existence of PTAs of i and j with "third countries" to influence the net welfare gains from and likelihood of the pair having a PTA; Egger and Larch (2008) demonstrated the significance of this interdependence. To address this, we also constructed for every country-pair a (ten-year-lagged) index of "third-country PTAs." We also constructed for each pair a similar index of "third-country BITs." Also, as addressed in BB and Egger and Larch (2008), the welfare gains from and probability of PTA_{ij} are larger the more "remote" the pair ij is from the *ROW* (other third-country-pairs). We also constructed $REMOTE_{ij}$, as defined in BB, which is an index of how remote (using bilateral distances) pair ij is from other countries.

Table 2 presents summary statistics for all the variables used in this study.

6. Empirical results

6.1. Main empirical results

Table 3 presents the main empirical results based on seemingly unrelated bivariate probit models for BITs and PTAs. These models allow for correlation of BIT_{ij} and PTA_{ij} through two sources: (i) the observed determinants of such agreements as included in the specification of the latent process determining bivariate binary outcomes,[40]

[37] Both BIT_{ij} and PTA_{ij} are constructed for each country-pair. If a country was part of a plurilateral agreement, this did not affect the variable's construction. Also, whether a country was a member of the WTO or not had no bearing on the determination of PTA_{ij} or BIT_{ij}.

[38] We calculate K_i by using the perpetual inventory method, following Leamer (1984). For this, we calculate an initial stock of capital for year 0 in each country i, $K_{i0} = \sum_{t=-5}^{-1} I_{it}$, where t is a time index. This provides an estimate of the initial capital stock for a chosen year 0 equivalent to the sum of gross fixed capital investments in the five years prior to that. We chose 1980 as the base year for all countries to make sure that the weight of measurement error of the initial capital stock is negligible by 2000. Then, we calculate the capital stock in year 1 as $K_{i1} = 0.87K_{i0} + I_{i1}$, where 0.87 is one minus the depreciation rate and I_{i1} is i's real gross investments in year 1, and so forth, until we obtain K_i as a measure of the capital stock in the year 2000.

[39] For a robustness analysis, we also construct and include two additional variables for political stability and inverse expropriation risk for the *more stable* and *less risky* of the two countries, respectively.

[40] The latent processes underlying BIT_{ij} and PTA_{ij} could be interpreted as the net gains for country-pair ij from concluding one or the other type of agreement.

Table 2
Summary statistics for bilateral investment treaties (BITs) and preferential trade agreements (PTAs) and their key determinants.

Variable	Acronym	Unconditional		At BIT = 1		At PTA = 1	
		Mean	Std. dev.	Mean	Std. dev.	Mean	Std. dev.
Dependent variables							
Bilateral investment treaty indicator	BIT_{ij}	0.115	0.319	1.000	0.000	0.273	0.446
Preferential trade agreement indicator	PTA_{ij}	0.158	0.365	0.376	0.485	1.000	0.000
Independent variables							
Log sum of *i*'s and *j*'s real GDP	$GDPSum_{ij}$	24.995	1.834	26.532	1.390	25.468	1.575
Log similarity of *i*'s and *j*'s real GDP	$GDPSim_{ij}$	−0.537	1.597	−0.793	1.790	−0.474	1.291
Log bilateral distance between *i*'s and *j*'s economic centers	$DIST_{ij}$	8.193	0.789	7.752	0.965	7.566	1.064
Adjacency indicator between *i* and *j*	ADJ_{ij}	0.021	0.142	0.045	0.207	0.084	0.277
Common official language indicator between *i* and *j*	$LANG_{ij}$	0.128	0.334	0.110	0.313	0.162	0.369
Political stability between *i* and *j*	$PolStab_{ij}$	72.875	11.764	80.010	9.473	73.907	11.673
Inverse expropriation risk between *i* and *j*	$IExpRisk_{ij}$	8.484	1.830	9.017	1.556	8.666	1.687
Log absolute difference in relative capital–unskilled labor ratios between *i* and *j*	$KURatio_{ij}$	2.349	1.713	2.010	1.536	1.615	1.231
Log absolute difference in capital and unskilled labor shares between *i* and *j*	$KUDiff_{ij}$	−2.727	2.388	−2.466	2.155	−2.431	2.027
Log similarity of *i*'s and *j*'s skilled labor endowment shares	$Ssim_{ij}$	−2.406	1.156	−2.390	1.149	−2.153	0.858
Log distance of *i* and *j* to the rest of the world	$REMOTE_{ij}$	8.436	0.153	8.385	0.163	8.403	0.180
BITs of *i* and *j* other than with each other (third-country BITs)		7.688	15.018	21.644	21.395	12.267	17.151
PTAs of *i* and *j* other than with each other (third-country PTAs)		31.961	29.764	37.927	29.091	48.572	32.577

and (ii) unobserved characteristics as included in the disturbances. Table 3 has several columns presenting the results of including variables suggested by our discussion above, similar to the presentation in Baier and Bergstrand (2004) for only PTAs. We will refer below to "a" to denote a specification associated with BIT_{ij} and "b" refers to results associated with PTA_{ij}.

Specifications 1a and 1b are reported to examine the effects on the likelihood of a BIT and a PTA, respectively, of variables from Section 3,

Table 3
The determinants of bilateral investment treaties (BITs) and preferential trade agreements (PTAs) in seemingly unrelated bivariate probit models: main results.

Determinants	Acronym	Model 1		Model 2		Model 3		Model 4	
		BITs	PTAs	BITs	PTAs	BITs	PTAs	BITs	PTAs
Log sum of *i*'s and *j*'s real GDPs	$GDPSum_{ij}$	0.374***	0.147***	0.327***	0.160***	0.353***	0.203***	0.286***	0.129***
		(0.010)	(0.007)	(0.011)	(0.008)	(0.012)	(0.010)	(0.014)	(0.012)
Log similarity of *i*'s and *j*'s real GDPs	$GDPSim_{ij}$	0.035***	0.058***	0.029***	0.060***			0.124***	0.124***
		(0.008)	(0.007)	(0.008)	(0.007)			(0.012)	(0.0126)
Log bilateral distance between *i*'s and *j*'s economic centers	$DIST_{ij}$	−0.529***	−0.617***	−0.509***	−0.614***	−0.475***	−0.542***	−0.472***	−0.775***
		(0.022)	(0.020)	(0.022)	(0.021)	(0.023)	(0.021)	(0.030)	(0.028)
Adjacency indicator between *i* and *j*	ADJ_{ij}	−0.341***	0.398***	−0.242**	0.342***	−0.233*	0.280***	−0.429***	0.008
		(0.116)	(0.099)	(0.123)	(0.100)	(0.126)	(0.101)	(0.14)	(0.116)
Common official language indicator between *i* and *j*	$LANG_{ij}$	−0.091*	0.087**	−0.087	0.048	−0.064	0.091**	0.081	−0.042
		(0.053)	(0.041)	(0.054)	(0.042)	(0.056)	(0.046)	(0.060)	(0.053)
Political stability between *i* and *j*	$PolStab_{ij}$	–	–	0.017***	−0.005***	0.015***	−0.007***	0.018***	−0.001
		–	–	(0.002)	(0.001)	(0.002)	(0.002)	(0.002)	(0.002)
Inverse expropriation risk between *i* and *j*	$IExpRisk_{ij}$							−0.051***	0.007
								(0.013)	(0.012)
Log absolute difference in capital and unskilled labor shares between *i* and *j*	$KUDiff_{ij}$	–	–	–	–	0.029***	–	0.029***	
		–	–	–	–	(0.009)	–	(0.009)	
Log absolute difference in relative capital–unskilled labor ratios between *i* and *j*	$KURatio_{ij}$	–	–	–	–	–	−0.166***		−0.151***
		–	–	–	–	–	(0.010)		(0.012)
Log similarity of *i*'s and *j*'s skilled labor endowment shares	$Ssim_{ij}$	–	–	–	–	0.169***	0.226***	0.117***	0.154***
		–	–	–	–	(0.021)	(0.017)	(0.020)	(0.018)
Log distance of *i* and *j* to the rest of the world	$REMOTE_{ij}$							−0.109	0.759***
								(0.142)	(0.130)
BITs of *i* and *j* other than with each other (third-country BITs)								0.024***	0.0099***
								(0.001)	(0.001)
PTAs of *i* and *j* other than with each other (third-country PTAs)								0.004***	0.0168***
								(0.001)	(0.001)
Constant		−6.436***	0.296	−6.679***	0.334	−7.018***	−0.333	−4.717***	−4.352***
		(0.272)	(0.233)	(0.286)	(0.236)	(0.299)	(0.253)	(1.112)	(1.015)
Observations		12,880		12,561		11,325		11,325	
Countries		161		159		151		151	
Correlation between disturbances in BITs and RTA processes		0.219		0.222		0.161		0.099	
Standard error of correlation coefficient above		0.023		0.024		0.025		0.025	
Log-likelihood of model		−8123.94		−7972.69		−7434.08		−6676.72	
Log-likelihood of constant-only model		−9968.14		−9968.14		−9312.86		−9312.86	
McFadden pseudo-R^2		0.185		0.200		0.202		0.283	

Notes: Standard errors in parentheses are robust to heteroskedasticity of unknown form.
*** Statistically significant at the 1% level, using 2-tailed tests.
** Statistically significant at the 5% level, using 2-tailed tests.
* Statistically significant at the 10% level, using 2-tailed tests.

in particular, measures of economic size, economic similarity, distance, and natural trade and investment costs. We consider first economic size and similarity. We find that the sum and similarity of the two countries' GDPs ($GDPSum_{ij}$, and $GDPSim_{ij}$) have positive and statistically significant impacts on the likelihood of a BIT and of a PTA, as our theoretical model suggested.[41] This is the first study to find and explain the positive association between the economic size and similarity of a pair of countries and the likelihood of their having a BIT. Other things the same, country-pairs that are economically larger and more similar in size tend to have more FDI so that these economies' welfare will tend to rise more from a BIT, increasing the likelihood of their forming one. Moreover, country-pairs that are economically larger and more similar in size tend to have more trade so that these economies' welfare will tend to rise more from a PTA, increasing the likelihood of their forming one. Hence, Hypotheses 1 and 2 are confirmed.

We now turn to $Distance_{ij}$, $Adjacency_{ij}$ and $Language_{ij}$. As in Baier and Bergstrand (2004), $Distance_{ij}$ was included as a proxy for "natural" trade costs.[42] However, bilateral distance is well-known from the gravity-equation literature to have a negative, economically significant, and statistically significant impact both on bilateral trade flows *and* bilateral FDI flows. Consequently, one might argue that bilateral distance is not capturing "trade" costs per se but rather trade as well as other "information" costs.

However, although the marginal response probabilities will be provided later, there is some information content in the relative coefficient estimates for $Distance_{ij}$ from Specifications 1a and 1b, consistent with gravity equations of FDI and trade. For instance, typically in gravity equations estimated using ordinary least squares (absolute values of) coefficient estimates on $Distance_{ij}$ are smaller for FDI flows relative to trade flows (cf., Berden et al, 2011), even though there are very few studies that estimate both trade and FDI gravity equations in the same study using a common specification.[43] This result is consistent with the following notion. FDI flows are motivated from two sources, with "trade costs" having opposite effects. Much vertical FDI is to set up plants abroad which serve as export platforms back to the home country; trade costs (as proxied by distance) should have a negative effect on this FDI. However, horizontal FDI sets up plants abroad to "jump-over" trade costs, so such costs should have a positive effect on this FDI. The smaller negative coefficient estimate for bilateral distance in gravity equations for FDI relative to trade flows is consistent with the presence of both horizontal and vertical FDI. Since BITs are intended to enhance FDI flows, the smaller negative coefficient estimate for $Distance_{ij}$ is consistent with this explanation.[44]

Specifications 1a and 1b reveal *opposite* coefficient signs between the BITs and PTA probits for $Adjacency_{ij}$ and $Language_{ij}$. These two variables are the most commonly used dummies in gravity equations of trade flows and typically have economically and statistically significant positive effects. It is interesting to find that these two variables have statistically significant *negative* coefficient estimates in the BIT equation but positive coefficient estimates in the PTA equation. These results are consistent with (the trade-cost portions of) Hypotheses 3 and 4. As Fig. 3A suggests, the likelihood of a PTA should be greater between two countries the lower their trade costs, which implies a positive relationship between $Adjacency_{ij}$ and $Language_{ij}$ with $Pr(PTA_{ij}=1)$. But lower trade costs discourage horizontal FDI, which suggests (as in Fig. 3B) that the net utility change for a pair of countries from a BIT is a positive (negative) function of τ_{ij} ($Adjacency_{ij}$ and of $Language_{ij}$). Thus, the results are consistent with inferring that sharing a common land border and a common language reduces trade costs.

However, it would be useful to have a measure of natural investment costs in order to determine if the remaining (investment-cost) portions of Hypotheses 3 and 4 are confirmed. Specifications 2a and 2b augment Specifications 1a and 1b to include a measure of natural investment costs (γ_{ij}). The measure employed here is the index $PolStab_{ij}$ described above, which is increasing in the perceived degree of political *stability* (of the less stable of the country-pair), and hence a measure of the *inverse* of γ_{ij}. In a recent study of several governance indicators and their relationships to FDI and trade flows (cf., Berden et al., 2011), the measure of political stability had a positive and statistically significant effect on FDI flows and an estimated zero effect on trade flows, suggesting a plausible (inverse) measure of natural investment costs; moreover, this variable had an economically and statistically significant effect on FDI relative to trade. Specification 2a reveals that greater political stability (in the less stable country), by lowering natural investment costs and enlarging FDI, leads country-pairs to be more likely to form a BIT. This confirms Hypothesis 3. We also tried, for robustness, political stability in the more stable of the country-pair; this variable was not statistically significant. Together, these results suggest that greater political stability (in the less stable country) increases the likelihood of a BIT to motivate *vertical* FDI. Moreover, $PolStab_{ij}$ has the opposite effect on the likelihood of a PTA. An increase in political stability reduces investment costs, which decreases the net utility gains from a bilateral PTA, consistent with Fig. 3A and Hypothesis 4.

Figs. 4A and 5A and Hypotheses 5 and 6 suggest relationships between k_i and u_i with the welfare effects (and, hence, likelihoods) of PTAs and BITs. Fig. 4A suggests a negative relationship between differences in k_i/u_i relative to k_j/u_j ($KURatio_{ij}$) and the utility gains to i and j from a PTA. Fig. 5A suggests a positive relationship between differences in k_i and u_i with k_j and u_j ($KUDiff_{ij}$) and the utility gains to i and j from a BIT, as a higher value of $KUDiff_{ij}$ is associated with a larger relative abundance of skilled labor in either i or j, which favors more MNEs and FDI. Wider relative K/U ratios between i and j lead to more NE trade, but a large decline in HMNE activity, such that on net a PTA is welfare decreasing. Specifications 3a and 3b confirm the qualitative impacts of these two variables on their respective probabilities as consistent with these two hypotheses. Higher skilled labor abundance of either i or j ($KUDiff_{ij}$) leads to a higher probability of a BIT between them as expected. A wider K/U ratio between i and j ($KURatio_{ij}$) leads to a lower probability of a PTA between them as expected. Thus, all six hypotheses suggested by the numerical comparative statics discussed earlier are supported empirically.

Table 3 provides one more specification, Model 4. In the interest of brevity, we combine four issues in this last specification in Table 3.[45] First, we include the BERI measure of *inverse* expropriation risk (of the riskier country of the pair), $IExpRisk_{ij}$, which is negatively related to g_{ij}. As discussed above, higher bilateral expropriation risk (higher g_{ij}) should increase the gains from BIT_{ij}, especially to motivate vertical FDI; hence, a higher value of $IExpRisk_{ij}$ should have a *negative* effect on the probability of BIT_{ij}. Specification 4 confirms this and the coefficient estimate is statistically significant. Second, the net welfare gains and probability of BIT_{ij} should not be influenced by economic characteristics of i and j alone; *third-country* effects matter also. BB showed that the net welfare gains from and probability of PTA_{ij} were influenced by the "remoteness" of pair ij from third-country pairs. For robustness, we included $REMOTE_{ij}$, defined earlier, to account for the influence of the distance of pair ij from the *ROW*.

[41] We discuss the economic significance of these and other coefficients later in the section on marginal response probabilities.

[42] $Distance_{ij}$ is the natural logarithm of the country-pair's bilateral distance. Baier and Bergstrand (2004) used the variable $NATURAL_{ij}$, which was simply the log of the inverse of bilateral distance.

[43] For an exception, see Bergstrand and Egger (2010).

[44] See also Egger and Pfaffermayr (2004b) on this issue. These authors find opposite effects of distance, negative for trade and positive for FDI, consistent with our interpretation.

[45] This consolidation was recommended by a referee.

Specification 4 reveals that, as in BB and Egger and Larch (2008), $REMOTE_{ij}$ has a positive and statistically significant effect on the probability of PTA_{ij}. However, $REMOTE_{ij}$ has no statistically significant effect on the likelihood of BIT_{ij}. Third, Egger and Larch (2008) raised the issue of PTA "interdependence." The results may be sensitive to omitting the effect of "third-country" BITs and PTAs on the probability of BIT_{ij} and of PTA_{ij}. Following the methodology in Egger and Larch (2008), we constructed (ten-year-lagged) indexes of "third-country" BITs and PTAs. Specification 4 reveals that *interdependence* matters; both indexes had statistically significant effects on the probabilities of BIT_{ij} and of PTA_{ij}. Fourth, when we introduced the two relative-factor-endowment variables in Specification 3, we omitted (for methodological reasons discussed earlier) the index of similarity of GDPs of *i* and *j*. To show that the results are not materially different with or without $GDPSim_{ij}$, we included it in Model 4. While the coefficient estimates are significant, they are also identical; however, in Table 5 later we will show that the marginal effect of GDP similarity for BITs is smaller than that for PTAs, as expected.

6.2. Robustness analysis

In this section, we discuss three sensitivity analyses pertaining to the robustness of the results just discussed for Model 4.

6.2.1. Robustness to preferential trade and investment agreements

As discussed under the Data description section, some of the PTAs in our sample are actually preferential trade *and investment* agreements (PTIAs), such as the European Union (EU) and NAFTA. Since our dependent variable for BITs is actual bilateral investment treaties, investment liberalizations covered under "trade" agreements are not included in our BITs' dependent variable. For instance, for Germany and France, PTA_{ij} is recorded as a 1 whereas BIT_{ij} is recorded as a 0. We approached this issue in two alternative ways. Specifications 5a and 5b in Table 4 comprise the bivariate probit model where we include an "adjusted" variable for *BIT*. The new variable – *AdjBIT* – includes also any bilateral investment agreements akin to BITs that are within country-pairs' PTIAs. We modified 108 "0s" to "1s" of the *BIT* variable to capture the influence of investment agreements in the EU and in NAFTA as representing BITs. A comparison of the results in Specifications 4a and 4b in Table 3 using BITs and PTAs with those in Specifications 5a and 5b in Table 4 using the adjusted-BITs variable and PTAs shows that the results are materially the same in the two sets of specifications.

Alternatively, we could simply remove all the PTIAs from our sample. However, we note that – if anything – the inclusion of PTIAs in our sample of PTAs would tend to bias the results against us. For instance, the coefficient estimates for *Adjacency*, *Common Language*, *Political Stability*, and *Inverse Expropriation Risk* are expected to have

Table 4
The determinants of bilateral investment treaties (BITs) and preferential trade agreements (PTAs): sensitivity analyses.

Determinants	Acronym	Model 5 (bivariate probit)		Model 6 (recursive)		Model 7 (dynamic)	
		AdjBITs	PTAs	BITs	PTAs	ΔBITs	ΔPTAs
Log sum of *i*'s and *j*'s real GDPs	$GDPSum_{ij}$	0.333***	0.129***	0.279***	0.129***	0.301***	0.154***
		(0.014)	(0.012)	(0.014)	(0.012)	(0.012)	(0.012)
Log similarity of *i*'s and *j*'s real GDPs	$GDPSim_{ij}$	0.148***	0.124***	0.117***	0.123***	0.186***	0.061***
		(0.012)	(0.013)	(0.012)	(0.013)	(0.018)	(0.015)
Log bilateral distance between *i*'s and *j*'s economic centers	$DIST_{ij}$	−0.611***	−0.776***	−0.420***	−0.774***	−0.342***	−0.332***
		(0.030)	(0.028)	(0.038)	(0.028)	(0.041)	(0.029)
Adjacency indicator between *i* and *j*	ADJ_{ij}	−0.376***	0.007	−0.436***	0.017	−0.171	0.030
		(0.133)	(0.116)	(0.140)	(0.118)	(0.168)	(0.112)
Common official language indicator between *i* and *j*	$LANG_{ij}$	0.067	−0.041	0.086	−0.043	−0.107	0.444***
		(0.062)	(0.053)	(0.060)	(0.053)	(0.097)	(0.054)
Political stability between *i* and *j*	$PolStab_{ij}$	0.023***	−0.001	0.019***	−0.001	0.022***	−0.018***
		(0.002)	(0.002)	(0.002)	(0.002)	(0.004)	(0.003)
Inverse expropriation risk between *i* and *j*	$IExpRisk_{ij}$	−0.047***	0.007	−0.052***	0.007	−0.002	−0.008
		(0.014)	(0.012)	(0.013)	(0.012)	(0.021)	(0.014)
Log absolute difference in capital and unskilled labor shares between *i* and *j*	$KUDiff_{ij}$	0.035***		0.027***		0.061***	
		(0.010)		(0.010)		(0.016)	
Log absolute difference in relative capital–unskilled labor ratios between *i* and *j*	$KURatio_{ij}$		−0.148***		−0.153***		−0.088***
			(0.012)		(0.012)		(0.013)
Log similarity of *i*'s and *j*'s skilled labor endowment shares	$Ssim_{ij}$	0.137***	0.154***	0.107***	0.154***	0.343***	0.165***
		(0.021)	(0.018)	(0.021)	(0.018)	(0.037)	(0.022)
Log distance of *i* and *j* to the rest of the world	$REMOTE_{ij}$	−0.130	0.766***	−0.183	0.750***	0.202	0.268*
		(0.145)	(0.130)	(0.146)	(0.131)	(0.215)	(0.151)
BITs of *i* and *j* other than with each other (third-country BITs)		0.027***	0.010***	0.024***	0.010***	0.042***	0.006*
		(0.001)	(0.001)	(0.001)	(0.001)	(0.004)	(0.003)
PTAs of *i* and *j* other than with each other (third-country PTAs)		0.005***	0.017***	0.003***	0.017***	0.006***	0.002**
		(0.001)	(0.001)	(0.001)	(0.001)	(0.001)	(0.001)
PTA between *i* and *j*				0.218*		−0.171	
				(0.116)		(0.124)	
BIT between *i* and *j*							−0.249
							(0.230)
Constant		−4.961***	−4.395***	−4.409***	−4.288***	−9.499***	−3.164***
		(1.150)	(1.014)	(1.123)	(1.018)	(1.718)	(1.194)
Observations		11,325		11,325		11,325	
Countries		151		151		151	
Correlation between disturbances in BITs and RTA processes		0.164		−0.021		−0.243	
Standard error of correlation coefficient above		0.027		0.060		0.050	
Log-likelihood of model		−6516.54		−6675.77		−3526.99	
Log-likelihood of constant-only model		−9312.86		−9312.86		−4391.58	
McFadden pseudo-R^2 (in Model 7); R^2 (in Models 8 and 9)		0.300		0.283		0.197	

Notes: Standard errors in parentheses are robust to heteroskedasticity of unknown form. In Model 6a, PTA on the RHS is current year (2000); in Models 7a and 7b, PTA and BIT on the RHS are lagged values (from 1990).

*** Statistically significant at the 1% level, using 2-tailed tests.

** Statistically significant at the 5% level, using 2-tailed tests.

* Statistically significant at the 10% level, using 2-tailed tests.

opposite signs for PTAs and BITs. The inclusion of PTIAs in our PTA sample would tend to bias the coefficient estimates for these variables toward similar signs for PTAs and BITs. Nevertheless, we also re-ran Specifications 4a and 4b in Table 3 deleting the 108 observations associated with the EU members and NAFTA members, and the results do not change materially enough to be presented.

6.2.2. Robustness to recursive simultaneous bivariate probit estimation

It is possible that the latent variable influencing the probability of a PTA for two countries also influences the latent variable influencing the probability of a BIT between the pair, or vice-versa. That is, the determination of the probabilities of PTA_{ij} and BIT_{ij} may be better represented by a *simultaneous equations* probit model. However, there is no econometric theoretical foundation for estimating a simultaneous equations probit model where *both* endogenous variables appear as explanatory variables (*PTA* affecting *BIT* in one equation and *BIT* affecting *PTA* in the other equation, cf., Wooldridge, 2002). However, there is econometric theory for estimating a *recursive* simultaneous equations model with one of the endogenous variables entering one of the equations, cf., Schmidt (1981) and Wooldridge (2002, pp. 477–478). Moreover, in order to evaluate which equation should have the endogenous explanatory variable, we turn for guidance to a three-stage least squares (3SLS) estimation of two linear probability models first.

First, we estimated the linear probability versions of Model 4 of *BIT* and *PTA* using 3SLS. The notable finding from the 3SLS estimation is that *PTA* does have a statistically significant effect on the existence of *BIT* (and the other coefficient estimates remain plausible), but the *PTA* equation has no statistically significant coefficient estimates, including that for *BIT*. Given that there is only empirical evidence that *PTA* causes *BIT* using the 3SLS estimates, we estimated a recursive simultaneous probit equations model of *BIT* and *PTA*, where *PTA* was allowed to be an endogenous explanatory variable for the *BIT* equation. These estimates are reported in Specifications 6a and 6b of Table 4. The main finding is that *PTA* does have a statistically significant positive effect on the existence of *BIT*. However, *none* of the other coefficient estimates of the *BIT* equation are materially different from those in bivariate probit Specifications 4a and 4b in Table 3. The *BIT* equation is basically robust to including the endogenous explanatory variable *PTA*. Also, the *PTA* equation in Specification 6b is very similar to that in Specification 4b; the *PTA* equation is also robust and we find no evidence of (current) BITs affecting PTAs.

6.2.3. Robustness to dynamic effects

While the previous section explored the effects of *current* PTAs (BITs) on concurrent BITs (PTAs) using a recursive simultaneous equations approach, it is possible that PTAs (BITs) formed *earlier* – specifically, in 1990 – have caused *changes* in PTA (BIT) status from 1990 to 2000. We explored this possibility as well. Specifications 7a and 7b are the analogs to Specifications 4a and 4b, respectively, but include on the RHS ten-year-lagged values of PTAs (BITs) in the BIT (PTA) equation. Moreover, the dependent variable is now the *change* in BIT (PTA) status from 1990 to 2000 in Specification 7a (7b). Qualitatively, the results in Specifications 7a and 7b are remarkably similar to those in Specifications 4a and 4b, despite the change in the dependent variables. Note, however, that ten-year-lagged levels of PTAs (BITs) had no statistically significant effect on the change in BIT (PTA) status in the subsequent decade.

6.3. Marginal response probabilities and predictions

In this section, we report two sets of findings. We discuss the marginal response probabilities of one-standard-deviation changes in the right-hand-side variables as well as some interactive effects. Then, we summarize the percentages of correctly predicted bivariate observations on BIT and PTA, BIT but no PTA, PTA but no BIT, and no BIT or PTA from the model.

6.3.1. Marginal response probabilities

Probit coefficient estimates cannot reveal the quantitative (economic) effect of a change in any RHS variable on the probability of a BIT or PTA. Given the standard bivariate normal distribution, we can calculate the marginal response probabilities to unit- or one-standard-deviation changes in the RHS variables. For brevity, we report in Table 5 only the marginal response probabilities to one-standard-deviation changes in the RHS variables, although the other results are available upon request. Since it is a bivariate probit model, we report both the unconditional and conditional response probabilities.

First, the variable that has the largest quantitative effect on either the probability of a BIT or a PTA is economic size. Moreover, a one-standard-deviation change in GDP size has a larger effect on the likelihood of a BIT than on that of a PTA. This result accords well with an empirical result in Bergstrand and Egger (2007) that FDI flows are more elastic with respect to changes in economic size than are trade flows.

Second, GDP similarity has an economically and statistically significant effect on BITs and PTAs, consistent with our theoretical findings. Moreover, the quantitative effect of a one-standard-deviation change in GDP similarity is larger for PTAs than for BITs, as our theoretical results predicted.

Third, distance has a larger (negative) impact on the likelihood of a PTA than on that for a BIT. This is consistent with the discussion earlier; the influence of distance on the likelihood of BITs is likely muted by the trade-cost-jumping role of horizontal FDI. Also, of *Adjacency* and *Language*, only *Adjacency* has a significant marginal response probability, and it is in the BIT equation. *Adjacency* has a clearer economic interpretation, as an inverse natural-trade-cost measure. Lower trade costs associated with adjacent economies increase trade, reduce horizontal FDI, and lower the likelihood of a BIT.

Fourth, both measures of investment costs have economically and statistically significant marginal response probabilities in the expected direction for likelihood of BITs; more expropriation risk (higher g) increases $Pr(BIT_{ij}=1)$ and more political instability (higher γ) decreases $Pr(BIT_{ij}=1)$. A one-standard-deviation increase in the political stability index has a larger (in absolute terms) quantitative effect on the probability of a BIT than a one-standard-deviation increase in the inverse expropriation risk index.

Fifth, both relative factor endowment variables have economically and statistically significant marginal response effects on their respective probabilities. The negative effect on the probability of a PTA of a one-standard-deviation increase in relative *K/U* ratios is larger quantitatively (in absolute terms) than the positive effect on the probability of a BIT of a one-standard-deviation increase in the relative skilled-labor abundance of countries *i* and *j*. This actually accords well with Figs. 4A and 5A, where the negative welfare effect from a PTA of widening *K/U* ratios was considerably larger (in absolute terms) than the positive welfare effect from a BIT of a widening of k_i and u_i relative to k_j and u_j (and consequently larger skilled-labor abundance of *i* or *j*).

Finally, we discuss the interactive effects suggested by theoretical Fig. 5B and C. A comparison of Fig. 5B with Fig. 5A reveals a disproportionately greater effect of relative skill abundance on the net utility gains from a BIT when natural investment costs are lower ($\gamma_{ij}=$ 0.35 in Fig. 5B, rather than 0.40 in Fig. 5A), as the underlying level of FDI between *i* and *j* is larger. In our model, $PolStab_{ij}$ is the proxy for the inverse of γ_{ij}. The (unconditional) marginal response probability of a one-standard-deviation increase in $PolStab_{ij}$ is 3.2%. However, if $KUDiff_{ij}$ is one standard deviation higher, the $PolStab_{ij}$ marginal response probability is 5.4%, consistent with our theoretical conjecture of a negative interaction effect between γ_{ij} and $KUDiff_{ij}$ on the welfare gains from a BIT.

Moreover, a comparison of Fig. 5C with Fig. 5A reveals a disproportionately greater effect of relative skill abundance on the net utility gains from a BIT when the level of expropriation risk is higher ($g_{ij}=$ 0.15 in Fig. 5C, rather than 0.10 in Fig. 5A). In our model, $IExpRisk_{ij}$ is a measure of the inverse of g_{ij}. The (unconditional) marginal response

Table 5
Impact of one-standard-deviation change in the determinants of BITs and PTAs on marginal and conditional response probabilities (parameters are based on Model 4 in Table 3).

Determinants	Acronym	Uncond. responses		Conditional responses	
		BITs	PTAs	BITs|PTA = 1	PTAs|BIT = 1
Log sum of i's and j's real GDPs	$GDPSum_{ij}$	0.076***	0.042***	0.073***	0.030***
		(0.004)	(0.004)	(0.004)	(0.003)
Log similarity of i's and j's real GDPs	$GDPSim_{ij}$	0.029***	0.035***	0.025***	0.042***
		(0.003)	(0.004)	(0.003)	(0.005)
Log bilateral distance between i's and j's economic centers	$DIST_{ij}$	−0.054***	−0.108***	−0.074***	−0.145***
		(0.003)	(0.004)	(0.005)	(0.006)
Adjacency indicator between i and j	ADJ_{ij}	−0.009***	0.000	−0.020***	0.002
		(0.003)	(0.003)	(0.007)	(0.005)
Common official language indicator between i and j	$LANG_{ij}$	0.004	−0.002	0.005	−0.003
		(0.003)	(0.003)	(0.004)	(0.003)
Political stability between i and j	$PolStab_{ij}$	0.032***	−0.003	0.037***	−0.005
		(0.004)	(0.005)	(0.005)	(0.004)
Inverse expropriation risk between i and j	$IExpRisk_{ij}$	−0.013***	0.002	−0.014***	0.004
		(0.004)	(0.004)	(0.004)	(0.004)
Log absolute difference in capital and unskilled labor shares between i and j	$KUDiff_{ij}$	0.007***		0.006***	
		(0.002)		(0.002)	
Log absolute difference in relative capital–unskilled labor ratios between i and j	$KURatio_{ij}$		−0.063***		−0.066
			(0.005)		(0.006)
Log similarity of i's and j's skilled labor endowment shares	$Ssim_{ij}$	0.020***	0.031***	0.015***	0.034***
		(0.003)	(0.004)	(0.003)	(0.004)
Log distance of i and j to the rest of the world	$REMOTE_{ij}$	−0.002	0.021***	−0.005	0.026***
		(0.003)	(0.004)	(0.004)	(0.004)
BITs of i and j other than with each other (third-country BITs)		0.009***	0.044***	0.008***	0.072***
		(0.001)	(0.001)	(0.002)	(0.003)
PTAs of i and j other than with each other (third-country PTAs)		0.105***	0.052***	0.129***	0.047***
		(0.005)	(0.006)	(0.007)	(0.007)**,*
Political stability between i and j (at 1 std. dev. higher $GDPSum_{ij}$)	$PolStab_{ij}$	0.047***		0.052***	
		(0.006)		(0.006)	
Political stability between i and j (at 1 std. dev. higher $KUDiff_{ij}$)	$PolStab_{ij}$	0.054***		0.059***	
		(0.010)		(0.010)	
Inverse expropriation risk between i and j (at 1 std. dev. higher $GDPSum_{ij}$)	$IExpRisk_{ij}$	−0.020***		−0.020***	
		(0.005)		(0.005)	
Inverse expropriation risk between i and j (at 1 std. dev. higher $KUDiff_{ij}$)	$IExpRisk_{ij}$	−0.023***		−0.023***	
		(0.007)		(0.007)	

Notes: Standard errors in parentheses.
*** Statistically significant at the 1% level, using 2-tailed tests.
** Statistically significant at the 5% level, using 2-tailed tests.
* Statistically significant at the 10% level, using 2-tailed tests.

probability of a one-standard-deviation *decrease* in $IExpRisk_{ij}$ is 1.3%. However, if $KUDiff_{ij}$ is one standard deviation higher, the response probability is 2.3%, consistent with our theoretical conjecture of a positive interaction effect between g_{ij} and $KUDiff_{ij}$ on the welfare gains from a BIT.

6.3.2. Explanatory power and predicted probabilities

One of the interesting results from the original Baier and Bergstrand (2004) study was the high pseudo-R^2 value of 73% in their fullest specification of explaining the likelihood of PTAs. However, this study examined only 1145 pairings of 54 countries. In a much larger and less selective cross-section using 146 countries and 10,585 country-pairs, Egger and Larch (2008) showed that the Baier–Bergstrand results held up, but the overall explanatory power, as captured by the pseudo-R^2, was much smaller at 27%. In this study, we use an even larger data set than Egger–Larch, with 161 countries and 12,880 observations. Moreover, explaining the likelihood of PTAs *and* BITs *simultaneously* is a larger challenge. Hence, our pseudo-R^2 of 28% in our main specification, Model 4 in Table 3, is a strong result, in this context.

In the spirit of these papers, we also consider here the percent of correctly predicted, both for "true positives" and for "true negatives." However, in this bivariate model, we are calculating percent correctly predicted for each of the *four* outcomes: BIT and PTA, BIT but no PTA, PTA but no BIT, and no BIT or PTA. Baier and Bergstrand (2004) conducted this statistical summary for their cross-section analysis of the year 1996 for PTAs and found that their model predicted correctly 243 of 286 PTAs, or 85% (using a cutoff probability of 0.5). They also predicted 1114 of the 1145 pairs without PTAs correctly, or 97%. However, this sample was quite small, and Egger and Larch conducted a similar analysis using their larger cross-section of 10,585 country-pairs. Also using a cutoff probability of 0.5 for the year 2000, the percent of PTAs correctly predicted was 62% and the percent of "No-PTAs" correctly predicted was 98%.

It is important to note, however, that a cutoff probability of 0.5 is not a very relevant one. The reason is that PTAs and BITs are still rare events. As Table 1 showed, of 12,880 country-pairs in year 2000 in our sample, only 556 country-pairs had a BIT and PTA, which implies an unconditional probability of only 4.3%. The unconditional probability of a BIT but no PTA is only 7.2%, and that of a PTA but no BIT is 11.5%. Hence, a cutoff probability of 50% for any of these events is too extreme. Cohen et al. (2003) and Cameron and Trivedi (2005) suggest using a priori information about the proportion of (PTA and BIT) events and non-events in the sample for forming cutoff probabilities; hence, we use the unconditional probabilities. In the case of country-pairs with a BIT and PTA, we predict correctly 88.4% of the observations. In the case of pairs with a BIT but no PTA, we predict correctly 81.2% of the observations. In the case of pairs with a PTA but no BIT, we predict correctly 83.8% of the observations. Finally, in the case of pairs with no BIT or PTA, we predict correctly 56.5% of the observations.

7. Conclusions

The purpose of this study was to develop an econometric model that explains the "economic" determinants of BITs – at the same time as explaining PTAs. In the spirit of Baier and Bergstrand (2004), which explained PTAs in the context of a general equilibrium model of world trade with exporters, the model in this study is the first econometric model to explain BITs (along with PTAs) in the context of an explicit general equilibrium model of world production, consumption, trade, and FDI with national and multinational firms in multiple countries.

The main conclusions are that the potential welfare gains from and likelihood of a BIT (PTA) between a country-pair are higher: (1) the larger and more similar in GDP are the country-pair; (2) the closer in distance are the two countries; (3) if the two countries are not adjacent (are adjacent) and do not share (do share) a common language; (4) the higher (lower) the degrees of political stability and of expropriation risk of the pair; and (5) the relatively more skilled labor abundant (the wider the relative K/U ratio of) the pair. These factors have economically and statistically significant effects on the probability of a BIT (PTA).

While there exist choices of cutoff probabilities in determining the percent correctly predicted of the alternative outcomes, using the unconditional probabilities the preferred empirical model predicts correctly more than 80% of country-pairs with a BIT and PTA, with a BIT but no PTA, and with a PTA but no BIT. Consequently, the model provides a benchmark for incorporating other economic – and especially political science and legal variables – into understanding the determinants of BITs and PTAs.

Acknowledgments

We are very grateful to editor Robert Staiger, James Markusen, Keith Maskus, and two anonymous referees for excellent comments that enhanced the manuscript substantively. We are grateful also for comments from participants at presentations at the Asia-Pacific Trade Seminars in Singapore, the University of Colorado at Boulder, the Ifo Institute in Munich (CESifo Area Conference on the Global Economy), ETH University in Zurich, and the University of Notre Dame (Kellogg Institute for International Studies). Egger gratefully acknowledges financial support from GA CR grant number P402/12/0982.

Appendix A. Supplementary data

Supplementary data to this article can be found online at http://dx.doi.org/10.1016/j.jinteco.2012.11.004.

References

Ai, D., Norton, E.C., 2003. Interaction terms in logit and probit models. Economics Letters 80, 123–129.

Aisbett, Emma, 2009. Bilateral investment treaties and foreign direct investment: correlation versus causation. In: Sauvant, Karl P., Sachs, Lisa E. (Eds.), The Effect of Treaties on Foreign Direct Investment. Oxford University Press, Oxford, UK.

Alfaro, Laura, Charlton, Andrew, 2009. Intra-industry foreign direct investment. American Economic Review 99 (5), 2096–2119 (December).

Arkolakis, Costas, Costinot, Arnaud, Rodriguez-Clare, Andres, 2012. New trade models, same old gains? American Economic Review 102 (1), 94–130.

Baier, Scott L., Bergstrand, Jeffrey H., 2004. Economic determinants of free trade agreements. Journal of International Economics 64, 29–63.

Baldwin, Richard E., 1993. A domino theory of regionalism. National Bureau of Economic Research Working Paper No. 4465.

Baldwin, Richard E., Jaimovich, Dany, 2012. Are free trade agreements contagious? Journal of International Economics 88 (1), 1–16 (September).

Berden, Koen, Bergstrand, Jeffrey H., van Etten, Eva, 2011. Globalization and governance. Working Paper. University of Notre Dame.

Bergstrand, Jeffrey H., Egger, Peter, 2006. Trade costs and intra-industry trade. Review of World Economics 142 (3), 433–458 (October).

Bergstrand, Jeffrey H., Egger, Peter, 2007. A knowledge-and-physical-capital model of international trade flows, foreign direct investment, and multinational enterprises. Journal of International Economics 73, 278–308.

Bergstrand, Jeffrey H., Egger, Peter, 2010. A general equilibrium theory for estimating gravity equations of bilateral FDI, final goods trade, and intermediate trade flows. In: van Bergeijk, Peter A.G., Brakman, Steven (Eds.), The Gravity Model in International Trade. Cambridge University Press, Cambridge, UK.

Bergstrand, Jeffrey H., and Egger, Peter, in press. Shouldn't physical capital also matter for multinational enterprise activity? Review of International Economics.

Bergstrand, Jeffrey, Egger, Peter, Larch, Mario, 2011. Economic determinants of the timing if preferential trade agreement formations and enlargements, unpublished manuscript. University of Notre Dame, December.

Blonigen, Bruce A., Piger, Jeremy, 2011. Determinants of foreign direct investment. National Bureau of Economic Research Working Paper No. 16704 (January).

Braconier, Henrik, Norback, Pehr-Johan, Urban, Dieter, 2005. Reconciling the evidence on the knowledge–capital model. Review of International Economics 13 (4), 770–786.

Buthe, Tim, Milner, Helen V., 2009. Bilateral investment treaties and foreign direct investment: a political analysis. In: Sauvant, Karl P., Sachs, Lisa E. (Eds.), The Effect of Treaties on Foreign Direct Investment: Bilateral Investment Treaties, Double Taxation Treaties, and Investment Flows. Oxford University Press, Oxford, UK.

Cameron, A. Colin, Trivedi, Pravin K., 2005. Microeconometrics: Methods and Applications. Cambridge University Press, Cambridge, UK.

Carr, David, Markusen, James R., Maskus, Keith E., 2001. Estimating the knowledge–capital model of the multinational enterprise. American Economic Review 91 (3), 693–708 (June).

Chen, Maggie Xiaoyang, Joshi, Sumit, 2010. Third-country effects on the formation of free trade agreements. Journal of International Economics 82, 238–248.

Cohen, Jacob, Cohen, Patricia, West, Stephen G., Aiken, Leona S., 2003. Applied Multiple Regression/Correlation Analysis for the Behavioral Sciences, Third edition. Lawrence Erlbaum Associates, Mahwah, NJ.

Eaton, Jonathan, Kortum, Samuel, 2002. Technology, geography, and trade. Econometrical 70, 1741–1779.

Egger, Peter, Larch, Mario, 2008. Interdependent preferential trade agreement memberships: an empirical analysis. Journal of International Economics 76, 384–399.

Egger, Peter, Pfaffermayr, Michael, 2004a. The impact of bilateral investment treaties on foreign direct investment. Journal of Comparative Economics 32, 788–804.

Egger, Peter, Pfaffermayr, Michael, 2004b. Distance trade, and FDI: a Hausman–Taylor SUR approach. Journal of Applied Econometrics 19, 227–246.

Freund, Caroline and Ornelas, Emanuel, 2009. Regional trade agreements, unpublished manuscript. London School of Economics.

Gallagher, Kevin P., Birch, Melissa B.L., 2006. Do investment agreements attract investment? Evidence from Latin America. Journal of World Investment and Trade 7 (6), 961–976.

Greene, William H., 1997. Econometric Analysis, third edition. Prentice-Hall International, Inc., New York.

Greene, William H., 2010. Testing hypotheses about interaction terms in nonlinear models. Economics Letters 107 (2), 291–296.

Hallward-Driemeier, Mary, 2003. Do bilateral investment treaties attract FDI? Only a bit and they could bite. World Bank Policy Research Paper WPS 3121.

Leamer, Edward E., 1984. Sources of International Comparative Advantage: Theory and Evidence. MIT Press, Cambridge, MA.

Lutz, Wolfgang, Cuaresma, Jesus Crespo, Sanderson, W., 2008. The demography of educational attainment and economic growth. Science 319, 1047–1048.

Markusen, James R., 2002. Multinational Firms and the Theory of International Trade. MIT Press, Cambridge, Massachusetts.

Markusen, James R., Maskus, Keith E., 2001. Multinational firms: reconciling theory and evidence. In: Blomstron, Magnus, Goldberg, Linda (Eds.), Topics in Empirical International Economics: A Festschrift in Honor of Robert E. Lipsey. University of Chicago Press, Chicago, IL.

Markusen, James R., Maskus, Keith E., 2002. Discriminating among alternative theories of the multinational enterprise. Review of International Economics 10 (4), 694–707.

Markusen, James R., Venables, Anthony J., Eby-Konan, Denise, Zhang, Kevin H., 1996. A unified treatment of horizontal direct investment, vertical direct investment, and the pattern of trade in goods and services. National Bureau of Economic Research Working Paper No. 5696 (August).

Moser, Christoph, Rose, Andrew K., 2011. Who benefits from regional trade agreements? The view from the stock market. National Bureau of Economic Research Working Paper No. 17415 (September).

Neumayer, E., Spess, L., 2005. Do bilateral investment treaties increase foreign direct investment to developing countries? World Development 33 (10), 1567–1585.

Ramondo, Natalia and Rodriguez-Clare, Andres, in press. Trade, Multinational production, and the gains from openness. Journal of Political Economy.

Salacuse, Jeswald W., 1990. BIT by BIT: the growth of bilateral investment treaties and their impact on foreign investment in developing countries. HeinOnline 24, 655–675.

Salacuse, Jeswald W., Sullivan, Nicholas P., 2005. Do BITs really work? An evaluation of bilateral investment treaties and their grand bargain. Harvard International Law Journal 46 (1).

Sauvant, Karl P., Sachs, Lisa E. (Eds.), 2009. The Effect of Treaties on Foreign Direct Investment. Oxford University Press, New York, NY.

Schmidt, Peter, 1981. Constraints on the parameters in simultaneous tobit and probit models. In: Manski, Charles, McFadden, Daniel (Eds.), Structural Analysis of Discrete Data and Econometric Application. MIT Press, Cambridge, Massachusetts.

Swenson, Deborah, 2005. Why do developing countries sign BITs? U.C. Davis Journal of International Law and Policy 131.

Tobin, Jennifer, Rose-Ackerman, Susan, 2005. Foreign direct investment and the business environment in developing countries: the impact of bilateral investment treaties. Yale Law School Center for Law, Economics, and Public Policy Research Paper No. 293.

United Nations Conference on Trade and Development, 2007. Bilateral Investment Treaties: 1995–2006. UNCTAD, New York, New York.

Vandevelde, Kenneth J., 1998. Investment liberalization and economic development: the role of bilateral investment treaties. Columbia Journal of Transnational Law 36, 501–527.

Vandevelde, Kenneth J., 2000. The economics of bilateral investment treaties. Harvard International Law Journal 41, 469–502.

Wooldridge, Jeffrey M., 2002. Econometric Analysis of Cross Section and Panel Data. MIT Press, Cambridge, Massachusetts.

Appendix: Calibration of Model

The underlying theoretical model is described in Bergstrand and Egger (2007), or Chapter 14. The complexity of the model (including the complementary-slackness conditions) introduces a high degree of nonlinearity, and it cannot be solved analytically. Consequently, as in Markusen (2002) we provide numerical solutions to the model. With three countries, we have several potential types of asymmetries, e.g., large vs. small GDPs, developed vs. developing economies. We focus initially on bilateral flows between three identical economies (in absolute and relative factor endowments). We then introduce absolute and relative factor endowment asymmetries. We use *GAMS* for our numerical analysis. The calibration of the model is very similar to that in Bergstrand and Egger (2007).

1. *Values of (exogenous) factor endowment, trade cost, and investment cost variables*

We assume a world endowment of capital (K) of 500 units, skilled labor (S) of 200 units, and unskilled labor (U) of 2000 units. Initially, countries i and j together have half of the world's endowments of each factor, and i's and j's factor endowments are identical. In the remaining summary of parameter choices, we note that we have tried to base selections upon empirical observations (as much as data availability allowed) or upon widely-known regression estimates of elasticities.

"Trade costs" include both the costs of shipping and distributing goods, as well as trade policies. Initially, we set the former costs for good X and good Y at (*ad valorem* equivalents of) 30 percent and 45 percent, respectively (for τ). This reflects recent estimates that homogeneous goods' transport costs are higher than those of differentiated goods, cf., Bergstrand and Egger (2006). Both values exceed estimated (c.i.f.-f.o.b.)/f.o.b. factors in that paper of 15 percent and 20 percent, respectively. However, values used are in the range of levels discussed in Anderson and van Wincoop (2004) on trade costs. For simplicity, we set tariff rates initially at *ad valorem* equivalents of 20 percent (for b).

In reality, of course, informational costs and policy barriers to FDI exist between countries. However, *ad valorem* empirical measures of such FDI cost are not available. We assumed initially a "tax-rate" equivalent (for γ) of 40 percent for FDI and a value for g of 10 percent.

2. *Utility and technology parameter values*

Consider first the utility function. The only two parameters are the Cobb–Douglas share of income spent on differentiated products from various producers (η) and the CES parameter (ε) influencing the elasticity of substitution between differentiated products ($\sigma \equiv 1 - \varepsilon$). Initially, we use 0.71 for the value of η, based upon an estimated share of manufactures trade in overall world trade averaged between 1990 and 2000 using 5-digit SITC data from the UNs' COMTRADE data set, which is a plausible estimate. The initial value of ε is set at -5, implying an elasticity of substitution of 6 among differentiated final goods, consistent with a wide range of recent empirical studies estimating the elasticity between 2 and 10, cf., Feenstra (1994).

Consider next the production function for differentiated goods. Labor's share of differentiated goods gross output is assumed to be 0.8; the Cobb–Douglas formulation implies the elasticity of substitution between capital and labor is unity. Griliches (1969) proposed — in a three-factor world with unskilled labor, skilled labor, and physical capital — that skills were more complementary with physical capital than with unskilled labor in production. Griliches found convincing econometric evidence that physical capital and skilled labor were relatively more complementary in production than physical capital and unskilled labor. Most evidence to date suggests that human and physical capital are relatively complementary in production, cf., Goldin and Katz (1998). In the only empirical study of MNE behavior considering this issue, Slaughter (2000) finds statistically significant evidence in favor of capital–skill complementarity. Initially, we assume $\chi = -0.25$, implying a technical rate (elasticity) of substitution of 0.8 [$= 1/(1 - \chi)$] and complementarity between physical and human capital.

As in the $2 \times 2 \times 2$ KC model in CMM (2001), a firm (or headquarters) setup uses only skilled labor. For national final goods producers, we assume a headquarters setup requires one unit of skilled labor per unit of output ($a_{\mathrm{Sn},1} = a_{\mathrm{Sn},2} = a_{\mathrm{Sn},3} = 1$). As in the knowledge–capital model, we assume "jointness" for MNEs; that is, services of knowledge-based assets are joint inputs into multiple plants. Markusen suggests that the *ratio* of fixed headquarters setup requirements for a horizontal or vertical MNE relative to a domestic firm ranges from 1 to 2 (for a two-country model). We assume initially a headquarters cost for MNEs of 1.01 ($a_{\mathrm{Sh},1} = a_{\mathrm{Sh},2} = a_{\mathrm{Sh},3} = a_{\mathrm{Sv},1} = a_{\mathrm{Sv},2} = a_{\mathrm{Sv},3} = 1.01$); hence, we assume the additional firm setup cost of an MNE over a national firm is quite small. We assume that every plant (national or MNE) requires two units of home physical capital ($a_{\mathrm{K}} = 2$); however, MNEs setting up plants abroad face additional natural investment cost (γ), for which we assumed a value of 0.40 (40 percent), and an investment cost (g) of 0.1 (10 percent), representing expropriation risk.

www.ingramcontent.com/pod-product-compliance
Ingram Content Group UK Ltd.
Pitfield, Milton Keynes, MK11 3LW, UK
UKHW022108170926
8624IPUK00024B/293

9 789811 202261